Canadian Red Cross

Emergency Care Manual

StayWell

Cette publication est disponible en français.

The terms "he" and "she" have been used throughout the manual to ensure representation of both genders and to correspond to any photos within a particular section.

Illustrations by Scott Mooney
Composition by Tinge Design Studio Inc.
Printing/binding by Transcontinental

Printed in Canada by:
The StayWell Health Company Ltd.
2 Quebec Street, Suite 107, Guelph, ON N1H 2T3
A division of
StayWell
780 Township Line Road, Yardley, PA 19067-4200 USA

ISBN: 978-1-58480-404-8

08 09 10 11 12 / 5 4 3 2 1

Contents

Acknowledgements

For over 50 years, the Canadian Red Cross First Aid Programs have grown and flourished. Each time a program undergoes a revision or the first aid and CPR standards change, the changes are started with a foundation of the great work done by previous revisions. In 1997, the original version of the *First Responder* manual was developed and produced through a joint effort of the American Red Cross and Mosby-Year book Inc. In 2005, the Canadian Red Cross developed an *Emergency Medical Responder Supplement* for the *First Responder* manual, which created the first Canadian Red Cross Emergency Medical Responder Program. Red Cross would like to recognize anyone who worked on developing these programs in the past; their hard work and dedication set the foundations for revising and updating these First Responder and Emergency Medical Responder programs.

There was excellent market research that guided the project's direction and vision. We would like to thank our Authorized Providers, Instructor Trainers, and Instructors who participated in the market research. Their input and guidance helped shape the new look of our programs and products.

This incredible project required the hard work and dedication of the many teams who put in countless hours to contribute to its success. Canadian Red Cross extends its thanks to each team and its members.

The Canadian Red Cross National Medical Advisory Team reviewed the content of the program and thanks go to: Brendan J. Hughes, MD, CCFP; Andrew MacPherson, BSc, MD, CCFP-EM, Chief, Department of Emergency Medicine, Vancouver Island Health Authority, Victoria; Ernest Prégent, MD, CCFP(em), CSPQ, FCCFP; and Ronald Stewart, OC, ONS, BA, BSc, MD, FACEP, DSc(hon) and Officer of the Order of Canada.

The Volunteer Technical Committee Members were responsible for developing the technical content and direction that laid the foundation for the program: Dan Anton (Yukon), John Boulay (Quebec), Jason Brinson (Ontario), Jonathan Britton (Ontario), Marc Côté (Quebec), Ian Fitzpatrick (British Columbia), Sioban Kennedy (Ontario), Ken Lane (Nova Scotia), and Dave Monilaws (Alberta).

The Primary Project Team was responsible for providing the overall leadership, and direction for the project and was made up of: Project Manager: Cathy Forner; Publishing Coordinator: Eric Ritterrath; French Verification: Michèle Bourcier, Mike Bourcier, Norm Robillard; Marketing Leadership: Carolyn Tees; and Technical Advisor: Janel Swain.

The Zone Project Advisory Teams were made up of: Tracey Braun, Kathy Cseff, Laura McNamara, Tannis Nostedt, Elizabeth Ramlogan, Sylvie Santerre, and Ann Thain.

As well, we extend thanks to the following volunteers for their review and contributions to the manual or for helping with the photo shoot: Jennifer Anderson, Robbie Anderson, Cora-Andree Martin, Alain Archambault, Frédérick Beauchamp, Mélanie Beauchamp, Anne Beaudry, Paul Beaudry, Patrick Boucher, Elena Bowell, Susan Brennan, Ken Brunton, Jeremy Calhoun, Liz Ciesluk, Heather Cliff, Alana Couvrette, Lauren Couvrette, Jonah Davidson, Andrew Davis, Martin De Vries, Lindsay Dods, Angelo Federico, Giuseppe Federico, Pam Ferguson, Krista Fewtrell, Serge Fournier, Sébastien Gagnon, François Gamache-Asselin, Maryse Glaude-Beaulieu, Janet Goldie, Jamie Hall, Madeline Jolicoeur, Geneviève Kingsley, Spencer Koeus, Kurt Kritsch, Kris Kurs, Luc Lauzon, Marie-Claude Lemire, Mehdi Louzouaz, Sheila Lurette, Gerald Lyon, Erica Mallett, Jessica Mallett, Rob Mallett, Thomas Mallett, Amy Mapara, Constantin Marango, Don Marentette, David Matschke, Gary R. McHugh, Daniel Mendonca, Andrea Norg, Ann Odgers, Tara O'Reilly, Dave Perras, Andre Poirier, Roman Popadiouk, Donovan Rota, Marie-Claire Savard-Mills, Jeff Shanks, Mike Silvestre, Kevin Smith, Caroline Sparks, Ingrid Taylor, Norah Taylor, Dean Turner, Vicky Wallace, Janis Watson, Adam Whiteford, and Robert Willson.

The following organizations reviewed, provided guidance, endorsed the program, or provided a location for the photo shoot. We thank them for their valuable contributions: Canadian Athletic Therapists Association (CATA); Canadian Ski Patrol; Industrial Accident Prevention Association (IAPA); Philip Groff, PhD, SMARTRISK; National Gallery of Canada; Ottawa Fire Services; Ottawa Paramedic Service; Rideau Canoe Club Securitas Canada; and Jill Skinner, Canadian Medical Association (CMA).

  The Canadian Medical Association (CMA) is pleased to support the important work of the Canadian Red Cross in developing this manual.

 The Industrial Accident Prevention Association (IAPA) is pleased to support the Canadian Red Cross and the review of this manual.

 Philip Groff, PhD, from SMARTRISK was pleased to review this manual and supports the work of the Canadian Red Cross.

 The Canadian Athletic Therapists Association (CATA) was pleased to review Chapter 12, Musculoskeletal Injuries, of this manual.

The Canadian Ski Patrol System recognizes the importance of First Responder training.

This project was possible because of the creative vision, ongoing support, and dedication of our publisher partner: StayWell; the Project Executive Sponsor: Yvan Chalifour; and Project Sponsor: Rick Caissie.

Index services provided by Frances Robinson.

The Red Cross

Henry Dunant— The Red Cross Founder

In June 1859, Henry Dunant saw an unforgettable scene: 40,000 dead and wounded soldiers left on the field after the Battle of Solferino in Italy. He organized local villagers into first aid teams to help as many of the wounded as possible, saving thousands of lives.

To prevent this horror from happening again, he decided to create a neutral organization to care for wounded soldiers and prisoners–an organization that would be respected and protected by both sides in any conflict. The result was the Red Cross. Dunant spent the rest of his life trying to reduce the suffering caused by war.

He lobbied governments, organized Red Cross Societies in different countries, and spoke to the public. In 1901, Dunant won the first Nobel Peace Prize. By founding the International Red Cross and Red Crescent Movement, he saved the lives of millions of people over the years.

Henry Dunant

The Red Cross—Fundamental Principles

There are Red Cross or Red Crescent Societies in over 184 countries around the world.

In every country, our programs and services are guided by seven Fundamental Principles. The Tanzanian Red Cross has created a short, simple version of these principles:

Humanity: We serve people, but not systems.

Impartiality: We care for the victims and the aggressors alike.

Neutrality: We take initiatives, but never take sides.

Independence: We bow to needs, but not rulers.

Voluntary Service: We work around the clock, but never for personal gain.

Unity: We have many talents, but a single idea.

Universality: We respect nations, but our work knows no bounds.

Essentially, we provide help to people in need, whatever their race, political beliefs, religion, social status, or culture.

Who We Are—Canadian Red Cross

Our Mission

The Canadian Red Cross mission is to improve the lives of vulnerable people by mobilizing the power of humanity in Canada and around the world.

Our Vision

The Canadian Red Cross is the leading humanitarian organization through which people voluntarily demonstrate their caring for others in need.

Our Values

Our actions and decisions will be based on:

- Humanitarian values.
- Respect, dignity, and care for one another within and outside Red Cross.
- Integrity, accountability, effectiveness, and transparency.

How We Help

Disaster Management

Canadian Red Cross helps people affected by emergencies and disasters. We work with governments and other humanitarian organizations to meet people's basic needs. We provide shelter, clothing, food, first aid, and emotional support. When families have been separated by disasters, we help bring them back together.

International Programs

Canadian Red Cross works in other countries to help people who have been affected by wars and natural disasters. We bring urgently needed supplies, reunite families, and help rebuild communities.

First Aid Programs

The Canadian Red Cross First Aid Program has been training Canadians in first aid for more than 60 years. Our courses prepare people to make safe choices, prevent injury, and help in emergency situations.

Water Safety Programs

More than 30 million Canadians have learned how to swim and safely enjoy water activities since 1946 through our swimming and Water Safety Programs.

RespectED: Violence and Abuse Prevention

Since 1984, this award-winning program has helped more than one million Canadian youth and adults understand abuse, harassment, and interpersonal violence issues.

Homecare Services

These in-home community services help frail and older adults, children at risk, people with disabilities, and people receiving palliative care live as independently as possible. Canadian Red Cross has provided these services for more than 70 years.

Part *1*

Preparing to Respond

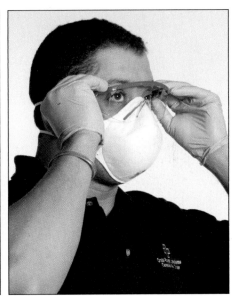

| 1 |

The Responder

| 2 |

The Emergency Scene

| 3 |

Preventing Disease Transmission

Chapter *1*

The Responder

You are called to the scene at a bathroom in a mall. A man has slipped and fallen on the bathroom floor. The man is breathing but unresponsive. He was found by other mall patrons, who are now upset and concerned. You have been summoned to help. What do you do?

INTRODUCTION

As a responder, you are a key part of the emergency medical services (EMS) system. You provide a link between the first actions of bystanders and more advanced care. A responder is a person, paid or volunteer, who is often summoned to provide initial care in an emergency. As the first trained professional on the scene, your actions are often critical. They may determine whether a seriously ill or injured person survives.

According to the Paramedic Association of Canada (PAC), "first responders" may be included within the emergency medical responder (EMR) level, although in many settings, first responders do not transport people.

According to PAC, the EMR "has successfully completed a recognized training program in emergency patient care and transportation." As part of the foundation of the Canadian emergency systems, EMRs are often linked with volunteer emergency services organizations in rural and remote areas and in some communities may be the sole provider of emergency services.

Responders across the country have different roles to perform, including primary and secondary surveys, the provision of safe and prudent care, and the transport of an ill or injured person to the most appropriate health-care facility.

By taking this course, you will gain the knowledge, skills, and confidence to give appropriate care when you are called to help someone who has become injured or suddenly ill. You will learn how to assess a person's condition and how to recognize and care for life-threatening emergencies. You will also learn how to minimize a person's discomfort and prevent further complications until you can obtain more advanced medical care.

Components of an EMS System

The EMS system is a network of community resources and medical personnel that provides emergency care to people with injury or sudden illness. When people at an emergency scene recognize an emergency and take action, they activate this system. The care provided by more highly trained professionals continues until an ill or injured person receives the level of care he needs. An effective EMS system includes the following components:

- Communications
- Transportation
- Facilities
- Medical control
- Trauma systems
- Public information and education
- Human resources, training, and continuing education
- Resource management
- Regulation and policy
- Evaluation

EMS systems throughout Canada vary by region and, in many cases, by city. In 2001, PAC, with the support of Human Resources Development Canada and the Canadian Medical Association, established the National Occupational Competency Profiles (NOCPs) to promote national consistency in paramedic training and practice.

Levels of Training for Providers

An EMS system may utilize emergency care providers with many different levels of training. PAC has developed four levels of pre-hospital EMS training: emergency medical responder, primary care paramedic (PCP), advanced care paramedic (ACP), and critical care paramedic (CCP). By meeting minimum competency profiles, EMS systems can attain consistency throughout the country, which will allow for portability and achieving an appropriate standard of professional care.

Medical Control

Certification as a first responder or emergency medical responder is not a licence to perform all the skills in the Emergency Care course or manual. These should be performed if you have been delegated these acts by a physician. Physicians provide medical direction in EMS systems, through a process called medical control. This process allows a physician to direct the care given to ill or injured people by pre-hospital care professionals. Usually, a medical director, who assumes responsibility for the care given, does this monitoring.

The medical director also oversees training and the development of protocols (standardized procedures to be followed when providing care to people with illness or injury). Since it is impossible for the medical director to be present at every incident outside the hospital, he can still direct care through standing orders. Standing orders allow responders to provide certain types of care or treatments without consulting the physician. This type of medical control is called indirect or off-line medical control and it includes education,

protocol review, and quality improvement of emergency care professionals. Other procedures not covered by standing orders require the responder to speak directly with the physician. This contact can be made via cellphone, radio, or telephone. This kind of medical control is called direct or on-line medical control.

THE EMERGENCY RESPONSE SUPPORTING THE EMS SYSTEM

The survival of an ill or injured person depends on all people performing their roles correctly and promptly to make the EMS system work. People must recognize emergencies and quickly get help by activating the system. They must learn what actions to take in the first critical minutes. They must also learn to prevent emergencies and prepare for them. They need to support the EMS system in their community.

When they are summoned, professionals must respond sensitively, quickly, and effectively to emergencies. They must keep their training current and stay abreast of new issues in emergency response. When each component of the system works effectively, this enhances the ill or injured person's chances for a full recovery.

So what happens if one of these components breaks down? Since the person's life may depend on each or all of these components, a break can cause serious consequences.

For instance, if a person does not recognize a lifethreatening emergency, such as the early signals of a heart attack, and does not quickly call EMS personnel, the person may not live. Poor information given to the EMS dispatcher may delay advanced care. Improper care of the ill or injured person before more advanced medical care is obtained can result in the person's condition worsening, possibly leading to permanent disability or death.

In a serious injury or illness, survival and recovery are not a matter of chance. Survival results from a carefully orchestrated continuum of events in which all participants fulfill their roles. The EMS system can make the difference between life and death or a partial or full recovery. You as a responder play a critical role in this system.

COMPONENTS OF AN EMERGENCY RESPONSE

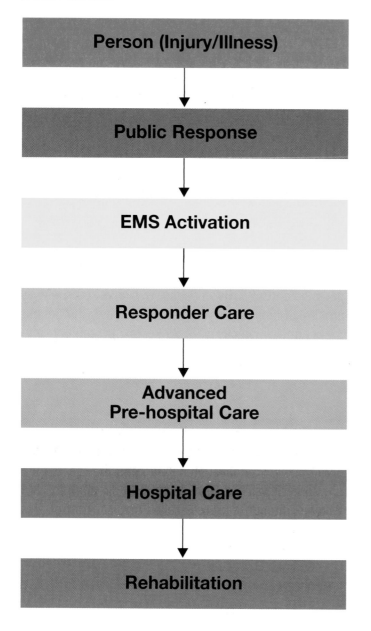

Person (Injury/Illness)

Public Response

EMS Activation

Responder Care

Advanced Pre-hospital Care

Hospital Care

Rehabilitation

THE RESPONDER

Responders, unlike lay people, are more likely to respond to the scene of a medical emergency and to provide emergency medical care to an ill or injured person while on duty. They should have ready access to supplies and equipment for providing care until more advanced emergency care is obtained. More advanced care refers to someone with a higher level of training, who takes over the care of the ill or injured person.

Some occupations, such as law enforcement and fire fighting, require personnel to respond to and assist at the scene of an emergency. These personnel are dispatched through an emergency number, such as 9-1-1 or the local EMS number, and often share common communication networks. When a person dials 9-1-1 or the local EMS number, he will contact police, fire, or ambulance personnel. These are typically considered public safety personnel. However, responders do not necessarily work in public safety agencies. People in many other occupations are called to help in the event of an injury or sudden illness, for example:

- Athletic therapists
- Disaster team members
- Emergency management personnel
- First aid station attendants
- Industrial safety personnel
- Lifeguards
- Ski patrol members
- Workplace first aid attendants

As a responder, you have a duty to quickly and safely respond to the scene of an emergency. Your duty is also to assess the ill or injured person's condition and provide necessary care, act as the person's advocate, make sure that any necessary additional help has been summoned, assist other medical personnel at the scene, and document your actions.

Personal Characteristics

As an emergency care provider who deals with the public, you must be willing to take on responsibilities beyond giving care. These responsibilities require you to demonstrate certain characteristics that include:

- *Maintaining a caring and professional attitude.*

  Ill or injured people are sometimes difficult to work with. Be compassionate; try to understand their concerns and fears. Realize that any anger an injured or ill person may show is often the result of fear. Someone who helps at the emergency may also be afraid. Try to be reassuring. Even though a person may not have done everything perfectly, be sure to thank him for taking action. Recognition and praise help affirm people's willingness to act. Also, be careful about what you say. Do not give distressing news about the emergency to the person or his family or friends.

- *Controlling your fears.*

  Try not to reveal your anxieties to the injured or ill person or bystanders. The presence of blood, vomit, unpleasant odours, or torn or burned skin is disturbing to most people. You may need to compose yourself before acting. If you must, turn away for a moment and take a few deep breaths before providing care.

- *Presenting a clean and professional appearance.*

  This helps ease a person's fears and inspires confidence.

- *Keeping your skills and knowledge up to date.*

  Involve yourself in continuing education, professional reading, and refresher training.

- *Staying fit with daily exercise and a healthy diet.*

  Job stresses can adversely affect your health. Exercise and diet can help you manage physical, mental, and emotional stress.

- *Maintaining a safe and healthy lifestyle.*

  As a responder, it is important to maintain a safe and healthy lifestyle both on and off the job.

  Identify the risk factors in your life so that you can take steps to reduce them.

Responsibilities

Since you will often be the first trained professional to arrive in many emergencies, your primary responsibilities centre on safety and early emergency care. Your six major responsibilities are to:

1. *Ensure safety for yourself and any bystanders.*

   Your first responsibility is to not make the situation worse by getting hurt yourself or letting bystanders get hurt. By making sure the scene is safe as you approach it, you can avoid unnecessary injuries.

2. *Gain access to the injured or ill person.*

   Carefully approach the person unless the scene is too dangerous to handle without help. Electrical hazards, unsafe structures, and other dangers may make it difficult to reach the person. Recognize when a rescue requires specially trained emergency personnel and know how to activate this response.

3. *Determine any threats to the person's life.*

   Check first for immediate life-threatening conditions and care for any you find. Next, look for other conditions that could eventually threaten the person's life or health if not cared for.

4. *Obtain more advanced medical care as needed.*

   After you quickly assess the person, notify more advanced medical personnel of the situation if someone has not already done so. Transport the person if it is necessary and you are trained and able to do so.

5. *Provide needed care for the ill or injured person.*

   Remain with the person and provide whatever care you can until more advanced personnel take over.

6. *Assist more advanced personnel.*

   Transfer your information about the ill or injured person and the emergency to more advanced personnel. Tell them what happened, how you found the person, any problems you found, and any care you gave. Assist them as needed and help with care for any other ill or injured people. When possible, try to anticipate the needs of those giving care.

In addition to these major responsibilities, you have secondary responsibilities that include:

- Summoning additional help when needed, such as special rescue teams.
- Controlling or directing bystanders or asking them for help.
- Taking additional steps, if necessary, to protect bystanders from dangers such as traffic or fire.
- Recording what you saw, heard, and did at the scene.
- Reassuring the person's family or friends.

Interpersonal Communication

Medical emergencies can be frightening to people. When speaking to the ill or injured person and family, be sure to speak slowly and clearly. Use language they can understand. Avoid technical terms that will confuse and possibly frighten them.

When speaking to people, get down to their level, if possible, to avoid appearing threatening. Make eye contact. Use body language that shows you are open and interested in what people have to say. One way to put people at ease is to address them by name, whenever possible. Note, however, that if the person is an older adult, you should not call him by his first name unless invited to do so.

Listen carefully to what the ill or injured person tells you. Observe the person when he talks. Provide reassurance if someone appears reluctant to speak about a topic. Tell him that any information the person may have about the problem is important, even if it is upsetting to talk about.

Listen to what bystanders tell you. They may have seen or heard something that will help you in determining how you will treat the person. Many times, people will want to stay with the person or watch to see what is going on. Be firm but reasonable with bystanders. Ask them to move away for the safety and comfort of everyone. Consider allowing a parent of a child or an immediate family member to stay, although this is not always possible. If there are hostile bystanders, ensure your safety, and the safety of the ill or injured person, and call for help from the appropriate source, if required.

You can also learn a lot about physical problems just by observing the person while he talks. If someone can only speak a few words before needing to take a breath, for example, he may be having a breathing emergency. Be observant. If someone is holding his stomach or clutching his chest—and may do so without being aware of it—this might give you information. Someone who winces with pain should be questioned about the pain.

From the person's perspective, nothing is more annoying than not being listened to. Consider the last time you had to repeat information to someone several times; it is not a pleasant experience. Listening lets a person know that you believe he is important. If you ask someone a question, listen for the answer. Make notes, if necessary, so you do not forget what the person said. If you forget too often, the person may stop answering your questions altogether.

Remember that everyone deserves equal care. One person should be treated with the same respect and dignity afforded to any other. If you are called to care for someone who does not speak a language you understand, call for someone who can translate. A family member or neighbour, for example, may be able to speak both your language and that of the ill or injured person.

Watch the person's body language, whether he speaks your language or another. Non-verbal clues can help you determine what is wrong. Be sensitive to cultural differences; in some cultures or religions, it may be inappropriate to make eye contact or for someone of the opposite gender to help the person. Respect this and do what you can to help.

LEGAL AND ETHICAL ISSUES

Many people are concerned about lawsuits. Lawsuits against those who give care at the scene of an emergency are highly unusual and rarely successful. By being aware of some basic legal principles, you may be able to avoid the possibility of legal action in the future (Figure 1–1).

The following sections address, in general terms, the legal principles that concern emergency care. Because laws vary between provinces, territories, and possibly regions, your instructor may need to update you on the laws that apply to you or tell you where you can find such information.

Duty to Act

Most responders, either by case law, statute, or job description, have a duty to act at the scene of an emergency. This duty applies to public safety officers, government employees, licenced and certified professionals, and paraprofessionals while on duty. For instance, members of a volunteer fire department have a duty to act based on their agreement to participate in the fire department. An athletic therapist has a duty to give care to an injured athlete. Failure to adhere to these agreements could result in legal action.[1]

If your actions do not meet the standards set for you, you may be successfully sued if your actions harm someone.

Scope of Practice

A responder's scope of practice is defined as the range of duties and skills he is allowed and expected to perform when necessary to his level of training and using reasonable care and skill. The responder is governed by legal, ethical, and medical standards. Be aware that when you practise a medical act, you may be doing so as an extension of your medical director. These standards establish the scope and the limits of care the responder provides. Since practices may differ by region, responders must be aware of the variations existing for their level of training and licencing in their region.

- **Duty to act**
- **Consent**
- **Competence**
- **Negligence**
- **Laws that protect responders**
- **Refusal of care**
- **Abandonment**
- **Confidentiality**
- **Documentation**

Figure 1–1 Responders should be aware of these basic legal considerations.

[1]Canadian Criminal Code, Articles 45, 215, 216, and 217.

Ethical Responsibilities

As a responder, you have an ethical obligation to carry out your duties and responsibilities in a professional manner. This includes showing compassion when dealing with an ill or injured person's physical and mental needs and communicating sensitively and willingly at all times. You should never become satisfied with meeting minimum training requirements but rather strive to develop your professional skills to surpass the standards for your region. Doing so includes not only practising and mastering the skills taught in the course, but also seeking further training and information through workshops, continuing medical education, conferences, and supplemental or advanced educational programs. In addition, be honest in reporting your actions and the events that occurred at a scene or when responding to an emergency. You have not only an ethical responsibility but also a legal one to document events accurately. Make it a personal goal to be a person whom others trust and can depend on to give accurate reports and provide effective care. You should address your responsibilities to the ill or injured person at each and every emergency. You must also periodically conduct a self-review of performance, including skills such as providing care to the ill or injured person, communication with him, and documentation to help improve any weaknesses.

Consent

An individual has a basic right to decide what can and cannot be done with his body. Therefore, to provide care for an ill or injured person, you must first obtain that person's consent. Usually, the person needs to tell you clearly that you have permission to provide care.

To obtain consent, you must:

1. Identify yourself to the person.

2. State your level of training.

3. Explain what you think may be wrong.

4. Explain what you plan to do.

After you have provided this information, the person can decide whether to grant his informed (or actual) consent. A person can withdraw consent for care at any time.

There is no specific age at which one is old enough to give or reject first aid treatment. In general, the person to receive the treatment must be mature enough to understand the circumstances he is in, the nature of the treatment to be provided, and the consequences of refusal.

A person who is unconscious, confused, or seriously ill or injured may not be able to grant informed consent. In these cases, the law assumes that the person would grant consent for care if he were able to do so. This is termed *implied consent*. Implied consent also applies to minors who obviously need emergency assistance when a parent or guardian is not present.

Consent: Special Situations

Unless an illness or injury is life-threatening, a parent or guardian must be present and give consent for minors before care can be given. If you encounter a parent or guardian who refuses to let you provide care, try to explain the consequences to the ill or injured child if care is not given. Use terms that the parent or guardian will understand. A law enforcement officer can help obtain the necessary legal authority to provide care. Do not argue with the parent or guardian as doing so can create a potentially unsafe scene. If the ill or injured person is an adult whom you know or learn is under a legal guardian's care, you must also get the guardian's consent to give care. In certain situations, a person's cultural or religious beliefs may prevent that person from receiving care or being cared for by strangers or members of the opposite sex. In such a situation, you should respect the person's wishes and obtain other trained personnel to deal with the situation.

Competence

Competence refers to the ill or injured person's ability to understand the responder's questions and to understand the implications of decisions. Responders must obtain permission from competent people before providing any care. Before receiving consent or refusal of care, the responder should determine if the person is competent. A person may not be competent to make rational decisions if he is intoxicated or on drugs, has a serious injury that might affect his judgment, or has a mental illness or disability. In such cases, call additional or appropriate personnel to evaluate the person. A law enforcement officer may need to be present to obtain the necessary legal authority so that care can be provided by the responder or advanced medical personnel.

Advance Directives and Do Not Resuscitate (DNR) Orders

Advance directives and do not resuscitate (DNR) orders are documented instructions from a person or his substitute decision maker and signed by a medical authority that protect a person's right to refuse efforts to resuscitate him in the case of cardiac arrest. Advance directives and DNR orders may differ by province, territory, or region. You must be aware of your relevant legislation and protocols relative to these orders. In some provinces/territories, a "No CPR" bracelet has been introduced to assist in identifying those wishes.

Negligence

Negligence is the failure to follow a reasonable standard of care, thereby causing injury or damage to another. A person could be negligent either by acting wrongly or failing to act at all.

The following scenario is an example of a case in which negligence may be suspected. A responder is called to the scene at a construction site, where a construction worker fell from a scaffolding several flights above. When the responder arrives, the worker is lying on the ground, moaning in pain, with both his hands holding his lower back.

The arriving responder notes the severity of the incident but fails to consider that the worker may have a spinal injury. The responder attempts to get the injured person to stand up and move away from the construction area, even though there is no immediate threat of danger. This movement causes him to experience severe pain, and he suddenly loses feeling in his legs. In this case, the responder may be negligent because he failed to follow a reasonable standard of care.

Four components must be present for a lawsuit charging negligence to be successful:

- Duty of care
- Breach of duty

A 16-year-old boy is star defenceman for his hockey team. During a game, one of his teammates accidentally smacks him on the side of the head with his stick, sending him falling to the ice. He loses consciousness for 30 seconds, and when he wakes up, he is confused and disoriented. The coach assesses him despite his protesting that he's feeling fine and is keen to get back to the game. After a few minutes, the coach and parents agree that he can go back and play. What is your responsibility in this case?

- Cause of harm due to what someone did or failed to do
- Damage caused

As a responder, you have a duty to respond in a professional manner, obeying traffic laws and protocols that govern your action. If you fail to act within this duty, then you commit a breach of duty. Sometimes your actions can cause improper care to be rendered, which can result in further harming an injured person.

Laws That Protect Responders

Most provinces and territories have enacted laws that protect people providing emergency care. These laws, which differ across Canada, are often called "Good Samaritan Laws" and will generally protect you from legal liability as a responder as long as you act in good faith, are not negligent and act with reasonable care and skill, and act within the scope of your training. In times when you have a duty to respond, these laws may not be applicable.

Refusal of Care

Some ill or injured people, even those who desperately need care, may refuse the care you offer. Even though the person may be seriously injured, you should honour his refusal of care. Try to convince the person of the need for care but do not argue. Allow other trained personnel to evaluate the situation. If possible, to make it clear that you did not abandon the person, have a witness hear the person's refusal and document it. Many EMS systems have a "Refusal of Care" form that you can use in these situations.

Before allowing a person to refuse care:

- Ensure that the person is competent and can make a rational decision.

- Try to persuade the person to accept care; repeat your offer to help at least once.

- Advise the person of the risks associated with refusing care.

- Consult the medical director (if required).

These factors should all be documented, and, as always, follow local protocol.

Abandonment

Just as you must have consent from a person before beginning care, you must also continue to give care once you have begun. Once you have started emergency care, you are legally obligated to continue that care until a person with equal or higher training relieves you. Usually, your obligation for care ends when more advanced medical personnel take over. If you stop your care before that point, you can be legally responsible for the abandonment of a person in need.

Confidentiality

While providing care, you may learn things about the person that are generally considered private and confidential. Information such as previous medical problems, physical problems, and medications being taken is personal to the individual. Respect his privacy by maintaining confidentiality, including any documentation you may create. Television and newspaper reporters may ask you questions. Lawyers may also approach you at the scene. Never discuss the person or the care you gave with anyone except law enforcement personnel or other personnel caring for the individual. Once transfer of care has taken place, your responsibilities for data gathering terminate, unless asked to act further. Any information gathered to that point must be documented.

Documentation

Documenting your care is as important as the care itself. Your record will help healthcare professionals assess and continue care for the person. Because a person's

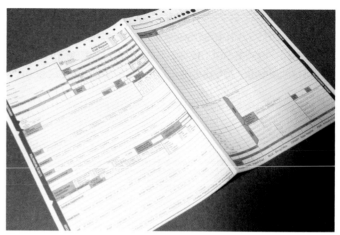

Figure 1–2 Printed care report form.

condition may change before he arrives at the hospital, a record of the condition immediately after the emergency will provide useful information for healthcare providers. They can compare the current condition with what you recorded earlier.

Your record is a legal document and is important if legal action occurs. Should you be called to court for any reason, your record will support what you saw, heard, and did at the scene of the emergency. It is important to write the record as soon as possible after the emergency, while all the facts are fresh in your memory. Many systems have printed forms for responders to use (Figure 1–2).

Reasons for Documentation

- Medical—To document care you provided

- Legal—To defend against lawsuits, as well as possible evidence in court proceedings (e.g., if an act of violence was involved)

- Administration—To transfer information about the individual from one person to another

- Research—To improve your EMS system

Elements of Good Documentation

- Completeness and accuracy (see Appendix B: Common Abbreviations for Documentation)

- Legibility

- Timeliness

- Absence of alterations

There are some situations when other documentation, or variance in the usual documentation, may be required, such as in the care of injury to responders, multiple casualty incidents, infectious disease exposure, and other such reasons.

It may be necessary to provide a verbal report of information about the ill or injured person to another healthcare provider. To do this, report the facts. Tell the other person what you found and what you have done up to that point. See Chapter 23 on communications for more information about a verbal report.

SUMMARY

The survival and recovery of a severely ill or injured person depend on all parts of the EMS system working together efficiently. Early response by the public, rapid EMS response, responder care, advanced pre-hospital care, hospital care, and extended care are the components for survival. The responder, the first trained person to arrive on the emergency scene, takes over care of the ill or injured person from any member of the public present.

After arriving on the scene, the responder must make sure the scene is safe and then reach the ill or injured person, give care for any life-threatening conditions, and obtain more advanced medical care, if needed. The responder should give more advanced medical personnel any assistance they need.

In your role as a responder, you are guided by certain legal parameters, such as the duty to act, and professional standards of care. Part of this professionalism includes effective documentation, which is important for maintaining the standard of care for an ill or injured person and provides legal protection for you and the organisation you represent. If you are a responder who falls under medical direction, you must follow protocols and standing orders within your scope of practice. In addition, there are legal and ethical requirements you must carry out, such as determining competence, obtaining consent, and adhering to advance directives when providing care. Since legal and medical standards and licensure can vary by region, it is important that you become knowledgeable about the standards in your area and the variations that exist for your level of training.

Regardless of your profession, when you are called to help a person with an injury or sudden illness, you assume the role of an emergency care provider. When an emergency occurs, the people in your care, as well as assisting bystanders, will expect you to know what to do. Be prepared to think and act accordingly. What to do, however, often involves more than giving emergency care. Chapter 2 provides an overview of the responder's role in assessing and managing emergency scenes.

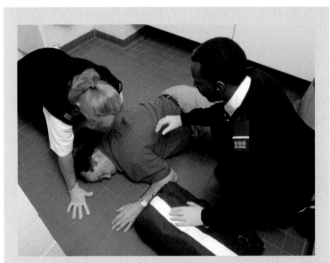

As you survey the scene, you think about everything at once: How seriously is the man injured? What do I need to do first to make it easier to help the man? How do I get the information I need in the quickest way so that I can get to work? What are my responsibilities as a responder?

Chapter 2

The Emergency Scene

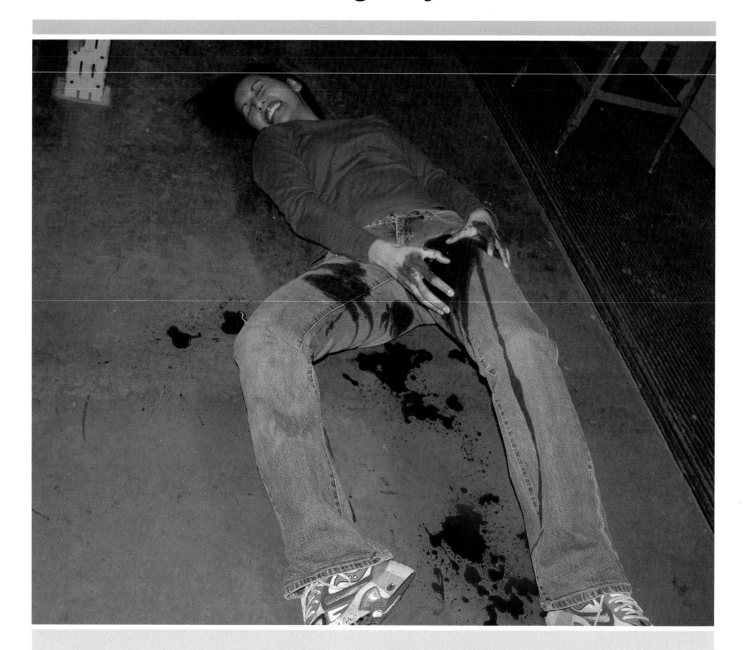

You are called to a factory and find a woman bleeding profusely from a deep wound in her upper thigh. She is in obvious pain and appears to be losing consciousness. Her breathing is rapid and her skin looks paler than normal. The factory is filled with loud machines, and you find it hard to communicate with anyone due to the noise. There are no witnesses to the incident. What do you do?

INTRODUCTION

As a responder, you have a duty to respond to an emergency when summoned. Although you should immediately proceed to the scene of an emergency when notified, you must do so safely. When you arrive, carefully evaluate the entire scene. Emergency scenes are often dangerous. Never enter a dangerous emergency scene unless you have been trained to do so and have the necessary equipment. Follow your established operating procedures, including when and how to access the EMS system.

This chapter describes the responsibilities for preparing for an emergency response and for identifying and managing initial dangers at an emergency scene.

PREPARING FOR THE EMERGENCY RESPONSE

Equipment and Personnel

The emergency response begins with the preparation of the vehicle/equipment and personnel before an emergency occurs. The first aid kit, or trauma kit, for the responder should be a standard part of your equipment for performing your duties. It should be checked on a regular schedule to ensure that it is well stocked at all times. You should be familiar with the location of all equipment within the kit. Emergency equipment must always be clean and in good working condition. Dressings, bandages, and other supplies kept in kits should be restocked as soon as possible after use. Automated external defibrillators (AEDs) must be properly maintained as per manufacturers' guidelines, making sure batteries are charged. Oxygen cylinders should be kept full. The quantity of specific items should be determined by individual need, local protocol, or legislation.

Plan of Action

To respond most efficiently to certain emergencies, you need a plan of action. A plan of this type is prepared in advance and rehearsed with personnel. Emergency plans should be established based on anticipated needs and available resources. All personnel should become familiar with these plans. For example, many businesses and industrial sites have emergency plans

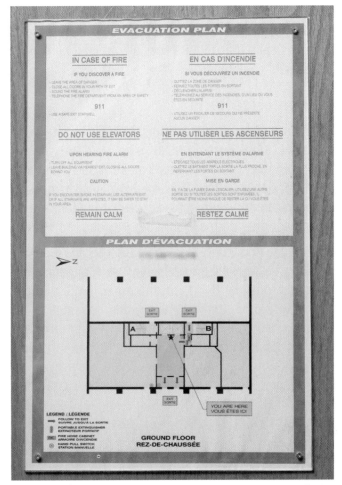

Figure 2–1 Posted evacuation routes may be part of an emergency plan.

that identify trained personnel, locations of supplies and equipment, a communication network, and evacuation routes (Figure 2–1).

Many fire departments and EMS systems plan responses for large facilities requiring special resources, such as sports stadiums, public buildings, and facilities with hazardous materials. These are generally referred to as emergency response plans. A plan for evacuating a stadium crowded with fans, for example, could save thousands of lives in an emergency. Developing the plan involves inspecting the site, noting potential dangers, and identifying the type of equipment and personnel that will probably be needed. Once developed, plans must be rehearsed, evaluated, and modified periodically.

Learn about the real or potential dangers in your area and familiarize yourself with existing emergency response plans. Evaluate your role and the available local resources. Know the resources in your community for handling special situations, such as a hazardous materials spill, that require specially trained personnel and special equipment.

Communications

Emergency response depends on a reliable and efficient communication system. Make sure you are always able to contact more advanced medical personnel and other special resources. This means having a backup communication system in place. Check communications equipment often to make sure it is working.

Be sure you know how to contact the special resources in your area. Some responders may use communication networks outside 9-1-1 or the local EMS number system. Become familiar with your communication networks and develop an alternative plan in case regular communications fail. Some types of communication devices are Family Radio Service (FRS), pagers, computers, two-way radios, cellphones, satellite phones, CB radios, and personal digital assistants (PDAs). For more information on communications, see Chapter 23.

Training

An important part of being prepared for emergencies is keeping your training current. Continue to practise the skills you use less often. Pursue activities that will help you perform your job better, including reading appropriate articles and publications and participating in workshops, emergency response exercises, and seminars.

RESPONDING TO THE EMERGENCY SCENE

Mental and Emotional Aspects

Just as it is important to keep equipment ready for emergencies, it is also important for you to be prepared psychologically. You can never predict how the next emergency may affect you. Certain injuries, smells, sights, and sounds can make you feel weak, nauseated, or faint the first time you encounter them. The sight of blood or gaping wounds, cries of pain, the threat of

danger, or other factors may so distress well-intentioned responders that they become barriers to prompt action.

You may never get used to some sights and sounds. With experience and by being prepared, however, you can learn to cope with your feelings. To calm yourself, take a deep breath and look away for a moment. Stay relaxed. Remind yourself that the person needs you and you need to be in full control of yourself to give the required care. If you feel nauseated, step back, take several deep breaths, mentally review your task, and then proceed. The person's life may depend on you.

Recognizing your emotions and the emotions of others will help you manage the situation in a more understanding and responsive way.

Notification and Transportation

If you are in a police department, fire department, or rescue squad, for example, you may be notified to go to an emergency by telephone, pager, or radio. Lifeguards, ski patrollers, and athletic therapists may already be near or at the scene when an emergency occurs. If you are at a distance from the scene, you will probably need to use a vehicle to get there. Laws and established procedures govern the use of emergency vehicles and their warning equipment, such as lights and sirens. You must remember that emergency vehicles do not have an absolute right-of-way.

Never drive a private vehicle as if it were an emergency vehicle. Even if you have lights and sirens, people do not always see you, hear you, or yield the right-of-way. People hurrying to an emergency or a hospital sometimes cause vehicle collisions because they fail to drive safely.

MANAGING DANGERS AT THE EMERGENCY SCENE

Some emergency scenes are immediately dangerous. Others may become dangerous while you are providing care. Sometimes the dangers are obvious, such as fire or hostile ill or injured people or bystanders. Other dangers may be less obvious, such as the presence of a hazardous material or unstable structures. Table 2-1 lists a number of hazards you may find at an emergency scene.

Primary Responsibilities of the Responder
1. Ensure safety for yourself and any bystanders.
2. Gain access to the ill or injured person.
3. Determine any threats to the person's life.
4. Obtain more advanced medical care, as needed.
5. Provide needed care for the ill or injured person.
6. Assist advanced medical personnel, as needed.

Personal Safety

Of the six primary responsibilities of the responder below, safety should always be foremost. You cannot overlook the importance of ensuring your own safety. Often it requires only simple tasks to make an emergency scene safe. Approach all emergency scenes cautiously until you can size up the situation. If you arrive at the scene by vehicle, park a safe distance away. If the scene appears safe, continue to evaluate the situation as you approach.

Pay particular attention to the:

- Location of the emergency

- Extent of the emergency

- Apparent scene dangers

- Apparent number of ill or injured people

- Behaviour of the person/people and bystanders

If at any time the scene appears unsafe, retreat to a safe distance. Notify additional personnel and wait for their arrival. Never enter a dangerous scene unless you have the training and equipment to do so safely. Well-meaning responders have been injured or killed because they forgot to look for scene hazards. If your training has not prepared you for a specific emergency, such as a fire or an incident involving hazardous materials, notify appropriately trained personnel.

When arriving on an emergency scene, always follow these four guidelines to ensure your personal safety and that of anyone else at the scene:

- Take time to evaluate the scene. This will enable you to recognize existing and potential dangers.

- Wear appropriate protective equipment.

- Perform only the skills you are trained to do. Know what resources are available to help.

- Get the help you need. If you have not already done so, notify additional personnel. Be able to describe the scene and the type of additional help required.

TABLE 2-1 POTENTIAL HAZARDS AT AN EMERGENCY SCENE

• Pets (or other animals)	• Debris	• Weather
• Weapons	• Confined spaces	• Ice
• Low lighting	• Pathogens	• Terrain
• Furniture scattered about	• People	• Hazardous materials
• Blocked or cluttered exits	• Unstable/unsafe structures	• Downed electrical lines
• Loud noise	• Fire	• Low-oxygen
• Traffic	• Water	• Sharp glass or metal

Safety of Others

You have a responsibility for the safety of others at the scene, as well as for your personal safety. Discourage bystanders, family members, or unprepared responders from entering an area that appears unsafe. You can use these well-intentioned individuals to help you keep unauthorized people away from unsafe areas and to summon more appropriate help. Some dangers may require you to take special measures, such as placing physical barriers to prevent onlookers from getting too close. Other situations may require you to act quickly to free someone who is trapped or move an ill or injured person in immediate danger to safety.

Ideally, you should move people only after you have assessed and properly cared for them. If, however, immediate dangers threaten their life, you must decide whether to move them. If the situation is dangerous and you cannot move them, retreat to safety yourself. If you can move them, do so quickly and safely.

Situations that may require an emergency move include:

- The presence of dangerous or hazardous materials or situations

- Moving a person with more minor injuries to reach someone who may have a life-threatening condition

- Moving a person to provide appropriate care

Chapter 21 provides more detailed information about how to move injured or ill people safely.

Specific Emergency Situations

Certain emergency scenes present a special set of problems. These situations include crime scenes, scenes with hazards, and scenes with multiple injured people.

Since every emergency scene has potential dangers, always expect the unexpected. Never attempt a rescue for which you are not properly trained and equipped. Always wear appropriate protective gear, such as gloves and goggles. Be aware that at any time even a seemingly safe emergency scene can turn dangerous. Always take the necessary precautions when you suspect or identify certain dangers. Several of the following situations are also discussed in Chapters 21 and 22.

Crime Scene

If you arrive at the scene of a crime or potential suicide, do not try to reach any ill or injured person until you are sure the scene is safe. A person who has been shot, stabbed, or beaten may have severe injuries, but until the scene is safe, there is nothing you can do to provide care. For the scene to be safe, law enforcement personnel must have made it secure.

Police usually gather evidence at a crime scene, so do not touch anything except what you must to give care. Use one path of entrance and exit. Your duty is to the ill or injured person; provide necessary care and then vacate the crime scene area. Once you enter a crime scene to give care, make sure that police are aware of your presence and actions. Document what you did, moved, and touched.

If you happen to be on the scene when an unarmed person threatens suicide, try to reassure and calm the person. Make sure that appropriate personnel have been notified. You cannot physically restrain a suicidal person without medical or legal authorization. Listen to her and try to keep her talking until help arrives. Try to be understanding. Many suicide attempts are a call for help. Do not dare the person to act or trivialize her feelings. Unless your personal safety is threatened, never leave a suicidal person alone.

Drug Labs

Drug labs are places where people illegally manufacture drugs. Clues such as the possession of chemical glassware, or unusual chemicals, by someone not working in the chemical field may indicate the presence of a drug lab.

Specific dangers in illegal drug lab situations are:

- Booby traps

- Electrical hazards

- Fire and explosion hazards

- Air quality, due to moulds or chemical reactions

- Biohazards

- General existence of large volumes of potentially hazardous materials

Wait until trained personnel arrive; this is an unsafe environment.

Traffic

Traffic is often the most common danger you and other emergency personnel will encounter. If you drive to the collision scene, always try to park where your vehicle will not block other traffic, such as an emergency vehicle that needs to reach the scene. The only time you should park in a roadway or block traffic is to:

- Protect an injured person.

- Protect any responders, including yourself.

- Warn oncoming traffic if the situation is not clearly visible.

Others can help you put reflectors, flares, or lights along the road. These items should be placed well back of the scene to enable oncoming motorists to stop or slow down in time.

Emergency personnel have been injured or killed by traffic at emergency scenes. If you are not a law enforcement officer and dangerous traffic makes the scene unsafe, wait for more help to arrive before giving care.

Fire

Any fire can be dangerous. Make sure that the local fire department has been summoned. Only fire fighters, who are highly trained and use equipment that protects them against fire and smoke, should approach a fire. Do not let others approach. Gather information to help the responding fire and EMS units. Give this information to emergency personnel when they arrive. If you are not trained to fight fires or lack the necessary equipment, follow these basic guidelines:

- Stay away from a burning vehicle.

- Never enter a burning or smoke-filled building.

- If you are in a building that is on fire, always check doors before opening them. If a door is hot to the touch, do not open it.

- Since smoke and fumes rise, stay close to the floor and put a moist cloth over your mouth and nose.

- Never use an elevator in a building that may be burning.

Electricity

Downed electrical lines also present a major hazard to responders. Always look for downed wires at a scene and always treat them as dangerous. If you find downed wires, follow these guidelines:

- Move any crowd back from the danger zone. The safe area should be established at a point twice the length of the span of the wire.

- Never attempt to move downed wires.

- Notify the fire department and power company immediately. Always assume that the wires are energized.

- If downed wires contact a vehicle, do not touch the vehicle and do not let others touch it. Tell anyone in the vehicle to stay still and stay inside the vehicle. Never attempt to remove people from a vehicle with downed wires across it, no matter how seriously injured they may seem.

- Do not touch any metal fence, metal structure, or body of water in contact with a downed wire. Wait for the power company to shut off the power source.

Water and Ice

Water and ice can also be serious hazards. To help a conscious person in the water, reach out to her with a branch, a pole, or even your hand, being careful not to be pulled into the water. When the person grasps the object, pull her to safety.

If you cannot reach the person, try to throw her something nearby that floats. If you have a rope available, attach a floatable object, such as a life jacket, plastic jug, ice chest, or empty gas can, to one end. Never enter a body of water to rescue someone unless you have been trained in water rescue and then enter only as a last resort.

Fast-moving water is extremely dangerous and often occurs with floods, hurricanes, and low-head dams. Ice is also treacherous. It can break under your weight, and the cold water beneath can quickly overcome even the best swimmers. Never enter fast-moving water or venture out on ice unless you are trained in this type of rescue. Such rescues require careful planning and proper equipment. Wait until trained personnel arrive.

Figure 2–2 Hazardous material placard.

Hazardous Materials

Hazardous materials are common and are a special risk for responding personnel. When you approach an emergency scene, look for clues that indicate the presence of hazardous materials. These include:

- Signs (placards) on vehicles, storage facilities, or railroad cars identifying the presence of hazardous materials

- Clouds of vapour

- Spilled liquids or solids

- Unusual odours

- Leaking containers, bottles, or gas cylinders

- Chemical transport tanks or containers

Those who transport or store hazardous materials in specific quantities are required to post placards identifying the specific hazardous material, by name or by number, and its dangers (Figure 2–2). This information is available from various reference materials. If you do not see a placard but suspect that a hazardous material is present, try to get information before you approach the scene.

Unsafe Structures

Buildings and other structures, such as mines, wells, and unreinforced trenches, can become unsafe because of fire, explosions, natural disasters, deterioration, or other causes. An unsafe building or structure is one in which:

- The air may contain debris or hazardous gases

- There is a possibility of being trapped or injured by collapsed walls, weakened floors, and other debris

Try to establish the exact or probable location of anyone in the structure. Gather as much information as you can, call for appropriate help, and wait for the arrival of properly trained and equipped personnel.

Wreckage

The wreckage of automobiles, aircraft, or machinery may contain hazards such as sharp pieces of metal or glass, fuel, and moving parts. The wreckage may be unstable. Do not try to rescue someone from wreckage unless you have the proper equipment and training. Rescue is made only after the wreckage has been stabilized. Gather as much information as you can and be sure that advanced medical personnel have been called.

Natural Disasters

Natural disasters include tornadoes, hurricanes, earthquakes, forest fires, ice storms, and floods (Figure 2–3). Rescue efforts after a natural disaster are usually coordinated by local resources until they become overwhelmed. Then the rescue efforts are coordinated by government agencies. Typically, you would report to the person or people in charge at the scene and then work with the disaster response team and follow the rescue plan.

Figure 2–3 A natural disaster.

Natural disasters pose more risks than you might be aware of. A large number of injuries and deaths result from electricity, hazardous materials, rising water, and other dangers as opposed to the disaster itself. When responding to a natural disaster, be sure to carefully survey the scene, avoid obvious hazards, and use caution when operating rescue equipment. Never use gasoline-powered equipment, such as chain saws, generators, and pumps, in confined spaces.

Multiple People Injured

Scenes that involve more than one person are referred to as multiple casualty incidents. Such scenes make your task more complex since you must determine who needs immediate care and who can wait for more help to arrive. To make these decisions, you use a process called triage that helps you prioritize the care you give to the people involved.

A large multiple casualty incident, such as a plane or train crash or natural disaster, may overwhelm the capabilities of the local EMS system. To effectively handle any emergency involving multiple people, EMS uses an incident command system (ICS). An ICS establishes a chain of command at the scene that permits one person to direct all the agencies helping. For example, when police, fire, and ambulance personnel are called to a major urban fire, the fire chief takes charge and all other resources report to her. These resources may include police evacuating nearby buildings, fire fighters fighting the blaze, and ambulance personnel providing emergency care and transportation for injured people. In this way, all available resources will be used effectively and efficiently.

Hostile Situations

Environmental factors, such as hazardous materials, electricity, and unsafe structures, are not the only dangers you may encounter. You may sometimes encounter a hostile ill or injured person or family member. Any unusual or hostile behaviour may be a result of the emergency. A person's rage or hostility may be caused by the injury or illness or by fear. Many ill or injured people are afraid of losing control and may show this as anger. Hostile behaviour may also result from the use of alcohol or other drugs, lack of oxygen, or an underlying medical condition.

If a person needing care is hostile toward you, try to explain calmly who you are and that you are there to help. Remember that you cannot give care without the person's consent. If the person accepts your offer to help, keep talking to her as you assess her condition. When she realizes that you are not a threat, the hostility usually goes away.

If the person refuses your care or threatens you, withdraw from the scene. Never try to restrain, argue with, or force your care on a person. If she does not let you provide care, wait for additional help. Sometimes a close friend or a family member will be able to reassure a hostile person and convince her to accept your care.

Family members or friends who are angry or hysterical, however, can make your job more difficult. Sometimes they may not allow you to provide care. At other times, they may try to move the ill or injured person before you have stabilized her. A terrified parent may cling to a child and refuse to let you help. When family members act this way, they often feel confused, guilty, and frightened. Be understanding and explain the care you are giving. By remaining calm and professional, you will help calm them. Hostile crowds are a threat that can develop when you least expect it. If you decide the crowd at a scene is hostile, wait at a safe distance until law enforcement and other trained personnel arrive. Approach the scene only when police officers declare it safe and ask you to help. Never approach a hostile crowd unless you are trained in crowd management and supported by other trained personnel.

Hostage Situations

If you encounter a hostage situation, your first priority is to not become a hostage yourself. Assess the scene from a safe distance and call for law enforcement personnel. A police officer trained in hostage negotiations should take charge.

Try to get any information from bystanders that may help law enforcement personnel. Ask about the number of hostages, any weapons seen, and other possible hazards. Report any information to the first law enforcement official on the scene. Remain at a safe distance until law enforcement personnel summon you.

SUMMARY

Emergency scenes by their nature can be dangerous, so never approach a scene until you are sure it is safe. Your personal safety is always your first concern. Potential hazards at emergency scenes include traffic, fire, electricity, water, ice, and unsafe structures. Other dangers include ill or injured people or family members who are violent or hostile or hostile crowds.

If you have any doubt about the safety of a scene or if you are not trained and equipped to handle the situation, stay back. Be sure that appropriate help has been called and wait for properly trained and equipped personnel.

Once you are sure the scene is safe, you will be expected to provide care to ill or injured people. Information on how the human body normally functions, which you will learn in Chapter 4, will help you assess an ill or injured person's condition and provide the appropriate emergency care.

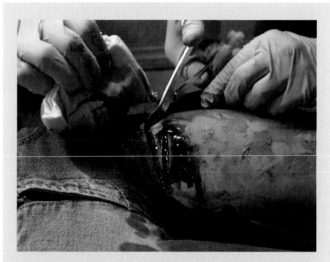

You are treating a wound that is spurting blood uncontrollably. There is a crowd of workers gathered around trying to see what is going on. There is blood and blood-soaked dressings all over the floor. What do you do?

Chapter 3

Preventing Disease Transmission

A woman has collapsed in her office. As the first trained person on the scene, you find her bleeding from the mouth. Vomit and blood are around her. She is not breathing. What do you do?

INTRODUCTION

It is not unusual to be faced with a situation in which you are concerned about disease transmission. You may encounter such concerns during everyday tasks you carry out within your job or other activities. It is important to understand how infections occur, how they are passed from one person to another, and what you can do to protect yourself and others from disease.

The types of diseases that can be contracted from other people, objects, animals, or insects are referred to as infectious diseases. Some of these infectious diseases can be transmitted more easily than others. During this course, you will learn how to recognize situations with the potential for disease transmission and how to protect yourself and others from contracting disease.

HOW INFECTIONS OCCUR

Disease-Causing Pathogens

The disease process begins when a pathogen gets into the body. When pathogens enter the body, they can sometimes overpower the body's defence systems and cause illness. This illness is an infection. Most infectious diseases are caused by one of the six types of pathogens identified in Table 3-1. The most common pathogens are bacteria and viruses.

Bacteria are everywhere. They do not depend on other organisms for life and can live outside the human body. Most bacteria do not infect humans. Those that do may cause serious illness. Meningitis, scarlet fever, and tetanus are examples of disease caused by bacteria.

TABLE 3-1 DISEASE-CAUSING PATHOGENS

Pathogen	Definition	Condition They Cause
Viruses	A disease-causing agent that requires another organism in order to live and reproduce	Hepatitis, measles, mumps, chicken pox, meningitis, rubella, influenza, warts, colds, herpes, shingles, HIV infection including AIDS, genital warts
Bacteria	Single-celled microorganism that may cause infection	Tetanus, meningitis, scarlet fever, strep throat, tuberculosis, gonorrhea, syphilis, chlamydia, toxic shock syndrome, legionnaires' disease, diphtheria, food poisoning
Fungi	A single-celled or multicellular organism	Athlete's foot and ringworm
Protozoa	A single-celled organism that can only divide within a host organism	Malaria and dysentery
Rickettsia	A group of microorganisms (like viruses) that require other living cells for growth but (like bacteria) use oxygen, have metabolic enzymes and cell walls, and are susceptible to antibiotics	Typhus, Rocky Mountain spotted fever
Parasitic worms	A worm classified as a parasite, which is a disease-causing organism that lives on or in a human or other animal and derives its nourishment from its host	Abdominal pain, anemia, lymphatic vessel blockage, lowered antibody response, respiratory and circulatory complications

The body has difficulty fighting infections caused by bacteria. Doctors may prescribe medications called antibiotics that either kill the bacteria or weaken them enough for the body to get rid of them.

Unlike bacteria, viruses depend on other organisms to live and reproduce. Viruses cause many diseases, including the common cold. Once they become established within the body, they are difficult to eliminate because very few medications are effective against them. Antibiotics do not kill or weaken viruses. The body's immune system is the main defence against them.

The Body's Natural Defences

The body's immune system is very good at fighting disease. Its basic tools are the white blood cells. Special white blood cells travel around the body and identify invading pathogens. Once they detect a pathogen, these white blood cells gather around it and release antibodies that fight infections.

These antibodies attack the pathogen and weaken or destroy it. Antibodies can usually get rid of pathogens; however, some pathogens can thrive and, under ideal conditions, overwhelm the immune system. To minimize

this possibility, the body depends on the skin for protection to keep pathogens out.

This combination of trying to keep pathogens out of the body and destroying them once they get inside is necessary for good health. Sometimes the body cannot fight off infection. When this occurs, an invading pathogen can become established in the body, causing serious infection. Fever and exhaustion often signal that the body is fighting an infection. Other common signals include headache, nausea, and vomiting.

How Diseases Are Transmitted

You need to understand these four conditions to understand how infections occur. Think of these conditions as the pieces of a puzzle. All the pieces have to be in place for the picture to be complete (Figure 3–1). If any one of these conditions is missing, an infection cannot occur:

1. A pathogen is present
2. There is enough of the pathogen to cause disease
3. A person is susceptible to the pathogen
4. There is a route of entry

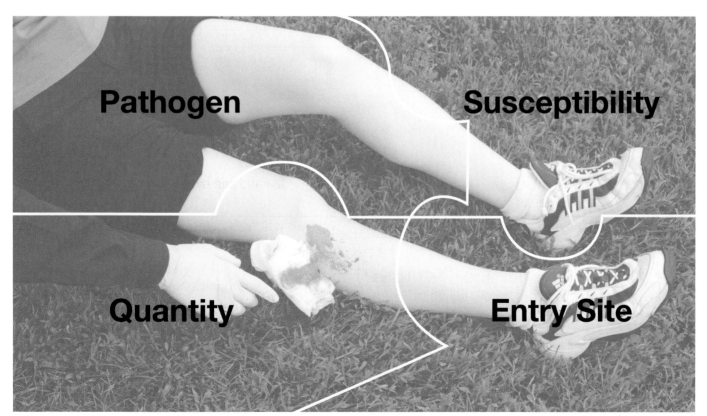

Figure 3–1 For an infection to occur, all four conditions must be present.

TABLE 3-2 HOW DISEASES ARE TRANSMITTED

Mode of Transmission	Example of Disease	Definition	Route of Entry	Signs and Symptoms
Direct contact	Herpes	Family of viruses; infection with one of the human herpes viruses, especially herpes simplex types 1 and 2	Broken skin, mucous membranes	Lesions, general ill feeling, sore throat
Airborne, direct, and indirect contact	Meningitis	Inflammation of the membranes that envelop the central nervous system (meninges), usually due to a bacterial infection but sometimes from viral, protozoan, or other causes	Food and water, mucus	Respiratory illness, sore throat, nausea, vomiting
Airborne, direct, and indirect contact	Tuberculosis	A highly contagious infection caused by the bacterium *Mycobacterium tuberculosis*	Mucus, broken skin	Weight loss, night sweats, occasional fever, general ill feeling
Direct and indirect contact	Hepatitis	Inflammation of the liver from any cause; most often viral due to infection with one of the hepatitis viruses (A, B, C, D, and E) or another virus	Blood, saliva, semen, feces, food, water, other products	Flu-like, jaundice
Direct and indirect contact	HIV/AIDS	Disease due to infection with the human immunodeficiency virus (HIV)	Blood, semen, vaginal fluid	Fever, night sweats, weight loss, chronic diarrhea, severe fatigue, shortness of breath, swollen lymph nodes, lesions

Pathogens enter the body in four ways (Table 3-2):

1. *Direct contact*

   Direct contact transmission (Figure 3–2) occurs when a person touches body fluids from an infected person.

2. *Indirect contact*

   Indirect contact transmission (Figure 3–3) occurs when a person touches objects that have touched the blood or another body fluid, such as saliva and vomit, of an infected person. These include soiled dressings, equipment, and work surfaces with which an infected person comes in contact. Sharp objects present a particular risk. If sharp objects have contacted the blood or body fluids of an infected person and are handled carelessly, they can pierce the skin and transmit infection.

3. *Airborne*

Airborne transmission (Figure 3–4) occurs when a person breathes in droplets that become airborne when an infected person coughs or sneezes. Exposure to these droplets is generally too brief for transmission to take place; however, it may if a person is coughing heavily.

4. *Vector-borne*

Vector-borne transmission (Figure 3–5) occurs when an animal, such as a dog or raccoon, or an insect, such as a tick, transmits a pathogen into the body through a bite. A bite from an infected human is also a vector-borne transmission. The carrier is a vector and passes the infection to another animal or person. Rabies and Lyme disease are transmitted this way.

Immunization

Most people receive immunization as babies against common childhood diseases such as measles and mumps. Immunization is the introduction of a substance that contains specific weakened or killed pathogens into the body. The body's immune system then builds resistance to a specific infection.

You should also be immunized against several other diseases. The following immunizations are recommended:

- DPT (diphtheria, pertussis, tetanus)
- Polio
- Hepatitis B
- MMR (measles, mumps, rubella)
- Influenza
- Chicken pox

You might not have been immunized against some of the childhood diseases. If you are not sure about which immunizations you have received or may need to update, contact your doctor or local community health nurse.

Figure 3–2 Direct contact transmission.

Figure 3–3 Indirect contact transmission.

Figure 3–4 Airborne transmission.

Figure 3–5 Vector-borne transmission.

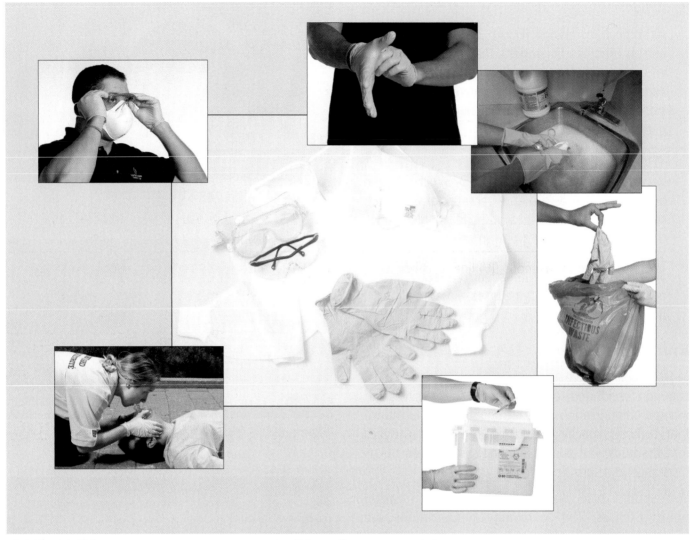

Figure 3–6 There are many ways to protect yourself from disease transmission.

PROTECTING YOURSELF FROM DISEASE TRANSMISSION

Precautions

Sometimes we might like to vary the level of protection we use based on what a person looks like, the circumstances surrounding the incident, or where he is at the time of the incident. However, the world is not that simple. Often you will not know the health status of the people you work with or care for. The one time you stop being careful may be the very time that you become infected. Each time you prepare to provide care, you must follow basic precautions, which include the following:

- Protective clothing and equipment (Figure 3–6)
- Personal hygiene
- Engineering and work practice controls
- Equipment cleaning and disinfecting

Protective clothing and equipment should be used to prevent skin and mucous membrane exposure when contact with blood or other body fluids is anticipated (Table 3-3). Protective equipment keeps you from direct contact with infected materials and includes disposable gloves, gowns, masks and shields, protective eyewear, and mouthpieces and resuscitation devices. To minimize your risk of contracting or transmitting an infectious disease, follow these universal precautions:

TABLE 3-3 RECOMMENDED PROTECTIVE EQUIPMENT FOR PRE-HOSPITAL SETTINGS

Task or Activity	Disposable Gloves	Gown	Mask	Protective Eyewear
Bleeding control with spurting blood	Yes	Yes	Yes	Yes
Bleeding control with minimal bleeding	Yes	No	No	No
Childbirth	Yes	Yes	Yes, if splash is likely	Yes, if splash is likely
Helping with an intravenous (IV) line	Yes	No	No	No
Oral/nasal suctioning, manually clearing airway	Yes	No	Yes	Yes, if splash is likely
Handling and cleaning contaminated equipment and clothing if body fluids are present	Yes	No, unless soiling is likely	No, unless cleaning after transporting a person with transmissible respiratory illness	No, unless gross amounts of bodily fluid are present
Transporting or caring for a person with signs of transmissible respiratory illness	Yes	No	Yes	Yes

Adapted from the Emergency Health Services Branch of the Ministry of Health and Long-Term Care (Ontario Government): Infection Prevention and Control - Best Practices Manual for Land Ambulance Paramedics. March 2007.

Protective Clothing and Equipment

- Handle all blood and other body fluids as if infectious.

- Handle all people in a way that minimizes exposure to blood and other body fluids.

- Wear disposable (single-use) gloves when it is possible you will contact blood or body fluids. This may happen directly through contact with an ill or injured person or indirectly through contact with soiled clothing or other personal articles.

- Remove gloves by turning them inside out, beginning at the wrist and peeling them off. When removing the second glove, do not touch the soiled surfaces with your bare hand. Hook the inside of the second glove at the wrist and peel the glove off (Figure 3–7, a-c).

- Discard gloves that are peeling, discoloured, torn, or punctured.

- Do not clean or reuse disposable gloves.

- Avoid handling items such as pens, combs, or radios, yours or another person's, when wearing soiled gloves.

- Change gloves for each person you contact.

- Wear protective coverings, such as a mask, eye-wear, and a gown, whenever you are likely to contact blood or other body fluids that may splash.

- Cover any cuts, scrapes, or skin irritations you may have with protective clothing or bandages.

- Use breathing devices, such as resuscitation masks with one-way valves. These should be readily available in settings where the need for resuscitation can be anticipated.

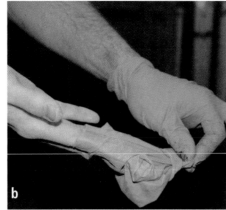
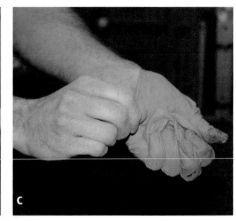

Figure 3–7, a-c Glove removal.

Personal Hygiene

Personal hygiene habits, such as frequent hand-washing (Figure 3–8, a-f), are as important in preventing infection as any equipment you might use. These habits and practices can prevent any materials that might have gone through the protective equipment from staying in contact with your body.

Engineering and Work Practice Controls

Engineering controls are controls that isolate or remove the hazard from the workplace. These include puncture-resistant containers for sharp equipment and mechanical needle recapping devices. To ensure that they work well, engineering controls should be examined and maintained or replaced on a regular basis.

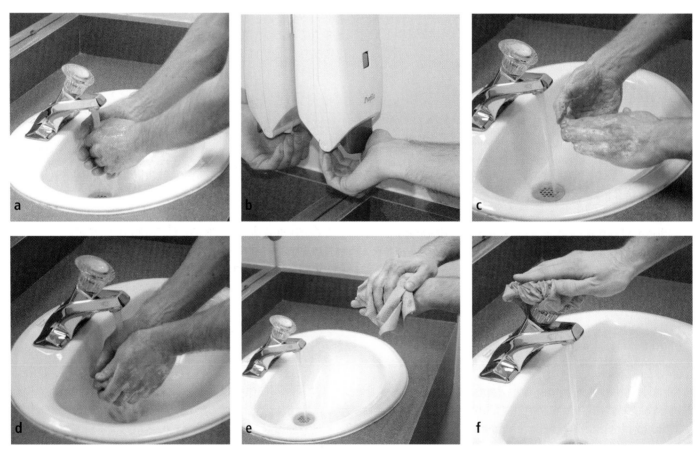

Figure 3–8, a-f Thoroughly, and properly, washing your hands helps protect you against disease transmission.

Work practice controls reduce the likelihood of exposure by changing the way a task is carried out. The protection provided by work practice controls is based on the way people behave rather than on a physical device.

Engineering controls and work practice controls are established to ensure good industrial hygiene. Following certain guidelines for engineering controls and work practice controls can greatly cut down your risk of contracting or transmitting an infectious disease.

- Ensure that all response kits are fully stocked with several pairs of disposable gloves, pocket masks or face shields, and antibacterial hand cleanser.

- Ensure that response kits are readily available and easily accessible to everyone.

- Maintain all protective equipment in good working order. Immediately dispose of any protective equipment that is peeling, discoloured, torn, or punctured.

- Check and restock response kits on a regular basis.

- Use dressings and tissues to minimize direct contact with blood, other body fluids, and wounds. If possible, have the ill or injured person wash the wound first and assist you, for example, holding a dressing in place or applying pressure if necessary.

- Avoid needle-stick injuries by not trying to bend or recap any needles.

- If a procedure requires the recapping of a needle, use mechanical devices or one-handed techniques to recap or remove contaminated needles.

- Place sharp items (e.g., needles, scalpel blades) in puncture-resistant, leak-proof, labelled containers.

- Perform all procedures in a way that cuts down on splashing, spraying, splattering, and producing droplets of blood or other potentially infectious materials.

- Remove soiled protective clothing as soon as possible.

- Avoid eating, drinking, smoking, applying cosmetics or lip balm, handling contact lenses, and touching your mouth, nose, or eyes in work areas where exposure to infectious materials may occur.

- Handle all soiled equipment, supplies, or other materials with great care until they are properly cleaned and disinfected. Place all contaminated disposable items in labelled containers. Place all soiled clothing in properly marked plastic bags for disposal or washing.

- Wash your hands thoroughly with soap and water immediately after providing care. Use a utility or restroom sink, not one in a food preparation area.

- If something occurs that creates disposable waste or soiled laundry, the materials should be stored in appropriate containers until they are disposed of or laundered. The containers must have warning labels or signs, such as "biohazard," to eliminate or minimize exposure of individuals. In addition, training should be provided to ensure that everyone understands and avoids the hazard.

Equipment Cleaning and Disinfecting

- Clean and disinfect equipment and work surfaces possibly soiled by blood or other body fluids to prevent infections.

- For cleaning equipment and surfaces, gloves should be worn.

- Surfaces such as floors, woodwork, vehicle seats, and countertops must be cleaned with soap and water first, using disposable towels, and then disinfected. To disinfect equipment soiled with blood or body fluids, wash thoroughly with a solution of common household chlorine bleach and water. Each EMS system may have protocols and solution ratios for various decontamination techniques. Many decontaminating solutions are available. Follow the directions on the label.

- Wash and dry protective clothing and work uniforms according to the manufacturer's instructions. Scrub soiled boots, leather shoes, and other leather goods, such as belts, with soap, a brush, and hot water.

- Work areas should be kept in a clean and sanitary condition based on a written schedule for cleaning and decontamination. The schedule should be based on the location in the facility, the type of surface to be cleaned, the type of soil present, and the tasks or procedures being done.

Spill Management

In addition, there should be a plan in place to deal with any spill that might occur. The plan should include a system to report a spill and the action taken to resolve the spill. It should also include a list of people responsible for containment, instructions for cleanup, and the final disposition of the spill. The first step in dealing with a spill is containment. Spill containment units designed for hazardous materials are available for purchase. However, any absorbent material, such as paper towels, can be used if the material is disposed of properly.

The steps for spill management are as follows:

• Wear gloves and other appropriate personal protective equipment when cleaning spills.

• Clean up spills immediately or as soon as possible after the spill occurs.

• If the spill is mixed with sharp objects, such as broken glass and needles, do not pick these up with your hands. Use tongs, a broom and a dust pan, or two pieces of cardboard.

• Dispose of the absorbent material used to collect the spill in a labelled biohazard container.

• Flood the area with disinfectant solution and allow it to stand for at least 20 minutes.

• Use paper towels to absorb the solution and put the towels in the biohazard container.

Following these precautions will usually remove at least one of the four conditions necessary for disease transmission. Remember, if only one condition is missing, infection will not occur.

The Exposure Control Plan

Preventing infectious disease transmission begins with preparation and planning. An exposure control plan is an important step in removing or reducing exposure to blood and other possibly infectious materials. The exposure control plan is a system to protect people in a given environment from infection and should be placed where it can easily be used. The plan should be updated each year or more often if changes in exposure occur.

An exposure control plan should contain the following elements:

• Exposure determination

• Identification of who will receive training, protective equipment, and vaccination

• Procedures for evaluating details of an exposure incident

Exposure determination is one of the key elements of an exposure control plan. It includes identifying and making a written record of tasks in which exposure to blood or other body fluids can occur.

The following Health Canada recommendations for healthcare providers can be applied to individuals at risk in any environment:

• There should be initial orientation and continuing education on modes of transmission and prevention of infections and the need for routine use of personal protective equipment for all people.

• Equipment and supplies necessary to minimize the risk of infection with pathogens should be provided.

• Adherence to recommended protective measures should be monitored. When monitoring reveals a failure to follow recommended precautions, counselling, education, or retraining should be provided.

• Health Canada also recommends that particular vaccinations, such as hepatitis B, be offered to all susceptible healthcare providers, particularly those who work in high-risk areas.

• The exposure control plan should include reporting procedures for any first aid incidents. The procedures must ensure that incidents are reported before the end of the shift in which they occur.

• Reports of first aid incidents should include the names of all responders involved and the details of the incident. The report should also include the date and time of the incident and if an exposure incident has occurred.

• Exposure reports should be included on lists of first aid incidents.

• Responders should be trained in reporting procedure specifics.

IF AN EXPOSURE OCCURS

If you suspect you have been exposed to an infectious disease, wash any area of contact as quickly as possible and write down what happened. Exposures usually involve contact with potentially infectious blood or other fluids through a needle stick, broken or scraped skin, or the mucous membranes of the eyes, nose, or mouth. Inhaling potentially infected airborne droplets also may be an exposure. Most organizations have protocols (standardized procedures) for reporting infectious disease exposure. Be aware of provincial/ territorial Occupational Health and Safety guidelines and Workers' Compensation guidelines.

The procedures should include the following elements:

- Be easy to access and user-friendly

- Ensure confidentiality

- Instill confidence in the exposed worker

- List events covered by the procedure

- List immediate actions to be taken by the exposed individual to reduce the chances of infection

- Provide direction on when or how quickly the individual should report the exposure incident

- Provide direction on where and to whom the individual should report the exposure incident

- Indicate which forms the individual should complete

- Provide directions for investigating the incident

- List information required from healthcare providers

- Indicate medical follow-up, including post-exposure vaccination

If you think you have been exposed to an infectious disease, you should report the exposure immediately. A test may be done to see if the infection was present. Even before a disease is confirmed, you should receive medical evaluation, counselling, and post-exposure care. Your medical personnel or supervisor is responsible for notifying any other personnel who might have been exposed. If your system does not have a designated physician or nurse at a local hospital for follow-up care, see your personal physician.

SUMMARY

Although the body's natural defence system defends well against disease, pathogens can still enter the body and sometimes cause infection. These pathogens can be transmitted in four ways:

- By direct contact with an infected person

- By indirect contact with a soiled object

- By inhaling air exhaled by an infected person

- By vector-borne contact, through a bite from an infected animal, insect, or even a person

Infectious diseases that you should be aware of include hepatitis, herpes, meningitis, tuberculosis, and HIV infections. You should know how the diseases are transmitted and take appropriate measures to protect yourself from them. Remember that all four conditions of infection must be present for a disease to be transmitted:

1. A pathogen is present

2. There is enough of the pathogen to cause disease

3. A person is susceptible to the pathogen

4. There is an entry route

One of the best defences against disease and infection is to wash your hands frequently. It has been determined that individuals face a significant risk as a result of exposure to blood and other potentially infectious materials because they may contain blood-borne pathogens. This hazard can be reduced or removed using a combination of engineering and work practice controls, personal protective clothing and equipment, training, medical surveillance, vaccinations, signs and labels, and other provisions.

Organizations have responsibilities that include:

- Identifying positions or tasks potentially at risk

- Developing an annual training system for all at-risk individuals

- Offering the opportunity for individuals to get counselling and medical care, such as hepatitis vaccinations, at no cost

- Using work practices, such as following universal and other precautions to minimize the possibility of infection

- Using engineering controls, such as puncture-resistant containers for sharp objects, to minimize the possibility of infection

- Creating a system for easy identification of soiled material and its disposal

- Creating an exposure control plan to minimize the possibility of exposure

- Establishing clear procedures to follow for reporting an exposure

- Creating a system of record keeping that includes updates in protocols and exposure control plans, training, medical records, and follow-up

Following these guidelines, especially the precautions, greatly decreases your risk of contracting or transmitting an infectious disease. If you suspect you have been exposed to such a disease, always document it and notify appropriate personnel. Seek medical help and participate in any follow-up procedures.

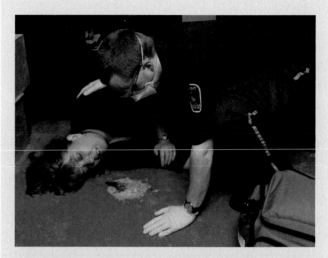

You approach the woman lying on the floor in her office. You see that her nose is bloody and blood is coming out of her mouth. The man who found her is visibly upset and asks you if you're going to be able to save her life. What do you do?

NOTES:

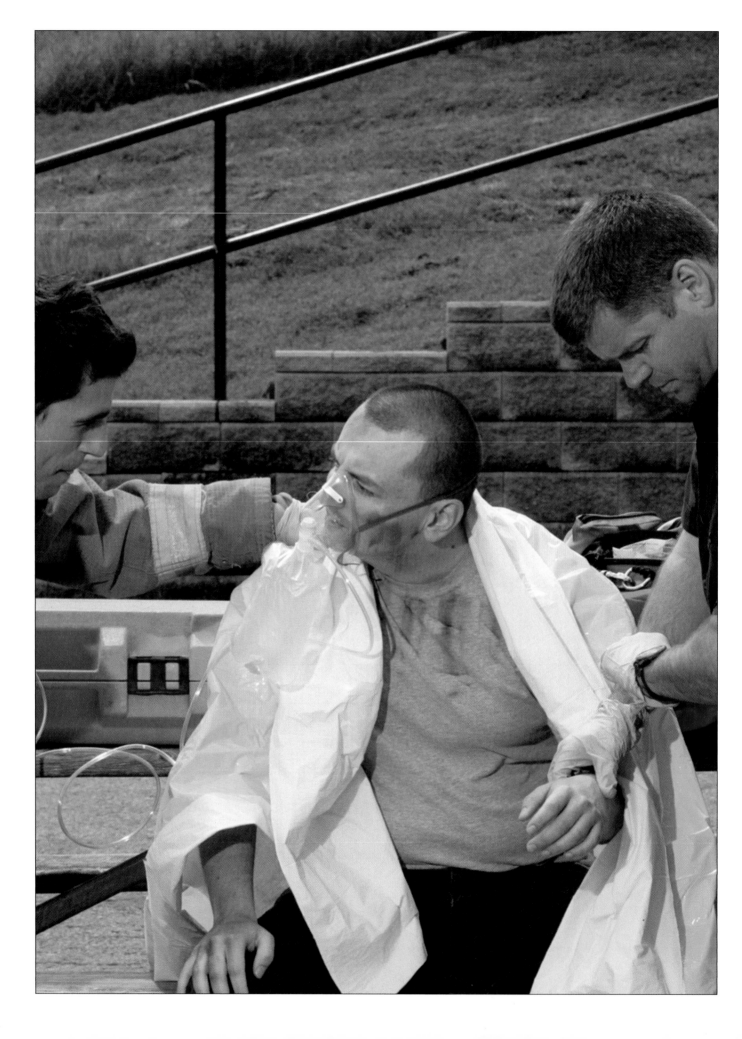

Part *2*

Establishing Priorities of Care

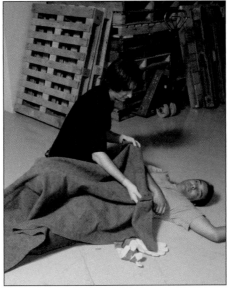
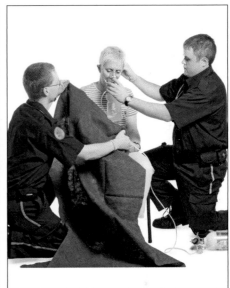

Human Body Systems

You are the responder at the scene of a motor vehicle collision involving a car with two occupants and a van driven by a woman with small children in car seats. At first glance, three people appear to be injured. The first person, a woman, was driving one of the cars, and she is going in and out of consciousness. You suspect her injuries may have crushed some of her ribs. The second person, a passenger in the same car, has injuries on the right side of his body. The third person, the driver of the van, appears to have chest and abdominal injuries, but she is conscious and you can speak to her. She is distraught because her children are in the back of the van and she is concerned about them. How would you describe the injuries and the body systems involved?

INTRODUCTION

As a responder, you need a basic understanding of normal human structure and function. Knowing the body's structures and how they work will help you more easily recognize and understand illnesses and injuries. Body systems do not function independently. Each system depends on other systems to function properly. When your body is healthy, your body systems are working well together. But an injury or illness in one body part or system will often cause problems in others. Knowing the location and function of the major organs and structures within each body system will help you to more accurately assess a person's condition and provide the best care.

To remember the location of body structures, it helps to learn to visualize the structures that lie beneath the skin. The structures you can see or feel are reference points for locating the internal structures you cannot see or feel. For example, to locate the pulse on either side of the neck, you can use the Adam's apple on the front of the neck as a reference point. Using reference points will help you describe the location of injuries and other problems you may find. This chapter provides you with an overview of important reference points, terminology, and the functions of eight body systems.

ANATOMICAL TERMS

You do not need to be an expert in human body structure and function to provide effective care. Neither should you need a medical dictionary to effectively describe an injury. By knowing a few key structures, their functions, and locations, you can recognize a serious illness or injury and accurately communicate with other emergency care personnel about a person's condition.

To use terms that refer to the body, you must first understand "anatomical position." All medical terms that refer to the body are based on the position shown in Figure 4–1, a-c.

The simplest anatomical terms are based on an imaginary line running down the middle of the body from the head to the ground, dividing it into two mirror-image right and left halves. This line is called the midline. In medical terms, right and left always refer to the person in question's right and left, not the responder's.

Other terms related to the midline include lateral and medial. Anything away from the midline is called lateral. Anything toward the midline is called medial.

Another reference line can be drawn through the side of the body, dividing it into front and back halves. Anything toward the front of the body is called anterior; anything toward the back is called posterior.

Other terms that refer to direction can also be useful. When comparing any two structures, such as two body parts, any part toward the person's head is described as superior. Any part toward the person's feet is described as inferior.

Two other terms are generally used when referring to the arms and legs. These terms are proximal and distal. To understand these terms, you must think of the chest, abdomen, and pelvis as those areas that make up the trunk of the body. The arms and legs are the attachments to the trunk. Points on the body closer to the trunk are described as proximal. Points away from the trunk are described as distal.

Figure 4–2 shows other basic terms used for body regions and their specific parts. These are all standard terms used by people who provide emergency care. Some terms will be familiar, whereas others may be new to you. Study these terms and learn to use them correctly when describing body parts.

Special anatomical terms are used for the abdomen, the part of the trunk below the ribs and above the pelvis. By drawing two imaginary lines, one from the breastbone down through the navel to the lowest point in the pelvis and another line horizontally through the navel, you divide the abdomen into four areas called quadrants (Figure 4–3). These terms are important when describing injuries to the abdomen because different organs may be injured depending on the quadrant involved.

Of all these terms, it is most important to correctly use left and right, lateral and medial, and the basic terms that refer to body parts. Even though you may not use the other terms, you should know what they mean. You may need to understand what other emergency care personnel are saying when they use these terms to refer to injuries.

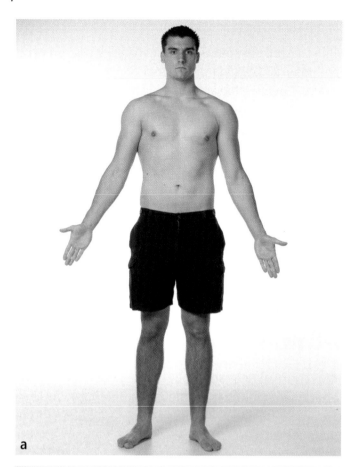

a

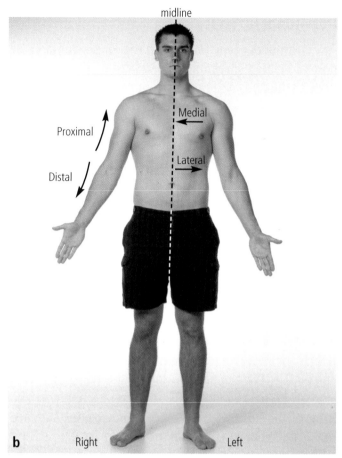

midline

Proximal

Distal

Medial

Lateral

b   Right   Left

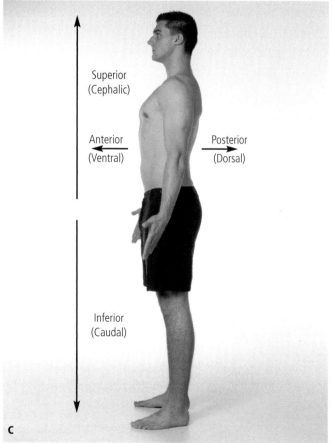

Superior
(Cephalic)

Anterior
(Ventral)

Posterior
(Dorsal)

Inferior
(Caudal)

c

Figure 4–1, a-c a, the anatomical position; **b**, medical use of the terms *right* and *left* refers to the ill or injured person's right and left. *Medial* refers to anything toward the midline; *lateral* refers to anything away from the midline. *Proximal* and *distal* are usually used to refer to extremities; and **c**, *anterior* refers to the front of the body; *posterior* refers to the back of the body; *superior* refers to anything toward the head; *inferior* refers to anything toward the feet.

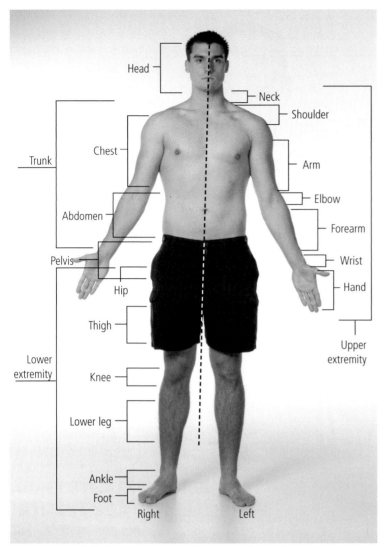

Figure 4–2 It is important to refer correctly to the parts of the body.

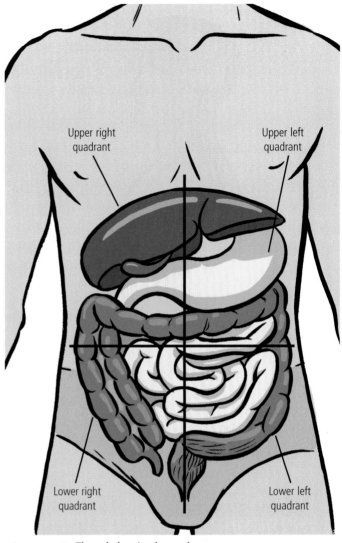

Figure 4–3 The abdominal quadrants.

BODY CAVITIES

A body cavity is a hollow place in the body that contains organs such as the heart, lungs, and liver. The five major cavities, illustrated in Figure 4–4, are the:

- Cranial cavity, located in the head, which is protected by the skull

- Spinal cavity, extending from the bottom of the skull to the lower back, protected by the bones of the spine

- Thoracic cavity, also called chest cavity, which is located in the trunk between the diaphragm and the neck. The thoracic cavity is protected by the rib cage and the upper portion of the spine

- Abdominal cavity, located in the trunk between the diaphragm and the pelvis

- Pelvic cavity, located in the pelvis, which is the lowest part of the trunk. It is protected by the pelvic bones and the lower portion of the spine

Knowing the general location of major organs in each cavity will help you assess a person's injury or illness. The major organs and their functions are more fully described in the next section of this chapter and in later chapters.

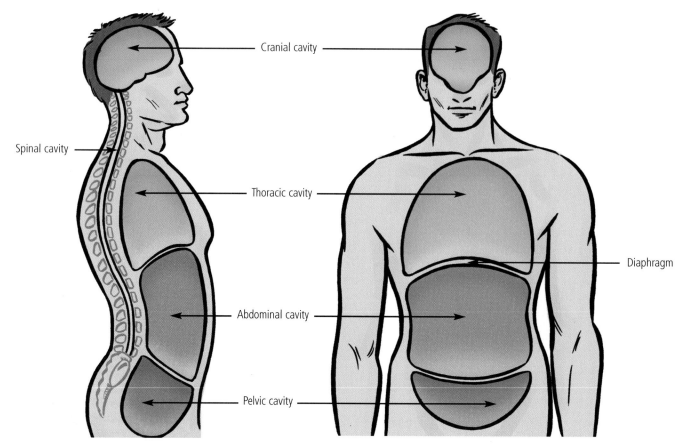

Figure 4–4 The five major cavities of the body.

BODY SYSTEMS

The human body is a miraculous machine. It performs many complex functions, each of which helps us live. Vital organs are organs whose functions are essential for life, such as the brain, heart, and lungs.

A body system is a group of organs and other structures that are especially adapted to perform specific body functions (Table 4-1). They work together to carry out a function needed for life. For example, the heart, blood, and blood vessels make up the circulatory system. The circulatory system keeps all parts of the body supplied with oxygen-rich blood.

For the body to work properly, all of the following systems must work well together:

- Respiratory
- Circulatory
- Nervous
- Musculoskeletal
- Integumentary (the skin, hair, and nails)
- Endocrine
- Digestive
- Genitourinary

TABLE 4-1 BODY SYSTEMS

Systems	Major Structures	Primary Functions	How the System Works With Other Body Systems
Respiratory system	Airway and lungs	Supplies the body with oxygen through breathing	Works with the circulatory system to provide oxygen to cells; is under the control of the nervous system
Circulatory system	Heart, blood, and blood vessels	Transports nutrients and oxygen to body cells and removes waste products	Works with the respiratory system to provide oxygen to cells; works in conjunction with the urinary and digestive systems to remove waste products; helps give skin colour; is under the control of the nervous system
Nervous system	Brain, spinal cord, and nerves	One of two primary regulatory systems in the body; transmits messages to and from the brain	Regulates all body systems through a network of nerves
Musculo-skeletal system	Bones, ligaments, muscles, and tendons	Provides body's framework; protects internal organs and other underlying structures; allows movement; produces heat; manufactures blood components	Provides protection to organs and structures of other body systems; muscle action is controlled by the nervous system
Integumentary system	Skin, hair, and nails	An important part of the body's communication network; helps prevent infection and dehydration; assists with temperature regula-tion; aids in production of certain vitamins	Helps protect the body from disease-producing organisms; together with the circulatory system, helps regulate body temperature under control of the nervous system; communicates sensation to the brain by way of the nerves
Endocrine system	Glands	Secretes hormones and other substances into blood and onto skin	Together with the nervous system, coordinates the activities of other systems
Digestive system	Mouth, esophagus, stomach, intestines	Breaks down food into a usable form to supply the rest of the body with energy	Works with the circulatory system to transport nutrients to the body
Genitourinary system	Uterus and genitalia	Performs the processes of reproduction	
	Kidneys, bladder	Removes wastes from the circulatory system and regulates water balance	

The Cell

The cell is the basic unit of life (Figure 4–5). Energy, DNA, and enzymes are examples of what is created within a human cell. From cells, tissues are formed, which then form organs. Organs are grouped together to form body systems.

Respiratory System

The body must have a constant supply of oxygen to stay alive. The respiratory system supplies the body with oxygen through breathing. When you inhale, air fills the lungs, and the oxygen in the air is transferred to the blood. The blood carries oxygen to all cells of the body. This same system removes carbon dioxide. Carbon dioxide is transferred from the blood to the lungs. When you exhale, air is forced from the lungs, expelling carbon dioxide and other waste gases. This breathing process is called respiration.

The respiratory system includes the airway and lungs. Figure 4–6 shows the parts of the respiratory system. The airway, the passage through which air travels to the lungs, begins at the nose and mouth. The nose and mouth form the upper airway. Air passes through the nose and mouth and through the pharynx (the throat), larynx (the voice box), and trachea (the windpipe) on its way to the lungs (Figure 4–7). The lungs are a pair of organs in the chest that provide the mechanism for taking in oxygen and removing carbon dioxide during breathing. Behind the trachea is the esophagus. The esophagus carries food and liquids from the mouth to the stomach. A small flap of tissue, the epiglottis, covers the trachea when you swallow to keep food and liquids out of the lungs.

Air reaches the lungs through two tubes called bronchi. The bronchi branch into increasingly smaller tubes (Figure 4–8, a). These eventually end in millions of tiny air sacs called alveoli (Figure 4–8, b). Oxygen and carbon dioxide pass into and out of the blood through the thin cell walls of the alveoli and tiny blood vessels called capillaries.

Air enters the lungs when you inhale and leaves the lungs when you exhale. When you inhale, the chest muscles and the diaphragm contract. This expands the chest and draws air into the lungs. When you exhale, the chest muscles and diaphragm relax, allowing air to exit from the lungs (Figure 4–9, a-b). This ongoing breathing process is involuntary and is controlled by the brain.

DID YOU KNOW?

In a lifetime, the air you breathe could fill two balloons the size of the Hindenburg, which held almost 200,000 cubic metres (7 million cubic feet) of gas.

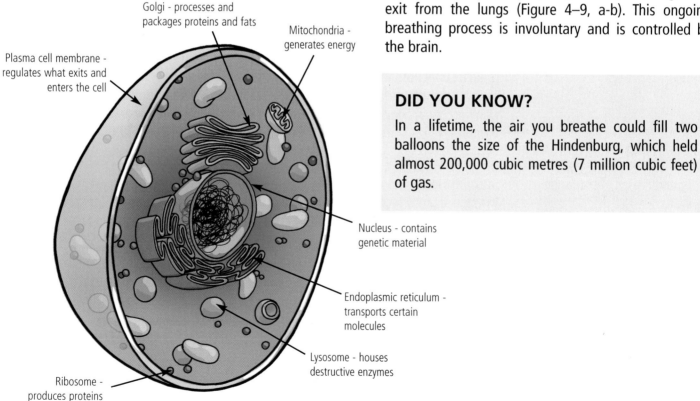

Golgi - processes and packages proteins and fats

Mitochondria - generates energy

Plasma cell membrane - regulates what exits and enters the cell

Nucleus - contains genetic material

Endoplasmic reticulum - transports certain molecules

Lysosome - houses destructive enzymes

Ribosome - produces proteins

Figure 4–5 The basic human cell.

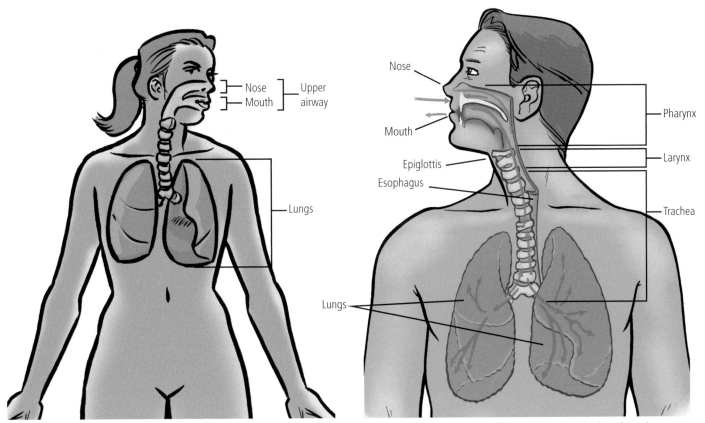

Figure 4–6 The respiratory system.

Figure 4–7 The respiratory system includes the pharynx, larynx, and trachea.

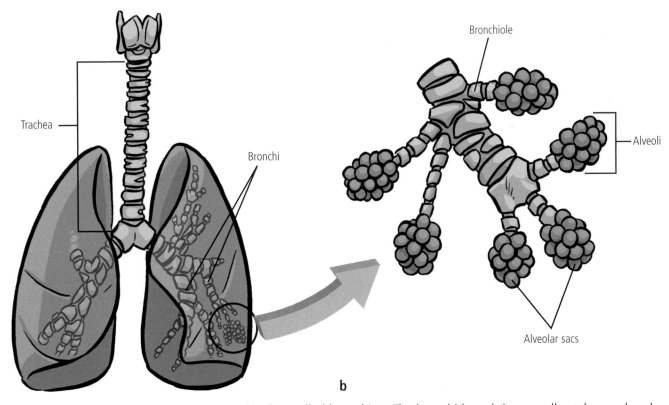

Figure 4–8, a-b **a**, Air reaches the lungs through tubes called bronchi; **b**, The bronchi branch into smaller tubes and end in air sacs called alveoli.

a   b

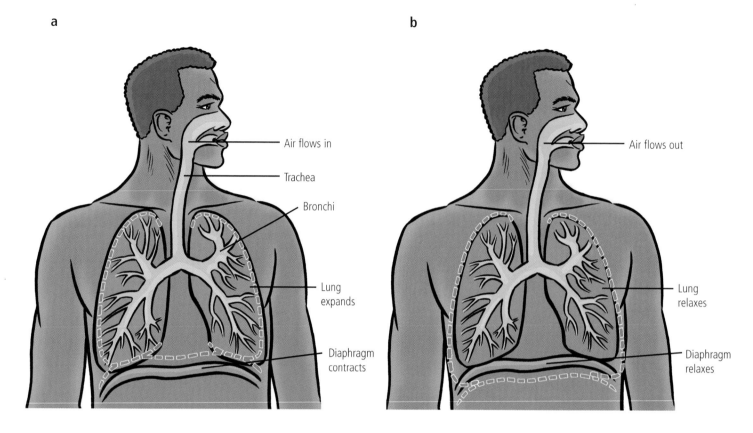

Air flows in

Trachea

Bronchi

Lung expands

Diaphragm contracts

Air flows out

Lung relaxes

Diaphragm relaxes

Figure 4–9, a-b The chest muscles and the diaphragm; **a**, contract as you inhale; and **b**, relax as you exhale.

Circulatory System

The circulatory system works with the respiratory system to carry oxygen to every body cell. It also carries other nutrients throughout the body and removes waste.

The circulatory system includes the heart, blood, and blood vessels. Figure 4–10 shows this system.

The heart is a muscular organ behind the sternum, or breastbone. The heart pumps blood throughout the body through veins and arteries. Arteries are large blood vessels that carry oxygen-rich blood from the heart to the rest of the body. The arteries subdivide into smaller blood vessels and ultimately become tiny capillaries. The capillaries transport blood to all the cells of the body and nourish them with oxygen.

After the oxygen in the blood is transferred to the cells, veins carry the oxygen-poor blood back to the heart. The heart pumps this oxygen-poor blood to the lungs to pick up more oxygen before pumping it to other parts of the body. This cycle is called the circulatory cycle.

The cross-section of the heart in Figure 4–11 shows how blood moves through the heart to complete the circulatory cycle.

The pumping action of the heart is called a contraction. Contractions are controlled by the heart's electrical system, which makes the heart beat regularly. You can feel the heart's contractions in the arteries that are close to the skin, for instance, at the neck or the wrist. The beat you feel with each contraction is called the pulse. The heart must beat regularly to deliver oxygen to body cells to keep the body functioning properly.

Nervous System

The nervous system is the most complex and delicate of all body systems. The brain, the centre of the nervous system, is the master organ of the body. It regulates all body functions, including the respiratory and circulatory systems. The primary functions of the brain can be divided into three categories: the sensory functions, the motor functions, and the integrated functions of consciousness, memory, emotions, and use of language.

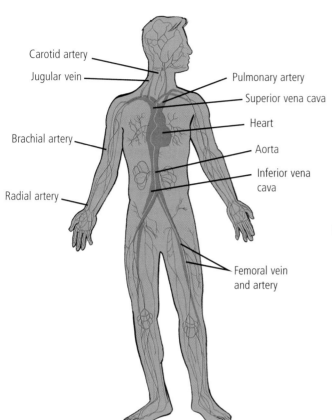

Carotid artery
Jugular vein
Brachial artery
Radial artery
Pulmonary artery
Superior vena cava
Heart
Aorta
Inferior vena cava
Femoral vein and artery

Figure 4–10 The circulatory system.

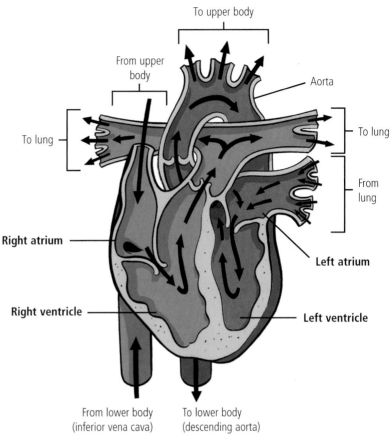

To upper body
From upper body
To lung
Aorta
To lung
From lung
Right atrium
Left atrium
Right ventricle
Left ventricle
From lower body (inferior vena cava)
To lower body (descending aorta)

Figure 4–11 The heart is a pump made up of four chambers. Various one-way valves keep the blood moving in the proper direction in order to complete the circulatory cycle.

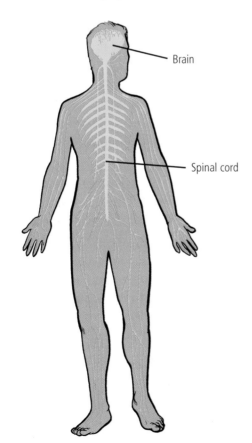

Brain
Spinal cord

Figure 4–12 The nervous system.

DID YOU KNOW?

An elephant's heart beats 25 times a minute and weighs 15 kilograms (40 pounds). A man's heart beats about 70 times a minute and weighs about 1/3 kilogram (1 pound). A mouse's heart beats about 700 times a minute and weighs approximately 1/2 gram (0.0175 ounce).

In a month, blood will have taken its journey around the human body 43,000 times. Blood vessels form a branching network of more than almost 100,000 km, almost 3 times the distance around the earth.

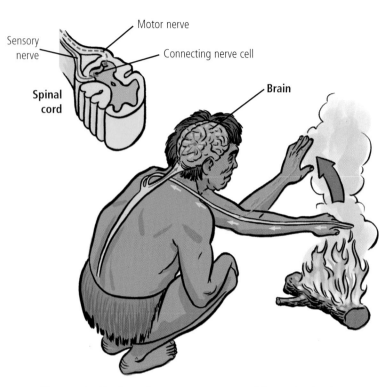

Sensory nerve

Motor nerve

Connecting nerve cell

Spinal cord

Brain

Figure 4–13 Impulses are sent to and from the brain by nerves.

The brain transmits and receives information through a network of nerves. Figure 4–12 shows the nervous system. The spinal cord, a large bundle of nerves, extends from the brain through a canal in the spine, or backbone. Nerves extend from the brain and spinal cord to every part of the body.

Nerves transmit information as electrical impulses from one area of the body to another. Some nerves conduct impulses from the body to the brain, allowing you to see, hear, smell, taste, and feel. These are the sensory functions. Other nerves conduct impulses from the brain to the muscles to control motor functions, or movement (Figure 4–13).

DID YOU KNOW?

A nerve impulse can travel 110 metres per second, fast enough to cover the length of a football field in less than a second.

Illness or injury to the brain may change a person's level of consciousness and/or alter memory, emotions, and the ability to use language.

Brain cells, unlike other body cells, cannot regenerate or grow back. Once brain cells die or are damaged, they are not replaced. Brain cells may die from disease or injury. When a particular part of the brain is diseased or injured, a person may lose the body functions controlled by that area of the brain forever. For example, if the part of the brain that regulates breathing is damaged, the person may stop breathing.

The integrated functions of the brain are more complex. One of the functions of the brain, particularly the brain stem, is consciousness. When your brain stem is fully functioning and oxygenated, you are conscious. Decreased oxygen supply results in a decreased level of consciousness; at this point, you may be roused by tactile or painful stimuli. The level of consciousness may degrade to a point of unconsciousness where there is no response to any stimuli.

Musculoskeletal System

The musculoskeletal system consists of the bones, muscles, ligaments, and tendons. This system performs the following functions:

• Supporting the body

• Protecting internal organs

• Allowing movement

• Storing minerals and producing blood cells

• Producing heat

Bones and Ligaments

The adult body has over 200 bones. Bone is hard, dense tissue that forms the skeleton. The skeleton forms the framework that supports the body (Figure 4–14). Where two or more bones join, they form a joint. Figure 4–15 shows a typical joint. Bones are usually held together at joints by fibrous bands called ligaments. Bones vary in size and shape, allowing them to perform specific functions.

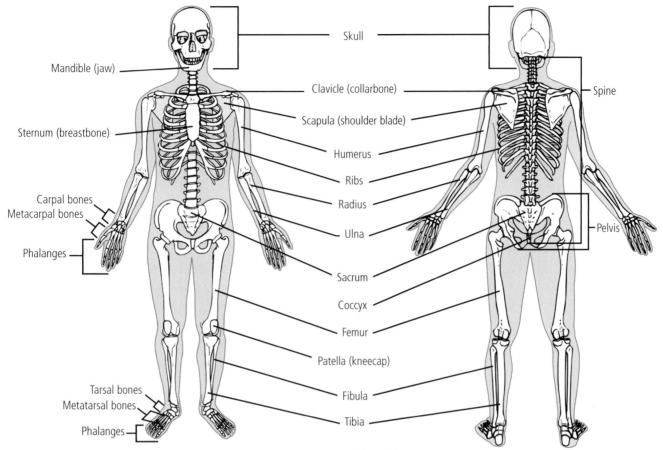

Figure 4–14 The skeleton.

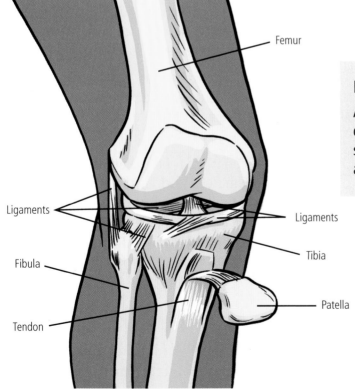

Figure 4–15 A typical joint consists of at least two bones that are held together by ligaments.

DID YOU KNOW?

A baby is born with approximately 300 bones. Why do adults have fewer bones? Some bones that are separate at birth, such as the skull, fuse together as a person grows.

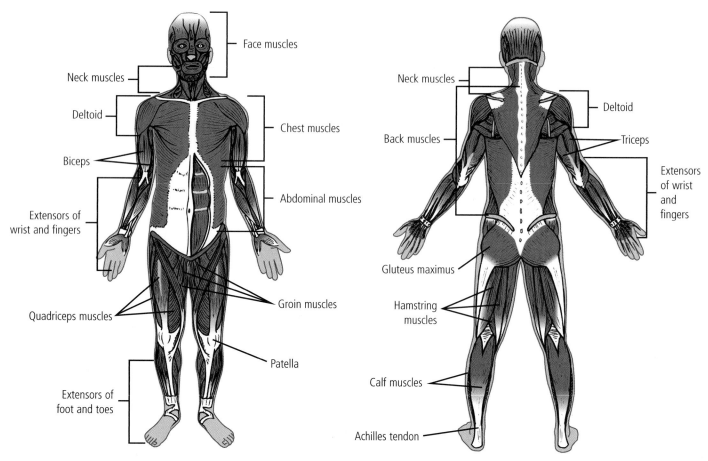

Figure 4–16 Major muscles of the body.

The bones of the skull protect the brain. The spine is made of bones called vertebrae that protect the spinal cord. The ribs are bones that attach to the spine and to the breastbone, forming a protective shell for vital organs such as the heart and lungs.

In addition to supporting and protecting the body, bones aid movement. The bones of the arms and legs work like a system of levers and pulleys to position the hands and feet so they can function. Bones of the wrist, hand, and fingers are progressively smaller to allow for fine movements such as writing. The small bones of the feet enable you to walk smoothly. Together they work as shock absorbers when you walk, run, or jump. Bones also store minerals and produce certain blood cells.

Muscles and Tendons

Muscles are made of special tissue that can lengthen and shorten, resulting in movement. Figure 4–16 shows the major muscles of the body. Tendons are tissues that attach muscles to bones. Muscles band together to form muscle groups. Muscle groups work together to produce movement (Figure 4–17). Working muscles also produce heat. Muscles protect underlying structures, such as bones, nerves, and blood vessels.

Muscle action is controlled by the nervous system. Nerves carry information from the muscles to the brain. The brain takes in this information and directs the muscles through the nerves (Figure 4–18).

Muscle actions can be voluntary or involuntary. Involuntary muscles, such as the heart and diaphragm, are automatically controlled by the brain. You don't have to think about them to make them work. Voluntary muscles, such as leg and arm muscles, are most often under your conscious control. You are aware of telling them to move.

DID YOU KNOW?

When we smile, we use 17 of our 30 facial muscles.

Figure 4–17 Muscles work together to produce movement.

Figure 4–18 The brain controls muscle movement.

Integumentary System

The integumentary system consists of the skin, hair, and nails (Figure 4–19). Most important among these is the skin because it protects the body. The skin helps keep fluids in. It prevents infection by keeping out disease-producing microorganisms, or germs. The skin is made of tough, elastic fibres that stretch without easily tearing, protecting it from injury. The skin also helps make vitamin D and stores minerals.

The outer surface of the skin consists of dead cells that are continually rubbed away and replaced by new cells. The skin contains the hair roots, oil glands, and sweat glands. Oil glands help keep the skin soft, supple, and waterproof. Sweat glands and pores help regulate body temperature by releasing sweat. The nervous system monitors blood temperature and causes you to sweat if blood temperature rises even slightly. Although you may not see or feel it, sweat is released to the skin's surface.

Blood supplies the skin with nutrients and helps provide its colour. When blood vessels dilate (become wider), the blood circulates close to the skin's surface. This makes some people's skin appear flushed and red and makes the skin feel warm. The redding may not appear with darker skin. When blood vessels constrict (become

narrower), not much blood is close to the skin's surface, causing the skin to look pale and feel cool.

Nerves in the skin make it very sensitive to sensations such as touch, pain, and temperature. Therefore, the skin is also an important part of the body's communication network.

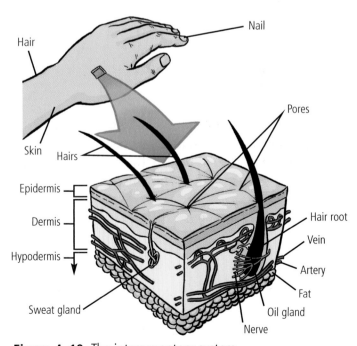

Figure 4–19 The integumentary system.

Endocrine System

The endocrine system is one of the body's two regulatory systems. Together with the nervous system, it coordinates the activities of other systems. The endocrine system consists of several glands (Figure 4–20). Glands are organs that release fluid and other substances into the blood or onto the skin. Some produce hormones, chemical messengers that enter the bloodstream and influence tissue activity in various parts of the body. For example, the thyroid gland makes a hormone that controls metabolism, the process by which all cells convert nutrients to energy. Other glands include the sweat and oil glands in the skin.

Problems in the endocrine system usually develop slowly and are seldom emergencies. Knowing how hormones work in general, however, helps you understand how some illnesses seem to develop suddenly, such as in the case of diabetic emergencies.

Digestive System

The digestive system, also called the gastrointestinal system, consists of organs that work together to break down food and eliminate waste. Figure 4–21 shows the major organs of the digestive system. Food entering the system is broken down into a form the body can use. As food passes through the system, the body absorbs nutrients that can be converted for use by the cells. The unabsorbed portion continues through the system and is eliminated as waste.

Since most digestive system organs are in the unprotected abdominal cavity, they are very vulnerable to injury. Damaged organs may bleed internally, causing severe loss of blood, or spill waste products into the abdominal cavity.

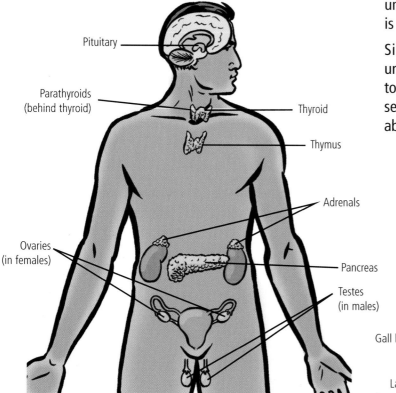

Figure 4–20 The endocrine system.

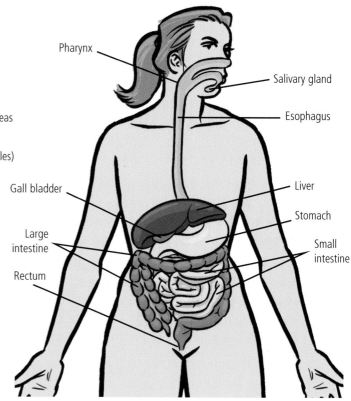

Figure 4–21 The digestive system.

DID YOU KNOW?

The skin weighs about 2.6 kilograms (7 pounds). If spread out flat, it would cover about 1.9 square metres (20 square feet).

Genitourinary System

The genitourinary system is made up of two organ systems: the urinary system and the reproductive system. The urinary system consists of organs that eliminate waste products filtered from the blood (Figure 4–22). The primary organs are the kidneys and the bladder. The kidneys are located behind the abdominal cavity just beneath the chest, one on each side. They filter wastes from the circulating blood to form urine. Urine is then stored in the bladder, a small muscular sac. The bladder stretches as it fills and then shrinks back when the urine is released.

The kidneys are partially protected by the lower ribs, making them less vulnerable to injury. But the kidneys may be damaged by a significant blow to the back just below the rib cage or a penetrating wound, such as a stab or gunshot wound. Because of the kidney's rich blood supply, such an injury may cause severe bleeding.

The bladder is injured less frequently than the kidneys, but injuries to the abdomen can rupture the bladder, particularly when it is full. Bone fragments from a fracture of the pelvis can also pierce or rupture the bladder.

The male and female reproductive systems include the organs for sexual reproduction (Figure 4–23, a-b). Because these organs are close to the urinary system,

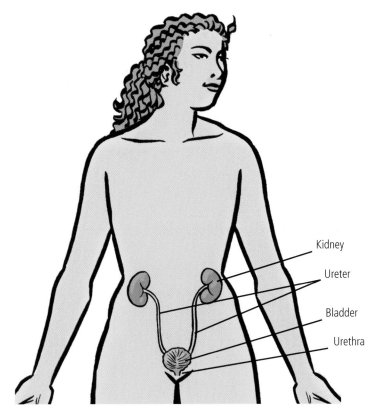

Figure 4–22 The urinary system.

injuries to the abdominal or pelvic area can injure organs in either system.

The female reproductive organs are smaller than many major organs and are protected by the pelvic bones. The soft tissue external structures are more susceptible to injury, although such injury is uncommon. The male reproductive organs are located outside the pelvis and are more vulnerable to injury.

The external reproductive organs, called genitalia, have a rich supply of blood and nerves. Injuries to these organs may cause heavy bleeding but are rarely life-threatening. Injuries to the genitalia are usually caused by a blow to the pelvic area but may be the result of sexual assault.

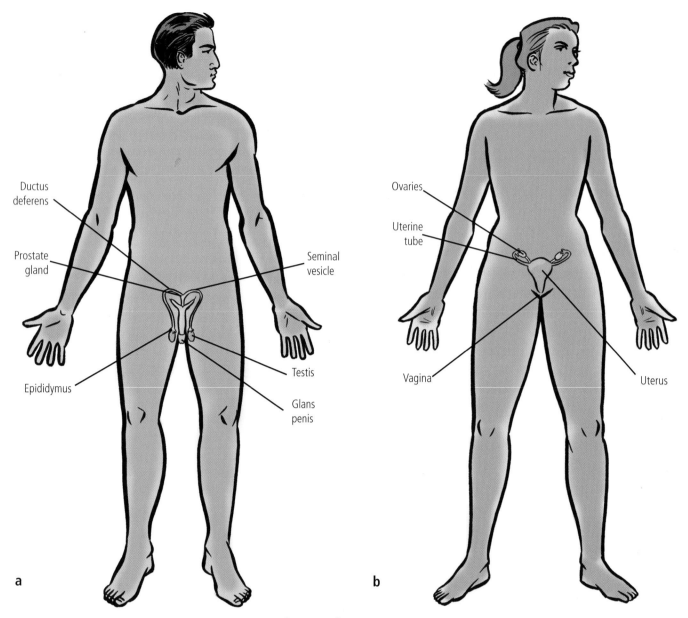

Figure 4–23, a-b The reproductive systems, **a**, male; **b**, female.

INTERRELATIONSHIPS OF BODY SYSTEMS

Each body system plays a vital role in survival. Body systems work together to help the body maintain a constant healthy state. When the environment changes, body systems adapt to the new conditions. For example, because your musculoskeletal system works harder when you exercise, your respiratory and circulatory systems must also work harder to meet your body's increased oxygen demands. Your body systems also react to the stresses caused by illness or injury.

Body systems do not work independently of each other. The impact of an injury or a disease is rarely restricted to one body system. For example, a broken bone may result in nerve damage that may impair movement and feeling. Injuries to the ribs can make breathing difficult. If the heart stops beating for any reason, breathing will also stop.

In any significant illness or injury, body systems may be seriously affected. This may result in a progressive failure of body systems called shock. Shock results from the inability of the circulatory system to provide adequate oxygen to all body cells, especially those of the vital organs.

Generally, the more body systems involved in an emergency, the more serious the emergency. Body systems depend on each other for survival. In serious injury or illness, the body may not be able to keep functioning. In these cases, regardless of your best efforts, the ill or injured person may die.

SUMMARY

The body includes a number of systems, all of which must work together for the body to function properly. The brain, the centre of the nervous system, controls all body functions, including those of the other body systems. Knowing a few key structures, their functions, and their locations helps you understand more about these body systems. Knowing certain anatomical terms helps you communicate with more advanced medical personnel about any injury or illness you may encounter.

Illness or injury that affects one body system can have a serious impact on other systems. Fortunately, basic care is usually all you need to give to support injured body systems until more advanced care is available. By learning the basic principles of care described in later chapters, you may be able to make the difference between life and death.

As you get closer to the first woman, you see that she is clutching one side of her abdomen, near the top. Her passenger is holding his right hip and looks dazed. The driver of the van has shallow breathing and her pulse is weak. How will you describe their injuries and which body systems are involved?

Chapter 5

Assessment

During a basketball game, two players collide while diving for a loose ball. Both players fall to the ground. One player is holding her knee, screaming in pain. Her leg appears to be twisted to one side. The second player is lying still but is moaning. What do you do?

INTRODUCTION

In previous chapters, you learned how to prepare for an emergency, the precautions to take when approaching the scene, and how to recognize a dangerous situation. You also learned about your roles and responsibilities as a responder. You learned that you can make a difference in an emergency—you may even save a life. But to do this, you must learn how to provide care for an ill or injured person. More important, you need to learn how to set priorities for the care you provide.

When an emergency occurs, you must determine if the person has any life-threatening conditions while conducting a primary survey, which includes assessing the person's level of consciousness (responsiveness) and checking the person's airway, breathing, and circulation. You can obtain more information about the person through a secondary survey, which includes interviewing the person and bystanders, monitoring vital signs, and conducting a physical exam.

In this chapter, you will learn a plan of action to guide you through any emergency. When an emergency occurs, at first you may feel confused. But you can train yourself to remain calm and to think before you act. Ask yourself, "What do I need to do? How can I help most effectively?" The following steps answer these questions. They are your plan of action for any emergency.

These principles, conducted in this order, can ensure your safety and that of the ill or injured person and bystanders. They will also increase the person's chance of survival if he has a serious illness or injury.

SCENE SURVEY

Once you recognize that an emergency has occurred and decide to act, you must make sure the emergency scene is safe for you, the ill or injured person/people, and any bystanders. Take time to survey the scene and answer these questions:

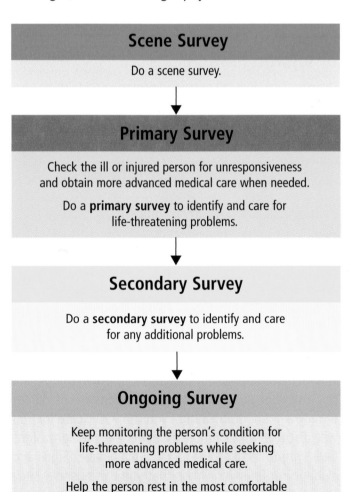

> What are the potential hazards at the scene?
> Weather conditions, people, animals, weapons, dangerous surfaces or objects, biohazards, tripping hazards, debris

> What happened?
> What is the mechanism of illness or injury (MOI)?
> A fall? A sudden illness? Were vehicles involved?
> Was there a collision? Are there pill containers?
> Are there bottles?

> How many people are ill or injured?

> What other resources might I need?
> Law enforcement, Poison Control Centre, utilities, more advanced medical care, fire fighters

Before You Approach the Ill or Injured Person

When you survey the scene, look for anything that may threaten your safety or that of bystanders or the ill or injured person. Examples of hazards that may be present are given in Chapter 2. Take the necessary precautions when working in a hazardous environment. If you are not properly trained and do not have the necessary equipment, do not approach the person. Summon the necessary personnel.

Nothing is gained by risking your safety. An emergency that begins with one ill or injured person could end up with two if you are hurt. If you suspect the scene is unsafe, wait and watch until the necessary personnel and equipment arrive. If conditions change, you may then be able to approach the person.

As You Approach the Ill or Injured Person

Try to find out what happened. Look around the scene for clues to what caused the emergency (the mechanism of injury) and the extent of the damage. Doing this will cause you to think about the possible type and extent of the person's injuries. You may discover a situation that requires you to act immediately. As you approach the person, take in the whole picture. Nearby objects, such as shattered glass, a fallen ladder, or a spilled medicine container, may suggest what happened (Figure 5–1). If the person is unconscious, surveying the scene may be the only way you can determine what happened.

When you survey the scene, always look carefully for more than one ill or injured person. You may not see everyone at first. For example, in a vehicle collision, an open door may be a clue that an injured person has left the car or was thrown from it. If one person is bleeding or screaming loudly, you may overlook another person who is unconscious. It is also easy in any emergency situation to overlook a baby or small child. Ask anyone present how many people may be involved. If you find more than one person, ask bystanders to help you provide care.

Look for bystanders who can help. Bystanders may be able to tell you what happened or help in other ways.

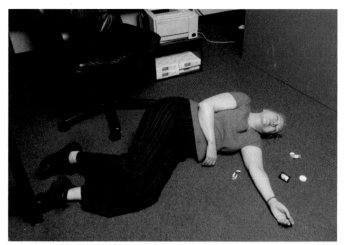

Figure 5–1 Look for nearby clues as to what might have happened.

A bystander who knows the ill or injured person may know whether he has any medical conditions or allergies. Bystanders can meet and direct further personnel to your location, help keep the area free of unnecessary traffic, and help you provide care.

Once You Reach the Ill or Injured Person

Once you reach the ill or injured person, quickly survey the scene again to see if it is still safe. At this point, you may see other dangers, clues to what happened, and other injured people or bystanders that you did not notice before. Determine the level of risk and put on personal protective equipment if you have not done so already.

Forming a General Impression

Once you reach the ill or injured person and begin your assessment, you will be able to form a general impression of his condition. This includes determining:

• The person's complaint or problem

• If the person is injured or ill

• The person's gender and approximate age

This general impression may alert you that the person has a serious problem that requires additional resources or only a minor problem that you can easily care for. You will discover these problems by looking for any signs and symptoms that the person may have. Signs are evidence of injury or illness that you can observe, such as bleeding or unusual skin appearance. Symptoms are

Figure 5–2 When talking to an ill or injured person, try to position yourself at eye level and speak in a calm and positive manner.

Figure 5–3 Determine if the person is responsive by asking "Are you okay?" and gently tapping him.

what the person tells you he is experiencing, such as pain, nausea, headache, or shortness of breath.

Do not move an ill or injured person unless there is an immediate danger, such as a fire, poisonous fumes, or an unstable structure. If the area is dangerous and the person does not seem to be seriously injured, ask the person to move to safety where you can help him. If the area is dangerous and the person cannot move, you may try to move the person as quickly as possible without making his condition worse. If there is no immediate danger, identify yourself, tell the person not to move, and obtain consent to give care. If the mechanism of injury indicates a head or spine injury, initiate manual spinal precautions, as described in Chapter 13.

Throughout, try not to alarm the person. Try to position yourself close to his eye level (Figure 5–2).

PRIMARY SURVEY

Check the Ill or Injured Person for Unresponsiveness and Obtain More Advanced Medical Care

Quality care begins with a primary survey. This is a check for conditions that are an immediate threat to the ill or injured person's life. The primary survey has several components:

• Assessing level of consciousness (LOC)

• Assessing airway, breathing, and circulation

• Checking for severe bleeding

First, determine if the person is responsive. Do this by gently tapping him and asking, "Are you okay?" (Figure 5–3). Do not jostle or move the person. A person who can speak or cry is conscious, is breathing, and has a pulse.

If the person is unable to respond, he may be unconscious. Unconsciousness can indicate a life-threatening condition. When a person is unconscious, the tongue relaxes and may fall to the back of the throat, blocking the airway. This can cause breathing to stop. Soon after, the heart will stop beating. With an unconscious person, more advanced medical care is needed.

One of the most important indicators of a person's condition is his LOC. A person's LOC can range from being fully alert to being unconscious (Table 5-1). In describing a person's LOC, a four-level scale is used. The letters **A**, **V**, **P**, and **U** each refer to a stage of awareness.

A = Alert: If a person is conscious and able to speak to you, this indicates the person is alert. It is important to note that a person can be deemed alert but still be confused or disoriented. If the person is not alert, proceed to check his response to verbal stimuli.

V = Verbal: Sometimes a person only reacts to sounds, such as your voice. This person may appear to be lapsing into unconsciousness. State a command or ask a question. If the person responds, the person is said to be responsive to verbal stimuli. If the person is not responsive to verbal stimuli, proceed to check response to painful stimuli.

P = Painful: If a person responds only when someone inflicts pain, he is described as responding to painful

TABLE 5-1 LEVELS OF CONSCIOUSNESS

Level of Response	Characteristic Behaviour
Alert	Eyes are open; able to verbalize
Verbal	Responds to commands or questions
Painful	Facial grimace; flexion, extension, or withdrawal of body part; moan or groan
Unresponsive	No response

stimuli. Pinching the nail bed or inside the arm is an example of a painful stimulus used to try to get a response. Avoid pinching anywhere above the collarbone as this could cause the person to move his head.

U = Unresponsive: A person who does not respond to any stimuli is considered to be unconscious, or unresponsive to stimuli.

Any change in the level of consciousness constitutes a possible life-threatening condition, and it is important to obtain more advanced medical care.

If your communication network is not directly linked to advanced medical personnel, you will need to use a telephone to call. If possible, ask another responder or a bystander to call the emergency number for you. Sending someone else to make the call will enable you to stay with the ill or injured person to provide care.

Whether placing the call yourself or sending someone to call, the following should be done:

1. Dial the local emergency number. This number is 9-1-1 in many communities. Sometimes the emergency number is on the inside front cover of telephone directories and on pay phones.

2. Be prepared to provide the dispatcher with the following information when asked:

    a. Where the emergency is located—Give the exact address or location and the name of the city or town. It is helpful to give the names of nearby intersecting streets (cross streets), landmarks, the name of the building, the floor, and the room number.

    b. Telephone number from which the call is being made

    c. Caller's name

    d. What happened—for example, a motor vehicle collision, fall, or fire

    e. The number of people involved

    f. Condition of the ill or injured person/people —for example, chest pain, difficulty breathing, no pulse, bleeding

    g. Care being given

3. Hang up only when the dispatcher has told you to do so. It is important to make sure the dispatcher has all the information needed to send the appropriate help immediately.

If you must leave the person for any reason, such as to call your emergency number, place him in the recovery

---

NOTE:

Obtain more advanced medical care if the primary survey determines a life-threatening condition and if you have not already called for help.

Figure 5–4 The recovery position.

position to help keep the airway open (Figure 5–4). Place the person on one side, bend the top leg, and move it forward to hold the person in that position. Support the head so that it is angled toward the ground. In this position, if the person vomits, the airway will stay clear.

Assessing the Person's Airway, Breathing, and Circulation

If you can, try to check the ABCs in whatever position you find the person, especially if you suspect he has a head or spine injury. Sometimes, however, the person's position prevents you from checking the ABCs. In this case, you may roll the person gently onto his back, keeping the head and spine in as straight a line as possible.

Check A: Airway

Be sure the person has an open airway, the pathway for air from the mouth and nose to the lungs. If a person is speaking or crying, he has an open airway, is breathing, and has a pulse. If a person is unconscious, it may be difficult to tell if he has an open airway. Open an unconscious person's airway by tilting the head back and lifting the chin. These two complementary motions move the tongue and epiglottis, opening the airway. If there is any possibility of head or spinal trauma, open the airway by using the two-handed jaw thrust technique (Figure 5–5). After opening the airway, check for breathing.

Sometimes opening the airway does not result in a free passage of air. This happens when a person's airway is blocked by liquid, food, or other objects. In this case, you will need to remove the obstruction. Chapter 6 describes how to care for an obstructed airway.

Check B: Breathing

Position yourself so that you can hear and feel air from the person's nose and mouth. At the same time, watch the chest rise and fall. If the person is breathing normally, you will observe the rise and fall of the chest, ease of breathing, and approximate respiratory rate. Someone who is having trouble breathing may have the following signs and symptoms:

- Inadequate rise and fall of the chest
- Increased effort on respiration
- Decreased LOC
- Difficulty breathing
- Blue or grey colour to the skin, lips, or nail beds (cyanosis)
- Very slow or fast breathing rates

Look, listen, and feel for breathing for no more than 10 seconds (Figure 5–6). A person with a breathing difficulty needs oxygen immediately (see Chapter 7). By assessing the quality of respirations, you can determine if this is needed.

If the person is not breathing or is not breathing adequately, you must breathe for him. Begin by giving two breaths, each lasting one second in length. Each breath should be given just until the chest rises. This will get air into the person's lungs. The longer someone goes without oxygen, the more likely he is to die. This process of breathing for the person is called rescue breathing. You will learn rescue breathing in Chapter 6.

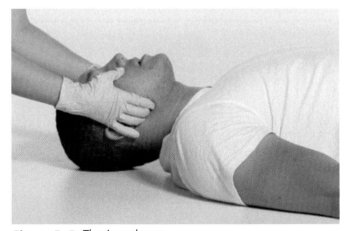

Figure 5–5 The jaw thrust.

Figure 5–6 Look, listen, and feel for breathing for no more than 10 seconds.

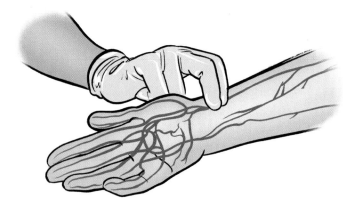

Figure 5–7 The location of the radial artery.

Check C: Circulation

The last step in the primary survey is checking for blood circulation. If the heart has stopped, blood will not circulate throughout the body. If blood does not circulate, the person will die in just a few minutes because the brain will not get any oxygen.

If the ill or injured adult or child is conscious and breathing, check his pulse using the radial artery on the thumb side of his wrist (Figure 5–7). If the adult or child is unconscious or not breathing, or you cannot feel a radial pulse, check the pulse at either of the carotid arteries located in the neck. You can also look for any movement of the person, normal breathing (more than an occasional gasp), coughing, and appropriate skin colour.

To find the pulse, feel for the Adam's apple at the front of the neck and then slide your fingers into the groove at the side of the neck (Figure 5–8). Sometimes the pulse may be difficult to find since it may be slow or weak. If at first you do not find a pulse, relocate the

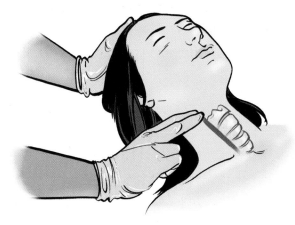

Figure 5–8 The location of the carotid artery.

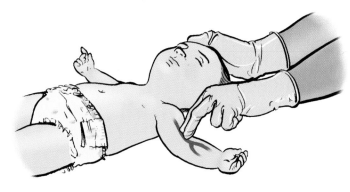

Figure 5–9 The location of the brachial artery.

Adam's apple and again slide your fingers into place. When you think you are in the right spot, keep feeling for no more than 10 seconds.

To find a baby's pulse, place your fingers over the brachial artery, located on the inside of the upper arm, midway between the shoulder and elbow (Figure 5–9).

If you do not observe the presence of signs of circulation, you need to keep oxygen-rich blood circulating. This

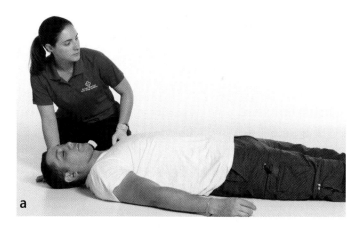

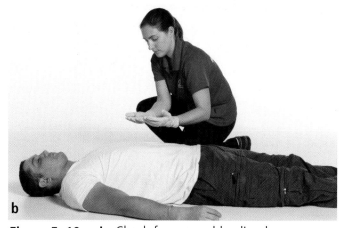

Figure 5–10, a-b Check for severe bleeding by **a**, visually inspecting then; **b**, physically checking for blood.

involves doing rescue breathing to get oxygen into the person's lungs and chest compressions to circulate the oxygen to the brain.

This procedure is called cardiopulmonary resuscitation (CPR) and is described in Chapter 8.

Checking circulation also means looking for severe bleeding. Bleeding is severe when blood spurts from the wound or cannot be controlled, and it is life-threatening. Check for severe bleeding by doing a quick visual check of the person from head to toe (Figure 5–10, a), then quickly feel each major part of the body for signs of severe external bleeding. Inspect your gloves often for blood (Figure 5–10, b). This is also known as a "wet check." Severe bleeding must be controlled before you provide any further care as, if left untreated, it can become fatal. Techniques for controlling severe bleeding are described in Chapter 9.

NOTE:

At this point, it may be appropriate to administer oxygen and treat for shock (see Chapter 10).

Decision Point

Initiate care for life-threatening emergencies as required, based on the primary assessment. If you are trained to do so, transport should also be initiated at this point. Otherwise, begin the secondary survey. Information regarding care for life-threatening emergencies and transport is found later in this manual.

SECONDARY SURVEY

If you are certain the person has no life-threatening conditions, you can begin the secondary survey. The secondary survey is a systematic method of gathering additional information about injuries or conditions that may need care. These injuries or conditions are not immediately life-threatening but could become so if not cared for. For example, you might find possible broken bones, minor bleeding, or a specific medical condition, such as diabetes. The secondary survey is made up of the following three steps:

1. Interview the ill or injured person and bystanders.
2. Check vital signs.
3. Do a head-to-toe examination.

As you do the secondary survey, try not to move the person. Most injured people will find the most comfortable position for themselves. For example, a person with a chest injury who is having trouble breathing may be sitting up and supporting the injured area. Let the person continue to do this. Do not ask him to change positions unless it is necessary.

Interview the Ill or Injured Person and Bystanders

Begin by asking the ill or injured person and bystanders simple questions to learn more about what happened and the person's condition. Asking about existing conditions and the incident itself, as well as what the chief complaint is (what is bothering the person), is commonly known as obtaining a person's "history." This should not take much time. You are looking not only for signs of the person's condition but also for symptoms. A symptom is something the person tells you about his condition, such as "I am dizzy" or "my head hurts." A sign is any evidence you can see of injury or illness, such as bleeding or unusually pale skin colour.

If you have not done so already, remember to identify yourself and to get the person's consent before helping. Begin the interview by asking the person's name. Using his name will make the person more comfortable. First ask what happened and whether the person feels any pain. Use the acronym **SAMPLE** to remember to ask the following questions:

S = Signs and symptoms (What things are bothering you?)

A = Allergies (What allergies do you have?)

M = Medications (What medications do you take?)

P = Past medical history (What medical conditions do you have?)

L = Last meal (When did you last eat or drink? What did you last eat or drink?)

E = Events before the incident (What happened to cause the problem?)

TABLE 5-2 QUESTIONS ABOUT PAIN: OPQRST

Mnemonic	Question to Ask
Onset	Did it start suddenly?
Provoke	What provokes the pain or causes it to get worse?
Quality	What does the pain feel like? (Sharp, dull, stabbing, moving, etc.)
Region (or Radiate)	Where exactly is the pain located? Does it radiate to other areas?
Severity	How bad is the pain?
Time	When did the pain begin?

If the person has pain, ask him to describe it. You may use the mnemonic OPQRST to remember the questions to ask (Table 5-2). You can expect to get descriptions such as burning, throbbing, aching, or sharp pain. Ask when the pain started. Ask how bad the pain is.

Assessing a Conscious Child or Baby

Be aware that babies and young children might not be able to respond to methods used to assess the level of consciousness in adults. For example, they may not be able to respond to your questions because of an inability to speak or understand your questions, fear of a stranger, or they are crying. If possible, assess a baby or small child in his parent's or caregiver's arms or lap. When assessing a baby or child:

• Approach the baby or child slowly.

• Kneel so that you are at eye level with the baby or child.

• Give the baby or child a few minutes to get used to you, if possible.

• Use the child's name.

• Demonstrate what you are going to do on a stuffed animal or doll, if possible.

• Allow a child to inspect items such as bandages.

• Let a school-aged child know if you are going to do anything painful.

Sometimes the person will be unable to give you the information. This is often the case with a child or with an adult who momentarily lost consciousness and may not be able to recall what happened or is disoriented. These people may be frightened. Be calm and patient. Speak normally and in simple terms. Offer reassurance. Ask family members, friends, or bystanders what happened. They may be able to give you helpful information, such as telling you if the person has a medical condition you should be aware of. They may also be able to help calm the person if necessary.

Check Vital Signs

The first set of vital signs is considered to be the baseline vital signs. These may include:

• Level of consciousness
• Breathing
• Pulse
• Skin characteristics
• Blood pressure
• Pupils

These vital signs can tell you how the body is responding to injury or illness. Look for changes in vital signs. Note anything unusual. Recheck vital signs every five minutes. Subsequent vital signs taken may depend on the conditions presented by the ill or injured person.

Level of Consciousness

You learned how to assess a person's LOC earlier in the chapter using the AVPU scale. Another measure, typically used for assessing people with head trauma, is the Glasgow Coma Scale.

Glasgow Coma Scale

The Glasgow Coma Scale (GCS) is a standardized system used to determine a person's level of consciousness and is considered a good indicator of eventual clinical outcome for head trauma. The scale is often performed on people with neurological damage. The assessment process involves assigning a score based on the person's motor and verbal responses and his ability to open his eyes. This scale is divided into three sections. The sections are scored individually and then added together (Table 5-3). To assess the person using the GCS, do the following:

TABLE 5-3
GLASGOW COMA SCALE

Eye Opening	E
spontaneous	4
to voice	3
to pain	2
no response	1
Best Verbal Response	**V**
oriented and converses	5
disoriented and converses	4
inappropriate words	3
incomprehensible sounds	2
no response	1
Best Motor Response	**M**
To Verbal Command:	
obeys command	6
To Painful Stimulus:	
localizes pain	5
withdrawal	4
abnormal flexion	3
abnormal extension	2
no response	1
E + V + M = 3 to 15	

Eye Opening

If a person spontaneously opens his eyes, he receives a score of 4. If he does not spontaneously open his eyes, give a verbal command, such as "Open your eyes." If he still does not open his eyes, apply a painful stimulus, as with the AVPU assessment.

Best Verbal Response

Ask a question. If the person responds coherently, he receives a score of 5. If the answer is not coherent, or the person does not respond, the response (or lack of response) can be put into one of the other categories and the appropriate score assigned.

Best Motor Response

Give the person a command, such as "wiggle your fingers." If he responds to your command, a score of 6 is given. If he does not follow your command, apply a painful stimulus, as described earlier, and score the response accordingly. If he pushes away the stimulus, this is localizing the pain.

A score of 13 to 15 is associated with mild head injury; 8 to 12, moderate head injury; and less than 8, severe head injury.

Breathing

A healthy person breathes regularly, quietly, and effortlessly. The normal breathing rate for an adult is between 12 and 20 breaths per minute. However, some people breathe slightly slower or faster. Excitement, fear, and exercise cause breathing to increase and become deeper. Certain injuries or illnesses can also cause both the breathing rate and quality to change.

During the secondary survey, watch and listen for any changes in breathing. Abnormal breathing may indicate a potential problem. The signs and symptoms of abnormal breathing include:

- Gasping for air
- Noisy breathing, including whistling sounds, crowing, gurgling, or snoring
- Excessively fast or slow breathing
- Painful breathing

In the primary survey, you are concerned with whether a person is breathing at all, whereas in the secondary survey, you are concerned with the rate, rhythm, and quality of breathing. Look, listen, and feel again for breathing. Look for the rise and fall of the person's chest or abdomen. Listen for sounds as the person inhales and exhales. Count the number of times a person breathes (inhales or exhales) in 15 seconds and multiply that number by 4. This is the number of breaths per minute. As you check for the rate and quality of breathing, try to do it without the person's knowledge. If a person realizes that you are checking his breathing, he may change his breathing pattern without being aware of doing so. Maintain the same position you would be in when you are checking the pulse.

Pulse

With every heartbeat, a wave of blood moves through the blood vessels. This creates a beat called the pulse. You can feel it with your fingertips in arteries near the skin. In the primary survey, you are concerned only with whether a pulse is present. To determine this, you check the carotid arteries. In the secondary survey, you are trying to determine pulse rate, rhythm, and quality. This is most often done by checking the radial pulse located on the thumb side of the person's wrist.

When the heart is healthy, it beats with a steady rhythm. This beat creates a regular pulse. A normal pulse for an adult is between 60 and 100 beats per minute. A well-conditioned athlete may have a pulse of 50 beats per minute or lower. Table 5-4 lists average pulses at different ages. If the heartbeat changes, so does the pulse. An abnormal pulse may be a sign of a potential problem. These signs include:

- Irregular pulse

- Weak and hard-to-find pulse

- Excessively fast or slow pulse

When severely injured or unhealthy, the heart may beat unevenly, producing an irregular pulse. The rate at which the heart beats can also change. The pulse speeds up when a person is excited, anxious, in pain, losing blood, or under stress. It slows down when a person is relaxed. Some heart conditions can also speed up or slow down the pulse rate. Sometimes changes may be very subtle and difficult for you to detect. The most important change to note is a pulse that changes from being present to no pulse at all.

Checking a pulse is a simple procedure. It merely involves placing two fingers on top of a major artery where it is located close to the skin's surface. Pulse sites that are easy to locate are the carotid arteries in the neck, the radial artery in the wrist, and, for babies, the brachial artery in the upper arm (Figure 5–11, a-c). There are other pulse sites you may use. Figure 5–12 shows these sites. To check the pulse rate, count the number of beats in 15 seconds and multiply that number by 4. The number you get is the number of heartbeats per minute. If you find the pulse is irregular, you may need to check it for more than 15 seconds.

An ill or injured person's pulse may be hard to find. If you have trouble finding a pulse, keep checking periodically. Take your time. Remember, if a person is breathing, his heart is also beating. However, there may be a loss in circulation to the injured area, causing a loss of pulse. If you cannot find the pulse in one place, check it in another major artery, such as in the other wrist.

TABLE 5-4 AVERAGE* VITAL SIGNS BY AGE

Age	Pulse	Respirations	Blood Pressure
Up to 28 days	120–160	40–60	80/40
1–12 months	100–120	30–40	80/40
1–8 years	80–120	16–24	90/50
Over age 8	60–100	12–20	120/80

These values vary among individuals and should not be considered "normal" values. They are averages for each age group.

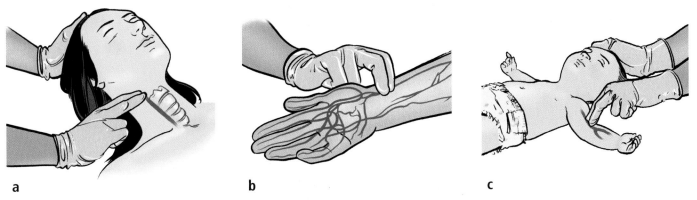

Figure 5–11, a-c Checking for **a**, the carotid pulse; **b**, the radial pulse; and **c**, the brachial pulse.

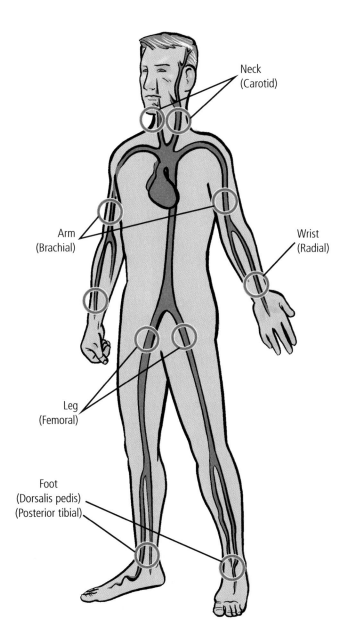

Neck
(Carotid)

Arm
(Brachial)

Wrist
(Radial)

Leg
(Femoral)

Foot
(Dorsalis pedis)
(Posterior tibial)

Figure 5–12 Easily located pulse sites.

Skin Characteristics

The colour, temperature, and condition of the skin often indicate something about the person's condition. For example, a person with a breathing problem may have a flushed or pale face.

The skin looks red when the body is forced to work harder. The heart pumps faster to get more blood to the tissues. This increased blood flow causes reddened skin and makes the skin feel warm. In contrast, the skin may look pale or bluish and feel cool and moist if the blood flow is directed away from the skin's surface. When a person with darker skin becomes pale, the skin turns ashen, a greyish colour. Illness and/or injury may also cause the skin to become dry, moist, or clammy, for example. Any changes in these skin characteristics may indicate a problem.

Blood Pressure

Blood pressure (BP) is the force exerted by the blood against the blood vessel walls as it travels throughout the body. Blood pressure is necessary to move the oxygen and nutrients in the blood to the body's organs and muscles. It is also necessary to move waste products, such as carbon dioxide, to various parts of the body for removal. Blood pressure is a good indicator of how the circulatory system is functioning.

Blood pressure is created by the pumping action of the heart. The pumping action involves two phases: the working (contracting) phase and the resting (refilling) phase. During the working phase, the ventricles (lower chambers) of the heart contract. This causes blood to be pumped through the arteries to all parts of the body.

During the resting phase, the ventricles relax and refill with blood before the next contraction.

Stress, excitement, illness, and injury often affect blood pressure. When a person is ill or injured, a single blood pressure measurement is often of little value. A more accurate picture of a person's condition immediately following an injury or the onset of an illness is whether his blood pressure changes over time while you provide care. For example, a person's initial blood pressure reading could be uncommonly high due to the stress of the emergency. Providing care, however, usually relieves some of the fear, and blood pressure may return to a normal range. At other times, blood pressure will remain unusually high or low. For example, an injury resulting in severe blood loss may cause blood pressure to remain unusually low. You should be concerned about unusually high or low blood pressure whenever symptoms of injury or illness are present.

To accurately assess a person's blood pressure, you need a blood pressure cuff. Cuffs come in sizes for small, average, and large arms. Inside the cuff is a rubber bladder, similar to an inner tube, that can be inflated. A pressure gauge, inflation bulb, and regulating valve are connected to the bladder by rubber tubing.

Blood pressure is measured in units called millimetres of mercury (mmHg). These units, written on the blood pressure gauge, range from 20 mmHg to 300 mmHg. In measuring blood pressure, two different numbers are usually recorded. The first number reflects the pressure in the arteries when the heart is working, or contracting. This pressure is called the systolic blood pressure. The second number reflects the pressure in the arteries when the heart is at rest and refilling. This is called the diastolic blood pressure.

You report blood pressure by giving the systolic number first and then the diastolic (S/D). Write this as BP 120/80.

The process of using a blood pressure cuff and stethoscope to listen for characteristic sounds is called auscultation. To auscultate means to listen. This method allows you to get accurate systolic and diastolic pressures. To auscultate blood pressure, begin by determining the systolic pressure using the palpation method (described on next page). Next, locate the brachial pulse. Place the earpieces of the stethoscope in your ears and

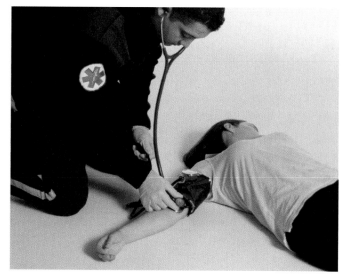

Figure 5–13 To auscultate blood pressure, position the cuff, find the brachial pulse, and position the stethoscope over it.

the other end, the diaphragm, over the spot where you found the brachial pulse (Figure 5–13). Close the valve and begin to inflate the cuff. Inflate the cuff to 20 mmHg above the approximate systolic blood pressure.

Slowly deflate the cuff at a rate of about 2 mmHg per second. As you deflate the cuff, listen carefully for the pulse. In some instances, it may sound like a tapping sound. The point at which the pulse is first heard is the systolic pressure.

As the cuff deflates, the pulse sound will fade. The point at which the sound disappears is the diastolic pressure. Release the remaining air quickly. Record the blood pressure as two numbers, such as 130/80. Also record whether the person was sitting or lying down.

To determine both the systolic and the diastolic pressure, you need a stethoscope. The stethoscope enables you to hear the pulsating sounds of blood moving through the arteries with each contraction of the heart. Sometimes you may not have a stethoscope or, because of noise, are unable to use one. You can still determine the systolic blood pressure through a method known as palpation. Palpation requires you to feel (palpate) the radial artery as you inflate the blood pressure cuff (Figure 5–14).

To determine blood pressure by palpation, begin by having the person sit or lie down. Wrap the blood pressure cuff around the person's arm so that the

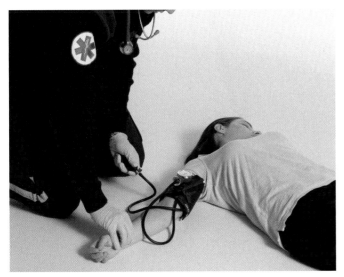

Figure 5–14 Estimating a systolic blood pressure requires you to feel for a radial pulse.

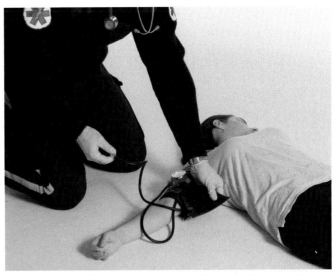

Figure 5–15 The centre of the cuff should be placed over the brachial artery, about 2.5 cm (1 in) above the crease of the elbow.

lower edge is about 2.5 cm (1 in) above the crease of the elbow. The centre of the cuff should be over the brachial artery, the major artery of the arm (Figure 5–15). Next, locate the radial pulse. Close the regulating valve by turning the valve clockwise and begin to inflate the cuff. Inflate the cuff until you can no longer feel the radial pulse. Note the number on the gauge.

Continue to inflate the cuff for another 20 mmHg beyond this point. Slowly release the pressure in the cuff by turning the regulating valve counter-clockwise. Allow the cuff to deflate at a rate of about 2 mmHg per second. Continue to feel for the radial pulse as the cuff deflates. The point at which the pulse at the wrist returns is the approximate systolic blood pressure by palpation. The systolic pressure found using this method is on average 10 to 20 mmHg less than the systolic pressure found by auscultation. This blood pressure reading is expressed as one number only, such as 130/P. In this example, the systolic pressure is 130, and P refers to palpation. Once you know the approximate systolic pressure, quickly deflate the cuff. Record the systolic pressure and whether the person was sitting or lying down when the blood pressure was taken.

Pupils

Look closely at the size of the pupils, as well as whether they react to light and are of equal size. You can check the reaction to light by shading each eye and then allowing light to enter. You can also check by shining a

Pulse Points

There are a number of pulse points on the body where the arteries are close to the surface of the skin and a pulse can be found. Some of these include radial, brachial, carotid, femoral, and pedal pulse points. These points can be used to estimate the systolic blood pressure, without the use of equipment. The further away from the core the pulse is found, the higher the systolic blood pressure will be.

light into each eye and then removing the light. Pupils should be equal, round, and reactive to light.

Pupils that are unequal, fully dilated or constricted, or unresponsive to light indicate a serious injury or illness (Figure 5–16).

Head-to-Toe Physical Examination

Once you are certain that the person has no life-threatening injuries or medical conditions that require your care, you can begin the physical exam.

If you find life-threatening injuries or medical conditions, such as unconsciousness, no breathing, no pulse, or severe bleeding during the primary survey, do not waste time with the physical exam. Instead, focus your attention on providing care for the life-threatening conditions.

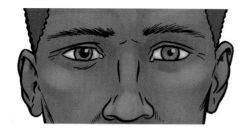

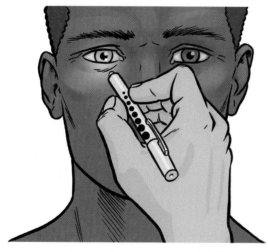

Figure 5–16 Pupils that are unequal, fully dilated, fully constricted, or unresponsive to light may indicate a serious head injury or illness.

The physical exam is a systematic "head-to-toe" examination that helps you gather additional information about injuries or conditions that may need care. These injuries or conditions are not immediately life-threatening but could become so if not cared for. For example, you might find minor bleeding or possible broken bones as you conduct your examination of the

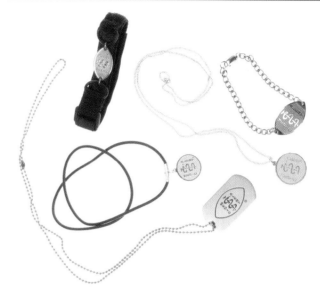

Figure 5–17 There are many forms of MedicAlert® medical identification products.

person. Begin the physical exam by telling the person what you are going to do and asking him for consent.

The physical exam process involves the use of looking (inspection), listening (auscultation), and feeling (palpation). You may even smell something that you can gather as information, such as the smell of bleach on the breath, which may indicate poisoning. After telling the person exactly what you are going to do and asking him to hold still, inspect and palpate each part of the body, starting with the head, before you move on to the next area.

Ask the person to tell you if any areas hurt. Avoid touching any painful areas or having the person move any area in which there is discomfort. Watch facial expressions; listen for a tone of voice that may reveal pain. Look for a MedicAlert® medical identification product on jewelery like a necklace or bracelet (Figure 5–17). This tag may help you determine what is wrong, whom to call for help, and what care to give.

As you do the head-to-toe examination, think about how the body normally looks and feels. Be alert for any sign of injuries—anything that looks or feels unusual. If you are uncertain whether your finding is unusual, check the other side of the body.

Check the head. Look for blood or clear fluid in or around the ears, nose, and mouth. Blood or clear fluid can indicate a serious head injury. Check the level of consciousness again and note any change. Check the pupils again and note any changes.

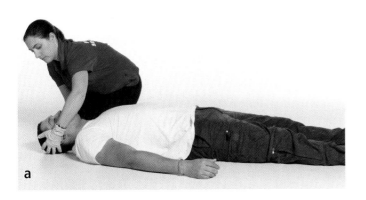

a

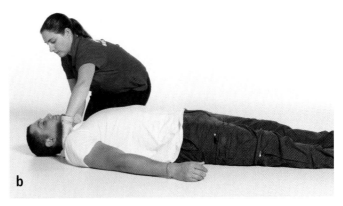

b

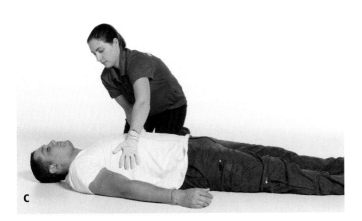

c

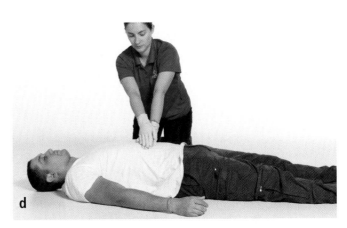

d

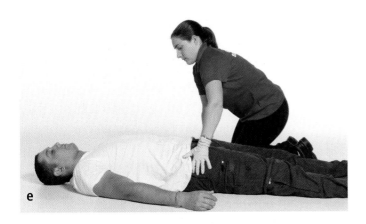

e

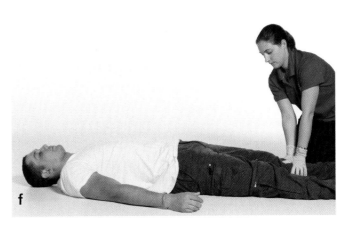

f

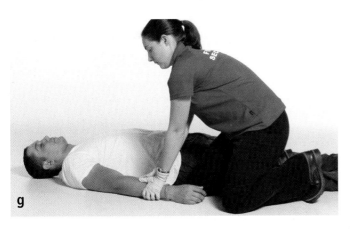

g

Figure 5–18, a-g To do a secondary survey **a**, check the neck; **b**, check the shoulders and collarbones; **c**, check the chest and the person's breathing; **d**, apply light pressure to the abdomen, then check the four quadrants; **e**, check the hips and pelvis; **f**, check the legs, feet, and toes; and **g**, check the arms, hands, and fingers.

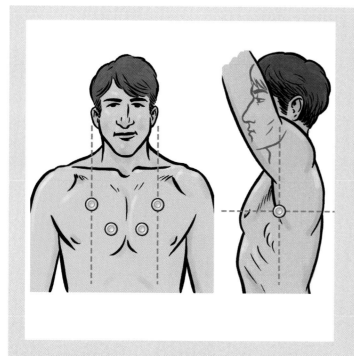

You may be required to auscultate for lung sounds using a stethoscope. When doing this, listen for present and equal breath sounds in both lungs, at the top and bottom. To do this:

- Place the stethoscope approximately 5 cm (2 in) below the clavicle at the mid-clavicular line. Listen to one full inhalation and exhalation on both sides of the chest.

- Place the stethoscope at the fourth or fifth intercostal space on the mid-axillary line. Listen to one full inhalation and exhalation on both sides of the chest.

Absent, diminished, or abnormal breath sounds may indicate abnormal or inadequate breathing. Your local protocol may indicate a specific auscultation pattern to follow.

To check the neck, look and feel for any abnormalities (Figure 5–18, a). If the person has not suffered an injury involving the head or trunk and does not have any pain or discomfort in the head, neck, or back, then there is little likelihood of a spinal injury. You should proceed to check other body parts. If, however, you suspect a possible head or spine injury because of the mechanism of injury, such as a motor vehicle collision or a fall from a height, minimize movement to the person's head and spine. If you suspect head or spine injuries, take care of these first. Do not be concerned about finishing the secondary survey. You will learn techniques for stabilizing and immobilizing the head and spine in Chapter 13.

If you do not suspect injury, check the collarbones and shoulders by feeling for deformity (Figure 5–18, b). Ask the person to shrug his shoulders. Check the chest by asking the person to take a deep breath and then blow the air out. Ask the person if he is experiencing pain. Auscultate for lung sounds if you are trained to do so. Look and listen for more subtle signs of breathing difficulty, such as wheezing or diminished lung sounds. Feel the ribs for deformity (Figure 5–18, c).

Next, ask if the person has any pain in the abdomen. Expose the abdomen; look for discolouration, open wounds, or distension. Look at the abdomen for any pulsating. If there is no pulsating, apply slight pressure

to each of the abdominal quadrants (Figure 5–18, d), avoiding any areas where the person had indicated pain. The abdomen should be soft. If it is rigid, this indicates a problem. Check the hips, asking the person if he has any pain. Place your hands on both sides of the pelvis and push in on the sides and down on the hips (Figure 5–18, e).

Next, look and feel each leg for any deformity (Figure 5–18, f). If there is no apparent sign of injury, ask the person to move his toes, foot, and leg. Finally, determine if the person has any pain in the arms or hands. Feel the arms for any deformity (Figure 5–18, g). It is best to check only one extremity at a time. If there is no apparent sign of injury, ask the person to move his fingers, hand, and arm. Repeat this procedure on the other arm. Check for distal circulation and sensation in both arms and legs.

NOTE:

As you perform the physical exam, try not to move the person. Most injured people will find the most comfortable position for themselves. For example, a person with a chest injury who is experiencing difficulty with his breathing may be sitting up and supporting the injured areas.

TABLE 5-5 WHEN TO OBTAIN MORE ADVANCED MEDICAL CARE

Condition	Signs and Symptoms
Unconscious or decreased level of consciousness	Person does not respond to tapping, loud voices, or other attempts to awaken
Difficulty breathing	Noisy breathing, such as wheezing or gasping Person feels short of breath Skin has a flushed, pale, or bluish appearance
No breathing	You cannot see the person's chest rise and fall You cannot hear and feel air escaping from the nose and/or mouth
No pulse or signs of circulation	You cannot feel the carotid pulse in the neck or the pulses in the arms and legs
Severe bleeding	Person has bleeding that spurts or gushes from the wound
Persistent pain or pressure in the chest or abdomen	Person has persistent pain or pressure in the chest or abdomen that is not relieved by resting or changing positions
Vomiting blood or passing blood	You can see blood in vomit, urine, or feces
Suspected poisoning	Person shows evidence of swallowed, inhaled, or injected poison, such as presence of drugs, medications, or cleaning agents Mouth or lips may be burned
Sudden illness requiring assistance	Person has seizures, severe headaches, slurred speech, or changes in level of consciousness, unusually high or low blood pressure, or a known diabetic condition
Head, neck, or spine injuries	How the injury happened; for example, a fall, severe blow, or collision suggests a head injury Person complains of severe headaches or neck or back pain Person is unconscious Bleeding, clear fluid, or deformity of the scalp, face, or neck
Possible broken bones	How the injury happened; for example, a fall, severe blow, or collision suggests a fracture Evidence of damage to blood vessels or nerves, for example, slow capillary refill, no pulse below the injury, loss of sensation in the affected part Inability to move body part without pain or discomfort Fractures associated with open wounds

If the person can move all his body parts without pain or discomfort and there are no other apparent signs or symptoms of injury, have him attempt to rest for a few minutes in a sitting position. If more advanced help is not needed, continue to check the signs and symptoms and monitor the ABCs.

Take note of the information you find during the physical exam. Sometimes you may need to have a partner fill out the form with the information you gather. This will help you when it is time to give a verbal report to the next level of care as you transfer the person.

ONGOING SURVEY

If you have completed the secondary survey and have given care for any injuries and illness, provide ongoing survey and care while you wait to obtain advanced medical care. The person's condition can gradually worsen, or a life-threatening condition, such as respiratory or cardiac arrest, can occur suddenly. Do not assume that the person is out of danger just because there were no serious problems at first. Keep watching the person's level of consciousness, breathing, and skin colour. Appropriate vital signs should be checked every 5 minutes if the person has a life-threatening emergency; otherwise, check vital signs every 15 minutes. The physical exam and history do not need to be repeated unless there is a specific reason to do so. If any life-threatening emergencies develop, stop whatever you are doing and provide appropriate care immediately.

Record additional findings and turn this information over to the next level of care.

While waiting for more advanced medical care (Table 5-5), help the ill or injured person stay calm and as comfortable as possible.

These conditions by no means make a complete list. It is impossible to describe every possible condition since there are always exceptions. Trust your instincts. If you think there is an emergency, there probably is. It is better to obtain more advanced medical care than wait until it is too late to help.

SUMMARY

A primary survey serves to determine if any life-threatening conditions are present so they can be treated rapidly. The secondary survey helps determine any other conditions that may not be a threat to life at the moment but still require care. Problems that are not an immediate threat to life can become serious if you do not recognize them and provide care. By following the appropriate steps when conducting primary and secondary surveys, you will give the person with a serious illness or injury the best chance for survival.

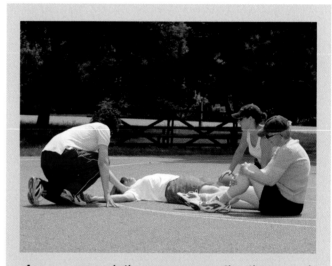

As you approach the scene, you notice the second basketball player falls silent and appears to go limp. What do you do?

Skills Summary

Primary Survey

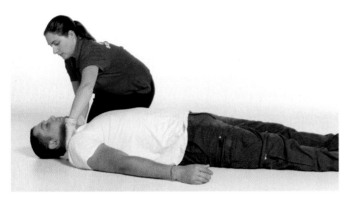

1. Check for responsiveness.

2. Open airway with head-tilt/chin-lift or jaw thrust and check for breathing.

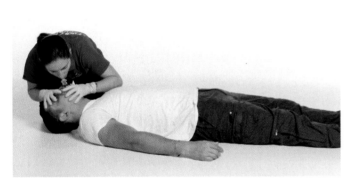

3. If not breathing, give two one-second breaths.

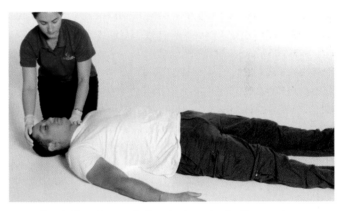

4. Check for signs of circulation, including pulse.

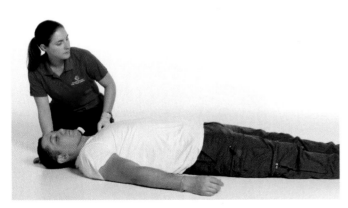

5. Visually inspect for bleeding.

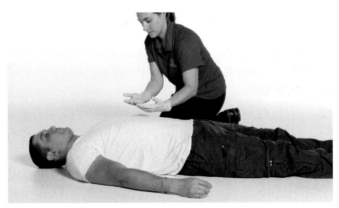

6. Physically check for bleeding.

Skills Summary

Measuring Blood Pressure (Palpation)

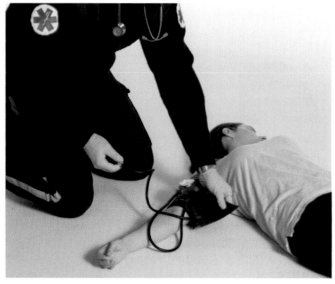

1. Position cuff.

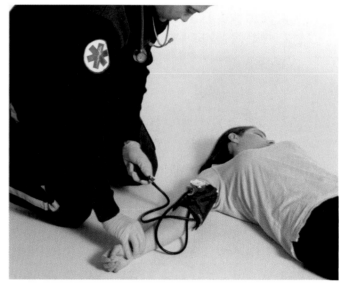

2. Locate radial pulse.

Inflate 20 mmHg

Pulse disappears

3. Inflate cuff beyond where pulse disappears.

Deflate slowly

4. Deflate cuff slowly until pulse returns. This is the approximate systolic blood pressure.

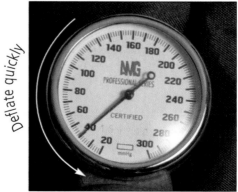

Deflate quickly

5. Quickly deflate cuff by opening valve.

Measuring Blood Pressure (Auscultation)

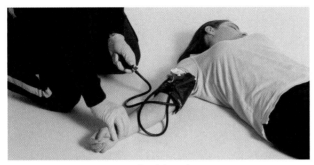

1. Approximate systolic blood pressure.

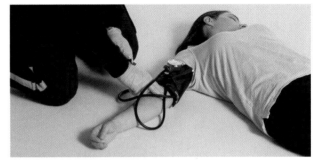

2. Locate brachial pulse.

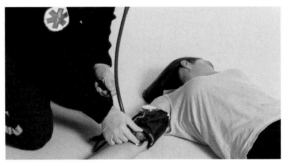

3. Position stethoscope.

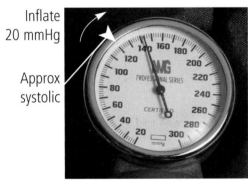

4. Inflate cuff 20 mmHg beyond approximate systolic blood pressure.

5. Deflate cuff slowly until pulse is heard.

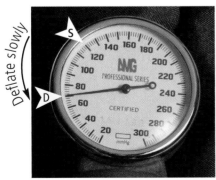

6. Continue deflating cuff until pulse disappears (diastolic).

7. Quickly deflate cuff.

Skills Summary

Head-to-Toe Examination

1. Check head and neck.

2. Check collarbones and shoulders.

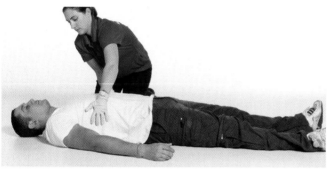

3. Check chest and ribs.

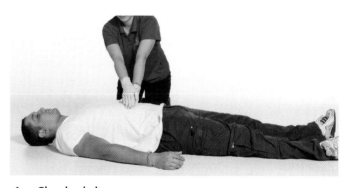

4. Check abdomen.

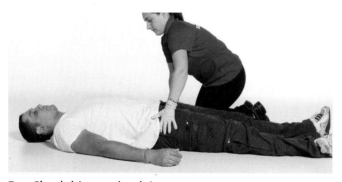

5. Check hips and pelvis.

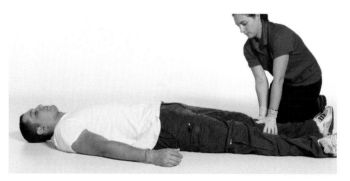

6. Check legs and feet.

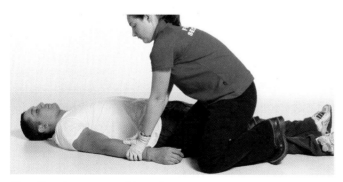

7. Check arms and hands.

Chapter 6

Respiratory Emergencies

It's a beautiful summer day. You are called to a family having a picnic.
A three-year-old girl is gasping for air and has a panicked look on her face.
Her mother is crying and doesn't know what to do. "She was just eating
her lunch when this happened!" she cries. You survey the scene.
What do you do?

INTRODUCTION

In this chapter, you will learn how to care for respiratory, or breathing, emergencies. Because oxygen is vital to life, you must always ensure that the person has an open airway and is breathing. You will often detect a breathing emergency during the primary survey. In a breathing emergency, a person's breathing is so impaired that life is threatened. This kind of emergency can occur in two ways: breathing becomes difficult or breathing stops. A person who is having difficulty breathing is having a breathing emergency. A person who has stopped breathing is in respiratory arrest.

THE BREATHING PROCESS

Air enters the respiratory system through the nose and mouth and passes through the pharynx (Figure 6–1). The pharynx divides into two passageways: one for food, the esophagus, and one for air, the trachea. The epiglottis protects the opening of the trachea when a person swallows so that food and liquid do not enter the lungs.

The body requires a constant supply of oxygen for survival. The supply required depends on the needs of the body, which are affected by variables such as activity level. A body fighting off an illness, even the common cold, uses more energy and oxygen than a body in its healthy state. With illness, the body must carry out all regular functions and also fight the illness. Some tissues, such as brain tissue, are very sensitive to oxygen starvation. Without oxygen, brain cells begin to die in as few as four to six minutes (Figure 6–2). Other

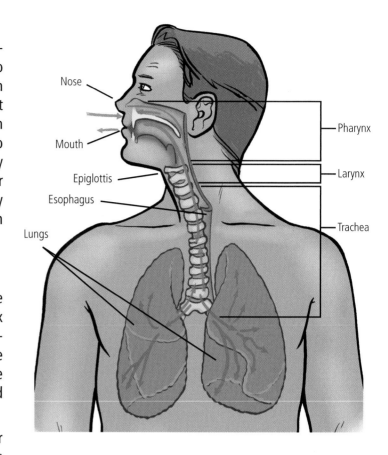

Figure 6–1 The respiratory system includes the pharynx, larynx, and trachea.

vital organs will also be affected unless oxygen supplies are restored.

The brain is the control centre for breathing. It adjusts the rate and depth of breaths according to the oxygen and carbon dioxide levels in the body. Breathing

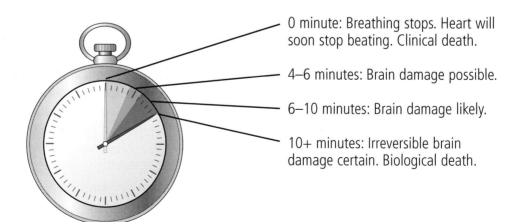

0 minute: Breathing stops. Heart will soon stop beating. Clinical death.

4–6 minutes: Brain damage possible.

6–10 minutes: Brain damage likely.

10+ minutes: Irreversible brain damage certain. Biological death.

Figure 6–2 In clinical death the heart and breathing stops. Clinical death can lead to biological death, which is the irreversible death of brain cells.

requires the respiratory, circulatory, nervous, and musculoskeletal systems to work together. Injuries or illnesses that affect any of these systems may cause breathing emergencies. For example, in the event of severe bleeding, where there has been a loss of blood, the body will compensate by increasing the blood flow to the tissue and therefore increasing the respiratory rate.

Respiratory emergencies can be caused by the following:

- Choking
- Illness, such as pneumonia
- Respiratory conditions, such as emphysema and asthma
- Electrocution
- Shock
- Drowning
- Heart attack or heart disease
- Injury to the chest or lungs
- Allergic reactions, such as to food or insect stings
- Drugs
- Poisoning, such as inhaling or ingesting toxic substances

CHOKING

Choking, caused by airway obstruction, is one of the most common causes of respiratory emergencies. The two types of airway obstruction are anatomical and mechanical.

An anatomical obstruction occurs when the airway is blocked by an anatomical structure, such as the tongue or swollen tissues of the mouth and throat. This type of obstruction may result from injury to the neck or a medical emergency such as anaphylaxis. The most common obstruction in an unconscious person is the tongue, which may drop to the back of the throat and block the airway. This occurs because muscles, including the tongue, relax when deprived of oxygen.

A mechanical obstruction occurs when the airway is blocked by a foreign object, such as a piece of food or a small toy, or fluids, such as vomit, blood, mucus, or saliva.

Common causes of choking include:

- Trying to swallow large pieces of poorly chewed food
- Drinking alcohol before or during meals (alcohol dulls the nerves that aid swallowing, making choking on food more likely)
- Wearing dentures (dentures make it difficult for you to sense whether food is fully chewed before you swallow it)
- Eating while talking excitedly or laughing or eating too fast
- Walking, playing, or running with food or objects in the mouth

A person whose airway is blocked by a piece of food or another object can quickly stop breathing, lose consciousness, and die. You must be able to recognize that the airway is obstructed and give care immediately. This is why checking the airway comes first in the ABCs of the primary survey.

A person who is choking may have either a mild or severe airway obstruction. A person with a severe airway obstruction is not able to pass a sufficient amount of air to maintain the breathing process. With a mild airway obstruction, the person's ability to breathe depends on how much air can get past the obstruction into the lungs.

Mild Choking

A person with a mild airway obstruction can still move air to and from the lungs. This air allows the person to cough, in an attempt to dislodge the object. The person may also be able to move air past the vocal cords to speak. The narrowed airway causes a wheezing sound as air moves in and out of the lungs. As a natural reaction to choking, the person may clutch at the throat with one or both hands (Figure 6–3). If the person is coughing forcefully, do not interfere with attempts to cough up the object. A person who has enough air to cough forcefully or speak also has enough air entering the lungs to breathe. Stay with the person and encourage her to continue coughing to clear the obstruction. If coughing persists, obtain more advanced medical care.

Figure 6–3 Clutching the throat with one or both hands is recognized as a distress signal for choking.

Severe Choking

A mild airway obstruction can quickly become a severe airway obstruction. A person with a severely blocked airway is unable to speak, cry, breathe, or cough effectively. Sometimes the person may cough weakly and ineffectively or make high-pitched noises. All of these signs tell you the person is not getting enough air to the lungs to sustain life. Act immediately. If you have not already done so, have a bystander call for more advanced medical care while you begin to give care.

Care for a Person Who Is Choking

When someone is choking, you must try to reopen the airway as quickly as possible.

The method you use depends on whether the person is conscious or unconscious and whether the person is an adult, a child, or a baby. Variations are used for large adults or pregnant women who are conscious.

Care for a Conscious Choking Adult

To give abdominal thrusts to a conscious choking adult, stand behind the person and wrap your arms around his waist (Figure 6–4, a). The person may be seated or standing. Make a fist with one hand and place the thumb side against the middle of the person's abdomen just above the navel and well below the lower tip of the breastbone (Figure 6–4, b). Grab your fist with your other hand and give quick upward thrusts into the abdomen (Figure 6–4, c).

Figure 6–4, a-c To give abdominal thrusts: **a**, stand behind the person and wrap your arms around his waist; **b**, place the thumb side of your fist against the middle of the person's abdomen; and **c**, grasp your fist with your other hand and give quick upward thrusts into the abdomen.

Abdominal thrusts compress the abdomen, increasing pressure in the lungs and airway. This simulates a cough, forcing trapped air in the lungs to push the object out of the airway like a cork from a bottle of champagne. Repeat these thrusts until the object is dislodged or the person becomes unconscious.

If the person becomes unconscious, lower him to the floor, ensuring you protect the head. Have someone obtain advanced medical care if this has not already been done.

After abdominal thrusts, it is best that the person be examined by a physician.

NOTE:

Treat a child as you would an adult, though you may need to kneel down to the child's level. Care for an unconscious choking child is the same as an adult.

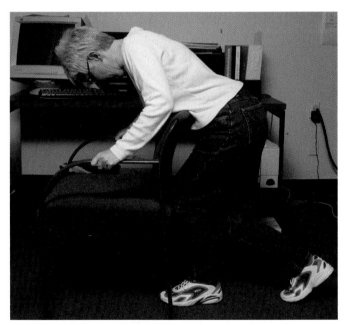

Figure 6–5 To give yourself abdominal thrusts, press your abdomen onto a firm object, such as the back of a chair.

If You Are Alone and Choking

If you are choking and no one is around who can help, you can give yourself abdominal thrusts in two ways:

1. Make a fist with one hand and place the thumb side on the middle of your abdomen slightly above your navel and well below the tip of your breastbone.

Figure 6–6 Chest compressions for unconscious choking are done just as they are in CPR.

Grasp your fist with your other hand and give a quick upward thrust.

2. Lean forward and press your abdomen over any firm object, such as the back of a chair, a railing, or a sink (Figure 6–5). Be careful not to lean over anything with a sharp edge or a corner that might injure you.

Care for an Unconscious Choking Adult

During your primary survey, you may discover that an unconscious adult is not breathing and that the first breath you give will not go in. If this happens, re-tilt the head and attempt to ventilate again. You may not have tilted the person's head back correctly. If air still does not go in, assume that the person's airway is obstructed and begin the CPR sequence (30 chest compressions).

Chest compressions are performed just as they are in CPR (Figure 6–6) and are proven to be effective in dislodging an object in the throat. Many people who have an obstructed airway will also not have circulation, so chest compressions will not only be effective in dislodging the obstruction but will also provide necessary care for absence of circulation.

After giving 30 chest compressions, look in the mouth. If you see an object, it should be carefully removed. Grasp the tongue and lower jaw and lift (Figure 6–7, a). Sweep the object out using a finger sweep (Figure 6–7, b); then attempt to ventilate. Remember, if

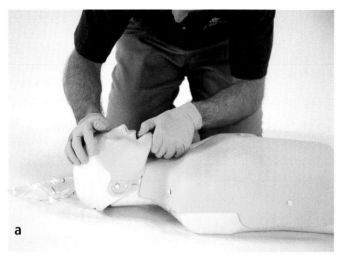
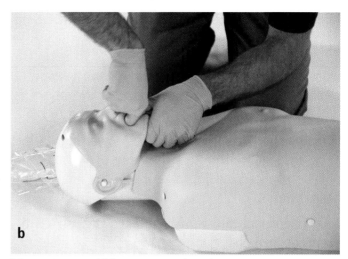

Figure 6–7, a-b To do a finger sweep: **a**, grasp the tongue and lower jaw and lift; **b**, sweep the object out using a finger sweep.

necessary, to reposition the head to adjust the airway. If you do not see an object, or you are still not able to breathe air into the person's lungs, repeat the CPR sequence. Always look in the mouth prior to the ventilation attempt.

If your first attempt to clear the airway is unsuccessful, do not stop. The longer the person goes without oxygen, the more the muscles will relax, making it easier to clear the airway.

Repeat the sequence until the object is expelled, you can breathe into the person, or other trained personnel take over.

Once you are able to breathe air into the person's lungs, give two one-second breaths. Then complete the primary survey by checking the person for signs of circulation and checking and caring for any severe bleeding. If there are no signs of circulation, have someone get an automated external defibrillator (AED) (if you don't already have one) and begin CPR (see Chapter 8). If the person has signs of circulation but is not breathing on his own, continue rescue breathing.

If the person starts breathing on her own, maintain an open airway and continue to monitor both breathing and circulation until you can obtain more advanced medical care. Place the person in the recovery position, as described in Chapter 5.

When to Stop Care

Stop immediately if the object is dislodged or if the person begins to breathe or cough. Make sure the object is cleared from the airway and the person is breathing freely again. Even after the object is coughed up, the person may still have breathing problems that you do not immediately see. You should also realize that abdominal thrusts, chest compressions, and chest thrusts may cause internal injuries. Therefore, anytime this type of care is used to dislodge an object, you should obtain more advanced medical care for follow-up, even if he seems to be breathing without difficulty.

Special Considerations for a Person Who Is Choking

In some instances, abdominal thrusts are not the best method of care for someone who is choking. Some people who are choking need chest thrusts. For example, if you cannot reach far enough around the person to give effective abdominal thrusts, you should give chest thrusts. You should also give chest thrusts instead of abdominal thrusts to noticeably pregnant choking women.

Chest Thrusts for a Conscious Person

To give chest thrusts to a conscious person, stand behind the person and place your arms under her

Figure 6–8 Give chest thrusts if you cannot reach around the person to give abdominal thrusts or if the person is noticeably pregnant.

armpits and around the chest. As for abdominal thrusts, make a fist with one hand, placing the thumb side against the centre of the person's breastbone. Be sure that your thumb is centred on the breastbone, not on the ribs. Also, make sure that your fist is not near the lower tip of the breastbone. Grab your fist with your other hand and thrust inward (Figure 6–8). Repeat these thrusts until the object is dislodged or the person becomes unconscious.

If the person becomes unconscious, position the person on his or her back. Once positioned, use the same techniques as described earlier in this chapter.

Babies

Choking emergencies are common in children and babies. Care for babies who are choking includes a combination of chest thrusts given with two fingers and back blows. Abdominal thrusts are not used for a choking baby because of their potential to cause injury.

Care for a Conscious Choking Baby

If, during the primary survey, you determine that a conscious baby cannot breathe, cough, or cry, give care for a severe airway obstruction. Begin by giving five back blows followed by five chest thrusts.

Start by positioning the baby face up on your forearm. Place your other arm on top of the baby, using your thumb and fingers to hold the baby's jaw while sandwiching the baby between your forearms (Figure 6–9, a). Turn the baby over so that she is face down on your forearm (Figure 6–9, b). Lower your arm onto your thigh so that the baby's head is lower than her chest. Give five firm back blows with the heel of your hand between the shoulder blades (Figure 6–9, c). Maintain support of the head and neck by firmly holding the jaw between your thumb and forefinger.

To give chest thrusts, you will need to turn the baby back over. Start by placing your free hand and forearm along the baby's head and back so that the baby is sandwiched between your two hands and forearms. Continue to support the head between your thumb and fingers from the front while you cradle the back of the head with your other hand.

Turn the baby onto her back. Lower your arm that is supporting the back onto your thigh. The head should be lower than her chest. Give five chest thrusts (Figure 6–10).

To locate the correct place to give chest thrusts, place your two fingers in the middle of the chest, just below the nipple line.

Use the pads of the two fingers to compress the breastbone. Compress the breastbone $1/3$ to $1/2$ the depth of the chest and then let the breastbone return to its normal position. Keep your fingers in contact with the baby's breastbone. Compress five times. You can give back blows and chest thrusts effectively whether you stand up or sit. If the baby is large or your hands are too small to adequately support the baby, you may prefer to sit. Place the baby in your lap to give back blows and chest thrusts. The baby's head should be lower than the chest.

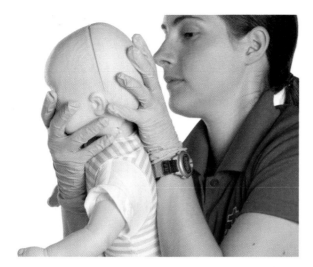

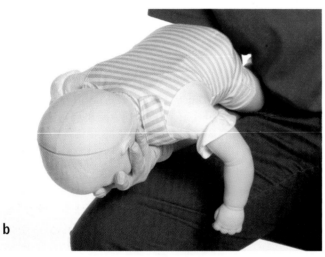

Figure 6–9, a-c To care for a conscious choking baby: **a**, sandwich the baby between your forearms; **b**, turn the baby over so she is face down along your forearm on your lap; and **c**, give 5 firm back blows with the heel of your hand between the shoulder blades.

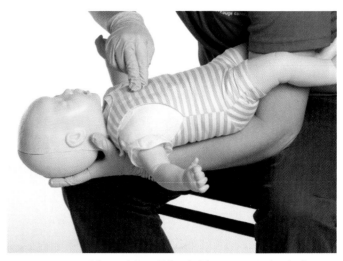

Figure 6–10 After giving 5 back blows, turn the baby onto her back, lower your arm onto your thigh, and give 5 chest thrusts.

Keep giving back blows and chest thrusts until the object is coughed up, the baby begins to breathe or cough, or the baby goes unconscious. Obtain more advanced medical care if you have not already done so. Even if the baby seems to be breathing well, she should be examined by more advanced medical personnel.

Care for an Unconscious Choking Baby

Like the care for an adult and a child, the care for an unconscious baby with a severe airway obstruction begins with a primary survey. If, while doing the ABC steps, you determine that you cannot get air into the lungs, re-tilt the head and reattempt the ventilation. Do not tilt the head back too far. If you still cannot breathe air into the baby, start the CPR sequence. Give 30 chest compressions; then look in the mouth for a foreign body. Next, open the airway, and attempt to ventilate. Remember, if necessary, to reposition the head to adjust the airway.

To do a foreign-body check, open the baby's mouth using your hand that is nearer the baby's feet (Figure 6–11). Grasp both the tongue and lower jaw and lift. Look for an object. If you can see it, try to remove it by sweeping the object out using a finger sweep with the little finger (Figure 6–12).

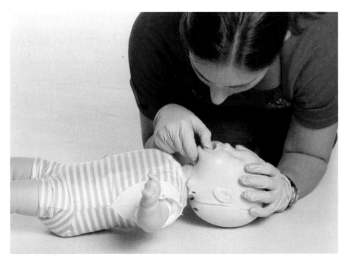

Figure 6–11 To do a finger sweep on a baby, put your thumb into the baby's mouth and hold the tongue and lower jaw between the thumb and fingers. Lift the jaw upward.

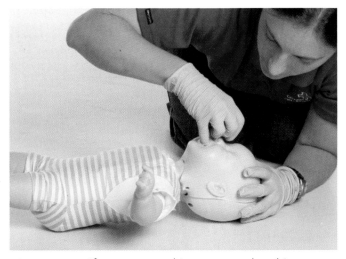

Figure 6–12 If you see an object, sweep the object out using your little finger.

If your first attempt to clear the airway is unsuccessful, do not stop. Repeat the CPR sequence until you are able to get air in the baby's lungs.

If you are able to breathe air into the baby's lungs, finish the primary survey. Give two breaths and check the baby's signs of circulation. Next, check and care for any severe bleeding. If the baby has no circulation, begin CPR,

which you will learn in Chapter 8. If the baby has signs of circulation and is not breathing on her own, continue rescue breathing, which is taught later in this chapter.

If the baby starts breathing on her own, complete a secondary survey, continue to maintain an open airway, and monitor breathing and circulation until you obtain more advanced care.

PREVENTION OF CHOKING

Choking can usually be prevented if you are careful when eating. Follow these guidelines:

- Chew food well before swallowing; eat slowly and calmly.

- Avoid talking or laughing with food in your mouth.

- Minimize alcohol consumption before and during meals.

- Avoid walking or other physical activity with food in your mouth.

- Keep other objects out of the mouth. For example, do not hold a pen cap or nails in your mouth when your hands are busy.

Babies and children are particularly at risk for choking. Parents and other supervisors should follow these guidelines:

- Feed children only when they are seated in a high chair or a secure seat. Do not let children move about with food in their hands or mouth.

- Feed a baby or young child appropriate soft food in small pieces. Constantly watch the child when eating.

- Check the environment and all toys to be sure there are no small objects or parts that the baby or young child may put in her mouth.

- Keep young children away from balloons, which can burst into small pieces that can be easily inhaled.

TABLE 6-1 SIGNS AND SYMPTOMS OF BREATHING EMERGENCIES

Conditions	Signs and Symptoms
Abnormal breathing	Breathing is unusually slow, rapid, deep, or shallow Person is gasping for breath Person is wheezing or gurgling or making high-pitched shrill noises
Abnormal skin appearance	Skin is unusually moist Skin has a flushed, pale or ashen, or bluish appearance
How the person feels	Short of breath Restless and anxious Dizzy or lightheaded Pain in the chest or tingling in hands and feet
How the person looks	Using accessory muscles to breathe, in the tripod position

BREATHING EMERGENCIES

Although breathing emergencies are often caused by injury, several other conditions can also cause them. These include anaphylaxis, chronic obstructive pulmonary disease (COPD), emphysema, chronic bronchitis, asthma, pneumonia, acute pulmonary edema, pulmonary embolism, and hyperventilation.

Signs and Symptoms of Breathing Emergencies

The signs and symptoms of breathing emergencies are usually obvious. People may look as if they cannot catch their breath, or they may gasp for air (Figure 6–13). Their breaths may be unusually fast, slow, deep, or shallow. They may make unusual noises, such as wheezing or gurgling or high-pitched, shrill sounds.

The person's skin may also signal a breathing emergency. At first, the skin may be unusually moist and appear flushed. Later, it may appear pale or bluish as the oxygen level in the blood falls. When the person's skin, lips, or nail beds appear blue, the condition is called cyanosis.

The person may say he feels dizzy or lightheaded. He may feel pain in the chest and tingling in the hands and feet. He may be apprehensive or fearful (Figure 6–14). Any of these symptoms is a clue that the person

may be having a breathing emergency. Table 6-1 lists the signs and symptoms of breathing emergencies.

Figure 6–13 People with breathing emergencies may look as if they cannot catch their breath, or they may gasp for air.

Figure 6–14 There are many signs and symptoms of breathing emergencies.

Specific Types of Breathing Emergencies

Anaphylaxis

Anaphylaxis, also known as anaphylactic shock, is a severe allergic reaction. The air passages constrict and restrict the person's breathing. Anaphylaxis may be caused by insect bites or stings or contact with drugs, medications such as penicillin, food, and chemicals.

Anaphylaxis usually occurs suddenly, within seconds or minutes after contact with the substance. The skin or area of the body that came in contact with the substance usually swells and turns red. This breathing difficulty can progress to an obstructed airway as the tongue and throat swell. The person may also feel dizzy or confused. Other signs and symptoms include hives, itching, rash, weakness, nausea, vomiting, dizziness, and breathing difficulty that includes tightness in the chest and throat, coughing, and wheezing (Figure 6–15).

Anaphylaxis is a life-threatening emergency requiring advanced medical care. Death from anaphylaxis usually occurs because the person's breathing is severely impaired.

If an unusual inflammation or rash is noticeable

Figure 6–15 A person in anaphylaxis may have many signs and symptoms including swelling of the face.

immediately after contact with a possible source, it could be an allergic reaction. Assess the person's airway and breathing. If the person has any breathing difficulty or complains that their throat is closing, obtain more advanced medical care immediately. Help the person into the most comfortable position for breathing. Administer oxygen if available. Monitor the ABCs and try to keep the person calm.

People who know they are extremely allergic to certain substances usually try to avoid them, although this is sometimes impossible. These people may carry an epinephrine auto-injector in case they have a severe allergic reaction (Figure 6–16). These are available most often by prescription. The injector contains a single dose of the drug epinephrine that can be injected into the body to counteract the reaction.

How to use an epinephrine auto-injector:

1. Make sure that you check the rights of medication.
2. Remove the grey safety cap.
3. Place the black tip against the outer thigh and push the epinephrine auto-injector firmly against the thigh with a quick motion. You should hear a click. Hold for 10 seconds.

Figure 6–16 An epinephrine auto-injector.

4. Remove the epinephrine auto-injector.

5. Return the auto-injector to the container.

6. Massage the injection area for several seconds.

There are epinephrine auto-injectors that have multiple doses in one injector. If a person has an injector of this type, be very careful when handling it and have the person recap the needle himself.

NOTE:

See Appendix A for information regarding pharmacology.

Chronic Obstructive Pulmonary Disease

Chronic obstructive pulmonary disease (COPD) is a disease of the airways that is characterized by a loss of lung function. This disease affects both men and women. The average Canadian with COPD is 65 years old and has a long history of smoking. However, the disease has been diagnosed in individuals as young as 40 years of age. COPD has also been reported to occur more often among people residing in urban centres compared with rural populations. The term COPD is used for emphysema or chronic bronchitis, two closely related diseases of the respiratory system.

People diagnosed with COPD may get colds or the flu often, and they also experience shortness of breath under conditions that do not tax most healthy people. Signs and symptoms of a person suffering from COPD are:

- Shortness of breath, gasping for air with sudden onset

- Sitting upright, leaning forward

- Barrel-chested

- Coarse rattling sounds in the lungs

- Distended neck veins

- Cyanosis

- Prolonged exhalation through pursed lips

- Person has oxygen system in his or her residence, either stationary or portable

Emphysema

Emphysema is a disease in which the alveoli lose their

General Guidelines for Medications

When administering or assisting a person with medication, the responder should use proper technique, know how to observe drug effects, and take careful drug histories for the person. Prior to having the person take any medication, it is the responder's responsibility to ensure that the six rights of medication administration have been met. Observe carefully and document any side effects other than those indicated for the drug administered, if any.

1. Right person. Make sure the person getting the medication is the one whose name is on the label of the medicine container.

2. Right medication. Read the label of the medication.

3. Right dosage. Use an accurately marked measuring container (if applicable).

4. Right time. Give the medication at the right time.

5. Right route. Read the directions carefully and administer with the correct method.

6. Right documentation. Completely document all of your care, including:

   - Time
   - Dose
   - Route
   - Effect

   Always follow local protocol.

elasticity, become distended with trapped air, and stop working. This results in the lungs losing their ability to efficiently exchange carbon dioxide and oxygen. Emphysema is often caused by smoking and usually develops over many years.

People with emphysema suffer from shortness of breath. As the total number of alveoli decreases, breathing becomes more difficult. Exhaling is extremely difficult. They may cough and may have cyanosis or fever. People with advanced cases may be restless, confused, and weak and can go into respiratory or cardiac arrest. Emphysema can get worse over time.

Chronic Bronchitis

Bronchitis is a disease causing excessive mucous secretions and inflammatory changes to the bronchi. These secretions make breathing difficult. Bronchitis is often caused by prolonged exposure to irritants (most commonly, cigarette smoke).

People with bronchitis suffer from shortness of breath and the presence of a cough with sputum. Chronic bronchitis is characterized by a productive cough that has persisted for at least three months in a given year and over two consecutive years. There may also be narrowing of the large and small airways, making it more difficult for air to move in and out of the lungs. This disease gets worse over time.

People with emphysema and/or chronic bronchitis may eventually develop a hypoxic drive to breathe. In healthy individuals, the drive to breathe is from the amount of carbon dioxide in the blood. People with emphysema and/or chronic bronchitis build up high levels of carbon dioxide in the blood. Due to the consistently high levels, the body looks to the oxygen levels to determine the need to breathe. If oxygen levels are low, the breathing rate increases. People with COPD who are not acutely short of breath may be receiving low concentrations of oxygen from their home oxygen unit.

In a person with COPD who has a true "hypoxic drive," increased levels of oxygen could signal the body to slow down or stop breathing entirely. However, this is rarely encountered in the field because EMS is usually called for a person who is acutely short of breath. In this case, you should administer high-flow oxygen to the person.

Asthma

Asthma is a condition that narrows the air passages and makes breathing difficult. During an asthma attack, the air passages become constricted or narrowed by a spasm of the muscles lining the bronchi or by swelling of the bronchi themselves. People may become anxious or frightened because breathing is difficult.

Asthma is more common in children and young adults. It may be triggered by an allergic reaction to food, pollen, a drug, cold weather, or an insect sting. Emotional distress may also trigger it. For some people, physical activity induces asthma. Normally, someone with asthma easily controls attacks with medication.

These medications stop the muscle spasm, opening the airway and making breathing easier.

A characteristic sign of asthma is wheezing when exhaling due to constricted air passages. This also leads to air being trapped in the lungs. This trapped air may also make the person's chest appear larger than normal, particularly in small children.

How to Help Someone Use a Metered Dose Inhaler (MDI)

1. Make sure that you have the inhaler prescribed to that particular person.

2. Shake the inhaler three or four times.

3. Remove the cap from the inhaler. If the person uses a spacer and it has a cap, remove it.

4. If the person uses a spacer, put the inhaler into the spacer (Figure 6–17).

5. Have the person breathe out, away from the inhaler and spacer.

6. Bring the spacer or inhaler to the person's mouth, put the mouthpiece between his or her teeth, and tell the person to close his or her lips around it.

7. Tell the person to press the top of the inhaler once. If the person can't do it, you may do it instead.

8. Tell the person to take one slow, full breath, hold it for about 10 seconds, and then breathe out.

This may need to be repeated multiple times.

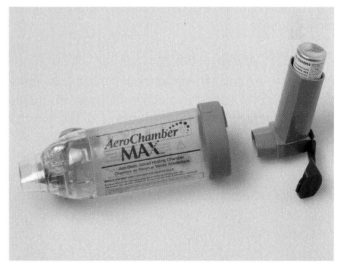

Figure 6–17 An inhaler prescribed for asthma and a spacer.

Pneumonia

Pneumonia is a term used to describe a group of illnesses characterized by lung infection and fluid- or pus-filled alveoli, resulting in inadequate oxygen in the blood. Pneumonia is caused by bacteria or a virus but also can be caused by irritants, such as smoke, or aspirated materials, such as vomit. The type of illness caused by chemical irritation or aspiration is called pneumonitis. People with pneumonia may complain of fever and chills.

The following signs and symptoms may be found in a person suffering from pneumonia:

- Difficulty breathing
- Rapid breathing
- Pleuritic chest pain, usually worse with breathing
- Productive cough with pus in the sputum or mucus
- Fever, usually exceeding 38°C (100°F)
- Chills

There may be other symptoms as well, such as:

- Nausea
- Vomiting
- Headache
- Tiredness
- Muscle aches

Have the person with a suspected case of pneumonia assume a comfortable position and administer supplemental oxygen.

Acute Pulmonary Edema

Pulmonary edema can be caused by heart or lung damage. For example, a number of heart disorders (e.g., heart attack, left-sided heart failure, dysrhythmias) can cause fluid to back up in the blood vessels (pulmonary veins) that carry blood away from the lungs to the heart. As a result of a buildup of pressure in these veins, excess fluid leaks out into the alveoli. Congestive heart failure (CHF) is the most common condition to cause pulmonary edema.

However, other causes include pneumonia, smoke or toxin inhalation, narcotic overdose, drowning, and high-altitude illness. You may find people with pulmonary edema sitting upright, leaning forward. If you find a person lying down, instruct her to sit up and dangle her legs to encourage fluid to pool in the legs.

As the fluid builds up in the lungs, the amount of oxygen entering the blood decreases (Figure 6–18). You should give high-flow oxygen to anyone with acute pulmonary edema. In some cases, you may need to assist the person's ventilations.

Signs and symptoms of pulmonary edema are:

- Shortness of breath with sudden onset
- Rapid, laboured breathing
- Cyanosis
- Frothy sputum (later stage)
- Restlessness
- Anxiety
- Exhaustion
- Rapid pulse
- Cool, clammy skin

Pulmonary Embolism

Pulmonary embolism is caused by a blockage (embolus) of a pulmonary artery by a clot or other foreign material that has travelled from another part of the circulatory system. It is a surprisingly common disorder that usually begins as a venous disease. It is most often

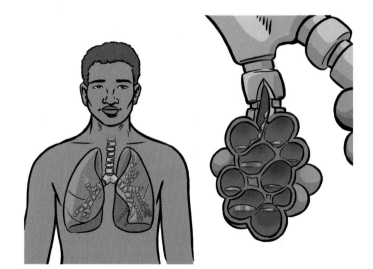

Figure 6–18 Pulmonary edema is a buildup of fluid in the lungs.

caused by a blood clot (thrombus) breaking free in the large veins of the lower extremities but can also be caused by fat, air, amniotic fluid, or tumour tissue. The embolus flows to the right side of the heart. From there it enters the pulmonary arteries, obstructing blood supply to that part of the lung.

An embolus may range in size from small to massive; therefore, the signs and symptoms may be varied (Figure 6–19). They depend on the location of the blockage and the size of the clot and may include the following:

- Shortness of breath
- Cough
- Pain
- Anxiety
- Fainting (syncope)
- Drop in blood pressure (hypotension)
- Cool, clammy skin
- Rapid pulse
- Fever
- Distended neck vein

If you suspect a person has a pulmonary embolism, help her to a comfortable position and administer high-flow oxygen. Definitive care requires hospitalization and thrombolytic or heparin therapy.

Figure 6–19 A pulmonary embolus may range in size from small to massive; therefore, the signs and symptoms may be varied.

Hyperventilation

Hyperventilation occurs when someone breathes faster than normal. This rapid breathing upsets the body's balance of oxygen and carbon dioxide. Hyperventilation is often the result of fear or anxiety and is more likely to occur in people who are tense and nervous. But it is also caused by injuries such as head injuries, by severe bleeding, or by conditions such as high fever, heart failure, lung disease, or diabetic emergencies. It can be triggered by asthma or exercise.

A characteristic sign of hyperventilation is shallow, rapid breathing. Despite their breathing efforts, people say that they cannot get enough air or that they are suffocating. Therefore, they are often fearful and apprehensive or may appear confused. They may say they feel dizzy or that their fingers and toes feel numb or tingly.

General Care for Breathing Emergencies

Recognizing the signs and symptoms of breathing emergencies and providing emergency care are often the keys to preventing other emergencies. Breathing emergencies may signal the beginning of a life-threatening condition. For example, it can be the first signal of a more serious breathing emergency or even a heart attack. Some breathing emergencies can lead to respiratory arrest, which, if not cared for, will result in death.

Many of the signs and symptoms of different kinds of breathing emergencies are similar. You do not need to know the specific cause to provide care. If the person is breathing, you know the heart is beating. Make sure the person is not bleeding severely. Help her rest in a comfortable position. Usually, sitting is more comfortable than lying down because breathing is easier. Open a window to provide more air if necessary. Provide ongoing survey and care. Have bystanders move back. Obtain more advanced medical care.

When you are able, do a secondary survey. Remember that a person experiencing breathing difficulty may have trouble talking. Ask questions to any bystanders who may know about the person's problem. The person can confirm answers or answer yes-or-no questions by nodding. If possible, try to help reduce any anxiety; it may contribute to the person's breathing difficulty. Help the person take any prescribed medication for the condition if it is available. This may be oxygen or an inhalant (bronchial dilator). Continue to provide ongoing survey and care. Help maintain normal body temperature by preventing chilling or overheating. Administer oxygen if available and indicated.

If the person's breathing is rapid and there are signs of an injury or an underlying illness, obtain more advanced medical care or transport immediately. If the person's breathing is rapid and you suspect that it is caused by emotion, such as excitement, try to calm the person to slow her breathing. Reassurance is often enough to correct hyperventilation. But you can also ask the person to try to breathe with you. Breathe at a normal rate, emphasizing inhaling and exhaling.

If the condition does not improve, the person may become unconscious. Obtain more advanced medical care if this has not already been done. Keep the person's airway open and monitor breathing.

RESPIRATORY ARREST

Respiratory arrest is the condition in which breathing stops. It may be caused by illness, injury, or an obstructed airway. The causes of breathing emergencies can also lead to respiratory arrest. In respiratory arrest, the person gets no oxygen. The body can function for only a few minutes without oxygen before body systems begin to fail. Without oxygen, the heart muscle stops functioning. This causes the circulatory system to fail. When the heart stops, other body systems will also start to fail. However, you can keep the person's respiratory system functioning artificially with rescue breathing.

Rescue Breathing

Rescue breathing is a technique of breathing air into a person to supply her with the oxygen needed to survive. Rescue breathing is given to people who are not breathing but still have a pulse.

Rescue breathing works because the air you breathe into the person contains more than enough oxygen to keep that person alive. The air you take in with every breath contains about 21 percent oxygen, but your body uses only a small part of that. The air you breathe out of your lungs and into the lungs of the person contains

about 16 percent oxygen, enough to keep someone alive.

A responder should always use a resuscitation mask when giving rescue breaths. In this chapter, you will learn how to do rescue breathing. You will learn how to use a resuscitation mask as well as other ventilatory devices in Chapter 7.

You will discover whether you need to give rescue breathing during the first two steps of the ABCs in the primary survey, when you open the airway and check for breathing. If you cannot see, hear, or feel signs of breathing, give two one-second breaths immediately to get air into the person's lungs. Then check for signs of circulation and look for severe bleeding. Obtain advanced medical care if you have not already done so.

If the person is not breathing but has a pulse, begin rescue breathing. To give breaths, keep the airway open with the head-tilt/chin-lift. Next, using a mask, make a tight seal over the person's mouth. If using a breathing barrier device that does not cover the nose, gently pinch the person's nose shut with the thumb and index finger of your hand that is on the person's forehead. Breathe into the person just until you see his chest rise (Figure 6–20). Each breath should last one second, with a pause between breaths to let the air flow back out. Watch the person's chest rise each time you breathe to make sure that your breaths are actually going in.

Figure 6–20 When giving a rescue breath, breathe into the person just until you see his chest rise.

If you do not see the person's chest rise and fall as you give a breath, you may not have the head tilted back far enough to open the airway adequately. Re-tilt the person's head and attempt to ventilate again. If air still does not go in, the person's airway is obstructed. You must give the care for an obstructed airway described earlier in this chapter.

Once you are able to give two breaths, check for signs of circulation. If the person has signs of circulation but is not breathing, continue rescue breathing by giving one breath every five to six seconds (for an adult).

After two minutes of rescue breathing, recheck for signs of circulation to make sure the heart is still beating. If the person still has circulation but is not breathing, continue rescue breathing. Check for signs of circulation every few minutes thereafter. Do not stop rescue breathing unless one of the following occurs:

• The person begins to breathe on her own

• The person has no signs of circulation—begin CPR (described in Chapter 8)

• Another responder with training equal to or greater than yours takes over

• You are too exhausted to continue

• The scene suddenly becomes unsafe

Special Considerations for Rescue Breathing

Air in the Stomach

When you do rescue breathing, air normally enters the person's lungs. Sometimes air may enter the person's stomach. There are several reasons why this may occur. First, breathing into the person longer than for one second may cause extra air to fill the stomach. Do not overinflate the lungs. Stop the breath when the chest starts to rise. Second, if the person's head is not tilted back far enough, the airway will not open completely. As a result, the chest may only rise slightly. This will lead

you to breathe more forcefully, causing air to enter the stomach. Third, breaths given too quickly create more pressure in the airway, causing air to enter the stomach.

Air in the stomach is called gastric distension. Gastric distension can be a serious problem because it can make the person vomit. When an unconscious person vomits, stomach contents may get into the lungs, obstructing breathing. Taking such foreign material into the lungs is called aspiration. Because aspiration can hamper rescue breathing due to an airway obstruction, it may require the responder to perform CPR or unconscious choking techniques.

To avoid forcing air into the stomach, be sure to keep the person's head tilted back far enough. Give one-second breaths, with just enough volume to make the chest rise. Pause between breaths long enough for the person's lungs to empty and for you to take another breath.

Vomiting

When you give rescue breathing, the person may vomit. If this happens, turn the person's head and body together as a unit to the side. This helps prevent vomit from entering the lungs. Quickly wipe the person's mouth clean, carefully reposition the person on her back, and reassess ABCs.

Mouth-to-Nose Breathing

Sometimes you may not be able to make an adequate seal over a person's mouth to perform rescue breathing. For example, the person's jaw or mouth may be injured or shut too tightly to open, or your mouth may be too small to cover the person's. If so, provide mouth-to-nose rescue breathing as follows:

• Maintain the head-tilt position with one hand on the forehead. Use your other hand to close the person's mouth, making sure to push on the chin, not on the throat.

• Seal your mouth tightly around the person's nose, and breathe full breaths into the person's nose (Figure 6–21). Open the person's mouth between breaths, if possible, to let air escape.

As with other rescue breathing situations, use a resuscitation mask if you are able to seal it properly on the face.

Figure 6–21 If giving mouth-to-nose breathing, seal your mouth around the person's nose, and breathe in. Ensure the person's mouth remains closed.

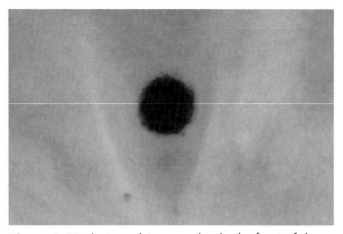

Figure 6–22 A stoma is an opening in the front of the neck that someone breathes through.

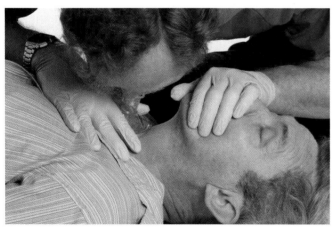

Figure 6–23 When giving rescue breaths to a person with a stoma, breathe directly into the stoma.

Mouth-to-Stoma Breathing

Some people have had an operation to remove all or part of the larynx, the upper end of the windpipe. They breathe through an opening in the front of the neck called a stoma (Figure 6–22). Air passes directly into the trachea through the stoma instead of through the mouth and nose.

To give rescue breathing to someone with a stoma, you must give breaths through the stoma instead of the mouth or nose. Follow the same basic steps as in mouth-to-mask breathing, except:

1. Look, listen, and feel for breathing with your ear over the stoma.

2. Give rescue breaths into the stoma (Figure 6–23).

If the chest does not rise when you give rescue breaths, suspect that the person may have had only part of the larynx removed. That means that some air continues to flow through the larynx to the lungs during normal breathing. When giving mouth-to-stoma breathing, air may leak through the nose and mouth, diminishing the amount of oxygen that reaches the lungs. If this occurs, you need to seal the nose and mouth with your hand to prevent air from escaping during rescue breathing.

People With Dentures

If you know or see the person is wearing dentures, do not automatically remove them. Dentures help rescue breathing by supporting the person's mouth and cheeks during mouth-to-mask breathing. If the dentures are loose, the head-tilt/chin-lift may help keep them in place. Remove the dentures only if they become so loose that they block the airway or make it difficult for you to give breaths.

Suspected Head or Spine Injuries

You should suspect head or spine injuries in people who have suffered a violent force, such as that caused by a motor vehicle crash, a fall, or a diving or other sports-related incident. If you suspect the person may have an injury to the head, neck, or spine, you should try to minimize movement of the head and neck when opening the airway. This requires you to change the way you open the airway.

Open the airway by placing your fingers under the angles of the jaw and lifting. Next, using a mask, make

Figure 6–24 Use a jaw thrust when giving rescue breaths to a person with a suspected head or spine injury.

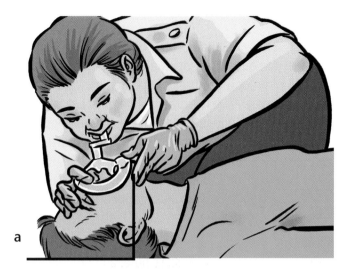

a tight seal over the person's mouth and breathe (Figure 6–24). This technique allows you to open the airway and provides rescue breathing without moving the head. If using a face shield, use your cheek to block the nose. If you are unable to ventilate properly with a jaw thrust, perform a head-tilt/chin-lift.

Babies and Children

Rescue breathing for babies and children follows the same general procedure as that for adults. The minor differences take into account the baby's or child's undeveloped physique, moderately faster pulse, and breathing rate. Rescue breathing for babies and children uses less air in each breath, and breaths are delivered at a slightly faster rate.

You do not need to tilt a child's or baby's head as far back as an adult's to open the airway. Tilt the head back only far enough to allow your breaths to go in. Tipping the head back too far in a child or baby may cause injury that will obstruct the airway. Using a mask, give one breath every three to five seconds for both a child and a baby. Figure 6–25, a-c, shows rescue breathing for an adult, a child, and a baby.

If using a face shield, cover the baby's mouth and nose with you mouth. Remember to breathe slowly into the baby or child. Each breath should last about one second. Be careful not to overinflate a child's or baby's lungs. Breathe only until you see the chest rise. After two minutes of rescue breathing, recheck for signs of circulation.

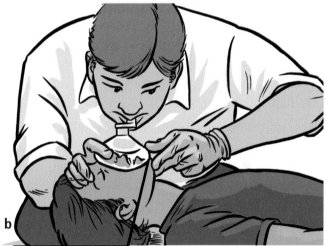

Figure 6–25, a-c Rescue breathing for **a**, an adult; **b**, a child; and **c**, a baby is similar. Often, the older the person, the farther the head needs to be tilted back in order to open the airway.

SUMMARY

Because oxygen is vital to life, you must always ensure that the person has an open airway and is breathing. You will often detect a breathing emergency during the primary survey. In a breathing emergency, a person's breathing is so impaired that life is threatened. This kind of emergency can occur in two ways: breathing becomes difficult or breathing stops. A person who is having difficulty breathing is having a breathing emergency. A person who has stopped breathing is in respiratory arrest.

The body requires a constant supply of oxygen for survival. The brain is the control centre for breathing. It adjusts the rate and depth of breaths according to the oxygen and carbon dioxide levels in the body. Breathing requires the respiratory, circulatory, nervous, and musculoskeletal systems to work together. Injuries or illnesses that affect any of these systems may cause breathing emergencies.

Respiratory emergencies can be caused by choking, illness such as pneumonia, respiratory conditions such as emphysema and asthma, electrocution, shock, drowning, heart attack or heart disease, injury to the chest or lungs, allergic reactions such as to food or insect stings, drugs, and poisoning such as inhaling or ingesting toxic substances.

Recognizing the signs and symptoms of breathing emergencies and providing emergency care are often the keys to preventing other emergencies. Breathing emergencies may signal the beginning of a life-threatening condition. For example, it can be the first signal of a more serious breathing emergency or even a heart attack. Some breathing emergencies can lead to respiratory arrest, which, if not cared for, will result in death.

Many of the signs and symptoms of different kinds of breathing emergencies are similar. You do not need to know the specific cause to provide care. If the person is breathing, you know the heart is beating. Make sure the person is not bleeding severely. Help her rest in a comfortable position. Usually, sitting is more comfortable than lying down because breathing is easier. Open a window to provide more air if necessary. Provide ongoing survey and care. Have bystanders move back. Obtain more advanced medical care.

The little girl begins to make a high-pitched wheezing sound. What do you do?

Conscious Choking Adult or Child

1. Position yourself behind the person who is choking. Make a fist and place the thumb side on the person's abdomen, just above the bellybutton.

2. Grab your fist with your other hand.

3. Give quick upward thrusts into the abdomen.

Continue thrusts until obstruction is relieved or person goes unconscious.

Skills Summary

Conscious Choking Baby

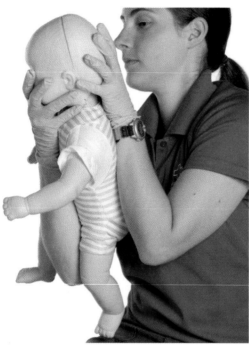

1. Sandwich the baby between your forearms, supporting the head and neck.

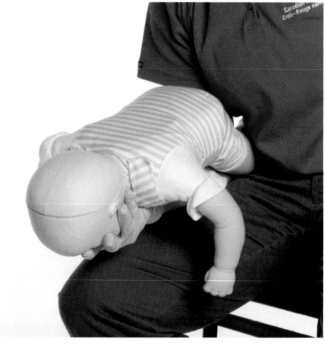

2. Turn the baby so she is face down on your forearm and your arm is supported by your thigh.

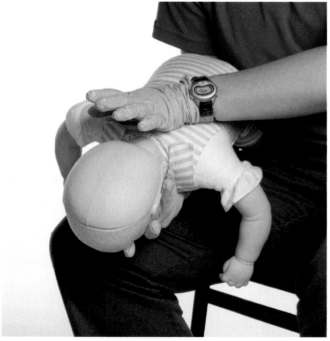

3. Give five firm back blows with the heel of your hand between the shoulder blades.

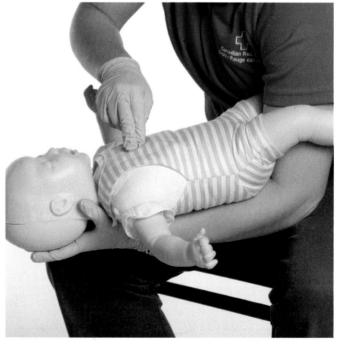

4. Turn the baby over so she is face up. Give five chest thrusts.

Continue until the obstruction is relieved or baby goes unconscious.

Skills Summary

Unconscious Choking Adult or Child

1. Check for responsiveness.

2. Open airway and check for breathing for no more than 10 seconds.

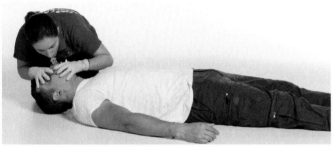

3. If no breathing, give two one-second breaths.

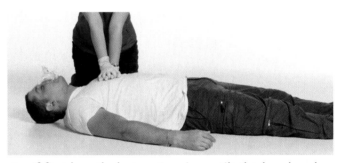

4. If first breath does not go in, re-tilt the head and attempt another breath. If it still does not go in, begin chest compressions (30).

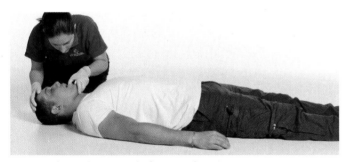

5. Look in the mouth for an object.

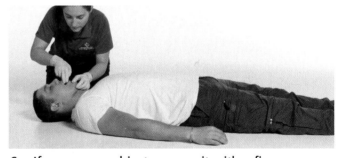

6. If you see an object, remove it with a finger sweep.

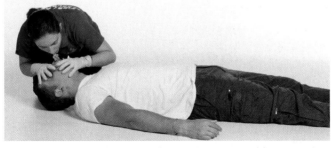

7. Attempt to ventilate. If breath goes in, give another breath; then proceed to check for signs of circulation. If breath does not go in, continue CPR sequence.

Skills Summary

Unconscious Choking Baby

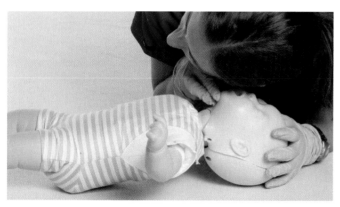

1. Open airway and check for breathing for no more than 10 seconds.

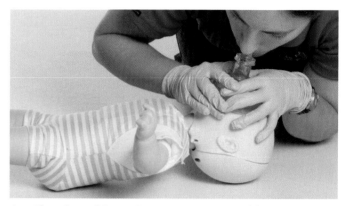

2. If no breathing, give two one-second breaths.

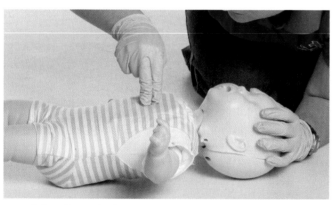

3. If first breath does not go in, re-tilt the head and attempt another breath. If it still does not go in, begin chest compressions (30).

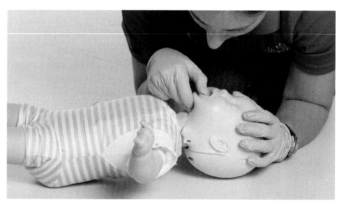

4. Look in the mouth for an object.

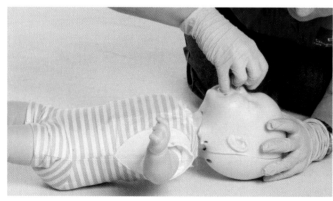

5. If you see an object, remove it with a finger sweep.

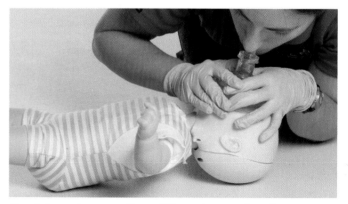

6. Attempt to ventilate. If breath goes in, give another breath; then proceed to check for signs of circulation. If breath does not go in, continue CPR sequence.

Rescue Breathing for an Adult or Child

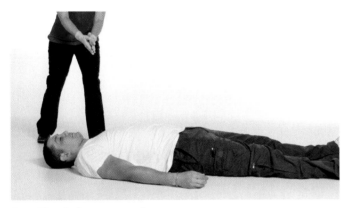

1. Check for responsiveness.

2. Open airway and check for breathing for no more that 10 seconds.

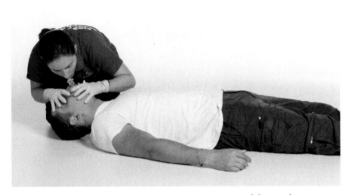

3. If no breathing, give two one-second breaths.

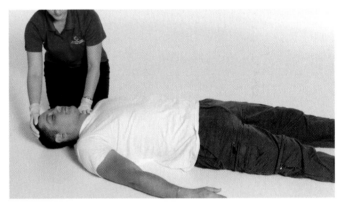

4. Check for signs of circulation (including a pulse) for no more than 10 seconds.

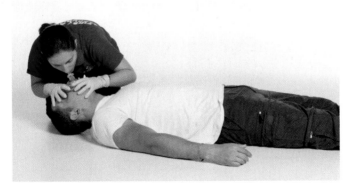

5. If circulation is present but no breathing, give one breath every 5–6 seconds for an adult (every 3–5 seconds for a child).

Recheck breathing and circulation after two minutes and every few minutes thereafter.

Skills Summary

Rescue Breathing for a Baby

1. Open airway and check for breathing for no more than 10 seconds.

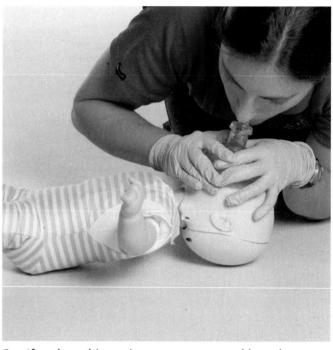

2. If no breathing, give two one-second breaths.

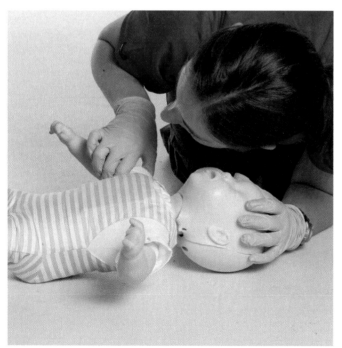

3. Check for signs of circulation (including a pulse) for no more than 10 seconds.

4. If circulation is present but no breathing, give one breath every 3–5 seconds.

Recheck breathing and circulation after two minutes and every few minutes thereafter.

Chapter 7

Airway and Ventilation

At the scene of an industrial fire, a young man is lucky to escape from the burning building. However, after he leaves the building, he finds that he has difficulty breathing. He clutches his chest and gestures to you for assistance. What do you do?

INTRODUCTION

Airway and ventilation management can contribute significantly to the survival and recovery of a seriously ill or injured person. A number of devices can help you maintain an open airway, perform rescue breathing, and increase the oxygen concentration in a person's bloodstream. In addition, these devices also limit the potential for transmitting disease.

CLEARING THE AIRWAY

Sometimes injury or sudden illness results in foreign matter, such as mucus, vomitus, water, or blood, collecting in a person's airway. The most appropriate initial method of clearing the airway is to roll the person onto his side and sweep the foreign matter from the mouth. A more effective method is to suction the airway clear. Suctioning is the process of removing foreign matter by means of a mechanical or manual device. A variety of manual and mechanical devices are used to suction the airway.

Manual suction devices are lightweight, compact, and relatively inexpensive (Figure 7–1, a-b). Mechanical suction devices use either battery-powered pumps or oxygen-powered aspirators. These devices are normally found on ambulances. Attached to the end of any suction device is a suction tip. These come in various sizes and shapes. Some are rigid and others are flexible. A "tonsil tip" catheter can be used for clearing the mouth and throat of an unconscious adult, child, or baby, whereas a "French" catheter can be used to clear the nose.

Whether using a manual or mechanical suction device, perform these six steps:

1. Turn the person's head to one side. (If you suspect spinal injury, roll the person's body onto one side.)

2. Open the person's mouth.

3. Sweep large debris out of the mouth with your finger before suctioning it.

4. Measure the distance of insertion from the person's earlobe to the corner of the mouth (Figure 7–2).

5. Insert the suction tip into the back of the mouth (Figure 7–3).

6. Suction until the airway is clear, without causing trauma to the airway.

Suctioning removes not only fluids and foreign matter but also oxygen from the person. After you have completed suctioning, administer supplemental oxygen.

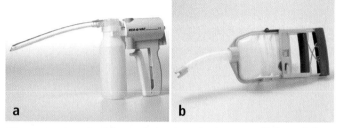

Figure 7–1, a-b Manual suction devices are lightweight and compact.

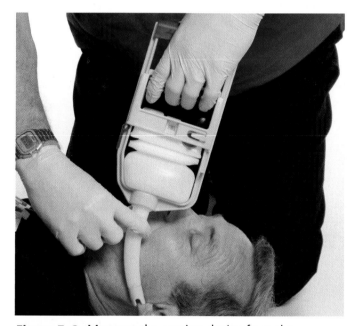

Figure 7–2 Measure the suction device from the person's earlobe to the corner of their mouth.

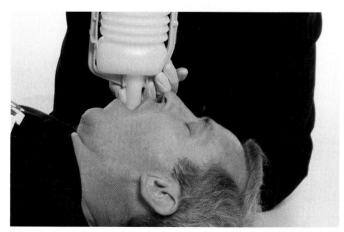

Figure 7–3 Insert the suction tip into the back of the mouth.

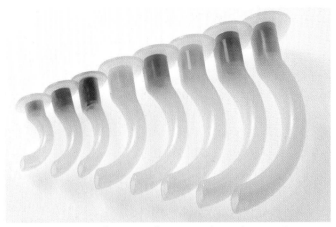

Figure 7–4 Oropharyngeal airways (OPAs) come in a variety of sizes.

OROPHARYNGEAL AIRWAYS

The tongue is the most common cause of airway obstruction in an unconscious person. An oropharyngeal airway (OPA) is a device that is inserted into the mouth of an unconscious person and positioned to assist in keeping the tongue off of the back of the throat. An improperly placed airway device can compress the tongue into the back of the throat, further blocking the airway.

OPAs come in a variety of sizes (Figure 7–4). The curved design fits the natural contour of the mouth and throat. Once you have positioned the device, you can use a resuscitation mask or bag-valve-mask (BVM) resuscitator to ventilate a non-breathing person.

If you have determined the person is unconscious, based on finding no response to painful stimuli, the person should be able to have an OPA inserted without causing a gag reflex.

Proper Sizing and Insertion of an OPA

Measure the device on the person to see that it extends from his earlobe to the corner of the mouth (Figure 7–5). Grasp the person's lower jaw and tongue and lift upward. With the person's jaw raised, insert the OPA with the curved end along the roof of the mouth (Figure 7–6). As the tip of the device approaches the back of the throat, rotate it a half-turn (Figure 7–7). If the person begins gagging as the device is positioned in the back of the throat, remove the device. The OPA should drop into the throat without resistance. The flange end should rest on the person's lips (Figure 7–8).

OPAs in Children and Babies

Younger children and babies have delicate airways, and caution must be taken when inserting an airway, to avoid damage, also being careful not to overextend the neck, which could close or even damage the airway.

On rare occasions, such as when inserting an OPA into a child's mouth, you may not be able to insert the OPA using the technique described above. As a secondary method, you can attempt to insert with the tip of the device pointing toward the cheek and then rotating it 90° to place it into the throat (Figure 7–9).

For babies, it may be required that you insert the OPA directly into position, without rotating it, by using a tongue depressor to open the back of the oral cavity. As always, follow local protocol.

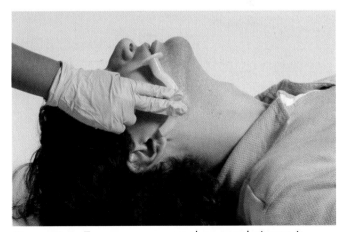

Figure 7–5 To measure an oropharyngeal airway, it should extend from the earlobe to the corner of the mouth.

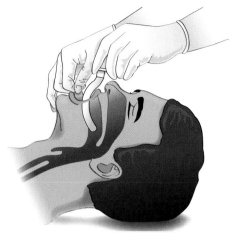

Figure 7–6 To insert the OPA, grasp the person's lower jaw and tongue and lift upward. Insert the OPA with the curved end along the roof of the mouth.

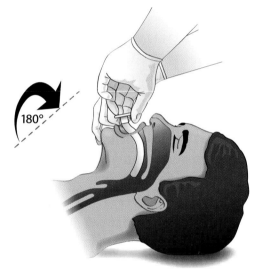

Figure 7–7 As the tip of the device approaches the back of the throat, rotate it a half-turn.

Figure 7–8 The flange end of the OPA should rest on the person's lips.

Figure 7–9 You may attempt to insert the OPA by pointing the tip of the device toward the cheek, then rotating it 90°.

An Alternate Way to Open the Airway: The Crossed-Finger Technique

One method of opening the mouth to assess the airway, insert an OPA, or suction the person's mouth is known as the crossed-finger technique.

1. Cross the thumb and index finger of one hand.

2. Place the thumb on the ill or injured person's lower front teeth and the index finger on the upper front teeth.

3. Open the mouth using a scissor motion.

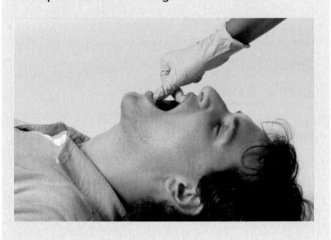

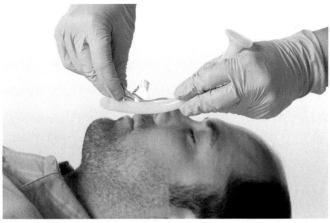

Figure 7–10 Lubricate a nasopharyngeal airway (NPA) with a water-soluble lubricant.

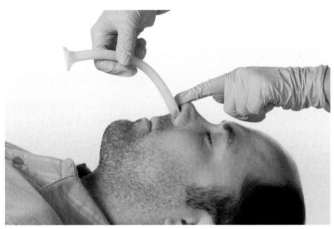

Figure 7–11 Insert the NPA into a nostril, with the bevel toward the septum.

NASOPHARYNGEAL AIRWAYS

A nasopharyngeal (nasal) airway (NPA) is used to assist in maintaining an airway in an unconscious adult. An NPA may also be used on responsive adults who need help keeping the tongue from obstructing the airway. Nasal airways are available in a variety of sizes.

Inserting an NPA

When using an NPA, determine the correct size by measuring the device on the person to see that it extends from his earlobe to the tip of the nose. Also make sure the diameter of the NPA is not larger than the diameter of the nostril.

Lubricate the airway with a water-soluble lubricant (Figure 7–10). Insert the NPA into a nostril, with the bevel toward the septum (Figure 7–11). Advance the airway gently, straight in, not upward, until the flange rests on the nose (Figure 7–12, a-b). If you feel even minor resistance, do not try to force the airway. If you

cannot get the airway to pass easily, remove it and try the other nostril. Unlike the OPA, the NPA should not cause the person to gag. Do not use an NPA on someone with a suspected skull fracture, active bleeding from the nose, or facial fractures.

OXYGEN DELIVERY DEVICES

Many different oxygen delivery devices are commonly used in the pre-hospital setting. Which devices are routinely available to you will depend on your local standards and protocols. This section focusses on those devices that you are likely to have immediately available or be asked to assist with in providing care. You should not delay care because a specific device is not available. Instead, you should start basic care, adding any devices when they become available.

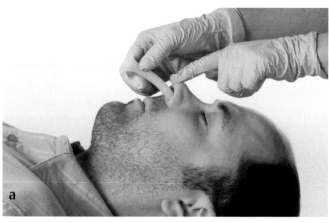
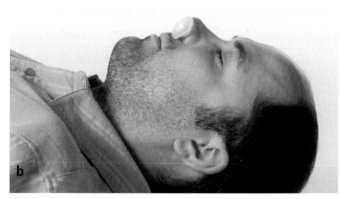

Figure 7–12, a-b a, Advance the airway gently, straight in, not upward; **b**, until the flange end rests on the nose.

Some of these devices include resuscitation masks and BVM resuscitators. They provide several advantages. They can help you:

• Maintain an open airway

• Perform rescue breathing

• Limit the potential for disease transmission

• Increase the oxygen concentration in a person's bloodstream

With all delivery devices, give the same number of ventilations as you would for CPR, or rescue breathing.

Resuscitation Masks

One of the most readily available, simple ventilation devices for responders is the resuscitation mask. Resuscitation masks are pliable, dome-shaped devices that fit over a person's mouth and nose, aiding ventilation (providing oxygen to the lungs). Several types of resuscitation masks are available, varying in size, shape, and features.

Resuscitation masks offer you several advantages. These include:

• Increasing the flow of air to the lungs by permitting air to travel through a person's mouth and nose at the same time

• Providing an adequate seal for ventilation, even when a person has facial injuries

• Providing an effective and easily accessible alternative to other methods of ventilation

• Permitting easy delivery of supplemental oxygen to either a breathing or a non-breathing person

• Reducing the possibility of disease transmission by providing a barrier between the responder and the person

Selecting a Resuscitation Mask

For a resuscitation mask to be most effective, it should meet the following criteria:

• Be made of a transparent, pliable material that allows you to make a tight seal on the person's face when you perform rescue breathing or supply supplemental oxygen

• Have a one-way valve for redirecting a person's exhaled air

• Have an inlet for the delivery of supplemental oxygen

• Work well under a variety of environmental conditions, such as extreme heat or cold

• Be easy to assemble and use

Figure 7–13 shows the features of an effective resuscitation mask.

Figure 7–13 A resuscitation mask should meet specific criteria.

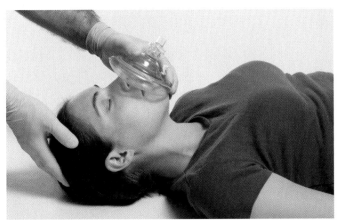

Figure 7–14 A resuscitation mask should be positioned over the mouth and nose, with the lower rim placed between the person's lower lip and chin.

Using a Resuscitation Mask

When using a resuscitation mask, begin by attaching the one-way valve to the mask. Next, place the mask so that it covers the person's mouth and nose. Position one rim of the mask between the person's lower lip and chin. The opposite end of the mask should cover the nose. Figure 7–14 shows how to position the resuscitation mask.

When you use a resuscitation mask to give rescue breathing, you must maintain a good seal to prevent air from leaking at the edges of the mask. Use both hands to hold the mask in place and to maintain an open airway. You do this by:

1. Tilting the person's head back.

2. Lifting the jaw upward

Figure 7–15, a-b, shows two methods for using a resuscitation mask.

If you suspect the person has a head or spinal injury, use the two-handed jaw thrust technique without head-tilt (Figure 7–16).

Bag-Valve-Mask Resuscitators

There may be times when you will have a bag-valve-mask (BVM) available or be asked to assist with one. A BVM is a hand-held device, like the resuscitation mask, primarily used to ventilate a non-breathing person. It is also used to assist ventilation of someone who is breathing too slowly or too quickly.

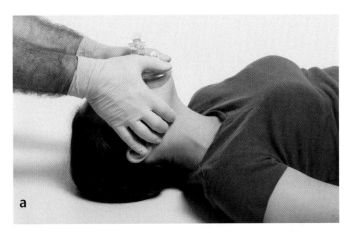

a

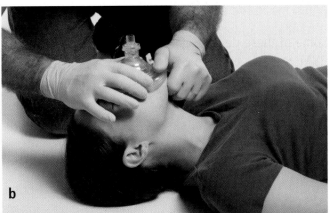

b

Figure 7–15, a-b To use a resuscitation mask: **a**, position yourself behind the person's head and hold the two sides tightly against the face or; **b**, position yourself beside the person and hold the mask in place.

Figure 7–16 If you suspect a head or spine injury, use the two-handed jaw thrust technique and hold the mask to the face without tilting the head.

Figure 7–17 A bag-valve-mask (BVM).

The device has three main components: a bag, a valve, and a mask. The bag is self-inflating. Once compressed, it reinflates automatically. The one-way valve allows air to move from the bag to the person but prevents his exhaled air from entering the bag. The mask is similar to the resuscitation masks described earlier in this chapter. An oxygen reservoir bag should be attached to the BVM when supplemental oxygen is administered (Figure 7–17).

The principle of the BVM is simple. By placing the mask on the person's face and squeezing the bag, you open the one-way valve, forcing air into the person's lungs. When you release the bag, the valve closes and air from the atmosphere refills the bag. At approximately the same time, the person exhales. This exhaled air is diverted into the atmosphere through the closed one-way valve.

Using a Bag-Valve-Mask Resuscitator

In the hands of a well-practised rescue team, the BVM is effective. For this reason, using a BVM is a two-rescuer skill. When using a BVM on a non-breathing person, make sure an OPA or NPA is in place.

When using a BVM, one responder positions the mask and opens the person's airway. This is done in the same way as previously described for resuscitation masks. While the first responder maintains a tight seal with the mask on the person's face, the second responder provides ventilations by squeezing the bag just until the person's chest rises (Figure 7–18). The bag should always be squeezed smoothly, not forcefully. This two-person technique maintains an open airway and a tight mask seal, while a second responder provides ventilations.

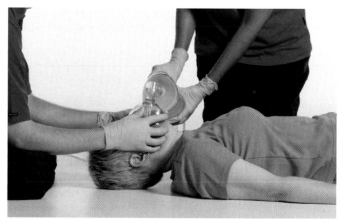

Figure 7–18 When using a BVM, one responder maintains a tight seal of the mask on the person's face, and a second responder provides ventilations.

Using the BVM has distinct advantages and disadvantages:

Advantages

- It delivers a higher concentration of oxygen than that delivered during mouth-to-mask rescue breathing.
- It limits the potential for disease transmission.

Disadvantages

- Without regular practice, you cannot stay proficient.
- It may take longer to assemble than other ventilation devices.

BVMs for Children and Babies

Some BVMs are designed specifically for children and babies. These devices have a smaller mask, and the bag is designed to hold a smaller volume of air, for a better fit on the face, and to limit the amount of air able to be squeezed into the lungs. The mask of the BVM should extend from the bridge of the nose to the cleft of the chin, which will ensure a proper seal on the face. A number of these BVMs also include a valve that stops the forced entrance of air once a certain pressure has been reached, avoiding overinflation of the lungs. As always, ventilate just until the chest starts to rise.

Cricoid Pressure

Cricoid pressure is pressure put on the cricoid cartilage (the prominent cartilage ring just below the thyroid cartilage, or Adam's apple) of an unresponsive person using the responder's thumb and index finger and can be used reduce complications associated with ventilating a person. This pressure pushes the trachea posteriorly, compressing the esophagus against the vertebrae, and preventing gastric distension during artificial ventilations. It also protects the airway from vomit and prevents aspiration. It is important to note that, during CPR, up to three responders are required to use this technique: one to seal the BVM on the face, one to squeeze the bag and do chest compressions, and one to apply cricoid pressure.

Supplemental Oxygen

The normal concentration of oxygen in the air is approximately 21 percent, which is what we inhale. Under normal conditions, this is more than enough oxygen to sustain life. However, when serious injury or sudden illness occurs, the body does not function properly and can benefit from additional, or supplemental, oxygen. Without adequate oxygen, hypoxia will result. Hypoxia is a condition in which insufficient oxygen reaches the cells. Hypoxia causes increased breathing and heart rate, cyanosis, changes in consciousness, restlessness, and chest pain.

For example, delivery of a higher concentration of oxygen may reduce breathing discomfort and chest pain caused by a heart attack or angina. Someone with shortness of breath or chest pain should always receive supplemental oxygen. Supplemental oxygen delivered to the person's lungs may help meet the increased demand for oxygen for all body tissues.

If a person who has had a heart attack suddenly suffers cardiac arrest, then you must use rescue breathing to supply air into his lungs. When you perform rescue breathing using the mouth-to-mask method, the oxygen concentration you deliver to the person is only 16 percent. This is adequate to sustain life in a healthy person, but since chest compressions only circulate one third of normal blood flow under the best of conditions, some body tissues will not receive the oxygen required for short-term survival.

Using a BVM alone only improves this situation slightly since it delivers atmospheric air (21 percent oxygen). Administering supplemental oxygen allows a substantially higher oxygen concentration, in some cases nearly 100 percent, to be delivered to the person (Figure 7–19).

To deliver supplemental oxygen, you must have:

- An oxygen cylinder
- A pressure regulator with flowmeter
- A delivery device

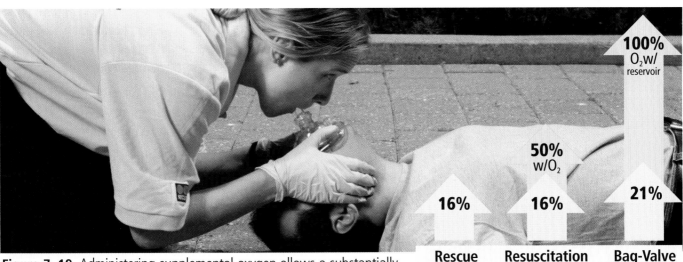

Figure 7–19 Administering supplemental oxygen allows a substantially higher oxygen concentration to be delivered to the person.

Figure 7–20 shows an oxygen cylinder, pressure regulator, and flowmeter.

Oxygen Cylinder

It is easy to recognize an oxygen cylinder because of its distinctive green or white colour and yellow diamond marking that says oxidizer. These cylinders are made of steel or an alloy. Depending on their size, those used in the pre-hospital setting can hold between 350 and 625 litres of oxygen. These cylinders have internal pressures of approximately 2,000 pounds per square inch (psi). Oxygen cylinders should never be left free-standing.

Pressure Regulator with Flowmeter

The pressure inside the oxygen cylinder is far too great for you to simply open the cylinder and administer the oxygen. Instead, a device must be attached to the cylinder to reduce the delivery pressure of the oxygen to a safe level. This regulating device is called a pressure regulator. The pressure regulator reduces the pressure from approximately 2,000 psi inside the cylinder to a safe pressure range from 30 to 70 psi.

A pressure regulator has a gauge that indicates how much pressure is in the cylinder. By checking the gauge, you can determine if a cylinder is full (2,000 psi), nearly empty (200 psi), or somewhere in between.

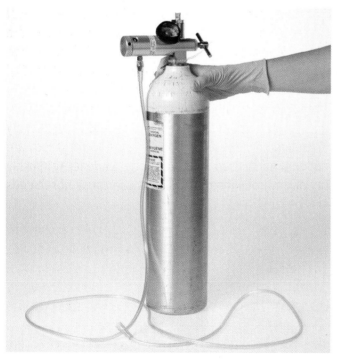

Figure 7–20 An oxygen cylinder, pressure regulator, and flowmeter.

> **NOTE:**
>
> *For more information on indications and contraindications of oxygen, see Appendix A.*

A pressure regulator has two metal prongs that fit into the valve at the top of the oxygen cylinder. To ensure a tight seal between the regulator and the tank, a gasket, commonly called an "O-ring," must be used.

A flowmeter controls the amount of oxygen administered in litres per minute (lpm). Flowmeters normally deliver from 1 to 25 lpm.

Using Oxygen Delivery Devices

Some oxygen delivery devices can deliver oxygen to either breathing or non-breathing people. Two devices, the resuscitation mask and the BVM, can deliver oxygen to both. For this reason, these devices are the most appropriate for you to use. Regardless of the device being used, a section of tubing is attached to the device at one end and to the flowmeter at the other end to create an oxygen-enriched environment for the person.

A resuscitation mask is capable of delivering approximately 50 percent oxygen to a breathing person when delivered at 6 lpm or more. This is substantially higher than the normal 21 percent that the person would get from the atmosphere. Some resuscitation masks have elastic straps attached to the mask. The elastic strap can be placed over the person's head and tightened to help keep the mask securely in place (Figure 7–21, a). If the mask does not have a strap, either you or the ill person can hold it in place. When a resuscitation mask is used on a non-breathing person, it will deliver an oxygen concentration of approximately 35 percent. The oxygen concentration is reduced because oxygen mixes with your exhaled air as you perform mouth-to-mask rescue breathing.

The BVM resuscitator with an oxygen reservoir bag is capable of supplying a minimum oxygen concentration of 90 percent when used at 10 lpm or more.

The BVM can be held against the person's face, allowing a breathing person to inhale the supplemental oxygen (Figure 7–21, b). A person breathing at a rate of less than 10 breaths per minute, or more than 30 per minute, should have his breathing assisted. For someone breathing less than 10 times per minute, squeeze the bag

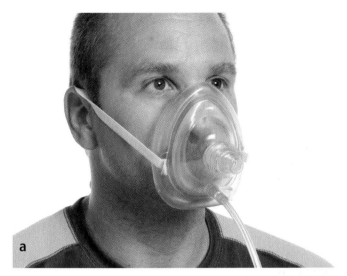

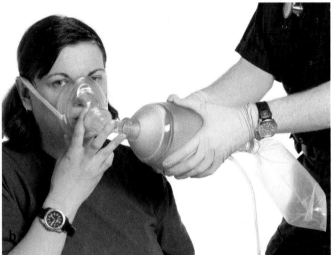

Figure 7–21, a-c Common oxygen delivery devices include: **a**, a resuscitation mask; **b**, a BVM; and **c**, a non-rebreather mask.

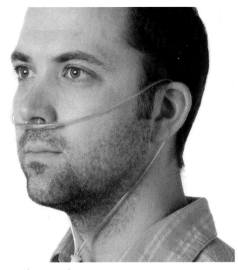

Figure 7–22 A nasal cannula.

each time the person breathes and once inbetween each breath. To assist a person breathing more than 30 times per minute, squeeze the bag on every second breath.

The high-concentration non-rebreather mask needs to have a flow rate of 10 lpm or more to ensure the proper reservoir bag inflation. This device allows the person to inhale air from the bag and exhale through the holes in the sides of the mask (Figure 7–21, c).

Some devices, such as the nasal cannula, can be used only to administer oxygen to breathing people. A nasal cannula is a device that delivers oxygen through the person's nostrils (Figure 7–22). It is a plastic tube with two small prongs that are inserted into the nose. The use of a nasal cannula is limited since it is normally used at a flow rate of 1 to 4 lpm. Under these conditions, it delivers a peak oxygen concentration of only approximately 36 percent. Flow rates above 4 lpm are not commonly used because of the tendency to quickly dry out mucous membranes. This can cause nosebleeds and headaches.

Because of its limitations, the nasal cannula is commonly used for people with only minor breathing difficulty. This device is not appropriate for people experiencing a serious breathing emergency since they are generally breathing through their mouth and need a device that can supply a greater concentration of oxygen. In addition, the nasal cannula can be ineffective if the person has a nasal airway obstruction, nasal injury, or

TABLE 7-1 OXYGEN DELIVERY DEVICES

Device	Common Flow Rate	Oxygen concentration	Function
Nasal cannula	1–4 lpm	24–36 %	Breathing persons only
Resuscitation mask	6+ lpm	35–55 %	Breathing and non-breathing persons
Bag-valve-mask resuscitator	10+ lpm	90+ %	Breathing and non-breathing persons
Non-rebreather mask	10+ lpm	90+ %	Breathing persons only

bad cold causing blocked sinus passages. It should, however, be used if the person cannot tolerate a mask over his face.

Table 7-1 provides an overview of each of the delivery devices presented.

Administering Oxygen

Begin by examining the cylinder to be certain that it is labelled "Oxygen" (Figure 7–23, a). Next, check to see that the cylinder is full. Full cylinders come with a protective covering over the tank opening. Remove this covering and save the "O-ring." While pointing the cylinder away from you, open the cylinder for one second (Figure 7–23, b). This will remove any dirt or debris from the cylinder valve. Position the gasket (Figure 7–24, a).

Next, examine the pressure regulator. Check to see that the pin index corresponds to an oxygen tank (Figure 7–24, b). Attach the pressure regulator to the cylinder, seating the prongs inside the holes in the valve stem (Figure 7–24, c). Hand-tighten the screw until the regulator is snug (Figure 7–24, d). Open the cylinder one full turn and listen for leaks (Figure 7–24, e).

Check the pressure gauge to determine how much pressure is in the cylinder. A full cylinder should have approximately 2,000 psi. Attach the chosen delivery device to the oxygen port near the flowmeter. Attach the device to the tank using the appropriate tubing.

Turn on the flowmeter to the desired flow rate. Listen and feel to make sure that oxygen is flowing into your

a

b

Figure 7–23, a-b **a**, an oxygen cylinder is usually green or white, with a yellow diamond indicating oxygen; **b**, open the cylinder for one second, pointing it away from you.

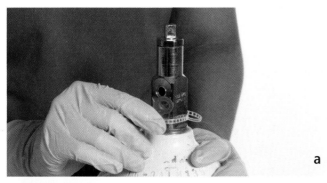

a

b

c

d

e

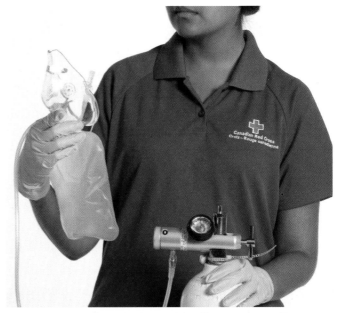

Figure 7–25 After turning on the flowmeter to the desired rate, check to ensure the oxygen is flowing into the delivery device.

delivery device. Ensure that the reservoir bag is full before placing the device on the person (Figure 7–25). Finally, place the delivery device on the person.

Precautions

When administering oxygen, safety is a primary concern. Remember the following precautions:

- Do not operate oxygen equipment around an open flame or sparks or in close proximity to an AED. Oxygen causes fire to burn more rapidly.

- Do not stand oxygen cylinders upright unless they can be well secured. If the cylinder falls, it could damage the regulator or possibly loosen the cylinder valve.

- Do not use grease, oil, or petroleum products to lubricate any pressure regulator parts. Oxygen does not mix with these products, and a severe chemical reaction could cause an explosion.

Figure 7–24, a-e To attach the pressure regulator to the cylinder; **a**, insert the gasket into the opening of the cylinder; **b**, check to see that the regulator is for use with oxygen; **c**, seat the three prongs of the regulator inside the cylinder; **d**, hand-tighten the screw until the regulator is snug; and **e**, turn on the oxygen.

SUMMARY

Although they are not required, oxygen delivery devices can make the emergency care you provide safer, easier, and more effective. OPAs and NPAs help maintain an open airway by elevating the tongue away from the back of the throat. Suction equipment helps clear the airway of substances such as water, blood, saliva, or vomitus. The use of supplemental oxygen can relieve pain and breathing discomfort. The resuscitation mask and BVM are the most appropriate devices for responders. They can significantly increase the oxygen concentration that an ill or injured person needs, help ventilate a non-breathing person, and reduce the likelihood of disease transmission.

Oxygen delivery devices are appropriate for almost all types of injury or illness in which breathing may be impaired. Knowing how to use these devices will enable you to provide more effective care until more advanced medical care has been obtained.

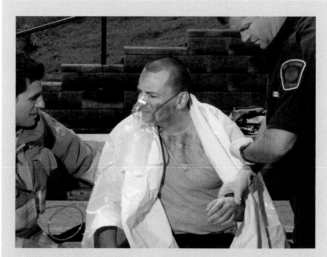

The man's breathing gets worse. What do you do?

Skills Summary

Clearing an Airway with Manual Suction

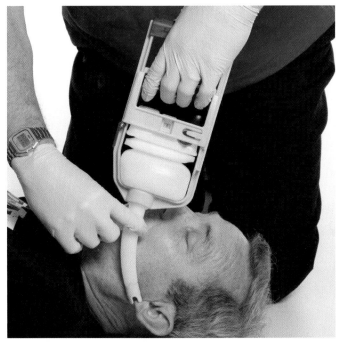

1. Measure suction device.

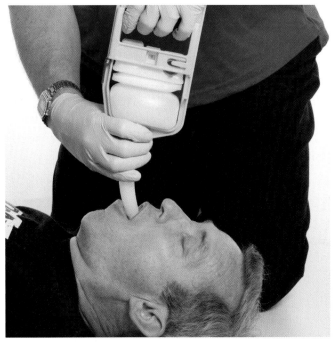

2. Insert device into mouth.

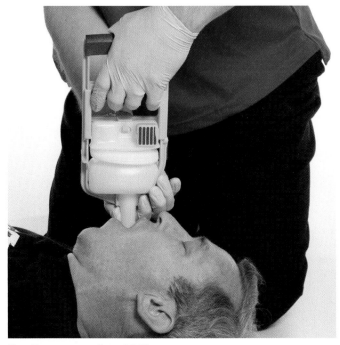

3. Rotate suction 180º.

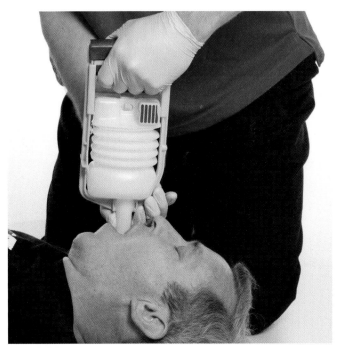

4. Suction until airway is cleared.

Skills Summary

Oxygen Administration

1. Check cylinder.

2. Clear valve.

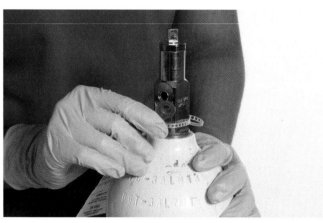

3. Insert gasket into cylinder.

4. Check pressure regulator.

5. Attach pressure regulator.

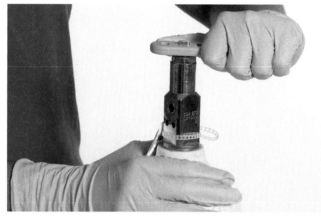

6. Tighten pressure regulator.

Skills Summary

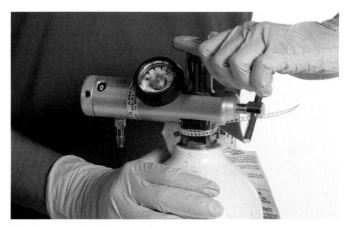

7. Open cylinder one full turn.

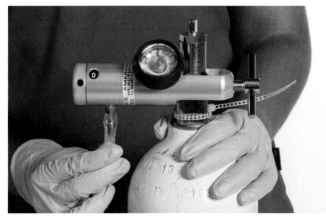

8. Attach oxygen delivery device.

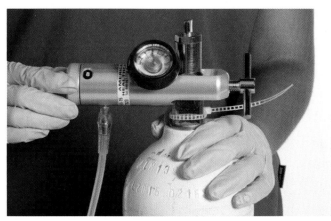

9. Adjust flowmeter.

10. Verify oxygen flow.

Caution: When breaking down the oxygen equipment, remove the delivery device from the person's face, turn off the flowmeter, close the cylinder, and then turn on the flowmeter to bleed the line. Finally, remove the regulator from the cylinder.

Skills Summary

Inserting an Oropharyngeal Airway

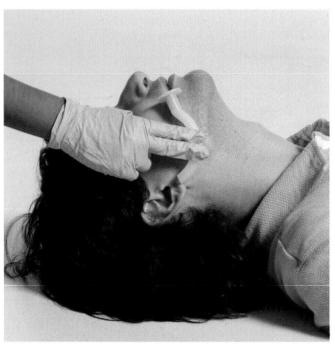

1. Measure from earlobe to corner of mouth.

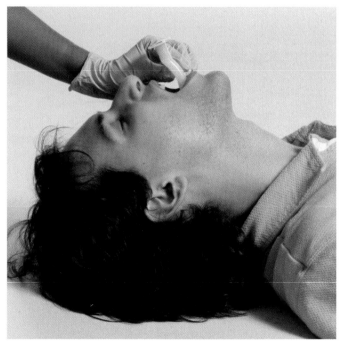

2. Insert airway with curved end along the roof of the mouth.

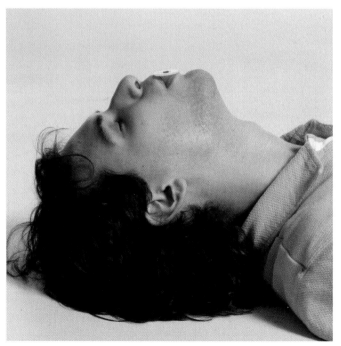

3. Rotate airway 180° so it drops into the throat. Flange end should rest on the lips.

Inserting a Nasopharyngeal Airway

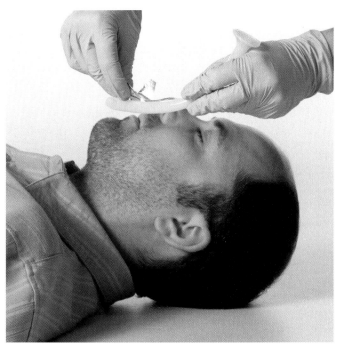

1. Apply lubrication to nasal airway.

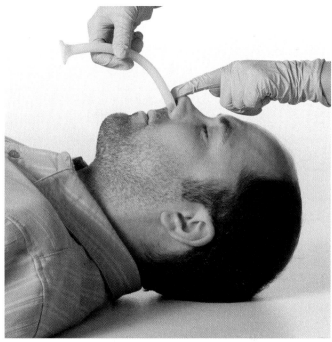

2. Insert airway into the nostril with the bevel toward the septum.

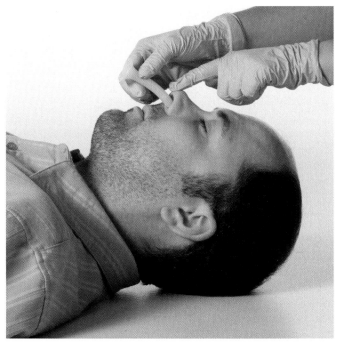

3. Advance the airway straight in, not upward.

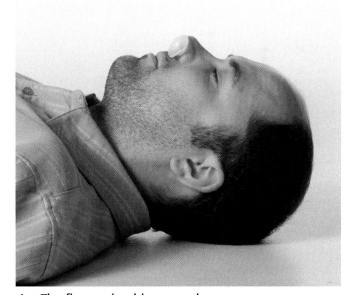

4. The flange should rest on the nose.

Skills Summary

Using a Bag-Valve-Mask Resuscitator

1. Assemble BVM while second responder performs a primary survey.

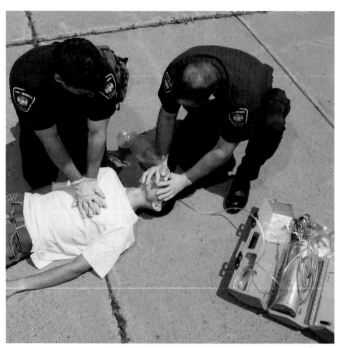

2. Position mask on person's face.

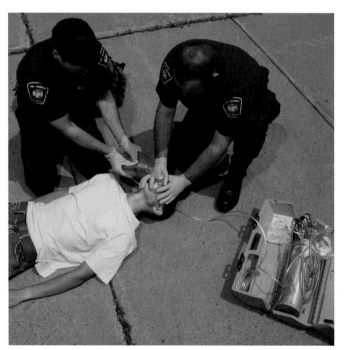

3. Second responder gives ventilations as required.

Chapter 8

Circulatory Emergencies

A 59-year-old woman is experiencing chest pain. She states that it started about 30 minutes ago as a mild, squeezing sensation. Now the pain is severe, and she is gasping for breath. You recognize that these signs and symptoms suggest a serious condition. While waiting to obtain more advanced medical care, what do you do?

INTRODUCTION

In this chapter, you will learn how to recognize and provide care for circulatory emergencies. You will learn the care for someone with persistent chest pain and for someone whose heart stops beating, as well as for someone who has had a stroke. The condition in which the heart stops, known as cardiac arrest, sometimes results from a heart attack. To provide care for someone with cardiac arrest, you need to learn how to perform cardiopulmonary resuscitation (CPR). Properly performed, CPR can keep someone's vital organs supplied with oxygen-rich blood until more highly trained personnel arrive to provide advanced care.

This chapter also identifies the important risk factors for cardiovascular disease. It is as important to prevent stroke, heart attack, and cardiac arrest as it is to learn how to recognize them when they occur and provide appropriate care. You will also learn to modify your behaviour to prevent cardiovascular disease.

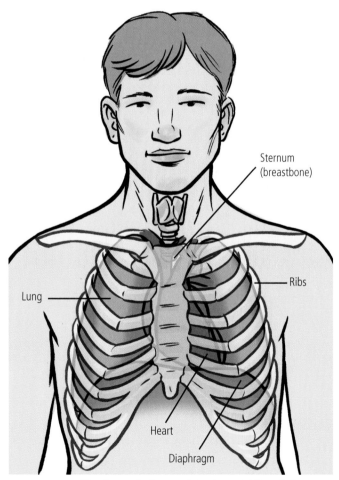

Sternum
(breastbone)

Ribs

Lung

Heart

Diaphragm

Figure 8–1 The heart is located in the middle of the chest, behind the lower half of the sternum.

HEART ATTACK

The heart is a muscular organ about the size of your fist, which functions like a pump. It lies between the lungs, in the middle of the chest, behind the lower half of the sternum (breastbone). The heart is protected by the ribs and sternum in front and by the spine in back (Figure 8–1). It has four chambers and is separated into right and left halves. Oxygen-poor blood enters the right side of the heart and is pumped to the lungs, where it picks up oxygen. The now oxygen-rich blood returns to the left side of the heart, from where it is pumped to all parts of the body. One-way valves direct the flow of blood as it moves through each of the heart's four chambers (Figure 8–2). For the circulatory system to be effective, the respiratory system must also be working so that the blood can pick up oxygen in the lungs.

Like all living tissue, the cells of the heart need a continuous supply of oxygen. The coronary arteries supply the heart muscle with oxygen-rich blood (Figure 8–3, a). If heart muscle tissue is deprived of this blood, it dies, and the person often develops certain signs and symptoms. When a great deal of tissue is deprived of oxygen and dies, it is called a heart attack.

A heart attack interrupts the heart's electrical system. This may result in an irregular heartbeat, which prevents blood from circulating effectively.

Common Causes of Heart Attack

Heart attacks usually result from cardiovascular disease. Cardiovascular disease—disease of the heart and blood vessels—is one of the leading causes of death in Canadians. About 80,000 deaths in Canada each year are attributed to cardiovascular disease. Of these, more than half are due to heart attack, and most of them are sudden deaths.

Cardiovascular disease develops slowly. Deposits of cholesterol, a fatty substance made by the body, and other material may gradually build up on the inner walls of the arteries. This condition, called atherosclerosis, is the progressive narrowing of these vessels. Narrowing of the coronary arteries is a common form of coronary artery disease. When coronary arteries narrow, a heart attack may occur (Figure 8–3, b). Atherosclerosis can also involve arteries in other parts of the body, such as the brain. Diseased arteries in the brain can lead to stroke, a disruption of blood flow to a part of the brain.

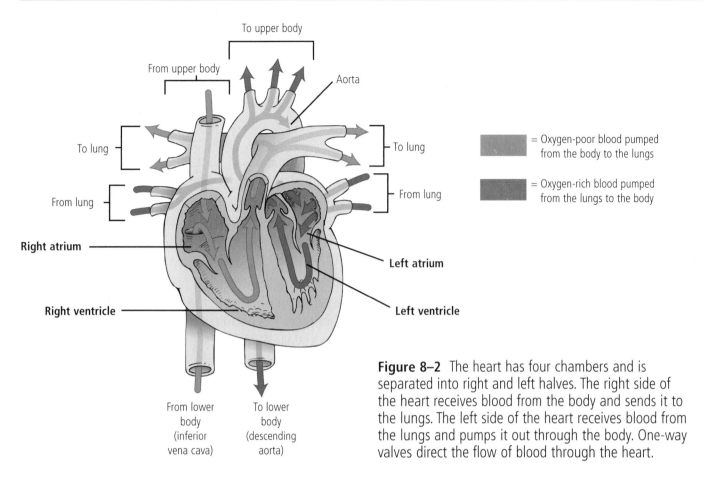

To upper body

From upper body

Aorta

To lung

To lung

From lung

From lung

= Oxygen-poor blood pumped from the body to the lungs

= Oxygen-rich blood pumped from the lungs to the body

Right atrium

Left atrium

Right ventricle

Left ventricle

From lower body (inferior vena cava)

To lower body (descending aorta)

Figure 8–2 The heart has four chambers and is separated into right and left halves. The right side of the heart receives blood from the body and sends it to the lungs. The left side of the heart receives blood from the lungs and pumps it out through the body. One-way valves direct the flow of blood through the heart.

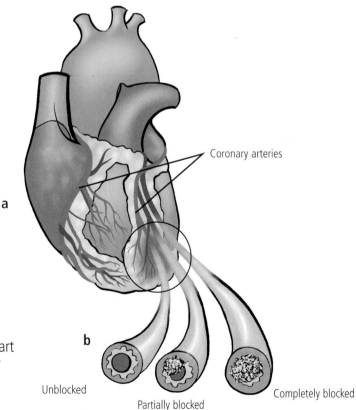

Coronary arteries

a

b

Unblocked

Partially blocked

Completely blocked

Figure 8–3, a-b a, the coronary arteries supply the heart muscle with blood; **b**, build-up of material on the inner walls of these arteries reduces blood flow to the heart muscle and may cause a heart attack.

Because atherosclerosis develops gradually, it can go undetected for many years. Even with significantly reduced blood flow to the heart muscle, there may be no signs and symptoms of heart trouble. Most people with atherosclerosis are unaware of it. As the narrowing progresses, some people experience symptoms such as chest pain, an early warning sign that the heart is not receiving enough oxygen-rich blood. Others may suffer a heart attack or even cardiac arrest without any previous warning. Fortunately, this process can be slowed or stopped by lifestyle changes, such as forming healthy eating habits.

Arteriosclerosis is the thickening, loss of elasticity, and calcification of the walls of arteries. This results in a decrease in blood flow. Most commonly affected are the cerebrum and the lower extremities.

Signs and Symptoms of a Heart Attack

The most prominent symptom of a heart attack is persistent chest pain or discomfort (Figure 8–4). However, it may not always be easy for you to distinguish between the pain of a heart attack and chest pain caused by indigestion, muscle spasms, or other conditions. Brief, stabbing chest pain or pain that feels more intense when the person bends or breathes deeply is usually not caused by a heart attack.

The pain of heart attack can range from mild discomfort to an unbearable crushing sensation in the chest. The person may describe it as an uncomfortable pressure, squeezing, tightness, aching, constricting, or heavy sensation in the chest. Often the person feels pain in the centre of the chest behind the sternum. It may spread to the shoulder, arm, neck, or jaw (Figure 8–5). The pain is constant and usually not relieved by resting, changing position, or taking oral medication. Any severe chest pain, chest pain that lasts longer than 10 minutes, or chest pain that is accompanied by other heart attack signs and symptoms should receive immediate emergency medical care.

Although a heart attack is often dramatic, someone experiencing a heart attack can have relatively mild symptoms. The person often mistakes the symptoms for indigestion. Sometimes the person feels little or no chest pain or discomfort. During a heart attack, many women, older adults, and people with diabetes tend

Figure 8–4 The most prominent symptom of a heart attack is chest pain.

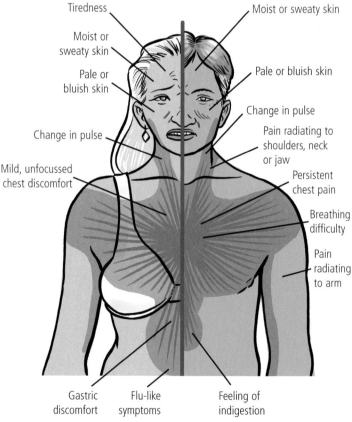

Figure 8–5 Signs and symptoms of a heart attack may be different for men and women.

to experience "soft signs," including tiredness, gastric discomfort, flu-like symptoms, and mild unfocussed chest discomfort that comes and goes, gets better with rest, gets worse with activity, and starts mild and gets continually stronger.

Another sign of a heart attack is difficulty breathing. The person may be breathing faster than normal because the body tries to get much-needed oxygen to the heart. Depending on the person's general condition, her pulse may be faster or slower than normal or irregular. The person's skin may be pale or bluish, particularly around the face. The face may also be moist from perspiration. Some people with a heart attack sweat profusely. These signs result from the stress the body experiences when the heart does not work effectively. Nausea and vomiting may also occur.

Since any heart attack may lead to cardiac arrest, it is important to recognize and act on these signs and symptoms. Prompt action may prevent cardiac arrest. Most people who die from a heart attack die within one to two hours after the first signs and symptoms appear. Many could have been saved if bystanders or the person herself had been aware of the signs and symptoms of a heart attack and acted promptly. Many people who have had a heart attack delay seeking care. Nearly half of them wait two or more hours before going to the hospital. Often they do not realize they are having a heart attack. They may dismiss the symptoms as indigestion or muscle soreness.

Since most heart attacks result from blood clotting within arteries, early treatment of an attack with medication that dissolves clots has been helpful in minimizing damage to the heart.

Remember, the key symptom of a heart attack is persistent chest pain. If the person states that chest pain is severe or chest discomfort has been present for more than 10 minutes, obtain more advanced medical care immediately and begin to care for the person.

A "silent MI" (myocardial infarction) is a heart attack that is not recognized; therefore, advanced care is not obtained. This can happen to anyone but occurs most often in those who experience "soft signs," such as women, people with diabetes, and older adults.

ANGINA

Some people with coronary artery disease may experience chest pain or pressure that comes and goes and is not generally caused by a heart attack. This type of pain is called angina pectoris, a medical term for pain in the chest. Angina pectoris, commonly referred to as angina, develops when the heart needs more oxygen-rich blood than it gets, such as during physical activity or emotional stress. This lack of oxygen can cause a constricting chest pain that may spread to the neck, jaw, and arms.

Pain associated with angina usually lasts less than 10 minutes. Someone who knows she has angina will often have a prescribed medication to help relieve the pain. Reducing the heart's demand for oxygen, such as by stopping physical activity, and taking prescribed medication often relieve angina. Administering oxygen to someone experiencing angina may help relieve chest pain.

Care for a Heart Attack and Angina

The most important step in providing care is to recognize the signs and symptoms of a heart attack. You must take immediate action if any of these appear. Someone having a heart attack will probably deny the seriousness of the symptoms she is experiencing. Do not let this influence you. If you think there is a possibility that the person is having a heart attack, you must act. First, have the person stop what she is doing and rest comfortably. Many people having a heart attack find it easier to breathe while sitting (Figure 8–6). Second, obtain more advanced medical care.

Figure 8–6 Many people having a heart attack find it easier to breathe when they are sitting.

Figure 8–7 Nitroglycerin spray is one of the common forms this medication comes in.

Continue with your secondary survey. Talk to the person and bystanders, if possible, to get more information. If the person continues to experience chest pain, ask her SAMPLE and OPQRST questions (see Chapter 5).

You may assist the person in taking her prescribed nitroglycerin if needed. If under medical direction to do so, you may administer nitroglycerin.

> **NOTE:**
>
> *For further information on nitroglycerin, refer to the drug profile in Appendix A.*

Nitroglycerin is a medication often prescribed for angina, which may come in pill or spray form (Figure 8–7). Once absorbed into the body (under the tongue), nitroglycerin enlarges the blood vessels to make it easier for blood to reach heart muscle tissue, which results in a drop in blood pressure. Because of this, it is important to take a blood pressure before and after the person takes nitroglycerin. Nitroglycerin may relieve the pain because the heart does not have to work so hard and it increases oxygen delivery to the heart.

> **NOTE:**
>
> *Locol protocol may dictate that it is not recommended that a person take nitroglycerin if the systolic blood pressure is too low, often below 100 mmHg, and/or pulse is below 60 bpm. In all cases, the person should be resting, preferably in a supine position, before taking nitroglycerin. As always, follow local protocol.*

A person will often know when they should take their prescribed nitroglycerin. If the person answers "yes" when you ask, "Would you normally take your medication at this time?" (taking into consideration their signs and symptoms), this is a good indication that this circumstance warrants use of their nitroglycerin.

Before suggesting that the person take nitroglycerin, ask if he or she has taken any medications for erectile dysfunction (such as Viagra®, Levitra®, or Cialis®) in the last 48 hours. If the person has, advise him or her not to take the nitroglycerin.

The nitroglycerin dose may be repeated every five minutes until the pain is relieved or until a maximum of three doses has been administered. If the person doesn't carry nitroglycerin, or the first dose does not make the pain go away, suggest that the person chew a minimum of 160 mg up to a maximum of 325 mg of acetylsalicylic acid (ASA), depending on what is available. ASA is an anti-clotting agent that will reduce the formation of a clot in the coronary artery at the site of the blockage. This will possibly decrease the damage to the heart muscle. Administer oxygen if it is available.

> **NOTE:**
>
> *Before offering ASA, ask if the person has an allergy to ASA, if she has asthma with no previous ASA use, or if she has had recent significant bleeding. If the answer is yes to any of these questions, do not suggest that the person take ASA.*

> **NOTE:**
>
> *Acetaminophen (e.g., Tylenol®) and ibuprofen (e.g., Advil®) do not have the same effect as ASA in reducing damage due to heart attacks. Do not substitute.*

Obtain more advanced medical care. Surviving a heart attack often depends on how soon the person receives advanced medical care (that being the special equipment and medications needed for someone experiencing a cardiac emergency).

Be calm and reassuring when caring for someone experiencing a heart attack. Comforting the person helps reduce anxiety and eases some of the discomfort.

TABLE 8-1 CARE FOR A HEART ATTACK AND ANGINA

- Recognize the signals of a heart attack.
- Convince the person to stop activity and rest.
- Help the person to rest comfortably.
- Try to obtain information about the person's condition.
- Comfort the person.
- Administer oxygen if available.
- Obtain more advanced medical care.
- Assist with medication.
- Monitor vital signs.
- Be prepared to perform CPR.

Provide ongoing survey and care until you can obtain advanced medical care. Watch for any changes in appearance or behaviour. Since the heart attack may lead to cardiac arrest, be prepared to perform CPR. Table 8-1 summarizes the care for heart attacks and angina.

CONGESTIVE HEART FAILURE

Congestive heart failure (CHF) is an abnormal condition in which the heart loses its pumping ability. This may be the result of a heart attack (acute myocardial infarction, or MI), valvular disease, ischemic heart disease, or any disease that affects the heart muscle or myocardium (cardiomyopathy). The result is that fluids and blood back up into the lungs or body tissues.

In acute MI, usually the left ventricle is damaged. Also, in chronic hypertension, the left ventricle suffers the long-term effects of having to pump against restricted arteries in the extremities (peripheral arteries). As a result, the left ventricle doesn't pump as effectively and can't pump with enough force to push enough blood through the body. Blood coming into the left chamber of the heart from the lungs backs up, causing fluid to leak into the lungs, which causes fluid in the lungs (pulmonary edema).

Signs and symptoms of left-sided heart failure may include:

- Shortness of breath
- Increased respiratory rate
- History of severe shortness of breath at night when the person is lying down, which gets better when standing
- Cyanosis
- Coughing up foamy sputum (sometimes blood-tinged)
- Increased heart rate
- Wheezing
- Pale, cool, clammy skin
- Panic, restlessness, agitation
- Normal to high blood pressure
- Confusion and disorientation

RIGHT-SIDED HEART FAILURE

Right-sided heart failure usually occurs due to left-sided failure. When the left ventricle fails, increased fluid pressure is transferred back through the lungs. Eventually, the right side is unable to keep up with the increased workload, it becomes damaged, and heart failure results. Right-sided heart failure may also occur as a result of a pulmonary embolism, long-standing chronic obstructive pulmonary disorder (COPD), or MI. When the right side fails and loses its pumping power, blood backs up into the body's veins. This usually causes pooling of fluid in the tissues, resulting in swelling of the extremities (peripheral edema). This will be most noticeable in the feet when the person is sitting or standing or in the lower back if the person is bedridden.

Signs and symptoms of right-sided heart failure may include:

- Shortness of breath
- Swelling of feet and ankles

- Urinating more frequently at night
- Pronounced neck veins (also known as jugular venous distension [JVD])
- Heart palpitations
- Irregular fast heartbeat
- Weakness and fatigue
- Fainting

Right-sided heart failure by itself is seldom a life-threatening emergency. A change in lifestyle and possibly medications are the definitive treatments for this condition.

PREVENTING CARDIOVASCULAR DISEASE

Although a heart attack seems to strike suddenly, the conditions that lead to it may develop over years. Many people's lifestyle may gradually be endangering their heart, which can eventually result in cardiovascular disease. Potentially harmful behaviours frequently begin early in life.

Risk Factors of Heart Disease

Scientists have identified many factors that increase a person's chances of developing heart disease. These are known as risk factors. Some risk factors for heart disease cannot be changed. For instance, men have a higher risk for heart disease than do women. Having a history of heart disease in your family also increases your risk.

But people can control many risk factors for heart disease. Smoking, diets high in fats, high blood pressure, obesity, and lack of routine exercise are all linked to increased risk of heart disease (Table 8-2). When one risk factor, such as high blood pressure, is combined with other risk factors, such as obesity or cigarette smoking, the risk of heart attack or stroke is greatly increased.

Controlling Risk Factors
Smoking

Cigarette smokers are more likely to have a heart attack than non-smokers and are also more likely to have

TABLE 8-2 CARDIOVASCULAR DISEASE RISK FACTORS

Uncontrollable	Controllable
Gender Men have a higher risk than women	**Smoking** Smokers are twice as likely to have a heart attack
Family History A history of heart disease in the family increases the risk	**Diet** A diet high in saturated fats and cholesterol increases the risk of atherosclerosis
Age The risk of heart attack increases with age	**Blood Pressure** High blood pressure can damage blood vessels throughout the body
	Weight Individuals who are overweight have a significantly higher risk of fatal heart attack
	Exercise Level Low exercise levels lead to increased weight and decreased muscle tone

cardiac arrest. The earlier a person starts using tobacco, the greater the risk to her future health. Giving up smoking will rapidly reduce the risk of heart disease. After a number of years, the risk becomes the same as if the person had never smoked. If you do not smoke, do not start. If you do smoke, quit. Living and working in a smoke-free environment will also control the risk of heart disease.

Diet

Eating healthy fats, such as omega-3 fats, will help combat the buildup of fatty materials. Some cholesterol in the body is essential. The amount of cholesterol in the blood is determined by how much your body produces and by the food you eat. Foods high in cholesterol include egg yolks, shrimp, lobster, and organ meats such as liver.

A more important contributor to an unhealthy blood cholesterol level is saturated fat. Saturated fats raise the blood cholesterol level by interfering with the body's ability to remove cholesterol from the blood. Saturated fats are found in beef, lamb, veal, pork, ham, whole milk, and whole milk products.

Rather than eliminating saturated fats and cholesterol from your diet, limit your intake. This is easier than you may think. Moderation is the key. Make changes whenever you can by substituting low-fat milk or skim milk for whole milk and margarine for butter, trimming visible fat from meats, and broiling or baking rather than frying. Read labels carefully. A "cholesterol-free" product may be high in saturated fat.

Blood Pressure

You can often control high blood pressure by losing excess weight and by changing your diet. When these are not enough, medications can be prescribed. It is important to have regular checkups to guard against high blood pressure and its harmful effects.

Weight and Exercise

Two additional ways to help prevent heart disease are to control your weight and exercise regularly. You store excess calories in your diet as fat. In general, overweight people have a shorter life expectancy.

Routine exercise has many benefits, including increased muscle tone and weight control. Exercise can also help you survive a heart attack because the increased circulation of blood through the heart develops additional channels for blood flow. If the primary channels that supply the heart are blocked in a heart attack, these additional channels can supply the heart tissue with oxygen-rich blood.

Routine exercise will often decrease stress and reduce your risk of heart disease. You can also develop a new hobby, set realistic goals for yourself, practise relaxation exercises, and avoid caffeinated products.

DID YOU KNOW?

Did you know that second-hand smoke...

- Can lead to heart disease?
- Can cause the formation of blood clots that can lead to heart attacks and stroke?
- Raises your heart rate?
- Damages your heart muscle?
- Lowers the level of protective cholesterol in your blood?

DID YOU KNOW?

Too often we take our hearts for granted. The heart is extremely reliable. It beats about 70 times each minute, or more than 100,000 times a day. During the average lifetime, the heart will beat nearly 3 billion times. The heart moves about 4 litres of blood per minute through the body. This is about 160 million litres in an average lifetime. The heart moves blood through about 100,000 kilometres of blood vessels.

Results of Managing Risk Factors

Managing your risk factors for cardiovascular disease really works. Over the past number of years, deaths from cardiovascular disease have decreased substantially.

Why did deaths from these causes decline? Probably they declined as a result of improved detection and treatment, as well as lifestyle changes. People are becoming more aware of their risk factors for heart disease and are taking action to control them. If you do this, you can improve your chances of living a long and healthy life. If you suffer a cardiac arrest, your chances of survival are poor. Begin today to reduce your risk of cardiovascular disease.

CARDIAC ARREST

What Is Cardiac Arrest?

Cardiac arrest occurs when the heart stops beating or beats too irregularly or too weakly to circulate blood effectively. Without a heartbeat, breathing soon ceases. The condition when the heart stops beating and breathing stops is referred to as clinical death.

Cardiac arrest is a life-threatening emergency because the body's vital organs, including the brain, are no longer receiving oxygen-rich blood. The irreversible damage caused by brain cell death is known as biological death (Figure 8–8). Every year, tens of thousands of Canadians die of cardiac arrest before reaching a hospital.

Common Causes of Cardiac Arrest

Cardiovascular disease is the most common cause of cardiac arrest. Other causes include drowning, suffocation, certain drugs, severe injuries to the chest, severe blood loss, and electrocution. Stroke and other types of brain damage can also stop the heart.

Signs of Cardiac Arrest

Someone in cardiac arrest is not breathing and does not have a pulse. The person's heart has either stopped beating or is beating so weakly or irregularly that it cannot produce a pulse. The signs of cardiac arrest include unconsciousness, no signs of normal breathing, and a lack of pulse. If you cannot feel a carotid pulse, no blood is reaching the brain. The person will be unconscious, and breathing will stop.

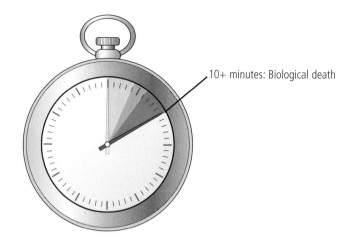

10+ minutes: Biological death

Figure 8–8 Biological death is the irreversible damage caused by brain-cell death.

Although cardiac arrest can result from a heart attack, cardiac arrest can also occur suddenly, from other causes. Therefore, the person may not have shown the signs and symptoms of a heart attack before the cardiac arrest.

Care for Cardiac Arrest

Someone in cardiac arrest needs cardiopulmonary resuscitation (CPR). The term "cardio" refers to the heart, and "pulmonary" refers to the lungs. CPR is a combination of rescue breathing and chest compressions. Chest compression is a method of making the blood circulate when the heart is not beating. Given together, rescue breathing and chest compressions artificially take over the functions of the lungs and heart.

For the person in cardiac arrest, CPR increases the chances of survival by keeping the brain supplied with oxygen until she receives advanced medical care. Without CPR, the brain will begin to die within four to six minutes. Be aware that, at best, CPR generates only about one third of the normal blood flow to the brain.

CPR alone is not enough to help someone survive cardiac arrest. Advanced medical care is needed immediately. Trained emergency personnel can provide advanced cardiac life support (ACLS). Acting as an extension of a hospital emergency department, some responders can administer medications or use a defibrillator as part of their emergency care.

A defibrillator is a device that sends an electric shock through the chest to allow the heart to resume its normal rhythm. Defibrillation given as soon as possible is the key to helping some people survive cardiac arrest. Immediate CPR must be combined with early defibrillation and other forms of ACLS to give the person in cardiac arrest the best chance for survival.

Responders in some communities are trained to use defibrillators called automated external defibrillators (AEDs). Today, AEDs are available for use by individuals in places such as factories, stadiums, airports, recreation facilities, casinos, and other places where large numbers of people gather. The use of defibrillators is described in a later section.

In all cases of cardiac arrest, it is very important to start CPR promptly and continue it until a defibrillator is available. When a defibrillator is not available, CPR should be continued. Effective rescue breathing and chest compressions can help keep the brain, heart, and other vital organs supplied with oxygen-rich blood. Any delay in starting CPR, or unnecessary delay in continuing it, reduces the person's chance for survival.

Starting CPR and defibrillation promptly, as well as ensuring advanced medical care is obtained, greatly increases the chance for survival.

CPR FOR ADULTS AND CHILDREN

Chest Compressions

Chest compressions create pressure within the chest cavity that moves blood through the circulatory system. For compressions to be most effective, the person should be flat on her back, on a firm surface.

Finding the Correct Hand Position

Placing your hands in the middle of the person's chest allows you to give the most effective compressions without causing injury.

- Once the heel of your hand is in position on the chest, place your other hand directly on top of it.

- Use the heel of your hand to apply pressure on the sternum.

If you have arthritis or a similar condition in your hands or wrists, you may use an alternative hand position. Find the correct hand position, as above; then grasp the

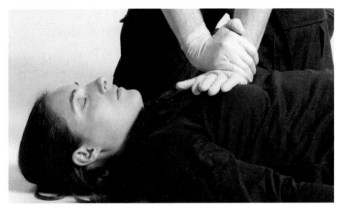

Figure 8–9 One-handed compressions can be done by grasping the wrist of the hand on the chest with the other hand.

NOTE:

Use two hands to compress a child's chest, unless the child is very small in comparison with the responder. With a small child, using two hands may create too much pressure. If this is the case, compress with only one hand.

---

wrist of the hand on the chest with the other hand (Figure 8–9).

If you can position your hands without removing thin clothing, such as a T-shirt, do so. The person's clothing will not necessarily interfere with your ability to position your hands on the chest.

Position of the Responder

Your body position is important when giving chest compressions. Compressing the chest straight down provides the best blood flow. The correct body position is also less tiring for you.

Kneel at the person's chest with your hands in the correct position. Straighten your arms and lock your elbows so that your shoulders are directly over your hands (Figure 8–10). When you press down in this position, you are pushing straight down onto the person's sternum. Locking your elbows keeps your arms straight and prevents you from tiring quickly.

Compressing the chest requires less effort in this position. When you press down, the weight of your upper body creates the force needed to compress the

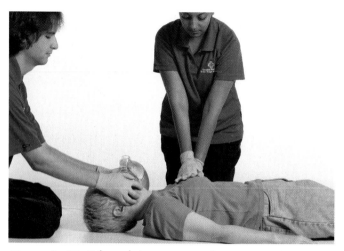

Figure 8–10 When doing compressions, your arms should be straightened and locked so your shoulders are directly over your hands.

chest. Push with the weight of your upper body, not with the muscles of your arms. Push straight down. Do not rock back and forth. Rocking results in less effective compressions and uses unnecessary energy. If your arms and shoulders tire quickly, you are not using the correct body position. After each compression, release the pressure on the chest without losing contact with it

NOTE:

For a child, compress 1/3 to 1/2 the depth of the chest.

and allow the chest to return to its normal position before you start the next compression (Figure 8–11).

Compression Technique

Each compression should push the sternum of an adult down 4 to 5 cm (1 1/2 to 2 in). The downward and upward movement should be smooth, not jerky. Maintain a steady down-and-up rhythm and do not pause between compressions. When you press down, the chambers of the heart empty. When you come up, release all pressure on the chest, which lets the chambers of the heart fill with blood between compressions.

Give compressions at the rate of about 100 per minute and "Push hard. Push fast." You should be able to do the 30 compressions in about 18 seconds. Even though you are compressing the chest at a rate of about 100 times per minute, you will not actually perform 100 compressions in a minute. This is because you must take

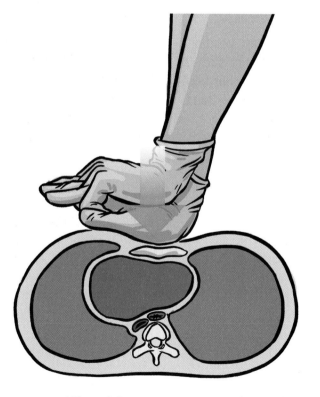
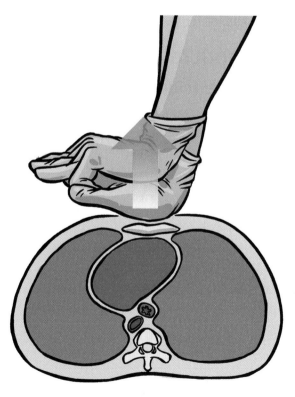

Figure 8–11 When doing compressions, push straight down, then release, allowing the chest to return to its normal position.

the time to do rescue breathing, giving two breaths between each group of 30 compressions.

Compression/Breathing Cycles

When you perform CPR, do cycles of 30 compressions and two breaths. You should be positioned midway between the chest and the head to move easily between compressions and breaths. For each cycle, do 30 chest compressions; then open the airway and give two one-second breaths, with just enough volume to make the chest rise.

After doing five cycles (2 minutes) of continuous CPR, recheck signs of circulation, including a pulse, and breathing. Tilt the person's head to open the airway and take no more than 10 seconds to check for signs of circulation. If there are no signs of circulation or you are unsure, continue CPR, beginning with compressions. Check circulation and breathing again every few minutes. If the person has a pulse but is not breathing, give rescue breathing. If the person is breathing, keep her airway open and provide ongoing survey and care.

CPR for Pregnant Women

When performing CPR on a visibly pregnant woman, putting a blanket or cushion under her right hip will help blood return to the heart. However, do not interrupt CPR to find an object.

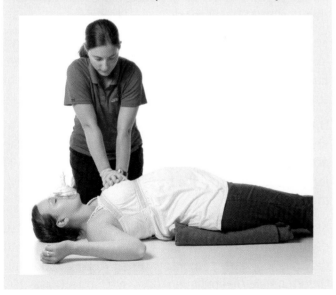

When to Stop CPR

Once you begin CPR, do not interrupt the blood flow you are creating artificially. However, you can stop CPR if:

- The person's heart starts beating
- Another responder with training equal to or greater than yours takes over (Continue to assist by obtaining advanced medical care if this has not already been done.)
- You are prompted to do so by an AED
- You are too exhausted to continue
- The scene suddenly becomes unsafe

The Heart's Electrical System

To better understand both the limitations of CPR and how defibrillators work, it is helpful to understand how the heart's electrical system functions. The electrical system determines the pumping action of the heart. Under normal conditions, specialized cells of the heart initiate and carry on electrical activity. The normal point of origin of the electrical impulse is the sinoatrial (SA) node, which is situated in the upper part of the heart's right atrium.

The electrical impulse moves to the atrioventricular (AV) node, which is situated between the two atria and ventricles, through conduction pathways within the heart muscle. From the AV node, the electrical signal is sent to the ventricles through other pathways.

These electrical impulses are the stimuli that cause the heart muscle to contract and pump the blood out of its chambers and throughout the body (Figure 8–12).

Cardiac monitors are used to read the electrical impulses in the heart to produce an electrocardiogram (ECG), which is a reading of the conduction of the electrical current through the pathways of the heart. The normal conduction of electrical impulses without any disturbances is called normal sinus rhythm (NSR) (Figure 8–13).

In NSR, the impulse is initiated in the SA node and transmitted to the atria. The stimulus from the electrical impulse causes the atria to contract and expel the blood to the ventricles. Meanwhile, the electrical current continues to travel through the

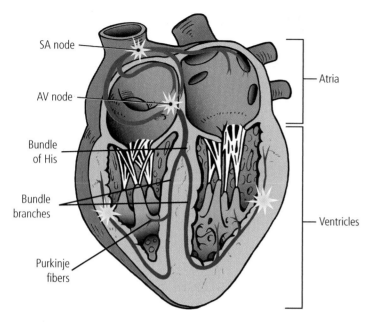

Figure 8–12 Conduction system of the heart.

atria and the AV node to the ventricles. When the ventricles receive the impulse, they contract to expel the blood throughout the body's blood vessels. This process normally takes place 60 to 100 times per minute.

Disturbances in Heart Rhythm

The healthy adult heart usually displays NSR on the ECG. Disturbances or variations in the conduction of electrical impulses within the heart are called dysrhythmias. Although dysrhythmias can either be benign or have serious consequences, there are three major conduction disturbances that are immediately life-threatening: asystole, ventricular tachycardia (VT), and ventricular fibrillation (VF).

Asystole

Asystole is the absence of electrical activity in the heart. AEDs are not able to shock this rhythm (Figure 8–14).

Ventricular Tachycardia

VT is a rhythm of fast-paced contractions of the heart's ventricles. The contractions are too rapid to allow the ventricles to fill with blood to pump an adequate supply of blood to the body (Figure 8–15). Someone experiencing this type of dysrhythmia can still have a pulse.

Ventricular Fibrillation

VF is a chaotic discharge of electrical activity that causes the heart muscle to quiver (Figure 8–16). People

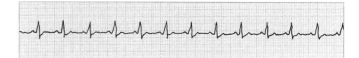

Figure 8–13 Normal sinus rhythm.

Figure 8–14 Asystole.

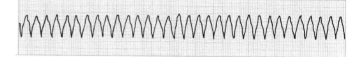

Figure 8–15 Ventricular tachycardia.

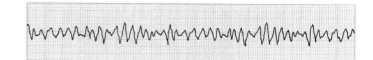

Figure 8–16 Ventricular fibrillation.

with this dysrhythmia have no pulse. VF will deteriorate to asystole within a few minutes if not treated promptly.

Correcting the Problem

In over 80 percent of all sudden cardiac arrests, the initial rhythm is VT or VF, which are the only two rhythms an AED will shock.

Studies show that early CPR and defibrillation are most likely to improve the survival of adults in cardiac arrest. Each minute that defibrillation is delayed, the chance of survival is reduced by about 7 to 10 percent.

During defibrillation, an electrical shock is delivered to the heart. The shock is intended to briefly stop the abnormal electrical activity (e.g., VF or pulseless VT) long enough to allow the heart to develop an effective rhythm on its own.

Because the treatment of choice for both of these rhythms in cases of cardiac arrest is CPR along with defibrillation, early response with an AED is important. Unfortunately, defibrillation does not correct asystole, and CPR must continue until more advanced help is obtained. CPR may cause an unshockable rhythm to become a shockable rhythm. The successful resuscitation of people in cardiac arrest with a shockable dysrhythmia (i.e., VF or VT) depends greatly on how much time has passed from the start of the dysrhythmia until defibrillation is initiated, as well as whether CPR was initiated. The availability of AEDs to a wider range of responders could greatly reduce the time from collapse to defibrillation, thereby increasing the chance for survival.

NOTE:

If the cardiac arrest was not witnessed by the responder, perform five cycles (two minutes) of CPR before starting the AED. This will increase the chances of the AED finding a shockable rhythm.

Using an AED

In a situation involving a cardiac arrest that is witnessed by the responder, an AED should be put to use as soon as it is available. To defibrillate someone in cardiac arrest by using an AED, take the following steps.

1. Confirm cardiac arrest. Check for responsiveness and ABCs.

2. Turn on the AED.

3. Expose and prepare the chest. Wipe the person's chest dry and shave if needed.

4. Attach electrode pads to the chest. Place one pad on the upper-right side of the chest and the other pad on the lower-left side of the chest (Figure 8–17).

5. Plug electrode pads into AED, if needed.

6. Let the AED analyze the heart rhythm (or push the "analyze" button if required).

7. Make sure no one is touching the person.

8. Deliver a shock if indicated by the AED.
   - Say "I'm clear, you're clear, everybody's clear"; ensure that no one is touching the person.
   - Deliver a shock by pushing the "shock" button when prompted by the AED.
   - After the shock, the AED will prompt you to provide five cycles (two minutes) of CPR.
   - After the two minutes, the AED will analyze again.

If the AED advises no shock is needed:
- Check for signs of circulation.
- If there are no signs, do five cycles of CPR (two minutes).

NOTE:

Use an AED only on someone without a pulse.

Figure 8–17 One electrode pad should be placed on the upper-right side of the chest, and the other pad on the lower-left side of the chest.

- Follow the prompts of the AED.

Responders using AEDs may fall under medical direction provided on a local, regional, or province/territory-wide basis. You must follow local protocols that establish how many shocks are delivered, the energy setting of each shock, and how CPR and other lifesaving measures are used.

Special Resuscitation Situations

Some situations require responders to pay special attention when using an AED. It is important that responders be familiar with these situations and be able to respond appropriately.

Hypothermia

Check the pulse of a person suffering from severe hypothermia for up to 45 seconds. If AED is indicated, give only one shock. Following the shock, continue with the CPR sequence. Follow local protocol.

Babies

Babies under one year of age should not be defibrillated.

Transdermal Medications

AED electrodes should not be placed over a transdermal medication patch (e.g., a patch of nitroglycerin, nicotine, pain medication, hormone replacement therapy, or antihypertensive medication) as the patch may block the transfer of the energy to the heart and

Canadian Red Cross AED Protocol

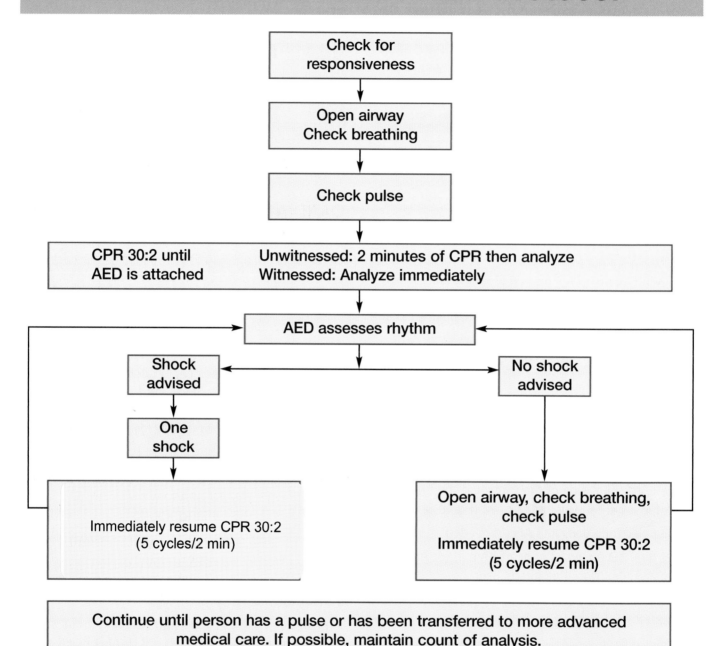

Check for
responsiveness

↓

Open airway
Check breathing

↓

Check pulse

↓

| CPR 30:2 until AED is attached | Unwitnessed: 2 minutes of CPR then analyze Witnessed: Analyze immediately |

↓

AED assesses rhythm

Shock advised ← → No shock advised

↓

One shock

↓

Immediately resume CPR 30:2
(5 cycles/2 min)

Open airway, check breathing,
check pulse

Immediately resume CPR 30:2
(5 cycles/2 min)

Continue until person has a pulse or has been transferred to more advanced
medical care. If possible, maintain count of analysis.

may cause small burns to the skin. With a gloved hand, remove any patches from the chest and wipe the area before attaching the electrode pads.

Implanted Pacemakers and Implanted Cardioverter-Defibrillators

The person may have a pacemaker or implanted cardioverter-defibrillator (ICD) implanted in the chest area where one of the electrode pads is intended to go. If you observe a small scar and a matchbox-sized lump on the chest, reposition the electrodes at least 2.5 cm (1 in) away. If an ICD is already in shock sequence (e.g., the person's muscles contract in a manner similar to that observed during external defibrillation), allow 30 to 60 seconds for the ICD to complete the treatment cycle before delivering a shock from the AED.

Body Jewellery

If a necklace or other body jewellery is in the way or within 2.5 cm (1 in) of electrode pad placement, remove the jewellery before AED use.

Trauma to the Torso

Place electrode pads on the chest if the trauma does not interfere with the placement.

Ice, Snow, and Water

If the person is lying in a puddle or other pool of water, do the "splash test." If you jump in the water and it splashes, it is deep enough to conduct an electrical charge, so you must remove the person from the water before you use the AED.

Maintenance

For defibrillators to perform optimally, they must be maintained like any other machine. The AEDs available today require minimal maintenance. These devices have various self-testing features. However, it is important that operators are familiar with any visual or audible warning or prompts that the AED may feature to warn of a malfunction or low battery. It is important to read the operator's manual thoroughly and check with the manufacturer to obtain all necessary information regarding maintenance.

Other Precautions

The following precautions must be taken when using an AED:

- As alcohol is flammable, avoid using alcohol pads to clean the chest before attaching the pads.

- Stand clear of the person while analyzing and defibrillating.

- Do not analyze the heart rhythm or defibrillate in a moving vehicle.

- Do not defibrillate a person in the presence of flammable materials (such as gasoline).

- Avoid radio transmissions while defibrillating, including cellphones within two metres (six feet) of the person.

- Keep breathing devices with free-flowing oxygen away from the person during defibrillation.

- Avoid the use of supplemental, free-flowing oxygen while using an AED in a confined space.

NOTE:

In general for first aid, someone is considered to be a child from the age of one year until the onset of puberty, except when using an AED. In the case of AED, someone is considered to be a child when between the ages of one and eight. For a child in this age range, child electrode pads should be used. Follow the directions for electrode pad placement. If there is less than 2.5 cm (1 in) between the electrode pads when on the chest, place one on the front of the chest (anterior) and one on the back (posterior).

CARDIAC EMERGENCIES IN BABIES AND CHILDREN

A child's heart is usually healthy. Unlike adults, children do not often initially suffer a cardiac emergency. Instead, the child suffers a respiratory emergency, which can lead to a cardiac emergency.

Common causes of cardiac emergencies for both babies and children include injuries from near-drowning, smoke inhalation, burns, poisoning, airway obstruction, and falls.

Most cardiac emergencies in babies and children are preventable. One way to prevent them in this age group is to prevent injuries. Another is to make sure that babies and children receive proper medical care. A third is to recognize the early signs of a breathing emergency. These signs include:

- Agitation
- Drowsiness
- Change in skin colour (to pale blue or grey)
- Difficulty breathing
- Increased heart and breathing rates

If you recognize that a baby or child is having a breathing emergency, provide necessary care. If the baby or child is in cardiac arrest, start CPR immediately. In either event, obtain more advanced medical care.

CPR FOR BABIES

The CPR technique for babies is similar to that for adults. As in rescue breathing, you need to modify the techniques to accommodate the smaller body size and faster breathing and heart rates. Figure 8–18 compares the adult, child, and baby CPR techniques.

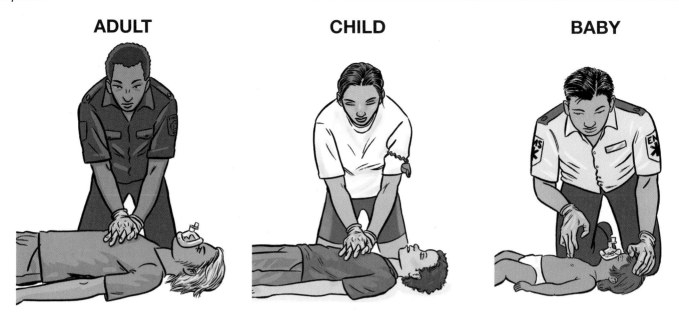

	ADULT	CHILD	BABY
HAND POSITION:	Two hands on lower half of sternum	One or two hands on lower half of sternum	Two fingers on lower half of sternum (just below nipple line)
COMPRESS:	4–5 cm (1$\frac{1}{2}$–2 in)	$\frac{1}{3}$–$\frac{1}{2}$ of chest depth	$\frac{1}{3}$–$\frac{1}{2}$ of chest depth
BREATHE:	Until chest gently rises (about 1 second per breath)	Until chest gently rises (about 1 second per breath)	Until chest gently rises (about 1 second per breath)
CYCLE:	30 compressions 2 breaths	30 compressions 2 breaths	30 compressions 2 breaths
RATE:	30 compressions in about 18 seconds	30 compressions in about 18 seconds	30 compressions in about 18 seconds

Figure 8–18 The technique for chest compressions is very similar for adults, children, and babies.

To find out if a baby needs CPR, begin with a primary survey to check the ABCs. To check the pulse in a baby, locate the brachial pulse in the arm. If the baby has no signs of circulation, including lack of a brachial pulse, begin CPR.

Position the baby face up on a firm, flat surface. Stand or kneel facing the baby from the side. Keep one hand on the baby's head to maintain an open airway. Use your other hand to give compressions.

To find the correct place to give compressions, place your two fingers in the middle of the chest, just below the nipple line.

Use the pads of two fingers to compress the chest (Figure 8–19). Compress the chest $\frac{1}{3}$ to $\frac{1}{2}$ the depth of the chest and then let the sternum return to its normal position. When you compress, push straight down. The down-and-up movement of your compressions should be smooth, not jerky. Keep a steady rhythm. Do not pause between compressions. When you are coming up, release pressure on the baby's chest completely but do not let your fingers lose contact with the chest (Figure 8–20). Keep your fingers in the compression position. Use your other hand to keep the airway open using a head-tilt.

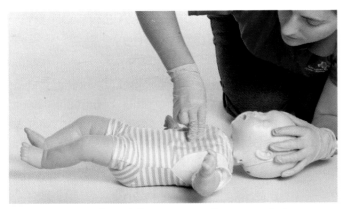

Figure 8–19 When doing compressions on a baby, use the pads of two fingers.

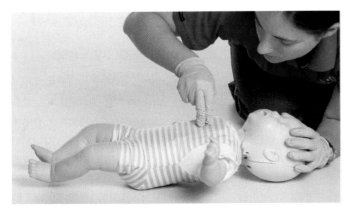

Figure 8–20 Allow the chest to return to its normal position between compressions.

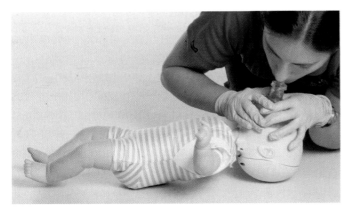

Figure 8–21 Continue cycles of 30 compressions and two breaths.

When you give CPR, do cycles of 30 compressions and two breaths (Figure 8–21). Compress at a rate of at least 100 compressions per minute. When you complete 30 compressions, give two one-second breaths, with just enough volume to make the chest rise, covering the baby's nose and mouth with your mask. Keep repeating cycles of 30 compressions and two puffs.

Recheck for signs of circulation, including brachial pulse, and breathing after about five cycles (two minutes) of continuous CPR. Check for signs of circulation for no more than 10 seconds with the hand that was giving compressions. If there are no signs of circulation or you are unsure, continue CPR, starting with compressions. Recheck circulation and breathing every few minutes.

If the baby has a pulse but is not breathing, give rescue breaths. If the baby is breathing, keep the airway open and provide ongoing survey and care.

TWO-RESCUER CPR

When two professional responders are available, they give two-rescuer CPR. They share the responsibility for performing rescue breathing and chest compressions (Figure 8–22).

Two-Rescuer CPR for an Adult

The cycle involves 30 compressions and two breaths (a ratio of 30:2). During two-rescuer CPR, the person giving breaths (the ventilator) checks the effectiveness of the compressions by feeling for the carotid pulse while the compressor is giving chest compressions. If the person has lost a significant amount of blood, a carotid pulse may not be felt even though compressions are effective.

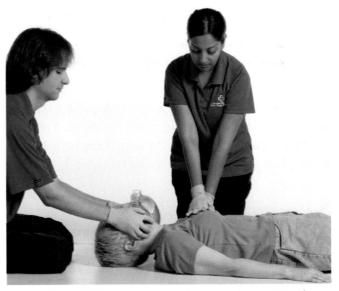

Figure 8–22 When two responders are doing CPR, they share the responsibility of performing rescue breathing and chest compressions.

The ventilator also checks for signs of circulation, including pulse, after the five cycles (two minutes) of compressions and repeats the check every few minutes after that to determine if circulation has returned. This is done by communicating that he is performing a circulation check; then the compressor stops after the 30th compression. The ventilator checks for signs of circulation for no more than 10 seconds. If there is no circulation or he is unsure, CPR is continued, starting with compressions.

Two-Rescuer CPR for a Child

Follow the same technique as described above but change the CPR ratio to 15 compressions to two breaths. In two minutes, 10 cycles of CPR should be done.

Two-Rescuer CPR for a Baby

One responder encircles the baby's chest with both hands, spreading her fingers around the baby's back and placing both thumbs on the lower half of the baby's breastbone (Figure 8–23). Compressions are performed by compressing the sternum with the hands in this position. The other responder monitors the baby's pulse to check whether the compressions are effective and gives rescue breaths. For a baby, if there are two responders, use a ratio of 15 compressions to two breaths. In two minutes, 10 cycles of CPR should be done.

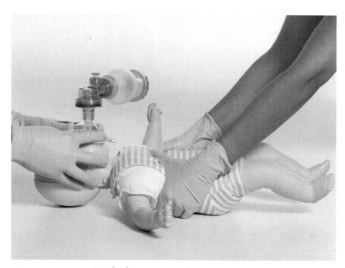

Figure 8–23 For baby CPR with two responders, the responder doing compressions circles their hands around the baby's chest, with the fingers at the back, and the thumbs on the lower half of the baby's breastbone.

When Two Responders Arrive on the Scene at the Same Time

If CPR is not being performed when you arrive, one responder should do a primary survey and, if appropriate, begin CPR. The other responder should manage other responsibilities at the scene and get an AED if available; then she can assist with CPR and AED. If both responders begin CPR at the same time, the first responder does a primary survey. While the first responder is doing the primary survey, the second responder gets into position to give chest compressions. She should begin chest compressions when the first responder communicates that there are no signs of circulation. Both responders continue CPR together.

When CPR Is in Progress by One Responder

When a responder is giving CPR and a second responder arrives, that responder should ask whether more advanced medical care has been obtained. If not, she should call, or send someone else to call, and have the person get an AED if available. Then the second responder should either replace the first responder or assist in giving two-rescuer CPR by providing ventilations or compressions.

Changing Positions

It is recommended that responders change every two minutes (between cycles) to maintain quality CPR. When the responders change, the responder at the person's head completes two breaths and then moves immediately to the chest. The responder at the chest moves immediately to the head. Both responders move quickly into position without changing sides. The person who is now at the chest begins compressions immediately.

STROKE

A stroke, also called a cerebrovascular accident (CVA), is a disruption of blood flow to a part of the brain that is serious enough to damage brain tissue (Figure 8–24).

There are three causes of stroke. Two of these are caused by a moving blood clot that forms or lodges in the arteries that supply blood to the brain, and the third is a rupture of the arteries.

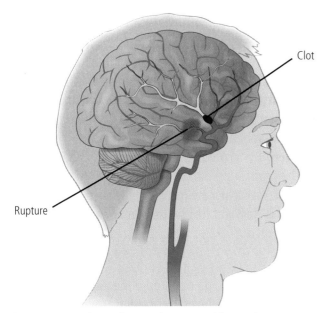

Clot

Rupture

Figure 8–24 A stroke can be caused by a clot or rupture.

1. *Embolic strokes.* A mass known as an embolus—which could be a solid, liquid or gas—can be carried to a blood vessel from another site in the body. The most common type is a clot coming from diseased carotid blood vessels or from abnormally contracting chambers in the heart.

2. *Thrombotic strokes.* A thrombus is a gradually developing blood clot that leads to an obstruction of a cerebral artery. Plaque deposits forming on the inner walls of arteries causes a narrowing of the arteries and reduces blood flow.

3. *Bleeding from a ruptured artery in the brain.* A head injury, high blood pressure or a weak area in an artery wall can result in this type of stroke.

Less commonly, a tumour or swelling from a head injury may cause a stroke by compressing an artery.

A transient ischemic attack (TIA) is a temporary episode that is like a stroke. TIAs are sometimes called "mini-strokes." Like a stroke, a TIA is caused by reduced blood flow to part of the brain. Unlike a stroke, the signs and symptoms of a TIA disappear within a few minutes or hours, although the person is not out of danger. Someone who experiences a TIA has a significantly increased risk of having a stroke in the future.

Signs and Symptoms of Stroke and TIA

As with other sudden illnesses, the primary signs and symptoms of stroke or TIA are looking or feeling ill, changes in consciousness, and abnormal behaviour.

Others signs and symptoms may include:

- Sudden weakness and/or numbness of the face, arm, or leg, usually only on one side of the body
- Difficulty talking or understanding speech
- Blurred or dimmed vision
- Pupils of unequal size
- Sudden, severe headache
- Dizziness
- Confusion
- Changes in mood
- Ringing in the ears
- Unconsciousness or temporary loss of consciousness
- Loss of bowel or bladder control

Remember FAST:

FACE – facial numbness or weakness, especially on one side

ARM – arm numbness or weakness, especially on one side

SPEECH – slurred speech or difficulty speaking or understanding

TIME – time is critically important; obtain more advanced care immediately

Assessing Someone Who Has Had a Suspected Stroke

To assess facial droop, arm weakness, and speech abnormalities, responders can use a tool such as the Cincinnati Pre-hospital Stroke Scale (CPSS).

Facial droop: Have the person show her teeth or smile.

If both sides of the face move equally, this is normal.

If one side of the face does not move as well as the other side, this is abnormal.

Arm weakness: Have the person close both eyes and hold her arms out straight for 10 seconds.

If both arms move the same or both arms do not move at all, this is normal.

If one arm does not move or one arm drifts down compared with the other, this is abnormal.

Speech abnormalities: Have the person say, "You can't teach an old dog new tricks."

If the person uses the correct words and does not slur, this is normal.

If the person uses the incorrect words, slurs the words, or does not speak at all, this is abnormal.

Care for Stroke and TIA

If the person is unconscious, make sure she has an open airway and care for any life-threatening conditions that may occur. If there is fluid or vomitus in the person's mouth, position her on the unaffected side to allow any fluids to drain out. You may have to use a finger sweep to remove some of the material from the mouth. Obtain more advanced medical care.

A stroke can make the person fearful and anxious; therefore, it is important to comfort and reassure the person. Often she does not understand what has happened. Have the person rest in a comfortable position. Do not give her anything to eat or drink. Rapid access to advanced medical care is very important. Provide ongoing survey and care.

Prevention of Stroke and TIA

The risk factors for stroke and TIA are similar to those for heart disease. Some risk factors are beyond your control, such as age, gender, or a family history of stroke, TIA, or diabetes. To prevent stroke, follow the same guidelines as those for preventing cardiovascular disease.

SUMMARY

It is important to recognize signs and symptoms that may indicate a circulatory emergency. If you think someone is suffering from a circulatory emergency or if you are unsure, obtain more advanced medical care without delay. Provide care by helping the ill person to rest in the most comfortable position and administering oxygen. If you are qualified to transport the person, do so safely and efficiently.

When heartbeat and breathing stop, it is called cardiac arrest. Someone who suffers a cardiac arrest is clinically dead since no oxygen is reaching the cells of vital organs. Irreversible brain damage will occur from a lack of oxygen. By starting CPR immediately, you can help keep the brain supplied with oxygen. By obtaining more advanced medical care rapidly, you can increase the chances for survival for the person in cardiac arrest.

If the person does not have signs of circulation, start CPR.

Once you start CPR, do not stop unnecessarily. Continue CPR until you are relieved by another trained responder, you are exhausted, the person's heart starts beating, you obtain more advanced medical care and they take over, or an AED is available.

When blood flow to the brain is interrupted, either due to a blockage or rupture of an artery in the brain, this is called a stroke. The part of the brain that was supplied by that artery is starved of oxygen and suffers damage. This can cause muscle weakness or numbness, difficulty speaking, or a range of other problems throughout the body. It is critical to obtain advanced medical care immediately as there are steps that will minimize that damage or even prevent it.

You find out that she has medication in her purse for this type of emergency. What do you do?

CPR for an Adult or Child

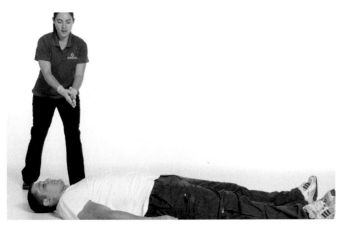

1. Check for responsiveness.

2. Open airway and check for breathing for no more than 10 seconds.

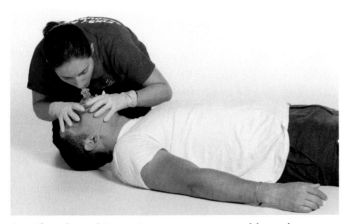

3. If no breathing, give two one-second breaths.

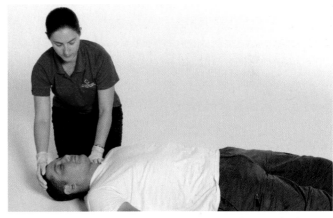

4. Check for signs of circulation (including pulse) for no more than 10 seconds.

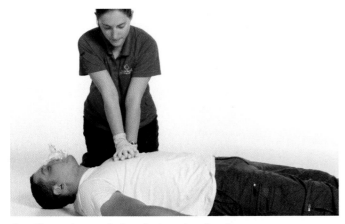

5. If no signs of circulation, begin chest compressions (30).

6. After 30 compressions, give two breaths.

Repeat cycle of 30 compressions and two breaths.

Skills Summary

CPR for a Baby

1. Open airway and check for breathing for no more than 10 seconds.

2. If no breathing, give two one-second breaths.

3. Check for signs of circulation (including pulse) for no more than 10 seconds.

4. If no signs of circulation, begin chest compressions (30).

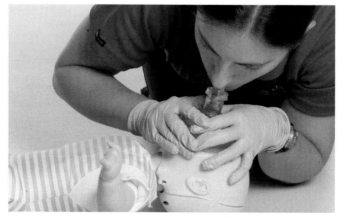

5. After 30 compressions, give two breaths.

Repeat cycle of 30 compressions and two breaths.

Two-Rescuer CPR for an Adult or Child

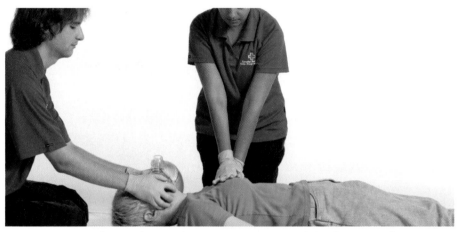

1. One responder performs chest compressions while the second responder keeps the head tilted and the mask sealed against the face.

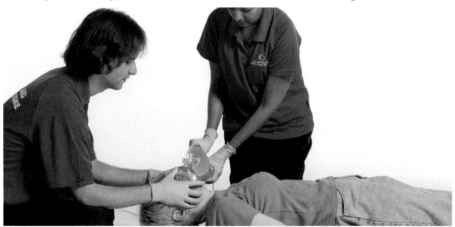

2. The first responder provides two ventilations after each set of 30 compressions (15 for a child).

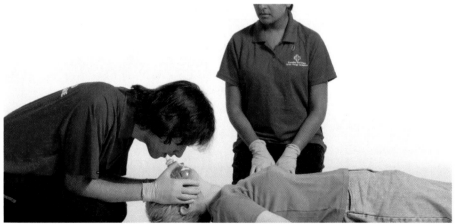

3. If using a resuscitation mask, the second responder provides ventilations.

Responders should switch every two minutes (between cycles) to ensure quality CPR.

Two-Rescuer CPR for a Baby

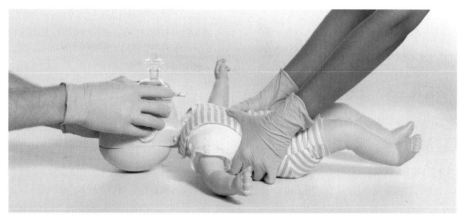

1. One responder performs chest compressions using the thumb-encircling technique while the second responder keeps the head tilted and the mask sealed against the face.

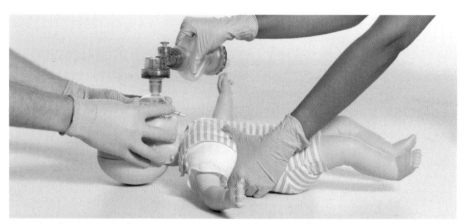

2. The first responder provides two ventilations after each set of 15 compressions.

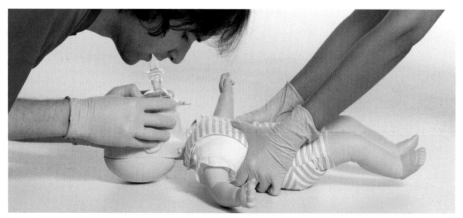

3. If using a resuscitation mask, the second responder provides ventilations.

Responders should switch every two minutes (between cycles) to ensure quality CPR.

Chapter 9

Bleeding

You are called to the scene of a construction site. A worker has fallen from some heavy equipment and has been impaled by a sharp metal fence post. He is bleeding profusely from a wound in his side. He's pale and his skin is moist. His voice is weak and he's starting to lose consciousness. What do you do?

INTRODUCTION

Bleeding is the loss of blood from arteries, veins, or capillaries. A large amount of bleeding occurring in a short time is called a hemorrhage. Bleeding is either internal or external. Internal bleeding is often difficult to recognize. External bleeding is usually obvious because it is typically visible. Uncontrolled bleeding, whether internal or external, is a life-threatening emergency.

Severe bleeding can result in death. Check for and control severe bleeding during the primary survey once you have checked for a pulse. You may not identify internal bleeding, however, until you perform a more detailed check during the secondary survey. In this chapter, you will learn how to recognize and care for both internal and external bleeding.

BLOOD AND BLOOD VESSELS

Blood Components

Blood consists of liquid and solid components and comprises approximately eight percent of the body's total weight, to a volume of approximately five litres. The liquid part of the blood is called plasma. The solid components are the red and white blood cells and cell fragments called platelets.

Plasma makes up about half of the blood volume circulating within the body. Composed mostly of water, plasma maintains the blood volume that the circulatory system needs to function normally. Plasma also contains nutrients essential for energy production, growth, and cell maintenance and carries waste products for elimination.

White blood cells are a key disease-fighting component of the immune system. They defend the body against invading microorganisms. They also aid in producing antibodies that help the body resist infection.

Red blood cells account for most of the solid components of the blood. They are produced in the marrow in the hollow centre of large bones such as the large bone of the arm (humerus) and of the thigh (femur). Red blood cells number nearly 260 million in each drop of blood. The red blood cells transport oxygen from the lungs to the body cells and carbon dioxide from the cells to the lungs. Red blood cells outnumber white blood cells about 1,000 to 1.

Platelets are disc-shaped cells in the blood. Platelets are an essential part of the blood's clotting mechanism because they tend to bind together. Clotting is the process by which whole blood thickens at a wound site. Platelets help stop bleeding by forming blood clots at wound sites. Blood clots form the framework for healing. Until blood clots form, bleeding must be controlled.

Blood Functions

The blood has three major functions:

- Transporting oxygen, nutrients, and wastes
- Protecting against disease by producing antibodies and defending against germs
- Helping to maintain constant body temperature by circulating throughout the body

Blood Vessels

Blood is channeled through blood vessels. There are three major types of blood vessels: arteries, capillaries, and veins (Figure 9–1). Arteries carry blood away from the heart. Arteries become narrower the farther they extend from the heart until they connect to the capillaries. Capillaries are microscopic blood vessels linking arteries and veins that transfer oxygen, nutrients, and carbon dioxide. The veins carry blood back to the heart. Waste products from the cells move through the blood to the organs that eliminate waste from the body, such as the kidneys and lungs.

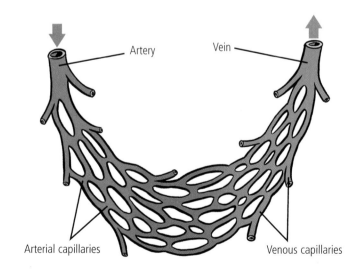

Figure 9–1 Blood flows through the three major types of blood vessels: arteries, veins, and capillaries.

Blood in the arteries travels faster and is under greater pressure than blood in the capillaries or veins. Blood flow in the arteries pulses with the heartbeat; blood in the veins flows more slowly and evenly.

WHEN BLEEDING OCCURS

When bleeding occurs, the body begins a complex chain of events. The brain, heart, and lungs immediately attempt to compensate for blood loss to maintain the flow of oxygen-rich blood to the body, particularly to the vital organs.

Other important reactions also occur. Platelets collect at the wound site in an effort to stop blood loss through clotting. White blood cells try to prevent infection by attacking microorganisms that commonly enter through breaks in the skin. The body manufactures extra red blood cells to help transport more oxygen to the cells.

Blood volume is also affected by bleeding. Normally, excess fluid is absorbed from the bloodstream by the kidneys, lungs, intestines, and skin. However, when bleeding occurs, this excess fluid is reabsorbed into the bloodstream as plasma. This helps maintain the critical balance of fluids needed by the body to keep blood volume constant.

Bleeding severe enough to critically reduce the blood volume is life-threatening. Severe bleeding can be either external or internal (Figure 9–2, a-b).

EXTERNAL BLEEDING

External bleeding occurs when a blood vessel is opened externally, such as through a tear in the skin. You can usually see this type of bleeding. Most external bleeding you will encounter will be minor. Minor bleeding, such as small cuts, usually stops by itself within 10 minutes, when the blood clots. Sometimes the damaged blood vessel is too large or the blood is under too much pressure for effective clotting to occur. In these cases, you will need to recognize and control bleeding promptly. Look for severe bleeding during the check for circulation as part of the primary survey.

Recognizing Severe External Bleeding

The signs of severe external bleeding include:

- Blood spurting or flowing freely from a wound

- Blood that fails to clot after you have taken all measures to control bleeding

Each type of blood vessel bleeds differently. Bleeding from arteries is often rapid and profuse and is life-threatening. This is because arterial blood is under direct pressure from the heart, so it usually spurts from the wound, making it difficult for clots to form. Because clots do not form rapidly in arteries, this type of bleeding is harder to control than bleeding from veins and capillaries. Its high concentration of oxygen gives arterial blood a bright red colour.

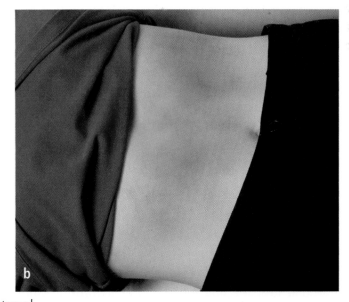

Figure 9–2, a-b Severe bleeding can be: **a**, external; or **b**, internal.

Veins are damaged more often than arteries because they are closer to the skin's surface. Bleeding from veins (venous bleeding) is easier to control than arterial bleeding. Venous blood is under less pressure than arterial blood and flows from the wound at a steady rate without spurting. Only damage to veins deep in the body, such as those in the trunk or thigh, produces profuse bleeding that is hard to control. Because it is oxygen poor, venous blood is dark red or maroon.

Capillary bleeding is usually slow because the vessels are small and the blood is under low pressure. It is often described as "oozing" from the wound. Clotting occurs easily with capillary bleeding. The blood from capillaries is usually dark red in colour.

Controlling External Bleeding

External bleeding is usually easy to control. Generally, you can control it by applying a pressure dressing with your gloved hand directly on the wound. This is called applying direct pressure. Pressure on the wound restricts the blood flow through the wound and allows normal clotting to occur. You can maintain pressure on a wound by snugly applying a bandage to the injured area.

In a few cases, direct pressure may not control severe bleeding. In these cases, other measures may have to be taken. To further slow bleeding, you may compress the artery supplying the area against an underlying bone at specific sites on the body. These sites are called pressure points (Figure 9–3, a).

The main pressure points used to control bleeding in the arms and legs are the brachial and femoral arteries (Figure 9–3, b). Pressure points in other areas of the body may also be used to control blood flow. A tourniquet, a tight band placed around an arm or leg to constrict blood vessels to stop blood flow to a wound, can be used as a last resort in controlling severe external bleeding. Use tourniquets only if trained to do so.

To control external bleeding, follow these general steps:

1. Place direct pressure on the wound with a sterile gauze pad or any clean cloth, such as a washcloth, towel, or handkerchief. Using gauze or a clean cloth keeps the wound free from germs. Place a gloved hand over the gauze pad and apply firm pressure

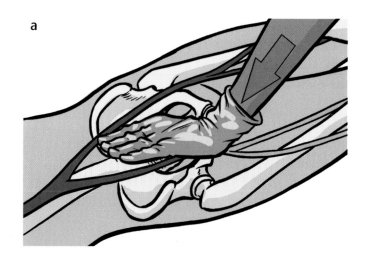

a

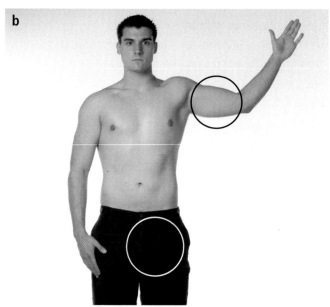

b

Figure 9–3, a-b a, pressure points are specific sites on the body where arteries lie close to the bone and the body's surface; **b**, two of the main pressure points used to control bleeding in the arms and legs are the brachial and femoral arteries.

(Figure 9–4, a). If gauze or cloth is not available, apply pressure with your gloved hand or, if necessary, have the injured person apply pressure with his own hand.

2. Have the person sit or lie down and rest.

3. Apply a pressure bandage. This bandage will hold the gauze pads or cloth in place while maintaining direct pressure (Figure 9–4, b). If blood soaks through, add additional dressings and bandages with additional direct pressure. Do not remove any blood-soaked dressings or bandages.

Figure 9–4, a-c To control external bleeding: **a**, place direct pressure on the wound; **b**, apply a pressure bandage; and **c**, apply pressure at a pressure point if bleeding continues.

4. If bleeding continues, apply pressure at a pressure point proximal to the injury to slow the flow of blood (Figure 9–4, c).

Continue to monitor the injured person's airway and breathing. Observe him closely for signs that indicate a worsening condition. If bleeding is severe, administer supplemental oxygen to the person if available. More advanced medical care must be obtained if not already done.

INTERNAL BLEEDING

Internal bleeding is the escape of blood from arteries, veins, or capillaries into spaces in the body. Capillary bleeding, indicated by mild bruising, is just beneath the skin and is not serious. Deeper bleeding, however, involves arteries and veins and may result in severe blood loss.

Severe internal bleeding usually occurs in injuries caused by a violent blunt force, such as when the driver is thrown against the steering wheel in a car crash or when someone falls from a height. Internal bleeding may also occur when a sharp object, such as a knife, penetrates the skin and damages internal structures.

Recognizing Internal Bleeding

Because internal bleeding is more difficult to recognize than external bleeding, you should always suspect internal bleeding in any serious injury. For example, if you find a motorcycle rider thrown from a bike, you may not see any serious external bleeding, but you should consider that the violent forces involved indicate the likelihood of internal injuries. Internal bleeding can occur from a fractured bone that ruptures an organ or blood vessels.

The body's inability to adjust to severe internal bleeding will eventually produce signs and symptoms that indicate shock. These signs and symptoms are less obvious and may take time to appear. They include:

• Discolouration of the skin (bruising) in the injured area

• Soft tissues that are tender, swollen, or firm

• Anxiety or restlessness

• Rapid, weak pulse

• Rapid breathing

• Skin that feels cool or moist or looks pale or bluish

• Nausea and vomiting

- Excessive thirst
- Declining level of consciousness
- Drop in blood pressure

Shock is discussed in detail in Chapter 10.

Controlling Internal Bleeding

How you control internal bleeding depends on the severity and site of the bleeding. For minor internal bleeding, such as a bruise on an arm, apply ice or a chemical cold pack to the injured area to help reduce pain and swelling. When applying ice, always remember to place something, such as a gauze pad or a towel, between the source of cold and the skin to prevent skin damage due to freezing.

If you suspect internal bleeding caused by serious injury, you must obtain more advanced medical care. There is little you can do to control bleeding effectively. The injured person must be transported rapidly to the hospital. The person will often need immediate surgery to correct the problem. While awaiting more advanced medical care, treat the person for shock and provide ongoing survey and care.

SUMMARY

One of the most important things you can do in any emergency is to recognize and control severe bleeding.

External bleeding is easily recognized and should be cared for immediately. Check and care for severe bleeding during the primary survey. Severe external bleeding is life-threatening. Although internal bleeding is less obvious, it also can be life-threatening. Recognize when a serious injury has occurred and suspect internal bleeding. You may not identify internal bleeding until you perform the secondary survey. When you identify or suspect severe bleeding, you must obtain advanced medical care.

Because of the nature of the injury, you suspect internal bleeding as well. What do you do?

Blood: A Timeline

The Ice Age

Primitive man draws a giant mammoth on a cave, with a marking resembling a heart in its chest.

3000 B.C.

Egyptians believe that blood is created in the stomach and that vessels running from the heart are filled with blood, air, feces, and tears.

500 B.C.

Ancient Greek physicians propound the theory of the humours, associating man's personality and health with four substances: blood, black bile, yellow bile, and phlegm. An imbalance can cause diseases or emotional problems. A curious practice called bloodletting develops in which physicians open a patient's vein and let him bleed to fix an imbalance in the humours.

Circa 200 A.D.

Galen, doctor of Roman Emperor Marcus Aurelius, theorizes that blood is continuously formed in the liver and then moves in two systems: one that combines with the air and a second that forms from food to nourish the body.

900 to 1400

Bloodletting flourishes, and astrology's influence grows, leading doctors to use astrological charts to determine when and where to open a vein.

1628

Dr. William Harvey cuts into live frogs and snakes to observe the heart. Through his studies, Harvey determines that blood circulates through the heart, the lungs, and the rest of the body.

1661

The invention of the microscope allows Italian-born physician Malpighi to see capillaries for the first time.

1665

The first blood transfusion mixes the blood of one dog with that of another. Transfusions range from successful to disastrous. One scientist proposes a transfusion between unhappily married people to try to reconcile the couple. After a man who receives sheep's blood dies, transfusion is outlawed in France.

Early 1900s

Dr. Karl Landsteiner discovers that all human blood is not compatible and names the blood types.

1953

Dr. John H. Gibbon invents a heart-lung machine to recirculate blood and provide oxygen during open-heart surgery, enabling more complex surgical techniques to develop.

1967

The first heart transplant is attempted by Dr. Christiaan Barnard in Cape Town, South Africa. A 54-year-old grocer receives the heart of a woman hit by a speeding car. The grocer survives 18 days.

1982

Dr. William DeVries implants the first artificial heart, called the Jarvik-7, in Barney Clark, which lasts 112 days and beats 12,912,499 times before Clark dies. In the 1980s, five artificial hearts are implanted. The longest survival period lasts 620 days.

2001–2003

483 heart transplants are performed in Canada.

2006

In May 2006, doctors at Papworth Hospital in Cambridgeshire, England, perform the U.K.'s first successful "beating heart" transplant (normally the heart's beating is stopped while the transplant is occurring). As of 2006, the heart of the world's longest living heart transplant patient is still beating and has been for 18 years. The 5-year survival rate for heart transplant patients is 71.2 percent for males and 66.9 percent for females.

The Future

Many millions of people throughout the world receive blood transfusions each year. Thousands of people are living with another person's heart inside their chest. The early medical experiments of yesterday have now become lifesaving procedures.

Shock

You are dispatched to a motor vehicle collision on a busy road. You arrive to see that one of the cars has been hit on the side near the driver. The passenger door is open and the passenger is out and walking around the car. As you survey the scene, the man says he is fine. He appears agitated and directs you to help his friend, the driver, who appears to be unconscious. What do you do?

INTRODUCTION

Both medical emergencies and injuries can cause life-threatening conditions, such as cardiac and respiratory arrest and severe bleeding. Medical emergencies and injuries also can become life-threatening as a result of shock. When the body experiences injury or sudden illness, it responds in a number of ways. Survival depends on the body's ability to adapt to the physical stresses of illness or injury. When the body's measures to adapt fail, the ill or injured person can progress into a life-threatening condition called shock. Shock complicates the effects of injury or sudden illness. In this chapter, you will learn to recognize the signs and symptoms of shock and to provide care to minimize it.

SHOCK

What Is Shock?

Shock is a condition in which the circulatory system fails to adequately circulate oxygen-rich blood to all cells of the body. When vital organs such as the heart, lungs, brain, and kidneys do not receive oxygen-rich blood, they fail to function properly. This triggers a series of responses that produces specific signs and symptoms known as shock. These responses are the body's attempt to maintain adequate blood flow to the vital organs, preventing their failure.

When the body is healthy, three conditions are necessary to maintain adequate blood flow:

1. The heart must be working well.

2. An adequate amount of blood must be circulating in the body.

3. The blood vessels must be intact and able to adjust blood flow.

Injury or sudden illness can interrupt normal body functions. In cases of minor injury or illness, this interruption is brief because the body is able to compensate quickly. With more severe injuries or illnesses, however, the body may be unable to adjust. When the body is unable to meet its demands for oxygen because the blood fails to circulate adequately, shock occurs.

How Shock Develops

There are different types of shock, as shown in Table 10-1. Although the responder does not have to be able to identify each of these different types of shock, it may

TABLE 10-1 TYPES OF SHOCK

Type	Cause
Anaphylactic	Life-threatening allergic reaction to a substance; can occur from insect stings or from foods or drugs
Cardiogenic	Failure of the heart to effectively pump blood to all parts of the body; occurs with heart attack or cardiac arrest
Hypovolemic	Severe bleeding
Neurogenic	Failure of nervous system to control size of blood vessels, causing them to dilate; occurs with brain or nerve injuries
Psychogenic	Factors such as emotional stress cause blood to pool in the body in areas away from the brain because of vessels dilating
Respiratory	Failure of the lungs to transfer sufficient oxygen into the bloodstream; occurs with breathing emergencies or respiratory arrest
Septic	Poisons caused by severe infections that cause blood vessels to dilate

be helpful to know that there are different ways in which people can develop shock. Each causes a decrease in the amount of blood that effectively circulates in the body. Regardless of the cause, when the body cells receive inadequate oxygen, it triggers shock.

You learned in Chapter 4 that the heart pumps blood by contracting and relaxing in a consistent, rhythmic pattern. The heart adjusts its speed and the force of its contractions to meet the body's changing demands for oxygen. For instance, when a person exercises, the heart beats faster and more forcefully because the working muscles demand more oxygen (Figure 10–1).

NOTE:

Hypovolemic shock is also commonly caused by dehydration and is the most common cause of shock in children.

Similarly, when someone suffers a severe injury or sudden illness that affects the flow of blood, the heart beats faster and stronger at first, to adjust to the increased demand for more oxygen.

Because the heart is beating faster, breathing must also speed up to meet the body's increased demands for oxygen. You can detect these changes by feeling the

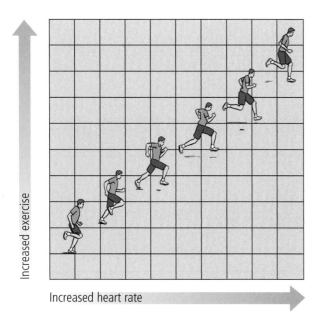

Figure 10–1 The heartbeat changes to meet the body's demand for oxygen.

pulse and listening to breathing when you check vital signs during the secondary survey.

For the heart to do its job properly, an adequate amount of blood must circulate within the body. The body can compensate for some decrease in blood volume. Consider what happens when you donate blood. You can lose 500 mL of blood over a 10- to 15-minute period without any real stress to the body. Fluid is reabsorbed from the kidneys, lungs, and intestines to replace lost fluid. The body immediately begins to manufacture the blood's solid components. With severe injuries involving greater or more rapid blood loss, the body may not be able to adjust adequately. Body cells do not receive enough oxygen, and shock occurs.

For the circulatory system to function properly, blood vessels must remain intact to maintain blood volume. Normally, blood vessels decrease or increase the flow of blood to different areas of the body by constricting (decreasing their diameter) or dilating (increasing their diameter). This ability ensures that blood reaches the areas of the body that need it most, such as the vital organs. Injuries or illnesses, especially those that affect the brain and spinal cord, can cause blood vessels to lose this ability to change size, causing a drop in blood volume (Figure 10–2). Blood vessels can also be affected if the nervous system is damaged by infections, drugs, or poisons.

Regardless of the cause, a significant decrease in blood volume affects the function of the heart. The heart will eventually fail to beat rhythmically. The pulse will become irregular or be absent altogether. With some irregular heart rhythms, blood does not circulate at all.

When shock occurs, the body attempts to prioritize its needs for blood by ensuring adequate flow to the vital organs. The body does this by reducing the amount of blood circulating to the less important tissues of the arms, legs, and skin. This is why the skin of a person in shock appears pale and feels cool. When checking capillary refill, you may find it to be slow. In later stages of shock, the skin, especially on the lips and around the eyes, may appear blue from a prolonged lack of oxygen. Increased sweating is also a natural reaction to stress caused by injury or illness, which makes the skin feel moist.

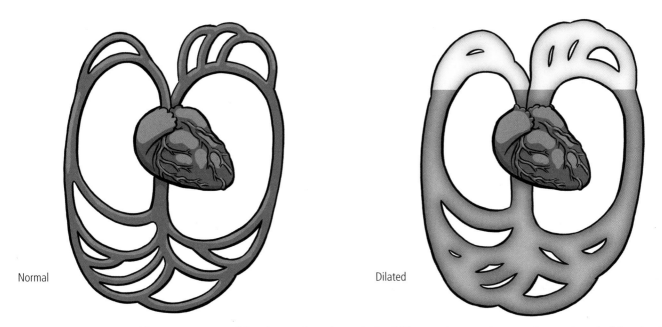

Normal   Dilated

Figure 10–2 Injury or illness can cause blood vessels to lose their ability to change size, causing a drop in blood volume.

Signs and Symptoms of Shock

Although you may not always be able to determine the cause, remember that shock is a life-threatening condition. You should learn to recognize its signs and symptoms (Figure 10–3).

People in shock usually show many of the same signs and symptoms. A common one is restlessness or irritability. This is often the first indicator that the body is experiencing a significant problem. More clearly recognizable signs are pale, cool, moist skin; rapid breathing; a rapid and weak pulse; and changes in the level of consciousness. Often a recognizable symptom is nausea. Conditions that affect blood volume or cause the blood vessels to work improperly can cause significant changes in blood pressure.

Figure 10–3 The signs and symptoms of shock may not be obvious immediately.

Shock: The Domino Effect

- An injury causes severe bleeding.

- The heart attempts to compensate for the disruption of blood flow by beating faster, which causes a rapid pulse in the injured person. This causes more blood to be lost, and as blood volume drops, the pulse becomes weak or hard to find.

- The increased workload on the heart results in an increased oxygen demand. Therefore, breathing becomes faster.

- To maintain circulation of blood to the vital organs, blood vessels in the arms and legs and in the skin constrict. Therefore, the skin appears pale and feels cool. In response to the stress, the body perspires heavily and the skin feels moist.

- Since tissues of the arms and legs are now without oxygen, cells start to die. The brain now sends a signal to return blood to the arms and legs in an attempt to balance blood flow between these body parts and the vital organs.

- Vital organs are now without adequate oxygen. The heart tries to compensate by beating even faster. More blood is lost, and the person's condition worsens.

- Without oxygen, the vital organs fail to function properly. As the brain is affected, the person becomes restless and drowsy and eventually loses consciousness. As the heart is affected, it beats irregularly, resulting in an irregular pulse. The rhythm then becomes chaotic, and the heart fails to pump blood. There is no longer a pulse. When the heart stops, breathing stops.

- The body's continuous attempt to compensate for severe blood loss eventually results in death.

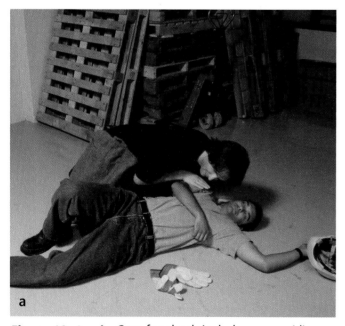 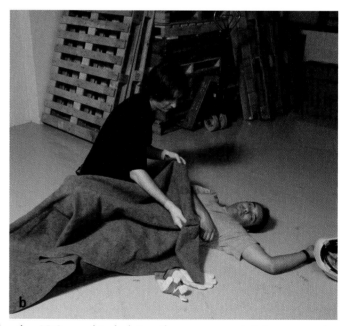

Figure 10–4, a-b Care for shock includes: **a**, providing care for the ABCs; and **b**, helping the person maintain a normal body temperature.

If the person does not show the telltale signs and symptoms of specific injury or illness, such as the persistent chest pain of heart attack or obvious external bleeding, it can be difficult to know what is wrong. Remember, you do not have to identify the specific nature of illness or injury to provide care that may help save the person's life. If the signs and symptoms of shock are present, assume that there is a potentially life-threatening injury or illness.

Care for Shock

After your scene survey, do a primary survey by checking the ABCs. Caring for life-threatening conditions, such as severe bleeding, will minimize the effects of shock. If you do not find any life-threatening conditions, perform a secondary survey. During the secondary survey, the signs and symptoms of shock will most likely become evident. Always follow the general care steps you learned in Chapter 5 for any emergency:

- Assess the ABCs and provide care for any airway, breathing, or circulation problem you find (Figure 10–4, a).
- Provide care for specific conditions.
- Help the person rest comfortably. This is important because pain can intensify the body's stress and accelerate the progression of shock. Helping the person rest in a more comfortable position may minimize the pain. Often having the person lay down will increase blood flow to the vital organs, especially the brain.
- Help the person maintain normal body temperature (Figure 10–4, b).
- Provide ongoing survey and care.

The general care you provide in any emergency will always help the person's body adjust to the stresses imposed by any injury or illness, thus reducing the effects of shock.

You can further help the person manage the effects of shock if you:

- Control any external bleeding as soon as possible to minimize blood loss.

- Administer oxygen if the equipment is available.
- Avoid giving the person anything to eat or drink, even though she is likely to be thirsty. The person's condition may be severe enough to require surgery, in which case, it is better for her to have an empty stomach.
- Obtain more advanced medical care. Shock cannot be managed effectively by emergency care alone.

SUMMARY

Do not wait for shock to develop before providing care to a person with an injury or sudden illness. Always provide prompt care to minimize the effects of shock. Care for life-threatening conditions, such as breathing problems or severe external bleeding, before caring for lesser injuries. Remember that the key to managing shock effectively begins with recognizing a situation in which shock may develop and giving appropriate care.

Remember that shock is a factor in serious injuries and illnesses, particularly if there is blood loss or if the normal function of the heart is interrupted. You cannot always prevent shock by administering emergency care, but you can usually slow its progress. Advanced medical care must be obtained immediately if there are signs and symptoms of shock.

While you are assisting the driver, the passenger passes out. What do you do?

Part 3

Injuries

 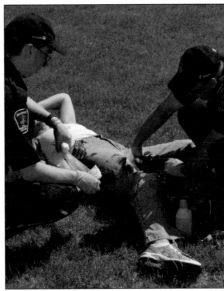 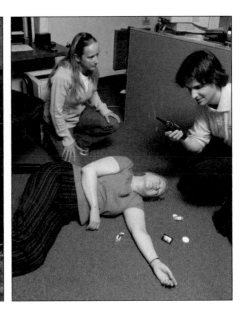

11 Soft Tissue Injuries

12 Musculoskeletal Injuries

13 Head and Spine Injuries

14 Chest, Abdominal, and Pelvic Injuries

INTRODUCTION

Several pairs of figure-skating partners are on the ice, practising for the championships. Pairs perform all types of spins, step sequences, and jumps. One of the men performs a throw jump, in which he throws his partner into a jump, and she bumps into another skater, slashing his leg with her blade. The injured skater cries out and falls to the ice, gripping his leg, which is bleeding badly. All the skaters skate to his side, horrified, and look around for help.

You go out onto the ice to help him. As you do, thoughts and questions rush through your mind: "Will I be able to control the bleeding? I'll need to obtain advanced medical care. Who can help? How will I make sure bystanders don't slow my care? I must act quickly to avoid complications."

Injury is a leading cause of death and disability in people aged 1 to 44 years. It greatly surpasses all major disease groups (cancer, heart disease, stroke) as a cause of death and disability in this age group. Injury is the leading reason for people to contact physicians and the most common cause of hospitalization among people under 45 years old. Statistics indicate that most people will have a significant injury at some time in their life. Some, because of their chosen professions, are more likely to be injured than others.

INJURIES

How Injuries Occur

The body has a natural resistance to injury. However, when certain external forms of energy produce forces that the body cannot tolerate, injuries occur. Mechanical forms of energy and the energy from heat, electricity, chemicals, and radiation can damage body tissues and disrupt normal body function. Superficial injuries include minor wounds or burns. Deep injuries include wounds caused by penetrating objects.

Some tissues, such as the soft tissues of the skin, have less resistance and are at greater risk of injury if exposed to trauma than the deeper, stronger tissues of muscle and bone. Some organs, such as the brain, heart, and lungs, are better protected by bones than other organs, such as those in the abdominal cavity. Understanding the forces that cause injury and the kinds of injury that each force can cause will help you recognize certain injuries someone may have.

Mechanical Energy

Mechanical energy produces the following forces: direct, indirect, twisting, and contracting. A direct force is the force of an object striking the body and causing injury at the point of impact. Direct forces can be either blunt or penetrating. For example, a fist striking the chin can break the jaw, or penetrating objects, such as bullets and knives, can injure structures beneath the skin at the point where they penetrate. Direct force can cause internal and external bleeding, head and spinal injuries, fractures, and other problems, such as crushing injuries.

An indirect force is the force of a blunt object striking the body in one body part and causing injury to another. For example, a fall on an outstretched hand may result in an injury to the arm, shoulder, or collarbone.

In twisting, one part of the body remains stationary while another part of the body turns. A sudden or severe twisting action can force body parts beyond their normal range of motion, causing injury to bones, tendons, ligaments, and muscles. For example, if a ski and its binding keep the lower leg in one position while the body falls in another, the knee may be forced beyond its normal range of motion. Twisting injuries are not always this complex. They more often occur as a result of simple actions such as stepping off a curb or turning to reach for an out-of-the-way object.

Sudden or powerful muscle contractions often result in injuries to muscles and tendons. These commonly occur in sports activities, such as throwing a ball far or hard without properly warming up or preparing your muscles. Although it happens rarely, sudden, powerful muscle contractions can even pull a piece of bone away from the point at which it is normally attached. Figure P3–1 shows how these forces can result in injuries. These four forces, products of mechanical energy, cause the majority of injuries. Soft tissue injuries and injuries to muscle and bone (musculoskeletal injuries) are most often the result.

Direct

Indirect

Twisting

Contracting

Figure P3–1 Four forces—direct, indirect, twisting, and contracting—cause the majority of all injuries.

Energy from Heat, Electricity, Chemicals, and Radiation

Together, the energy from heat, electricity, chemicals, and radiation accounts for a significant proportion of all injuries in Canada. Exposure to any of these can result in burns. Thermal burns, burns caused by heat, are the most common. Sources of electricity, such as common household current or lightning, can penetrate the body, causing external and internal damage. Electrical current can also affect the part of the brain that controls breathing and heartbeat. When certain chemicals contact the skin, they cause burns. Solar radiation from the sun's rays causes sunburn. The average person is rarely exposed to other forms of radiation.

Factors Affecting Injury

A number of factors affect the likelihood of injury—among them age, gender, geographic location, economic status, and alcohol use and abuse. The type and frequency of injuries can also be affected by fads and seasonal activities. As certain activities gain and lose popularity or as activities such as softball or skiing change with the seasons, the injury statistics reflect these changes.

Injury statistics consistently show that:

- Injury rates are higher among people under age 45.
- Males are at greater risk than females for most types of injury.
- Motor vehicle crashes are the leading cause of deaths in Canada.

Many factors influence injury statistics. Whether people live in a rural or an urban area, whether a home is built of wood or brick, the type of heat used in the home, and the climate all affect the degree of risk. Death rates from injury are typically higher in rural areas. The death rate from injuries is higher in low-income areas than in high-income areas.

The use and abuse of alcohol is a significant factor in many injuries and fatalities, even in young teenagers. The deaths of almost half of all fatally injured drivers involve alcohol, as do those of many adult passengers and pedestrians. Alcohol use also contributes to other injuries. It is estimated that a significant number of people who die as a result of falls, motor vehicle collisions, drownings, fires, assaults, and suicides have high blood alcohol concentrations.

Table P3-1 shows the leading causes of death from injuries.

TABLE P3-1 LEADING CAUSES OF DEATH FROM INJURIES IN CANADA (2003–2004)

Cause	Percentage
Motor vehicle collisions	38.6
Falls	34.8
Assault and purposely inflicted injury	8.2
Suicide and self-inflicted injury	5.6
Miscellaneous	4.8
Fire and flames	3.1
Motor vehicles (non-traffic)	2.1
Other road vehicles	1.1
Drowning	0.7
Natural and environmental factors	0.6
Air and water transport	0.2
Choking/suffocation	0.1
Railway	0.1

Note: Poisoning is not included in these data.

Injury Prevention

Many people believe that injuries just happen—their targets are unfortunate results of circumstance. However, overwhelming evidence shows that injury, like disease, does not occur at random. Rather, many injuries are predictable, preventable events resulting from the interaction of people and hazards, whether at home, at work, or during recreation.

Preventing injuries is everyone's responsibility. As a responder, injury prevention may be part of your job.

As an athletic therapist, you are responsible for preventing athletic injuries. As an emergency team member, you may be responsible for ensuring that safety codes and regulations are met. As a lifeguard, you are responsible for preventing drowning and other injuries. A fire fighter or police officer who supervises or instructs others may be responsible for their safety. In any event, responders should take all precautions to ensure their personal safety and to be role models of safe behaviour.

There are three general strategies for preventing injuries:

- Persuade people to alter risky behaviour.

- Require behaviour change by law and regulation.

- Provide automatic protection through product and environmental design.

Laws and regulations that require you to conform to safety measures, such as wearing safety belts when driving and wearing protective clothing when on the job, are only moderately effective. The most successful injury prevention strategy is the built-in protection of product design. For instance, automatic protection, such as airbags in motor vehicles, does not require people to make choices.

Typically, people who engage in risky behaviours are the hardest to influence, regardless of whether safer behaviours are required. For example, despite the overwhelming evidence of alcohol-related injuries and fatalities, people still drink when driving and when operating equipment.

Many people view laws or regulations that require certain behaviours as an infringement of their rights— even though these laws and regulations are intended to protect them from injury. Product designs are equally difficult to influence because of manufacturers' reluctance to bear the costs of design changes.

It has been estimated that if everyone worked to prevent injuries, about half of all injuries would not occur. Everyone has a personal responsibility to promote safety, both in their own life and in the lives of others. Taking the following steps could significantly reduce the risk of injury:

1. Know your injury risk.

2. Take measures that can make a difference. Adopt behaviours that decrease your risk of injury and the risk of others, both on and off the job.

3. Think safety. Be alert for and avoid potentially harmful conditions or activities that increase your injury risk or that of co-workers. Take precautions, such as wearing appropriate protective clothing— helmets, outer garments, and effective barriers—to prevent disease transmission and buckle up when driving or riding in motor vehicles.

4. Encourage others to take a Red Cross first aid course. This can decrease their risk of injury significantly.

Chapter *11*

Soft Tissue Injuries

You are dispatched to the scene of a building on fire. Four people are being assisted out of the burning structure. One woman has burns on her arms and chest. One man has soot on his face, mouth, and nostrils and appears to be having problems breathing, while the other woman is coughing and holding her chest. The baby does not appear to be burned anywhere. What do you do?

INTRODUCTION

A baby falls off a couch and gets jabbed in the abdomen on the sharp corner of a glass table; a toddler grabs a knife off the counter and cuts her finger; a child gets a black eye when he's banged in the head by a swing; an adolescent gets stabbed in the chest during a gang fight; and an adult cuts her hand while working in a tool and die shop. What do these injuries have in common? They are all soft tissue injuries.

In the course of growing up and in our daily lives, soft tissue injuries occur often and in many different ways. Fortunately, most soft tissue injuries are minor, requiring little attention. Often only an adhesive bandage or ice and rest are needed. Some injuries, however, are more severe and require immediate medical attention. In this chapter, you will learn how to recognize and care for the most common type of injuries: soft tissue injuries.

SOFT TISSUES

The soft tissues include the layers of skin, fat, and muscles that protect the underlying body structures (Figure 11–1). The skin is the largest single organ, and without it, the human body could not function. It provides a protective barrier for the body, helps regulate the body's temperature, and absorbs information about the environment through nerves in the skin.

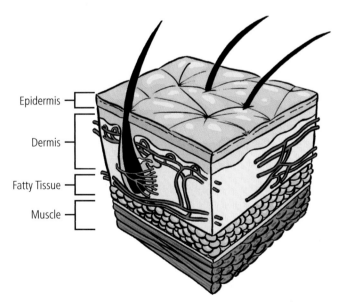

Figure 11–1 The soft tissue includes the layers of skin, fat, and muscle.

Epidermis

Dermis

Fatty Tissue

Muscle

The skin has two layers. The outer layer of skin, the epidermis, provides a barrier to bacteria and other organisms that can cause infection. The deeper layer, called the dermis, contains the important structures of the nerves, sweat and oil glands, and blood vessels. Because the skin is well supplied with blood vessels and nerves, most soft tissue injuries are likely to bleed and be painful.

Beneath the skin layers lies a layer of fat. This layer helps insulate the body to help maintain body temperature. The fat layer also stores energy. The amount of fat varies in different parts of the body and in different people.

The muscles lie beneath the fat layer and comprise the largest segment of the body's soft tissues. Most soft tissue injuries involve the outer layers of tissue. However, deep burns or violent forces that cause objects to penetrate the skin can injure all the soft tissue layers. Although the muscles are considered soft tissues, muscle injuries are discussed more thoroughly in the next chapter, with other musculoskeletal injuries.

Types of Soft Tissue Injuries

An injury to the soft tissues is called a wound. Soft tissue injuries are typically classified as either closed or open wounds. A wound is closed when the soft tissue damage occurs beneath the surface of the skin, leaving the outer layer intact. A wound is open if there is a break in the skin's outer layer. Open wounds usually result in external bleeding.

Burns are a special kind of soft tissue injury. A burn occurs when intense heat, caustic chemicals, electricity, or radiation contacts the skin or other body tissues. Burns are classified as either superficial, partial-thickness, or full-thickness. Superficial burns affect only the outer layer of skin. Partial-thickness burns damage both skin layers. Full-thickness burns penetrate the layers of skin and can affect other soft tissues and even bone. Burns are discussed in more detail later in this chapter.

Closed Wounds

The simplest closed wound is a bruise, also called a contusion (Figure 11–2, a-b). Contusions result when the body is subjected to a blunt force, such as when you

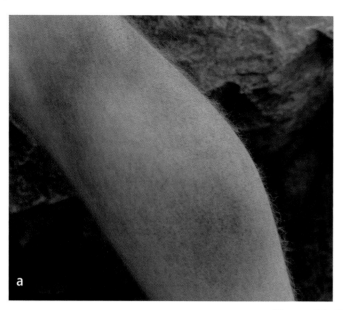

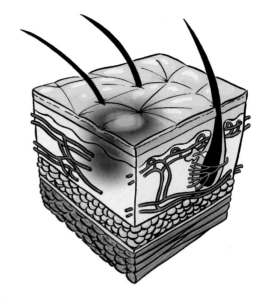

Figure 11–2, a-b A bruise.

bump your leg on a table or chair. This usually results in damage to soft tissue layers and blood vessels beneath the skin, causing internal bleeding. When blood and other fluids seep into the surrounding tissues, the area discolours and swells. The amount of discolouration and swelling varies depending on the severity of the injury. At first, the area may only appear red. Over time, more blood may leak into the area, making it appear dark red or purple. Violent forces can cause more severe soft tissue injuries involving larger blood vessels, the deeper layers of muscle tissue, and even organs deep within the body. These injuries can result in profuse internal bleeding. With deeper injuries, a responder may or may not immediately see bruising.

Crush Injury

A crush injury can occur when a crushing force is applied to any part of the body. These injuries can be severe and cause internal bleeding, fractures, and organ damage with the skin still intact. This type of injury may occur from force that has been applied over a short or relatively long period of time. The latter is seen most often when the injured person has been trapped with his limbs compressed for a long period of time. When the crushing object has been removed from a person, toxins that may have built up in the crushed area can be released into the bloodstream, causing further damage.

Unless the object is hindering the ABCs or you are trained to remove it, leave the object in place. Allow more advanced medical personnel to remove the object or extricate the person.

Compartment Syndrome

When pressure builds up to dangerous levels within the muscles, this is called compartment syndrome. The pressure blocks circulation to the cells. This can affect muscle groups in the arms, hands, legs, feet, and buttocks because they are covered by tough membranes that do not readily expand. Within the muscle compartment, swelling and/or bleeding creates pressure on capillaries and nerves. The capillaries collapse when the pressure in the compartment becomes greater than the blood pressure within the capillaries, disrupting blood flow to muscle and nerve cells. Without a steady supply of oxygen and nutrients, nerve and muscle cells begin to die within hours. Unless the pressure is relieved quickly, this syndrome can cause permanent disability or death.

Compartment syndrome can be caused by a traumatic injury, such as a fracture of one of the long bones in the body, or other conditions, such as a badly bruised muscle, complication after surgery, blockage of circulation, a crush injury, or anabolic steroid use.

Signs and Symptoms

The classic sign of compartment syndrome is pain, especially when the muscle is stretched. Other signs and symptoms may be present:

- The pain may be intensely out of proportion to the injury, especially if no bone is broken.

- There may also be a tingling or burning sensation in the muscle.

- The muscle may feel tight or full.

- If the area becomes numb or paralysis sets in, this means that cell death has begun; in this case, efforts to lower the pressure in the compartment may not be successful in restoring function to the muscle.

Acute compartment syndrome is a medical emergency requiring immediate treatment. Obtain more advanced medical care.

Blast Injuries

Blast injuries occur when pressure waves generated by an explosion strike the body surfaces. Blast injuries can occur from bombing, underwater blasts, natural gas explosions, or explosions in a mine, shipyard, or chemical plant. Blasts release large amounts of energy in the form of pressure and heat. Injuries due to the blast are almost exclusively confined to the ear, the respiratory system, and the gastrointestinal tract. As a result, injuries can include loss of hearing, pulmonary hemorrhage, pulmonary edema, pneumothorax, pulmonary embolism, abdominal hemorrhage, and bowel perforation. Thermal burns may also occur from the release of energy in the form of heat. Blast injuries may be difficult to identify because sometimes there are no visible external injuries, whereas internal injuries may be severe.

There are three mechanisms of injury resulting from blasts:

1. Injuries from the blast itself
2. Injuries from flying debris (shrapnel) from the blast
3. Trauma from being thrown by the blast

Myocardial Contusion

The heart muscle may be bruised after blunt force to the chest (motor vehicle collision, CPR, a fall, etc.). The person may have some pain in the chest (from the blunt force) and may feel the heart racing. More advanced medical care should be obtained as the person may require monitoring over a period of time.

Open Wounds

Open wounds are injuries that break the skin. These breaks can be as minor as a scrape of the surface layers or as severe as a deep penetration. The amount of bleeding depends on the severity of the injury. Any

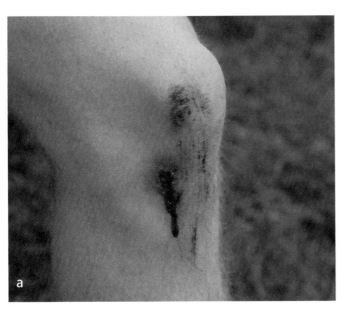

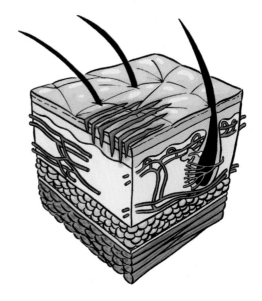

Figure 11–3, a-b An abrasion.

break in the skin provides an entry point for disease-producing microorganisms. There are four main types of open wounds:

- Abrasions
- Lacerations
- Avulsions
- Punctures

An abrasion is the most common type of open wound. It is characterized by skin that has been rubbed or scraped away (Figure 11–3, a-b). This often occurs when a person falls and scrapes his hands or knees. An abrasion is sometimes called a rug burn, or road rash. Because the scraping of the outer skin layers exposes sensitive nerve endings, an abrasion is usually painful. Bleeding is easily controlled and not severe since only the capillaries are affected. Because of the way the injury occurs, dirt and other matter can easily become embedded in the skin, making it especially important to clean the wound.

A laceration is a cut, usually from a sharp object. The cut may have either jagged or smooth edges (Figure 11–4, a-b). Lacerations are commonly caused by sharp-edged objects, such as knives, scissors, or broken glass. A laceration can also result when a blunt force splits the skin. This often occurs in areas where bone lies directly under the skin's surface, such as the eyebrow. Deep lacerations can also affect the layers of fat and muscle, damaging both nerves and blood vessels. Lacerations usually bleed freely and, depending on the structures involved, can bleed profusely. Because the nerves may also be injured, lacerations are not always immediately painful.

An avulsion is an injury in which a portion of the skin and sometimes other soft tissue is partially or completely torn away (Figure 11–5, a-b). A partially avulsed piece of skin may remain attached but hangs like a flap. Bleeding is usually significant because avulsions often involve deeper soft tissue layers. Sometimes a force is so violent that a body part, such as a finger, may be severed.

A complete severing of a part is called an amputation (Figure 11–6). Although damage to the tissue is severe, bleeding is usually not as bad as you might expect. The blood vessels usually constrict and pull in (retract) at the point of injury, slowing bleeding and making it relatively easy to control with direct pressure. With today's technology, reattachment is often successful, making it important to send the severed part to the hospital with the injured person.

A puncture wound results when the skin is pierced with a pointed object such as a nail, a piece of glass, a splinter, or a knife (Figure 11–7, a-b). A bullet wound is also a puncture wound. Because the skin usually closes around the penetrating object, external bleeding is

a

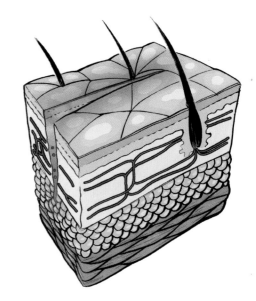

b

Figure 11–4, a-b A laceration.

Figure 11–5, a-b An avulsion.

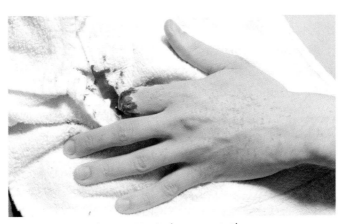

Figure 11–6 An amputation.

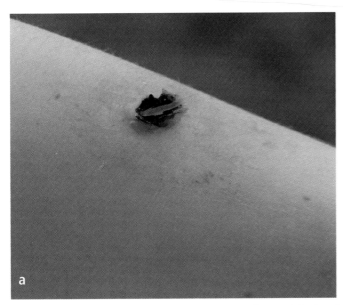
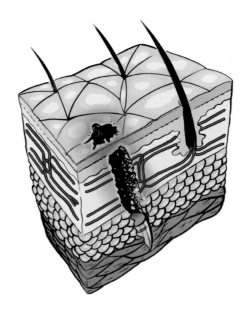

Figure 11–7, a-b A puncture wound.

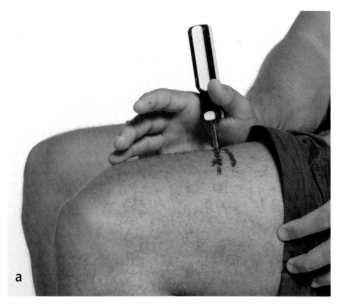

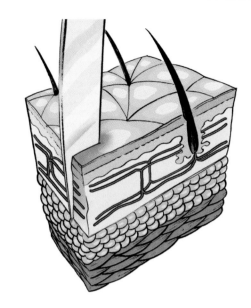

Figure 11–8, a-b An impaled object.

generally not severe. However, internal bleeding can be severe if the penetrating object damages major blood vessels or internal organs. An object that remains in the open wound is called an impaled object (Figure 11–8, a-b). An object may also pass completely through a body part, making two open wounds: one at the entry point and one at the exit point.

Although puncture wounds generally do not bleed profusely, they are potentially more dangerous than wounds that do because they are more likely to become infected. Objects penetrating the soft tissues carry microorganisms that cause infections. Of particular danger is the microorganism that causes tetanus, a severe infection.

Infection

Injuries causing breaks in the skin carry great risk of infection. Since the skin tends to collect microorganisms, injuries involving breaks in the skin can become infected unless properly cared for.

The best initial defence against infection is to cleanse the area thoroughly. For minor wounds—those that

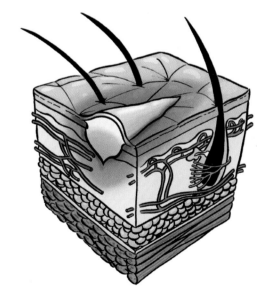

Figure 11–9, a-b An infected wound.

are small and do not bleed severely—wash the area with soap and water. Most soaps are effective in removing harmful bacteria. Do not use alcohol because it can damage tissues. Once washed, rinse the wound under running water for five minutes (if possible); then apply an antibiotic cream or ointment (as long as the injured person has no allergy or sensitivities to antibiotics). Wounds that require medical attention because of more extensive tissue damage or bleeding need not be washed immediately. These wounds will be cleaned thoroughly in the medical facility as a routine part of the care. It is more important for you to control bleeding. Some soft tissue injuries warrant having a tetanus shot, such as if the person was injured with a rusty piece of metal. In these cases, the person should seek more advanced care.

Signs of Infection

Sometimes even the best care for a soft tissue injury is not enough to prevent infection. When a wound becomes infected, the area around the wound becomes swollen and red. The area may feel warm or throb with pain. Some wounds have a pus discharge (Figure 11–9, a-b). Red streaks may develop that progress from the wound toward the heart. More serious infections may cause the injured person to develop a fever and feel ill. Infections require a physician's care.

Tetanus

- A serious infection can cause severe medical problems. One such infection is tetanus, caused by the organism *Clostridium tetani*. This organism, commonly found in soil and the feces of cows and horses, can infect many kinds of wounds. Worldwide, tetanus kills thousands of people annually.

- Tetanus is introduced into the body through a puncture wound, abrasion, laceration, or burn. Because the organism multiplies in an environment that is low in oxygen, puncture wounds and other deep wounds are at particular risk for tetanus infection. It produces a powerful toxin, one of the most lethal poisons known, that affects the central nervous system and specific muscles. People at risk for tetanus include drug addicts, people with burns, and people recovering from surgery. Newborn babies can be infected through the stump of the umbilical cord.

- Signs and symptoms of tetanus include difficulty swallowing, irritability, headache, fever, and muscle spasms near the infected area. Later, as the infection progresses, it can affect other muscles, such as those in the jaw, causing the condition called "lockjaw." Once tetanus gets into the nervous system, its effects are irreversible.

- The best way to prevent tetanus is to be immunized against it and then receive periodic booster shots.

Immunizations assist the natural function of the immune system by building up antibodies, disease-fighting proteins that help protect the body against specific bacteria. Because the effects of immunization do not last a lifetime, booster shots help maintain the antibodies that protect against tetanus. Booster shots are recommended every 5 to 10 years, whenever a wound has been contaminated by dirt, or whenever an object, such as a rusty nail, causes a puncture wound. Most children in Canada receive an immunization known as DPT, which includes the tetanus toxoid. Always contact your physician if you are unsure how long it has been since you received a tetanus immunization or booster.

- If an injury occurs, the best defence against tetanus is to thoroughly clean an open wound. Major wounds should be cleaned and treated at a medical facility. Clean a minor wound with soap and water and apply a clean or sterile dressing. If signs of wound infection develop, seek medical attention immediately. Infected wounds of the face, neck, and head should receive immediate medical care since the tetanus toxin can travel rapidly to the brain. A physician will determine whether a tetanus shot or a booster shot is needed, depending on the person's immunization status.

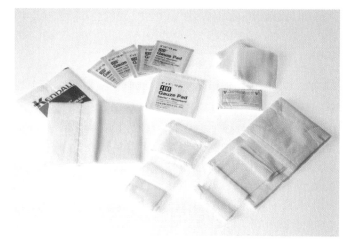

Figure 11–10 Dressings come in various sizes.

Dressings and Bandages

All open wounds need some type of covering to help control bleeding and prevent infection. These coverings are commonly referred to as dressings and bandages. There are many different types of both.

Dressings

Dressings are pads placed directly on the wound to absorb blood and other fluids and to prevent infection. To minimize the chance of infection, dressings should be sterile. Most dressings are porous, allowing air to circulate to the wound to promote healing. Standard dressings include varying sizes of cotton gauze, commonly ranging from 5 to 10 cm (2 to 4 in) square. Much larger dressings called universal dressings are used to cover very large wounds and multiple wounds in one body area (Figure 11–10). Some dressings have non-stick surfaces to prevent the dressing from sticking to the wound.

A special type of dressing, called an occlusive dressing, does not allow air to pass through. Aluminum foil, plastic wrap, and petroleum jelly–soaked gauze are examples of this type of dressing. These dressings are used for certain chest and abdominal injuries that are discussed in Chapter 14.

Bandages

A bandage is any material used to wrap or cover any part of the body. Bandages are used to hold dressings in place, to apply pressure to control bleeding, to help protect a wound from dirt and infection, and to provide support to an injured limb or body part. Many different

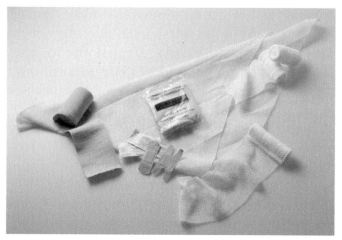

Figure 11–11 Different types of bandages are used to hold dressings in place, apply pressure to control bleeding, help protect a wound from dirt and infection, and provide support to an injured body part.

types of bandages are available commercially (Figure 11–11). A bandage applied snugly to create pressure on a wound or injury is called a pressure bandage.

A common type of bandage is a commercially made adhesive compress. Available in assorted sizes, it consists of a small pad of non-stick gauze (the dressing) on a strip of adhesive tape (the bandage) that is applied directly to small injuries. Also available is the bandage compress, a thick gauze dressing attached to a gauze bandage. This bandage can be tied in place. Because it is specially designed to help control severe bleeding, the bandage compress usually comes in a sterile package.

A roller bandage is usually made of gauze or gauze-like material. Some gauze bandages are made of a self-adhering material that easily conforms to different body parts. Roller bandages are available in assorted

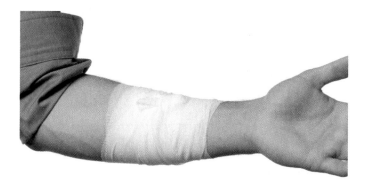

Figure 11–12 Roller bandages are wrapped around a body part, over a dressing, using overlapping turns until the dressing is completely covered.

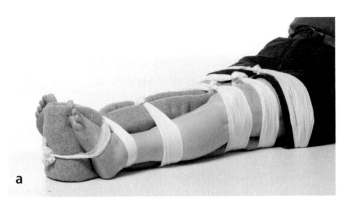

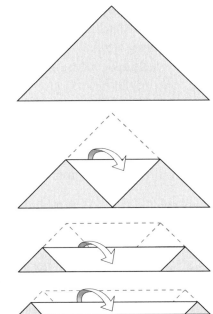

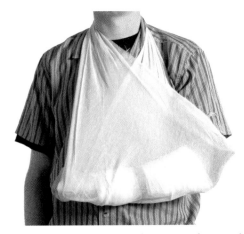

Figure 11–14 Triangular bandages can be used to support an injured shoulder, arm, or hand.

Figure 11–13, a-b **a**, triangular bandages can be used to hold a splint in place; **b**, folding a triangular bandage.

widths from 1 to 30 cm (1/2 to 12 in) and lengths from 5 to 10 metres. A roller bandage is generally wrapped around the body part, over a dressing, using overlapping turns until the dressing is completely covered (Figure 11–12). It can be tied or taped in place. A folded strip of roller bandage may also be used as a dressing or compress. In the next chapters, you will learn to use roller bandages to hold splints in place.

Another commonly used bandage is the triangular bandage. Folded, it can hold a dressing or splint in place on most parts of the body (Figure 11–13, a-b). Used as a sling, the triangular bandage can support an injured shoulder, arm, or hand (Figure 11–14).

Applying a Bandage

To apply a roller bandage, follow these general guidelines:

- Secure the end of the bandage in place (Figure 11–15, a). Wrap the bandage around the body part until the dressing is completely covered and the bandage extends several centimetres beyond the dressing (Figure 11–15, b). Tie or tape the bandage in place (Figure 11–15, c).

- Do not cover the fingers or toes, if possible. By keeping these parts uncovered, you will be able to tell if the bandage is too tight (Figure 11–15, d). If the fingers or toes become cold or begin to turn pale or blue, the bandage is too tight and should be loosened slightly.

- If blood soaks through the bandage, apply additional dressings and another bandage. Leave the blood-soaked ones in place.

Care for Wounds

Closed Wounds

Most closed wounds do not require special medical care. Cold can be effective in helping control both pain and swelling. When applying ice or a chemical cold pack, place a gauze pad, towel, or other cloth between the ice and the skin to protect the skin (Figure 11–16). Apply the cold for 20 minutes every hour until pain is relieved.

Do not dismiss a closed wound as "just a bruise." Be aware of possible serious injuries to internal organs or other underlying structures, such as the muscles or bones. Take the time to evaluate how the injury happened and whether more serious injuries could be present. If a person complains of severe pain or cannot

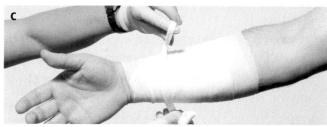

Figure 11–15, a-d When applying a bandage: **a**, secure the end of the bandage in place; **b**, wrap the bandage around the body part until the dressing is completely covered; **c**, tie or tape the bandage in place; and **d**, ensure the bandage is not too tight by checking distal circulation.

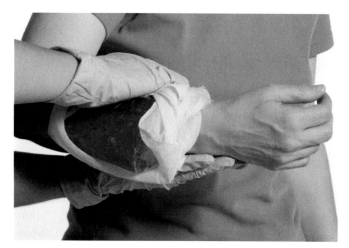

Figure 11–16 Ice can reduce pain and swelling. Ensure it is not placed directly on the skin.

move a body part without pain, or if you think the force that caused the injury was great enough to cause serious damage, obtain more advanced medical care immediately. Care for these injuries is described in later chapters.

Major Open Wounds

A major open wound is one with severe bleeding, deep destruction of tissue, or a deeply impaled object. To care for a major open wound, follow these general guidelines:

- Quickly control bleeding using direct pressure. Apply direct pressure by placing a sterile dressing over the wound with your gloved hand. If nothing sterile is available, use any clean covering, such as a towel or a handkerchief. If you do not have a glove and a cloth is not available, have the injured person use his hand.

- Continue direct pressure by applying a pressure bandage.

- Obtain more advanced medical care.

- Wash your hands immediately after completing care, even though you wore gloves.

If the person has an injury in which a body part has been amputated, try to retrieve the severed body part. Wrap the part in sterile gauze, if any is available, or in any clean material, such as a washcloth. Place the wrapped part in a plastic bag. If possible, keep the part cool by placing the bag on ice (Figure 11–17). Be careful to keep the ice from directly contacting the amputated part so that it does not freeze. Make sure the part is transported to the medical facility with the injured person.

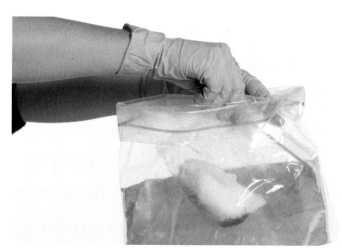

Figure 11–17 Wrap a severed body part in a sterile gauze, put it in a plastic bag, and put the bag on ice.

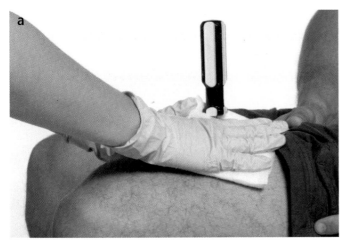
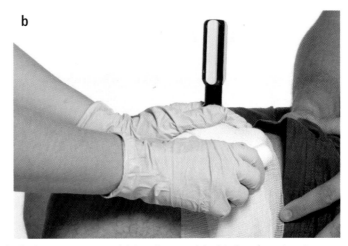

Figure 11–18, a-b **a**, use bulky dressings to support an impaled object; **b**, control bleeding and hold the dressing in place by applying a bandage.

If the person has an impaled object in the wound:

- Leave the object in place unless it involves the cheek or interferes with breathing.
- Use bulky dressings to stabilize the object (Figure 11–18, a). Any movement of the object can result in further tissue damage.
- Control bleeding by bandaging the dressings in place around the object (Figure 11–18, b).

Stitches

It can be difficult to judge when a wound should be seen by a doctor for stitches. A quick rule of thumb is that stitches are needed when the edges of skin do not fall together or when the wound is more than 2.5 cm (1 in) long. Stitches speed the healing process, lessen the chances of infection, and improve the look of scars. The wound should be stitched within the first few hours after the injury. The following major injuries may require stitches:

- Bleeding from an artery or uncontrollable bleeding
- Deep cut or avulsion that shows the muscle or bone, involves joints near the hands or feet, gapes widely, or involves the thumb or the palm of the hand
- Large or deep puncture
- Large or deeply embedded object
- Human or animal bite

- Wound that, if left unattended, could leave a conspicuous scar, such as one that involves the lip or eyebrow

If you are caring for a wound and think it may need stitches, it probably does.

Minor Open Wounds

A minor wound, such as an abrasion, is one in which damage is only superficial and bleeding is minimal. To care for a minor wound, follow these general guidelines:

- Cleanse the wound with soap and water.
- Rinse the wound with running water for five minutes (if possible).
- Apply an antibiotic cream or ointment to the wound (as long as the person has no allergy or sensitivity to antibiotics).
- Place a sterile dressing over the wound.
- Hold the dressing in place with a bandage or tape.

Burns

Burns are another type of soft tissue injury, caused primarily by heat. Burns can also occur when the body is exposed to caustic chemicals, electricity, or solar or other forms of radiation.

When burns occur, they first affect the top layer of skin. If the burn progresses, the dermis can also be affected. Deep burns can damage underlying tissues. Burns that

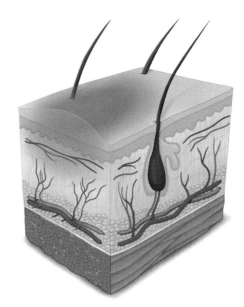

Figure 11–19, a-b A superficial burn.

break the skin can cause infection, fluid loss, and loss of temperature control. Burns can also damage the respiratory system and the eyes.

The severity of a burn depends on the:

• Temperature of the source of the burn

• Length of exposure to the source

• Location of the burn

• Extent of the burn

• Person's age and medical condition

In general, people under age 5 and over age 60 have thinner skin and often burn more severely. People with acute trauma or chronic medical problems such as fractures, heart or kidney problems, or diabetes tend to have more complications resulting from burns; the effects of burns in these people may be more severe.

Severity of Burns

Burns are classified by their cause, such as heat, chemicals, electricity, or radiation. They are also classified by depth. The deeper the burn, the more severe it is. Generally, three depth classifications are used: superficial, partial-thickness, and full-thickness.

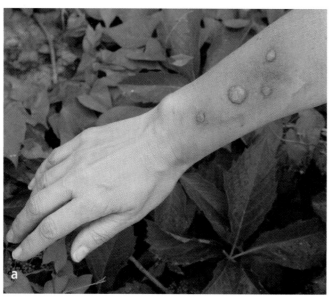

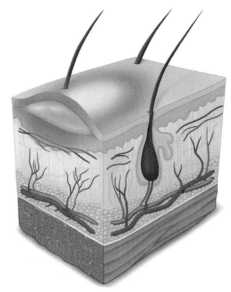

Figure 11–20, a-b A partial-thickness burn.

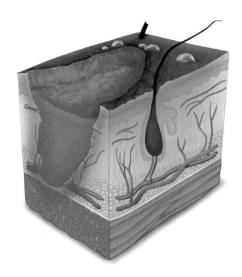

Figure 11–21, a-b A full-thickness burn.

Superficial Burns

A superficial burn involves only the top layer of skin (Figure 11–19, a-b). The skin is red and dry, and the burn is usually painful. The area may swell. Most sunburns are superficial burns. Superficial burns generally heal in five to six days without permanent scarring.

Partial-Thickness Burns

A partial-thickness burn involves both the epidermis and the dermis (Figure 11–20, a-b). These injuries are also red and have blisters that may open and weep clear fluid, making the skin appear wet. The burned skin may look blotched. These burns are usually painful, and the area often swells. Although the burn usually heals in three or four weeks, a skin graft may still be necessary. Extensive partial-thickness burns can be serious, requiring more advanced medical care. Scarring may occur from partial-thickness burns.

Full-Thickness Burns

A full-thickness burn destroys both layers of skin, as well as any or all of the underlying structures—fat, muscles, bones, and nerves (Figure 11–21, a-b). These burns may look brown or charred, with the tissues underneath sometimes appearing white. They can be either extremely painful or relatively painless if the burn destroys nerve endings in the skin. Full-thickness burns are often surrounded by painful partial-thickness burns.

Full-thickness burns can be life-threatening. Because the burns are open, the body loses fluid, and shock is likely to occur. These burns also make the body highly prone to infection. Scarring occurs and may be severe. Skin grafts are usually required.

Identifying Critical Burns

It is important that you be able to identify a critical burn. A critical burn is one that requires immediate, more advanced medical care. Critical burns are potentially life-threatening, disfiguring, or disabling. Knowing whether you should obtain more advanced medical care for a burn injury can sometimes be difficult. It is not always easy or possible to assess the severity of a burn immediately after injury. Even superficial burns to large areas of the body or to certain body parts can be critical. You cannot judge severity by the pain the person feels because nerve endings may have been destroyed. More advanced medical care must be obtained for the following burns:

- Inhalation injuries causing breathing difficulty or signs of burns around the mouth and nose

- Flame burns that occurred in a confined space

- Burns covering more than one body part

- Burns to the head, neck, hands, feet, or genitals

- Any partial-thickness or full-thickness burns to a child or an older adult

- Burns resulting from chemicals, explosions, or electricity

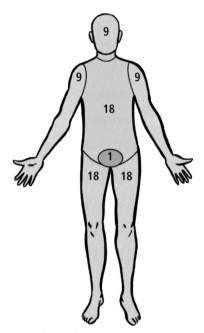

Figure 11–22 The Rule of Nines is one method to help determine how much of the body is burned.

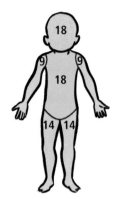

Figure 11–23 The Rule of Nines is modified when determining the percent of body burned on a baby.

Expect that burns caused by flames or hot grease will require medical attention, especially if the injured person is under 5 or over 60 years of age. Hot grease is slow to cool and difficult to remove from the skin. Burns that involve hot liquid or flames contacting clothing will also be serious since the clothing keeps the heat in contact with the skin. Some synthetic fabrics melt and stick to the body. They may take longer to cool than the soft tissues. Although these burns may appear minor at first, they can continue to worsen over a period of time.

Estimating the Extent of Burns

When communicating with more advanced medical personnel about a burned person, you may be asked how much of the body is burned. The Rule of Nines is a common method for estimating what percentage of the body is affected by burns (Figure 11–22).

In an adult, the head equals 9 percent of the total body surface. Likewise, each arm also equals 9 percent of the body. Each leg equals 18 percent, as does the front or back of the trunk. For example, if the front of the trunk (18 percent) and one entire arm (9 percent) are burned, you would estimate that 27 percent of the body's surface area has been burned.

If you do not remember the Rule of Nines, simply communicate how the burn occurred, the body parts

involved, and the approximate degree of burn. For example, "The person was injured when an overheated car radiator exploded. The person has partial-thickness burns on his face, neck, chest, and arms." The Rule of Nines is most useful when determining body surface area for large burns.

If someone has small burns on his body, you may want to use the Rule of Palms. The Rule of Palms is another method for estimating what percentage of the body is affected by burns. The palm of the injured person's hand is roughly equivalent to 1 percent of his body surface area.

Estimating the Extent of Burns for Babies

The Rule of Nines is modified when determining the extent of body surface area for a baby. For a baby, the head and neck equal 18 percent of the total body surface. Additionally, each upper extremity equals 9 percent, each lower extremity equals 14 percent, and each surface of the trunk equals 18 percent (Figure 11–23).

Care for Thermal Burns

Look for fire, smoke, downed electrical wires, and warning signs for chemicals or radiation. If the scene is unsafe and you have not been trained to manage the situation, summon other specially trained personnel.

If the scene is safe, approach the person cautiously. If the source of heat is still in contact with the person, take steps to remove and extinguish it. This may require you to smother the flames or extinguish them with water or to remove smoldering clothing. If the burn is caused by hot tar, cool the area with water but do not attempt to remove the tar.

If the burn is superficial, you may not need to obtain more advanced medical care unless the person is in a great deal of pain or becomes unconscious. More advanced medical care should be obtained if a partial-thickness burn covers more than 10 percent of the body or the person is in a great deal of pain, becomes unconscious, or has a full-thickness burn.

Do a primary survey. Make sure ABCs are present. Pay close attention to the person's airway.

As you do a secondary survey, look for additional signs of burn injuries. Look also for other injuries, especially if there was an explosion or electric shock. Treat any non-life-threatening injuries.

If thermal burns are present, follow these three basic care steps:

1. Cool the burned area.

2. Cover the burned area.

3. Minimize shock.

NOTE:

If the eyes have been burned due to a flash burn, rinse them with saline or water; then have the person close the eyes and cover them with moist, sterile dressings.

Cool the Burned Area

Even after the source of heat has been removed, soft tissue will continue to burn for minutes afterward, causing more damage. Therefore, it is essential to cool burned areas immediately with large amounts of cool water (Figure 11–24, a). If a partial- or full-thickness burn covers more than 10 percent of the body, cool only a small area at a time. Cooling the person too quickly may cause the person to go into shock. Do not use ice or ice water as ice can cause critical body heat loss. Instead, flush or immerse the area using whatever resources are available—a tub, shower, or garden hose. You can apply soaked cloths to any area that cannot be immersed or is too painful to be immersed. Be sure to keep these compresses cool by adding more water until the site has returned to body temperature.

Allow adequate time for the burned area to cool. If pain continues or if the edges of the burned area are still warm to the touch when the area is removed from the water, continue cooling. When the burn is cool, remove any remaining clothing from the area by carefully removing or cutting material away. Do not try to remove any clothing that is sticking to skin.

In some regions, you may be provided with more specific directions for when and how to cool burns.

Cover the Burned Area

Burns often expose sensitive nerve endings. Cover the burned area to keep out air and help reduce pain (Figure 11–24, b). Use non-stick, sterile dressings and loosely bandage them in place. The bandage should not put

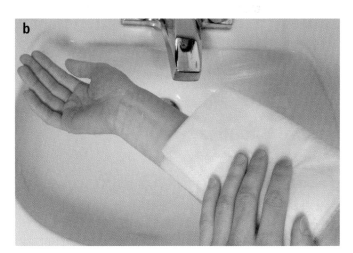

Figure 11–24, a-b a, it is important to cool a burn with large amounts of cool water; **b**, cover the burned area.

pressure on the burn surface. If the burn covers a large area of the body, cover it with clean, dry sheets or other cloth. Small burns (under 10 percent of the body) may be covered with a moist dressing.

Covering the burn helps prevent infection. For a small, superficial burn, you can put an antibiotic cream or ointment on a burn after it is cooled (if the person has no allergy or sensitivity to it). Do not put other ointments, butter, oil, or other commercial or home remedies on any burn. Oils and ointments seal in heat and do not relieve pain or can contaminate open skin areas, causing infection. Do not break blisters. Intact skin helps prevent infection.

For small superficial burns or small burns with open blisters that are not sufficiently severe or extensive to require medical attention, care for the burned area as an open wound. Wash the area with soap and water. Immerse the burn in water if possible, instead of using running water, as running water can damage tissues. Ensure that the water you are immersing the burn in is clean and stays cool. Cover the burn with a non-stick dressing and bandage. Tell the person to watch for signs of infection.

For a large partial-thickness burn, after cooling the skin, cover it loosely with a dry, sterile dressing, preferably non-stick gauze. If the person has full-thickness burns, cover the burn with a dry sterile dressing and obtain more advanced medical care if necessary.

Minimize Shock

Pain and loss of body fluids from full-thickness and large partial-thickness burns can cause shock. Lay the person down unless he is having difficulty breathing. People with burns tend to chill. Help the person maintain normal body temperature by protecting him from drafts. Administer oxygen if it is available and it is safe to do so.

Special Situations

Chemical Burns

Chemical burns are common in industrial settings but also occur in the home. Cleaning solutions, such as household bleach, oven or drain cleaners, toilet bowl cleaners, paint strippers, and lawn or garden chemicals, are common sources of caustic chemicals. Caustic chemicals destroy tissues and cause chemical burns.

Typically, burns result from chemicals that are strong acids or alkalis. These substances can quickly injure the skin. As with heat burns, the stronger the chemical and the longer the contact, the more severe the burn. The chemical will continue to burn as long as it is on the skin. You must remove the chemical from the skin as quickly as possible and then obtain more advanced medical care immediately.

With a chemical powder or granules, brush the chemical from the skin before flushing. Whether the substance is liquid, granular, or powder, flush the burn continuously with large amounts of cool, running water. A continuous flow of water will remove a dry substance before the water can activate it. Continue flushing until you can obtain more advanced medical care. Have the person remove contaminated clothing if possible. Take steps to minimize shock.

Chemical burns to the eyes can be exceptionally traumatic. If an eye is burned by a chemical, flush the affected eye until you can obtain more advanced medical care (or for at least 20 minutes) (Figure 11–25). Flush the affected eye from the nose outward to prevent washing the chemical into the unaffected eye.

With all chemicals, ensure that you protect yourself from the chemicals and avoid contaminating any unaffected areas of the injured person.

Electrical Burns

The human body is a good conductor of electricity. When someone comes in contact with an electrical source, such as a power line, a malfunctioning household appliance, or lightning, he conducts the electricity through his body. Some body parts, such as the skin, resist the electrical current. Resistance produces heat, which can cause electrical burns along the flow of the current (Figure 11–26). The severity of an electrical burn depends on the type and amount of contact, the current's path through the body, and how long the contact lasted. Electrical burns are often deep. Although these wounds may look superficial, the tissues beneath may be severely damaged. Some electrical burns will be marked by characteristic entry and exit wounds indicating where current has passed through the body. In the secondary survey, look for two burn sites. Cover any burn injuries with a non-stick sterile dressing and give care to minimize shock.

Figure 11–25 Flush a chemical burn to the eye for at least 20 minutes.

Figure 11–26 An electrical burn.

With someone who was hit by lightning, look and care for life-threatening conditions, such as respiratory or cardiac arrest. The person may also have fractures, including spinal fracture, so do not move him unless necessary.

Inhalation Injuries

Note soot or burns around the mouth or nose or the rest of the face and singed hair and/or eyebrows, which may signal that air passages or lungs have been burned (Figure 11–27). Burns that resulted from a fire in an enclosed, confined space are likely to be associated with inhalation injuries of the airway and lungs. When possible, move the person to a well-ventilated place out of the confined area. If you suspect a burned airway or burned lungs, continually monitor breathing and obtain advanced medical care immediately. Air passages may swell, impairing or stopping breathing. Oxygen should be administered if available.

Radiation Burns

Solar radiation from both the sun and other sources can cause radiation burns. Radiation burns are often caused by the sun and are similar to thermal burns. Usually, they are mild, but they can be painful (Figure 11–28). They may blister, involving more than one skin layer. Care for sunburns as you would any other burn. Cool the burn and protect the burned area from further damage by keeping it out of the sun.

People working in special settings, such as certain medical, industrial, or research sites, may be exposed to other types of radiation. If this type of radiation causes a burn, treat it as you would any other burn.

Figure 11–27 Burns to the face may indicate an inhalation injury.

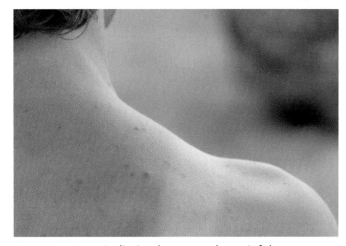

Figure 11–28 Radiation burns can be painful.

Lightning

Lightning causes more deaths than most other weather hazards. Lightning occurs when particles of water, ice, and air moving inside storm clouds lose electrons. Eventually, the cloud becomes divided into layers of positive and negative particles. Most electrical currents run between the layers inside the cloud. Occasionally, the negative charge flashes toward the ground. An electrical current snakes back and forth between the ground and the cloud many times in the seconds that we see a flash crackle down from the sky. Anything tall—a tower, a tree, or a person—becomes a path for the electrical current.

Travelling at speeds up to 500 kilometres per second, a lightning strike can hurl a person through the air, burn his clothes off, and sometimes cause the heart to stop beating. The most powerful lightning strikes carry up to 50 million volts of electricity, enough to keep 13,000 homes running. Lightning can "flash" over a person's body, or, in its more dangerous path, it can travel through blood vessels and nerves to reach the ground.

Besides burns, lightning can also cause brain and spinal damage, cardiac arrest, fractures, and ruptured ear drums.

If you see or hear a storm approaching in the distance:

- Go inside a large building or home.

- Get inside a car and roll up the windows.

- Stop swimming or boating as soon as you see or hear a storm; water conducts electricity.

- Stay away from the telephone, except in an emergency.

- Stay away from telephone poles and tall trees if you are caught outside.

- Stay off hilltops; try to crouch down in a ravine or valley.

- Stay away from farm equipment and small metal vehicles such as motorcycles, bicycles, and golf carts.

- Avoid wire fences, clotheslines, metal pipes, rails, and other conductors.

- Stay several metres apart if you are in a group.

You can also reduce the chances of being struck by lightning by assuming the "lightning position" in situations of risk. This position requires you to squat down and ball yourself up so you are as low to the ground as possible without lying down. Wrap your arms around your legs. This provides a safer path for electrons to flow from the ground rather than through your torso. It is also comfortable enough that you can hold this position for a bit of time. Close your eyes. Although this position doesn't guarantee your safety from lightning, it does reduce your risk.[1]

[1] http://www.nols.edu/resources/research/pdfs/lightningsafetyguideline.pdf

SUMMARY

Caring for wounds is not difficult. You need only follow the basic guidelines to control bleeding and minimize the risk of infection. Remember that with minor wounds your primary concern is to cleanse the wound to prevent infection. With major wounds, control the bleeding quickly using direct pressure and obtain more advanced medical care. Dressings and bandages, when correctly applied, help control bleeding, reduce pain, and minimize the danger of infection.

Burns damage the layers of the skin and sometimes the internal structures as well. Heat, smoke inhalation, chemicals, electricity, and radiation all cause burn injuries. When caring for a person with burns, always ensure your safety first. When the scene is safe, approach the person and do a primary survey and a secondary survey if necessary.

Once the person has been removed from the burn source and is in a well-ventilated area, follow the steps of burn care:

- Cool the burned area to minimize additional tissue destruction.

- Keep air away from the burned area by covering it with non-stick sterile dressings.

- To minimize shock, maintain the person's normal body temperature.

- Obtain more advanced medical care for any critical burn.

- If inhalation injury is possible, provide supplemental oxygen.

In addition, always check for inhalation injury if the person has a heat or chemical burn involving the face. With electrical burns, check carefully for additional problems such as breathing difficulty, cardiac problems, and fractures.

You notice the first woman is now having trouble breathing. What do you do?

Skills Summary

Care for an Open Leg Wound

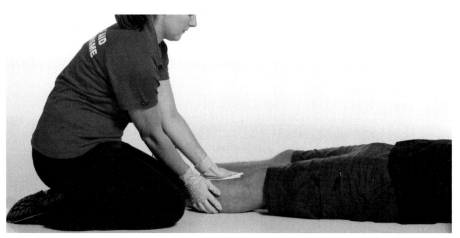

1. Apply direct pressure.

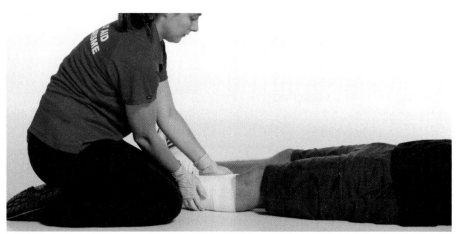

2. Apply pressure bandage.

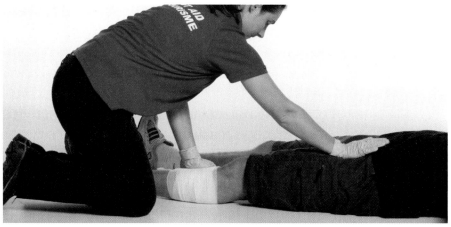

3. Use pressure point if necessary.

Skills Summary

Care for an Open Arm Wound

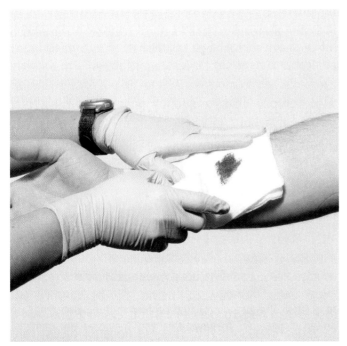

1. Apply dressing.

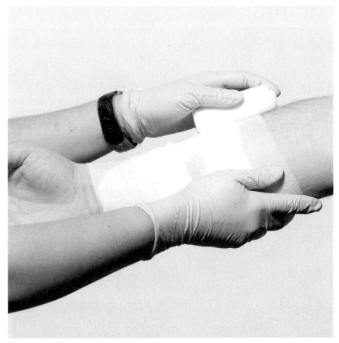

2. Apply pressure bandage.

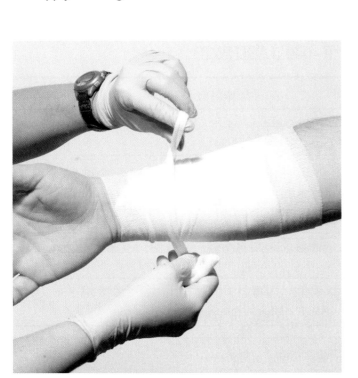

3. Tie or tape bandage.

4. Check circulation and sensation distal to the injury.

Musculoskeletal Injuries

A mountain biker goes over the handle bars. She hits the ground and screams in pain. Her leg is deformed and she cannot stand up. What do you do?

INTRODUCTION

Injuries to the musculoskeletal system are common. Millions of people at home, at work, or at play injure their muscles, bones, or joints. No age group is immune. An athlete may fall and bruise the muscles of the thigh, making walking painful. Heavy machinery may fall on a worker and break ribs, making breathing difficult. A person who braces a hand against a dashboard in a car crash may injure the bones at the shoulder, disabling the arm. A person who falls while snowboarding may fall and injure her wrist, tear the supportive ligaments, and make it impossible to use her hand.

Injuries to the extremities, the arms and legs, hands and feet, are quite common. They range from simple bruises to open fractures, where bone protrudes through the skin. With any injury to the extremities, the prompt care you give can help prevent further pain and damage.

Although musculoskeletal injuries are almost always painful, they are rarely life-threatening. However, when not recognized and taken care of properly, they can have serious consequences and even result in permanent disability or death. Developing a better understanding of the structure and function of the body's framework will help you assess musculoskeletal injuries and give appropriate care.

MUSCULOSKELETAL SYSTEM

The musculoskeletal system is made up of muscles and bones that form the skeleton, connective tissues, tendons, and ligaments. Together, these structures give the body shape, form, and stability. Bones and muscles connect to form various body segments. They work together to provide body movements.

Muscles

The body has more than 600 muscles. Most are skeletal muscles, which attach to the bones. Skeletal muscles account for most of your lean body weight (body weight without excess fat).

Muscles are able to shorten (contract) and lengthen (relax). All body movements result from skeletal muscles contracting and relaxing. Skeletal muscle actions are under your conscious control. Because you control the movement, skeletal muscles are also called voluntary muscles. Skeletal muscles also protect the bones, nerves, and blood vessels.

Most skeletal muscles are anchored to bone at each end by strong, cord-like tissues called tendons. Muscles and their adjoining tendons extend across joints. When the brain sends a command to move, electrical impulses travel through the spinal cord and nerve pathways to

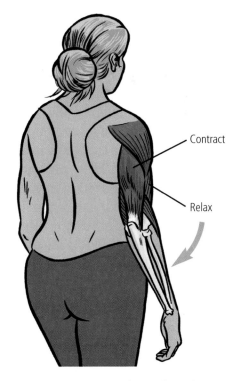

Contract

Relax

Contract

Relax

Figure 12–1 Movement occurs when one group of muscles contracts and an opposing group of muscles relaxes.

Adjacent muscle

Injured muscle

Figure 12–2 Adjacent muscles can often assume the function of an injured muscle.

the individual muscles and stimulate the muscle fibres to move. When a muscle contracts, the muscle fibres shorten, pulling the ends of the muscle closer together. The muscles pull the bones, causing motion at the joint the muscle crosses.

Motion is usually caused by a group of muscles close together pulling at the same time. For instance, the hamstring muscles are a group of muscles at the back of the thigh. When the hamstrings contract, the leg bends at the knee. The quadriceps are a group of muscles at the front of the thigh. When the quadriceps muscles contract, the leg straightens at the knee. Generally, when one group of muscles contracts, another group of muscles on the opposite side of the body part relaxes (Figure 12–1). Even simple tasks, such as bending to pick up an object from the floor, involve a complex series of movements in which different muscle groups contract and relax.

Injuries to the nervous system, brain, spinal cord, or peripheral nerves can affect muscle control. A complete loss of muscle control is called paralysis. Injuries to the nerves can also affect sensation, the ability to feel. When an isolated injury to a muscle or nerve occurs, the

adjacent muscles can sometimes assume some of the function of the injured muscle (Figure 12–2).

Skeleton

The skeleton is formed of over 200 bones of various sizes and shapes (Figure 12–3). These bones shape the skeleton, giving each body part a unique form. For example, the head is defined by the bones that form the skull, and the chest is defined by the bones that form the rib cage. Prominent bones, bones that can be seen or felt beneath the skin, provide landmarks for locating body parts.

The skeleton protects vital organs and other soft tissues. The skull protects the brain (Figure 12–4, a). The ribs protect the heart and lungs (Figure 12–4, b), as well as the liver, kidneys, and pancreas. The spinal cord is protected by the canal formed by the bones that form the spinal column (Figure 12–4, c). Two or more bones come together to form joints. Ligaments, fibrous bands that hold bones together at joints, give the skeleton stability and, with the muscles, help maintain posture.

Bones

Bones are hard, dense tissues. Their strong, rigid structure helps them withstand stresses that cause injuries. The shape of bones depends on what the bones do and the stresses on them. For instance, the surfaces of bones at the joints are smooth (Figure 12–5). Although similar to the bones of the arm, the bones of the leg are much larger and stronger because they carry the body's weight.

Bones are classified as long, short, flat, or irregular. Long bones are longer than they are wide. These include the bones of the upper arm (humerus), the forearm (radius and ulna), the thigh (femur), and the lower leg (tibia and fibula). Short bones are about as wide as they are long. Short bones include the small bones of the hand (metacarpals) and feet (metatarsals). Flat bones have a relatively thin, flat shape. Flat bones include the breastbone (sternum), the ribs, the shoulder blades (scapula), and some of the bones that form the skull. Bones that do not fit in these three categories are called irregular bones. Irregular bones include the vertebrae and the bones of the face. Bones are weakest at the points where they change shape, and fractures usually occur at these points.

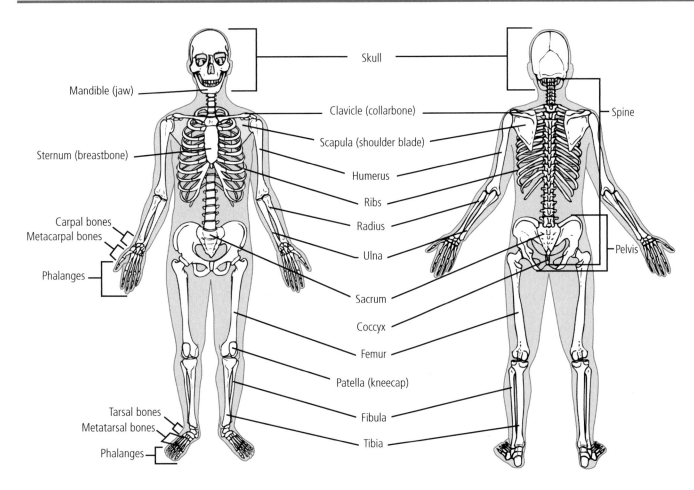

Figure 12–3 The bones of the skeleton give the body its shape and protect vital organs.

Bones have a rich supply of blood and nerves. Some bones store and manufacture red blood cells and supply them to the circulating blood. Bone injuries are usually very painful and can bleed excessively. The bleeding can become life-threatening if not properly cared for. Bones heal by forming new bone cells. Bone is the only body tissue that can regenerate in this way.

Bones weaken with age. Bones in young children are more flexible than in adults, so they are less likely to break. An older adult's less dense, more brittle bones are more likely to give way, even under everyday stresses. For example, an older adult may even break the strongest bone in the body, the femur, if enough stress is created on the bone when pivoting with all the body weight on one leg. When bones become gradually, progressively weaker and less dense, this is called osteoporosis.

Joints

A joint is a structure formed by the ends of two or more bones coming together at one place. Most joints allow motion. However, the bone ends at some joints are fused together, which restricts motion. Fused bones, such as the bones of the skull, form solid structures that protect their contents (Figure 12–6).

Joints are held together by tough, fibrous, connective tissues called ligaments. Ligaments resist joint movement. Joints surrounded by ligaments have restricted movement; joints that have few ligaments move more freely. For instance, the shoulder joint, with few ligaments, allows greater motion than the hip joint, although their structure is similar. Joint motion also depends on the bone structure.

Joints that move more freely have less natural support and are therefore more prone to injury. However, there

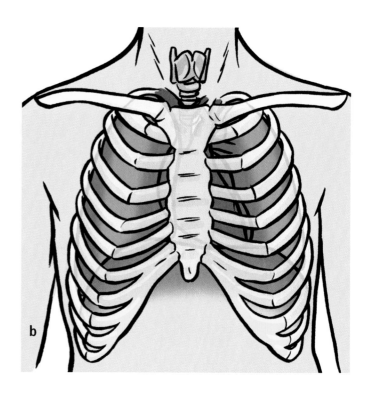

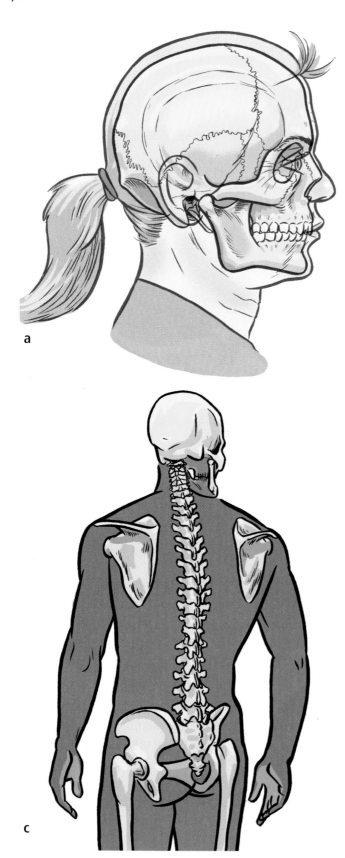

Figure 12–4, a-c **a**, the immovable bones of the skull protect the brain; **b**, the rib cage protects the heart and lungs; and, **c**, the vertebrae protect the spinal cord.

is a normal range of movement for each joint. When a joint is forced beyond its normal range, ligaments stretch and tear. Stretched and torn ligaments permit too much motion, making the joint unstable. Unstable joints can be disabling, particularly when they are weight bearing, such as the knee or ankle. Unstable joints are also prone to reinjury and often develop osteoarthritis, an inflamed condition of the joints, in later years.

Injuries to the Musculoskeletal System

Injuries to the musculoskeletal system occur in a variety of ways. They are more commonly caused by forces generated by mechanical forms of energy but can result from heat, chemical, or electrical forms of energy.

Types of Musculoskeletal Injuries

The four basic types of musculoskeletal injuries are fractures, dislocations, sprains, and strains. Injuries to the musculoskeletal system can be classified according to the body structures damaged. Some injuries may involve more than one type of injury. For example, a direct blow to the knee may injure both ligaments and bones. Injuries are also classified by the nature and extent of the damage.

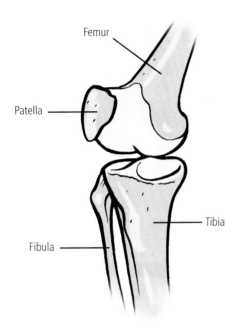

Figure 12–5 Bone surfaces at the joints are smooth.

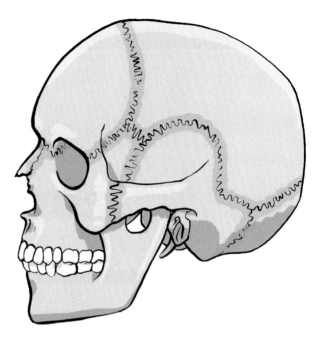

Figure 12–6 Fused bones, such as those of the skull, form solid structures that protect their contents.

Fracture

A fracture is a partial or complete break in bone tissue. Fractures include chipped or cracked bones, as well as bones that are broken all the way through (Figure 12–7). Fractures are commonly caused by direct and indirect bending forces. However, if strong enough, twisting forces and strong muscle contractions can cause a fracture, for example, a femur fracture.

Fractures are classified as open or closed. An open fracture involves an open wound. Open fractures often occur when the limb is severely angulated or bent, causing bone ends to tear the skin and surrounding soft tissues, or when an object, such as a bullet, penetrates the skin and breaks the bone. Closed fractures leave the skin unbroken and are more common than open fractures. Open fractures are more serious than closed fractures because of the risks of infection and severe blood loss. Although fractures are rarely an immediate threat to life, any fracture involving a large bone can cause hypovolemic shock because bones and soft tissue may bleed heavily.

Fractures are not always obvious unless there is a telltale sign, such as an open wound with protruding bone ends or a severely deformed body part. You must always consider the way in which the injury occurred, which is often enough to suggest a possible fracture.

Dislocation

A dislocation is a displacement or separation of a bone from its normal position at a joint (Figure 12–8). Dislocations are usually caused by severe forces such as twisting or falls. After repeated injury, joints may dislocate easily because their bones and ligaments do not provide adequate protection. Others, such as the elbow or the joints of the spine, are well protected and therefore dislocate less easily.

When bone ends are forced far enough beyond their normal position, ligaments stretch and tear. Subsequent dislocations are then more likely to occur. A force violent enough to cause a dislocation can also cause a fracture and can damage nearby nerves and blood vessels.

Dislocations are generally more obvious than fractures because the joint appears to be deformed. The displaced bone end often causes an abnormal lump, ridge, or depression, sometimes making dislocations easier to identify than other musculoskeletal injuries. An injured person is also unable to move a joint that is dislocated because the bones are out of place.

Sprain

A sprain is the stretching or tearing of ligaments and other tissues at a joint. A sprain usually results when the

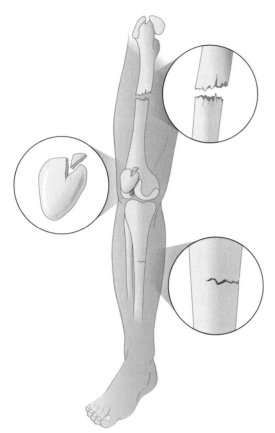

Figure 12–7 Fractures include chipped or cracked bones, as well as bones that are broken all the way through.

Figure 12–8 A dislocation is a displacement or separation of a bone from its normal position at a joint.

bones that form a joint are forced beyond their normal range of motion (Figure 12–9). The more ligaments that are torn, the more severe the injury. The sudden, violent forcing of a joint beyond its limit can completely rupture ligaments and dislocate the bones. Severe sprains may also involve a fracture of the bones that form the joint.

Mild sprains, which only stretch ligament fibres, generally heal quickly. The person may have only a brief period of pain or discomfort (7–10 days) and quickly return to activity with little or no soreness. For this reason, people often neglect sprains, and the joint is often reinjured. Severe sprains, or sprains that involve a fracture, usually cause pain when the joint is moved or used. It is important to take care of a sprain to aid in healing.

Often a sprain is more disabling than a fracture. When fractures heal, they usually leave the bone as strong as it was before; it is unlikely that a repeat break would occur at the same spot. On the other hand, once ligaments become stretched or torn, the joint may become less stable if the injury does not receive proper

care. A less stable joint makes the injured area more susceptible to reinjury.

Strain

A strain is the excessive stretching and tearing of muscle or tendon fibres. It is sometimes called a "muscle pull" or "tear." Because tendons are tougher and stronger than muscles, tears usually occur in the muscle itself or where the muscle attaches to the tendon. Strains are often the result of overexertion, such as lifting something too heavy or overworking a muscle. They can also result from sudden or uncoordinated movement. Strains commonly involve the muscles in the neck or back, the front or back of the thigh, or the back of the lower leg. Strains of the neck and lower back can be particularly painful and therefore disabling.

Like sprains, strains are often neglected, which commonly leads to reinjury. Strains sometimes recur chronically, especially to the muscles of the neck, lower

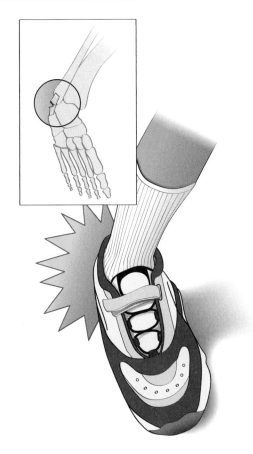

Figure 12–9 A sprain usually results when the bones that form a joint are forced beyond their normal range of motion.

back, and back of the thigh. Neck and back problems are two of the leading causes of absenteeism from work, accounting for millions of dollars in lost productivity annually. Using proper body mechanics and ergonomics, these injuries can often be prevented.

Signs and Symptoms of Musculoskeletal Injuries

Common Signs and Symptoms of Musculoskeletal Injuries

Five common signs and symptoms associated with musculoskeletal injuries are:

- Pain
- Swelling
- Deformity
- Discolouration of the skin

Tendonitis is an inflammation of a tendon due to overuse or systemic inflammatory diseases. It can present with pain and stiffness in the tendon area or a burning sensation around the whole joint.

- Inability to use the affected part normally

Pain, swelling, and discolouration of the skin commonly occur with any significant injury. Irritation to nerve endings that supply the injured area causes pain. Pain is the body's signal that something is wrong. The injured area may be painful to touch and to move.

Swelling is often caused by bleeding from damaged blood vessels and tissues in the injured area. It may also be due to excessive fluid production by the capsule surrounding the joint. However, swelling is often deceiving. It may appear rapidly at the site of injury, develop gradually, or not appear at all. Swelling by itself, therefore, is not a reliable sign of the severity of an injury. Nor is it a reliable way to determine which structures are involved as bleeding may discolour the skin in surrounding tissues (this may take hours or days to appear). At first, the skin may only look red. As blood seeps to the skin's surface, the area begins to look bruised.

Deformity may also be a sign of significant injury (Figure 12–10). Abnormal lumps, ridges, depressions, or unusual bends or angles in body parts are types of deformities. Marked deformity is often a sign of fracture or dislocation. Comparing the injured part with the uninjured side may help you detect deformity.

An injured person's inability or unwillingness to move or use an injured part may also indicate a significant injury. The person may tell you she is unable to move or that it is simply too painful to move. Moving or using injured parts can disturb tissues, further irritating nerve endings, which causes or increases pain. Often the muscles of an affected area will spasm in an attempt to keep the injured part from moving.

Similarly, an injured person often supports the injury in the most comfortable position. To care for musculoskeletal injuries, try to avoid causing additional pain.

Osteoporosis

Osteoporosis, a degenerative bone disorder, affects 1 in 4 women over the age of 50 and 1 in 8 men. Fair-skinned women with ancestors from northern Europe, the British Isles, Japan, or China are genetically predisposed to osteoporosis. Inactive people are also more susceptible to osteoporosis.

Osteoporosis occurs when there is a decrease in the calcium content of bones. Normally, bones are hard, dense tissues that endure tremendous stresses. Bone-building cells constantly repair damage that occurs as a result of everyday stresses, keeping bones strong. Calcium is a key to bone growth, development, and repair. When the calcium content of bones decreases, bones become frail, less dense, and less able to repair the normal damage they incur.

This loss of density and strength leaves bones more susceptible to fractures. Where once tremendous force was necessary to cause fractures, they may now occur with little or no aggravation, especially to hips, vertebrae, and wrists. Spontaneous fractures are those that occur without trauma. The person may be taking a walk or washing dishes when the fracture occurs. Some hip fractures thought to be caused by falls are actually spontaneous fractures that caused the person's fall.

Osteoporosis can begin at any age. The amount of calcium absorbed from the diet naturally declines with age, making calcium intake increasingly important. When calcium in the diet is inadequate, calcium in bones is withdrawn and used by the body to meet its other needs, leaving bones weakened.

Building strong bones at an early age is the key to preventing osteoporosis. Calcium and exercise are necessary to bone building. Many physicians recommend more than 1,000 milligrams of calcium per day for women age 19 and over. Three to four daily servings of low-fat dairy products should provide adequate calcium. Magnesium and vitamin D are also necessary because they aid in calcium absorption. Exposure to sunshine enables the body to make vitamin D. Fifteen minutes of sunshine on the hands and face of a young, light-skinned individual is enough to supply the recommended dietary allowance of 5 to 10 micrograms of vitamin D per day. Dark-skinned and older adults need more sun exposure. People who do not receive adequate sun exposure need to consume vitamin D. The best sources are vitamin-fortified milk and fatty fish, such as tuna and salmon.

Calcium and magnesium supplements combined with vitamin D are available for those who do not take in adequate calcium and/or magnesium. However, before taking a supplement, consult a physician. Many highly advertised supplements are ineffective because they do not dissolve in the body.

Exercise seems to increase bone density and the activity of bone-building cells. Regular exercise may reduce the rate of bone loss by promoting new bone formation and may also stimulate the skeletal system to repair itself.

Specific Signs and Symptoms of Serious Musculoskeletal Injuries

In the secondary survey, you may notice certain tell-tale signs and symptoms that help you determine the type of injury. Often what the injured person feels or can recall about the moment of injury provides important clues.

Sprains or strains are fairly easy to tell apart. Because a sprain involves the soft tissues at a joint, pain, swelling, and deformity are usually confined to the joint area. Strains involve the soft tissue structures that, for the most part, stretch between joints. In most strains, pain, swelling, and any deformity are generally in the areas between the joints (Figure 12–11).

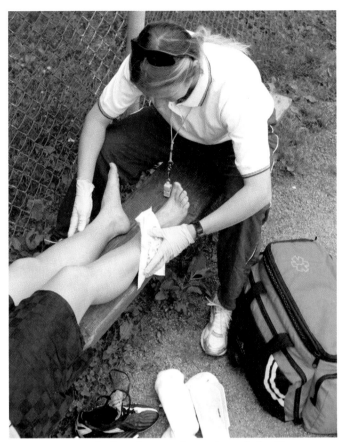

Figure 12–10 Deformity may be a sign of significant injury.

Figure 12–11 Strains generally involve an area between the joints.

However, it is not always easy to determine if a musculoskeletal injury is serious, requiring more advanced medical care. Always suspect a serious injury when the following signs and symptoms are present:

- Significant deformity
- Moderate or severe swelling and discolouration
- Inability to move or use the affected body part
- Bone fragments protruding from a wound
- Person feels bones grating or felt or heard a snap or pop at the time of injury
- Person reports a feeling of the affected joint "giving way"
- Loss of circulation or feeling in an extremity
- Cause of the injury suggests that the injury may be severe

Care for Musculoskeletal Injuries

Some musculoskeletal injuries are obvious because they involve severe deformities, such as protruding bones or bleeding. The injured person may also be in severe pain, although such injuries are rarely life-threatening. Complete the primary survey and care for any life-threatening conditions. Then do the secondary survey and care for any other injuries. When you find a musculoskeletal injury, immediately obtain more advanced medical care if:

- The injury involves severe bleeding
- The injury involves the head, neck, or back
- The injury impairs walking or breathing
- There is severe angulation with reduction or loss in sensation and/or circulation
- You see or suspect multiple musculoskeletal injuries

Figure 12–12 General care for all musculoskeletal injuries is similar—rest, immobilize, cold, elevate.

General Care

You identify and care for injuries to the musculoskeletal system during the secondary survey. Because they often appear similar, it may be difficult for you to determine exactly what type of injury has occurred. As you do the secondary survey, think about how the body normally looks and feels. Compare the injured side with the uninjured side.

During the interview, ask how the injury happened. The cause of injury is often enough to make you suspect a serious musculoskeletal injury. As the injured person or bystanders explain how the injury occurred, listen for clues, such as a fall from a height or another significant impact to the body that would have the potential to cause a serious injury. Also ask the person if any areas are painful.

Then do a head-to-toe examination of the entire body, beginning with the head. Check each body part. Start with the neck, followed by the shoulders, the chest, and so on. As you conduct the secondary survey, look and listen for clues that may indicate a musculoskeletal injury.

The general care for all musculoskeletal injuries is similar. Just remember the acronym RICE for rest, immobilize, cold, and elevate (Figure 12–12).

R – rest

I – immobilize

C – cold

E – elevate

Rest

Avoid any movements or activities that cause pain. Help the injured person find the most comfortable position. If you suspect head or spine injuries, leave the person lying flat and move him only if absolutely necessary.

Immobilize

If you suspect a serious musculoskeletal injury, you must immobilize the injured part before giving additional care, such as applying ice or elevating the injured part. To immobilize, use a splint or another method to keep the injured part from moving.

The purpose of immobilizing an injury is to:

- Lessen pain
- Prevent further damage to soft tissues
- Reduce the risk of serious bleeding
- Reduce the possibility of loss of circulation to the injured part
- Prevent closed fractures from becoming open fractures

If you are not able to transport the person and more advanced medical care is on the way, the ground can temporarily immobilize an injured area effectively. However, if necessary, you can further immobilize an injured part by applying a splint, sling, or bandages to keep the injured body part from moving. A splint is a device that maintains an injured part in place. To effectively immobilize an injured part, a splint must extend above and below the injury site (Figure 12–13).

When using a splint, follow these basic principles:

- Have the appropriate, effective equipment.
- Splint only if you can do it without causing further injury.
- Splint the injured area and the joints above and below the injury site.
- Check for proper circulation and sensation before and after splinting.

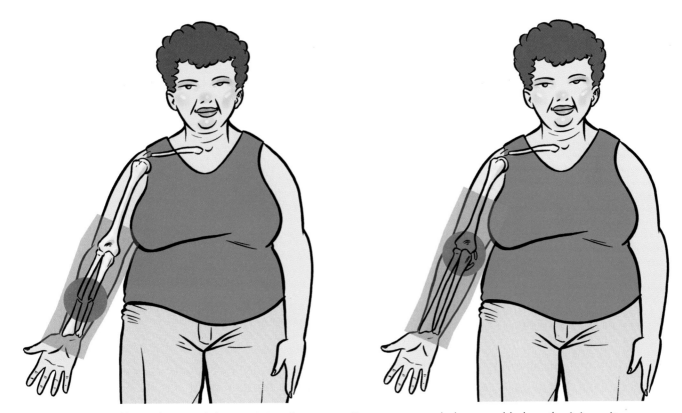

Figure 12–13 To effectively immobilize an injured part, a splint must extend above and below the injury site.

If splinting a part causes circulation or sensation to become impaired, loosen the splint and wait for advanced medical care.

Types of Splints

Splints are of four general types: soft, rigid, anatomical, and traction. Soft splints include folded blankets, towels, pillows, slings or cravats (Figure 12–14). A blanket can be used to splint an injured ankle (Figure 12–15). A sling, which can be made from a triangular bandage, is tied to support an arm, a wrist, or a hand (Figure 12–16). A cravat is a folded triangular bandage used to hold dressings or splints in place.

Rigid splints include boards, metal strips, and folded plastic or cardboard splints (Figure 12–17). For example, a padded rigid splint can be applied to an injured arm

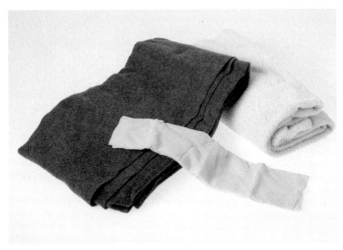

Figure 12–14 Soft splints include folded blankets, towels, and triangular bandages.

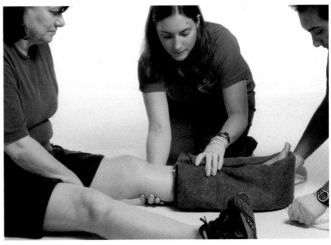

Figure 12–15 A blanket can be used to splint an injured ankle.

Figure 12–16 A triangular bandage can be tied to support an arm, wrist, or hand.

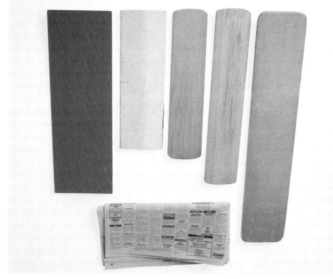

Figure 12–17 Rigid splints can include boards, folded newspaper, or cardboard.

(Figure 12–18). Anatomical splints refer to the use of the body as a splint. You may not ordinarily think of the body as a splint, but it works very well and requires no special equipment. For example, an arm can be splinted to the chest. An injured leg can be splinted to the uninjured leg (Figure 12–19).

A traction splint is a special type of splinting device used primarily to immobilize fractures of the femur. One end attaches to the hip and the other at the ankle. When traction is engaged, a constant, steady pull is applied against opposite ends of the leg, stabilizing the fractured bone ends and keeping them from causing

any further damage (Figure 12–20). Each commercial brand of traction splint has its own unique method of application, and responders must be thoroughly familiar with and proficient in the technique of applying the splint being used.

As a responder, you are likely to have commercially made splints immediately available to you. Commercial splints include padded board splints, air splints, specially designed flexible splints, vacuum splints, and traction splints (Figure 12–21). You should become familiar with the splinting devices you are likely to have before you use them.

Figure 12–18 A rigid splint can be used to support an injured arm.

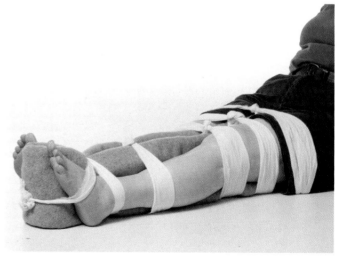

Figure 12–19 An injured leg can be splinted to the uninjured leg.

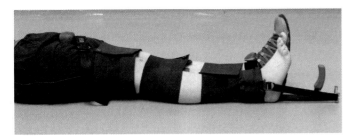
Figure 12–20 A traction splint is primarily used to immobilize femur fractures.

Figure 12–21 Commercial splints.

How to Splint

Follow these guidelines when splinting an injured body part:

1. Support the injured part. If necessary, have the injured person or a bystander help you.

2. Cover any open wounds with a dressing and bandage to help control bleeding and prevent infection.

3. If the injury involves an extremity, check for circulation and sensation at a site below (distal to) the injury. Expose the foot or hand if possible to check for distal circulation, check the colour of the digits below the injury, feel the hand or foot for warmth, or check for capillary refill in the fingers or toes. Ensure that the injured person has feeling in the fingers or toes; compare the injured side with the non-injured side in terms of pulse, skin colour, capillary refill, mobility, and sensation.

4. If using a rigid or anatomical splint, pad the splint so that it is shaped to the injured part. This will help prevent further injury and provide comfort to the person.

5. Secure the splint in place with folded triangular bandages (cravats) or straps provided with the splint.

6. Recheck circulation below the injury site to ensure that circulation has not been restricted due to the splint being applied too tightly. Loosen the splint if the person complains of numbness or if the fingers or toes turn blue (discolour) or become cold.

7. Elevate the splinted part, if possible.

One technique for checking how the body is reacting to illness or injury is to check the capillaries' ability to refill with blood. Capillary refill is an estimate of the amount of blood flowing through the capillary beds, such as those in the fingertips. The capillary beds in the fingertips are normally rich with blood, which causes the pink colour under the fingernails. When a serious illness or injury occurs, the body attempts to conserve blood in the vital organs. As a result, capillaries in the fingertips are among the first blood vessels to constrict, thereby limiting their blood supply. Also, when blood flow to an extremity is disrupted, due to injury, blood does not circulate to the capillaries appropriately.

To check capillary refill, squeeze the person's nail bed and then release. In a healthy person, the normal response is for the area beneath the nail to turn pale as you press it and turn pink again as you release and it refills with blood. If the area does not return to pink within two seconds, this indicates insufficient circulation.

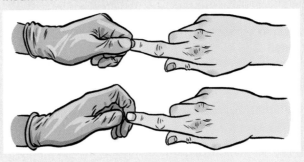

After the injury has been immobilized, recheck the ABCs and vital signs and take steps to care for shock. Shock is likely to develop as a result of a serious musculoskeletal injury. Help the injured person rest in the most comfortable position, apply ice or a cold pack, maintain normal body temperature, and reassure her. Determine what additional care is needed and whether to obtain more advanced medical care if it has not already been done. Provide ongoing survey and care.

If more advanced medical care is not available within 30 minutes, and there is decreased or absent distal circulation, sensation, and/or mobility; gross angulation of the limb; tenting of the skin; or great discomfort, a single attempt may be made to straighten the limb, with the person's willingness.

To do this, gently straighten the limb, using gentle traction, into anatomical position. Grasp the limb above and below the site of injury and pull gently. DO NOT attempt this if a joint injury, such as a dislocation, is suspected or you observe firm resistance to movement, a significant increase in pain, or the sound or feeling of bone fragments grating.

Cold

Regardless of whether the injury is a closed fracture, dislocation, sprain, or strain, apply ice or a cold pack.

Cold helps ease pain and discomfort. Commercial cold packs can be stored in a kit until ready to use, or you can make an ice pack by placing ice in a plastic bag and wrapping it with a towel or cloth. Place a layer of moistened gauze or cloth between the source of cold and the skin to prevent skin damage. Do not apply an ice or cold pack directly over the fracture because doing so would require you to put pressure on the fracture site and could cause discomfort to the injured person. Instead, place cold packs around the site. In general, cold should be applied for 20 minutes every hour for the first 24 to 48 hours after the injury.

Elevate

Elevating the injured area above the level of the heart helps slow the flow of blood, reducing swelling. Elevation is particularly effective in controlling swelling in extremity injuries. However, never attempt to elevate a seriously injured limb area unless it has been adequately immobilized.

Considerations for Transporting an Injured Person

Some musculoskeletal injuries are obviously minor, and the injured person may choose not to get emergency medical care. Others are more serious, requiring more advanced care. Obtain more advanced medical care

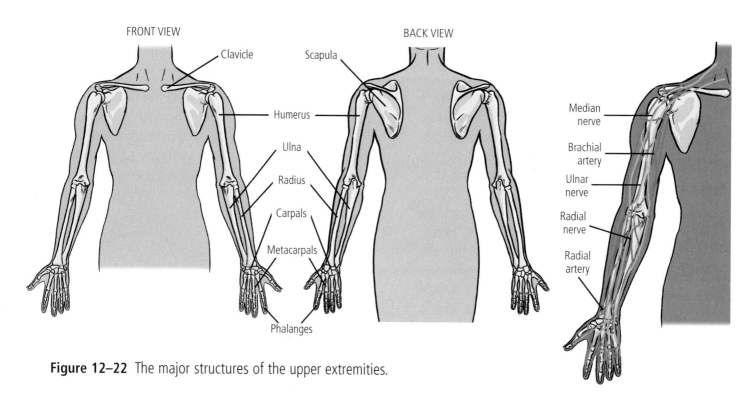

Figure 12–22 The major structures of the upper extremities.

Figure 12–23 A fall can cause a serious injury to the hand, arm, or shoulder.

immediately if you suspect an injury involving severe bleeding, injuries to the head or spine, or an injury that impairs breathing or if you see or suspect multiple musculoskeletal injuries. Fractures of large bones, or multiple fractures, can cause severe internal bleeding and may lead to shock.

Some situations may require you to move the person before an ambulance arrives. If possible, always splint the injury before moving the person. If you are in position in which you must transport the person to a medical facility, one person should monitor the person at all times.

UPPER EXTREMITY INJURIES

The upper extremities are the arms and hands. Upper extremity bones include the clavicle, scapula, humerus, radius and ulna, carpals and metacarpals, and phalanges. Figure 12–22 shows the major structures of the upper extremities.

The upper extremities are commonly the most injured area of the body. Injuries to the upper extremities occur in many different ways. The most frequent cause is falling on the hand of an outstretched arm. Since the hands are rarely protected, abrasions occur easily. A falling person instinctively tries to break the fall by extending the arms and hands, so these areas receive

the force of the body's weight. This can cause a serious injury to the hand, forearm, upper arm, or shoulder, such as a severe sprain, fracture, or dislocation (Figure 12–23).

When caring for serious upper extremity injuries, minimize any movement of the injured part. If an injured person is holding the arm securely against the chest, do not change the position. Holding the arm against the chest is an effective method of immobilization, keeping an injured body part from moving. Allow the person to continue to support the arm in this manner. You can further assist her by binding the injured arm to the chest. This eliminates the need for special splinting equipment and still provides an effective method of immobilization.

Injuries to the upper extremities may also damage blood vessels, nerves, and other soft tissues. It is particularly important to ensure that blood flow and nerve function have not been impaired. Always check for circulation and sensation below the injury site, both before and after splinting. Sometimes when a splint is applied too tightly, blood flow may be impaired. If this occurs, loosen the splint. If you suspect that either the blood vessels or the nerves have been damaged, minimize movement of the area and obtain more advanced medical care immediately.

Shoulder Injuries

The shoulder consists of three bones that meet to form the shoulder joint. These bones are the clavicle, scapula, and humerus. The most common shoulder injuries are sprains. However, injuries of the shoulder may also involve a fracture of one or more of these bones or dislocation of the shoulder joint.

The most frequently injured bone of the shoulder is the clavicle, injured more commonly in children than in adults. Typically, the clavicle is fractured as a result of a fall. The person usually feels pain in the shoulder area. The pain may radiate down the arm. A person with a fractured clavicle usually attempts to ease the pain by holding the arm against the chest. Since the clavicle lies directly over major blood vessels and nerves to the arm, it is important to immobilize the injured area to prevent injury to these structures.

Scapular fractures are not common. A fracture of the scapula typically results from violent force. The signs and symptoms of a fractured scapula are the same as for any other extremity fracture, although you are less

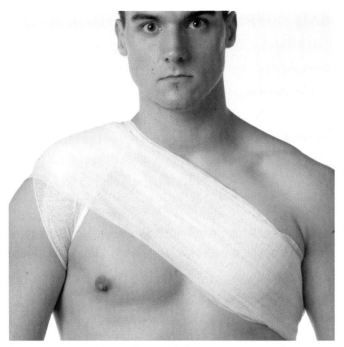

Figure 12–24 Use a figure-eight pattern to apply a pressure bandage to a shoulder.

likely to see deformity of the scapula. The most significant signs and symptoms are extreme pain and the inability to move the arm.

It takes great force to break the scapula, so you must consider that the force may have been great enough to injure the ribs or internal organs in the chest. If this is the case, the person may have difficulty breathing.

A dislocation is another common type of shoulder injury. Like fractures, dislocations often result from falls. This happens frequently in contact sports, such as football and rugby. A player may attempt to break a fall with an outstretched arm or may land on the tip of the shoulder, forcing the arm against the joint formed by the scapula and clavicle (this is commonly referred to as a separation). This can result in ligaments tearing, causing the end of the clavicle to displace. Dislocations also occur at the joint where the humerus meets the socket formed by the scapula. For example, when an arm in a throwing position is hit, it forces the arm to rotate backward. Ligaments tear, causing the upper end of the arm to dislocate from its normal position in the shoulder socket.

Shoulder dislocations are painful and can often be identified by the deformity present. As with other

shoulder injuries, the person often tries to minimize the pain by holding the arm in the most comfortable position.

Care for Shoulder Injuries

To care for shoulder injuries, first control any external bleeding with direct pressure. Apply a pressure bandage using a figure-eight pattern (Figure 12–24). Allow the person to continue to support the arm in the position in

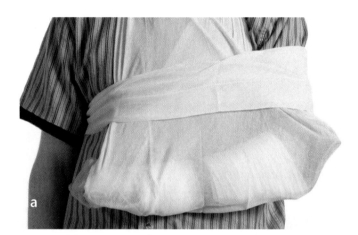
a

b

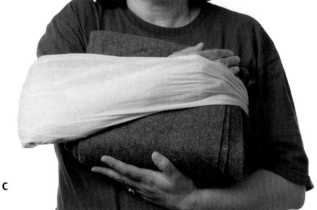
c

Figure 12–25, a-c Splint the arm against the chest in the position the person was holding it.

which she is holding it (usually the most comfortable position) and, if possible, splint it in that position. If the person is holding the arm away from the body, use a pillow, rolled blanket, or similar object to fill the gap between the arm and chest to provide support for the injured area. Check for circulation and sensation in the hand and fingers. Then splint the arm in place. This can be done by merely binding the arm to the chest or by placing the arm in a sling and binding the arm to the chest with a cravat (Figure 12–25, a-c). Recheck for circulation and sensation. Apply cold to the injured area to help minimize pain. Take steps to minimize shock.

Upper Arm Injuries

The humerus can be fractured at any point, although it is usually fractured at the upper end near the shoulder or in the middle of the bone. The upper end of the humerus often fractures in older adults and in young children as a result of a fall. Breaks in the middle of the bone occur mostly in young adults.

When the humerus is fractured, there is danger of damage to the blood vessels and nerves supplying the entire arm. Most humerus fractures are very painful and prevent the person from using the arm. A fracture can cause considerable arm deformity.

Care for Upper Arm Injuries

To care for a serious upper arm injury, immobilize the upper arm, from the shoulder to the elbow. This can be done in the same way as for shoulder injuries. Control any external bleeding with direct pressure. Place the arm in a sling and bind it to the chest with cravats. You

can use a short splint, if one is available, to give more support to the upper arm (Figure 12–26). Apply cold in the best way possible. Always check for circulation and sensation in the hand and fingers before and after immobilizing the injured area.

Elbow Injuries

Like other joints, the elbow can be sprained, fractured, or dislocated. Injuries to the elbow can cause permanent disability since all the nerves and blood vessels to the forearm and hand go through the elbow. Therefore, take elbow injuries seriously. Injuries to a joint such as the elbow can be made worse by movement.

Care for Elbow Injuries

If the injured person says that she cannot move the elbow, do not try to move it. Control any external bleeding with direct pressure and a pressure bandage using a figure-eight pattern (Figure 12–27). Check for circulation and sensation. Support the arm and immobilize it from the shoulder to the wrist.

Immobilize the elbow in the position in which you find it. Place the arm in a sling and secure it to the chest, as shown in Figure 12–25, a-c. If this is not possible, immobilize the elbow with a splint and two cravats. If the elbow is bent, apply the splint diagonally across the underside of the arm (Figure 12–28, a). The splint should extend beyond both the upper arm and the wrist. If the elbow is straight, apply the splint along the arm. Secure the splint at the wrist and upper arm with cravats or roller bandages (Figure 12–28, b). Recheck for circulation and sensation. Obtain more advanced

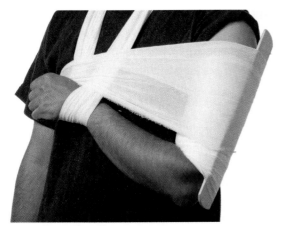

Figure 12–26 A short splint can provide additional support for an injury to the upper arm.

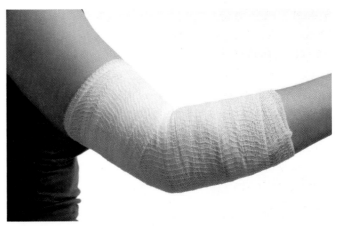

Figure 12–27 Use a figure-eight pattern to apply a pressure bandage to the elbow.

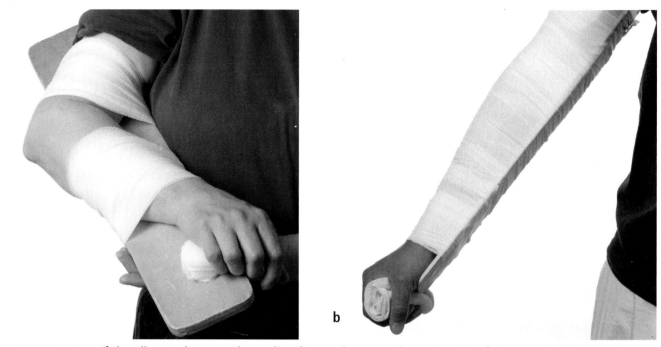

a   b

Figure 12–28, a-b a, if the elbow is bent, apply a splint diagonally across the underside of the arm; **b**, if the arm is straight, apply a splint along the underside of the arm.

medical care. Apply ice or a cold pack and take steps to care for shock. Provide ongoing survey and care.

Forearm, Wrist, and Hand Injuries

The forearm is the upper extremity from the elbow to the wrist. Fractures of the two forearm bones, the radius and ulna, are most common in children and older adults. If a person falls on the palmar surface of an outstretched arm, both bones of the lower arm may break, but not always in the same place. With forearm fractures, the arm may look S-shaped (Figure 12–29). Because the radial artery and nerve are near these bones, a fracture may cause severe bleeding or a loss of movement in the wrist and hand. The wrist is also a common site of sprains.

Because the hands are used in so many daily activities, they are very susceptible to injury. Most injuries to the hands and fingers involve only minor soft tissue damage. However, a serious injury may damage nerves, blood vessels, and bones. Home, recreational, and industrial mishaps often produce lacerations, avulsions, burns, and fractures of the hands. Because the hand structures are delicate, deep lacerations can cause permanently disabling injuries.

Care for Forearm, Wrist, and Hand Injuries

Begin by controlling any external bleeding with direct pressure. To bandage the hand, apply a pressure bandage using a figure-eight pattern (Figure 12–30). Check for circulation and sensation and then care for the injured forearm, wrist, or hand by immobilizing the injured part. When using a rigid splint, support the injured part by placing a splint underneath the forearm. Extend the splint beyond both the hand and elbow.

Figure 12–29 Fractures of both bones of the forearm may lead to an S-shaped deformity.

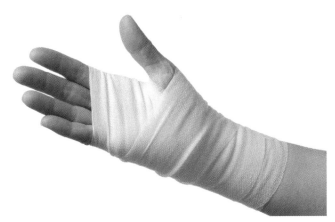

Figure 12–30 A pressure bandage for the palm of the hand.

Figure 12–31 If the forearm is fractured, place a splint under the forearm and secure it.

a

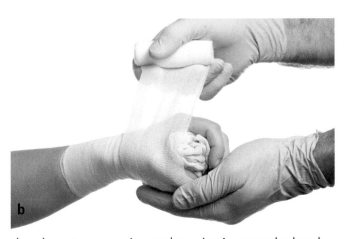

b

Figure 12–32, a-b A roll of gauze can be used to immobilize a hand: **a**, start wrapping at the wrist; **b**, cover the hand with the gauze.

Place a roll of gauze or a similar object in the palm to keep the palm and fingers in a normal position. Then secure the splint with cravats or roller gauze (Figure 12–31). Recheck circulation and sensation. Then put the arm in a sling and secure it to the chest.

You can immobilize injured hands and fingers using a soft splint made of a roll of gauze or rolled up cloth and bandages (Figure 12–32, a-b). You can splint an injured finger to an adjacent finger with tape (Figure 12–33). Do not attempt to put displaced finger or thumb bones back into place. Always apply ice or a cold pack to forearm, wrist, and hand injuries; elevate the injured area; and seek medical attention.

LOWER EXTREMITY INJURIES

Injuries to the leg, the entire lower extremity, can involve both soft tissue and musculoskeletal damage.

The major bones of the thigh and lower leg are large and strong enough to carry the body's weight. Bones of the leg include the femur, patella, tibia, and fibula, as well as the tarsals, metatarsals, and phalanges. Because

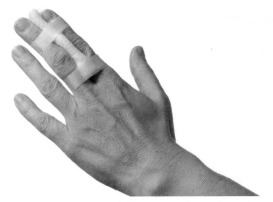

Figure 12–33 An injured finger can be splinted to an adjacent finger.

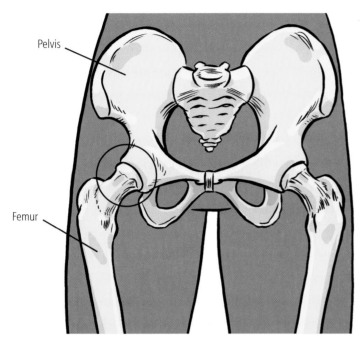

Figure 12–34 The upper end of the femur meets the pelvis at the hip joint.

of the size and strength of the bones in the thigh and lower leg, a significant amount of force is required to cause a fracture.

The femoral artery is the major supplier of blood to the legs and feet. If it is damaged, which may happen with a fracture of the femur, the blood loss can be life-threatening. If there is a very weak pulse or no pulse at all below the injury, this is a sign of damage to the femoral artery.

Serious injury to the lower extremities can result in their inability to bear weight. Since the injured person may be unable to walk, you should obtain more advanced medical care.

Thigh and Lower Leg Injuries

The femur is the largest bone in the body. Because it bears most of the weight of the body, it is most important in walking and running. Thigh injuries range from bruises and torn muscles to severe injuries such as fractures. The upper end of the femur meets the pelvis at the hip joint (Figure 12–34). Most femur fractures involve the upper end of the bone. Even though the hip joint itself is not involved, such injuries are often called hip fractures.

A fracture of the femur usually produces a characteristic deformity. When the fracture occurs, the thigh muscles contract. Because the thigh muscles are so strong, they pull the broken bone ends together, causing them to overlap. This may cause the injured leg to be noticeably shorter than the other leg. The injured leg may also be turned outward (Figure 12–35). Other signs and symptoms of a fractured femur may include severe pain and swelling and the inability to move the leg.

A fracture in the lower leg may involve one or both bones. Often both are fractured simultaneously. However, a blow to the outside of the lower leg can cause an isolated fracture of the fibula. Because these two bones lie just beneath the skin, open fractures are common. Lower leg fractures may cause a severe deformity in which the lower leg is bent at an unusual angle (angulated). These injuries are painful and result in an inability to move the leg. However, fractures of the fibula, and some very small fractures of the tibia, may not cause any deformity, and the person may be able to continue to use the leg.

Care for Thigh and Lower Leg Injuries

Initial care for the person with a serious injury to the thigh or lower leg is to stop any external bleeding, immobilize the injured area, and help the person rest in the most comfortable position (Figure 12–36). Obtain more advanced medical care immediately. They are much better equipped to care for and transport a person with a serious leg injury. Consider that the ground can adequately immobilize the legs, if the surface is relatively flat and firm, until you are able to obtain more advanced medical care.

However, there may be situations, such as moving the person, in which you will need to splint an injured leg. Securing the injured leg to the uninjured leg with several wide cravats is one simple method. If available, place a pillow or rolled blanket between the legs and bind the legs together in several places above and below the site of the injury (Figure 12–37). If rigid splints are available, apply one long splint to the outside of the injured leg, extending above the hip and beyond the foot. Place a shorter padded splint to the inside of the leg, also extending beyond the foot. Secure the splints to the leg with cravats (Figure 12–38). Other commercial splints,

Figure 12–35 A fractured femur often produces a characteristic deformity. The injured leg is shorter than the uninjured leg and may be turned outward.

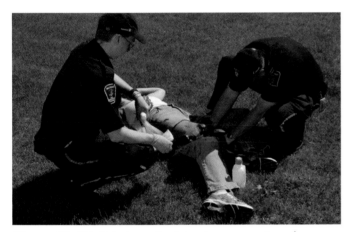

Figure 12–36 It is important to stop any external bleeding and help the person rest in the most comfortable position.

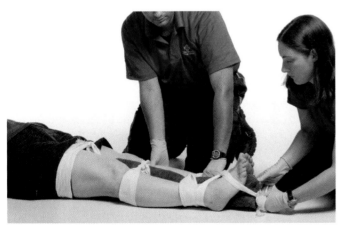

Figure 12–37 To splint an injured leg, secure the injured leg to the uninjured leg with cravats. A pillow or rolled blanket can be placed between the legs.

such as air splints or vacuum splints, can also be used if available. Regardless of the type of splint applied, always check and recheck the circulation and sensation of the foot. Apply ice or a cold pack to reduce pain.

A fractured femur can injure the femoral artery, and serious bleeding can result. The likelihood of shock is great. Therefore, take steps to minimize shock. Keep the person lying down and try to keep her calm. Maintain normal body temperature, administer oxygen if it is available, and obtain more advanced medical care. Provide ongoing survey and care.

Some fractures of the femur may require traction splinting. Traction helps prevent broken bone ends from causing further injury and helps reduce pain and minimize shock. However, not all responders are trained to use traction splints. If you are not trained or if you need assistance, immobilize the injured leg in the best way possible and provide ongoing survey and care until you can obtain advanced medical care. Figure 12–39, a-b, shows two types of traction splints.

Knee Injuries

The knee joint is very vulnerable to injury. The knee includes the lower end of the femur, the upper ends of the tibia and fibula, and the patella. The kneecap is a bone that moves on the lower front surface of the thigh bone. Knee injuries range from cuts and bruises to sprains, fractures, and dislocations. Deep lacerations in the area of the knee can later cause severe joint

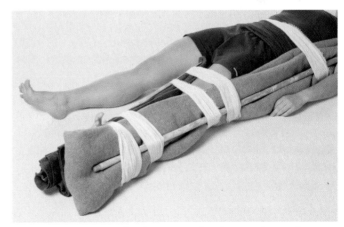

Figure 12–38 Rigid splints can also be used to splint an injured leg.

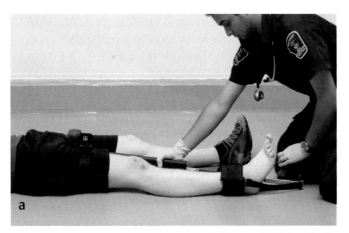
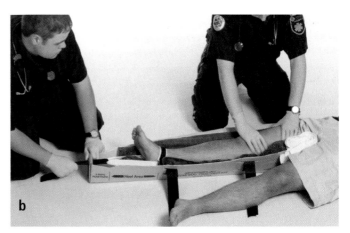

Figure 12–39, a-b Two types of traction splints.

infections. Sprains, fractures, and dislocations of the knee are common in athletic activities that involve quick movements or exert unusual force on the knee.

The most agile of joints, the knee is also the most vulnerable. It joins the two longest bones of the body. Four ligaments attach to the bones and hold the knee together. Two cartilage discs serve to increase joint stability, facilitate joint lubrication, and spread out the weight-bearing forces. The cartilage can be torn due to a torsion injury. Repeated and excessive shocks to the knee can also splinter the cartilage pads and stretch or fray ligaments.

The kneecap is unprotected in that it lies directly beneath the skin. This part of the knee is very vulnerable to bruises and lacerations, as well as dislocations. Violent forces

to the front of the knee, such as those caused by hitting the dashboard of a motor vehicle or by falling and landing on bent knees, can fracture the kneecap.

Care for Knee Injuries

To care for an injured knee, first control any external bleeding. Apply a pressure bandage using a figure-eight pattern (Figure 12–40). If the knee is bent and cannot be straightened without pain, support it in the bent position (Figure 12–41). If the knee is straight or can be straightened without pain, splint the leg as you would an injury of the thigh or lower leg or apply a long rigid splint to the leg. Other commercial splints can also be used if available. Apply ice or a cold pack. Help the person rest in a comfortable position. Obtain more advanced medical care. Provide ongoing survey and care.

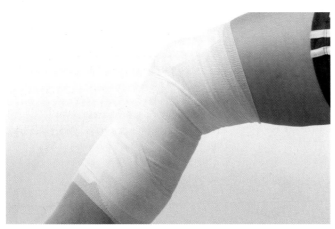

Figure 12–40 Use a figure-eight pattern to apply a pressure bandage to a knee.

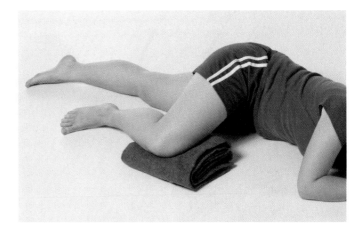

Figure 12–41 Support a knee injury in the bent position if the person cannot straighten the knee.

Arthroscopy

In 1994, *Sports Illustrated* magazine marked its 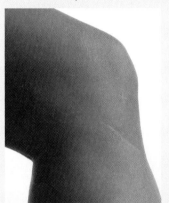 40th anniversary by selecting the 40 people who "most significantly altered or elevated the world of sports in the last four decades." One of those honoured was Canadian doctor Robert W. Jackson, an athlete in his own right but selected for this honour because he extended the careers of numerous professional athletes through a process known as arthroscopic surgery.

The train-track scars that once criss-crossed the injured knees of many athletes have almost disappeared. Both the scars and the trauma of knee surgery have been diminished with the advent of arthroscopy.

The recovery after arthroscopy is remarkable considering that about 20 years ago knee surgery meant a five-day hospital stay, a cast, and months of rehabilitation. With arthroscopic surgery, many athletes can have day surgery in a hospital or clinic setting and begin athletic therapy or physiotherapy within days of the procedure.

The arthroscope, a thin, flexible fibre-optic scope, allows physicians to perform delicate joint surgery without cutting muscles and ligaments and without lifting the kneecap to get to the injured area. After injecting a saline solution to distend the knee joint, the surgeon inserts the arthroscope through small puncture wounds into the space of the knee joint. By projecting magnified images inside the knee onto a screen, the arthroscope allows orthopedic surgeons to use microsurgical instruments to smooth arthritic surfaces, remove chipped bones and cartilage, and sew up torn ligaments.

Thousands of people undergo arthroscopic surgery each year. Arthroscopes, some less than 1.7 millimetres in diameter, are being used to repair shoulders, ankles, wrists, and even jaws. Not all joint problems can be repaired with arthroscopy, but most surgeons would agree that advances in arthroscopy have had a profound impact on the lives of people who might otherwise be incapacitated.

Ankle and Foot Injuries

Ankle and foot injuries are commonly caused by twisting forces. Injuries range from minor sprains with little swelling and pain that heal with a few days' rest to fractures and dislocations. As with other joint injuries, you cannot always distinguish between minor and severe injuries. You should initially care for all ankle and foot injuries as if they are serious. As with other lower extremity injuries, if the ankle or foot is painful to move, if it cannot bear weight, or if the foot or ankle is swollen, a physician should evaluate the injury. Foot injuries may also involve the toes. Although these injuries are painful, they are rarely serious.

Fractures of the feet and ankles can occur when a person forcefully lands on the heel. With any great force, such as falling from a height and landing on the feet, fractures are possible. The force of the impact may also be transmitted up the legs. This can result in an injury elsewhere in the body, such as the thigh, pelvis, or spine.

Care for Ankle and Foot Injuries

Care for ankle and foot injuries by controlling external bleeding and immobilizing the ankle and foot in the best way possible. Some commercial splints are specifically designed for ankle and foot injuries. Secure the splint to the injured area with two or three cravats or a roller bandage. Once it is splinted, elevate the injured ankle or foot to help reduce the swelling. Apply ice or a cold pack. Suspect that anyone who has fallen or jumped from a height may have additional injuries. Obtain more advanced medical care. Keep the person from moving until this care has been obtained. Provide ongoing survey and care.

SUMMARY

Injuries are a leading health problem in Canada. When the body experiences violent forces, many kinds of injuries can occur. Injuries may affect soft tissues, nerves, muscles, bones, ligaments, and tendons. These injuries can have permanent, disabling effects on the body and can even be life-threatening.

The musculoskeletal system is a complex group of structures that provide protection, support, and movement for the body. The musculoskeletal system has four main structures: bones, muscles, tendons, and ligaments. Sometimes it is difficult to tell whether an injury is a fracture, dislocation, sprain, or strain. Since you cannot be sure which injury someone might have, always care for the injury as if it were serious. If you're awaiting more advanced medical care, do not move the person. Control any bleeding first and take steps to minimize shock. Provide ongoing survey and care. If you are going to transport the person to a medical facility, be sure to first immobilize the injury before moving her.

You can care for serious musculoskeletal and soft tissue injuries to the extremities by focussing on minimizing pain, shock, and further damage to the injured area. You can do this by:

- Managing airway or breathing problems
- Controlling any external bleeding
- Checking circulation and sensation below the site of injury before and after immobilizing
- Immobilizing the injured area of the body
- Applying ice or a cold pack to the injured area
- Limiting movement of or by the injured person
- Calming and reassuring the person
- Maintaining normal body temperature
- Administering oxygen
- Obtaining more advanced medical care
- Providing ongoing survey and care

As you examine the biker, you find that her injured leg appears to be noticeably shorter than her other leg and her pulse is weak. What do you do?

Skills Summary

Applying a Splint to an Ankle

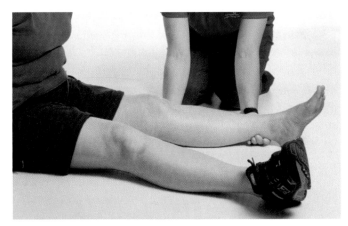

1. Support injured area.

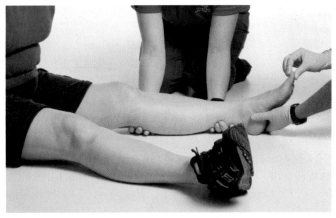

2. Check circulation and sensation distal to the injury.

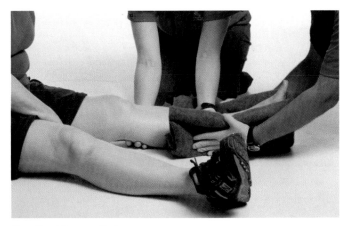

3. Position splint.

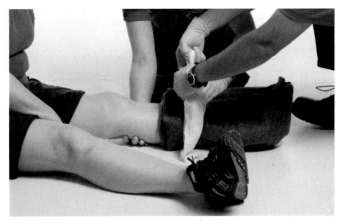

4. Position and tie cravats.

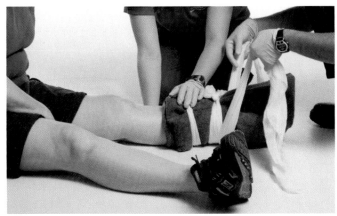

5. Complete securing splint.

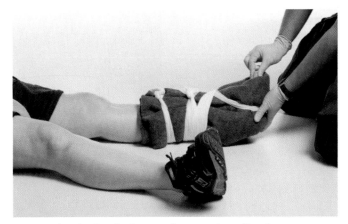

6. Recheck circulation and sensation distal to the injury.

Skills Summary

Applying a Splint to a Lower Arm

1. Support injured area. Check circulation and sensation distal to the injury.

2. Position splint.

3. Begin securing splint.

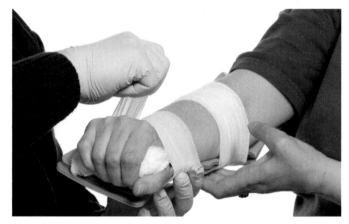

4. Complete securing splint.

5. Recheck circulation and sensation distal to the injury.

Skills Summary

Applying a Splint to a Leg

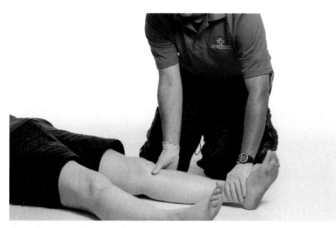

1. Support injured area.

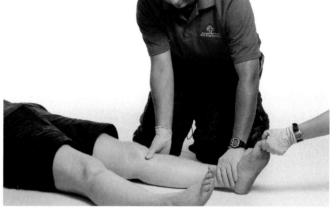

2. Check circulation and sensation distal to the injury.

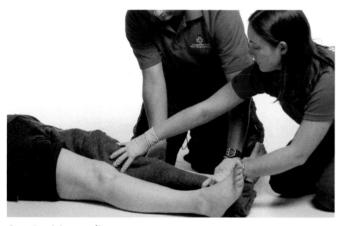

3. Position splint.

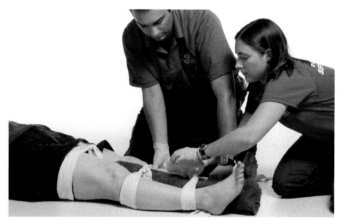

4. Position and tie cravats.

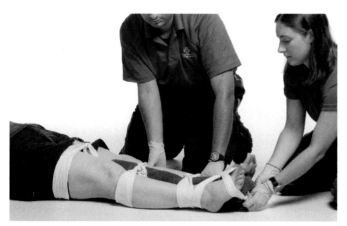

5. Complete securing splint.

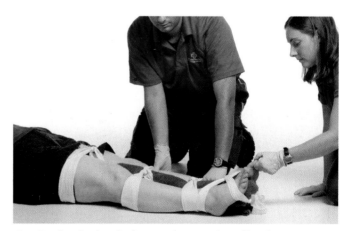

6. Recheck circulation and sensation distal to the injury.

Skills Summary

Applying a Traction Splint

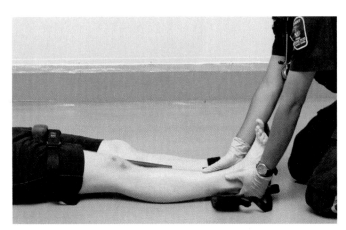

1. Support injured area.

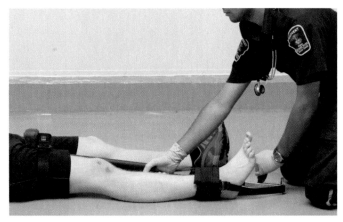

2. Secure ankle strap.

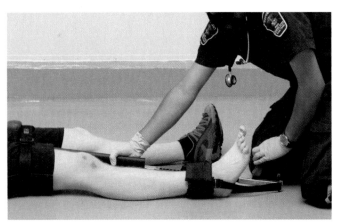

3. Apply traction.

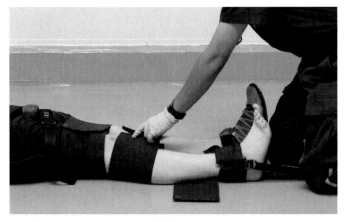

4. Secure upper and middle straps.

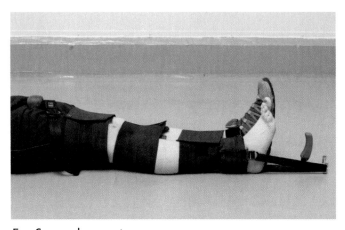

5. Secure lower strap.

Head and Spine Injuries

You respond to an industrial incident involving someone who has fallen from a height of approximately three metres. You arrive to find a man lying on the ground. He is unconscious. Looking at the scene, it is difficult to determine exactly what has happened and what his injuries might be. What do you do?

INTRODUCTION

It's summer vacation at the lake. A group of teenage boys are swimming around in the lake when one of them says he's going to dive off the edge of a cliff about 12 metres up. The water is normally a safe depth, about 5 metres deep, but it's been a drier season than usual and the lake is only about 3½ metres deep. He dives straight down and strikes his head on the sandy bottom. His friends rush to pull him out and find him unconscious, having broken his neck.

Each year, tens of thousands of Canadians suffer a head or spine injury serious enough to require medical care. Most of these people are males between the ages of 15 and 30. Motor vehicle collisions account for about half of all head and spine injuries. Other causes include falls, sports and recreational activities, and violent acts such as assault.

Besides those who die each year from head and spine injury, thousands become permanently disabled. Today there are many thousands of people in Canada permanently disabled from head or spine injuries. These survivors have a wide range of physical and cognitive impairments, including paralysis, behavioural disorders, and speech and memory problems.

Fortunately, prompt, appropriate care can help minimize the damage from most head and spine injuries. In this chapter, you will learn how to recognize when a head or spine injury may be serious. You will also learn how to provide the appropriate care to minimize injuries to the head and spine.

RECOGNIZING SERIOUS HEAD AND SPINE INJURIES

Injuries to the head and spine can damage both bone and soft tissue, including brain tissue and the spinal cord. It is usually difficult to determine the extent of damage in head and spine injuries. In most cases, the only way to assess the damage is by having an X-ray or scan done at a hospital. Since you have no way of knowing exactly how severe an injury is, always provide initial care as if the injury is serious. Remember your priorities of care to treat a spinal injury before minor bleeding. There is a significant difference between a head injury and an injury to the head. An injury to the head is often a superficial injury, for example, a cut to the face or scalp, whereas a head injury often involves brain trauma. Focus on treating the most serious injuries during the initial assessment.

The Brain

Injuries to the head can affect the brain. Blood from a ruptured vessel in the brain can accumulate in the skull (Figure 13–1). Because there is very little empty space in the skull, bleeding can build up pressure that can cause further damage to brain tissue.

Bleeding in the skull can occur rapidly or slowly over a period of days. This bleeding will affect the brain, causing changes in consciousness. An altered level of consciousness is often the first and most important sign of a serious head injury.

Bleeding in the skull is divided into three general types:

Epidural Hematoma

An epidural hematoma is an arterial bleed occurring between the skull and dura mater, usually resulting from a low-velocity blow (Figure 13–2). The signs and symptoms appear quickly, and the person usually presents with a brief loss of consciousness, then regained consciousness, and then a rapid decline in consciousness. As this decline occurs, pupils may become sluggish, dilated, or non-reactive. Motor function may also be impaired on one side of the body (the side opposite the injury).

Subdural Hematoma

A subdural hematoma is venous bleeding in the subdural space, resulting from a violent blow to the head (Figure 13–3). Neurological deficits may present themselves immediately after the blow or days later. The signs and symptoms may not appear immediately after the impact, although other signs of trauma can be seen. The signs and symptoms will appear as the pressure resulting from the bleed increases. Headaches, visual disturbances, personality changes, difficulty speaking, and deficits in motor function are all possible symptoms of someone with this type of bleeding.

Intracerebral Hematoma

An intracerebral hematoma is caused by damage to the blood vessels in the brain itself due to either blunt or penetrating trauma. There is often more than one

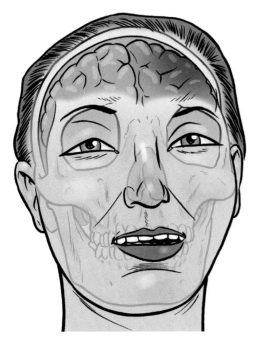

Figure 13–1 Blood from a ruptured vessel in the brain can accumulate in the skull.

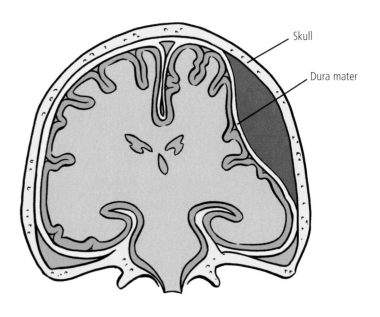

Figure 13–2 An epidural hematoma is an arterial bleed between the skull and the dura mater.

contusion, and they can enlarge over time. Specific neurological findings depend on the location and size of the hematoma.

The Spine

The spine is a strong, flexible column that supports the head and the trunk and encases and protects the spinal cord. The spinal column, which extends from the base of the skull to the tip of the tailbone, consists of small bones, vertebrae, with circular openings. The vertebrae are separated from each other by cushions of cartilage called discs (Figure 13–4, a). This cartilage, an elastic tissue, acts as a shock absorber when a person is walking, running, or jumping. The spinal cord, a bundle of nerves extending from the base of the skull to the lower back, runs through the hollow part of the vertebrae. Nerve branches extend to various parts of the body through openings on the sides of the vertebrae.

The spine is divided into five regions: the cervical or neck region, the thoracic or mid-back region, the lumbar or lower back region, the sacrum, and the coccyx, the small triangular bone at the lower end of the spinal column. Injuries to the spinal column include fractures and dislocations of the vertebrae, sprained ligaments, and compression or displacement of the discs between the vertebrae.

Injuries to the spine can fracture the vertebrae and sprain the ligaments. These injuries usually heal without problems. With severe injuries, however, the vertebrae may shift and compress or sever the spinal cord. This can cause temporary or permanent paralysis, even death. The extent of the paralysis depends on which area of the spinal cord is damaged (Figure 13–4, b).

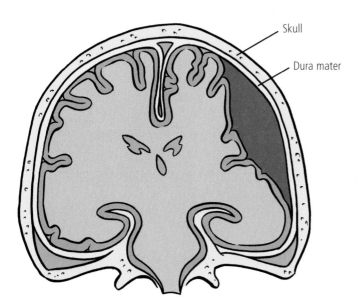

Figure 13–3 A subdural hematoma is a venous bleed in the subdural space.

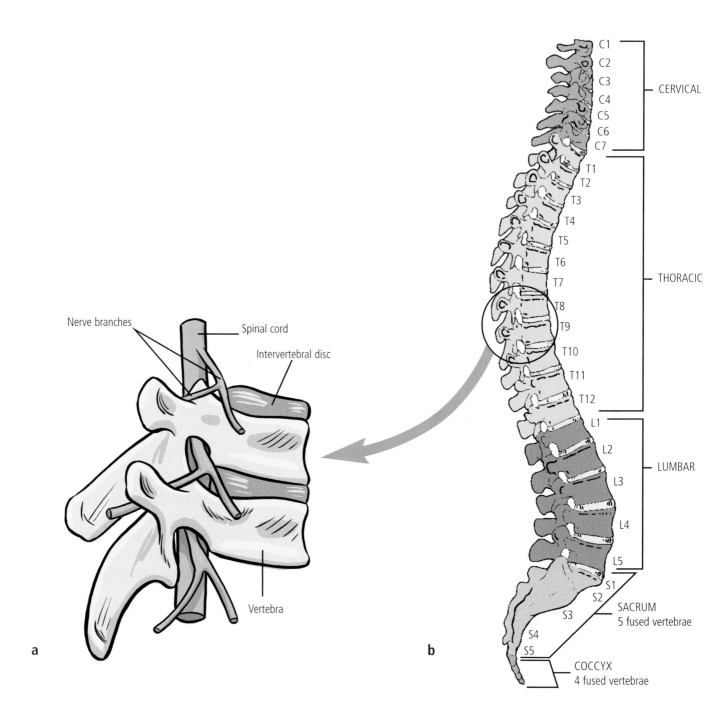

Figure 13–4, a-b **a**, vertebrae are separated by pads of cartilage called invertebral discs; **b**, the spine is divided into 5 regions. Injury to regions of the spine can cause paralysis of specific body areas.

Mechanism of Injury

Consider the mechanism of injury to help you determine whether someone has suffered a head or spine injury (Figure 13–5). Survey the scene and think about the forces involved in the injury. Strong forces are likely to cause severe injury to the head and spine. For example, a driver whose head breaks a car windshield in a crash may have a serious head or spine injury. A diver who hits his head on the bottom of a swimming pool may also have a serious head or spine injury. Evaluate the scene for clues as to whether a serious head or spine injury has occurred.

You should consider the possibility of a head or spine injury in a number of situations. These include:

- Any motor vehicle crash
- Any ejection from a motor vehicle
- A fall from a height greater than the individual's height
- Any injury in which the person's helmet is broken
- Any injury involving a severe blunt force to the head or trunk
- Any injury, such as a gunshot wound, that penetrates the head or trunk
- Any diving mishap
- Unconsciousness of unknown cause
- Any incident involving a lightning strike

Signs and symptoms that indicate a head or spine injury may be obvious right away or may develop later (Table 13-1). These signs and symptoms alone do not always suggest a head or spine injury, but they may when combined with the cause of the injury. Regardless of the situation, always obtain more advanced medical care when you suspect a head or spine injury.

CARE FOR SERIOUS HEAD AND SPINE INJURIES

Head and spine injuries can become life-threatening emergencies. A serious injury can cause someone to stop breathing. Care for serious head and spine injuries also involves supporting the respiratory, circulatory, and nervous systems. Provide the following care while waiting to obtain more advanced medical care:

TABLE 13-1 SIGNS AND SYMPTOMS OF HEAD AND SPINE INJURIES

- Changes in the level of consciousness
- Severe pain or pressure in the head or spine
- Swelling
- Tingling or loss of sensation in the extremities (arms and legs)
- Partial or complete loss of movement of any body part
- Unusual bumps or depressions on the head or spine
- Blood or other fluids draining from the ears, nose, mouth, or open wounds
- Profuse external bleeding of the head or spine
- Irregular breathing
- Open wounds to the scalp
- Seizures
- Sudden impaired breathing or vision
- Unusual or unequal pupil size
- Nausea or vomiting
- Persistent headache
- Loss of balance
- Incontinence
- Specific changes in blood pressure and pulse
- Bruising of the head, especially around the eyes ("raccoon eyes") or behind the ears ("Battle's sign")

- Minimize movement of the head and spine
- Maintain an open airway
- Control any external bleeding
- Provide ongoing survey and care
- Administer oxygen if available

Chapter 13

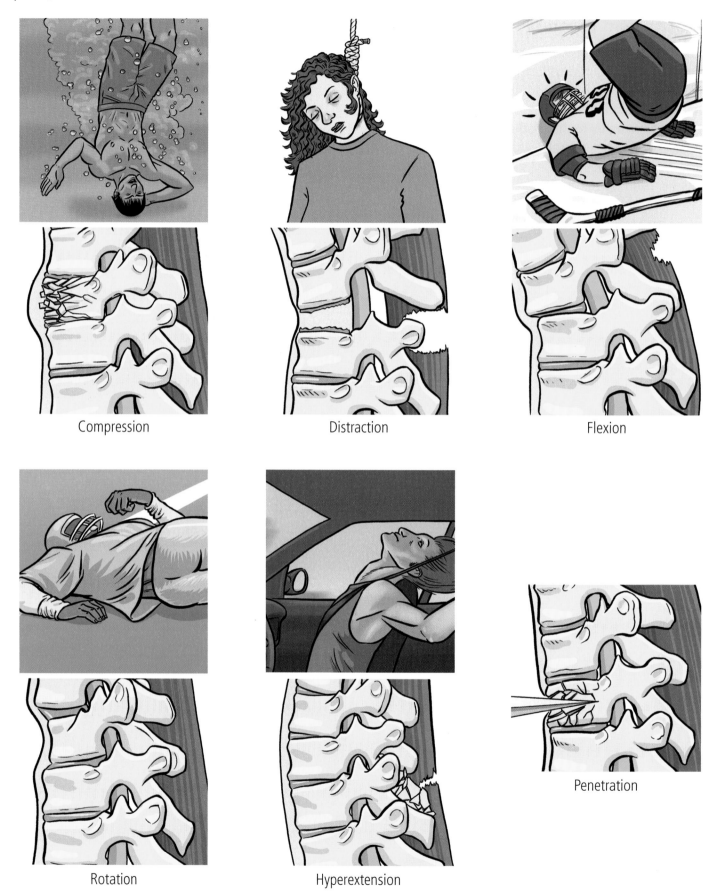

Compression Distraction Flexion

Rotation Hyperextension Penetration

Figure 13–5 The mechanism of injury may help you to determine if the person has suffered a head or spine injury.

224 Emergency Care Manual

Minimize Movement

Caring for a head or spine injury is similar to caring for any other serious soft tissue or musculoskeletal injury. Immobilize the injured area and control any bleeding. Because movement of an injured head or spine can damage the spinal cord irreversibly, keep the person as still as possible until you can obtain more advanced care. To minimize movement of the head and neck, use a technique called in-line stabilization:

1. Place your hands on both sides of the person's head.

2. Apply gentle traction to the head away from the body.

3. Slowly rotate the head until the chin is in line with the middle of the chest.

4. Maintain manual stabilization and continue care.

The head in this anatomically correct, neutral position helps prevent further damage to the spinal column (Figure 13–6, a-b). If a second responder is available, that person can give care for any other conditions while you keep the head and neck stable. There are, however, some circumstances in which you would not move the person's head in line with the body. These include:

• When the person's head is severely angled to one side

• When the person complains of pain, pressure, or muscle spasms in the neck when you begin to align the head with the body

• When the responder feels resistance when attempting to move the head in line with the body

In these circumstances, support the person's head in the position in which you found it, except when the person's airway cannot be maintained open in that position.

If the head is manually stabilized in anatomical position, a rigid cervical collar should be applied (Figure 13–7, a-b). This collar helps minimize movement of the head and neck and keeps the head in line with the body. It is important to note that these devices reduce movement and some range of motion but do not by

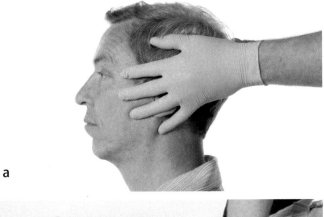

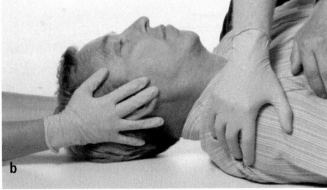

Figure 13–6, a-b Support the person's head in line with the body using in-line stabilization.

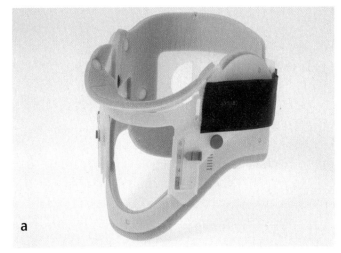

Figure 13–7, a-b **a**, an adjustable rigid cervical collar; **b**, non-adjustable rigid cervical collars.

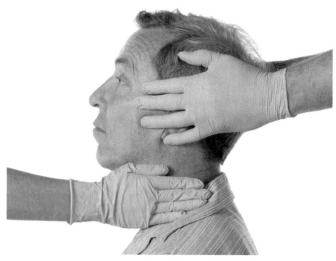

Figure 13–8 To select the correct size cervical collar, measure the distance from the top of the shoulders to the bottom of the chin.

themselves provide adequate immobilization of the spine. The collar must always be used in conjunction with manual in-line stabilization or a mechanical immobilization device.

Applying a cervical collar requires two responders. While one responder maintains in-line stabilization, another carefully applies an appropriately sized cervical collar. An appropriately sized collar is one that fits securely, with the person's chin resting in the proper position and the head maintained in line with the body. To appropriately size a collar, imagine a line across the top of the shoulders and a second one at the bottom on the chin. Measure the distance between the two lines using your fingers (Figure 13–8). Some cervical collars come with specific manufacturer's instructions for proper sizing.

Immobilize the Injured Person

Once the cervical collar has been applied and in-line stabilization maintained, the person's entire body should be immobilized. When a head or spinal injury is suspected, spinal immobilization should be considered to move a person out of a dangerous place, to rescue them, or to transport them. This can be done using the following equipment:

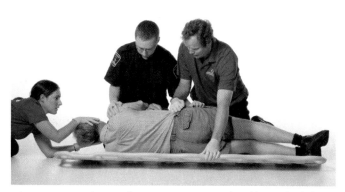

Figure 13–9 Log-roll a person onto a backboard while keeping the spine in as straight a line as possible.

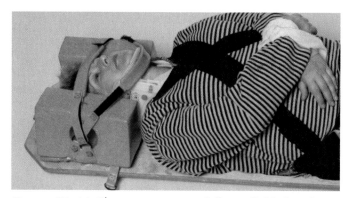

Figure 13–11 There are commercially available head immobilization devices.

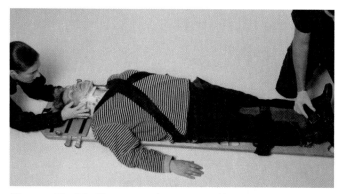

Figure 13–10 Use several straps and/or cravats to secure the person to the backboard.

Figure 13–12 Attaching the head straps on a Kendrick Extrication Device (K.E.D.®).

- Rigid splint, such as a backboard
- Large towel or blanket
- Straps or triangular bandage(s) folded into a cravat(s)

Local protocol may dictate what equipment is to be used.

If you do not have a backboard available, support the person in the position in which you found him until you can obtain more advanced medical care.

Once the cervical collar is in place, the person is positioned on a backboard. This is done by "log-rolling" the person onto the board. This technique keeps the head in line with the body. It requires a minimum of two responders: one to maintain in-line stabilization and another to position the backboard and roll the person's body. However, it is highly preferable to have three responders available to perform this technique. With three responders, one can provide in-line stabilization and the second and third can log-roll the person and position the backboard (Figure 13–9). When the person is in a position in which the back is visible, check the back quickly for signs of trauma such as bleeding, deformity, discolouration, or muscle spasms.

Before strapping the person to the backboard, ensure that he is in the correct position. If the person is too low, too high, or too far to one side of the board, you must move him.

Once the person is on the board properly, use several straps or cravats to secure her body to the backboard (Figure 13–10). There are several different configurations you can use to strap the person onto the board. A common one is to secure the chest by criss-crossing the straps. Regardless of which method is used, the straps should be snug, but not so tight as to restrict movement of the chest during breathing. With the remaining straps, secure the person's hips, thighs, and legs. If necessary, secure the hands in front of the body.

Once the person's body is secured to the backboard, secure his head. If the person's head does not appear to be resting in line with the body, you may need to place a small amount of padding, such as a small folded towel, to support the head. Normally, approximately 2.5 cm (1 in) of padding is all that is needed to keep the head in line with the body while at the same time providing comfort for the person. Next, place a folded or

Babies and children have large heads and may require padding under the body when being put on a board. Collars and other equipment specifically designed for children should be used when possible.

rolled blanket in a horseshoe shape around the person's head and neck. Use a cravat or tape to secure the forehead.

You may have a commercially made head immobilization device available (Figure 13–11). Many of these use Velcro® straps to secure the head. You should follow the manufacturer's directions when using these devices.

Use of an Upper Body Motion Restriction Device

You might be called upon to assist more advanced medical personnel to immobilize someone with an upper body motion restriction device, such as a Kendrick Extrication Device (K.E.D.®) (Figure 13–12). The steps are as follows:

1. After manual in-line stabilization and the application of a rigid cervical collar, the K.E.D.® or short backboard device can be placed behind the person. If using a K.E.D.®, it should be positioned snugly beneath the person's armpits to prevent it from moving up the torso.

2. The middle torso is immobilized by fastening the middle and lower chest straps. The straps should be snug so that fingers cannot be slipped beneath the straps.

3. When using a K.E.D.®, each groin strap is positioned and fastened separately, forming a loop. These straps prevent the device from moving up and the lower end from moving laterally.

4. The head is padded and secured to the device.

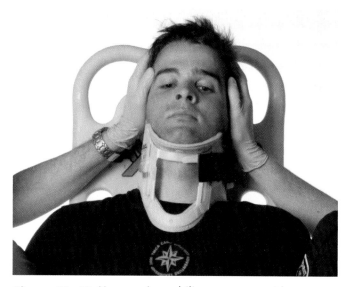

Figure 13–13 You can immobilize a person with a suspected spinal injury while they are standing.

5. The upper torso is then immobilized by securing the chest strap.

6. The person is carefully moved as a unit to a long backboard by rotating the person and K.E.D.® onto the board. The legs are held proximal to the knees and lifted during the transition.

7. The person is centred on the backboard, any groin straps are loosened, and the legs are slowly lowered to an in-line position.

8. The person is secured to the backboard, keeping the K.E.D.® in place.

If the person is standing and you suspect a spinal injury, you can immobilize him while standing. This technique takes at least two responders (Figure 13–13).

1. Have one responder apply a cervical collar while the other maintains manual in-line stabilization.

2. Place the long backboard behind the person. Check the placement of the board from in front of the person to ensure that it is aligned correctly.

3. With one responder on each side of the injured person, each should place his lower arm under the injured person's armpit and grasp the next highest handhold on the backboard. The responder's free hand should hold the injured person's elbows. If there is a third responder, that person is positioned behind the backboard with arms wrapped around

the board, maintaining manual in-line stabilization. If there are only two responders, the free hand of the responders on each side of the injured person can be used to hold the person's head in position.

4. Lower the person to the ground while holding the head stable.

5. After the person is completely immobilized and secured to the board, you can release manual in-line stabilization.

Rapid Extrication

In some cases, it may be necessary to move a person quickly using only manual in-line stabilization.

The circumstances in which this may be required are as follows:

• The scene is not safe.

• Life-saving care cannot be given due to the location or position of the person.

• It is necessary to move the person to gain access to another person with life-threatening emergencies.

A rapid extrication should be performed by at least two people in order to move a person to a sitting position to a long backboard. As with using a short backboard, ensure that the person's head is in a neutral position, apply a cervical collar, and use short, coordinated moves until the person can be moved and secured onto a backboard.

If the person must be removed quickly and there is no upper body motion restriction device available, you can do the following:

1. Responder 1 maintains manual in-line stabilization of the injured person's head.

2. Responder 2 places a cervical collar on the person.

3. Responder 2 places a blanket, which is pre-rolled, around the person, with the centre of the blanket placed at the anterior midline of the cervical collar.

4. Responder 2 wraps the ends of the blanket around the cervical collar and places them under the person's arms from the front.

5. Responder 2 turns the person using the ends of the blanket until the person's back is toward the door opening.

6. Responder 1 takes control of the blanket ends, which can be put under the person's shoulders, along with the motion of the upper body, while responder 2 takes control of the person's lower body.

If the situation requires immediate extrication due to dangers at the scene, just pull the person out of the situation, taking precautions to stabilize the head and spine in the best way possible.

Maintain an Open Airway

You do not always have to roll the person onto his back to check breathing. A cry of pain, regular chest movement, or the sound of breathing tells you the person is breathing. If the person is breathing, support him in the position in which you found him. If he begins to vomit, position him onto one side to keep the airway clear. Ask other responders to help move the person's body while you maintain in-line stabilization.

Monitor Vital Signs

After immobilizing the person, monitor the vital signs. Pay close attention to the person's level of consciousness and breathing. A serious head injury will often cause changes in consciousness. The person may give inappropriate responses when asked his name, the time, the place, or what happened or may speak incoherently. The person may be drowsy, appear to fall asleep, and then suddenly awaken or lose consciousness completely. Breathing may become rapid or irregular. Because injury to the head or spine can paralyze chest nerves and muscles, breathing can stop. If this happens, perform rescue breathing. People with serious head or spine injuries need supplemental oxygen. Administer oxygen if it is available.

Control External Bleeding

Some head and neck injuries include soft tissue damage. Because there are many blood vessels in the head and two major arteries—the carotid arteries—in the neck, the person with this type of injury can lose large amounts of blood quickly. If there is external bleeding, control it promptly. If applying a pressure dressing to the neck, be careful not to stop the carotid arteries from getting blood to the head.

Maintain Normal Body Temperature

A serious injury to the head or spine can disrupt the body's normal heating or cooling mechanism. When this happens, a person is more susceptible to shock. For example, a person suffering a serious head or spine injury while outside on a cold day will be more likely to suffer from hypothermia, a life-threatening cooling of the body. This is because the normal shivering response to rewarm the body may not work. It is always important to minimize shock by maintaining normal body temperature.

Special Situation—Removing a Helmet

There may be a time when you are responding to someone wearing a helmet, such as a motorcyclist or an athlete, who suffers a serious head and/or neck injury. Since most fitted helmets (e.g., football, motorcycle) fit snugly to the head, it is difficult to remove one without moving the head and neck. Hockey helmets, on the other hand, are usually easy to remove.

If the helmet has a face piece, such as a visor or mask, that interferes with normal breathing, maintaining an open airway, or performing rescue breathing, initially remove the mask or visor only. Usually, you can remove the face piece by unsnapping the visor or unscrewing the facemask snubbers (fasteners) on each side or, if unscrewing does not work, cutting the snubbers with anvil-type shears (pruner).

A helmet should be removed if it interferes with the care you are providing, such as stabilizing the head in-line with the body or performing rescue breathing. In these situations, two responders should carefully remove the helmet. To properly immobilize someone with a spinal injury, helmet removal is required. However, if you are not required to package and transport, then manual stabilization should be maintained until you obtain the next level of prehospital care. Helmet removal is a skill that should be practised. It is best to remove protective equipment on-site before packaging and transportation if two skilled personnel are present and the techniques can be performed in a controlled manner. This option is better than performing an emergency helmet removal with one responder in the back of a moving ambulance should the person's status change for the worse.

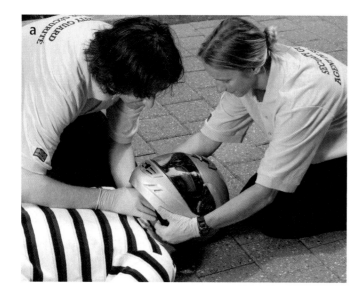

Figure 13–14, a-c To remove a helmet: **a**, one responder immobilizes the head by grasping the mandible and the base of the skull while the other responder spreads the sides of the helmet; **b**, the second responder slides the helmet off; and **c**, once the helmet is removed, the second responder applies in-line stabilization.

To remove a motorcycle helmet:

1. First remove the chin strap.

2. Next, as one responder supports the head by holding the jaw with one hand while the other hand supports the back of the head (occipital region), a second responder spreads the sides of the helmet to clear the ears (Figure 13–14, a).

3. While the first responder continues to support the head, the second responder slides the helmet off, causing as little motion as possible and watching as it clears the nose (Figure 13–14, b).

4. The responder who removed the helmet then replaces his or her hands on either side of the person's head and maintains in-line stabilization until immobilization is complete (Figure 13–14, c).

The procedure for a football helmet is similar; however, the sides of the helmet should not be overly spread (this may push the helmet up into the occipital region), and it is best to first remove the face mask (if time permits) as this facilitates helmet removal. Hockey helmets are fitted loosely and rarely provide adequate head and neck support. The responding team doing the transport can easily remove them prior to securing the person on a backboard.

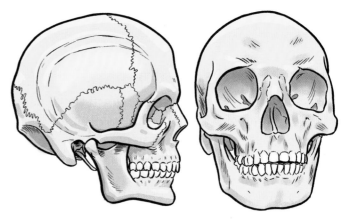

Figure 13–15 The head is easily injured because it lacks the padding of muscles and fat that are in other areas of the body.

Most sports teams should have personnel on hand who are familiar with and able to assist with equipment and extrication as required by the situation.

CARE FOR SPECIFIC HEAD AND FACIAL INJURIES

The head is easily injured because it lacks the padding of muscle and fat that are in other areas of the body. You can feel bone just beneath the surface of the skin over most of the head, including the chin, cheekbones, and scalp (Figure 13–15).

Skull Fracture

A skull fracture accompanied by a brain injury is very serious. The signs and symptoms include:

- Visible damage to the scalp

- Deformity of the skull or face

- Pain or swelling

- Fluid (clear or pinkish) coming from the nose, ears, mouth, or a head wound

- Unusual pupil size

- "Raccoon eyes" (bruising around the eyes)

- "Battle's signs" (behind-the-ear bruising)

With a skull fracture, it may be appropriate to take spinal precautions.

Injuries to the Brain

Brain damage can occur with an open or closed wound. The severity of the injury often depends on the mechanism of injury and the force involved. All head injuries should be considered serious. The signs and symptoms include:

- Changes in the level of consciousness

- Paralysis or flaccidity (limp, lacking tone) (usually on one side of the body)

- Unequal facial movements, disturbances in vision or pupils

- Ringing in the ears or disturbances in hearing

- Limb rigidity

- Loss of balance

- Pulse that becomes rapid and weak

- High blood pressure with slow pulse

- Breathing problems

- Vomiting

- Incontinence

When the brain sustains an acceleration (or moving) injury, there is usually damage at two points. The brain initially strikes the skull, called the "coup effect," and then there is a second point of damage when the brain strikes the skull on the opposite side, in what is called the "contre-coup effect."

Concussion

A concussion is a complex injury affecting the brain that usually does not result in permanent physical damage to the brain tissue. It can be caused by either a direct blow to the head, face, neck, or elsewhere, with an "impulse" force transmitted to the brain.

Concussions typically result in the rapid onset of short-lived symptoms such as memory loss, dizziness, balance problems, headache, or loss of consciousness. The person may say he "saw stars" or even "blacked out." You can even have a concussion without loss of consciousness.

The signs and symptoms include:

- Confusion

- Inability to recall what happened just before and after the injury

- Repetitive questioning

- Irritability, uncooperativeness, combativeness

- Inability to answer questions or follow commands

- Persistent vomiting

- Headache

- Balance problems

- Dizziness

- Nausea and/or vomiting

- Ringing in the ears

- Fatigue

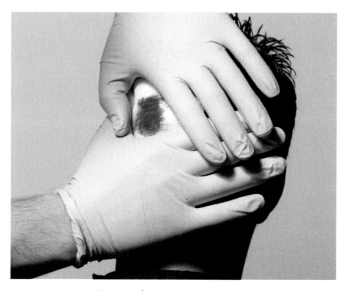

Figure 13–16 To avoid putting pressure on a deep scalp wound, apply pressure around the wound.

- Restlessness
- Seizures
- Brief loss of consciousness

In a sports situation, it is important that athletes showing any symptoms or signs of a concussion not be allowed to return to the current game or practise. The player should not be left alone and should be monitored. The person should be medically evaluated and follow a supervised return-to-play process that takes a minimum of a week to complete.[2] Anyone suspected of having a concussion should be examined by a physician.

Penetrating Wounds

If an object is impaled in the skull, leave it in place and stabilize it with bulky dressings. Dress the area around the wound with sterile gauze but allow blood to drain. Avoid putting direct pressure to a head injury that may involve a skull fracture.

Scalp Injury

Scalp bleeding can be minor or severe. The bleeding is usually easily controlled with direct pressure. Because the skull may be injured, be careful to press gently at first. If you feel a depression, a spongy area, or bone fragments, do not put direct pressure on the wound. Attempt to control bleeding with pressure on the area around the wound (Figure 13–16). Examine the injured area carefully because the person's hair may hide part of the wound. If you are unsure about the extent of a scalp injury, obtain more advanced medical care.

If the person has only an open wound, control the bleeding with direct pressure. Apply several dressings and hold them in place with your hand (Figure 13–17, a). Secure the dressings with a roller bandage (Figure 13–17, b).

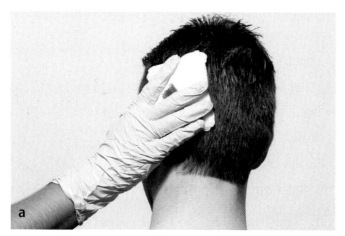
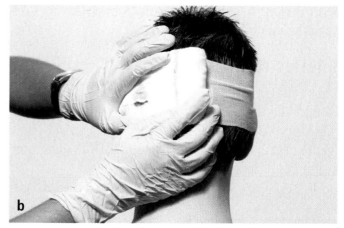

Figure 13–17, a-b a, apply pressure to control bleeding from a scalp wound by holding several dressings against the wound; **b**, secure the dressings with a bandage.

[2] Summary and Agreement Statement of the 2nd International Conference on Concussion in Sport, Prague, 2004, Clinical Journal of Sport Medicine, Vol 15, Number 2, March 2005.

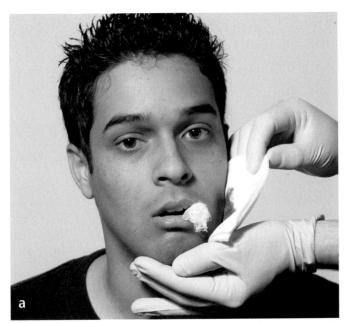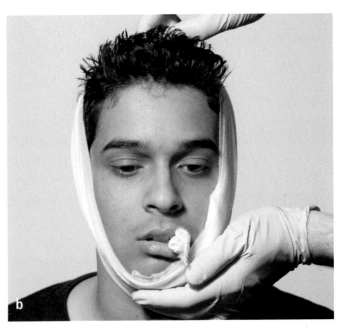

Figure 13–18, a-b a, apply pressure to control bleeding from a cheek wound by holding several dressings against the wound; **b**, secure the dressings with a bandage.

Cheek Injury

Injury to the cheek often involves soft tissue only. Control bleeding from the cheek in the same way as other soft tissue bleeding. Begin by examining both the outside and inside of the cheek. Bleeding from inside may result from a blow that caused the teeth to cut the inside of the cheek or from a laceration or puncture wound outside. To control bleeding, place several folded dressings inside the mouth, against the cheek. If possible, have the person hold them in place. If external bleeding is also present, place dressings on the outside of the cheek and apply direct pressure with your hand (Figure 13–18, a) or a pressure bandage (Figure 13–18, b).

An embedded object in the cheek cannot be easily stabilized, makes control of bleeding more difficult, and may become dislodged and obstruct the airway. You can remove the object by pulling it out the same way it entered. If doing this is difficult or is painful to the person, leave the object in place and stabilize it with bulky dressings and bandages.

If an object passes completely through the cheek and becomes embedded, you may have to remove it to control bleeding and keep the airway open. This circumstance is the only exception to the general rule of not removing embedded objects from the body.

If you remove the object, fold or roll several dressings and place them inside the mouth. Be sure not to obstruct the airway. Apply dressings to the outside of the cheek as well. The person may not be able to hold these in place, so you may have to hold them. Bleeding inside the cheek can cause the person to swallow blood. If the person swallows enough blood, nausea or vomiting could result, which would complicate the situation. When possible, place the person in a seated position, leaning forward slightly so that blood will not drain into the throat. As with any situation involving

Figure 13–19 To control a nosebleed, have the person lean forward while pinching the nostrils together.

serious bleeding or an embedded object, obtain more advanced medical care.

Nose Injury

Nose injuries are often caused by a blow from a blunt object. The result is often a nosebleed. In most cases, you can control bleeding by having the person sit with the head slightly forward while pinching the nostrils together (Figure 13–19). Other methods of controlling bleeding include applying an ice pack to the bridge of the nose or putting pressure on the upper lip just beneath the nose.

Once you have controlled the bleeding, tell the person to avoid rubbing, blowing, or picking the nose since this could restart the bleeding. Later, the person may apply a little petroleum jelly inside the nostril to help keep it moist.

If you think an object is in the nostril, look into the nostril. If you see the object and can easily grasp it with your fingers, then do so. However, do not probe the nostril with your finger. Doing so may push the object farther into the nose and cause bleeding or make it more difficult to remove later. If the object cannot be removed easily, the person should seek medical attention.

High blood pressure or changes in altitude can also cause nosebleeds. You should obtain more advanced medical care if the bleeding cannot be controlled within 10 to 15 minutes, it stops and then recurs, or the person says the bleeding is the result of high blood pressure. If the person loses consciousness, place him on his side to allow blood to drain from his nose.

Eye Injury

Although rarely life-threatening, eye injuries can be scary as the person can lose vision. Eyes can be injured in any manner. Cuts, impaled objects, and burns are among the ways eyes can be injured. Loss of vision; bruising; swelling; burning, tingling, or scratching sensations; and fluid coming from the eyes are all examples of indicators of eye injuries.

See Figure 13–20 for the anatomy of the eye. When you assess someone with an eye injury, you will need to obtain answers to a few questions: When did the injury occur? Were both eyes affected? What symptoms did the person first notice? Next, carefully examine each eye

separately and then together using a small penlight.

Here is the procedure for the examination:

- Orbits (the bones in the skull surround and create the structure that holds the eyeballs): Check for bruising, swelling, lacerations, tenderness, depression, and deformity.
- Eyelids: Check for bruising, swelling, and lacerations.
- Mucous membranes: Check for redness, pus, and foreign objects.
- Eyeballs (globes): Check for abnormal colouring, laceration, and foreign objects.
- Pupils: Check for size, shape, and equality. Also check for reaction to light. The pupils should be black, round, and equal in size. They should react to light by constricting.
- Eye movement: Check to see that the eyes can move in all directions. Check for abnormal gaze or pain upon movement.

Here are the basic rules for emergency care of an injured eye:

- Many EMS systems do not allow flushing of an injured eye, except for a chemical injury. Flushing would cause irreversible damage if the eye has been perforated. Follow local protocol.
- Do not put salves or medicines in the injured eye. If this is necessary, a physician will do so.
- Do not remove blood or blood clots from the eye.

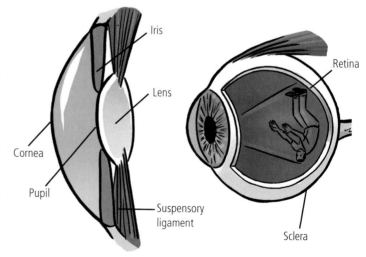

Figure 13–20 The anatomy of the eye.

Figure 13–21 Flushing the eye with clean water.

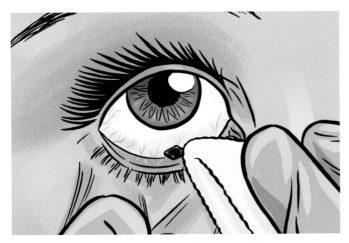

Figure 13–22 Use the corner of a piece of sterile gauze to remove an object under the lower eyelid.

However, you can sponge blood from the person's face to help keep him comfortable.

- Only force the eyelid open if you have to flush out chemicals.

- If someone has an eye injury, do not allow the person to walk without help, especially up or down stairs.

- Do not allow the person to eat or drink.

- Never panic. It will upset the person, and you may lose his trust.

- Reassure the person constantly.

- Ideally, the person should be transported in a supine position.

Foreign Objects

A foreign object can enter the eye usually by being blown or driven in. Examples of foreign objects may include particles of dirt, sand, cinders, coal dust, or fine pieces of metal. These must be removed or they may cause inflammation, scarring, or infection. They also may scratch the cornea. Signs and symptoms of foreign objects in the eye include pain, excessive tearing, and abnormal sensitivity to light.

Do not allow the person with a foreign object in the eye to rub his eyes. Rubbing can force a particle with sharp edges into tissues, making removal difficult.

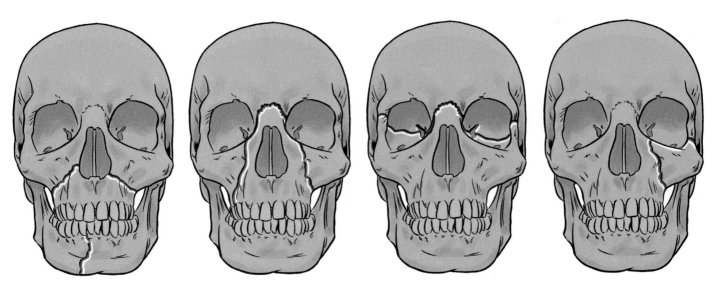

Figure 13–23 Facial trauma may result in a fracture of the eye sockets.

It is always safer for responders to allow EMS personnel with more training to remove a foreign object. However, if removal is necessary and local protocols allow it, there are several ways in which you might proceed. They are as follows:

- Hold the lids apart and flush the eye with clean water (Figure 13–21). Note that some EMS systems do not allow flushing except for chemical burns. Follow local protocol.

- If the object is under the upper eyelid, draw the upper lid down over the lower lid. When you let it return to its normal position, its undersurface will be drawn over the lashes of the lower lid, which will sweep away the foreign object.

- Grasp the eyelashes of the upper lid. Turn up the lid over a cotton swab. The foreign object may then be carefully removed with the corner of a piece of sterile gauze.

- If the object is under the lower eyelid, pull down the lower lid to expose the inner surface. Then use the corner of a piece of sterile gauze to remove the object (Figure 13–22).

Should a foreign object become lodged in the eyeball, do not try to remove it. Doing so may force the object deeper into the eye, causing further damage. In this case, place a rigid eye shield over the injured eye. Obtain more advanced medical care.

Orbits

Trauma to the face may result in fracture of the bones that form the orbits, or eye sockets (Figure 13–23). Someone with an orbit injury may complain of double or decreased vision, numbness above the eyebrow or over the cheek, or massive discharge from the nose.

Fractures of the lower part of the orbit are the most common. They can cause paralysis of the upward gaze, that is, the person's eyes would not be able to follow

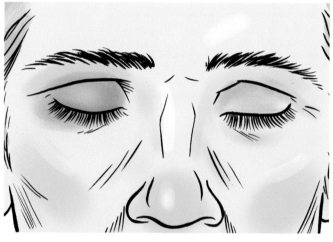

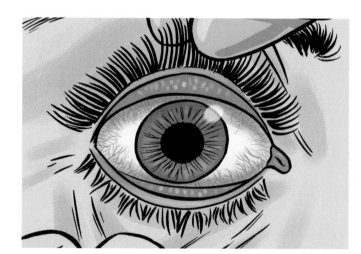

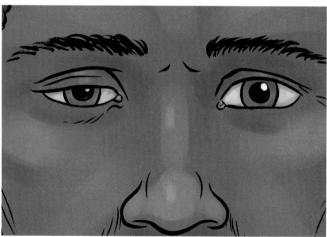

Figure 13–24 Eyelid injuries include bruising, burns, swelling or drooping, and lacerations.

Figure 13–25 Chemical burns to the eyes are quite common.

your finger upward. Someone with an orbit fracture needs hospitalization and surgery.

If there is no injury to the eyeball, place cold packs over the injured orbit to help reduce the swelling. However, if the eyeball is injured or you are in doubt, do not apply cold packs. Obtain more advanced medical care.

Eyelids

Lid injuries include bruising, burns, swelling or drooping, and lacerations (Figure 13–24). Anything that damages the lid may also damage the eyeball. In general, there is not much that can be done for these injuries in the field, beyond gentle patching.

To control bleeding from the eyelid, apply light pressure. Don't use any pressure if the eyeball itself is injured.

Never attempt to remove embedded material, such as gravel. Use sterile gauze soaked in saline to keep the wound from drying. If the lid is avulsed, preserve it and send it with the person for later grafting.

Globes

Injuries to the globe include bruises, lacerations, foreign objects, and abrasions. It is generally best to treat these in the hospital, where specialized equipment is available. In the field, keep the person with an injury to the globe supine.

Chemical Burns to the Eye

Chemical burns to the eye are quite common (Figure 13–25) and represent one of the most urgent emergencies related to the eyes. Permanent damage can occur within seconds of the injury. The first 10 minutes are crucial to the final outcome. Remember, burning and tissue damage will continue as long as the chemical remains in the eye, even if it is diluted.

To provide emergency care, begin immediate, continuous irrigation with water. Do not use anything other than water. The water does not need to be sterile, but it must be clean. You must wear protective glasses when provid-

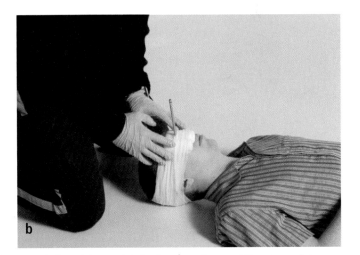

Figure 13–26, a-b For an impaled object in the eye: **a**, pack around the object with bulky dressings, without applying pressure; **b**, bandage over and around the dressings to secure them in place.

ing this care. Gently hold the person's eyelid open so that all the chemical can be flushed away. You may have to force the eyelid open because of the person's pain.

Pour water from the inside corner across the eyeball to the outside edge. This will help avoid contaminating the uninjured eye. Irrigate continuously for 10 to 15 minutes.

Remove any solid particles from the surface of the eye with a moistened cotton swab. Contact lenses must be removed or flushed out. If not, chemicals could be trapped between the lens and the cornea. Follow local protocol.

Following irrigation, wash your hands thoroughly to avoid contaminating your own eyes.

Impaled Objects

Only a physician should remove an object impaled in the eye. You must protect the person from further injury until he can reach a doctor. Therefore, you must stabilize the object in place.

Begin by stabilizing the person's head. Keep the person supine. Pack around the object with bulky dressings, without applying pressure (Figure 13–26, a). Bandage over and around the dressings to keep them in place (Figure 13–26, b).

After covering, stay with the person and ensure he knows someone is there. It is common for the injured person to panic.

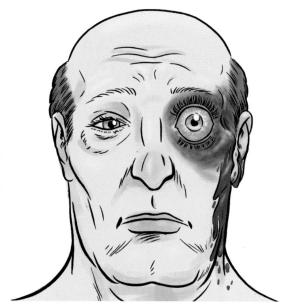

Figure 13–27 The eyeball may be extruded during a serious injury.

Extruded Eyeball

During a serious injury, the eyeball may be knocked out of the socket, or extruded (Figure 13–27). Do not try to replace it. Instead, cover it with a moist dressing and protective cup. Do not apply any pressure.

Other Eye Injuries

For all other emergencies involving the eye, patch the eye and arrange for transportation. Such emergencies may include eye infections, a black eye, corneal abrasions, light burns, and heat burns. Follow local protocol.

Removing Contact Lenses

Millions of people in Canada wear contact lenses. Some may wear a lens in one eye only, so be sure to examine both eyes carefully. Other people, especially older adults, wear both contact lenses and eyeglasses. To detect lenses, shine a penlight into each eye. A soft lens will show up as a shadow on the outer portion of the eye. A hard lens will show up as a shadow over the iris. In general, remove contact lenses only when there has been a chemical burn to the eye. Always follow local protocols.

Ear Injury

Ear injuries are common. Either the soft tissue of the outer ear or the eardrum within the ear may be injured. Open wounds, such as lacerations or abrasions, can result from recreational injuries, for example, falling off a bike. An avulsion of the ear may occur when a pierced earring catches on something and tears the earlobe. You can control bleeding from the soft tissues of the ear by applying direct pressure to the affected area.

If the person has a serious head or spine injury, blood or other fluid may be in the ear canal or draining from the ear. Cover the ear lightly with a sterile dressing without applying direct pressure, stabilize the head and spine, and obtain more advanced medical care.

The ear can also be injured internally. A direct blow to the head may rupture the eardrum. Sudden pressure changes, such as those caused by an explosion or a deep-water dive, can also injure the ear internally. The person may lose hearing or balance or experience inner ear pain. These injuries require more advanced medical care.

A foreign object, such as dirt, an insect, or a piece of cotton, can easily become lodged in the ear canal. If you can easily see and grasp the object, remove it. Do not try to remove any object by using a pin, a toothpick, or any sharp item. You could force the object farther back or puncture the eardrum. Sometimes you can remove the object if you pull down on the earlobe, tilt the head to the side, and shake or gently strike the head on the affected side. If you cannot easily remove the object, the person should be seen by a physician.

Mouth and Jaw Injuries

Your primary concern for any injury to the mouth or jaw is to ensure an open airway. Injuries in these areas may cause breathing problems if blood or loose teeth obstruct the airway. A swollen or fractured trachea may also obstruct breathing.

If the person is bleeding from the mouth and you do not suspect a head or spine injury, place him in a seated position with the head tilted slightly forward. This will allow any blood to drain from the mouth. If this position is not possible, place the person on his side to allow blood to drain from the mouth.

For injuries that penetrate the lip, place a rolled dressing between the lip and the gum. You can place another dressing on the outer surface of the lip. If the tongue is bleeding, apply a dressing and direct pressure. Applying cold to the lips or tongue can help reduce swelling and ease pain. If the bleeding cannot be controlled, obtain more advanced medical care.

If the injury knocked out one or more of the person's teeth, control the bleeding and save any teeth so that they can be reinserted. To control the bleeding, roll a sterile dressing and insert it into the space left by the missing tooth. Have the person bite down to maintain pressure (Figure 13–28). Put the tooth in a container of milk and keep the tooth with the injured person. A dentist may be able to reinsert the tooth.

If the injury is severe enough for you to need to obtain more advanced medical care, give the tooth to the appropriate personnel. If the injury is not severe, the person should immediately seek a dentist who can re-implant the tooth. Time is a critical factor if the tooth is to be successfully re-implanted. Ideally, it should be done within an hour after the injury.

Figure 13–28 If a person has a knocked out tooth, they can bite down on a sterile piece of gauze to maintain pressure.

Injuries serious enough to fracture or dislocate the jaw can also cause other head or spine injuries. Be sure to maintain an open airway. Check inside the mouth for bleeding. Control bleeding as you would for other head injuries.

PREVENTING HEAD AND SPINE INJURIES

Injuries to the head and spine are a major cause of death, disability, and disfigurement. However, many such injuries can be prevented by managing the risks in all parts of your life:

- Wearing seat belts
- When appropriate, wearing approved helmets, eyewear, faceguards, and mouthguards
- Preventing falls
- Obeying rules in sports and recreational activities
- Avoiding inappropriate use of drugs
- Inspecting work and recreational equipment periodically
- Thinking and talking about safety and managing risks

Figure 13–29 Helmets are designed for multiple purposes, and offer protection only for their intended use.

Wearing Safety Belts

Always wear safety belts, including shoulder restraints, when driving or riding in an automobile. Be sure all passengers also wear them. Airbags provide additional protection. All small children riding in a car must be in approved safety seats correct for the child's age, height, and weight.

Wearing Helmets and Eyewear

Helmets can prevent many needless injuries to the head. They are designed for different purposes, with varying degrees of protection, and offer protection only for their intended use (Figure 13–29). For example, the industrial work helmet, called a "hard hat," provides adequate protection against falling debris but does not offer the proper protection for riding a motorcycle.

Any open form of transportation, such as a motorcycle, moped, or all-terrain vehicle, exposes the head and spine to injury. Wearing a helmet can help reduce such injuries. The ideal helmet, sometimes called a "full-face helmet," protects the lower face and jaw and has a large clear or tinted face shield. In all cases, the helmet should be the correct size and fit comfortably and securely.

Eyewear can help prevent many needless injuries that result in loss of sight. Anytime you operate machinery or perform an activity that may involve flying particles or splashing chemicals, you should wear protective eyewear such as goggles.

Safeguarding Against Falls

Although most falls occur at home and involve young children and older adults, falls can and do occur in the workplace. There are precautions to take to prevent falls. Floor surfaces should be made of non-slip material. Stairs should have non-slip treads and handrails and be well lit. Rugs should be secured to the floor with double-sided tape. All spills should be cleaned up promptly.

In the workplace:

- Use all appropriate safety equipment when working above ground level.

- When using ladders, you should have three points of contact on the ladder at all times (e.g., two hands and a foot or two feet and a hand).

- Keep floors and aisles free of clutter and ensure that nothing is blocking stairwells, worksites, or exits.

- Check equipment, such as warehouse forklifts, ladders, and scaffolding, regularly for worn or loose parts.

Extra prevention for children:

- If there are small children in the home, gates should be placed at the top of the stairs.

- Babies and children should always ride in approved safety seats. Ensure that they are the right fit and have them properly installed.

- Ensure that children and adults wear an approved, properly fitting helmet for any activity in which a blow to the head may occur.

Managing Risks in Sports and Recreation

Participants in sports or recreational activities should know their physical limitations. Proper protective equipment is necessary for any activity in which serious injury may occur. In all sports involving physical contact, participants should wear mouthpieces. Most important, everyone must know and follow the rules. Rules not only make the activity fair, they also help prevent injuries. The coach, athletic therapist, or a more experienced participant may impose additional rules for the safety of newcomers. Participants should never engage in a new activity until they know the rules and risks involved.

Diving is one of the leading causes of head and spine injuries. Divers must always be careful around water.

- Ensure that the water is deep enough before diving.
- Enter unknown water and pools feet first.
- Check for objects below the surface, such as logs or piling, before diving.

Thinking and Talking About Managing Risks

People too often neglect thinking about managing risks in their daily lives, yet we are most vulnerable to injury at work, during recreational activities, or while travelling. Take the time to inspect and think about your daily environment. People should consider the following five questions:

1. Are there things you could do in your workplace or at home to help prevent injuries to yourself or others?

2. Are you taking unnecessary risks in any activities?

3. Do you follow rules meant for your safety?

4. Do you maintain your vehicle appropriately?

5. Do you ever attempt an activity without being in the physical condition that would allow you to do it without injury?

Talk with others about preventing injuries at work, at home, and in recreation. Everyone needs to know about managing risks. Seek guidance to help prevent injuries that could permanently affect your life or the lives of others. Discuss safety when using mechanical devices or equipment or when approaching a potentially dangerous scene.

SUMMARY

In this chapter, you have learned how to recognize and care for serious head and spine injuries and specific injuries to the head and face. To decide whether an injury is serious, you must consider its cause. If you think that an injury of this type might be serious, obtain more advanced medical care.

Like injuries elsewhere on the body, injuries to the head and spine often involve both soft tissues and bone. Control bleeding as necessary, usually with direct pressure on the wound. With scalp injuries, be careful not to apply pressure to a possible skull fracture. With eye injuries, remember not to apply pressure on the eyeball.

If you suspect that the person may have a serious injury to the head or spine, minimize movement of the injured area when providing care. This is best accomplished by using in-line stabilization. Administer oxygen if it is available. Secure the person to a backboard if you must move him.

As you read the next chapter about how to care for injuries to the chest, abdomen, and pelvis, remember the principles of care for head and spine injuries—serious injuries of the chest and abdomen can also affect the spine.

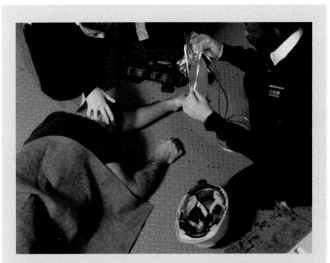

The man vomits while you are giving care. What do you do?

Skills Summary

Rolling a Person From a Supine Position Onto a Backboard

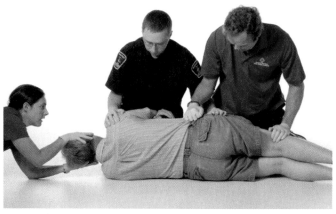

1. While maintaining manual stabilization, other responders position themselves at the torso and hips

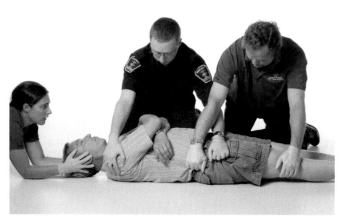

2. Roll the person toward the responders, maintaining manual stabliization. Check the back.

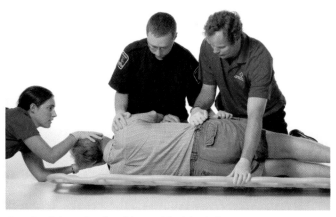

3. Position the backboard behind the person.

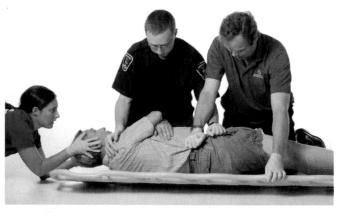

4. Roll person onto the backboard.

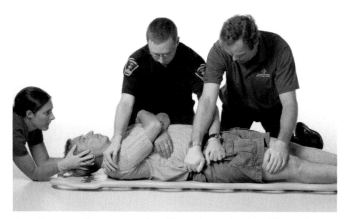

5. Ensure the person is aligned on the backboard.

Note: If there are only two responders, one should maintain manual stabilization while the other controls the injured person's torso.

Note: A cervical collar can be applied before the log roll.

Skills Summary

Rolling a Person From a Prone Position Onto a Backboard

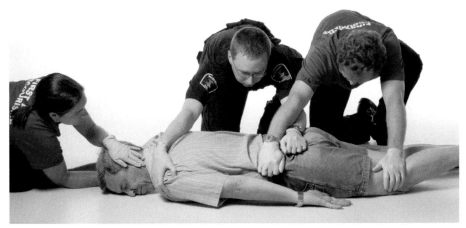

1. While maintaining manual stabilization, the other responders position a backboard between them and the injured person. Responders position themselves at the torso and hips.

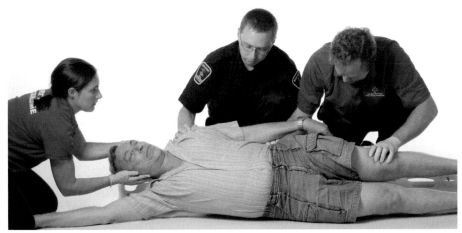

2. Roll the person onto the backboard.

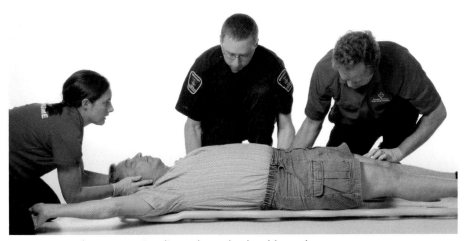

3. Ensure the person is aligned on the backboard.

Skills Summary

Rolling a Person From a Semi-Prone Position Onto a Backboard

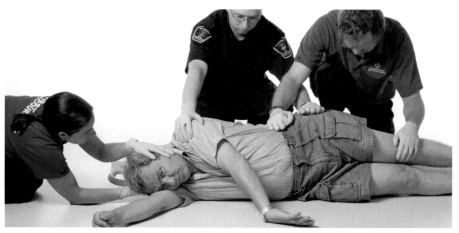

1. While maintaining manual stabilization, the other responders position the backboard between them and the injured person. Responders position themselves at the person's torso and hips.

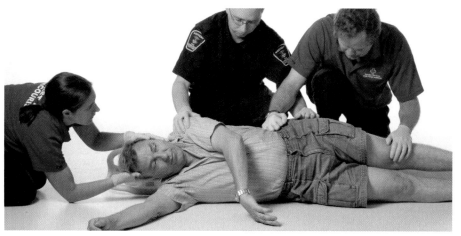

2. Roll the person onto the backboard.

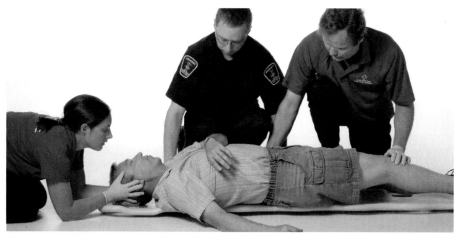

3. Ensure the person is aligned on the backboard.

Skills Summary

Immobilizing a Person on a Backboard

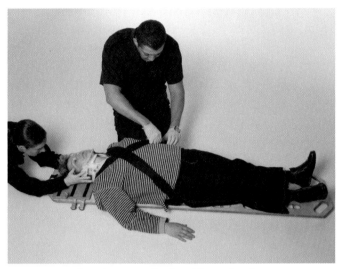

1. Secure the chest to the backboard using a cross-strap technique.

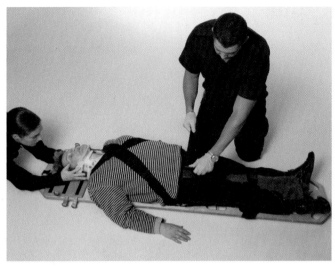

2. Secure the hips and legs, positioning padding between the legs if needed. Ensure that all straps are secure and tight.

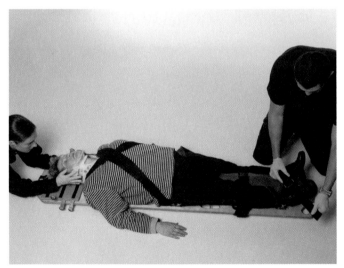

3. Secure feet together.

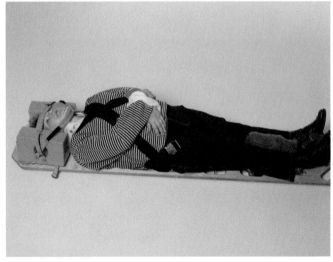

Note: You may also use a cross-strap technique for the lower body as well.

Skills Summary

Removing a Helmet

1. Apply manual stabilization.

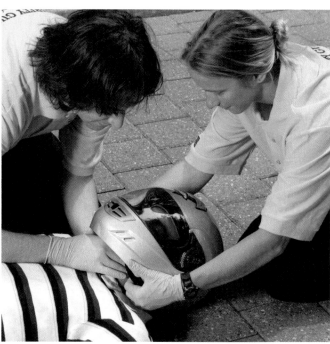

2. Remove the chin strap, then support the head by holding the jaw and the back of the head.

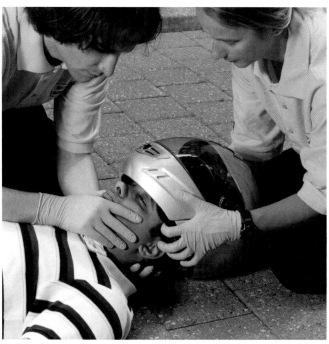

3. Spread the sides of the helmet and slide it off.

4. Maintain manual stabilization.

Skills Summary

Applying a K.E.D.®

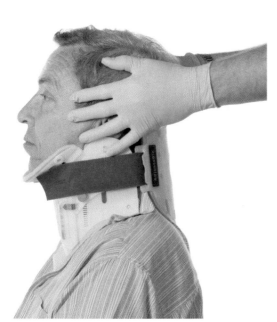

1. Apply a cervical collar.

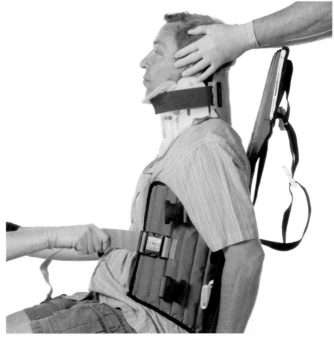

2. Fasten and tighten the middle torso strap.

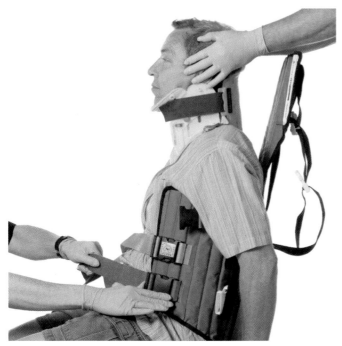

3. Fasten and tighten the lower torso strap.

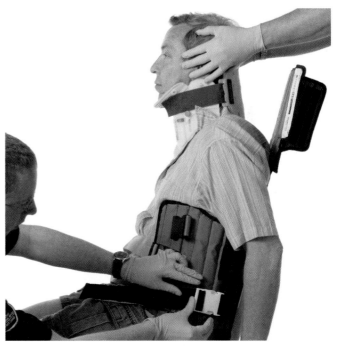

4. Fasten and tighten the leg straps.

Applying a K.E.D.®

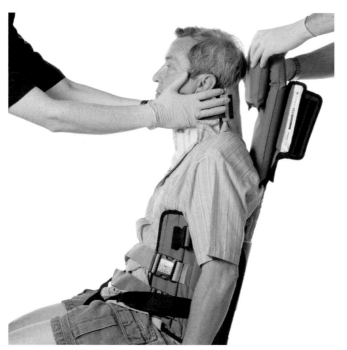

5. Pad the head if needed.

6. Secure the head.

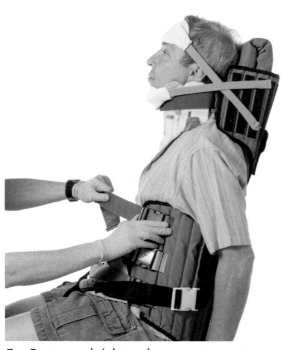

7. Fasten and tighten the upper torso strap.

Skills Summary

Standing Take-Down: 3 Responders

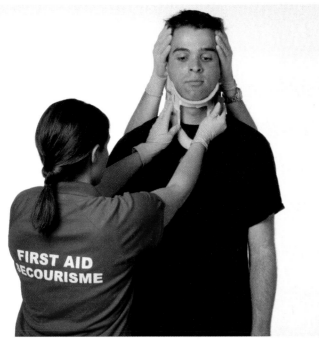

1. Apply a cervical collar.

2. One responder maintains manual stabilization while the other responder positions a backboard behind the person.

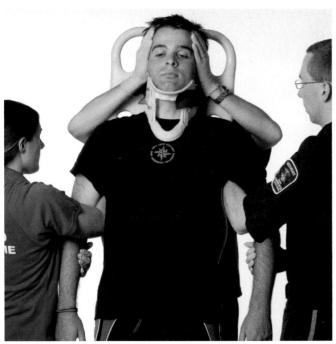

3. Grasp the backboard by reaching under the person's armpits. Hold the injured person's arm with the free hand.

4. Lower the person to the ground.

Skills Summary

Standing Take-Down: 2 Responders

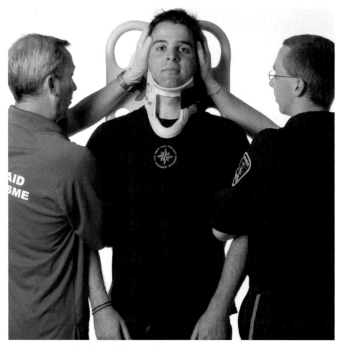

1. Grasp the backboard by reaching under the person's armpits. Hold the injured person's head with the free hand.

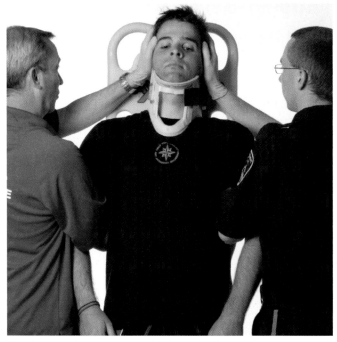

2. Lower the person to the ground.

Chest, Abdominal, and Pelvic Injuries

A man who has been shot is lying on a sidewalk in a busy urban setting. He is semi-conscious and in considerable pain. There is blood on his shirt, and he makes an abnormal sucking sound when he tries to breathe. The scene has been deemed safe for you to approach. What do you do?

INTRODUCTION

Injuries to the chest and abdomen may include minor soft tissue injuries, internal organ damage, or fractures. Fractures and lacerations often occur in motor vehicle collisions to occupants not wearing safety belts. Falls, penetration by objects such as bullets, and other forms of trauma may also cause such injuries.

Injuries to the pelvis may be minor soft tissue injuries or serious bone and internal structure injuries. The pelvis includes a group of large bones that form a protective girdle around the organs inside. A great force is required to cause serious injury to the pelvis.

Because the chest, abdomen, and pelvis contain many organs important to life, injury to these areas can be fatal. A force that causes severe injury in these areas may also cause injury to the spine. Care for these injuries includes:

• Controlling external bleeding

• Limiting movement

• Minimizing shock

• Administering oxygen if available

• Obtaining more advanced medical care

• Providing ongoing survey and care

This chapter describes the signs and symptoms of and care for injuries to the chest, abdomen, and pelvis. In all cases, perform your scene and primary survey and then care for all life-threatening injuries first. *All injuries described in this chapter are serious enough that you should always obtain more advanced medical care immediately.*

CHEST INJURIES

The chest is the upper part of the trunk. It is formed by 12 pairs of ribs, 10 of which attach to the sternum in front and the spine in back. The other 2 pairs attach only to the spine in the back and are sometimes called "floating" ribs. The rib cage is the cage of bones formed by the 12 pairs of ribs, the sternum, and the spine. It protects vital organs, such as the heart, major blood vessels, and the lungs (Figure 14–1). Also in the chest are the esophagus, the trachea, and the muscles of respiration.

Chest injuries are one of the leading causes of trauma deaths each year. Many traffic fatalities involve chest injuries. Injuries to the chest may also result from a wide variety of other causes, such as falls, sports mishaps, and crushing or penetrating forces (Figure 14–2).

Chest wounds are either open or closed. Open chest wounds occur when an object, such as a knife or bullet, penetrates the chest wall. Fractured ribs may break through the skin to cause an open chest injury. A chest wound is closed if the skin is not broken. Closed chest wounds are generally caused by a blunt force, such as that from a fall or a motor vehicle collision.

Signs and Symptoms of Chest Injury

You should know the signs and symptoms of a serious chest injury. These may occur with both open and closed wounds. You will recognize some of these signs and symptoms from Chapter 6. They include:

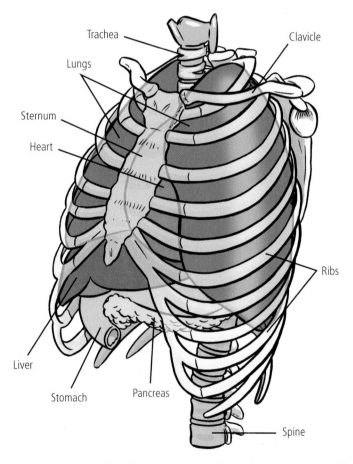

Figure 14–1 The rib cage surrounds and protects several vital organs.

Figure 14–2 Injuries to the chest may result from crushing forces, falls, or sports mishaps.

- Difficulty breathing
- Pain at the site of the injury that increases with deep breathing or movement
- Obvious deformity, such as that caused by a fracture
- Flushed, pale, or bluish discolouration of the skin
- Coughing up blood

Specific Types of Chest Injuries

Rib Fractures

Rib fractures are usually caused by a forceful blow to the chest (Figure 14–3). Although painful, a simple rib fracture is rarely life-threatening. Someone with a fractured rib often breathes shallowly because normal or deep breathing is painful. The person will usually attempt to ease the pain by leaning toward the side of the fracture and pressing a hand or arm over the injured area. Therefore, pain in the rib area, shallow breathing, and holding the area are signs and symptoms of a possible rib fracture.

However, serious rib fractures can be life-threatening. In severe blows or crushing injuries, multiple ribs can fracture in many places. This can produce a loose section of ribs that does not move normally with the rest of the

chest during breathing. Usually, the loose section will move in the opposite direction from the rest of the chest; this is called paradoxical movement. The portion of chest wall lying between the fractures is called flail chest. When a flail chest involves the sternum, the breastbone is separated from the rest of the ribs.

Care for Rib Fractures

If you suspect a fractured rib or ribs, have the person rest in a position that will make breathing easier. You can use an object, such as a pillow or rolled blanket, to help support and immobilize the injured area. Serious fractures often cause severe bleeding and difficulty breathing; shock is likely to develop. Administer oxygen if it is available and provide ongoing survey and care.

Care for Flail Chest

Have the person rest in a position that makes breathing easier, usually a semi-reclining position. Feel the chest area gently to locate the area of the flail segment and apply bulky dressings several centimetres thick.

Bandage the dressings in place with long strips of tape. If bulky dressings are not available, use a small pillow or other lightweight material. Do not try to bind, strap, or tape the flail section itself.

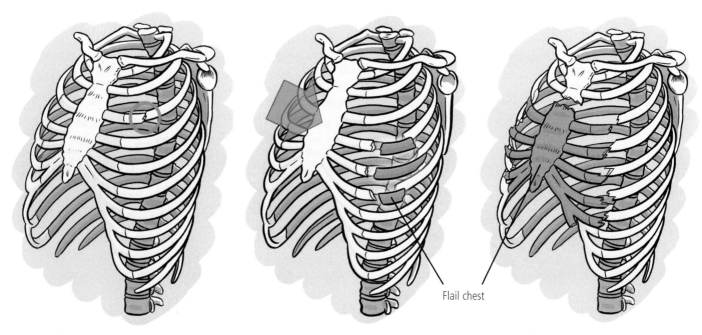

Figure 14–3 Forceful blows to the chest can cause rib fractures.

Flail chest

Puncture Injuries

Puncture wounds to the chest range in severity from minor to life-threatening. Stab and gunshot wounds are examples of puncture injuries. A forceful puncture may penetrate the rib cage and allow air to enter the chest through the wound (Figure 14–4). This prevents the lungs from functioning normally. The penetrating object can injure any structure within the chest, including the lungs, heart, or major arteries or veins.

Hemothorax

Hemothorax is bleeding into the pleural space (Figure 14–5). This can be caused by blunt or penetrating trauma resulting in a lacerated lung or laceration of a blood vessel to the chest. As the affected side of the chest begins to fill with blood, the person will have trouble breathing and will suffer from shock secondary to the blood loss. If bleeding continues, it will also create pressure on the heart and lungs.

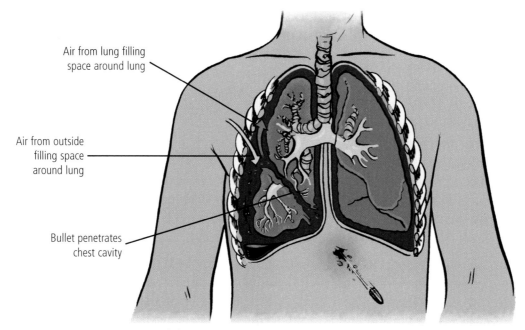

Air from lung filling space around lung

Air from outside filling space around lung

Bullet penetrates chest cavity

Figure 14–4 A puncture wound that penetrates the lung or the chest cavity surrounding the lung allows air to go in and out of the cavity.

Hemothorax can occur with closed or open chest wounds. The severity of the hemothorax depends on the amount of bleeding into the pleural space. Hemothorax is cared for by correcting the ventilatory and circulatory problems. High concentration oxygen should be administered, and if breathing is shallow or inadequate, ventilations should be assisted using a BVM. Control any external bleeding if necessary.

Pneumothorax

Pneumothorax is a condition caused by air entering the pleural space. It may occur as a result of blunt or penetrating trauma or spontaneously in certain individuals. The lung may be partially or totally collapsed, depending on how much air has entered the pleural space. A person's signs and symptoms will also depend on how much air has entered the space. Signs and symptoms of pneumothorax may include the following:

- Pleuritic chest pain, pain that is made worse by coughing or deep breaths

- Difficult and rapid breathing (dyspnea)

- Decreased or absent breath sounds on the affected side

There is always the possibility that a pneumothorax can progress to a tension pneumothorax.

Tension Pneumothorax

Tension pneumothorax is the continual flow of air into the pleural space, which cannot escape (Figure 14–6). This usually occurs when lung tissue is torn and air leaks into the pleural space, causing pressure on the lung, heart, and major blood vessels. The lung will eventually collapse, thereby diminishing the amount of air that can be inhaled or exhaled. As the condition worsens, the signs of hypoxia follow, and a breathing emergency is evident. Provide ongoing survey and care, administer oxygen, and ensure prompt transport to a medical facility.

Care for Puncture Injuries

Puncture wounds cause varying degrees of internal or external bleeding. If the injury penetrates the rib cage, air can pass freely in and out of the chest cavity and the person cannot breathe normally. With each breath the person takes, you may hear a sucking sound coming from the wound. This is the primary sign of a penetrating chest injury called a sucking chest wound.

Without proper care, the person's condition will worsen quickly. The affected lung or lungs will fail to function, and breathing will become more difficult. Your main concern is the breathing problem. To care for a sucking chest wound, cover the wound with an occlusive dressing—one that does not allow air to pass through

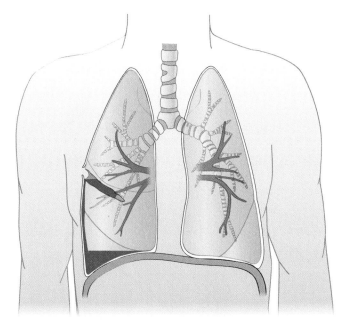

Figure 14–5 A hemothorax is bleeding into the pleural space.

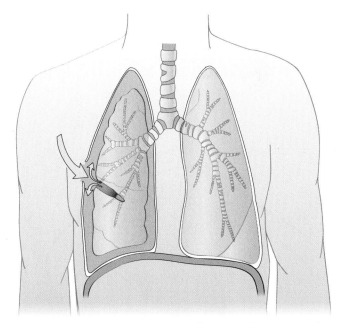

Figure 14–6 A tension pneumothorax is the continual flow of air into the pleural space, which cannot escape.

NOTE:
Subcutaneous emphysema: *If air or gas gets into the subcutaneous tissue of the body,* *the affected area may appear swollen and may make* *a "crackling" sound as air moves around.*

it. A plastic bag, a vinyl or nitrile glove, or a piece of plastic wrap or aluminum foil folded several times and placed over the wound can be substituted if a sterile occlusive dressing is not available. Tape the dressing in place, except for one corner or side that remains loose to let air escape as the person exhales (Figure 14–7, a-c). This keeps air from entering the wound during inhalation but allows it to escape during exhalation. There are some commercially made occlusive dressings for chest wounds, such as an Asherman Chest Seal (Figure 14–8). Administer oxygen if available and take steps to minimize shock. Provide ongoing survey and care.

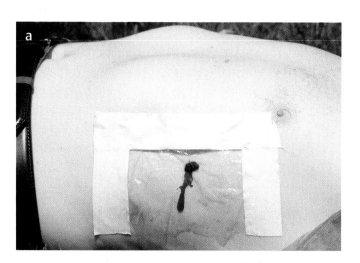

ABDOMINAL INJURIES

The abdomen is the area immediately under the chest and above the pelvis. It is easily injured because it is not surrounded by bones. It is protected at the back by the spine. The upper abdomen is only partially protected in front by the lower ribs. The muscles of the back and abdomen also help protect the internal organs, many of which are vital (Figure 14–9). Most important are the organs that are easily injured or tend to bleed profusely when injured, such as the liver, spleen, and stomach.

The liver is rich in blood. Located in the upper right quadrant of the abdomen, this organ is protected somewhat by the lower ribs. However, it is delicate and can be torn by blows from blunt objects or penetrated by a fractured rib. The resulting bleeding can be severe and can quickly be fatal. The liver, when injured, can also leak bile into the abdomen, which can cause severe infection.

The spleen is located in the upper left quadrant of the abdomen, behind the stomach, and is protected somewhat by the lower left ribs. Like the liver, this organ is easily damaged. The spleen may rupture when the abdomen is struck forcefully by a blunt object. Since the spleen stores blood, an injury can cause a severe loss of blood in a short time and be life-threatening.

The stomach is one of the main digestive organs. The upper part of the stomach changes shape depending on its contents, the stage of digestion, and the size and strength of the stomach muscles. It is lined with many blood vessels and nerves. The stomach can bleed severely when injured, and food contents may empty into the abdomen and possibly cause infection.

b Inhalation

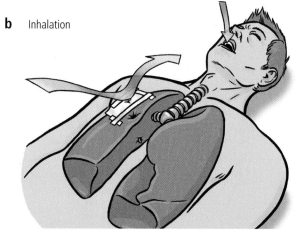

c Exhalation

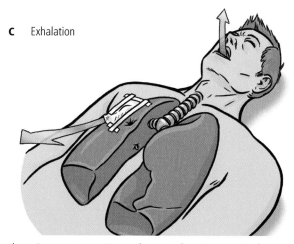

Figure 14–7, a-c With a sucking chest wound, use an occlusive dressing: **a**, tape it on three sides; **b**, so air does not enter the chest cavity when the person inhales; but **c**, air can escape when the person exhales.

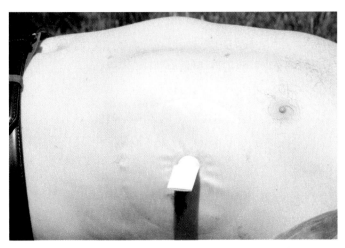

Figure 14–8 A commercially available occlusive dressing.

Signs and Symptoms of Abdominal Injury

The signs and symptoms of serious abdominal injury include:

- Severe pain
- Bruising
- External bleeding
- Nausea and vomiting (sometimes vomit containing blood)
- Pale, moist skin
- Weakness
- Thirst
- Pain, tenderness, or a tight feeling in the abdomen
- Distension in the abdomen
- Organs possibly protruding from the abdomen
- Signs and symptoms of shock

Care for Abdominal Injuries

Like a chest injury, an injury to the abdomen is either open or closed. Even with a closed wound, the rupture of an organ can cause serious internal bleeding that can quickly result in shock. Injuries to the abdomen can be extremely painful. Serious reactions can occur if organs leak blood or other contents into the abdomen.

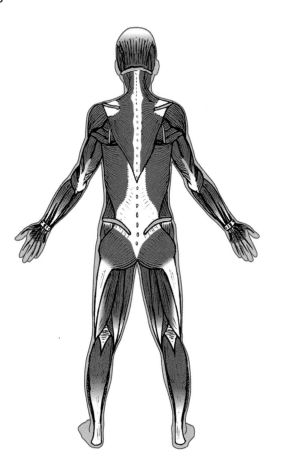
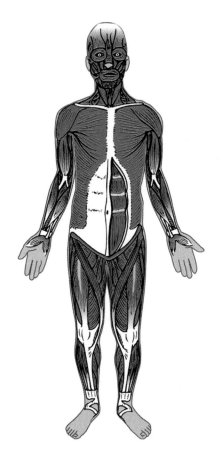

Figure 14–9 The muscles of the back and abdomen help to protect the internal organs.

With a severe open injury, abdominal organs sometimes protrude through the wound (Figure 14–10, a). To care for an open wound in the abdomen, follow these steps:

1. Carefully position the person on his back.

2. Bend the person's knees slightly. This allows the muscles of the abdomen to relax. Place rolled-up blankets or pillows under the person's knees. If the movement of the person's legs causes pain, leave the legs straight.

3. Do not apply direct pressure.

4. Do not push organs back in.

5. Remove clothing from around the wound.

6. Apply moist, sterile dressings loosely over the wound. (Figure 14–10, b). (Warm tap water can be used).

7. Cover dressings loosely with plastic wrap if available.

8. Cover dressings lightly with a folded towel to maintain warmth (Figure 14–10, c).

9. Maintain normal body temperature.

10. Administer oxygen if available.

11. Obtain more advanced medical care.

12. Provide ongoing survey and care.

To care for a closed abdominal injury:

1. Carefully position the person on her back.

2. Bend the person's knees slightly. This allows the muscles of the abdomen to relax. Place rolled-up blankets or pillows under the person's knees. If the movement of the person's legs causes pain, leave the legs straight.

3. Do not apply direct pressure.

4. Administer oxygen if available.

5. Take steps to minimize shock.

6. Obtain more advanced medical care.

7. Provide ongoing survey and care.

Abdominal Aortic Aneurysm

In an abdominal aortic aneurysm, the wall of the aorta weakens and bulges (like a bulge in a garden hose) until the vessel thins and ruptures. The risk factors are the same as those for heart disease or stroke.

Signs and symptoms:

• Abdominal pain

• Abdominal rigidity

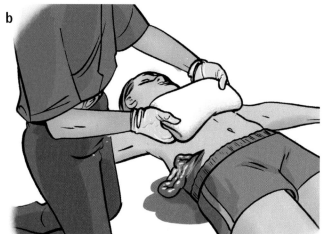

Figure 14–10, a-c a, severe injuries to the abdominal cavity can result in protruding organs; **b**, after removing clothing, apply moist, sterile dressings loosely over the wound; and **c**, cover dressings lightly with a folded towel to maintain warmth.

- Back pain
- Nausea and vomiting
- Pulsating mass in the abdomen
- Diminished or absent pulses in lower extremities
- Tingling or numbness in the lower extremities

NOTE:

If the aneurysm has ruptured, look for signs and symptoms of shock and internal bleeding. Treat as any other abdominal injury.

PELVIC INJURIES

The pelvis is the lower part of the trunk and contains the bladder, the reproductive organs in women, and the lower portion of the large intestine, including the rectum. Arteries and nerves pass through the pelvis. The organs within the pelvis are well protected on the sides and back but not in front (Figure 14–11). Injuries to the pelvis may include fractures to the pelvic bone and damage to structures within. Fractured bones may puncture or lacerate internal organs. These organs can also be injured when struck by forceful blows from blunt or penetrating objects.

Signs and Symptoms of Pelvic Injury

Signs and symptoms of injury to the pelvis are very similar to those of abdominal injury. There may also be pain on palpation, as well as a grating, crackling, or popping sound (crepitus). Certain pelvic injuries may also cause loss of sensation in the legs or inability to move them. This may indicate an injury to the lower spine.

Care for Pelvic Injuries

Care for pelvic injuries in the same way as for abdominal injuries. Do not move the person unless necessary and avoid putting any pressure on the pelvis. If possible, keep the person lying flat. If not, help

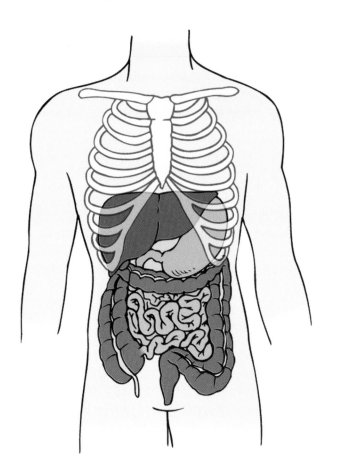
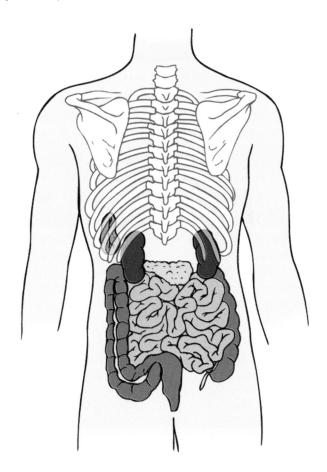

Figure 14–11 Unlike the organs of the chest or pelvis, organs within the abdominal cavity and front of the pelvic cavity are not well protected.

her become comfortable. Control any external bleeding and cover any protruding organs. Someone with a pelvic injury should be immobilized on a backboard. Always obtain more advanced medical care, administer oxygen if available, take steps to minimize shock, and provide ongoing survey and care.

An injury to the pelvis sometimes involves the genitals, the external reproductive organs. Genital injuries are either closed wounds, such as a bruise, or open wounds, such as an avulsion or laceration. Any injury to the genitals is extremely painful. It is also important to maintain the person's privacy the best you can. Care for a closed wound as you would for any closed wound. If the injury is an open wound, apply a sterile dressing and direct pressure with your hand or the injured person's hand. If any parts are amputated, wrap them appropriately and make sure they are transported with the person. Injuries to the genital area can be embarrassing for both the injured person and the responder. Explain briefly what you are going to do and do it. Act in a confident manner; this will make the situation easier for you and the person for whom you are providing care.

SUMMARY

Injuries to the chest, abdomen, or pelvis can be serious. They can damage soft tissues, bones, and internal organs. Although many injuries are immediately obvious, some may be detected only as the person's condition worsens over time. Watch for signs and symptoms of serious injuries that require medical attention.

Care for any life-threatening condition, such as a breathing emergency; then give any additional care needed for specific injuries. For open wounds to the chest, abdomen, or pelvis, control bleeding. If you suspect a fracture, immobilize the injured part. Use special dressings for sucking chest wounds and open abdominal wounds when these materials are available. Always obtain more advanced medical care as soon as possible, administer oxygen if it is available, and take steps to minimize shock. This gives the person with a serious injury the best chance for survival and full recovery.

The man begins to find breathing more difficult. What do you do?

NOTES:

Part 4

Medical Emergencies

15
Sudden Illnesses

16
Poisoning

17
Heat- and Cold-Related Emergencies

INTRODUCTION

You are summoned to assist with an emergency in an office building. When you arrive at the office, you find a middle-aged woman lying motionless on her side on the floor. A man is kneeling helplessly next to her; he identifies himself as her co-worker. Other co-workers are gathering, but no one is helping her. There is an empty pill bottle without a label on the floor beside her. You notice that her body is limp. Saliva is dribbling from her mouth. Her face seems distorted; her mouth droops to one side. The man tells you her name and then you speak to her, calling her name a few times and tapping her on the shoulder, but she doesn't respond. You observe that she is breathing rapidly. Her skin is cool, and she is sweating heavily.

You ask the man what happened and how long she has been lying like this, unresponsive. He says he's not sure. He came out of his office and found her lying face down on the floor. He then rolled her over. You obtain more advanced medical care. You ask the man and the bystanders if anyone knows whether she has any medical conditions, is taking any medications, or is allergic to anything. No one seems to know. You look for a MedicAlert® medical identification product but don't find one.

You scramble to think of all the possibilities to explain this woman's condition. Could she have had a heart attack? Could she have been poisoned? Did she have an allergic reaction? A stroke? A diabetic emergency? A head injury from a fall? Did she have a seizure?

You know that advanced medical care will arrive in about eight minutes. You try to remain calm. You ask bystanders for a blanket to help warm the woman's cool body and you cover her. You check to make sure her airway is clear. You administer oxygen. You don't move her but examine her carefully for any clues as to what the problem could be. You want to help the woman more, but because you do not know what the problem is, you are unsure about how to proceed. You feel as if you should do something. But what more should you do?

The Dilemma of Medical Emergencies

The dilemma in the preceding scenario is not rare. You could someday face a similar situation involving an unclear medical emergency. Unlike easily identifiable problems, such as external bleeding, medical emergencies are rarely as clear. Therefore, you may feel more uncertain about providing care.

When you face an emergency you do not understand, it is normal to feel helpless or indecisive. Yet, like everyone, you still want to help to the best of your ability. Take comfort from the fact that giving initial care, even for medical emergencies you do not understand, does not require extensive knowledge. You do not have to "diagnose" or choose among possible problems to be able to provide appropriate care. By conducting a proper assessment and using the guidelines for care in previous chapters, you can provide appropriate care until you are able to obtain more advanced medical care. Knowing this, you can approach an unclear medical emergency with confidence.

The woman could have been experiencing a stroke, a diabetic emergency, or some other medical emergency, but you could not have known this. None of the bystanders knew the nature of her problem, and she was not wearing a MedicAlert® medical identification product. Did it matter that you could not diagnose exactly what her condition was? Not at all. You correctly focussed on the following basics of care:

• Monitor the ABCs. Keeping her positioned on one side kept her airway clear by letting fluid drain from her mouth so that it would not obstruct her airway. You could easily determine that she was breathing by watching and listening to her inhale and exhale. Since she was breathing, you knew she had a pulse. She did not have any severe external bleeding.

• Obtain more advanced medical care. This ensured a rapid response for a person who needed more advanced attention.

- Do a secondary survey to check for any additional injuries. When you surveyed the woman's body looking for any clues to her condition or additional problems, you did not find any. Therefore, you did not need to give further care.

- Minimize shock. Maintaining normal body temperature with a blanket, keeping her positioned on the floor, and administering oxygen helped minimize shock.

In this instance, everything that needed to be done was done. What if other information had been available, such as a MedicAlert® medical identification product indicating that the woman had diabetes? Would that have helped you care for this person? No; even if you had known she had diabetes, it would not have affected the care you provided. Since she was not conscious, your care would have been the same. Almost all the care you will give someone having a medical emergency is as simple as following these basics of care, whether the person is conscious or unconscious.

The Onset of Medical Emergencies

Medical emergencies can be caused by widely varying conditions and illnesses. Some acute conditions can develop very rapidly, whereas chronic conditions may develop gradually and persist for a long time. Medical emergencies can result from illness, disease, or chronic problems caused by diseases such as heart and lung disease. Or they can involve hormone imbalances, such as diabetes. Sometimes a medical emergency can involve sudden unexplained conditions, such as fainting. A person may become seriously ill because of poisoning. Someone with epilepsy can become ill due to occasional seizures. In other instances, medical emergencies result from allergies, when someone is exposed to a certain substance that causes a severe reaction. Still other medical emergencies can be caused by serious illness brought on by overexposure to heat or cold.

Sudden Illnesses

On a hot afternoon at the lake, a little boy staggers and falls into the water. The mother pulls him out onto the dock, where he begins to have a seizure. His arms and legs flail wildly about. What do you do?

INTRODUCTION

Certain illnesses can occur suddenly. Sometimes there are no warning signs or symptoms to alert you or the ill person that something is about to happen. At other times, the person may feel ill or state that he feels something is wrong.

Sudden illnesses may have a variety of signs and symptoms. They may cause changes in a person's level of consciousness. The person may complain of feeling lightheaded, dizzy, or weak. He may feel nauseated or may vomit. Breathing, pulse, and skin characteristics may change. If a person looks and feels ill, there is a problem.

Several conditions, such as diabetes, epilepsy, poisoning, shock, and high-altitude illness, can cause a change in consciousness. In an emergency, you may not know what caused the change, but the cause is not important. You do not need to know the exact cause to provide appropriate care for the person.

Faced with an unknown illness, you should obtain more advanced medical care. Sometimes, as with simple fainting, the condition can pass quickly. At other times, the problem may not be resolved quickly and easily. The condition may get worse. Therefore, it is better to err on the side of caution and obtain more advanced medical care.

This chapter provides information about some sudden illnesses you may encounter. Even though each of the sudden illnesses occurs for a different reason, they present with many of the same signs and symptoms. The care for these illnesses follows the same general guidelines:

- Obtain more advanced medical care
- Maintain normal body temperature
- Administer oxygen if available
- Provide ongoing survey and care

SPECIFIC SUDDEN ILLNESSES

Fainting

One of the most common sudden illnesses is fainting. Fainting (syncope) is a partial or complete loss of consciousness. It is caused by a temporary reduction in blood flow to the brain, such as occurs when blood collects in the legs and lower body. When the brain is suddenly deprived of its normal blood flow, it momentarily shuts down and the person faints.

Fainting can be triggered by an emotional shock, such as the sight of blood. It may be caused by pain, by specific medical conditions such as heart disease, by standing for a long time, or by overexertion. Some people, such as pregnant women or older adults, are more likely to faint when suddenly changing positions, for example, when moving from lying to standing up. Anytime changes inside the body momentarily reduce the blood flow to the brain, fainting may occur.

Signs and Symptoms of Fainting

Fainting may occur with or without warning. Often the person may initially feel lightheaded or dizzy. Because fainting is one form of shock, he may show signs of shock, such as pale, cool, moist skin. The person may feel nauseated and complain of numbness or tingling in the fingers and toes. The person's breathing and/or pulse may become faster.

Care for Fainting

Fainting often resolves itself. When the person moves from an upright position to a horizontal position, normal circulation to the brain often resumes. The person usually regains full consciousness within a minute.

Fainting itself does not usually harm the person, but injury may occur from falling. If you suspect a head or spine injury, take the necessary precautions when providing care. If you reach a person starting to collapse, lower him to the ground or other flat surface and position him on the back. Loosen any restrictive clothing, such as a tie or collar. Check the ABCs. Do not give the person anything to eat or drink as this can increase the chance of vomiting. Do not splash water on the person's face. This does little to stimulate the person, and he could aspirate the water. Administer oxygen if it is available.

Usually, someone who has fainted recovers quickly, with no lasting effects. However, since you will not be able to determine whether the fainting is linked to a more serious condition, you should obtain more advanced medical care.

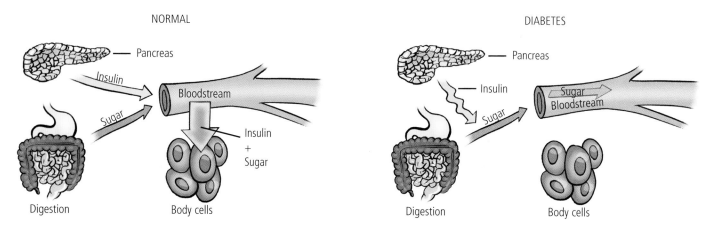

Figure 15–1 The hormone insulin is needed to take sugar from the blood into the body cells.

Diabetic Emergencies

To function normally, body cells need sugar as a source of energy. Through the digestive process, the body breaks down food into sugars, which are absorbed into the bloodstream. However, sugar cannot pass freely from the blood into the body cells; it needs an escort. Insulin, a hormone produced in the pancreas, takes sugar into the cells. Without a proper balance of sugar and insulin, the cells will starve and the body will not function properly (Figure 15–1).

The condition in which the body does not produce enough insulin is called diabetes mellitus or sugar diabetes.

There are two major types of diabetes. Type 1, insulin-dependent diabetes, occurs when the body produces little or no insulin. Since this type of diabetes tends to begin in childhood, it is often called juvenile diabetes. Most people with insulin-dependent diabetes have to inject insulin into their bodies daily.

Type 2, non-insulin-dependent diabetes, occurs when the body produces insulin but not in a quantity sufficient for the body's needs, or the body does not properly use the insulin that it produces. This condition is called maturity-onset diabetes.

Anyone with diabetes must carefully monitor his diet and exercise. People with insulin-dependent diabetes must also regulate their use of insulin (Figure 15–2). When someone with diabetes fails to control these factors, either of two problems can occur: too much or too little sugar in the body. This imbalance causes illness, which can become a diabetic emergency.

When the insulin level in the body is too low, the sugar level in the blood is high. This condition is called hyperglycemia (Figure 15–3, a). Sugar is present in the blood but cannot be transported from the blood into the cells without insulin. When this occurs, body cells become starved for sugar. The body attempts to meet its need for energy by using other stored food and energy sources, such as fats. However, converting fat to energy produces waste products and increases the acidity level in the blood, causing a condition called acidosis. As this occurs, the person becomes ill. If it continues, the hyperglycemic condition deteriorates into its most serious form, diabetic coma.

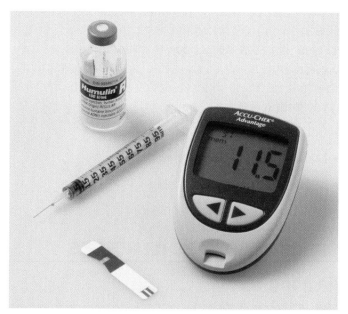

Figure 15–2 People with insulin-dependent diabetes must regulate their use of insulin. They may need to check their blood glucose level frequently.

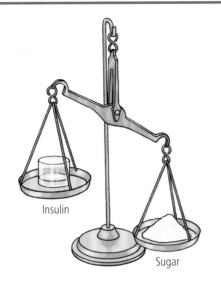

Figure 15–3, a-b a, hyperglycemia occurs when there is insufficient insulin in the body, causing a higher level of sugar in the blood; **b**, hypoglycemia occurs when the insulin level in the body is high, causing a low level of sugar in the blood.

On the other hand, when the insulin level in the body is too high, the person has a low sugar level. This condition is known as hypoglycemia (Figure 15–3, b). The sugar level can become too low if the person with diabetes:

• Takes too much insulin

• Fails to eat adequately

• Overexercises and burns off sugar faster than normal

• Experiences great emotional stress

In this situation, the small amount of sugar is used up rapidly and there is not enough for the brain to function properly. This results in an acute condition called insulin reaction, which can be life-threatening.

NOTE:

Many people with diabetes carry a glucometer, a device with which they can test their blood sugar level.

Signs and Symptoms of Diabetic Emergencies

The signs and symptoms of hyperglycemia and hypo-glycemia differ somewhat, but the major signs and symptoms are similar. These include:

• Changes in the level of consciousness, including dizziness, drowsiness, and confusion

• Rapid breathing

• Rapid pulse

• Feeling and looking ill

It is not important for you to differentiate between insulin reaction and diabetic coma. The basic care for both conditions is the same.

Care for Diabetic Emergencies

First, do a primary survey and care for any life-threatening conditions. If the person is conscious, do a secondary survey, asking and looking for anything visibly wrong. Ask if he has diabetes and look for a MedicAlert® medical identification product. If the person is known to have diabetes and exhibits the signs and symptoms previously stated, then suspect a diabetic emergency.

If the person is conscious and can take food or fluids, give him sugar (Figure 15–4). Most candy, fruit juices, and non-diet soft drinks have enough sugar to be effective. Common table sugar, either dry or dissolved in a glass of water, can restore the blood sugar level to normal. Commercially available sugar sources also work well. Sometimes a person who has diabetes will be able to tell you what is wrong and will ask for some-thing with sugar in it. If the person's problem is low sugar (hypoglycemia), the sugar you give will help quickly. If the person already has too much sugar (hyper-glycemia), the excess sugar will do no further harm.

Figure 15–4 Examples of types of sugar that can be given to someone having a diabetic emergency.

NOTE:

If local protocol requires you to carry oral glucose, see the drug profile in Appendix A.

Do not try to assist the person by administering insulin. Give something by mouth only if the person is fully conscious. Maintain normal body temperature, obtain more advanced medical care, and administer oxygen if available. If the person is conscious but does not feel better within approximately five minutes after taking sugar, obtain more advanced medical care. Oxygen should be administered if available. In both situations, provide ongoing survey and care.

Seizures

When the normal functions of the brain are disrupted by injury, disease, fever, or infection, the electrical activity of the brain becomes irregular. This irregularity can cause a loss of body control known as a seizure.

Seizures may be caused by an acute or a chronic condition. The chronic condition is known as epilepsy,

NOTE:

Diabetes can often be managed with diet, exercise, and medication. Checking your blood level regularly and keeping it in a target range, along with maintaining a healthy lifestyle, will prevent or delay the onset of diabetes-related complications such as vision loss, heart disease, and kidney problems.

which is usually controlled with medication. Still, some people with epilepsy have seizures from time to time. Others who go a long time without a seizure may think the condition has gone away and stop taking their medication. They may then have a seizure again. Seizures may also result when someone with epilepsy is changing his medication.

Signs and Symptoms of Seizure

Before a seizure occurs, the person may experience an aura. An aura is an unusual sensation or feeling, such as a visual hallucination; a strange sound, taste, or smell; or an urgent need to get to safety. If the person recognizes the aura, he may have time to tell bystanders and sit down before the seizure occurs.

Seizures range from mild blackouts that others may mistake for daydreaming to uncontrolled muscular contractions (convulsions) lasting several minutes.

The stages of generalized seizures are:

1. Aura phase—sensing something unusual
2. Tonic phase—unconsciousness then muscle rigidity
3. Clonic phase—seizures
4. Postictal phase—deep sleep with gradual recovery

Infants and young children are at risk for seizures brought on by high fever. These are called febrile seizures. When someone has a seizure, breathing may become irregular and even stop temporarily. There may also be frothing from the mouth or a loss of bowel and/or bladder control.

Care for Seizures

Although it may be frightening to see someone having a seizure, you can easily care for the person. Remember that he cannot control any muscular contractions that may occur. Allow the seizure to happen. Do not attempt to stop the seizure or restrain the person. This can cause musculoskeletal injuries.

Your objectives for care are to protect the person from injury and manage the airway. First, move away nearby objects, such as furniture, that might cause injury. Protect the person's head by placing a thin cushion, such as folded clothing, beneath it. If there is fluid, such as saliva or vomitus, in the person's mouth, position him on one side after the seizure so that the fluid can drain from the mouth.

Do not try to place anything between the person's teeth. People having seizures rarely bite their tongue or cheeks with enough force to cause any significant bleeding. However, some blood may be present, so positioning the person on his side will help any blood drain out of the mouth.

NOTE:

A continuous seizure, or two or more seizures without a period of consciousness, is called status epilepticus. This is a true medical emergency that can be fatal. Obtaining more advanced medical care must not be delayed.

In most instances, the seizure will be over by the time you arrive to help. The person will be drowsy and disoriented. Do a secondary survey, checking to see if the person was injured during the seizure. Offer comfort and reassurance. The person will be tired and want to rest. If the seizure occurred in public, the person may be embarrassed and self-conscious. Provide maximum privacy. Stay with the person until he is fully conscious and aware of his surroundings.

If the person is known to have periodic seizures, you do not necessarily need to obtain more advanced medical care immediately. The person will usually recover from a seizure in a few minutes. However, obtain more advanced medical care, if available, when:

- The seizure lasts more than a few minutes
- The person has repeated seizures (status epilepticus)
- The person appears to be injured

- You are uncertain about the cause of the seizure
- The person is pregnant
- The person is known to have diabetes
- The person is a baby or child
- The seizure takes place in water
- The person fails to regain consciousness after the seizure
- The person with a febrile seizure has a high fever

Appendicitis

Appendicitis is an acute inflammation of the appendix. This is a common abdominal emergency that occurs as a result of a viral or bacterial infection in the digestive tract or when the channel or cavity in the appendix becomes blocked. If untreated, the appendix may become gangrenous and rupture, which causes inflammation of the membrane that covers the abdominal wall (peritoneum).

The signs and symptoms of appendicitis include:

- Abdominal pain or cramping
- Nausea
- Vomiting
- Constipation
- Diarrhea
- Low-grade fever
- Abdominal swelling

The pain usually begins near the umbilical area and diffuses, later becoming intense and localized to the right lower quadrant. The pain becomes worse when moving, taking deep breaths, coughing, sneezing, and being touched in the area.

The goal of definitive care for appendicitis is surgical removal before rupture. Have the person rest in a comfortable position and help ensure prompt transport to a medical facility. Provide comfort measures by placing the person in a comfortable position, prevent life-threatening complications such as shock or aspiration (remember to give nothing by mouth), and obtain more advanced medical care. Provide ongoing survey and care.

Bowel Obstruction

Bowel obstruction is an occlusion of the intestinal cavity that results in blockage of normal flow of intestinal contents. This condition may be caused by a number of factors, including adhesions, hernias, fecal blockage, and tumours. Bowel obstruction in the small intestine is usually caused by adhesions and hernias, whereas obstruction in the large intestine is usually caused by tumours and fecal obstruction. The signs and symptoms of a bowel obstruction include:

- Abdominal pain
- Constipation
- Abdominal distension

The time of onset depends on whether the obstruction is in the small or large bowel. A danger of an obstructed bowel is perforation with generalized inflammation of the peritoneum and infection (sepsis).

Definitive treatment includes fluid replacement and antibiotics. Frequently, surgery is necessary to correct the obstruction. Provide supportive treatment, care for any life-threatening conditions, and ensure prompt transport to an appropriate medical facility. The person should not eat or drink anything.

Gastroenteritis

Gastroenteritis often results from infection of the gastrointestinal tract. It is often caused by poor hygiene or improper water disinfection or food preparation.

To prevent gastroenteritis, keep hydrated, eat balanced meals, do not restrain bowel movements, and ensure that all water is disinfected, food is prepared and stored properly, and you wash your hands frequently.

Signs and symptoms of gastroenteritis may include:

- Nausea and vomiting
- Diarrhea
- Headache (due to dehydration)
- Abdominal cramps
- Possible fever
- Rapid onset/short duration
- Pain associated with diarrhea

Definitive treatment includes fluid replacement and possibly antibiotics (if not viral) or other medications prescribed at a medical facility.

Other conditions may be confused with gastroenteritis. If a person has these signs and symptoms, he is not suffering from gastroenteritis, and you should obtain advanced medical care for them (see abdominal injuries in Chapter 14):

- Localized and constant pain
- Slow pain onset
- Rebound tenderness
- Abdominal rigidity
- Signs of internal bleeding or shock

> **NOTE:**
>
> *Looking at what the person last ingested and if there is anyone else experiencing similar symptoms may give you a clue as to what the cause might be.*

Kidney Stones

Kidney stones are solid concentrations of dissolved minerals found in the kidneys or ureters. These usually pass in the urine, but if they cause a blockage and obstruct the flow of urine, the person can present with:

- Pain in the flank, lower abdomen, and groin (usually radiating from the back to the front)
- Nausea, vomiting
- Restlessness
- Possible blood in the urine (if urine is present)

Kidney stones cause severe pain, and the person should be transported to a medical facility for removal of the stones, or wait until the stones pass.

Peptic Ulcers

A peptic ulcer is a small erosion in the gastrointestinal tract caused by destruction of the gastric or intestinal mucosal lining by hydrochloric acid. Infection by *Helicobacter pylori* is also thought to play a role, and ulcers caused by *Helicobacter pylori* are treated with medications prescribed by a doctor. Other major causes of ulcers include the chronic use of medications, such as ASA, and cigarette smoking.

The major symptom of an ulcer is a burning or gnawing feeling in the stomach area that lasts between 30 minutes and 3 hours. This pain is often misinterpreted as heartburn, indigestion, or hunger and usually occurs in the upper abdomen, although it may occur below the breastbone. In some individuals, the pain occurs immediately after eating; in others, it may not occur until hours after eating. The pain frequently awakens the person at night. Weeks of pain may be followed by weeks with no pain. Pain can be relieved by drinking milk, eating, resting, or taking antacids. Other symptoms include loss of appetite and weight loss.

Ulcers can also occur in the duodenum. People with duodenal ulcers may experience weight gain because they tend to eat more to help ease the discomfort. Other symptoms include recurrent vomiting, blood in the stool, and anemia.

More advanced medical care is required as prescription medication is often used to treat or relieve symptoms of ulcers.

Peritonitis

Peritonitis, an inflammation of the peritoneum, presents with acute abdominal pain and tenderness. Coughing, flexing the hips, and releasing manual pressure from the abdomen all tend to elicit more pain.

Peritonitis can be caused by infectious sources or non-infectious sources, such as sterile body fluids leaking into the peritoneum. Treatment includes rehydration, as well as possible antibiotics or surgery.

Urinary Tract Infection (UTI)

A UTI is an infection at any site within the urinary tract, usually bacterial. It can affect the urethra, bladder, or kidney, as well as the prostate gland in men. These infections are very common. Those at greater risk of UTIs include females, because of their shorter urethra, paraplegics, and those with nerve disruption to the bladder, for example, people with diabetes. As well, those with urinary stasis (incomplete emptying of the bladder, which may serve as nutrition for pathogens)

are also predisposed to the infection. This latter group includes pregnant woman and people with neurological impairment. More advanced care is needed as medication will most likely be prescribed.

High-Altitude Illness

When travelling in mountainous areas, people can become sick due to the change in altitude. At higher altitudes, it is harder for the oxygen to enter the bloodstream due to the lower atmospheric pressure. When ascending quickly above 2,133 metres (7,000 feet), people can experience high-altitude illness.

It takes the body time to adapt physiologically to altitudes. Some of these changes take place within 10 days. Within the first 10 days, the body adapts to altitudes by increased respiratory rate, increased heart rate, and fluid shifts.

Other adaptations take longer for the body to make. Later changes occur after anywhere from 10 days to up to 6 weeks and include increased red blood cell production, increased active capillaries, and gradually decreasing heart rate.

High-altitude illness can take one of three forms: acute mountain sickness (AMS), high-altitude pulmonary edema (HAPE), and high-altitude cerebral edema (HACE).

AMS is not a specific disease but a group of varied symptoms caused by altitude.

Signs and symptoms of AMS include:

- Headache and/or insomnia
- Vomiting and loss of appetite
- Coughing and/or tightness in the chest
- Irregular breathing or shortness of breath
- Swelling around eyes and face
- Reduced urine output
- Weakness, fatigue, and lethargy
- Peripheral edema
- Cyanosis at nail beds and around the mouth
- Difficulty maintaining balance (ataxia)

Care for AMS includes the following:

- Check and record vital signs on a regular basis.

- Stop and rest, with light activity, allowing up to two days for acclimatization.

- If signs and symptoms persist, rapid descent is necessary.

HAPE is a progressive stage of AMS and usually occurs one to four days after arrival at altitude. It is a serious, life-threatening condition in which fluid begins pooling in the lungs. The result is a breathing emergency.

Signs and symptoms of HAPE include:

- Fatigue with difficulty breathing at rest; wheezing

- General ache in the chest

- Continuous fast pulse

- Bluish colouring of the skin

- Gurgling cough accompanied by frothy sputum

- Mental confusion, delirium, and irrational behaviour (caused by reduced oxygen to the brain)

In more severe cases, the person may have a productive (fluid-generating) cough, extreme weakness, shortness of breath while at rest, heart rate greater than 110 at rest, breathing rate greater than 30 at rest, and frothy, blood-tinged sputum.

HACE is another progressive stage of AMS and is an accumulation of fluid between the brain and skull. It occurs two to three days after arrival at altitude. It is a serious condition that is difficult to diagnose but will usually accompany HAPE.

Signs and symptoms of HACE include:

- Increasingly severe headache, convulsions, stupor

- Nausea and/or vomiting

- Dizziness and/or lack of coordination, mental confusion

- Unconsciousness

- Ataxia

- Vision disturbances

- Paralysis

- Seizures

- Hallucinations

- Cyanosis

- Increased blood pressure

- Decreasing heart rate

Care for HAPE and HACE includes the following:

- Check and record vital signs on a regular basis

- Descend, prepare for evacuation if necessary, and obtain more advanced medical care

There are also steps you can take to help anyone with high-altitude illness of any type. First, descend to a significantly lower altitude. If available, and the person's condition remains poor, place him in a portable altitude chamber (hyperbaric bag). It is also important to hydrate the person regularly with four to six litres of fluids per day.

Prevention of High-Altitude Illness

There are steps to take to reduce the likelihood or severity of symptoms of high-altitude illness. These steps should be considered by anyone climbing to high altitudes:

- Assess in advance your ability to perform at high altitudes

- Plan your trip in stages, thereby allowing time for people to acclimatize at specific sleeping elevations

- Remember to descend to sleep

- Observe others in the party regularly, watching for signs and symptoms of altitude sickness

- Drink up to four litres of fluid per day (keep urine colour light)

- Avoid sleeping pills, alcohol, or any other respiratory depressants

SUMMARY

Sudden illness can strike anyone at any time. The signs and symptoms for each of the sudden illnesses described in this chapter are very similar. Recognizing their general signs and symptoms, such as changes in the level of consciousness, sweating, confusion, weakness, and appearing ill, will indicate to you the necessary initial care you should provide. Usually, you will not know the cause of the illness. Diabetic emergencies, seizures, and fainting are all sudden illnesses, each with an individual, specific cause. Fortunately, you can provide proper care without knowing the cause. High-altitude illness may present with some of the same signs and symptoms but with a known cause. Performing a proper assessment and following the general guidelines of care for any emergency will help prevent the condition from becoming worse. When providing care for sudden illnesses, you should:

- Obtain more advanced medical care

- Maintain normal body temperature

- Administer oxygen if available

- Provide ongoing survey and care

The boy's seizure soon stops. His rigid body goes limp. At this time, another responder asks if there is anything you would like him to do. What do you do?

Poisoning

You've been called to attend to a man feeling unwell, sitting on a bench in a shopping centre. You examine his leg where he says he's developed a rash. The centre of the rash is lighter in colour, and the outer edges are red and raised, giving the rash a bull's-eye appearance. He says he feels as if he's coming down with something, possibly the flu, but he's worried about the rash. What do you do?

INTRODUCTION

Poisoning is another type of sudden illness, but unlike sudden illnesses such as fainting and diabetic emergencies, poisoning results when an external substance enters the body. The substance may be a chemical, or it may be a germ or virus that enters the body through a bite or sting. In this chapter, you will learn how to recognize and care for poisoning.

HOW POISONS ENTER THE BODY

A poison is any substance that causes injury or illness when introduced into the body. Some poisons can cause death. Poisons include solids, liquids, and fumes (gases and vapours). A poison can enter the body in four ways: ingestion, inhalation, absorption, and injection (Figure 16–1).

To ingest means to swallow. Ingested poisons include foods, such as certain mushrooms and shellfish; substances, such as alcohol; medications, such as ASA; and household and garden items, such as cleaning products, pesticides, and plants. Many substances not poisonous in small amounts are poisonous in larger amounts.

Figure 16–1 A poison can enter the body by ingestion, inhalation, absorption, and injection.

Poisoning by inhalation occurs when a person breathes in toxic fumes. Inhaled poisons include:

- Gases such as carbon monoxide, from an engine or other combustion
- Gases such as carbon dioxide, which can occur naturally from decomposition
- Gases such as nitrous oxide, used for medical procedures
- Gases such as chlorine, found in commercial swimming facilities
- Fumes from household products, such as glues and paints
- Fumes from drugs, such as marijuana

An absorbed poison enters the body after coming in contact with the skin or other membranes (thin sheets of tissue that cover a structure or line a cavity, such as the mouth or nose). Absorbed poisons come from plants, such as poison ivy, poison oak, and poison sumac, and from fertilizers and pesticides used in lawn and plant care. They can also come from drugs, such as cocaine, that can be absorbed through the mucous membranes in the mouth and nose.

Injected poisons enter the body through bites or stings of insects, spiders, ticks, snakes, and other animals or as drugs or medications injected with a hypodermic syringe.

SIGNS AND SYMPTOMS OF POISONING

The most important thing with a poisoning is to recognize that it may have occurred. As with other serious emergencies, such as severe chest pain or head and spine injury, evaluate the scene, the condition of the person, and any information given by the person or bystanders. If you then have even a slight suspicion that the person has been poisoned, obtain more advanced medical care immediately.

As you approach the person, survey the scene. Be aware of any unusual odours, flames, smoke, open or spilled containers, an open medicine cabinet, an overturned or damaged plant, or other signs of possible poisoning.

When you reach the person, do a primary survey. If the person has no life-threatening conditions, do a secondary survey. Someone who has been poisoned generally displays signs and symptoms common to other sudden illnesses. These include nausea, vomiting, diarrhea, chest or abdominal pain, breathing difficulty, sweating, altered level of consciousness, and seizures.

Other signs of poisoning are burn injuries around the mouth or on the skin. You may also suspect a poisoning based on any information you have from or about the person. Look also for any drug paraphernalia, such as pipes, paper for rolling, syringes, or containers.

If you suspect a poisoning, try to get answers to the following questions:

• What type of poison was taken?

• How much was taken?

• When was it taken?

This information will help you provide the most appropriate initial care and provide more advanced medical personnel with valuable information that may affect additional care.

POISON CONTROL CENTRES

A poisoning emergency can sometimes pose a unique problem for those trying to provide appropriate care. The severity of the poisoning depends on the type and amount of the substance, how it entered the body, and the person's size, weight, and age. Some poisons act quickly and have characteristic signs and symptoms. Others act slowly and cannot easily be identified. Sometimes you will be able to identify the specific poison, sometimes not.

To help responders on all levels deal with poisonings, Poison Control Centres exist throughout Canada. Medical professionals in these centres have access to information about virtually all poisonous substances. They can tell you how to counteract the poison. You should know your closest Poison Control Centre number.

If the person is unconscious, obtain more advanced medical care immediately. The dispatcher may be able to link you with the Poison Control Centre. The dispatcher may also monitor your discussion with the Poison Control Centre and provide additional information to the responding medical care personnel. In some instances, this eliminates the need for a second call and saves time.

CARE FOR POISONING

Follow these general principles for any poisoning emergency:

• Survey the scene to make sure it is safe to approach and gather clues about what happened.

• Remove the person from the source of the poison.

• Do a primary survey to assess the person's airway, breathing, and circulation.

• Care for any life-threatening conditions.

• If the person is conscious, do a secondary survey to gather additional information. Look for containers, pills, etc.

• Contact the Poison Control Centre and/or obtain more advanced medical care.

• Follow the directions of the Poison Control Centre.

• Avoid giving the person anything by mouth unless advised to do so by medical professionals. If the poison is unknown and the person vomits, save some of the vomitus, which may be analyzed later to identify the poison.

• Provide ongoing survey and care.

Ingested Poisons

Besides following these general principles for any poisoning, you may also need to provide additional care for specific types of poisons. The Poison Control Centre may instruct you to induce vomiting. Unless local protol dictates otherwise, induce vomiting only upon the instruction of the Poison Control Centre.

The Poison Control Centre may ask you to neutralize the amount that remains with activated charcoal. Activated charcoal is available in both liquid and powder forms and may be part of your response equipment. Always follow local protocol and the directions from the Poison Control Centre.

If directed to do so by the Poison Control Centre, you can dilute some ingested poisons by giving the person water to drink. Examples of such poisons are corrosive chemicals, such as acids or alkalis, which damage or destroy tissues. Vomiting these corrosives could burn the esophagus, throat, and mouth. Diluting the corrosive substance decreases the potential for damaging tissues.

Diluting poisons taken in tablet or capsule form is usually not a good idea. The increased fluid could dissolve them more rapidly in the stomach, speeding the body's absorption of the poison. As always, follow the advice of the Poison Control Centre or other medical professionals.

Inhaled Poisons

Toxic fumes come from a variety of sources. Hydrogen sulfide (H_2S), for example, is an inhaled poison given off by decomposing organic matter, some wells, and sewers. It is also found in the fumes from certain industrial and home spray chemicals.

A more common inhaled poison is carbon monoxide (CO). It is present in car exhaust and can be produced by defective cooking equipment, fires, and charcoal grills. A pale or bluish skin colour that indicates a lack of oxygen may signal carbon monoxide poisoning.

For years, people were taught that carbon monoxide poisoning was indicated by a cherry-red colour of the skin and lips. This, however, is a poor initial indicator of carbon monoxide poisoning. The red colour occurs later, usually after death.

When someone has inhaled poison, the person needs to be removed from the poison as soon as possible. First and foremost, ensure your own safety. Survey the scene to determine if it is safe for you to help. If you can remove the person from the source of the poison without endangering your life, then do so. You can help a conscious person by just getting her to fresh air and then obtaining more advanced medical care. Remove an unconscious person from the environment and maintain an open airway. If the person is not breathing, begin rescue breathing. Administer oxygen, if available, to anyone who has inhaled a poison.

Absorbed Poisons

People often contact poisonous substances that can be absorbed into the body. Thousands of people each year suffer from contact with poison ivy (Figure 16–2, a), poison oak (Figure 16–2, b), and poison sumac (Figure 16–2, c). Other common poisons absorbed through the skin include dry and wet chemicals, such as those found in insecticides and toxic industrial chemicals, which may also burn the surface of the skin.

To care for poison contact, immediately wash the affected area with water. Rinse the area with cool water and pat dry. Keep the area clean and dry. Instruct the person to see a doctor if the condition gets worse. If poi-

Figure 16–2, a-c a, poison ivy; **b**, poison oak; and **c**, poison sumac.

Hantavirus

Hantavirus is found throughout North America, although it is most common in the southern United States. It is carried by various types of rodents. Hantavirus may be caused by inhaling microscopic particles of dried rodent saliva, urine, or feces. It can also be caused when someone touches her mouth or nose after handling contaminated materials. And it may occur after being bitten by a rodent.

There are steps to prevent acquiring hantavirus. Check sites for rodent droppings and burrows, avoid sleeping near areas where there may be rodents, and store food where rodents can't get at it. Thoroughly clean and disinfect areas (home, work, cabin, etc.) where there have been rodents, and use gloves if you have to pick up a rodent for any reason.

Signs and Symptoms of Hantavirus

A person with hantavirus will appear with flu-like symptoms: fever, headache, muscle aches, nausea, and vomiting. This can progress to breathing difficulties.

Care for Hantavirus

The care for hantavirus is the same as care for other poisons.

---

sons such as dry or wet chemicals contact the skin, flush the affected area continuously with large amounts of water. Obtain more advanced medical care immediately. Continue to flush the area until care is obtained.

If running water is not available, brush off dry chemicals, such as lime. Take care not to get any in your eyes or the eyes of the person or any bystanders. Dry chemicals are activated by contact with water, but if continuous running water is available, it will flush the chemical from the skin before activating it. Running water reduces the threat to you and quickly and easily removes the substance from the person.

Injected Poisons

Insect and animal stings and bites are among the most common sources of injected poisons. This text cannot consider all possible types of stings and bites that could result in poisoning. The following sections describe the care for common stings and bites of insects, spiders, marine life, snakes, warm-blooded animals, and ticks.

Insects

Although insect stings are painful, they are rarely fatal. Some people, however, have a severe allergic reaction to an insect sting, resulting in the life-threatening condition anaphylaxis, discussed in Chapter 6.

To care for an insect sting, first examine the sting site to see if the stinger is in the skin. If it is, remove it to prevent any further poisoning. Scrape the stinger away from the skin with your fingernail or a plastic card, such as a driver's licence or credit card. Often the venom sac will still be attached to the stinger. Do not remove the stinger with tweezers since putting pressure on the venom sac can cause further poisoning.

Next, wash the site with soap and water. Cover it to keep it clean. Apply a cold compress to the area to reduce the pain and swelling. Observe the person periodically for signs and symptoms of an allergic reaction.

Spiders

Few spiders in North America have venom that causes death. But the bites of the black widow and brown recluse spiders can be fatal. You can identify them by the unique designs on their bodies. The black widow spider is black with a reddish hourglass shape on its underbody (Figure 16–3). The brown recluse spider is light brown with a darker brown, violin-shaped marking on the top of its body.

Both spiders prefer dark, out-of-the-way places where they are seldom disturbed. Bites usually occur on the hands and arms of people reaching into places such as wood, rock, and brush piles or rummaging in dark storage areas. Often the person will not know that she has been bitten until signs or symptoms develop.

If the spider is identified as either a black widow or brown recluse, the person should get immediate care at a medical facility. The wound will be cleansed and medication provided to reduce the pain and inflammation. An antivenin, a substance used to counteract or reduce the poisonous effects of snake or other venom, is available for particular spider bites.

Signs and symptoms of spider bites include:

- Nausea and vomiting
- Difficulty breathing or swallowing
- Sweating and salivating profusely
- Irregular heart rhythms that can lead to cardiac arrest
- Severe pain in the sting or bite area
- Swelling on or around the site
- A mark indicating a possible bite or sting

To care for a spider bite, wash the wound and apply a cold compress to the site. A person who has these signs and symptoms needs to go to a medical facility.

Marine Life

Sting rays, sea anemones, certain fish, jellyfish, and some other marine animals can give painful stings that may cause serious problems, such as allergic reaction, paralysis, and cardiac and respiratory difficulties (Figure 16–4). Always remove the person who has been stung from the water as soon as possible. Obtain more advanced medical care if the person:

- Has a history of allergic reactions to marine life stings
- Is stung on the face or neck
- Develops severe problems, such as difficulty breathing

If the sting is from a jellyfish, sea anemone, or man-of-war, soak the injured part in vinegar. Vinegar often works best to deactivate the toxin. Rubbing alcohol or baking soda may also be used. Do not rub the wound or apply fresh water or ammonia since this will increase pain.

If the sting is from a stingray, sea urchin, or spiny fish, flush the wound with sterile saline or water. Tap or ocean water may also be used. Immobilize the injured part, usually the foot, and soak the affected area in non-scalding hot water (as hot as the person

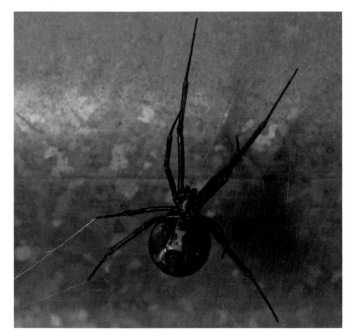

Figure 16–3 A black widow spider.

Figure 16–4 A sting ray.

can stand) for about 30 minutes or until the pain subsides. Then carefully clean the wound and apply a bandage. Remind the person to watch for signs of infection and check with a healthcare provider to determine if a tetanus shot is needed.

Snakes

Few people die of snakebites. Furthermore, a snake-bite does not mean that venom is injected. Rattlesnakes account for most snakebites and nearly all deaths from snakebites. Most deaths occur because the person has an allergic reaction or a weakened body system or because significant time passes before the person receives medical care. Elaborate care is usually unnecessary because, in most cases, the person can reach advanced medical care within 30 minutes.

Follow these guidelines to provide initial care for someone bitten by a snake:

• Wash the wound.

• Immobilize the affected part.

• Keep the affected area lower than the heart if possible.

• Obtain more advanced medical care.

• Provide ongoing survey and care.

You should follow your local protocols regarding care for someone bitten by a snake.

When caring for a snake bite, avoid:

• Applying ice. Studies show that cooling the bite can cause as much harm as good.

• Cutting the wound. Cutting the wound can further injure the person and has not been shown to remove any significant amount of venom.

• Applying a tourniquet. A tourniquet severely restricts blood flow to the extremity, which could result in the loss of the extremity.

NOTE:

If the person's arm or leg is bitten by an elapid snake (coral family), the responder should wrap the entire extremity with an elastic bandage. The bandage should immobilize the extremity. It should be wrapped snugly enough to allow one finger to slip between the bandage and the skin.

Animals

The bite of a domestic or wild animal carries the risk of infection, as well as soft tissue injury. The most serious possible result is rabies, a disease transmitted through the saliva of diseased animals such as skunks, bats, raccoons, cats, dogs, cattle, and foxes.

Animals with rabies may act in unusual ways. For example, nocturnal animals, such as raccoons, may be active in the daytime. A wild animal that usually tries to avoid humans may not run away when you approach. Rabid animals may salivate, appear partially paralyzed, or act irritable, aggressive, or strangely quiet. Avoid petting or feeding wild animals and do not touch the body of a dead wild animal.

If not treated, rabies is fatal. Anyone bitten by an animal suspected of having rabies must get medical attention. To prevent rabies from developing, the person receives a series of injections to build up immunity. In the past, caring for rabies meant a lengthy series of painful injections that had many unpleasant side effects. The vaccines used now require fewer injections and have less severe side effects.

If someone is bitten by an animal, try to get her away from the animal without endangering yourself. If possible, try to get a good description of the animal and the area in which it was last seen. If the wound is minor, wash it with soap and water and then control any bleeding. If the wound is bleeding seriously, control the bleeding first. The wound will be properly cleaned at a medical facility. Obtain more advanced medical care for any wounds with serious bleeding. Other authorities, such as animal control, may need to be notified. Any person who has been bitten by an animal must see her physician. Local laws or protocols may require you to report the bite to the proper authorities.

Ticks

Ticks can carry and transmit disease to humans. In the past, Rocky Mountain spotted fever was widely publicized as a tick disease. It is still occurring today, but attention has been focussed on another disease transmitted by ticks, known as Lyme disease or Lyme borreliosis. Lyme disease is an illness people get from the bite of an infected tick.

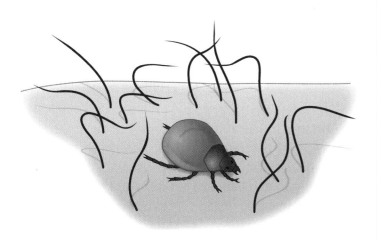

Figure 16–5 Ticks can be as small as a head of a pin.

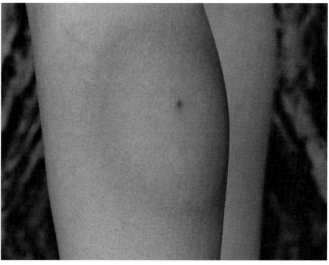

Figure 16–6 A rash in a bull's-eye pattern is a common sign of Lyme disease infection.

Not all ticks carry Lyme disease. Lyme disease is spread primarily by a type of tick that commonly attaches itself to field mice and deer. It is sometimes called a deer tick. This tick is found around beaches and in wooded and grassy areas. Like all ticks, it attaches itself to any warm-blooded animal that brushes by it, including humans.

Deer ticks are very tiny and difficult to see. They are much smaller than the common dog tick or wood tick. They can be as small as a poppy seed or the head of a pin (Figure 16–5). Even in the adult stage, they are only as large as a grape seed. A deer tick can attach to you without your knowledge. Many people who develop Lyme disease cannot recall having been bitten.

A person can get Lyme disease from the bite of an infected tick at any time of the year, but this occurs most often in summer, when ticks are most active and people spend more time outdoors.

The first sign of infection may appear a few days or a few weeks after a tick bite. Typically, a rash starts as a small red area at the site of the bite. It may spread up to 12 to 17 cm (5 to 7 in) across (Figure 16–6). In fair-skinned people, the centre is lighter in colour and the outer edges are red and raised, sometimes giving the rash a bull's-eye appearance. In dark-skinned people, the area may look black and blue, like a bruise.

Signs and symptoms of Lyme disease include fever, headache, weakness, and joint and muscle pain similar to

the pain of "flu." These signals may develop slowly and may not occur at the same time as a rash. In fact, a person can have Lyme disease without developing a rash.

Lyme disease can get worse if not treated. In its advanced stages, it may cause arthritis, numbness, memory loss, problems seeing or hearing, high fever, and a stiff neck. Some of these symptoms could indicate nervous system problems. An irregular or rapid heartbeat could indicate heart problems.

If you find a tick, remove it by pulling steadily and firmly. Grasp the tick with fine-tipped tweezers (or a hook designed for tick removal), as close to the skin as possible, and pull slowly (Figure 16–7). If you do not

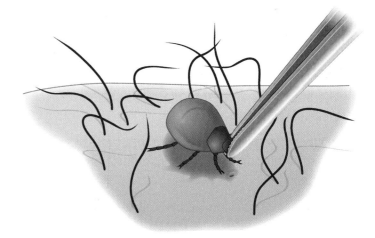

Figure 16–7 Remove a tick by grabbing it with tweezers as close to the skin as possible.

have tweezers, use a glove, plastic wrap, a piece of paper, or a leaf to protect your fingers. If you use your bare fingers, wash your hands immediately. If you are unable to remove the tick or if its mouth parts stay in the skin, the person should obtain medical care, such as from a family physician.

Once the tick is removed, wash the area immediately with soap and water. Unless the person is allergic, if an antiseptic or antibiotic ointment is available, apply it to prevent wound infection. The person should be told to observe the site periodically thereafter. If a rash or flu-like symptoms develop, she should seek medical help. A physician will usually use antibiotics to treat Lyme disease. Antibiotics work best and most quickly when taken early. Treatment is slower and less effective in advanced stages.

POISONING PREVENTION

Thousands of Canadians are admitted to hospitals each year due to poisoning. The best approach to poisoning emergencies is to prevent them from occurring in the first place.

By following these general guidelines, people will be able to prevent most poisoning emergencies:

- Keep all medications and dangerous products well out of the reach of children.

- Use childproof safety caps on medication containers and other potentially dangerous products.

- Keep products in their original containers with the labels in place.

- Use poison symbols to identify dangerous substances.

- Dispose of outdated products.

- Use potentially dangerous chemicals only in well-ventilated areas.

- When working with a poisonous substance, wear clothing that can prevent contact with the substance.

- Wear appropriate clothing and footwear when in an area where bites from insects, spiders, ticks, and snakes are possible.

SUBSTANCE MISUSE AND ABUSE

Alcohol and over-the-counter medications such as ASA, sleeping pills, and certain stimulants are among the most often misused or abused substances. The misuse or abuse of a substance results in the poisoning of the body.

Substance misuse is the use of a substance for unintended purposes or for appropriate purposes but in improper amounts or doses. Substance abuse is the deliberate, persistent, and excessive use of a substance without regard to health concerns or accepted medical practices. Many substances that are abused or misused are legal. Other substances are legal when prescribed by a physician. Some are illegal only for those under age. Figure 16–8 shows some commonly misused and abused substances.

A drug is any substance other than food taken to affect body functions. A drug used to prevent or treat a disease or condition or otherwise enhance mental or physical well-being is a medication.

An overdose occurs if someone takes enough of a substance that it has toxic (poisonous) or fatal effects.

Figure 16–8 Commonly misused and abused substances.

An overdose may occur if the person takes more of a drug than is needed for medical purposes. It may occur unintentionally when someone takes too much medication at one time, for example, if an older adult forgets that she has already taken the medication and takes another dose. Or a person with failing eyesight may mistake one medication for another.

An overdose may also be intentional, such as in a suicide attempt. Sometimes the person takes a sufficient quantity of a substance to cause certain death. Other times, to gain attention or help, the person takes enough of a substance to need medical attention but not enough to cause death.

The term "withdrawal" describes the condition produced when someone stops using or abusing a drug to which she is addicted. Withdrawal may occur because of someone's deliberate decision to stop or because she is unable to obtain the specific drug. Withdrawal from certain substances, such as alcohol, can cause severe mental and physical discomfort and can become a serious medical condition.

Commonly Misused and Abused Substances

Substances are categorized according to their effects on the body. The basic categories are stimulants, hallucinogens, and depressants. The category to which a substance belongs depends mostly on the effects it has on the central nervous system. Some substances depress the nervous system, whereas others speed up its activity. Some are not easily categorized because they have various effects. Designer drugs, those that don't fit into one of the other three drug categories, are also commonly used. Figure 16–9 shows a variety of illegal misused and abused substances.

Stimulants

Stimulants affect the central nervous system by speeding up physical and mental activity. They have limited medical value. They produce temporary feelings of alertness, improve task performance, and prevent sleepiness. They are sometimes used for weight reduction because they suppress appetite.

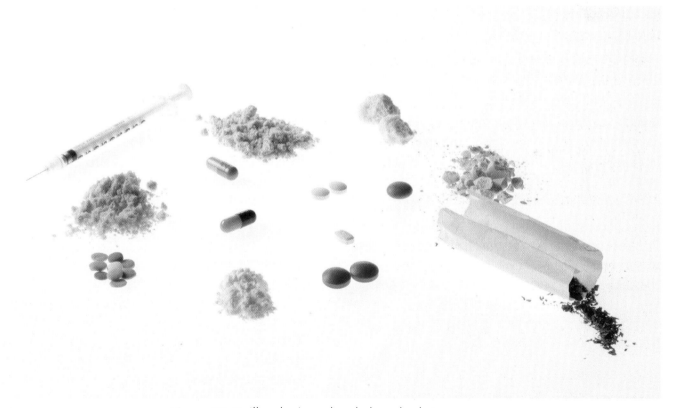

Figure 16–9 Illegal misused and abused substances.

Many stimulants are ingested as pills, but some can be absorbed or inhaled. Amphetamine, dextroamphetamine, and methamphetamine are stimulants. There are many street, or slang, names for stimulants, for example, "speed."

Cocaine is one of the most publicized and powerful stimulants. Cocaine can be taken into the body in different ways. The most common is sniffing it in powder form. In this method, the drug is absorbed into the blood through the capillaries in the nose. A purer and more potent form of cocaine is crack. Crack is smoked. The vapours that are inhaled into the lungs reach the brain within 10 seconds, causing immediate effects. Crack poses a serious threat because it is highly addictive.

The most common stimulants are legal. Leading the list is caffeine, present in coffee, tea, many kinds of sodas, chocolate, diet pills, and pills used to combat fatigue. Next is nicotine, found in tobacco products. Other stimulants used for medical purposes are inhaled to treat asthma.

Hallucinogens

Hallucinogens, at present, have no medical uses. They cause changes in mood, sensation, thought, emotion, and self-awareness. They alter perception of time and space and produce delusions.

Among the most widely abused are LSD (lysergic acid diethylamide), commonly called acid; psilocybin, called mushrooms; and PCP (phencyclidine), also known as angel dust. These substances are usually ingested, but PCP is also often inhaled.

Hallucinogens often have physical effects similar to those of stimulants but are classified differently because of the other effects they produce. Hallucinogens can sometimes cause intense fear, panic, paranoid delusions, vivid hallucinations, profound depression, tension, and anxiety. The person may be irrational and feel threatened by any attempt others make to help.

Depressants

Depressants affect the central nervous system to slow down physical and mental activity. Unlike stimulants and hallucinogens, which have limited or no medical value, depressants are commonly used for medical purposes. Common depressants are barbiturates, benzodiazepines, narcotics, alcohol, and inhalants. Most depressants are ingested or injected.

All depressants alter consciousness to some degree. They relieve anxiety, promote sleep, relieve pain, and relax muscles, but they also depress respiration and impair coordination and judgment. Like other substances, the larger the dose or the stronger the substance, the greater its effects.

Alcohol is the most widely used and abused depressant in Canada. In small amounts, its effects are fairly mild. In higher doses, its effects can be toxic. Alcohol is like other depressants in its effects and the risks for overdose. Frequent drinkers may become dependent on the effects of alcohol and increasingly tolerant of them.

Alcohol taken in large amounts or frequently has many unhealthy consequences. The digestive system may be irritated. Alcohol can cause the esophagus to rupture or can injure the stomach lining, causing the person to vomit blood. This type of consumption is life-threatening. Chronic drinking can affect the brain and cause a lack of coordination, memory loss, and apathy. Other problems include liver disease, such as cirrhosis. In addition, many psychological, family, social, and work problems are related to chronic drinking.

Narcotics have effects similar to those of other depressants. They are powerful and are used to relieve anxiety and pain. All narcotics are illegal without a prescription, and some are not prescribed at all. The most common natural narcotics are morphine and codeine. Most other narcotics, including heroin, are synthetic.

Substances inhaled to produce an intoxicating effect are called inhalants. Inhalants also have a depressing effect on the central nervous system. In addition, inhalant use can damage the heart, lungs, brain, and liver. Solvents, such as acetone, toluene, butane, gasoline, kerosene, lighter fluid, paints, nail polish and remover, and aerosol sprays, have been inhaled for their effects. The effects are similar to those of alcohol. The user, at first, appears to be drunk.

Designer Drugs

Designer drugs are substances that do not fit neatly into any of the three categories mentioned previously.

Designer drugs are variations of medically prescribed substances such as narcotics and amphetamines. Through simple and inexpensive methods, the molecular structure of substances produced for medicinal purposes can be modified by street chemists into extremely potent and dangerous street drugs—hence the name designer drug. One such designer drug, a form of the commonly used surgical anaesthetic fentanyl, can be made 2,000 to 6,000 times stronger than its original form.

When the chemical makeup of a drug is altered, as with designer drugs, the user may experience a variety of unpredictable and dangerous effects. In many cases, the chemist has no knowledge of what the effects of the new designer drug could be.

Signs and Symptoms of Substance Misuse or Abuse

Like other poisons, the general signs and symptoms of substance misuse and abuse are similar to those of other medical emergencies. The misuse or abuse of stimulants can have many unhealthy effects on the body. These can include moist or flushed skin, sweating, chills, nausea, vomiting, fever, headache, dizziness, rapid pulse, rapid breathing, high blood pressure, and chest pain. In some instances, it can cause a breathing emergency, disrupt normal heart rhythms, or cause death. The person may appear very excited, restless, talkative, irritable, or combative or may suddenly lose consciousness.

Specific signs and symptoms of hallucinogen abuse may include sudden mood changes and a flushed face. The person may claim to see or hear something not present. She may be anxious and frightened.

Specific signs and symptoms of depressant misuse or abuse may include drowsiness, confusion, slurred speech, slow heart and breathing rates, and poor coordination. An alcohol abuser may smell of alcohol. A person who has consumed a great deal of alcohol in a short time may be unconscious or hard to arouse. The person may vomit violently. Someone suffering alcohol withdrawal, a potentially dangerous condition, can be confused and restless. She may also tremble and experience hallucinations.

You may be able to find clues that suggest the nature of the problem. Often these clues will come from the person, bystanders, or the scene itself. Look for containers, drug paraphernalia, and signs and symptoms of other medical problems. Try to get information from the person or from any bystanders or family members. Since many of these physical signs and symptoms of substance abuse mimic other conditions, you may not be able to determine that a person has overdosed on a substance.

To provide care for the person, you need only recognize abnormalities in breathing, pulse, skin colour, temperature, moisture, and behaviour that may indicate a condition requiring professional help.

Care for Substance Misuse or Abuse

As with other medical emergencies, you do not have to diagnose substance abuse or misuse to provide care. Your initial care does not require that you know the specific substance taken. Since substance misuse or abuse is a form of poisoning, care follows the same general steps as for other types of poisoning:

- Survey the scene to be sure it is safe to help the person.

- Do a primary survey and care for any life-threatening conditions.

- Contact the Poison Control Centre and/or obtain more advanced medical care.

- Question the person or bystanders during your secondary survey to try to find out what substance was taken, how much was taken, and when it was taken.

- Try to keep the person calm by minimizing movement, loud noises, etc.

- If the person is unconscious, maintain an open airway.

- Maintain normal body temperature.

- If the person vomits or has vomited, place her on one side and clear any matter out of the mouth. Save a sample of the vomitus, if possible.

- Withdraw from the area if the person becomes violent or threatening.

- If you suspect that someone has used a designer drug, tell the responding advanced medical personnel. This is important because someone who has overdosed on a designer drug frequently does not respond to usual medical treatment.

- Provide ongoing survey and care.

SUMMARY

Poisonings can occur in four ways: ingestion, inhalation, absorption, and injection. Substance misuse and abuse are types of poisoning that can occur in any of these ways. Substance misuse and abuse can produce a variety of signs and symptoms, most of which are common to other types of poisoning. You do not need to be able to determine the cause of a poisoning to provide appropriate initial care. If you see any of the signs and symptoms of sudden illness, ensure your own safety and follow the basics of care for any sudden illness.

For suspected poisonings, contact your local or regional Poison Control Centre and/or obtain more advanced medical care. Beyond following the general guidelines for giving care for a suspected poisoning, medical professionals may advise you to provide some specific care, such as inducing vomiting. The best way to avoid poisoning is to take steps to prevent it.

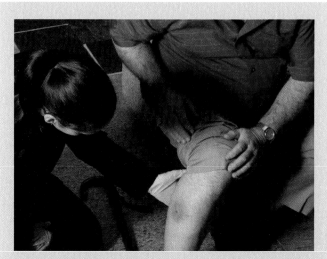

On questioning, the man tells you he was recently hiking in the woods and was not wearing long pants. Knowing this and his signs and symptoms, what do you do?

Chapter 17

Heat- and Cold-Related Emergencies

On a winter morning, you are summoned to the home of an older woman by her daughter, who tells you that her mother must have become confused the night before and had been wandering out in the cold overnight. When the daughter arrived in the morning to check on her, she found her mother sitting on the snowy steps, barely awake. She managed to wake her mother up and bring her into the house, where she covered her in blankets. You speak to her and ask how she is. She appears disoriented and responds weakly. She is shivering uncontrollably. What do you do?

INTRODUCTION

The lead runner enters his final lap and is approaching the finish line. You are part of the mobile aid team that has been following the front runners throughout the race. A few laps back, you remember seeing the person who is now in first place and noticing that he looked fresh and ready for the final few laps. You knew he had trained hard for this race. But now you observe that he looks exhausted. Urged forward by the cheering crowd, he appears to summon up his last reserves of energy to push ahead, but, instead, his legs begin to falter. He looks ill, and you suddenly see him shiver, even though the day is hot. Others begin to pass him. You hear him say he is dizzy and feeling nauseated.

Later, he says he can't remember falling. He barely remembers hearing voices shouting for help and people sponging him with cool water. He says things are now coming into focus. The sounds around him are becoming clearer. He says he hears a siren very near. Suddenly, he realizes he is the one in trouble. He is on his way to the hospital in an ambulance. His moment of glory ended just short of the finish line. He has fallen ill from the heat.

The human body is equipped to withstand extremes of temperature. Usually, its mechanisms for regulating body temperature work very well. However, when the body is overwhelmed by extremes of heat and cold, illness occurs.

Extreme temperatures can occur anywhere, both indoors and outdoors, but a person can develop a heat- or cold-related illness even if temperatures are not extreme. The effects of humidity, wind, clothing, living and working environments, physical activity, age, and an individual's health are all factors in heat- and cold-related illnesses.

Illnesses caused by exposure to temperature extremes are progressive and can become life-threatening. Once the signs and symptoms of a heat- or cold-related illness begin to appear, a person's condition can rapidly deteriorate and lead to death. If the person shows any of the signs and symptoms of sudden illness, notice the weather conditions and decide if they suggest the possibility of a heat- or cold-related emergency. If so, give the appropriate care. Immediate care can prevent the illness from becoming life-threatening. In

this chapter, you will learn how extremes of heat and cold affect the body, how to recognize temperature-related emergencies, and how to provide care.

HOW BODY TEMPERATURE IS CONTROLLED

Body temperature must remain constant for the body to work efficiently. Normal body temperature is 37°C (98.6°F). Body heat is generated primarily through the conversion of food to energy. Heat is also produced by muscle contractions, as in exercise or shivering.

Heat always moves from warm areas to cooler ones. Since the body is usually warmer than the surrounding air, it tends to lose heat to the air (Figure 17–1). The body maintains its temperature by constantly balancing heat loss with heat production. The heat produced in routine activities is usually enough to balance normal heat loss.

When body heat increases, the body removes heat through the skin. Blood vessels near the skin dilate (widen) to bring more warm blood to the surface. Heat then escapes, and the body cools (Figure 17–2, a).

The body is also cooled by the evaporation of sweat. When the air temperature is very warm, dilation of blood vessels is a less effective means of removing heat. Therefore, sweating increases. But when humidity is high, sweat does not evaporate as quickly. It stays on the skin longer and has little or no cooling effect.

When the body reacts to cold, blood vessels near the skin constrict (narrow), which moves warm blood to the centre of the body. Thus, less heat escapes through the skin, and the body stays warm (Figure 17–2, b). When constriction of blood vessels fails to keep the body warm, shivering results. Shivering produces heat through muscle action.

Three external factors affect how well the body maintains its temperature: air temperature, humidity, and wind. Humidity and wind multiply the effects of heat or cold. Extreme heat or cold accompanied by high humidity hampers the body's ability to effectively maintain normal body temperature (Figure 17–3). A cold temperature combined with a strong wind rapidly cools exposed body parts. The combination of temperature and wind speed forms the "wind chill factor."

Figure 17–1 Since the body is usually warmer than the surrounding air, it tends to loose heat to the air.

Other factors, such as the clothing you wear, how often you take breaks from exposure to extreme temperature, how much and how often you drink water, and how intense your activity is, also affect how well your body manages temperature extremes. These are all factors you can control to prevent heat- or cold-related emergencies.

PEOPLE AT RISK FOR HEAT- OR COLD-RELATED EMERGENCIES

People at risk for heat- or cold-related emergencies include:

- Those who work or exercise strenuously outdoors or in unheated or poorly cooled indoor areas
- Older adults
- Young children
- Those with health problems
- Those who have had a heat- or cold-related illness in the past
- Those who have respiratory or cardiovascular disease or other conditions that cause poor circulation
- Those who take medications to eliminate water from the body (diuretics)

a

b

Figure 17–2, a-b **a**, when body heat increases, the body removes heat by dilating blood vessels; **b**, when the body is cold, blood vessels near the surface constrict to conserve heat.

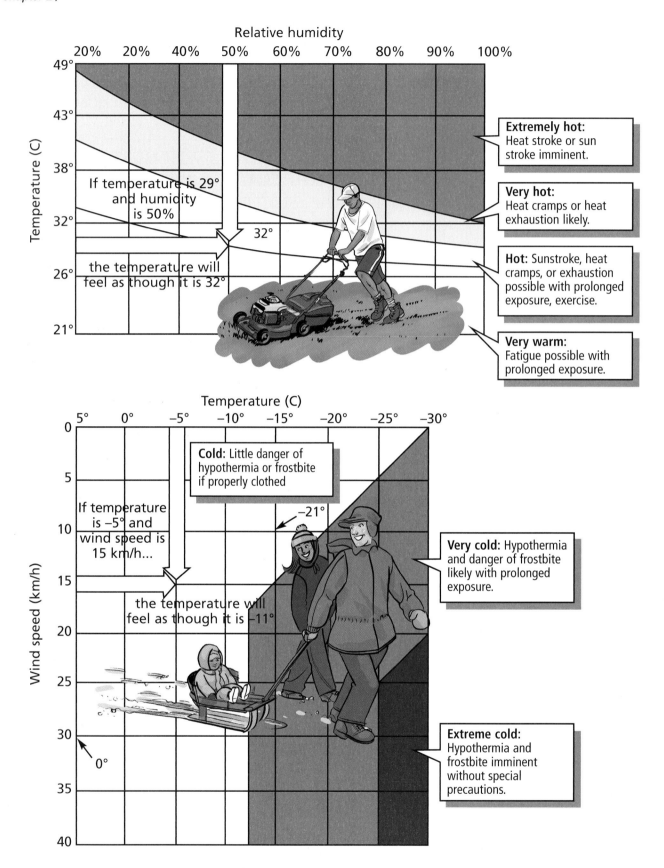

Figure 17–3 Extreme heat accompanied by humidity, or cold accompanied by wind, can hamper the body's ability to maintain normal body temperature.

Usually, people seek relief from an extreme temperature before they begin to feel ill. However, some people do not or cannot easily escape these extremes. Athletes and those who work outdoors or in hot, humid indoor conditions often keep working even after they develop the first signs or symptoms of illness, which they may not even recognize (Figure 17–4).

Heat- and cold-related emergenices occur more frequently in older adults, especially those living in poorly ventilated and insulated buildings or in buildings with poor heating or cooling systems. Young children and people with health problems are also at risk because their bodies do not respond as effectively to temperature extremes.

HEAT-RELATED EMERGENCIES

Heat cramps, heat exhaustion, and heat stroke are conditions caused by overexposure to heat. Heat cramps are the least severe but are often the first indicator of a problem. Heat exhaustion and heat stroke are more serious conditions.

Heat Cramps

Heat cramps are painful spasms of skeletal muscles. The exact cause is not known, although it is believed to be a combination of fluid and salt loss caused by heavy sweating. Heat cramps develop fairly rapidly and usually occur after heavy exercise or work outdoors in warm or even moderate temperatures. Heat cramps are characterized by severe muscle contractions, usually in the legs and the abdomen, but can occur in any voluntary muscle. Body temperature is usually normal, and the skin is moist. However, heat cramps may also indicate that a person is in the early stages of a more severe heat-related emergency.

To care for heat cramps, have the person rest comfortably in a cool place. Provide cool water or a commercial sports drink. Usually, rest and fluids are all the body needs to recover. Lightly stretch the muscle and gently massage the area (Figure 17–5).

Once the cramps stop and there are no other signs or symptoms of illness, the person can usually resume activity. Caution the person to be aware of signs and symptoms of developing heat-related illness. Tell the person to continue to drink plenty of fluids during and after activity.

Heat Exhaustion

Heat exhaustion is the early stage and the most common form of heat-related illness. It typically occurs

Figure 17–4 Athletes and those who work in hot, humid conditions often keep going after they develop the first signs or symptoms of heat illness.

Figure 17–5 Resting and lightly stretching the affected muscle may help relieve heat cramps.

after long periods of strenuous exercise or work in a hot environment. Although heat exhaustion is commonly associated with athletes, it also affects fire fighters, construction workers, factory workers, and others who work and wear heavy clothing in a hot, humid environment. Heat exhaustion is an early indication that the body's temperature-regulating mechanism is becoming overwhelmed. It is not always preceded by heat cramps. Over time, the person loses fluid through sweating, which decreases blood volume. Blood flow to the skin increases, reducing blood flow to the vital organs. Because the circulatory system is affected, the person goes into mild shock.

The signs and symptoms of heat exhaustion include:

- Normal or slightly raised body temperature
- Cool, moist, pale skin (skin may be red in the early stage, immediately following exertion)
- Headache
- Nausea
- Dizziness and weakness
- Exhaustion

In its early stage, heat exhaustion can usually be reversed with prompt care. Often the person feels better when he rests in a cool place and drinks cool

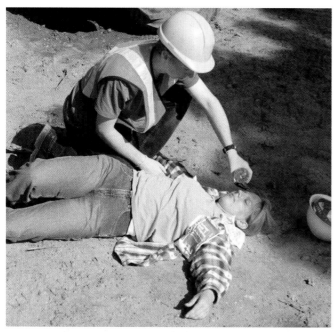

Figure 17–6 Cool the body of a person who has a heat-related emergency.

water. If heat exhaustion is allowed to progress, the person's condition will worsen. Body temperature will continue to climb. The person may vomit and begin to show changes in his level of consciousness. Without prompt care, heat exhaustion can quickly advance to a more serious stage of heat-related illness—heat stroke.

Heat Stroke

Heat stroke is the least common and most severe heat-related illness. It most often occurs when people ignore the signs and symptoms of heat exhaustion. Heat stroke develops when body systems are overwhelmed by heat and begin to stop functioning. Sweating stops because body fluid levels are low. When sweating stops, the body cannot cool itself effectively, and body temperature rapidly rises. It soon reaches a level at which the brain and other vital organs, such as the heart and kidneys, begin to fail. If the body is not cooled, seizures, coma, and death will result. Heat stroke is a serious medical emergency. You must recognize the signs and symptoms of this later stage of heat-related illness and provide care immediately.

The signs of heat stroke include:

- High body temperature (often as high as 41°C or 106°F)
- Red, hot, dry skin
- Progressive loss of consciousness
- Rapid, weak pulse
- Rapid, shallow breathing

Someone with heat stroke may at first have a strong, rapid pulse as the heart works hard to rid the body of heat by dilating blood vessels and sending more blood to the skin. As consciousness deteriorates, the circulatory system begins to fail and the pulse becomes weak and irregular. Without prompt care, the person will die.

Care for Heat-Related Emergenices

When signs or symptoms of sudden illness develop and you suspect the illness is caused by overexposure to heat, follow these general care steps immediately:

1. Cool the body
2. Give fluids

3. Minimize shock

4. Provide ongoing survey and care

When you recognize heat-related illness in its early stages, you can usually reverse it. Remove the person from the hot environment and give him cool water to drink. Moving the person out of the sun or away from the heat allows the body's own temperature-regulating mechanism to recover, cooling the body more quickly.

Remove any tight or heavy clothing. Cool the body by any means available (Figure 17–6). This can be done by applying cool, wet cloths, such as towels or sheets, to the skin. You can also fan the person to help increase evaporation. If you only have ice or cold packs, place them on areas such as the person's wrists and ankles, in each armpit, and on the neck to cool the large blood vessels. Do not apply rubbing (isopropyl) alcohol. Alcohol closes the skin's pores and prevents heat loss.

If the person is conscious, have him drink cool water slowly. This will help replenish the vital fluids lost through sweating. The person is likely to be nauseated, and water is less likely than other fluids to cause vomiting. It also is more quickly absorbed into the body from the stomach. Do not let the person drink too quickly. Give one half-glass (approximately 120 mL) about every 15 minutes. Let the person rest in a comfortable position and watch carefully for changes in his condition. A person with a heat-related emergency should not resume normal activities the same day.

Refusing water, vomiting, and changing level of consciousness are signs that the person's condition is worsening. Obtain more advanced medical care immediately, if you have not already done so. If the person vomits, stop giving fluids and position the person on one side. Make sure the airway is clear. Keep the person lying down and continue to cool the body. Someone with heat stroke may experience respiratory or cardiac arrest. Be prepared to do rescue breathing or CPR. Provide ongoing survey and care.

COLD-RELATED EMERGENCIES

Frostbite and hypothermia are two types of cold-related emergencies. Frostbite occurs in body parts exposed to the cold. Hypothermia is a general cooling of the body that develops when the body can no longer generate sufficient heat to maintain a normal temperature.

Frostbite

Frostbite is the freezing of body tissues. It usually occurs in exposed areas of the body, depending on the air temperature, length of exposure, and wind. Frostbite can affect superficial or deep tissues. In superficial frostbite, the skin is frozen, but the tissues below are not. In deep frostbite, also called freezing, both the skin and underlying tissues are frozen. Both types of frostbite are serious. The water in and between the body's cells freezes and swells. The ice crystals and swelling damage or destroy the cells. Frostbite can cause the loss of fingers, hands, arms, toes, feet, and legs.

The signs and symptoms of frostbite include:

- Lack of feeling in the affected area

- Skin that appears waxy

- Skin that is cold to the touch

- Skin that is discoloured (flushed, white, yellow, blue, or black)

Frost nip

Frost nip is a superficial injury caused by the freezing of the skin. The skin may appear pale, and there may be pain or stinging in the area. Treat it similarly to frostbite.

Care for Frostbite

When caring for frostbite, handle the area gently. Never rub an affected area. Rubbing causes further damage because of the sharp ice crystals in the skin.

Warm the area gently by soaking the affected part in water no warmer than 38°C to 40°C (100° to 105°F). Use a thermometer to check the water, if possible. If not, test the water temperature yourself. If the temperature is uncomfortable to your touch, the water is too warm. Keep the affected body part away from the bottom or sides of the container (Figure 17–7, a). Keep the frostbitten part in the water until it appears red and feels warm. Bandage the area with a dry, sterile dressing. If fingers or toes are frostbitten, place cotton or gauze between them (Figure 17–7, b). Avoid breaking any blisters. The person should seek professional medical attention as soon as possible.

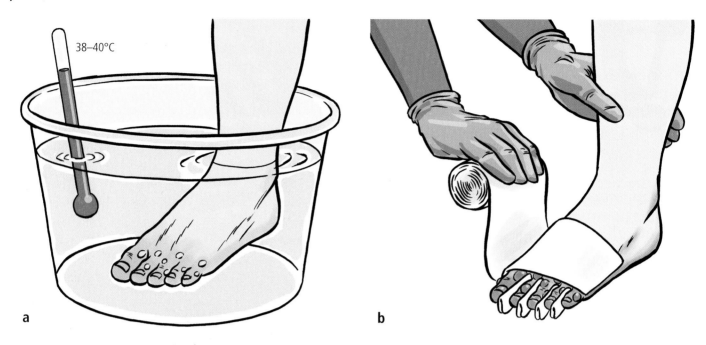

Figure 17–7, a-b a, warm the frostbitten area gently by soaking the area in water; **b**, after rewarming, bandage the area with dry, sterile dressings. Place gauze between frostbitten fingers or toes.

TABLE 17-1 PROGRESSION OF CLINICAL SIGNS AND SYMPTOMS OF HYPOTHERMIA

Class	Core Temperature		Signs and Symptoms
	°C	°F	
Mild	36	96.8	Increased metabolic rate, maximum shivering, thermogenesis
Moderate	34	93.2	Impaired judgement, slurred speech
	30	86.0	Respiratory depression, irregular heart rhythms
Severe	<30	<86.0	Loss of deep tendon reflexes, fixed and dilated pupils, spontaneous ventricular fibrillation

Note: Normal body temperature is 37°C

Do not thaw the area if transport may be delayed or if there is a possibility of the area refreezing. Provide ongoing survey and care.

Hypothermia

In hypothermia, the entire body cools when its warming mechanisms fail. The person will die if not given care. In hypothermia, body temperature drops below 35°C (95°F). Hypothermia progresses from mild to severe stages (Table 17-1). As the body temperature cools, the heart begins to beat erratically and eventually stops. Death then occurs.

Some signs and symptoms of hypothermia include:

- Shivering (may be absent in later stages)
- Slow, irregular pulse
- Numbness
- Glassy stare
- Apathy and decreasing level of consciousness
- Changes in skin colour
- Decreased blood pressure
- Slowly responding pupils
- Decreasing motor and/or sensory function

The air temperature does not have to be below freezing for people to develop hypothermia. Older adults in poorly heated homes, particularly people who have poor nutrition and get little exercise, can develop hypothermia at higher temperatures. People who are homeless or ill are at risk. Certain substances, such as alcohol and barbiturates, can also interfere with the body's normal response to cold, causing hypothermia to occur more easily. Medical conditions such as infection, insulin reaction, stroke, and brain tumours make a person more susceptible. Anyone remaining in cold water or wet clothing for a prolonged time may easily develop hypothermia.

Care for Hypothermia

To care for hypothermia, do a primary survey and care for any life-threatening conditions. Obtain more advanced medical care. Remove any wet clothing and dry the person.

Warm the body gradually by wrapping the person in blankets or putting on dry clothing and moving him to a warm environment. Hot water bottles, heating pads (if the person is dry), or other heat sources can aid in rewarming the body. Keep a barrier, such as a blanket, towel, or clothing, between the heat source and the person to avoid burning him. If the person is alert, give warm liquids to drink. Do not warm the person too quickly by immersing in warm water, for instance. Rapid rewarming can cause dangerous heart rhythms. Be extremely gentle in handling the person.

In cases of severe hypothermia, shivering will cease and the person may be unconscious. Breathing may have slowed or stopped. The pulse may be slow and irregular. The body may feel stiff as the muscles become rigid. Rescue breathing should be started immediately if the person is not breathing. Be prepared to start CPR. Before starting CPR, check the person's signs of circulation, including pulse, for up to 45 seconds. If you cannot detect signs of circulation, begin CPR. Obtain more advanced medical care. Provide ongoing survey and care.

Preventing Heat- or Cold-Related Emergencies

Generally, emergencies caused by overexposure to extreme temperatures are preventable. To prevent heat- or cold-related emergencies from happening to you or anyone you know, follow these guidelines:

- Avoid being outdoors in the hottest or coldest part of the day.
- Change your activity level according to the temperature.
- Take frequent breaks.
- Dress appropriately for the environment.
- Drink large amounts of fluids.

The easiest way to prevent emergencies caused by temperature extremes is to avoid being outside during the time of day temperatures are most intense. For instance, if you plan to work outdoors in hot weather, plan your activity for the early morning and evening hours when the sun is not as strong. Likewise, if you must be outdoors on cold days, plan your activities for the warmest part of the day.

However, not everyone can avoid extremes of temperature. Often work or other situations require exposure to extreme conditions. But you can take additional precautions, such as changing your activity level and taking frequent breaks. For instance, in very hot conditions, exercise only for brief periods; then rest in a cool, shaded area. Frequent breaks allow your body to readjust to normal body temperature, enabling it to better withstand brief periods of exposure to temperature extremes. Avoid heavy exercise during the hottest or coldest part of the day. Extremes of temperature promote fatigue, which hampers the body's ability to adjust to them.

Always wear clothing appropriate to the environmental conditions and your activity level. When possible, wear light-coloured cotton clothing in the heat. Cotton absorbs perspiration and lets air circulate through the material. This lets heat escape and perspiration evaporate, cooling the body. Light-coloured clothing reflects the sun's rays.

When you are in the cold, wear layers of clothing made of tightly woven fibres, such as wool, that trap warm air against your body. Wear a head covering in both heat and cold. A hat protects the head from the sun's rays in the summer and prevents heat from escaping in the winter. Also protect other areas of the body, such as the fingers, toes, ears, and nose, from cold exposure by wearing protective coverings.

Whether you're in heat or cold, always drink enough fluids. Drinking plenty of fluids is the most important thing you can do to prevent heat- or cold-related illnesses. Plan to drink fluids when you take a break. Just as you would drink cool fluids in the summer, drink warm fluids in the winter. Cool and warm fluids help the body maintain a normal temperature. If cold or hot drinks are not available, drink plenty of plain water. Avoid drinking beverages containing caffeine or alcohol. Caffeine and alcohol hinder the body's temperature-regulating mechanism.

SUMMARY

Overexposure to extreme heat and cold may cause a person to become ill. The likelihood of illness also depends on factors such as physical activity, clothing, wind, humidity, working and living conditions, and a person's age and physical condition.

Heat cramps are an early indication that the body's normal temperature-regulating mechanism is not working efficiently. They may signal that the person is in the early stage of a heat-related illness. For heat-related emergencies, it is important to stop physical activity, cool the body, and obtain more advanced medical care.

Frostbite and hypothermia are serious cold-related emergencies, and the person experiencing either needs professional medical care. Hypothermia can be life-threatening. For both hypothermia and frostbite, it is important to warm the person. For hypothermia, warm the entire body. For frostbite, warm the affected area.

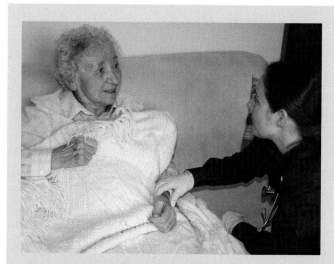

As you assess the woman, you find that she has a slow, irregular pulse. What do you do?

NOTES:

Part **5**

Special Populations and Situations

Special Populations

You're called to the scene at a playground where a young girl has been struck in the face by a moving swing seat. The girl's sister brings the bleeding child toward you. The child is crying and is bleeding from a laceration on her cheek. What do you do?

INTRODUCTION

You are summoned to assist an older woman who says she hasn't been feeling well. As you question her, you notice she seems distracted and her answers don't exactly fit with your questions. Is some condition causing her to be disoriented? Is she fully conscious? Is this the way she normally behaves? Are you missing something?

A seven-year-old boy has crashed his bicycle into a parked car. He was thrown on the ground, landing on his head. As you approach, you notice him clinging to his mother and he appears lethargic. Does he have a head injury? Is this a reaction to a stranger, or is this normal behaviour for him?

As a responder, you are likely to encounter individuals who fit the description of "special populations." What makes these people special are their needs and considerations. This chapter focusses on three special populations: children, older adults, and persons with mental or physical impairments or disabilities. By being able to understand the special needs of a particular person, you will be better able to communicate with him. As a result, you will be able to provide more effective care.

THE ILL OR INJURED CHILD

At some time, you will probably be summoned to assist an ill or injured child. If you are, you must keep several considerations in mind. The most important is that children are not simply small adults. They have unique needs and require special care. They do not readily accept strangers. This can make it difficult to accurately assess a child's condition. Young children can be especially difficult to assess since they often will not be able to tell you what is wrong.

It is often difficult for adults to imagine how a young child with a serious illness or injury feels. One of a child's primary emotions is fear. A child is afraid of the unknown. He is afraid of being ill or hurt, of being touched by strangers, and of being separated from his parents. Being aware of the fears of a child and knowing how to cope with them will enable you to provide more effective care.

Assessing the Child

When assessing a child, follow the same steps as for an adult. However, remember to get consent from the child's parent or guardian. Do the primary survey first. Any problems that threaten the child's airway, breathing, and circulation must be taken care of as soon as he is found. Once you have completed the primary survey, you can begin the secondary survey.

Keep in mind that there are differences in babies and children compared with adults (Table 18–1).

During the secondary survey, you will interview the child and any bystanders, such as the child's parent or guardian. How you interact with the child and the parent or guardian is very important. You must establish a good rapport. This means reducing anxiety and panic in both the child and the parent or guardian. There are a few basic guidelines that will help you assess an injured or ill child:

- Observe the child before touching him. Information can be obtained before actually touching the child. Look for signs that indicate changes in the level of consciousness, any breathing difficulty, and any apparent injuries or conditions. All may change as soon as you touch the child because he may become anxious or upset.

- Communicate clearly with the parent or guardian and the child. If the family is excited or agitated, the child is likely to be so, too. When you can calm the family, the child will often calm down as well. Explain what you wish to do. Get at eye level with the child (Figure 18–1). Talk slowly and use simple words when speaking with the child. Ask questions that can be easily answered.

- Remain calm. Caring for children, especially those who are seriously ill or injured, can be very stressful. Calmness on your part will show confidence and help keep the child and parent or guardian calm.

- Keep the child with loved ones, unless it's necessary to separate them. This is especially true for younger children (under age seven or eight). Often a parent or guardian will be holding a crying child. In this case, you can assess the child's condition while the parent or guardian continues to hold the child.

TABLE 18-1 ANATOMICAL AND PHYSIOLOGICAL DIFFERENCES IN BABIES AND CHILDREN COMPARED WITH ADULTS

Differences	Clinical Significance
Tongue is larger	Can cause airway to become blocked
Airway size is reduced	Can become easily blocked
Secretions are abundant	Can block airway
Nose and face are flat	Makes it more difficult to obtain good airway seal with mask
Head is bigger (proportionally)	Causes neck flexion or head to be displaced anteriorly when supine Increases potential for head injuries in trauma cases
Brain tissue is thinner and softer	Head injury is considered more serious
Neck is short	Stabilization is difficult
Trachea is shorter and narrower with incomplete cartilage development	Can close off trachea if overextended
Respiratory rate is faster	Muscles become easily fatigued
Breathing is done primarily through the nose (newborns)	Airway is more easily blocked
Abdominal muscles are used for breathing	Evaluating breathing is more difficult
Ribs are more flexible	Less protection of lungs May have significant injuries without external signs
A faster heart rate can be sustained for a longer time	Can compensate longer before signs of shock are evident Usually decompensates faster
Body surface is larger	More prone to hypothermia
Bones are softer	Bend and fracture easily
Skin is thinner	Burns are considered more serious

Adapted from Keith J. Karren, PhD, et al. *Emergency Medical Responder: A Skills Approach.* Toronto: Prentice Hall, 1998: 447.

- Gain trust through your actions. Explain to the child and parent or guardian what you are going to do before you do it. Be sure to use terms and language appropriate for the child's age.

In performing the secondary survey, it is often easier to do the head-to-toe examination before you check vital signs. Furthermore, the head-to-toe examination is often better performed in reverse order, as a toe-to-head examination, on a conscious child. The child is more likely to accept you first touching the feet and progressing to the head. You should still look and feel for the same things.

Children up to one year of age are commonly referred to as babies. Young babies, those less than six months old, are relatively easy to examine. Your presence will not generally bother this age group. Older babies, however, will often exhibit "stranger anxiety." They are uncomfortable around strangers and may cry and cling to a parent or guardian.

Children one to three years of age are called toddlers. These children are frequently uncooperative. As a result, they are often best examined in the parent's or guardian's lap. A toddler will be concerned that he will be separated from his parent or guardian. Reassurance that this will not happen will often comfort a concerned child of this age.

Figure 18–1 When communicating with a child, get down to their eye level.

Children aged three to five are generally referred to as preschoolers. Children in this age group are usually easy to examine if approached properly. Use their natural curiosity. Allow them to inspect equipment or supplies, such as oxygen tubing or bandages. This can allay many fears and distract them during your assessment.

School-aged children are those between 6 and 12 years of age. They are usually cooperative and can be a good source of information regarding what happened. You should be readily able to converse with them. Children in this age group are becoming conscious of their bodies and do not like exposure. Respect the child's modesty.

Adolescents are between 13 and 18 years of age. They are typically more of an adult than a child. Direct questions to them instead of toward parents or guardians. However, allow input from a parent or guardian. Occasionally, in the presence of a parent or guardian, it may not be possible to get an accurate history. Adolescents do not like having their bodies exposed and often respond better to a caregiver of the same gender. Respect the adolescent's modesty.

When checking a child's vital signs, such as breathing and pulse, during the secondary survey do not be alarmed at finding faster rates. A child's resting pulse and breathing are normally faster than those of an adult. A normal resting heart rate for an adult ranges from 60 to 100 beats per minute. Babies and toddlers, on the other hand, have normal resting heart rates from approximately 100 to 160 beats per minute. As the child ages, his resting heart rate will become slower. By the time the child reaches adolescence, his resting heart rate will be approximately the same as an adult's.

This is also true for a child's breathing rate. In response to a heart that is beating faster, the child also breathes faster. Average resting breathing rates for preadolescent children are 20 to 40 breaths per minute.

Special Problems

Injury

Injury remains the number one cause of death for children in Canada. Many of these deaths result from incidents involving motor vehicles. The greatest dangers to a child involved in a vehicle incident that results in serious injury are airway obstruction and bleeding. Because a child's head is usually large in proportion to the rest of the body, the head is often injured.

To prevent some of the needless deaths children suffer as a result of motor vehicle incidents, laws requiring safety seats and seat belts have been imposed. As a result, more lives will be saved, but also more injured children will need to be cared for while in car seats (Figure 18–2). A car seat does not normally pose any problem when you are trying to assess a child. A child involved in a motor vehicle crash and found in a car seat should be left in the car seat if the device has not been damaged. If the child is to be transported to a medical facility for evaluation, he can be easily secured in the car seat by putting rolled towels on each side of the head and wrapping two strips of tape around the car seat and the head—one over the forehead and one over the upper lip. Pad any spaces with blankets or towels.

High Fever

A high fever in a child indicates some type of infection. Because a young child's temperature-regulating mechanism has not fully developed, even a minor infection can result in a rather high fever. This is often defined as a temperature above 39°C (103°F). In this case, prolonged or excessively high fever can result in seizures known as febrile seizures. Obtain more advanced medical care. Your initial care for a child with

Figure 18–2 Children may need to be cared for while they are in a car seat.

high fever is to gently cool the child. This includes removing excessive clothing or blankets and sponging lukewarm water on the child. Provide ongoing survey and care.

Breathing Emergencies

Infections of the respiratory system are more common in children than adults. These can range from minor infections, such as the common cold, to life-threatening infections that block the airway. Signs and symptoms of a breathing emergency in children include:

• Unusually fast or slow breathing

• Noisy breathing

• Skin discolouration

• Retraction of the spaces between the ribs during breathing

• Diminished level of consciousness

Croup is a common childhood illness that causes a breathing emergency. It is a viral infection that causes swelling of the tissues below the vocal cords. Besides the basic signs and symptoms of a breathing emergency and a cough that sounds like the bark of a seal, croup is often preceded by one or two days of illness, sometimes with a fever. Croup occurs more often in the winter months, and the signs and symptoms of croup are often more evident in the evening. It is generally not life-threatening. The child will often improve when exposed to cool air, such as the air outdoors or cool steam from a vaporizer.

Another childhood problem is epiglottitis, a bacterial infection that causes severe inflammation of the epiglottis. The epiglottis is a flap of tissue above the vocal cords that protects the airway during swallowing. When it becomes infected, it can swell to a point at which the airway is completely obstructed. The child with epiglottitis will appear quite ill and have a high fever. He will often be sitting up and straining to breathe. The child will be very frightened. Saliva will often be drooling from his mouth. This is because swelling of the epiglottis prevents the child from swallowing.

You will not need to distinguish between croup and epiglottitis since the care you provide will be the same for either situation. To care for a child in a breathing emergency, allow him to remain in the most comfortable position for breathing and administer oxygen. Do not attempt to place any object in the child's mouth or examine the mouth. Obtain more advanced medical care immediately. This is extremely important because the child needs immediate transport to a medical facility. Provide ongoing survey and care.

Child Abuse

Child abuse is unfortunately an all-too-common occurrence in our society. Child abuse commonly refers to the physical, psychological, or sexual assault of a child, resulting in injuries and/or emotional trauma. Children of all ages and backgrounds are victimized. You should suspect child abuse if a child's injuries are not consistent with the explanation you are given by the child or parent or guardian as to what happened.

The child abuser can come from any geographic, ethnic, religious, occupational, or socioeconomic background. The abuser is often a person that the child or family knows and trusts. The signs of child abuse include:

- Obvious fractures in a child less than two years of age

- Signs of shaken baby syndrome

- Injuries in various stages of healing, especially bruises and burns

- More injuries than are usually seen in a child of the same age

- Injuries located in suspect parts of the body, such as the back, buttocks, genitals, upper thighs, torso, head, upper arms, or neck

- An injury that does not fit the description of what caused the injury

When caring for a child who may have been abused, always care for the child's injuries first. An abused child may be frightened, hysterical, or withdrawn. He may be unwilling to talk about the incident in an attempt to protect the abuser. As you provide care for any injuries, attempt to reassure the child and listen calmly and openly to what he tells you. Do not ask questions or make any accusations. Instead, explain your concerns to responding law enforcement or EMS personnel and follow organizational policies regarding making

a report of child abuse. In all provinces and most territories in Canada, suspected child abuse must be reported to the appropriate child protection agency or police. When in doubt, ask your local police department or child protection agency for advice. As a follow-up, accurately complete an incident report, noting in detail anything you were told and any injuries you noted when you first examined the child. Also ensure that you record any instructions provided by police or the child protection agency.

Sudden Infant Death Syndrome (SIDS)

Sudden infant death syndrome (SIDS) is defined as the sudden death of a seemingly healthy baby that occurs during the baby's sleep and without evidence of disease. Usually, a thorough medical examination fails to reveal a cause of death. SIDS is sometimes mistaken for child abuse because of the unexplained death of an otherwise normal child and the bruise-like blotches on the infant's body. However, SIDS is not related to child abuse. It is not caused by vomiting or aspiration of stomach contents. It is also not believed to be hereditary but does tend to recur in families. What causes SIDS is not yet clear. You will not be able to "diagnose" SIDS. When the baby is found, he will be in cardiac arrest. You should care for the baby as you would anyone in cardiac arrest.

Shaken Baby Syndrome

When a baby won't stop crying, some people get so angry and frustrated that they shake the baby. This can cause fractures, heavy bleeding, bruising, and brain swelling, which stops oxygen from getting to the brain. Treat the baby for the injuries found and obtain more advanced medical care. Treat the situation as a case of suspected child abuse.

OLDER ADULTS

Older adults are generally considered those 65 years of age and over. These individuals are quickly becoming the fastest growing population group in Canada. A major reason for this is an increase in life expectancy because of advances in health care. Since 1900, there has been a 53 percent increase in life expectancy. For example, in 1900, the average life expectancy was 49 years. Today, the average life expectancy exceeds 75 years.

TABLE 18-2 AGE-RELATED SYSTEMIC CHANGES

Body System	Changes with Age	Clinical Significance
Respiratory	Respiratory muscles weaker and less coordinated Lung function decreases Cough and gag reflex are reduced	More likely to have respiratory failure
Circulatory	Arteries harden and lose their elasticity Changes in heart rate, rhythm, efficiency Decrease in blood volume and/or red blood cells	Hypertension is common Higher potential for strokes/heart attacks More likely to have bleeding from minor trauma Recuperates more slowly from illness/injury Greater risk of complications from trauma
Nervous	Brain tissue shrinks Memory declines Clinical depression common Altered mental status common Balance is impaired Pain perception decreases Reaction time decreases	Symptoms from head injury may be delayed May be more difficult to assess More prone to falls
Endocrine	Lowered estrogen production (women) Decline in insulin sensitivity Increase in insulin resistance Decrease in glucose metabolism Less effective pituitary gland	Increased risk of fractures (bone loss) and heart disease Diabetes mellitus common and more likely to have hyperglycemia Decrease in energy
Gastrointestinal	Digestive functions are less effective	Constipation common More likely to suffer from malnutrition Vitamin and mineral deficiencies
Thermoregulatory	Reduced sweating Decreased shivering	Decreased heat/cold tolerance
Integumentary	Skin becomes thinner and more fragile	Skin more subject to tears and sores Bruising more common Heals more slowly
Musculoskeletal	Bones become weaker (osteoporosis) Joints become weaker and less flexible (osteoarthritis)	More prone to fractures Slower healing More prone to falls
Renal	Kidneys get smaller and function less effectively	Increased problems with drug toxicity
Genitourinary	Loss of bladder function Prostate enlarges	Increased urination/incontinence Increased urinary tract infection Urinary retention
Immune	Poorer immune response	More susceptible to infections Doesn't respond effectively to vaccines

Many changes occur with age (Table 18–2). Overall, there is a general decline in body function, with some changes beginning as early as age 30. One of the first body systems affected by age is the respiratory system. The capacity of the respiratory system begins to decrease around age 30. By the time we reach age 65, our respiratory system may be only half as effective as it was in our youth. The heart also suffers the effects of aging. The amount of blood pumped by the heart with each beat decreases, and the heart rate slows. The blood vessels harden, causing increased work for the heart. The number of functioning brain cells also decreases with age. Hearing and vision usually decline, often causing some degree of sight and hearing loss. Reflexes become slower, and arthritis may affect joints, causing movement to become painful.

As a result of slower reflexes, failing eyesight and hearing, arthritis, and problems such as numbness related to blood vessels, older adults are at increased risk of injury from falls. Falls frequently result in fractures because bone density decreases. Bones become weaker and more brittle with age.

An older adult is also at increased risk of serious head injuries due to trauma. This is primarily because of the difference in proportion between the brain and the skull. As we age, the size of the brain decreases, which results in increased space between the surface of the

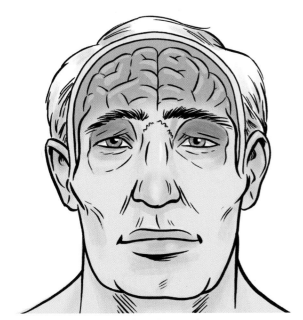

Figure 18–3 The size of the brain decreases as we age.

brain and the inside of the skull (Figure 18–3). This allows more movement of the brain within the skull, which can increase the likelihood of serious head injury. Occasionally, an older adult may not develop the symptoms of a head injury until days after a fall. Therefore, you should always suspect a head injury as a possible cause of unusual behaviour in an older adult, especially if there is a history of a fall or blow to the head. Burns are a special concern to older adults as their skin is thinner and more fragile. Their immune system is less effective in fighting infection, so infections become more frequent and the potential for localized infection becomes widespread. Bowel obstructions are common due to the weak muscles of the bowel. Older people are susceptible to problems involving the system that regulates body temperature, called the thermoregulatory system.

Alzheimer's Disease

Older adults are also prone to nervous system disorders. One of the most common of these disorders in older adults is stroke, discussed in Chapter 8. In addition, older adults are at increased risk of altered thinking patterns and confusion. Some deterioration in mental function caused by aging is normal.

Another common nervous system disorder is Alzheimer's disease, a progressive, degenerative disease that affects the brain. It results in impaired memory, thinking, and behaviour.

If you are providing care for a confused older adult, try to determine whether the confusion is the result of injury or a pre-existing condition. Get at the person's eye level so he can see and hear you more clearly. Sometimes confusion is actually the result of decreased vision or hearing.

Care for older adults requires you to keep in mind the special problems and concerns of older adults and to communicate appropriately. Often an older adult's problem will seem insignificant to him—he may not recognize the signs or symptoms of a serious condition. For example, an older adult may complain of weakness. On further questioning, you may learn that he has been having fainting episodes with periods of numbness and tingling in one side of the body. Some older adults may purposely minimize their symptoms for fear of losing their independence or of being placed in a nursing home or similar institution. If the person takes medications, you should gather them and see that they are with the person if he is being taken to a medical facility.

Elder Abuse

Elder abuse is a growing problem in our society. Elder abuse involves any of four types of abuse: the infliction of pain or injury (physical abuse), mental anguish or suffering (psychological abuse), financial or material abuse, or unnecessary confinement or willful deprivation (neglect) by an older adult's caretaker. Typically, the abuser is a relative and lives with the abused elder.

The signs and symptoms of elder abuse generally include any unexplained injury or any physical situation in which older adults seem to be neglected. Provincial/territorial laws may require the reporting of such abuse if suspected, so follow your local protocol.

THE TERMINALLY ILL PERSON

As a responder, you will respond to calls involving terminally ill people. Terminal illness can happen to anyone, at any age. Often these situations are emotionally charged and require empathy and compassion toward the ill person and his family and friends at the scene.

Cancer

Cancer is the general term used for a group of diseases in which there is an increased growth of cells in one or more organs or tissues. These cells most commonly develop in major organs such as the breasts, intestine, skin, lungs, stomach, brain, and pancreas but can also develop in cell-forming tissues of the bone marrow, muscle, or bone.

Not all people diagnosed with cancer become terminally ill; however, those who have cancer will often become very ill. The signs and symptoms will usually depend on the type, extent, and location of the disease. When responding to a person with cancer, try to obtain a thorough history from the person, including a list of all his medications. Caring for a terminally ill person also requires that you offer comfort and support for the person as well as his family and friends at the scene.

PERSONS WITH PHYSICAL OR MENTAL DISABILITIES

Other special populations include those with physical or mental disabilities. The terms "physical disability" and "mental disability" mean different things to different people. What comes to mind when you hear these words? A person who uses a wheelchair? An amputee? Someone with a mental health impairment?

A person who suffers a serious injury that results in the loss of a limb or who is born lacking a limb is often referred to as having a physical impairment. So is someone who suffers the paralyzing effects of a stroke.

A person with a mental disability has an impairment of mental function that may interfere with normal activity and participation in life. Anyone at any age can find himself challenged by a physical or mental impairment that may interfere to some degree with normal activities, causing an activity limitation or participation restriction.

Visually Impaired

People who are unable to see adequately, or at all, are often called blind or partially blind. These people are also said to be visually impaired. Blindness can occur from many causes. Some people are born blind. Others are born with the ability to see and then subsequently lose that ability through injury or illness. Visual impairment is not necessarily a problem in the eyes. It can occur because of problems in the visual centres of the brain.

Visually impaired people usually adapt well to their condition. It should be no more difficult to communicate with a visually impaired person than with a sighted person. It is not necessary to speak loudly or in overly simple terms. In fact, your assessment of the visually impaired person should be little different from that of a sighted person. The person may not be able to tell you certain things about how an injury occurred but can generally give you a good description based on his interpretation of sounds and touch.

If you are called to assist someone who is visually impaired, explain to him what is going on and what you are doing. This will help alleviate anxiety. It will also

Figure 18–4 You can help a person with a visual impairment by having them hold onto your arm.

allow the person to orient himself to the environment and then provide you with information regarding his care. If you must move a blind person who can walk, stand beside the person and have her hold on to your arm (Figure 18–4). Walk at a normal pace and alert her to any hazards, such as stairs, as you move. If the person has a guide dog, try to keep the dog with him. These dogs are usually not aggressive.

Hearing Impaired

People who are partially or completely deaf are referred to as hearing impaired. Deafness can occur as a result of injury or illness affecting the ear, the nerves leading from the ear to the brain, or the brain itself. As with blindness, deafness can be present at birth or can develop later because of injury or illness. Some responders become anxious when called to treat a hearing-impaired person. This anxiety is unfounded. People with a hearing impairment should be cared for in basically the same manner as hearing people. You may only have to modify your assessment somewhat so that you can obtain necessary information.

You may not even be aware initially that a person is deaf. Often the person will tell you. Others may point at their ear and shake their head, "No." A child may carry a card stating that he is deaf. You may see a hearing aid in a person's ear.

The biggest obstacle you must overcome in caring for the hearing-impaired person is how to best communicate. Most hearing-impaired people have adapted to their hearing loss by learning to speak, lip read, sign, or any combination of these.

Don't assume that hearing-impaired people can't speak; many can, although their speech may be unclear. If you do not understand what the person is saying, ask him to repeat. Do not pretend that you understand.

Often the person will be able to read lips. If the person's illness or injury does not detract from the ability to read your lips, then communicate in this manner. Position yourself where the person can see you, look at the person when you speak, and speak slowly and enunciate carefully (Figure 18–5, a).

Some hearing-impaired people communicate using sign language. Communicate in this way if you are able to (Figure 18–5, b).

If the person cannot speak, read lips, or communicate through sign language, you can write messages on paper and have the person respond (Figure 18–5, c). This system is slow but effective. Some hearing-impaired people have a machine called a Telecommunications Device for the Deaf (TDD), which is generally used for telephone communication. You can use this device to type messages and questions to the person, and the person can type replies to you.

Physically Disabled

The term "physically disabled" refers to a person who is unable to move normally. The impairments causing a disability can be diverse. Physical impairments are generally the result of problems with the muscles or bones or the nerves controlling them. Causes include stroke, cerebral palsy, multiple sclerosis, muscular dystrophy, and brain and spinal cord injuries. Depending on the nature and severity of the problem, you may care for the physically disabled person in

Figure 18–5, a-c There are many ways you can communicate with someone who has a hearing impairment: **a**, allow them to read your lips; **b**, use sign language; and **c**, write down what you want to say.

much the same way you would care for anyone else. In some situations, you will need to adapt to complex problems that may call for extra patience and compassion on your part. Many people have adapted to life without assistance, so be careful not to make assumptions about a person's ability.

The physically disabled person who is injured poses unique problems because it may be difficult to determine which problems are new and which are pre-existing conditions. If this situation occurs, care for any detected problems as if they are new.

Developmentally Disabled

Impairment of mental function occurs with greater frequency than you might expect. A person with a mental health impairment may be developmentally disabled. As with physical impairments, mental impairments also can be diverse. Some types of mental impairment, such as Down's syndrome, are genetic. Others result from injuries or infections that occur during pregnancy, after birth, or later in life. Some occur from undetermined causes.

Often you will be able to determine easily whether a person is developmentally disabled. However, in some situations, you will not be able to tell. Always approach the person as you would any other person in his age group. When you speak, try to determine the person's level of understanding. If the person is confused, rephrase your statement or question in simpler terms. Listen carefully to what the person is saying. A sudden illness or injury can interrupt the order in the person's life and cause a great deal of anxiety and fear. You should expect this and offer reassurance. Take time to explain to the person who you are and what you are going to do. Try to gain the person's trust. If a parent or guardian is present, ask him to assist you in providing care.

Behavioural or Psychiatric Disorders

Responding to an emergency involving someone with a behavioural or psychiatric disorder provides challenges that you should try to be equipped to handle. These people may be out of touch with reality, withdrawn, or even suicidal. As a responder, it is not your responsibility to diagnose a psychiatric disorder. In any behavioural emergency, first ensure the safety of responders and the scene. After determining that the scene is safe, your most important responsibility is to identify and care for any potentially life-threatening medical conditions the person may have.

The Person with a Behavioural or Psychiatric Disorder

Behavioural or psychiatric emergencies are those in which the person's chief complaint is some disorder of mood, thought, or behaviour that is dangerous or disturbing to the person or those around him. The cause of the disorder, either behavioural or psychiatric, can be classified into three categories:

1. Situational
2. Organic
3. Psychiatric

Situational disturbances can affect anyone if subjected to enough stress, but some people are more vulnerable than others. When a person's basic needs are threatened, that person faces a crisis. The severity of the crisis will depend on his ability to deal with his own feelings.

Organic disturbances can result in significant changes in behaviour. Examples include:

• Substance abuse

• Trauma

• Illness (e.g., diabetes, electrolyte imbalance, infection, tumour, dementia)

It is important for you to consider the possibility of organic causes in all behavioural emergencies.

Psychiatric problems may result in behavioural disturbances, that is, problems that arise within the mind of the person, by mechanisms we do not yet understand fully. Conditions that fall into this category are psychosis, anxiety, and depression.

Psychiatric disorders can also present with the appearance of a medical problem. For example, a person with an anxiety disorder may experience a panic attack, with signs and symptoms of hyperventilation and rapid heart rate and even chest pain, which suggests a medical emergency. Also, a person with a history of mental illness may experience a situational or physical problem unrelated to his psychiatric history.

In any behavioural emergency, first ensure the safety of responders and the scene. You may need to take special precautions for concerns that pose a threat to you or other responders. Then identify and care for the person's potentially life-threatening medical conditions. If the person has no obvious life-threatening conditions, take extra time to calm the person and develop a rapport before proceeding with your assessment. Avoid making judgments or subjective interpretations of the person's behaviour. You may need to look beyond the obvious to determine the true nature of the problem.

A good secondary survey will help you determine whether an underlying medical emergency exists and how to proceed. Transport decisions should be made in accordance with local protocols and based on medical control orders. Throughout management and transport, reassess the person's ABCs and mental status at frequent intervals.

Psychosis

Psychosis is a severe mental condition characterized by a loss of touch with reality. An individual who is psychotic is tuned into his internal reality of ideas and feelings, which he may mistake for the reality of the real world. The internal reality may make him belligerent and angry toward others. Or the individual may become mute and withdrawn as he gives all his attention to the voices and feelings within. Signs and symptoms of psychosis may include:

• Loss of touch with reality

• Hallucinations

• Mania

• Confusion

• Depression

• False beliefs

As you assess the person, his responses to your questions may reveal bizarre or disorganized thought processes, memory disturbance, and an inability to concentrate. Dealing with a psychotic person is often difficult. An attempt to reason with the person may be ineffective. Aggressive behaviour can also occur during psychotic episodes. Before approaching the person, assess the potential for violence. Consider the possibility of requesting police backup or other support when necessary.

Schizophrenia

This is a group of mental disorders that may present with distortions in language and thought. The person may also have delusions, hallucinations, and social withdrawal.

Anxiety

Anxiety is a term for mental disorders in which the dominant mood is fear and apprehension. All of us experience anxiety from time to time, and a certain amount of anxiety is useful and even necessary in helping us adjust to stress. But a person with an anxiety disorder may experience persistent, incapacitating anxiety in the absence of external threat. There are several types of anxiety disorders, but the two you are most likely to encounter are panic disorder and phobia.

Panic disorders, often called panic attacks, are unpredictable feelings of terror that strike suddenly and repeatedly. They can occur at any time, even during sleep. Signs and symptoms of panic attacks may include:

- Hyperventilation
- Feelings of weakness or faintness
- Chest discomfort
- Dizziness

- Rapid heart rate
- Sweating
- Nausea
- Smothering sensations
- Fear of loss of control

A phobia is a constant, irrational fear of something that compels a person to avoid it, causes stress, and impairs a person's ability to function normally. Phobias produce anxiety that is out of proportion to the actual threat. Signs and symptoms of phobias may include:

- Anxiety produced by exposure to an object or situation of phobia that may be overwhelming
- Sweating
- Rapid heart rate
- Feelings of weakness, cowardice

Calming and reassuring the person may be the only treatment necessary for a panic attack or phobia. However, a complete medical history may be necessary to rule out the possibility of an underlying disease. For example, the rapid heart rate often associated with panic attacks or phobias may indicate a pulmonary embolism.

Altered Mental States in Children

Some children may experience a change in their behaviour, personality, or responsiveness, beyond what is expected at that age. This type of change is referred to as altered mental status (AMS). These children may present with anxiety, agitation, or aggression/combativeness. Alternatively, they may be difficult to rouse, sleepy, or even unresponsive. It is not unusual for AMS to result in decreased muscle tone (hypotonia).

Common causes of AMS requiring immediate medical attention include respiratory failure, deficiency in oxygen concentration in arterial blood (hypoxemia),

shock, hypoglycemia, brain injury (including shaken baby syndrome), seizures, poisoning, intentional overdose, sepsis, meningitis, hyperthermia, and hypothermia.

Left untreated, this condition can lead to life-threatening problems, including inefficient respiration, hypoxemia, airway obstruction, and respiratory failure.

For care of children with AMS, take spinal precautions if the cause of the AMS is not clear or trauma is suspected. Treat any breathing emergency as outlined in Chapter 6 and care for any other injuries or conditions found. Obtain advanced medical care. Provide ongoing survey and care.

Depression

Depression or depressive behaviour in a person is often identified by a sad expression, bouts of crying, and listless or apathetic behaviour. Major depression, or clinical depression, is a mood disorder. The person may express feelings of worthlessness, hopelessness, guilt, and pessimism. Depressed individuals may also experience fatigue, a change in appetite with weight gain or loss, disruption of sleep patterns, and recurring thoughts of death or suicide. He may have difficulty concentrating or making decisions and may be restless or irritable. The person may want to be left alone, asserting that no one understands or cares. A depressive reaction can also arise in the wake of a stressful event, such as the loss of a close friend or relative.

Care for a person with depression includes calmly talking to the person about his interests and trying to direct responsiveness. Individuals experiencing depression are at risk for suicide. Any statements about suicide attempts or suicidal ideation should be taken seriously, documented, and reported to the receiving facility.

SUMMARY

As a responder, you will likely be called to assist a wide variety of special populations. When dealing with children, remember that they are not small adults. They must be approached gently and in a manner appropriate for their age. You need to recognize and try to alleviate their fears. Your assessment will be modified slightly because of the special needs of children. Certain illnesses, such as croup and epiglottitis, can cause a breathing emergency that should be cared for promptly. When caring for the child, do not forget the parent or guardian. They can make your job easier, so allow them to remain with the ill or injured child and to assist in care when appropriate.

Besides the ill or injured child, you are likely to encounter an older adult or a person with a physical or mental disability. Remember to care for these individuals based on individual need. You should recognize their limitations and work around them. As with the ill or injured child, proper communication will be the most important thing for you to establish.

After a little while, the girl stops crying, and she seems to be getting tired. What do you do?

Childbirth

A 32-year-old woman believes she is in labour. She says that this will be her third child and labour came on so fast she didn't have a chance to get to the hospital. She says she feels the need to move her bowels. Contractions are frequent, about two minutes apart. What do you do?

INTRODUCTION

A woman calls the local EMS number and asks for an ambulance. She says she is expecting a baby and is in labour now. She thinks the baby is coming fast. The woman lives in a rural area, and it will take the ambulance nearly 25 minutes to get there. A police officer nearby is dispatched to help until ambulance personnel arrive.

The officer knocks on the door, and there is no answer. She tries the door and finds it unlocked, so she enters the house and finds the woman lying on the floor, in obvious pain. She sees bloody fluid on the floor. When she examines the woman, she sees the baby's head at the opening of the birth canal and realizes that the birth is imminent. She knows that the baby will be born before the ambulance crew arrives. She prepares to help deliver the baby.

Someday you may be faced with a similar situation, requiring you to assist with childbirth. If you have never seen or experienced childbirth, your expectations probably consist of what others have told you.

Terms such as exhausting, stressful, exciting, fulfilling, painful, and scary are sometimes used to describe a planned childbirth, one that occurs in the hospital or at home under the supervision of a healthcare provider. If you find yourself assisting with the delivery of a baby, however, it is probably not happening in a planned situation. Therefore, your feelings, as well as those of the expectant mother, may be intensified by fear of the unexpected or the possibility that something might go wrong.

Take comfort in knowing that things rarely go wrong. Childbirth is a natural process. Thousands of children all over the world are born each day, without complications, in areas where no medical assistance is available during childbirth.

By following a few simple steps, you can effectively assist in the birth process. This chapter will help you better understand the birth process, how to assist with the delivery of a baby, how to provide care for both the mother and the newborn, how to recognize complications, and what complications could require more advanced care.

PREGNANCY

Pregnancy begins when an egg (ovum) is fertilized by a sperm, forming an embryo. The embryo implants itself within the mother's uterus, a pear-shaped organ that lies at the top centre of the pelvis. The embryo is surrounded by the amniotic sac. This is a fluid-filled sac also called the "bag of waters." The fluid is constantly renewed and helps protect the baby from injury and infection.

As the embryo grows, its organs and body parts develop. After about eight weeks, the embryo is called a fetus. To continue to develop properly, the fetus must receive nutrients. The fetus receives these nutrients from the mother through a specialized organ attached to the uterus called the placenta. The placenta is attached to the fetus by a flexible structure called the umbilical cord. The fetus will continue to develop for approximately 40 weeks (about 9 months), at which time the birth process will begin (Figure 19–1).

THE BIRTH PROCESS

The birth process begins with the onset of labour. Labour is the final phase of pregnancy. It is a process in which many systems work together to bring about birth. Labour begins with a rhythmic contraction of the uterus. As these contractions continue, they dilate the

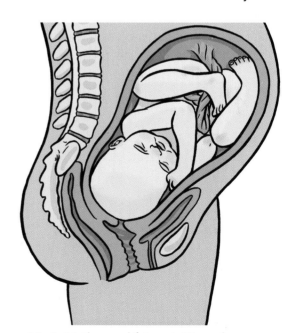

Figure 19–1 Mother and fetus at 40 weeks.

cervix—a short tube of muscle at the upper end of the birth canal, the passageway from the uterus to the vaginal opening. When the cervix is sufficiently dilated, it allows the baby to travel from the uterus through the birth canal. The baby passes through the birth canal and emerges from the vagina, the lower end of the canal, to the outside world. For first-time mothers, this process normally takes between 12 and 24 hours. Subsequent babies are usually delivered more quickly.

The Labour Process

The labour process has four distinct stages. The length and intensity of each stage vary.

Stage One—Preparation

In the first stage, the mother's body prepares for the birth. This stage covers the period of time from the first contraction until the cervix is fully dilated. A contraction is a rhythmic tightening of the muscles in the uterus. It is like a wave. It begins gently, rises to a peak of intensity, and then drops off and subsides. The muscles then relax, and there is a break before the next contraction starts. As the time for delivery approaches, the contractions become closer together, last longer, and feel stronger. Normally, when contractions are less than three minutes apart, childbirth is near.

Stage Two—Delivery of the Baby

The second stage of labour involves the actual delivery of the baby. It begins once the cervix is completely

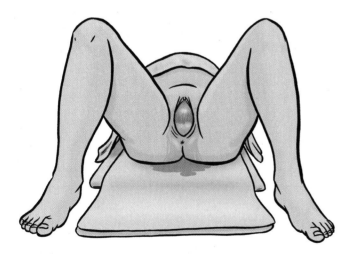

Figure 19–2 When crowning begins, birth is imminent.

dilated and ends with the birth of a baby. The baby's head will become visible as it emerges from the vagina. When the top of the head begins to emerge, it is called crowning (Figure 19–2). When crowning occurs, birth is imminent, and you must be prepared to receive the baby.

Stage Three—Delivery of the Placenta

Once the baby's body emerges, the third stage of labour begins. During this stage, the placenta usually separates from the wall of the uterus and exits from the birth canal. This process normally occurs within 20 minutes of the delivery of the baby.

Stage Four—Stabilization

The final stage of labour involves the initial recovery and stabilization of the mother after childbirth. Normally, this stage lasts for approximately one hour. During this time, the uterus contracts to control bleeding, and the mother begins to recover from the physical and emotional stress that occurred during childbirth.

Assessing Labour

If you are called to assist a pregnant woman, you will want to determine whether she is in labour. If she is in labour, you should determine how far along she is in the birth process and whether she expects any complications. You can determine these factors by asking a few key questions and making some quick observations. Ask the following:

- Is this your first pregnancy? The first stage of labour normally takes longer with first pregnancies than with subsequent ones.

- Has the amniotic sac ruptured? When this happens, fluid flows from the vagina in a sudden gush or a trickle. Some women think they have lost control of their bladder. The breaking of the sac usually signals the beginning of labour. People often describe the rupture of the sac as "the water breaking."

- What are the contractions like? Are they very close together? Are they strong? The length and intensity of the contractions will give you valuable information about the progress of labour. As labour progresses, contractions become stronger, last longer, and are closer together.

- Is there a bloody discharge? This pink or light red, thick discharge from the vagina is the mucous plug that falls from the cervix as it begins to dilate, also signalling the onset of labour.

- Does she have an urge to bear down? If the expectant mother expresses a strong urge to push, this signals that labour is far along.

- Is the baby crowning? If the baby's head is visible, the baby is about to be born.

PREPARING FOR DELIVERY

Preparing Yourself

There comes a time when you realize that you are about to assist with childbirth. Although this is often exciting, it is rarely comforting. Childbirth is messy. It involves a discharge of watery, sometimes bloody fluid at stages one and two of labour and what appears to be a rather large loss of blood after stage two. Try not to be alarmed at the loss of blood. It is a normal part of the birth process. Only bleeding that cannot be controlled after the baby is born is a problem. Take a deep breath and try to relax. Remember that you are only assisting in the process; the expectant mother is doing all the work.

Helping the Mother Cope With Labour and Delivery

Explain to the expectant mother that the baby is about to be born. Be calm and reassuring. A woman having her first child often feels fear and apprehension about the pain and the condition of the baby. Labour pain ranges from discomfort similar to menstrual cramps to intense pressure or pain. Many women experience something in between. Factors that can increase pain and discomfort during the first stage of labour include:

- Irregular breathing

- Tensing up because of fear

- Not knowing what to expect

- Feeling alone and unsupported

You can help the expectant mother cope with the discomfort and pain of labour. Begin by reassuring her that you are there to help. Explain what to expect as labour progresses. Suggest specific physical activities that she can do to relax, such as regulating her breathing. Ask her to breathe in slowly and deeply through the nose and out through the mouth. Ask her to try to focus on one object in the room while regulating her breathing. By staying calm, firm, confident and offering encouragement, you can help reduce fear and apprehension. This will aid in reducing pain and discomfort.

The use of slow, deep breathing through the mouth during labour can help in several ways:

- Aids muscle relaxation

- Offers a distraction from the pain of strong contractions as labour progresses

- Ensures adequate oxygen to both the mother and the baby during labour

Taking childbirth classes, such as those offered at local hospitals, can help you become more competent in techniques used to help the expectant mother relax.

ASSISTING WITH DELIVERY

It is difficult to predict how much time you have before the baby is delivered. However, if the expectant mother says that she feels the need to push or feels as if she has to have a bowel movement, delivery is near.

You should time the expectant mother's contractions from the beginning of one contraction to the beginning of the next. If they are less than two minutes apart, prepare to assist with the delivery of the baby.

Assisting with the delivery of the baby is often a simple process. The expectant mother is doing all the work. Your job is to create a clean environment and to help guide the baby from the birth canal, minimizing the possibility of injury to the mother and baby. Begin by positioning the mother. She should be lying on her back, with her head and upper back raised, not lying flat. Her legs should be bent, with the knees drawn up and apart (Figure 19–3, a). Positioning the mother in this way will make her more comfortable.

Next, establish a clean environment for delivery. Use items such as clean sheets, blankets or towels. To make the area around the mother as sanitary as possible, place these items over the mother's abdomen and under

a
b

Figure 19–3, a-b a, position the mother with her legs bent, and knees drawn up and apart; **b**, place clean sheets, blankets, towels, or even clothes under the mother.

her buttocks and legs (Figure 19–3, b). Keep a clean, warm towel or blanket handy to wrap the newborn. Because you will be coming in contact with the mother's and baby's body fluids, be sure to wear appropriate personal protective equipment.

Other items that can be helpful include a bulb syringe to suction secretions from the baby's mouth and nose, gauze or sanitary pads to help absorb secretions and vaginal bleeding, a large plastic bag or towel to hold the placenta after delivery, and oxygen if available.

As crowning occurs, place a hand on the top of the baby's head and apply light pressure (Figure 19–4). In this way, you allow the head to emerge slowly, not forcefully. This will help prevent tearing of the vagina and injury to the baby. At this point, the expectant mother should stop pushing. Instruct the mother to concentrate on her breathing techniques. Have her "pant like a dog." This technique will help her stop pushing and help prevent a forceful birth.

As the head emerges, the baby will turn to one side

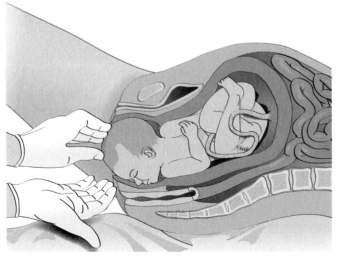

Figure 19–4 Place your hand on top of the baby's head and apply light pressure.

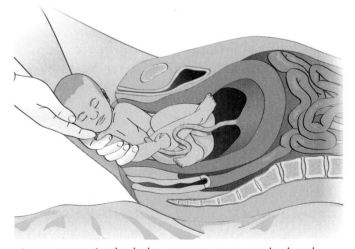

Figure 19–5 As the baby emerges, support the head.

(Figure 19–5). This will enable the shoulders and the rest of the body to pass through the birth canal. Check to see if the umbilical cord is looped around the baby's neck. If it is, gently slip it over the baby's head. If this cannot be done, slip it over the baby's shoulders as they emerge. The baby can slide through the loop.

Guide one shoulder out at a time. Do not pull the baby. As the baby emerges, she will be wet and slippery. Use a clean towel to catch the baby. Place the baby on its side, between the mother and you. In this way, you can provide initial care without fear of dropping the newborn. If possible, note the time the baby was born.

Leave the cord in place and do not pull on it. Clamp or tie the cord while waiting for the placenta to be delivered. Use strips of sterile cloth tied tightly at two different locations 10 and 15 cm (4 and 6 in) away from the baby. Do not cut the cord.

CARING FOR THE NEWBORN AND MOTHER

Caring for the Newborn

The first few minutes of the baby's life are a difficult transition from life inside the mother's uterus to life outside. You have two priorities at this point. Your first is to see that the baby's airway is open and clear. Since a newborn baby breathes primarily through the nose, it is important to immediately clear the mouth and nasal passages. You can do this by using your finger, a gauze pad, or a bulb syringe (Figure 19–6).

Most babies begin crying and breathing spontaneously. If the baby has not made any sounds, stimulate her to elicit the crying response by flicking your fingers on the soles of the baby's feet. Crying helps clear the baby's airway of fluids and promotes breathing. If the baby does not begin breathing on her own within the first minute after birth, begin rescue breathing. If the baby does not have a pulse, begin CPR. You can review these techniques in Chapters 6 and 8.

If the baby is having difficulty breathing, additional oxygen would be beneficial. If you have oxygen available, you can attach a section of tubing to the flowmeter and deliver oxygen at 4 litres per minute to the newborn. Do this by holding the other end of the tubing near the baby's face (Figure 19–7).

Your second responsibility is to maintain normal body temperature. Newborns lose heat quickly; therefore, it is important to keep her warm. Dry the newborn and wrap her in a clean, warm towel or blanket. If possible, record an initial set of vital signs. Most important are breathing, heart rate, and skin colour. You can review vital signs in Chapter 5.

Figure 19–6 It is important to clear the baby's mouth and nose of any secretions.

Figure 19–7 If you are delivering oxygen to a baby, do so by holding the end of the tubing near the baby's face.

TABLE 19-1 THE APGAR SCORE

Element	0	1	2	Score
Activity (muscle tone)	Limp	Some flexion of extremities	Active movement, flexed arms and legs	
Pulse	Absent	Below 100 bpm	100 bpm or above	
Grimace (irritability)	No response	Grimace	Cough, sneeze, cry	
Appearance (skin colour)	Body and extremities blue; pale	Body pink, extremities blue	Completely pink	
Respiration	Absent	Slow and irregular	Strong, crying	
				Total Score =

Assessing the Newborn

If the newborn's respiratory rate does not increase to a normal range with tactile stimulation, assess the heart rate. Do so using a stethoscope, feeling a pulse at the base of the umbilical cord, or palpating the brachial or femoral artery. Optimally, the heart rate should be between 140 and 160 bpm (normal is 100 to 180 bpm). If the pulse is in the normal range, continue to assess. If it is less than the normal range, or there is cyanosis around the chest and abdomen (after 100% oxygen has been administered), artificial ventilation is called for.

Newborns should be assisted to achieve between 40 and 60 breaths per minute. It may be necessary to place a cloth or small towel under the newborn's shoulders to maintain proper positioning. Use an appropriate BVM for ventilations; never use mechanical ventilation.

If the newborn's pulse rate is less than 60 bpm and she is not responding to ventilations, begin CPR. Continue to reassess frequently.

The APGAR score is a numerical system of rating the condition of the newborn (Table 19–1). It evaluates the newborn's heart rate, respiratory rate, muscle tone, reflex irritability, and colour. It is done at one minute after birth and five minutes after birth. A normal score is 7 to 10, 4 to 6 is fairly low, and 0 to 3 is critically low.

Caring for the Mother

You can continue to meet the needs of the newborn while caring for the mother. Allow the mother to begin nursing the newborn. This will stimulate the uterus to contract and help slow bleeding. The placenta will still be in the uterus, attached to the baby by the umbilical cord. Contractions of the uterus will usually expel the placenta within 20 minutes of delivery. Catch the placenta in a clean towel or container. Do not separate the placenta from the newborn or cut the clamped/tied umbilical cord. Leave the placenta attached to the newborn and place it in a plastic bag or wrap it in a towel for transport to the hospital.

Expect some additional vaginal bleeding when the placenta is delivered. Using gauze pads or clean towels, gently clean the mother. Place a sanitary pad or towel over the vagina. Do not insert anything inside the vagina. Have the mother place her legs together. Feel for a grapefruit-sized mass in the lower abdomen. This is the uterus. Gently massage the lower portion of the abdomen. Massage will help eliminate any large blood clots within the uterus, cause the uterus to contract, and slow bleeding.

Many new mothers experience shock-like signs or symptoms, such as cool, pale, moist skin; shivering; and slight dizziness, after childbirth. Keep the mother positioned on her back. Administer oxygen if available. Maintain normal body temperature and monitor vital signs.

COMPLICATIONS REQUIRING ADVANCED CARE

Complications During Pregnancy

Complications during pregnancy are rare. Since the nature and extent of most complications can only be determined by medical professionals during or after examination, you should not be concerned with trying to "diagnose" a particular problem. Instead, concern yourself with recognizing signs and symptoms that suggest a serious complication during pregnancy. You should be concerned with two important signs and symptoms: vaginal bleeding and abdominal pain. Any persistent or profuse vaginal bleeding, or bleeding in which tissue passes through the vagina during pregnancy, is abnormal, as is any abdominal pain.

For an expectant mother exhibiting these signs and symptoms, obtain advanced medical care quickly. While waiting or en route, take steps to minimize shock. These include:

- Helping the woman into the most comfortable position
- Controlling bleeding
- Maintaining normal body temperature
- Administering oxygen if available

Miscarriage

Miscarriage is the spontaneous termination of pregnancy from any cause before 20 weeks of gestation. This is a common cause of vaginal bleeding in the first trimester of pregnancy. This condition occurs in about 1 in 10 pregnancies. Signs and symptoms of miscarriage to check for include the following:

- Often the woman is anxious and apprehensive
- Vaginal bleeding, which may be minor or profuse

- "Cramp-like" pain that is similar to the pain of labour or menstruation

When assessing the woman, you should use sensitivity to obtain a detailed history, which should include:

- Time of onset of pain and bleeding
- Amount of blood loss
- Whether the woman passed any tissue during the bleeding episodes

Often the woman will tell you that she feels an urge to go to the bathroom. If this happens, make sure you check the contents for tissue or clot-like matter. You should collect and transport any tissue found for analysis at the hospital.

Pre-hospital management of all first-trimester emergencies includes close observation of vital signs for signs of shock from blood loss. If the woman is not in shock, have her rest in a comfortable position. Administer supplemental oxygen as necessary.

Premature Labour

Labour that begins between the 20th and 37th week of gestation is called premature or preterm labour and frequently requires medical intervention. This could be due to problems with the mother, baby, or placenta.

Many factors increase the chance of having a preterm birth, including a history of preterm births or miscarriages, carrying multiple births, and poor nutrition, as well as certain diseases and abnormalities.

Common signs and symptoms are:

- Contractions every 10 minutes (or less)
- Dull backache
- Feeling as if the baby is pushing down or has "dropped"
- Menstrual cramps or abdominal pain
- Possible diarrhea
- Cramps in the bowel
- Vaginal bleeding or discharge (out of the normal)

Treat as a regular childbirth.

For the premature baby, provide the following care:

- Keep the baby warm with a blanket or swaddle.
- Keep the baby's mouth and nose clear of fluids by gentle suctioning with a bulb syringe.
- Prevent bleeding from the umbilical cord.
- Administer passive oxygen, if local protocols permit, by blowing the oxygen gently across the baby's face.
- Do not let anyone breathe into the baby's face (to prevent infection).
- Obtain more advanced medical care.

Ectopic Pregnancy

An ectopic pregnancy is the leading cause of maternal death in the first trimester, which usually results from hemorrhage. It occurs when a fertilized ovum implants anywhere other than in the uterus. This occurs in about 1 in every 200 pregnancies. There are numerous causes of ectopic pregnancy; however, most involve factors that delay or prevent passage of the fertilized ovum to its normal place of implantation in the uterus. Predisposing factors include previous surgery, previous ectopic pregnancy, or if the woman has had her tubes blocked as a sterilization method. When conducting a secondary survey, it is important to get a thorough history from the woman. Most ruptures occur by 2 to 12 weeks of gestation.

The signs and symptoms of ectopic pregnancy include:

- Abdominal pain
- Referred pain to the shoulder
- Vaginal bleeding (spotty, minimal, or severe)
- Nausea
- Vomiting
- Fainting spells
- Signs of shock

A ruptured ectopic pregnancy is a true emergency. When administering care for a woman with a ruptured ectopic pregnancy, maintain the ABCs (which may deteriorate rapidly), administer supplemental oxygen, and help ensure prompt transport to the medical facility.

Remind the woman to take nothing by mouth in case she requires surgery. Provide ongoing survey and care.

Third Trimester Bleeding

Third trimester bleeding occurs in a very small percentage of pregnancies and is never normal. The causes of third trimester bleeding are usually abruptio placentae, placenta previa, or uterine rupture. Abruptio placentae is a partial or complete detachment of a normally implanted placenta at more than 20 weeks' gestation. Placenta previa is a condition in which the placenta is attached in the lower uterus, encroaching on the opening to the cervix. Uterine rupture is a spontaneous or traumatic rupture of the uterine wall. This condition may be a result of a previous scar from a Caesarean birth, prolonged or obstructed labour, or direct trauma.

The signs and symptoms of third trimester bleeding may include:

- Vaginal bleeding (may be sudden or painless)
- Uterine cramping
- Back pain

Treat the woman for shock, administer supplemental oxygen, and maintain the ABCs. Place the woman in the recovery position and help ensure prompt transport to the medical facility. Remind the woman to take nothing by mouth as she may require surgery. Provide ongoing survey and care.

Complications During Childbirth

The vast majority of births occur without complication. However, this fact is reassuring only if the one you are assisting with is not complicated. For the few that do have complications, delivery can be stressful and even life-threatening for the expectant mother and the baby. In all of these cases, obtain advanced medical care.

The most common complication of childbirth is persistent vaginal bleeding. Besides obtaining more advanced medical care, you should take steps to minimize shock. Other childbirth complications include prolapsed cord, premature birth, breech birth, and multiple births.

Prolapsed Cord

A prolapsed cord occurs when a loop of the umbilical cord protrudes from the vagina while the baby is still in the birth canal (Figure 19–8). If this occurs, it can threaten the baby's life. As the baby moves through the birth canal, the cord will be compressed against the unborn baby and the birth canal and blood flow to the baby will stop. Without this blood flow, the baby will die within a few minutes from lack of oxygen. If you notice a prolapsed cord, have the expectant mother assume a knee-chest position (Figure 19–9). This will help take the pressure off the cord. Administer oxygen to the mother if it is available. Obtain more advanced medical care if you have not done so already.

Breech Birth

Most babies are born head first. However, on rare occasions, the baby is delivered feet or buttocks first. This condition is commonly called breech birth. If you encounter a breech delivery, support the baby's body as it exits the birth canal while you are waiting for the head to deliver. Do not pull on the baby's body. This will not help to deliver the head.

If, after about three minutes, the head has not delivered, you will need to help create an airway for the baby to breathe. Because the weight of the baby's head lodged in the birth canal will reduce or stop blood flow by compressing the cord, the baby will be unable to get any oxygen. Should the baby try to take a spontaneous breath, she will also be unable to breathe because the face is pressed against the wall of the birth canal.

To help with a breech delivery, place the index and middle fingers of your gloved hand into the vagina next to the baby's mouth and nose. Spread your fingers to form a "V" (Figure 19–10). Although this will not lessen the compression on the umbilical cord, it may allow air to enter the baby's mouth and nose. You must maintain this position until the baby's head is delivered. Administer oxygen to the mother if it is available. Obtain more advanced medical care.

Multiple Births

Although most births involve only a single baby, a few will involve delivery of more than one. If the mother has had proper prenatal care, she will probably be aware that she is going to have more than one baby. Multiple births should be handled in the same manner as single births. The mother will have a separate set of contractions for each child being born. There may also be a separate placenta for each child, although this is not always the case.

Limb Presentation

In most births, the baby's head presents first and the rest of the body follows. Less frequently, the baby's arms or legs may present first, preventing the possibility of a normal delivery (Figure 19–11). This kind of delivery can be fatal. Never pull on the baby's arms or legs. This type of birth is an emergency, and you must transport the mother to the hospital without delay.

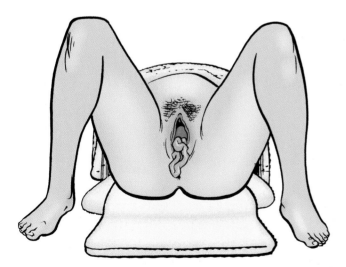

Figure 19–8 A prolapsed cord.

Figure 19–9 The knee-chest position will take pressure off the cord.

Figure 19–10 During a breech birth, position your index and middle fingers to allow air to enter the baby's mouth and nose.

Postpartum Bleeding

Postpartum bleeding is bleeding after the birth of the newborn that is characterized by more than 500 mL of blood loss. It may be caused by the uterine muscles

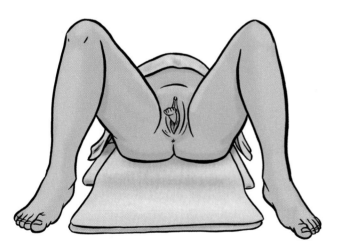

Figure 19–11 Limb presentation prevents the possibility of a normal birth and could be fatal. This type of birth is an emergency and the mother requires immediate transport.

not contracting fully after birth, pieces of placenta or membranes left in the uterus, or vaginal or cervical tears caused during delivery.

The signs and symptoms of postpartum bleeding include excessive bleeding (more than 500 mL) after giving birth. It frequently occurs within the first few hours after delivery but can be delayed for up to 24 hours after delivery.

If a woman experiences postpartum bleeding, care for any external bleeding from perineal tears. Do not attempt vaginal packing to control internal bleeding. Position the woman for shock and maintain her ABCs. Remind the woman to take nothing by mouth. Help ensure prompt transport to the medical facility. Provide ongoing survey and care.

SUMMARY

Ideally, childbirth should occur in a controlled environment under the guidance of healthcare professionals trained in delivery. In this way, the necessary medical care is immediately available for mother and baby should any problem arise. However, there will always be unexpected deliveries occurring outside the controlled environment that may require your assistance. By knowing how to prepare the expectant mother for delivery, assist in the delivery, and provide proper care for the mother and baby, you will be able to successfully assist in bringing a new child into the world.

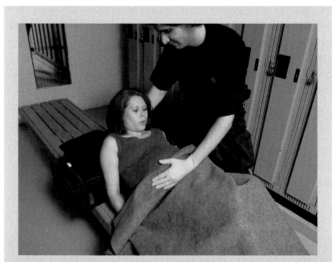

The woman's contractions are about two minutes apart. Now she tells you she feels a powerful urge to push. What do you do?

Chapter 20

Crisis Intervention

You are summoned to a home where a 49-year-old father of three children has attempted suicide by carbon monoxide poisoning. He was found unconscious inside his car in the garage by his oldest child. What do you do?

INTRODUCTION

In one way or another, a serious injury, sudden illness, or death has an emotional impact on everyone involved: the ill or injured person(s), family, friends, bystanders, responders, and others. The degree of impact varies from person to person. For some, the impact is minimal. The acceptance of injury or illness that results in hospitalization, disability, or even death is handled well. For others, however, even a minor injury can create an extreme emotional crisis, a highly emotional state resulting from stress. The way a person responds to an emergency largely depends on his emotional makeup and patterns of response. Therefore, the way one person responds to a stressful situation can differ substantially from the response of another person in a similar situation.

Sometimes it is not the fact that injury or illness has occurred that triggers emotional distress but how it occurred. The nature of an event, such as a sexual assault, can cause great emotional turmoil. A person's realization that he has been sexually violated can cause extreme stress. Events such as a suicide, self-inflicted death, or attempted suicide can cause great stress to the family and friends of the person. They often feel as if they could have done more or should have been able to help.

You may someday encounter a situation involving someone experiencing an emotional crisis. Besides providing care for any specific injury or illness, you may also need to provide emotional support. In some instances, the person will be so distraught that he will be entirely dependent on you and your directions. Being able to understand some of what the person is feeling can help you cope with the situation.

SPECIFIC EMOTIONAL CRISES

Many different situations can result in emotional crisis for the person or bystanders. Examples commonly encountered by emergency personnel include attempted suicide, sexual or physical assault, the sudden death of a loved one, or a dying person.

Suicide

Suicide is more common in Canada than most people realize. It is one of the leading causes of death among people aged 15 to 19, although it is common among adults and older adults as well. Many people who attempt suicide suffer from some form of mental or emotional problem or illness. Substance misuse or abuse, primarily of alcohol and barbiturates, plays a major role in attempted suicides.

What motivates a person to suddenly try to commit suicide? It is often a combination of unbearable underlying tensions caused by a major event in a person's life, such as:

- A failing or failed relationship with a spouse, other family member, or friend
- Serious illness or death of a close family member or friend
- Serious, prolonged, or chronic personal illness
- A long period of failure at work or school
- A long period of unemployment
- Failure to achieve sufficient occupational, educational, or financial success
- Dramatic change in the economy

Assault

Assault is an all-too-common occurrence in our society. It can be physical, sexual, or both. It results in injury and often emotional distress to the person.

Sexual Assault

Sexual assault occurs when one person takes advantage of another by rape or forces a person to take part in any unwanted sexual act. Rape is a crime of violence, or one committed under threat of violence, that involves a sexual attack. Rape is a devastating experience for the person. People who have been raped often feel degraded, extremely frightened, and at further risk for attack. They require significant emotional support.

Besides providing emotional support, you must care for any injuries the person may have received. When caring for a person who has been sexually assaulted, do the following:

- Cover the person and protect him or her from unnecessary exposure.
- Clear the area of any bystanders, except those friends or family able to help provide emotional support.

- Remove articles of clothing only if absolutely necessary to provide care for injuries.

- Care for any physical injuries.

- Discourage the person from bathing, showering, or douching before a medical examination can be performed.

- Treat the area as a crime scene.

- Do not question the person about the specifics of the assault.

- Obtain more advanced medical care and summon law enforcement personnel.

Physical Assault

Physical assault on a child, spouse or partner, or older adults occurs more frequently than reported. Unfortunately, when you are summoned, often the assault has resulted in more serious injuries. The emergency scene where a physical assault has occurred is not always safe. The attacker may still be present or nearby. If the scene involves domestic violence, it may not be clear what has happened. Substances such as alcohol may be involved. Remember that your first concern is always your safety. If you are not trained in law enforcement, do not approach the scene until it is determined to be safe. Wait for additional personnel. As with sexual assault, the scene is a crime scene. Therefore, do not handle items unrelated to the person's care. Reassure and comfort the person while providing care.

Death and Dying

You may be summoned to an emergency in which one or more people have died or are dying. Although your responses will vary according to the situation, you must recognize that death will have an emotional impact on you, as well as on others involved. Be prepared to handle your feelings and the feelings of others. Remember that reactions to death and dying range from anxiety to acceptance. How well you and others handle the situation will depend on both personal feelings about death and the nature of the incident.

One of the most disturbing situations is when there is sudden death. This could involve someone who suffers a sudden illness, becomes unconscious, and later dies. It could also be someone involved in what appeared to be a minor motor vehicle collision; the person may be alert and talkative when you arrive but suddenly suffers a cardiac arrest. Especially disturbing to new parents is the sudden unexplained death of an infant in the first few weeks of life. In situations such as these, there is no time to prepare for what has happened. Suddenly, a man, woman, or child who was alive only minutes earlier is now dead.

Sometimes you may be in a situation in which you think someone has been dead for a while and you are unsure whether you should attempt to resuscitate the person. The general rule is to always attempt to resuscitate and continue efforts to resuscitate until advanced medical personnel advise you to stop.

There are protocols to follow to determine whether a person is dead. When it is determined that the person has no heart rhythm, no pulse, no respiration, and no blood pressure, the person is declared dead by the appropriate authority. In some instances, this will be after prolonged resuscitation attempts. At other times, additional signs, such as decapitation, transection, gross evisceration, rigor mortis, lividity, and decomposition, may cause resuscitation attempts to be withheld.

Some people may have living wills, written legal documents saying that they do not wish to be resuscitated or kept alive by mechanical means. In most instances, the wishes of the person expressed in writing should be honoured. However, since provincial/territorial and local laws about these situations vary, you should obtain more advanced medical care immediately.

If you must confront the individual, his family and friends, or bystanders during or after a situation in which death is probable, be cautious about what you say. Avoid making statements about the person's condition. You can provide comfort with positive statements such as "We are doing everything we can."

STAGES OF GRIEF

Everyone involved in a sudden, unexpected, and undesired event, such as a life-threatening illness or injury or the death of a loved one, experiences grief. The grieving process involves an outpouring of emotions that often follows a common pattern with various stages. These stages are not separate entities and do not necessarily follow one after the other. Instead, they often blend together. These stages include:

- Anxiety—a stage characterized by a feeling of worry, uncertainty, and fear. Signs and symptoms include rapid breathing and pulse, increased activity, rapid speech, loud talking or screaming, and agitation.

- Denial/disbelief—a stage in which a person refuses to accept the fact that the event, such as the death of a loved one or suffering a debilitating injury, has occurred.

- Anger—a stage that involves the expression of aggressive verbal or physical behaviour. It is sometimes the result of the frustration of not being able to accept the event or a feeling that not enough was done or is being done to help.

- Bargaining—a stage that involves an unspoken promise of something in exchange for an extension of life or return to the pre-event condition.

- Guilt/depression—a stage that involves placing the blame for what happened on yourself, resulting in feelings of guilt or depression. A parent will often feel guilty for the event involving his child. A family member may feel guilty for not being of help to another family member who committed suicide.

- Acceptance—the final stage in the grieving process is when the pain and discomfort are eased. The person accepts the event and the outcome. For some people, arriving at the stage of acceptance takes weeks, months, or even years after the event. For others, such as friends or family members who are aware that a person's condition is terminal, this stage can occur much more rapidly.

CRISIS INTERVENTION

Regardless of the nature of the incident, caring for someone experiencing an emotional crisis involves offering emotional support, as well as caring for any specific injury. The most important initial step you can take is to communicate with the person in an open manner. Communication can be both verbal and nonverbal.

Nonverbal communication refers to your actions. Sometimes your actions (body language) say more than you intend. You should always be aware of the messages you are sending with your body. General body posture is an important aspect of nonverbal communication. Begin by assuming a non-threatening posture. This involves getting at eye level with the person and looking at him as you talk (Figure 20–1). Also, avoid positions such as placing your arms across your chest, your hands on your hips, pointing at the person, or leaning over and looking down at the person.

As you begin to communicate verbally, remember that communication involves stimulating discussion and listening as much as talking. When you do talk, speak in a calm, reassuring manner. Ask the person his name and use it frequently in conversation. One technique used to help you more fully communicate is "active listening." The process of active listening requires you to listen closely to what the person is saying. It involves four behaviours:

- Making every effort to understand fully what the person is trying to say

- Repeating back to the person, in your own words, what he said

- Avoiding criticism, anger, or rejection of the person's statements

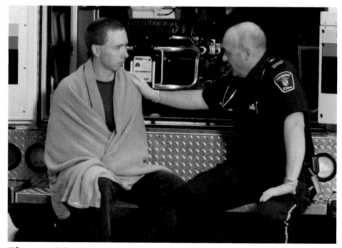

Figure 20–1 Assuming a non-threatening posture and getting at eye level are examples of nonverbal communication.

- Using open-ended statements/questions such as "You appear to be very sad" or "What problems are you having?" Generally, avoid questions that can be answered with "yes" or "no."

People in emotional crisis may be withdrawn or hysterical. Some may be entirely dependent on you to help. Avoid being judgmental. Do not place blame on the person. The person needs to be cared for gently and with respect. If care is needed for a minor injury, try to get the person to help you (Figure 20–2). By encouraging the person to participate, you may help him regain a sense of control that he had lost.

Do not be fooled into thinking you can manage a situation involving emotional crisis yourself. A suicidal person or someone who has been raped needs professional counselling. Obtain more advanced care. This could include law enforcement, EMS, or local mental health or rape crisis centre personnel. While waiting for others to arrive, continue to talk with the person. Never leave the person alone unless there is a threat to your safety.

CRITICAL INCIDENT STRESS MANAGEMENT

Researchers have recognized for years that individuals who provide emergency care can experience high levels of stress. Incidents involving multiple people, rescues, children, failed resuscitation attempts, and death or serious injury to co-workers tend to cause more stress than others. Critical incident stress can cause a number of signs and symptoms, some of which may appear as long as weeks after the incident:

- Confusion
- Lowered attention span
- Poor concentration
- Denial
- Guilt
- Depression
- Anger
- Change in interactions with others
- Increased or decreased eating
- Uncharacteristic, excessive humour or silence
- Unusual behaviour

NOTE:

Stress management techniques should also be used for children and adolescents.

From the time you begin to establish a rapport with someone, you become involved in the person's pain and stress. You share to some degree the thoughts and emotions of the person.

As a result, the emotional impact of a situation may be too great for you to handle alone. For this reason, you may need counselling to deal with the stress.

Counselling is not just for those incidents involving death or major disasters. Any incident is a potential source of emotional crisis for you. Even though the outcome of such an incident would be completely different from one involving death, the emotions and stress factors would all still be present.

Some people think that participating in counselling is an admission of weakness—quite the contrary. Counselling should be, and in many areas is, a routine part of any overwhelming incident, such as an airline

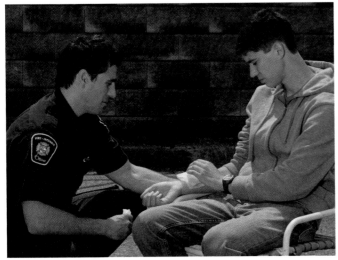

Figure 20–2 Having a person help care for their own injury may give them a sense of regained control.

disaster. Counselling can help in any situation, regardless of how minor you may think the event was. The most important thing you can do to minimize the effects of any emergency is to express your feelings and thoughts after the incident. Check with your local agency to see what resources are available to you.

While the man is being cared for by more advanced medical personnel, the daughter is trying to see what is going on. She is crying and shaking. What do you do?

NOTE:
Critical incident stress can affect anyone involved in an emergency.

SUMMARY

An emotional crisis often is the result of an unexpected, shocking, and undesired event, such as the sudden loss of a loved one. Although people react differently in different situations, each experiences some or all of the stages associated with grieving. By considering the nature of the incident, you can begin to prepare yourself to deal with its emotional aspects.

Regardless of the nature of the event, however, the care you provide to people in any emotional crisis is very similar. Your care involves appropriate verbal and nonverbal communication. It also requires you to

understand that in some cases death is inevitable. In some situations, you may be overcome by emotion. Remember that self-help involves sharing your feelings with others.

Reaching and Moving People

You arrive on the scene of a two-vehicle collision. Both people inside the smaller car appear to be unconscious and are bleeding. What do you do?

INTRODUCTION

You have learned how to care for injured and ill people when it is safe to do so; sometimes, however, you will not have easy access to the person. At other times, the person may be in a dangerous situation and must be moved before you provide care. In this chapter, you will learn how to quickly and safely reach and move people.

GAINING ACCESS

One of your primary responsibilities as a responder is to provide care for an ill or injured person. Sometimes, however, providing care is not possible because the person is inaccessible. One example is a situation in which someone is able to call 9-1-1 or another local emergency number for help but is unable to unlock the door of the home or office to let in the responders. This is also true in a large number of motor vehicle collisions. Vehicle doors are sometimes locked or crushed, windows may be tightly rolled up, or the vehicle may be unstable. In other instances, fire, water, or other elements may prevent you from reaching the person.

In these cases, you must immediately begin to think of how to safely gain access to the person before you can begin to provide care. If you cannot reach the person, you cannot help her. But remember, when attempting to reach a person, your safety is the most important consideration. Protect yourself and the ill or injured person by doing only what you are trained to do and by using equipment and clothing appropriate for the situation (Table 21–1). Items such as helmets, face shields, safety goggles, gloves, and heavy clothing will help keep you safe. Items such as blankets, reflective markers or flares, and flashlights will help keep the scene, as well as the ill or injured person, safe as you attempt to gain access to someone who is trapped. Simple tools such as a screwdriver, hammer, pocket knife, vehicle jack, rope, hatchet, pry bar, and chains can also be helpful. It is also important to take precautions to not cause the person further injury. Stay with the person and try to keep her calm—explain what is going on and monitor the person closely. It is also important to keep the spine immobilized during the extrication. If glass needs to be broken, ensure your safety and the safety of the injured person by using a thick blanket, tarp, or other object to prevent glass from being thrown at you or the injured person.

During any extrication, or when attempting to gain access to an injured person, ensure that all team members communicate clearly and develop a plan so that each team member knows the role she will play.

TABLE 21-1 RECOMMENDED EQUIPMENT AND CLOTHING FOR RESPONDERS

Warning Devices	Protective Items	Breaking Windows
• Flares	• Helmet	• Pry bar
• Reflective markers	• Safety goggle	• Hammer or hatchet
• Flashlights	• Face shield	• Window punch
	• Gloves	
	• Heavy clothing	
	• Blanket	

NOTE:

Local fire department and rescue squad personnel specially trained in vehicle stabilization and extrication will respond to the scene when available and notified.

Motor Vehicles

As with any emergency situation, begin by surveying the scene to see if it is safe. If it is not safe, determine whether you can make it safe so that you can attempt to gain access to the injured person. Well-intentioned responders and others are injured or killed every year while attempting to help injured people out of motor vehicle collisions. Often these responders are struck by oncoming vehicles. Such unfortunate instances can be prevented if you take adequate measures to make the scene safe before trying to gain access and provide care.

Upright Vehicles

Fortunately, most motor vehicle collisions you encounter will involve upright, stable vehicles. These vehicles are unlikely to move while you attempt to help their occupants. However, there are times when the vehicle will not be stable. Environmental factors can influence the stability of the vehicle. Vehicles on slippery surfaces, such as ice, water, or snow, or on inclined surfaces need to be stabilized. In addition, vehicles positioned where oil has been spilled should also be stabilized.

Stabilizing an upright vehicle is a simple task. Placing blocks or wedges against the wheels of the vehicle will greatly reduce the chance of the vehicle moving. This process is called chocking (Figure 21–1). You can use items such as rocks, logs, wooden blocks, and spare tires. If a strong rope or chain is available, these can be attached to the frame of the car and then secured to strong anchor points such as large trees, guard rails, or another vehicle. Letting the air out of the car's tires also reduces the possibility of movement.

Once you are certain the vehicle is stable, you should attempt to enter it. Begin by checking all the doors to see if they are unlocked. Although it may seem obvious to check the doors, sometimes in the excitement it is easy to forget this simple, time-saving step. If the doors are locked, the people inside may be able to unlock at least one door for you. If the windows are open, you may be able to unlock the door yourself.

Sometimes locked or jammed doors require you to enter the vehicle through a window. If the window is open or can be rolled down by someone inside the car, this is not a problem. If the window is rolled up, you can use specific equipment and techniques to get into the car (Figure 21–2). Once inside the vehicle, you can further stabilize it by placing the vehicle in "park," turning the key to the off position, and setting the parking brake.

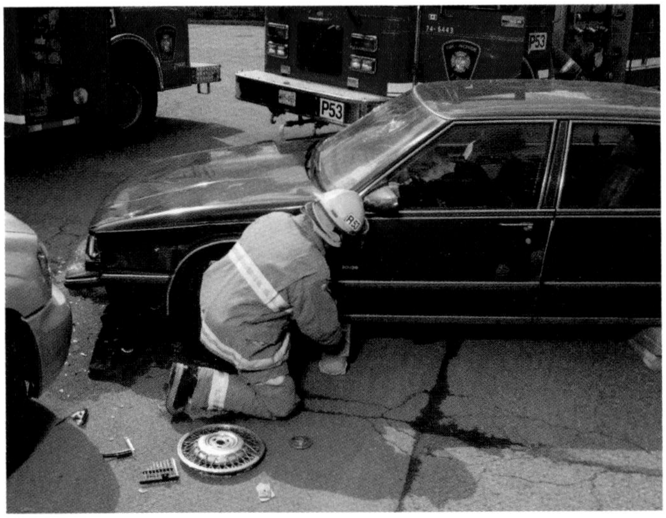

Figure 21–1 Chocking is used to stabilize a vehicle.

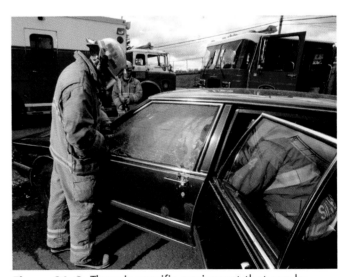

Figure 21–2 There is specific equipment that can be used to get into a car.

Overturned Vehicles

It is unusual to find a vehicle overturned or on its side. Consider any vehicle found in either position to be unstable. Although a vehicle on its side or overturned can be stabilized by using spare tires, jacks, wooden blocks, or other items, it is unlikely that you can adequately stabilize the vehicle.

NOTE:

It is important to beware of airbags. If they haven't gone off already, they may still be charged and ready to inflate. Ensure your own safety.

Vehicles and Electrical Hazards

When a vehicle is in contact with an electrical wire, you must consider the wire to be energized until you know otherwise. When you arrive on the scene, your first priority is to ensure your safety and that of others in the immediate area. A safety area should be established at a point twice the length of the span of the wire. Attempt to reach and move people only after the power company has been notified and has removed any electrical current from the downed wire. Do not touch any metal fence, metal structure, or body of water in contact with the downed wire. People inside the vehicle should be told to remain in the vehicle. You can tell them how to provide care for any injured people in the vehicle. Do not attempt to deal with electrical hazards unless you are specifically trained to do so.

Once the current has been removed from the wire, you can safely approach the vehicle. Since the vehicle and possibly the injured person/people were in contact with the current, electrical injury is possible.

Hazardous Materials Incidents

When approaching any scene, you should be aware of dangers involving chemicals. Whether a motor vehicle collision or an industrial emergency is involved, you should be able to recognize clues that indicate the presence of hazardous materials. These include:

- Signs (placards) on vehicles or storage facilities identifying the presence of hazardous materials
- Spilled liquids or solids
- Unusual odours

Figure 21–3 A hazardous material placard.

- Clouds of vapour
- Leaking containers

Placards, or signs, are required by law to be placed on any vehicles that contain specific quantities of hazardous materials (Figure 21–3). In addition, manufacturers and others associated with the production and distribution of these materials are required by law to display the appropriate placard. Placards often clearly identify the danger of the substance. Terms such as "explosive," "flammable," "corrosive," and "radioactive" are frequently used. Universally recognized symbols are also used.

Unless you have received special training in handling hazardous materials and have the necessary equipment, clothing, and personal protective equipment to deal with it without danger, you should stay well away from the area. Stay out of low areas where vapours and liquids may collect. Stay upwind and uphill from the scene. Be alert for wind changes that could cause vapours to blow toward you. Do not attempt to be a hero. It is not uncommon for responding paramedics approaching the scene to recognize a hazardous materials placard and immediately move to a safe area and summon more advanced help.

Many fire departments have specially trained teams to handle incidents involving hazardous materials. While awaiting help, keep people away from the danger zone.

Hazardous materials are not found only in industrial sites. They are often transported by rail or truck and may be exposed when a vehicle turns over or is in a collision. Homes contain many hazardous materials, such as natural gas, gasoline, kerosene, and pesticides.

Some hazardous materials, such as natural gas, are flammable and can cause an explosion. Even turning on a light switch or using a telephone or radio may create a spark that sets off an explosion. When you call for help, use a telephone or radio well clear of the scene.

Figure 21–4 A throwing assist.

WATER EMERGENCIES

Drowning

Drowning is death by suffocation when submerged in water. In a near-drowning situation, the person survives submersion, although sometimes only temporarily. The process of drowning begins whenever small amounts of water are inhaled into the lungs. This happens when a person is gasping for air while struggling to stay afloat. Stimulation by the water causes spasms of the muscles of the larynx, which closes the airway (laryngospasm). This is a natural body response to prevent more water from entering the lungs. As a result, the lungs of most people who drown or nearly drown are relatively dry unless the people are submerged for a long time. However, the spasms that block the airway to prevent water from entering also prevent air from entering. Without air, the person suffocates and soon becomes unconscious. At some point after unconsciousness, the muscles relax, and the person spontaneously breathes. If the person is submerged, more water can enter the lungs.

Assisting a Near-Drowning Person

A person who has been submerged in water for more than two or three minutes will suffer from a lack of oxygen and will need emergency care. The responder should get to the person as soon as possible without risking personal safety. The safest methods are throwing, reaching, and wading assists. In most cases, at least one of these methods will succeed.

Figure 21–5, a-b When using a throwing assist: **a**, try to throw the device beyond the person; **b**, keep your centre of gravity low when pulling the person back in.

You must always remember not to endanger yourself. Rescues that require swimming to a person require special training. If you swim to a person without this training, you are not likely to save the person. In fact, you only put yourself in danger and thus risk two lives. Likewise, leaping into water, even shallow water, to help someone may seem courageous, but choosing a less dramatic method is safer and usually more effective. You can help a person only if you remain safe yourself and in control of the situation. The throwing, reaching, and wading methods presented here help you do both.

Throwing Assists

With a throwing assist, you throw a heaving line, ring buoy, throw bag, rescue tube, or any other device that the person can grab to help stay afloat (Figure 21–4). If a line is attached, you can pull the person to safety.

When throwing a device, follow these general principles:

- Get into a safe position where you can keep your balance—keep low to the ground.

- Secure the non-throwing end of the line.

- Try to throw the device beyond the person (Figure 21–5, a).

- Throw the device so that the wind or current will bring it back within the person's reach.

- Once the person has grasped the device, slowly pull her to safety. Lie down or lean your body away from the person as you pull so that you are less likely to get pulled into the water (Figure 21–5, b).

Figure 21–6 You can use many things for a reaching assist such as a paddle, tree branch, belt, or towel.

- If there is no line on the device, tell the person to hold on and kick to safety.

Reaching Assists

With a reaching assist, you reach out to the person in the water while remaining in a safe position. First, firmly brace yourself. Extend your reach with any object that will reach the person, such as a pole, oar or paddle, tree branch, shirt, belt, or towel (Figure 21–6).

If you have no objects to extend your reach, try to extend your arm and grasp the person or extend your foot to the person. To avoid going into the water, lie flat on a pool deck or pier and reach with your arm. If you are in the water, use one hand to get a firm grasp on a pool ladder, overflow trough, piling, or other secure object and extend your free hand or one of your legs to the person.

Wading Assists

If you can enter the water without danger from currents, objects on the bottom, or an unexpected drop-off, wade in and reach to the person. If possible, extend your reach using a floatable item, such as a rescue tube, a ring buoy, a buoyant cushion, a raft, a kickboard, a personal flotation device (PFD), or a lifejacket. If you do not have a buoyant object, reach out with a tree branch, a pole, or another object.

Whatever object you have, use it for support in the water. Let the person grasp the other side of it. You can then pull the person to safety, or you can let go of an object that floats and tell the person to kick with it toward safety. Keep the safety device between you and the person so that a panicked person cannot grab you and pull you under.

After Reaching the Person

After reaching the person, remove her from the water as quickly as possible. If you suspect that the person may have a head or spine injury, you must support her neck and keep it aligned with the body. If it is necessary to turn the person on her back, the head, neck, chest, and the rest of the body must be aligned, supported, and turned as a unit. The person should be floated, on her back, onto a firm support, such as a backboard, before being moved from the water.

Once the person is out of the water, open the airway and check for breathing. Begin ventilation if the person is not breathing. If you are unable to get air into the person, the airway is probably obstructed. In this case, follow the procedure for an obstructed airway. Once you have been able to get your air in, check for signs of circulation. If you cannot detect a pulse, start CPR.

Basic life support should be continued until more advanced medical help is available. Every near-drowning person, regardless of how rapid the recovery, should be transported to a medical facility immediately for follow-up care.

You should attempt to resuscitate the person even if she has been submerged for a prolonged period. People have been successfully resuscitated even after being submerged in cold water for longer than 30 minutes. Continue CPR until advanced care can be started.

NOTE:

If you suspect a spinal injury,
treat as such.

Self-Rescue

Besides knowing the skills needed to rescue someone in trouble in the water, you should know what to do to help yourself if you suddenly get into trouble in the water. Whenever you attempt a water rescue in a dangerous water environment, you should wear a PFD.

However, if you unexpectedly fall into the water without a PFD, you may need to remove clothing to swim or

Figure 21–7 The Heat Escape Lessening Position.

float. But some clothing, such as a long-sleeved shirt that buttons, will actually help you float and protect you from cold. If your shoes are light enough for you to swim comfortably, leave them on. If they are too heavy, remove them.

Tread water to stay in an upright position while you signal for help or wait for rescue. You may need to tread water while you arrange your clothing to help you float. To tread water, stay vertical and submerge to your chin. Move your hands back and forth and use a kick that you can do effectively and comfortably, using the least amount of energy.

If you are wearing a PFD and help is nearby, you can wait for help using the Heat Escape Lessening Position (HELP). Hold the insides of your arms against your sides and place your forearms against your chest. Hold your thighs together and raise your knees toward your chest (Figure 21–7).

Ice Rescue

People needlessly die each year as a result of falling through ice. Unfortunately, some of these incidents also involve well-intentioned responders rushing to someone's aid. Ice rescues are dangerous because if someone has fallen in, this means the ice is unstable in that area. Ice rescues require special training and equipment.

Ice is not uniformly thick. Just because ice is safe enough to walk on in one area does not mean it is safe in other areas. While trying to reach the person, you could walk on an undetected thin spot and suddenly fall through the ice.

The safest methods of ice rescue are those that do not require you to make contact with the person. Using a reaching device, such as a stick or pole, is your best initial action to reach someone who is nearby. If the person is farther out on the ice, you should try to throw a line or floatable object to her. If the person is beyond your throwing distance or reach, do not venture onto the ice yourself. Summon necessary personnel, such as fire and rescue personnel, for assistance.

When attempting any ice rescue, you should always have the following:

- *Adequate personnel.* Never attempt a rescue by yourself. You will often need the assistance of several others to pull the person to safety.

- *Proper clothing.* Items such as wet suits or dry suits are required clothing if you are likely to enter the water.

- *Proper equipment.* PFDs for you and the person, rope, boat, paddle, and ice pick (screwdriver could substitute) are all necessary items.

- *Appropriate training.* Beyond the basic water rescue skills of throwing and reaching, responders should have the skills needed to operate a rescue boat or ice sled or to move properly over ice toward a person. These skills can be obtained through specialized ice rescue courses.

MOVING PEOPLE

Three general situations require you to perform an emergency move:

1. *Immediate danger.* This includes danger to you or the person being rescued from fire, a lack of oxygen, risk of drowning, possible explosion, a collapsing structure, or uncontrolled traffic hazards.

2. *Gaining access to other people.* A person with minor injuries may need to be moved quickly to reach other people who may have life-threatening conditions.

3. *Providing proper care.* Someone with a medical emergency, such as a cardiac arrest or heat stroke, may need to be moved to provide proper care. For example, someone in cardiac arrest needs CPR. It should be performed on a firm, flat surface. If the person collapses on a bed or in a small bathroom, the surface or space may not be adequate to provide appropriate care. You may have to move the person to give the proper care.

Usually, when you provide care, you will not face hazards that require moving the person immediately. In most cases, you can give care where you find the person. Moving someone needlessly can lead to further injury. For example, moving someone with a closed fracture of the leg without taking the time to splint it could result in an open fracture if the end of the bone tears the skin. Soft tissue damage, damage to nerves, blood loss, and infection could all result unnecessarily. Needless movement of someone with a head or spine injury could cause paralysis or even death.

Some rescue situations bring specialized challenges for gaining access to people, and these require responders with specialized training and equipment. One such situation is when the person needing rescue is in a confined space. Confined spaces are particularly challenging because they:

- Are not designed or intended to have people in them

- Have a restricted entrance or exit due to their location, size, or means

- Can present a risk to the health and safety of anyone who enters, including responders, due to one or more of the following factors:

  - Their design, construction, location, or atmosphere

  - The materials or substances in them

  - Work activities being carried out in them

  - They present mechanical, process, and/or safety hazards

Before you act, you must consider the limitations of the situation. Consider the following limitations to ensure that you move one or more people quickly and safely:

- Dangerous conditions at the scene

- The size of the person

- Your own physical ability

- Whether others can help you

- The person's condition

Failing to consider these limitations could result in injury. If you become injured, you may be unable to move the person and may risk making the situation worse. Due to the need to lift and carry a great deal of equipment, back injuries, as well as other musculoskeletal injuries, have a high potential of occurring in an EMS setting. If this occurs at a scene, you will have become part of the problem that arriving personnel with more advanced training will have to deal with. The situation will have become more complicated because now there is one more person to rescue.

To protect yourself and the ill or injured person, follow these guidelines when moving someone:

- Only attempt to move someone you are sure you can comfortably handle.
- Walk carefully, using short steps.
- When possible, move forward rather than backward.
- Look where you are going.
- Support the person's head and spine.
- Avoid bending or twisting someone with a possible head or spinal injury.

NOTE:

There are specific ways to deal with confined spaces (such as in a grain silo, vat, or pipe), and without appropriate training, you are putting yourself at risk. Ensure that the appropriate responders are on the way and manage the scene until they arrive. Only people with specialized training and equipment should enter confined spaces.

Body Mechanics

Some basic principles of body mechanics to be used for all lifts and moves are:

- Use your legs, not your back, to lift—use the muscles of your legs, hips, and buttocks, as well as your abdomen. Never use the muscles of your back to move or lift a heavy object.
- Keep the weight of the object as close to you as possible—reduce the distance you have to reach.
- Keep your body aligned—imagine a straight line from your shoulders, through your hips down to your feet. These should be stacked on top of each other, and always move them as a unit. This will reduce twisting forces.
- Reduce the height or distance you need to move an object—lift in stages if you need to.
- Keep a normal inward curve in your back and your wrists and knees in normal alignment.

Everyone on the team should use proper body mechanics, which will reduce the risk of injuring everyone else on the team, as well as themselves.

Reaching can also lead to injury of the back ligaments, if done incorrectly. When reaching, keep your back locked (avoid hyperextending it) and never twist your back. You should avoid reaching more than 15 to 20 cm in front of the body as your muscles in the upper back and shoulders can stay stretched in that position only for just seconds before they become fatigued and the risk of injury increases.

There are many different ways to move someone to safety, but no one way is best. As long as you can move the person to safety without injuring yourself or causing further injury to the person, the move is successful.

Moves used by responders include assists, carries, and drags. The most common of these are the:

- Walking assist
- Pack-strap carry
- Two-person seat carry
- Clothes drag
- Blanket drag
- Foot drag
- Extremity lift

All of these moves can be done by one or two people and without equipment. This is important because, with most moves, equipment is not often immediately available and time is critical.

Walking Assist

The most basic move is the walking assist. It is frequently used to help people who simply need assistance to walk to safety. Either one or two responders can use this method with a conscious person. To do a walking assist, place the person's arm across your shoulders and hold it in place with one hand. Support the person with your other hand around the person's waist (Figure 21–8). In this way, your body acts as a "crutch," supporting the person's weight while you both walk. A second responder, if present, can support the person in the same way from the other side (Figure 21–9).

Figure 21–8 A walking assist with one responder.

Figure 21–9 A walking assist with two responders.

Pack-Strap Carry

The pack-strap carry can be used on both conscious and unconscious people. To use it on an unconscious person requires a second responder to help position the person on your back. To perform the pack-strap carry, have the person stand or have a second responder help support the person. Position yourself with your back to the person, knees bent, so that your shoulders fit into the person's armpits. Cross the person's arms in front of you and grasp the person's wrists. Lean forward slightly and pull the person up onto your back. Stand up and walk to safety (Figure 21–10). Depending on the size of the person, you may be able to hold both of the person's wrists with one hand. This leaves your other hand free to help maintain balance, open doors, and remove obstructions.

Two-Person Seat Carry

The two-person seat carry is a method for moving a person who requires a second responder. To perform the two-person seat carry, put one arm under the person's thighs and the other across the person's back. Interlock

There are many different pieces of equipment on the market used to move ill or injured people. Use local protocol and manufacturers' directions when using this equipment.

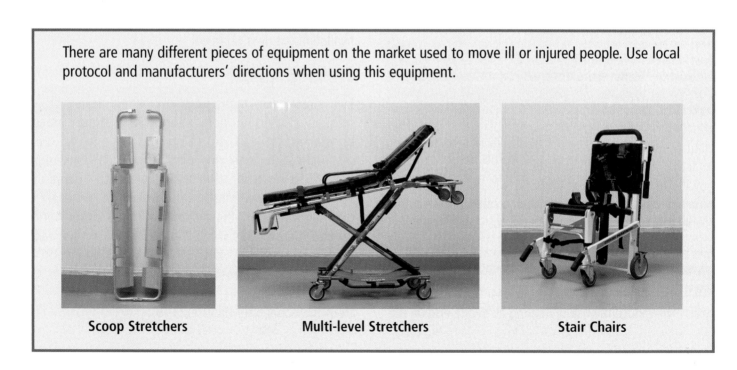

Scoop Stretchers   Multi-level Stretchers   Stair Chairs

Figure 21–10 A pack-strap carry.

your arms with those of a second responder under the person's legs and across the person's back. The person is then lifted in the "seat" formed by the responders' arms (Figure 21–11). The move should not be used for someone suspected of having a serious head or spine injury.

Clothes Drag

The clothes drag is an appropriate emergency move for someone suspected of having a head or spine injury. This move helps keep the head and neck stabilized. To do a clothes drag, gather the person's clothing, such as a jacket or shirt, behind the person's neck. Using

the clothing, pull the person to safety. During the move, the person's head is cradled by both the clothing and the responder's hands (Figure 21–12). This type of emergency move is exhausting and may result in back strain for the responder, even when done properly.

Blanket Drag

The blanket drag is an appropriate emergency move if you do not have a stretcher. To do a blanket drag, gather half a blanket and place the gathered side alongside the person. Roll the person toward you, tuck the blanket under the person as far as you can, and then roll the person back onto the blanket. Wrap the blanket around the person and then drag the person by pulling the part of the blanket at the person's head (Figure 21–13).

Foot Drag

To move someone who cannot otherwise be carried or moved, grasp the person's ankles and pull the person in a straight line, being careful not to bump the person's head (Figure 21–14).

Extremity Lift

The extremity lift, also called a fore-and-aft lift, is done with a partner when the person has no suspected spine injury and no injuries to the arms or legs (Figure 21–15). This can be used to lift an unconscious person from the floor to a chair.

Figure 21–11 A two-person seat carry.

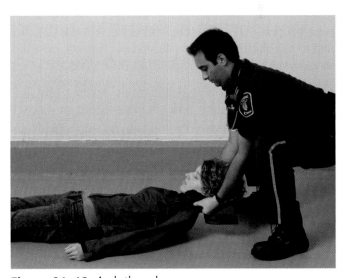

Figure 21–12 A clothes drag.

Positioning a Person

There are many ways to position a person:

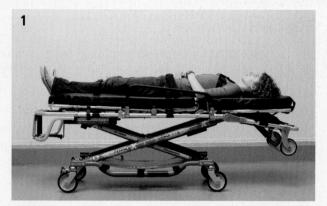

1

Supine

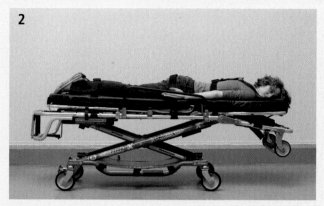

2

Prone

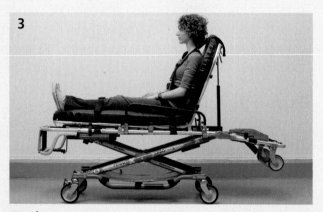

3

Fowler

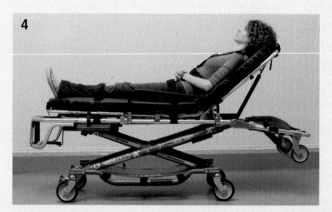

4

Semi-Fowler

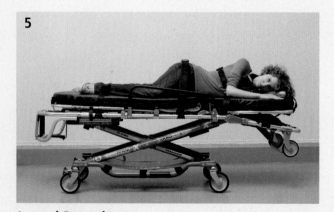

5

Lateral Recumbent

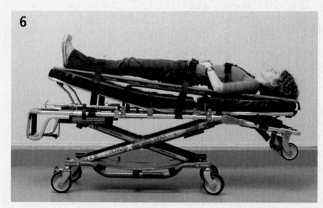

6

Trendelenburg

Figure 21–13 A blanket drag.

Figure 21–14 A foot drag.

1. Crouch at the person's head. The other responder should kneel at the person's side, by the knees.

2. Place one hand under each of the person's shoulders, reaching through to grab the person's wrists. Ensure that the person's back is close to your chest.

3. The responder at the knees should slip her hands under the person's knees.

4. On signal, both responders can then lift and move the person to the desired location.

Figure 21-15 An extremity lift.

SUMMARY

Take the time to survey the scene before attempting to gain access to or move the person. This is especially true in incidents involving hazardous materials. When gaining access, always try the simple approach first, such as checking all doors and windows for easy access into a building or vehicle. Check to see if anyone has keys. If you must forcibly gain access, several basic tools and techniques can be used.

A common mistake to avoid is forcibly gaining access or moving an ill or injured person unnecessarily. If you recognize a potentially life-threatening situation that requires a person to be moved, use one of the techniques described in this chapter. Use the safest and easiest method to rapidly move the person without causing injury to either yourself or the person.

In water emergencies, use the basics of throw, reach, or wade to rescue someone without endangering yourself. Enter the water only if you have been trained to do so and have the proper equipment.

As you extricate the driver, she begins to have a seizure. What do you do?

Chapter 22

Multiple Casualty Incidents

© Winnipeg Sun/The Canadian Press/Brian Donogh

A school bus carrying 30 students is involved in a collision and is severely damaged near the front. The students are scared and some are injured. People are starting to crowd around the area and the local fire department is already on scene. What do you do?

INTRODUCTION

In rush-hour traffic, during a rain storm, the driver of a tractor trailer loses control of the vehicle on a four-lane highway. The rig crosses the centre line, "jackknifes," and slides into an embankment. Numerous cars and a loaded tour bus try frantically to avoid colliding with the tractor trailer. Two cars collide head on. The bus plunges over an embankment, coming to rest 5 metres (15 feet) below in a ditch. Minor collisions occur farther back from the scene. Many people are injured; some are probably dead.

As a responder, you are likely to be among the first trained individuals nearby or summoned to assist with a serious incident such as this. The task of trying to create order out of chaos will initially fall on you. To respond most effectively to an emergency with multiple people, you need a plan of action. This plan must enable you to rapidly determine what additional resources are needed and how best to use them. During a serious incident, it is not uncommon for you to be on the scene for 15 minutes before any other trained personnel arrive. It could be up to an hour before adequate resources are available to care for the large number of injured people.

An appropriate initial response can eliminate potential problems for arriving personnel and possibly save the lives of several injured people. To accomplish this, you must thoroughly understand your plan of action. Your plan must enable you to take charge. This includes making the scene safe for you and others to work, delegating responsibilities to others, managing available resources, identifying and caring for the people most in need of care, and relinquishing command as more highly trained personnel arrive.

MULTIPLE CASUALTY INCIDENTS

As the term implies, a multiple casualty incident (MCI) refers to a situation involving two or more people. You are most likely to encounter small MCIs involving injury to only a few people, such as a motor vehicle crash involving the driver and a passenger. But MCIs can also be large-scale events, such as those caused by natural disasters or those from materials/structures made by humans. Examples include:

- Flood
- Fire
- Explosion
- Structure collapse
- Train derailment
- Airliner crash
- Hazardous materials incident
- Earthquake
- Tornado
- Hurricane

Incidents of this magnitude can result in hundreds or even thousands of injured or ill people. Whether small or large scale, MCIs can strain the resources of a local community. Coping effectively with an MCI requires a plan that enables you to acquire and manage additional personnel, equipment and supplies.

Organizing Resources

The Incident Command System

Providing appropriate help to one or more people in an emergency involves organisation. Different types of incidents vary in complexity. MCIs can strain the resources of the responding personnel and require additional resources from other areas, some far away. To ensure that the various resources operate in an orderly, united fashion to accomplish a task, the incident command system (ICS) was developed.

The ICS is a management system designed to be used for a wide variety of emergencies. It is especially useful in emergencies involving multiple ill or injured people because of its ability to handle several emergency situations at the same time. It is a common system that can be easily understood by different agencies working together at the scene of an emergency.

Originally developed in California to manage the large numbers of fire fighters necessary for major brush and forest fires, the ICS has subsequently been modified for use in a variety of MCIs. To understand the ICS, think of it as an organisation. An organisation is a group of people working together to achieve a common goal. To do this, the organisation must clearly define who is in charge, the scope of authority and responsibility, the goal, and the objectives to accomplish the goal. This same approach applies to the ICS. The advantages of the ICS for use in numerous situations include:

- Terms commonly understood by those taking part

- An integrated communications system

- One "boss" with the absolute authority to do what is necessary to accomplish the goal

- One unified command structure with well-established divisions, all working to accomplish the same goal

- Easily managed units normally consisting of not more than four people

The sectors, as designated by command, may include the following (Figure 22–1):

- Triage officer—supervises assessment, tagging, and moving of people to designated treatment areas

- Treatment officer—sets up a treatment area and supervises treatment, making sure the most seriously injured are transported first

- Transportation officer—arranges for ambulances while also tracking the priority, identity, and destination of all ill or injured people leaving the scene

- Staging officer—releases and distributes resources as needed and ensures that there is no transportation gridlock

- Safety officer—maintains scene safety by identifying potential dangers and taking action to prevent them from causing injury to all involved

Using the Incident Command System

A police officer is dispatched to a single motor vehicle collision. Since she is the first responder to arrive at the scene, she assumes the role of incident commander. She surveys the scene to determine the magnitude of the incident. She makes the scene safe for herself, bystanders, and any ill or injured people. Once the scene is safe, she approaches the vehicle. The driver has already left the vehicle and is seated on the curb next to the vehicle. The officer determines that the driver is the only injured person and approximates the type of injuries. The officer notifies the dispatcher of the situation, requesting only one ambulance as an additional resource. She gathers information from the injured person while providing care until more advanced medical personnel arrive. Once the person is turned over to the arriving paramedics, the officer reassesses scene safety, checks to make sure nothing else is needed, finishes gathering information, and completes any paperwork.

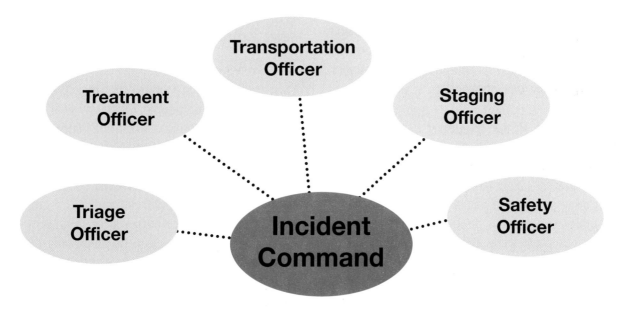

Figure 22–1 Basic structure of an incident command system.

In this situation, the resources needed were minimal. But what if the car had struck a utility pole and knocked down an electrical wire, the injured person had been trapped in a crushed vehicle, or multiple people had been injured? As the incident commander, the police officer would have notified the dispatcher of the situation and requested additional resources. She would have summoned the power company for the downed wire. If a person was trapped in the vehicle, resources such as the fire department or specialized rescue squad personnel would have been sent to the scene.

As these personnel arrive, the police officer could continue to act as the incident commander, or command could be turned over to other, more experienced personnel. These decisions are often based on the type of emergency and on local protocols. If the incident is beyond your scope, you should act as incident commander only until a more experienced person arrives. At this point, he will assume command.

At other times, you may be responding to a large-scale MCI because it requires additional personnel. Where you are placed and how your services are used will be based on your expertise and the needs at the time. This could include assisting medical personnel, aiding in crowd or traffic control, helping to maintain scene security, or helping to establish temporary shelter. By using the ICS in numerous emergencies, the tasks of reaching, caring for, and transporting ill or injured people are performed more effectively, thereby saving more lives. Since there are variations in the ICS throughout the country, you should become familiar with the ICS for your local community.

Caring for the Ill or Injured

Triage

In previous chapters, you learned how to conduct a systematic assessment of a person by doing a primary and secondary survey. This enabled you to care for life-threatening emergencies before minor injuries. You will recall that the primary survey has three steps that involve checking the person's airway, breathing, and circulation. You will also recall that the secondary

survey has three steps that include interviewing the person, checking vital signs, and doing a head-to-toe examination.

Although this approach is appropriate for one ill or injured person, it is not effective when there are fewer responders than ill or injured people. If you took the time to completely conduct each of these six steps and to correct all problems that you found, your entire time could be spent with only one person. An ill or injured person who is unconscious and not breathing, simply because the tongue is blocking the airway, could be overlooked and die while your attention is given to caring for someone with a less severe injury, such as a broken arm.

In an MCI, you must modify your technique for checking ill or injured people. This requires you to understand your priorities. It also requires that you accept death and dying because some people, such as those in cardiac arrest who would normally receive CPR and be a high priority, will be beyond your ability to help in this situation.

To identify which people require urgent care in an MCI, you use a process known as triage. Triage is an old French term that was first used to refer to the sorting and treatment of those injured in battle. Today, the triage process is used any time there are more ill or injured people than responders. Its common definition is the sorting of people into categories according to the severity of their injuries or illnesses.

The START System

Over the years, a number of systems have been used to triage ill or injured people. Most, however, required you to "diagnose" the exact extent of injury or illness. This was often time-consuming and resulted in delays in assessment and care for people in MCIs. As a result, the START system was created. START stands for Simple Triage And Rapid Treatment. It is a simple way to quickly assess and prioritize ill or injured people. The START system requires you to check only three items: breathing, circulation, and level of consciousness. As you check these items, you will classify ill or injured people into one of three levels that reflect the severity of injury or illness and need for care. These levels are "immediate," "delayed," and "dead/non-salvageable."

Using the START system requires the first responders on the scene to clear the area of all those people with only minor problems. These are sometimes called the "walking wounded." If someone is able to walk from the site of the incident, allow him to do so. Have these people walk to a designated area for evaluation by arriving medical personnel. This first action is critical to the success of START. It enables you to move people to safety, ensures higher-level medical care, and reduces the number of remaining people that you need to check.

Next, move quickly among the remaining people, assessing the severity of the problems. As you do so, you are attempting to classify each person into one of three categories for care.

The first of these categories is "immediate care." This categorization means that the person needs immediate transport to a medical facility. An example of an "immediate" ill or injured person is one who requires assisted ventilation as she is breathing more than 30 times a minute.

The second category is "delayed care." This category is assigned to a person who is breathing and has a pulse and level of consciousness within normal limits but who may not be able to move because of a broken leg or back injury.

The final category is "dead/non-salvageable." This category is assigned to those individuals who are obviously dead. People who are initially found not breathing and who fail to breathe after attempts are made to open and clear the airway are classified as dead/non-salvageable. This is also true for obvious mortal injury, such as decapitation.

As you classify each person into one of these three categories, you need to mark the person in some distinguishing manner so that responders coming behind you will be able to begin to care for and remove the most critical people first. This process of labelling people is easily done with commercial triage markers or multicoloured tape, which should be fastened to the person in an easily noticeable area, such as around the

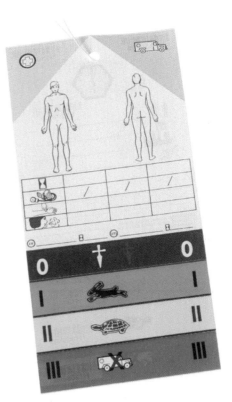

Figure 22–2 Example of a multiple casualty incident tag.

wrist (Figure 22–2). Colour codes are as follows:

- Immediate = red
- Delayed = yellow or green
- Dead/non-salvageable = black or grey

To make this decision, take the following steps:

Step one: Check breathing. When you locate a person, begin by assessing whether he is breathing. If he is not breathing, clear the mouth of any foreign object and make sure the airway is open. If he does not begin breathing on his own, even with the airway open, the person is classified as "dead/non-salvageable." There is no need to check the pulse. Place a black or grey marker on the person and move on.

On the other hand, if the person does begin to breathe on his own when you open the airway, this person should be classified as needing "immediate" care. Any individual who needs help maintaining an open airway is a high priority. Position the person in a way that will maintain an open airway, place a red tag on the person,

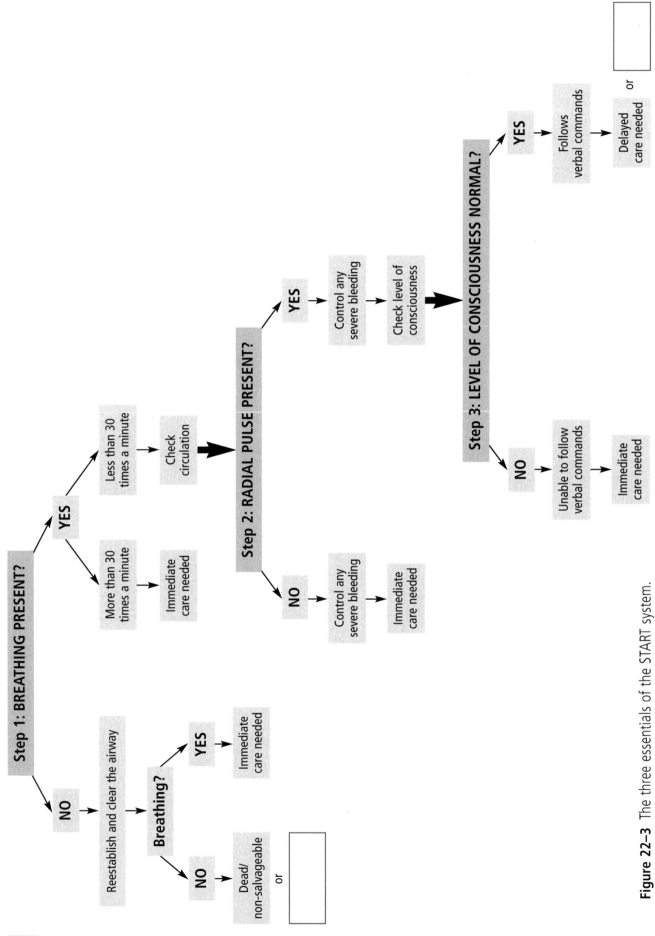

Figure 22–3 The three essentials of the START system.

TABLE 22-1 START CLASSIFICATION SYSTEM

Immediate (red)	Delayed (yellow/green)	Dead/non-salvageable (black/grey)
Breathing more than 30 times a minute	Breathing normal, radial pulse present, and level of consciousness normal	Not breathing
Breathing normal, but radial pulse absent		
Breathing normal, radial pulse present, but level of consciousness abnormal		

and move on to the next person. Once triage of all ill or injured people is complete, you may be able to come back and assist with their care.

If the person is breathing when you arrive, you must check the rate of the person's breathing. Someone breathing more than 30 times a minute should be classified "immediate." A person breathing less than 30 times a minute should be further evaluated. This requires you to move to the next check—circulation.

Step two: Check circulation. The next step is to evaluate the breathing person's pulse. You do this by checking the radial pulse. You are only checking for the presence of the radial pulse. If you cannot find the radial pulse in either arm, then the person's blood pressure is substantially low. Control any severe bleeding by using direct pressure and applying a pressure bandage. Classify the person as one requiring "immediate" care and move on to the next person. If the pulse is present and no severe bleeding is evident, conduct the final check—level of consciousness.

Step three: Check level of consciousness. The final step is to assess the person's level of consciousness. At this point, you know the following about the person:

• Breathing is normal (less than 30 times per minute).

• Radial pulse is present. (Severe bleeding may or may not be present.)

This final check will serve to classify this person. You determine the person's level of consciousness by using the AVPU scale. You give a person who is alert and responds appropriately to verbal stimuli a final classification of "delayed." This person has some injury that prevents him from moving to safety, but his present condition is not life-threatening. Someone who remains unconscious and responds only to painful stimuli or responds inappropriately to verbal stimuli is classified as "immediate."

By using the START system, you will be able to move quickly among ill or injured people, assessing and classifying them (Figure 22–3). Remember, your role is not to provide extensive care for the person. Instead, you are expected to get to as many people as possible. You should not at any time stop triaging people to begin CPR on one of them. This person is dead, and if you start CPR, you will need to continue. If you do, others who might have lived if you had done your job properly could now die as a result of delay. The likelihood that someone in a trauma situation in cardiac arrest will survive is extremely rare. Table 22–1 provides a simple overview of the START classification system.

SUMMARY

MCIs can be small- or large-scale operations. They can range from two people injured in a motor vehicle collision to hundreds injured in the collapse of a structure. Coping effectively with the magnitude of the problem requires an organized approach. The ICS provides this approach. The ICS provides for efficient use of resources, such as personnel, equipment, and supplies. When the ICS is used with an effective triage system such as START, the lives of many people can be saved because responders are able to reach, sort, and care for ill or injured people in the most efficient manner.

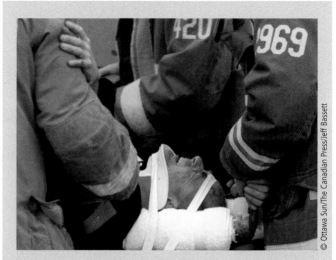

© Ottawa Sun/The Canadian Press/Jeff Bassett

A number of the students are yelling at you to help them and one of the firefighters asks you to come over and check the coach whose pain in his abdomen and chest seems to be getting worse. What do you do?

Chapter 23

Communications and Transportation

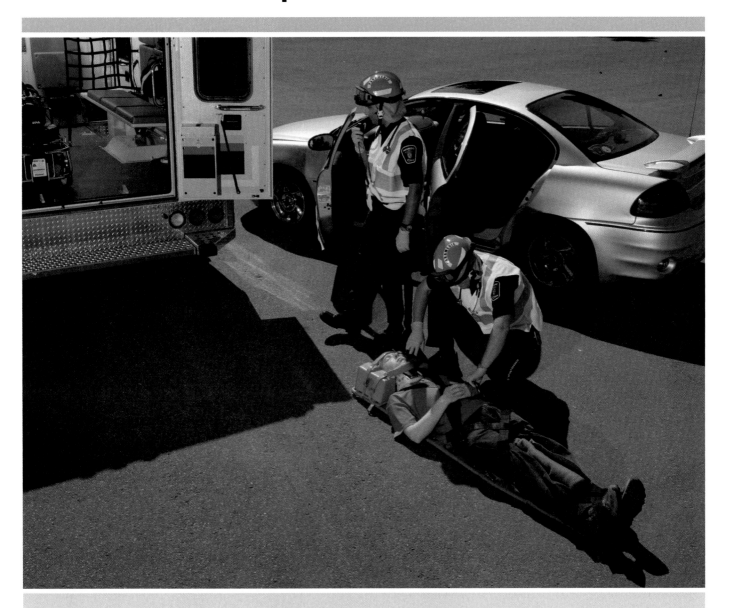

You are on the scene of a motor vehicle collision. One of the people injured has a head and spine injury and will need to be transported to a nearby hospital. Helicopter evacuation has been requested. What do you do?

INTRODUCTION

As an emergency medical responder (EMR), your responsibilities are not necessarily completed after you have provided assessment and treatment at the scene. You may be required to prepare and transport the ill or injured person to a hospital or medical facility.

Modern emergency vehicles are more than just vehicles for transporting someone to the hospital. They are well-equipped and efficiently organized vehicles or aircraft with advanced communications and technology that can bring needed medical supplies, personnel, and advanced life support (ALS) care to the scene.

Communication

There are several aspects to the EMR's role. You must be able to determine the person's major complaint, obtain a medical history, and properly reassure and comfort the ill or injured person. But just as important are tasks such as updating incoming EMS units on the person's status, requesting help from dispatch, asking the medical director for advice, and providing a hand-off report to any advanced care personnel who take over care. Both the former and latter types of tasks take skill; the latter depend on your skills as a good communicator.

Some of your communications with other EMS personnel will be on the radio or phone; others will be in person. In these situations, it is important for you to be accurate and speak slowly and clearly. Clear communication is critical to be able to provide accurate, complete information. Ineffective communication could result in harm to the person in your care.

Radio Communication

Radios operate on specific frequencies that are regulated and licenced by Industry Canada's Spectrum Management. Unauthorized people do not have access to these frequencies, so they cannot disrupt emergency radio traffic.

A radio system is made up of several components, usually including the following (Figure 23–1):

- *A base station.* The base system is the stationary radio located in a dispatch centre, station, or hospital.

- *Mobile radios.* These radios are mounted inside vehicles.

- *Portable radios.* These are hand-held radios that may be carried on your belt or in your pocket.

- *Repeaters.* Repeaters are devices that receive a low-power radio transmission and rebroadcast it with increased power.

- *Cellular phones.* In common use by the public, cellular phones are useful where radio coverage is unavailable to contact the medical director or the dispatcher.

During an emergency call, you will need to keep the dispatcher aware of your activities, assuming that your EMS system has a dispatch centre and radios. The specific times to report your activities are when you:

- Are en route to a call;

- Arrive at the scene of a call;

- Require additional assistance or specialized personnel; and

- Return to service and are available for the next call.

You will also use the radio to update incoming EMS units or to speak with the medical director.

It's important to become familiar with the use of a radio so that you don't have to learn how to use it during an emergency situation, when you'll be feeling anxious. Remember to speak slowly and clearly. When you are ready to speak, push the "push to talk" button and then wait one second before you begin to speak. Hold the microphone approximately 5 to 7 cm away from your

Figure 23–1 There are several components of a radio system.

mouth. Keep your transmission brief; others may be waiting to use the frequency. Listen before you transmit so that you don't disrupt another conversation.

Assume that anything you say over the radio can be heard by others. People with scanners can hear what you say, for example. So never say anything personal or confidential, such as a person's name. Of course, the public nature of radio transmission also means you should always keep your language and tone of voice professional.

Communicating with the Medical Director

While you are on the scene, you may need to consult with a physician, who can help you and the person in your care. Whenever you have questions about someone that cannot be resolved by protocols, consult with the medical director.

Since the physician may be far from the emergency scene, it is up to you to present the information clearly and concisely. Prepare yourself ahead of the call so that you're ready to provide the following information in your report:

- Your unit identifier and the fact that you are an EMR

- The ill or injured person's age, gender, and chief complaint

- A brief, pertinent history of the events leading to the injury or illness

- Results of the person's physical exam, including vital signs

- The care provided to the person and her response to that care

- The reason you are calling

If the physician gives you orders, repeat the orders back to verify them. Be sure that all orders and advice given to you by the physician are clear. If you have any questions, ask the physician for clarification.

> **NOTE:**
>
> *This information is what you would relay to any other healthcare provider when giving a verbal report.*

DOCUMENTATION

It is very important to properly document your assessment and care given to an ill or injured person. This documentation should include the following:

- Administrative information: names of the responders, as well as the unit number, call number, and address to which the responders were sent

- Ill or injured person's information: the person's name, age, gender, birth date, address, and any care given prior to the arrival of the responder

- Vital signs

- Chief complaint

- History (SAMPLE and OPQRST) and assessment findings

- Care given

Local protocols often dictate what specifics are to be included in a report, as well as in what format the information is to be documented.

> **NOTE:**
>
> *Reasons for documentation were discussed previously in this manual.*

TRANSPORTATION

Emergency Vehicle Maintenance and Safety Check

Completing an ambulance equipment and supply checklist at the beginning of every work shift is important for safety, patient care, and risk management issues and helps ensure the appropriate functioning of the vehicle for use in emergency and non-emergency responses. Some equipment on the ambulance (e.g., AEDs) requires routine maintenance and testing to ensure safe and effective operation when needed (Figure 23–2).

The vehicle and equipment must be disinfected and cleaned at times, both inside and out, to ensure that pathogens have been removed and that the vehicle represents your professional appearance. The procedure for vehicle maintenance and routine care varies by jurisdiction. The procedure for vehicle checks is often legislated by a governmental body, but specific EMS

Figure 23–2 Equipment on the ambulance requires routine maintenance and testing to ensure effective operation.

services may develop their own equipment checklists.

You should follow your operational guidelines for the safe and effective procedures for checking vehicles, equipment, and supplies. It is important to note and record any problems or deficiencies found when checking the emergency vehicle. Place any vehicle or piece of equipment out of service if an immediate safety issue arises.

Safe Vehicle Operations

Safe vehicle operation is important for the safety of people being rescued, the EMR crew, and the public in the vicinity of an emergency response. It is encouraged that all EMR agencies, where there is a requirement to transport people, require personnel to complete an emergency driving course and maintain that certification throughout their career. Never drive a private vehicle as if it were an emergency vehicle. Even if you have lights and sirens, people do not always see you, hear you, or yield the right-of-way. People hurrying to an emergency or a hospital sometimes cause collisions because they fail to drive safely.

When operating an emergency vehicle, follow these guidelines:

- Follow all laws and acts with respect to the operation of an emergency vehicle in your province or territory.

- Follow all operational guidelines for your jurisdiction.
- Be tolerant and observant of other motorists and pedestrians.
- Always use your seat belts and restraining devices.
- Be familiar with the characteristics of the emergency vehicle.
- Be alert to changes in weather and road terrain and conditions.
- Exercise caution in the use of audible and visible warning devices.
- Drive within the speed limit, except in circumstances allowed by law.
- Select the fastest and most appropriate route to and from the scene.
- Maintain a safe following distance.
- Drive with due regard for the safety of others.
- If possible, drive in a manner that allows the ill or injured person comfort.
- Always drive in a manner consistent with managing acceptable levels of risk.

In addition to the size and weight of the emergency vehicle and driver's experience level, factors that influence safe operation include:

- Attitude
- Environmental conditions
- Appropriate use of warning devices
- Proceeding safely through intersections
- Parking at the emergency scene
- Operating with due regard for the safety of all others

Attitude

Attitude is the mental framework that structures your day-to-day driving performance. It is the way you see yourself as a driver and how you view other drivers. Attitudes are influenced by experiences, emotions, values, feelings, prejudices, and personality. Being a safe driver requires an open mind, a willingness to learn, and a desire to improve.

Safe drivers are courteous and considerate. They are willing to yield the right-of-way and they keep a constant check on traffic and adapt to changing conditions. A positive attitude will help you drive amicably with others and help maintain the safe operation of your vehicle.

Environmental Conditions

Environmental conditions can pose significant dangers to EMRs when responding to calls. Factors that can affect safe operation include road and weather conditions, such as fog and heavy rain that decrease visibility, and slippery conditions caused by snow, ice, or water that can cause the vehicle to hydroplane. When hazardous environmental conditions are present, the driver should proceed at safe speeds appropriate to the conditions.

Appropriate Use of Warning Devices

When responding to an emergency call, the driver must use audible and visual warning devices according to local protocols and based on provincial/territorial motor vehicle laws. Use of warning devices while transporting someone should be based on assessment of the person and appropriate protocol for treatment and transportation. When responding to or from a call using warning devices, keep in mind that motorists who drive with car windows rolled up or who are using a radio, air conditioning, or heating system may not be able to hear the warning devices. It is important that you proceed with caution and never assume that the warning devices provide an absolute right-of-way to proceed. When backing up, take extra caution to ensure that there is nothing in your path and use backup signals if available.

Proceeding Safely Through Intersections

Most provinces and territories require all emergency vehicles to come to a complete stop at all controlled intersections (i.e., red light, stop sign) and proceed through the intersection when safe to do so. Take precautions when proceeding through controlled intersections to gain the attention of surrounding motorists such as:

• Changing the mode of the siren

• Using air horns

• Using legislated sirens

Parking at the Emergency Scene

When parking the emergency vehicle at the scene, consider any hazards such as leaking fuel, hazardous materials, or leaking gas. If any of these conditions are present, position the vehicle upwind and at a safe distance. In addition, position the vehicle so that it protects you and the ill or injured person from other motorists and hazards. When parking or positioning your vehicle, keep the following in mind:

• Vehicle exhaust fumes

• Downed electrical wires

• Poor lighting

• Blocking extrication vehicles and equipment

• The possibility of collapse of surrounding buildings due to fire or explosion

Operating With Due Regard for the Safety of All Others

Most provinces and territories allow privileges for drivers of emergency vehicles, such as driving slightly above the speed limit and proceeding through controlled intersections (after a complete stop) during an emergency response.

However, these privileges must take into consideration the safety of others. "Due regard for the safety of all others" carries legal responsibility and can result in liability for you and the agency you represent if damage, injury, or death results from its failure. As an EMR, you must be familiar and aware of local and provincial/territorial laws and regulations pertaining to the operation of an emergency vehicle.

Air Medical Transportation

In certain situations, it is sometimes best for the ill or injured person to be transported to the medical facility by a helicopter or a fixed-wing aircraft. This type of transport enables severely injured or ill people to be transported quickly to specialty centres and large treatment facilities. Geography and other circumstances play a large role in this type of transport decision, and emergency personnel should follow local and provincial/territorial protocols.

Air ambulance services typically use fixed-wing and/or rotary-wing (helicopter) aircraft throughout the country. Fixed-wing aircraft are not usually as high profile as helicopters but are particularly useful for long-distance (i.e., > 200 km) and inter-hospital transfers of people or vital organs. Fixed-wing aircraft can also operate in weather conditions that may restrict rotor-wing aircraft.

Landing Site Preparation

A helicopter landing zone should be approximately 30 metres X 30 metres (100 feet X 100 feet). It should have no vertical structures that can impair landing or takeoff and should be relatively flat and free of high grass, crops, or other factors that can conceal uneven terrain or hinder access. The landing site should also be free of debris that could injure people or damage structures or the aircraft. Rescue personnel close to the landing site should wear protective eyewear and helmets. Given the time of day, the landing site may need lighting such as portable lights and traffic cones with reflectors or may require positioning of the emergency vehicles, with warning lights on, around the perimeter of the landing zone. If white lights are used, point them toward the centre of the landing zone and not directly at the aircraft. If conditions are very dry, you may need to wet the landing zone to prevent the pilot and drivers of vehicles on the ground from being blinded. It may also be helpful to use radio communications with the pilot to advise her of conditions such as wind direction or any hazards or obstructions of which she needs to be aware. In some cases, when the helicopter is landing, it may be appropriate for you to use hand signals to guide the pilot.

Ground Safety Precautions

Keep the landing zone clear during takeoffs and landings. Maintain a distance of 30 to 60 metres (100 to 200 feet). In addition, adhere to the following guidelines:

- Never allow ground personnel to approach the helicopter unless requested to do so by the pilot or flight crew.

- Stay in view of the flight crew at all times.

- Stay away from propellers.

- Allow only necessary personnel to help load or unload people.

- Secure any loose objects or clothing that could be blown by rotor or downwash (e.g., stretcher, sheets, or blankets).

- Do not allow smoking.

- After the aircraft is parked, move to the front, beyond the perimeter of the rotor blades, and wait for a signal from the pilot to approach.

- Approach the helicopter in a crouched position, staying within view of the pilot or other crew members (Figure 23–3).

- Never approach the aircraft (rotary or fixed wing) from the rear (Figure 23–4). The tail rotors on most aircraft are near the ground and spin at high rpm, which makes them virtually invisible. Tail rotor injuries are often fatal.

- Carry long objects horizontally and no higher than waist height.

- Depart the helicopter from the front and within view of the pilot.

Medical Evacuation From a Ship

A helicopter should not be requested for evacuation from a ship unless the person is in a serious situation. In many cases, the decision to use aeromedical evacuation is made in consultation with the medical advisor, based on the medical information provided by the attendant.

Preparing the Person for Transfer

To prepare a person for transfer, follow these steps:

- Ensure that the person's airway, breathing, and circulation are under control. If indicated, strap the person in a stretcher to prevent her from slipping or falling out.

- Place the person's medical records (if any) with all necessary papers (including passport, if available) in a plastic envelope to be sent along with her.

Figure 23–3 Approach a helicopter in a crouched position.

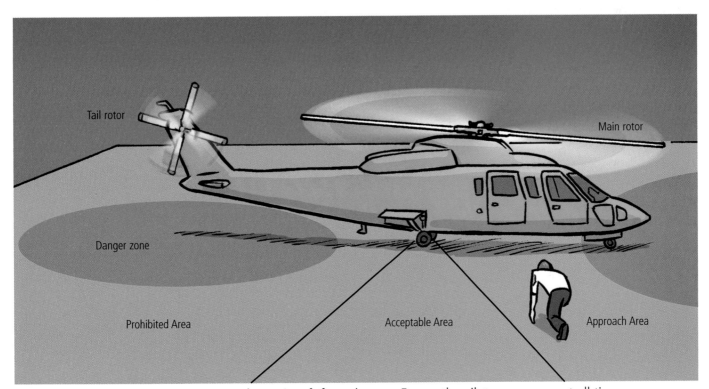

Figure 23–4 Never approach an aircraft from the rear. Ensure the pilot can see you at all times.

- Add notes of any treatment given.

- If possible, ensure that the person is wearing a PFD before moving her to the stretcher.

- Perform a concise but thorough assessment and relay all pertinent information directly to one of the flight crew members.

- Describe any bandaged or covered injury, or any physical finding, to the flight medical crew, along with a concise history of the event.

Ship-to-Ship Transfer

Ship-to-ship transfer involves difficult manoeuvring for two vessels. It is a seamanship problem demanding high standards of competence for its safe and efficient performance. Light (unloaded) ships must be approached slowly and with caution. Ships with the higher freeboard should provide the illumination and boarding facilities. The transfer should be performed quickly, and ships should not linger alongside for any reason.

SUMMARY

The ability to communicate clearly and accurately is one of the most critical skills for an EMR so that you can effectively update incoming EMS units on the status of the person in your care, request help from dispatch, ask the medical director for advice, and provide a hand-off report to the more advanced personnel who take over care. It's also important to learn how to use radio equipment competently.

Your job does not necessarily end after you have assessed and cared for a person at the emergency scene. In some circumstances, you may be required to transport the person to a medical facility or assist with air medical transportation or medical evacuation from a ship. This responsibility includes maintaining and safely operating an emergency vehicle as well as understanding how to prepare a landing zone for an air ambulance in any type of emergency situation.

The helicopter is on its way and you are told to get the landing zone ready. What do you do?

Chapter 24

Marine Advanced First Aid

One of your crew members has fallen overboard into frigid waters. It has only been a minute or two since he went in the water but he is quickly becoming less and less responsive. What do you do?

INTRODUCTION

As a marine advanced first aid attendant, you are required to hold a marine first certificate specified by Transport Canada, Marine Safety. This chapter references the need for specialized training for those responsible for the medical care of seafarers, particularly in oxygen administration, airway adjuncts, drug administration, Workplace Hazardous Materials Information System (WHMIS), and confined space entry. Although this chapter outlines procedures intended for those with specialized training, as a marine first aid attendant you may be requested to gather supplies and/or assist a ship's doctor or more advanced medical personnel with procedures. This information is being provided to familiarize you with the equipment and safety precautions required for each procedure.

NOTE:

Any procedure described in this chapter should be applied by the first aid attendant under appropriate supervision in accordance with professional standards of care used with regard to unique circumstances that apply to each situation.

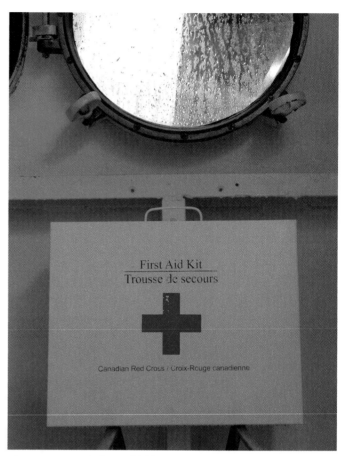

Figure 24–1 A first aid kit.

Preparing to Respond

First Aid Kits, Supplies, and Equipment

As a marine first aid attendant, it is important for you to be aware of the location of your ship's:

- first aid station(s), which are found in the Wheelhouse, Engine, Galley, and in lifesaving equipment such as lifeboats;

- first aid kits (Figure 24–1) and equipment; and

- medical supplies.

You should also be familiar with the contents and proper use of the supplies contained in each kit. First aid kit contents for vessels travelling in International waters are outlined in Table 24-1, whereas Table 24-2 outlines the kit contents for each vessel type when traveling in Canadian waters, as per the current version of the *Canadian Labour Code: Marine Occupational Safety and Health Regulations.* Survival crafts, such as lifeboats, require certain minimum kit contents as outlined in Table 24-3.

First aid attendants should also understand the importance of checking the expiry date of all first aid materials, having reliable supplies available, routinely checking the first aid stations, and ensuring that the first aid station and its contents are in a clean, dry, and serviceable condition. Throughout this chapter, specific equipment lists have been provided where appropriate.

NOTE:

Unless there is a person qualified on board the ship, such as a registered nurse or doctor, the Ship Captain is ultimately responsible for the administration of medicine. The Ship Captain is normally the custodian of the medical chest on board any ship; however, the decision whether to administer the medicine is made after consulting with the medical advisor. Also, the Captain must maintain a log book of all medicine administered during the voyage and for which type of illnesses. An official entry in the Ship's Log Book must also be made.

TABLE 24-1 INTERNATIONAL FIRST AID KIT CONTENTS*

	Category	Recommendation Item	Quantity per 10 crew
1	**RESUSCITATION EQUIPMENT**		
	Equipment for the administration of oxygen	Portable oxygen set, complete, containing:	1
		1 oxygen cylinder (D: 425 litres or E: 680 litres)	1
		1 spare oxygen cylinder (D: 425 litres or E: 680 litres)	1
		Pressure regulator and flowmeter, with tubes such that ship's industrial oxygen can also be used	1
		3 disposable face masks of choice including resuscitation mask and non-rebreather mask	3
	Oropharyngeal airway (OPA)	Sizes medium and large	2
	Suction device	Manual suction to clear upper airways, including 2 catheters	1
	Bag-valve-mask (BVM) resuscitator	BVM supplied with large, medium and small masks	1
	Barrier devices for mouth-to-mouth resuscitation	Pocket mask with one-way valve	1
2	**DRESSING MATERIAL AND SUTURING EQUIPMENT**		
	Adhesive bandages	Assorted sizes, water-resistant	200
	Sterile gauze compress	Gauze compress, 5 x 5 cm, sterile	100
		Gauze compress, 10 x 10 cm, sterile	100
	Gauze roll	Gauze roll, 5 cm and 90 cm (or 60 cm) x 100 m, non sterile	1
	Gauze dressing with non-adherent surface	Non-adherent gauze dressing, 10 cm x 10 cm, sterile	100
	Vaseline® gauze	Paraffin gauze dressing, 10 x 10 cm, sterile	50
	Elastic bandage	Elastic fixation bandage, 6 cm x 4 m	3
	Sterile pressure bandage	Sizes small/medium/large	5
	Tubular gauze for finger bandage	Tubular gauze bandage for finger bandage with applicator, 5 m	1

Adhesive elastic bandage	Adhesive elastic bandage, 6 cm x 4 m	10
Triangular bandages	Triangular bandages	5
Sterile sheet for burns	Sterile sheet for burns	1
Adhesive sutures (or zinc oxide bandages)	Adhesive tape, waterproof, skin-friendly, 5 x 1.25 cm	10
Q-tips®	Q-tips® (wooden)	100
Safety pins	Safety pins (stainless steel) 12 pcs	50
Butterfly sutures	Butterfly sutures, skin closures, sterile	20
Skin adhesive	2-octyl cyanoacrylate liquid, 0.5 mL	2
Suturing equipment	Sutures, absorbable with curved non-traumatic needles, 1-0, 3-0, & 4-0 (or 5-0)	10 each
Gloves (latex free)	Disposable examination gloves	50
	Surgical gloves sizes 6.5, 7.5, 8.5, sterile, in pairs	3 of each size
3	**INSTRUMENTS**	
Disposable scalpels	Scalpel, sterile, disposable	20
Stainless steel instrument box	Instrument box (stainless steel)	1
Scissors	Operating scissors, straight (stainless steel)	1
	Bandage scissors (stainless steel)	1
Forceps	Splinter forceps, pointed (stainless steel)	3
	Teeth tissue forceps (stainless steel)	1
Needle holder	Needle holder, 80 mm straight	1
Hemostatic clamps	Hemostatic clamp, 125 mm (stainless steel)	3
Disposable razors	Razor, disposable	50
4	**EXAMINATION AND MONITORING EQUIPMENT**	
Disposable tongue depressors	Tongue depressors, disposable	100
Reactive strips for urine analysis	Reactive strips for urine analysis (blood/glucose/protein/nitrite/leukocytes)	100
Microscope slides	Microscope slides	100
Stethoscope	Stethoscope	1

Blood pressure cuff	Blood pressure cuff, preferably automatic	1
Standard thermometer	Digital if possible	1
Rectal thermometer	Thermometer, digital if possible	1
Hypothermic thermometer	Thermometer 32°–34°C, digital if possible	1
Penlight	Penlight plus blue cover	1

5 EQUIPMENT FOR INJECTION, INFUSION, AND CATHETERIZATION

Equipment for injection	Syringes, Luer connection, 2 mL, sterile disposable	50
	Syringes, Luer connection, 5 mL, sterile, disposable	50
	Hypodermic subcutaneous needle, Luer connection, 16 x 0.5 mm, sterile, disposable	20
	Hypodermic intramuscular needle, Luer connection, 40 x 0.8 mm, sterile, disposable	20
	Needles, 19 gauge blunt, "drawing up" type	20
Equipment for infusion	Intravenous, infusion cannula 16 gauge (1.2 mm) and 22 gauge (0.8 mm), Luer-lock connection, sterile, non-recap type	10 each
	Intravenous giving set, Luer-lock connection, sterile	3
	Tourniquet, blood-taking type, to be used with intravenous infusion cannula	1
Bladder drainage equipment	Penile sheath set with condom catheter (Texas Catheter™), tube, and bag	2
	Short-term urine catheter with Soft Eye™ straight tip Thieman No. 12 and No. 16 or equivalent (Foley), sterile, individually packed, prelubricated or with additional lidocaine/chlorhexidine lubricant	2
	Urine collecting bag and tube	2

6 GENERAL MEDICAL AND NURSING EQUIPMENT

Eye protection	Plastic goggles or full-face masks	2
Plastic apron	Disposable	20
Kidney dish (basin)	Kidney dish, stainless steel, 825 mL	2
Plastic backed towels	Towels, plastic backed, absorbent, 600 x 500 mm	10
Safety box (sharps container)	Safety box for sharps disposal, 5 L	1

Masks	Masks, duckbill type, disposable	50
Tape measure	Tape measure, vinyl coated, 1.5 m	1
Draw sheets	Draw sheet, plastic 90 x 180 cm	2
Bedpan	Bedpan, stainless steel	1
Hot-water bottle	Hot-water bag	1
Urine bottle	Urinal, male (plastic)	1
Ice bag	Cold pack	1
Emergency blanket (aluminum foil blanket)	Aluminum foil blanket	1
Condoms	Male condoms	100
Wash bottle	Plastic wash bottle, 250 mL	1
Plastic bottle	Bottle, 1 litre, plastic with screw top	3
Dressing tray	Stainless steel dressing tray, 300 x 200 x 30 mm	1
Bowl	Bowl, stainless steel, 180 mL	3
Specimen jars	Jars, plastic, with lids and labels, 100 mL	10
Plaster-of-Paris bandage	Bandages, POP, 5 cm and 10 cm x 2.7 m	12 each
Stockinet	Sizes for arm and leg splints, 10 m roll	1 each
Cotton wool	Cotton wool roll, 500 g	10
Alcohol swabs	70% alcohol swabs for skin cleansing prior to injection	200
Nail brush	Nail brush	1
7 **IMMOBILIZATION AND TRANSPORTATION EQUIPMENT**		
Malleable splints	Malleable finger splint Malleable forearm/hand splint	1 of each

Source: Adapted with permission from World Health Organization, *International Medical Guide for Ships, 3rd Edition*. Geneva: World Health Organization, 2007.

TABLE 24-2 FIRST AID KIT CONTENTS AS PER THE CANADA LABOUR CODE*

ITEM SUPPLIES AND EQUIPMENT	TYPE OF FIRST AID KIT				
	ON A SHIP				AT A DETACHED WORK PLACE
	With 2-5 employees	With 6-19 employees	With 20-49 employees	With 50+ employees	
	Quantity per Type of First Aid Kit				
Antiseptic-wound solution, 60 mL or antiseptic swabs (10-pack)	1	2	3	6	1
Applicator-disposable (10-pack) (not needed if antiseptic swabs used)	1	2	4	8	—
Bag-disposable, waterproof, emesis	1	2	2	4	—
Adhesive bandages	12	100	200	400	6
Gauze rolls, 2.5 cm x 4.5 m (not needed if ties attached to dressing)	2	6	8	12	—
Triangular bandages (with 2 safety pins)	2	4	6	8	1
Container-First Aid Kit	1	1	1	1	1
Gauze compress, 7.5 x 12 cm, sterile	2	4	8	12	—
Gauze dressing, 7.5 x 7.5 cm, sterile	4	8	12	18	2
Forceps (splinter)	1	1	1	1	—
First Aid manual, English — current edition	1	1	1	1	—
First Aid manual, French — current edition	1	1	1	1	—
Pad with shield or tape for eye	1	1	2	4	1
Record-First Aid	1	1	1	1	1
Scissors — 10 cm	—	1	1	1	—
Roll of waterproof adhesive tape, 1.2 cm x 4.6 m (not needed if ties attached to dressings)	1	1	2	3	—
Antipruritic lotion, 30 mL or swabs (10-pack)	1	1	1	2	—
Elastic bandage, 7.5 cm x 5 m	—	—	1	2	—
Emergency blanket (aluminum foil blanket)	—	—	—	—	1

Dressing-burn, sterile, 10 x 10 cm	1	1	1	2	—
Hand cleanser or cleaning towelettes, 1 pack	1	1	1	1	—
Splint set with padding	—	1	1	1	—
Stretcher	—	—	1	1	—

Source: Adapted with permission from Marine Occupational Health and Safety Regulations, Canada Labor Code, Subsection 13.6(1)

TABLE 24-3 MINIMUM FIRST AID KIT CONTENTS ON SURVIVAL CRAFTS (INCLUDING LIFEBOATS AND RAFTS)*

Item Supplies and Equipment	Quantity
Adhesive bandages, 7.5 x 2.2 cm (individually wrapped)	32
Gauze rolls, 5 cm x 4.6 m	4
Compress bandages, 10 x 10 cm with 90-cm gauze tabs	8
Sterile abdominal pads, 15.2 x 20.3 cm	2
Triangular bandages	6
Sterile eye pads, 4.69 x 6.98 cm	10
Extra-ocular ophthalmic irrigating solution in an unbreakable bottle that shows a drug identification number and an expiry date	120 mL
Unbreakable plastic eyewash cup	1
Wire splint, 9.5 x 60 cm	1
Individual packs of ammonia inhalant	20
Pads impregnated with povidone and iodine that show an expiry date	20
Pocket guide to Emergency First Aid, in English and French, published by the Canadian Red Cross or St. John Ambulance	1
Waterproof contents list and instruction sheet in English and French	1
Safety pins	6
Bandage scissors (stainless steel)	1
Roll of waterproof adhesive tape, 2.5 cm x 4.5 m	1

The first aid kit shall be placed in a container that is:

Watertight;

Resealable;

Fitted with a gasket to ensure a tight seal; and

Made of a rigid plastic that is capable of withstanding temperatures of -30°C, such as acrylonitrile butadienestyrene (ABS) or high-impact polystyrene (HIPS).

Source: Adapted with permission from http://www.tc.gc.ca/acts-regulations/GENERAL/C/csa/regulations/030/csa032/csa_32-b.html#K

AIRWAY ADJUNCTS

Endotracheal Intubation

Advanced medical personnel prefer endotracheal intubation as the advanced technique for airway management for people who are unable to maintain an open airway. Endotracheal (ET) intubation provides a definitive means to control a person's airway. Intubation with a cuffed ET tube helps ensure that the airway remains open by preventing aspiration. Once an ET tube is placed properly within the trachea, it is possible to provide controlled ventilation with 100% oxygen without concern for pushing air into the stomach.

Indications for ET intubation include situations when

- the rescuer is unable to ventilate an unconscious person with conventional methods (e.g., mouth-to-mask, BVM);

- the person is unable to protect his own airway due to coma, or respiratory or cardiac arrest; and

- prolonged resuscitation is necessary.

In addition, ET intubation provides the following advantages:

- It isolates the airway, preventing aspiration of material, such as vomit, into the lower airway.

- It facilitates ventilation and oxygenation of the body.

- It facilitates suctioning of the trachea and bronchi.

- It prevents wasted ventilation and gastric distention during positive-pressure ventilation.

- It provides a route for the administration of some medications.

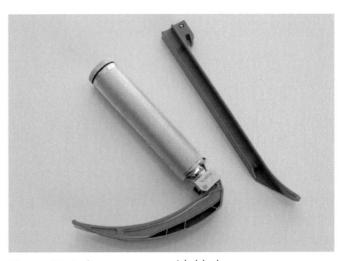

Figure 24–2 Laryngoscope with blades.

Although ET intubation provides many advantages, it is a technically challenging procedure that poses risks and potential complications that can be considered life-threatening. It is important to note that the priority for a nonbreathing person is ventilation, not intubation.

Preparing the Equipment

One of the first steps in ET intubation is to make careful preparations. To perform ET intubation, you may be requested to gather and prepare the intubation equipment outlined in Table 24-4.

> **NOTE:**
>
> *The ship medic, nurse, or doctor may be required to perform airway intervention. The information on the techniques and procedures for intubation is intended as a basic overview only. These skills require specialized training and are intended for those who provide advanced medical care.*

TABLE 24-4 EQUIPMENT NEEDED FOR ENDOTRACHEAL INTUBATION

• Gloves	• Water-soluble lubricant	• 10 mL syringe
• Goggles	• Suction unit	• Stylet
• Laryngoscope blades and handle	• BVM	• Assorted endotracheal tubes
• Towel	• Tape and/or commercial securing device	• Stethoscope

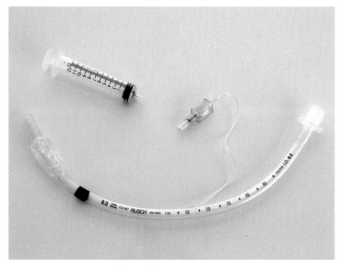

Figure 24–3 ET tube and syringe.

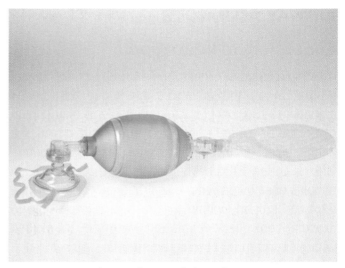

Figure 24–4 A bag-valve-mask (BVM).

A laryngoscope is an instrument used to visualize the vocal cords for ET tube placement (Figure 24–2). It consists of two parts: a handle (which contains the batteries) and a lighted blade. Two to three blades should be available to allow for differences in size and anatomy of different people. The blade has a notch that attaches to a locking bar on the laryngoscope handle. Locking the blade in place causes a light to turn on, allowing vocal cord visualization. Check the light. It should be bright white and steady.

ET tubes are available in several sizes. Sizes, in millimetres, are determined by the internal diameter of the tube (Figure 24–3). You will need two to three cuffed ET tubes in different sizes. A 7.5 mm tube usually fits an adult.

The ET tube cuff holds about 10–20 mL of air. Test the cuff for leaks prior to intubation attempts.

A stylet is used to provide stiffness to the ET tube during insertion. This allows the tube to be directed toward the vocal cords. Stylets are malleable metal rods that are inserted into the ET tube and moulded to the desired shaped curve. To place a stylet into the ET tube, first lubricate it with water-soluble jelly. Then, insert the stylet into the ET tube, ensuring that it does not extend beyond the end of the tube.

Intubating the Person

In preparation for ET intubation, place the person in the sniffing position (the head backward as if the person's nose is pointing up sniffing the air). This provides the best alignment for direct visualization of the larynx (vocal cords). The tube should be lubricated, and a stethoscope, stylet, and suction equipment should be readily available. As in all advanced airway procedures, you should ventilate the person's lungs with 100% oxygen for 1 to 2 minutes before intubation using a BVM (Figure 24–4) and supplemental oxygen.

To ventilate the person using ET intubation, begin by holding the laryngoscope in the left hand. Insert the blade into the right side of the mouth, displacing the tongue to the left. Advance the ET tube through the corner of the mouth, and under direct vision, through the vocal cords. First, inflate the cuff with 10 to 20 mL of air and then ventilate the person's lungs with a BVM. While ventilating the person, confirm ET placement by listening to the abdomen and chest with a stethoscope. Finally, secure the ET tube to the person's head and face with tape or a commercially available device designed for this use, and provide ventilatory support with supplemental oxygen.

ET Tube Removal

If the person begins to breathe on his own, the ET tube may need to be removed. To accomplish removal, first suction the person's mouth, nose, and back of the throat. Then, deflate the cuff of the ET tube. If the person is conscious, instruct the person to take a deep breath. Have them blow out while you withdraw the tube. Be prepared to suction the person's mouth in case of vomiting.

TOXICOLOGICAL HAZARDS ON BOARD A SHIP

Workplace Hazardous Materials Information System (WHMIS)

Many workers are exposed to chemical hazards in the workplace. To help protect employees, the federal, provincial, and territorial governments have legislated WHMIS, a nationwide class identification system that provides Canadian workers and employers with information on the hazardous materials they use on their job. WHMIS regulations require employers to (1) clearly label hazardous materials, including all toxic substances, and (2) inform employees about risks and precautions.

WHMIS uses the following three main approaches to help identify and handle hazardous materials safely:

1. Labels (risks, precautionary measures, and first aid to be given in case of exposure or poisoning)

2. Material Safety Data Sheets (MSDS)

3. Worker education

To minimize safety and health risks, workers should observe all warning labels, tags, and placards in the workplace and follow the required precautions. When both employer and employee follow these government guidelines, hazardous materials injuries in the workplace can be prevented.

Material Safety Data Sheets (MSDS)

Material Safety Data Sheets are documents containing important technical information for workers on the work site. An MSDS must be available for every hazardous material on the work site.

The employer must be aware of the following nine main sections:

1. Product information and use

2. Hazardous ingredients

3. Physical data

4. Fire and explosion data

5. Reactivity data

6. Toxicological properties

7. Preventive measures

8. First aid measures

9. Preparation information

It is recommended that **copies of all relevant MSDSs be kept in a location where the first aid attendant will have ready access to the information.** For worker reference, appropriate MSDSs must also be available at all locations where the products are used.

Potentially Toxic Substances

Toxic substances can cause death, illness, or serious injury. They can be harmful when they are swallowed or inhaled or come into contact with skin. Toxic substances can be gases, solids, or liquids.

Carbon monoxide gas can occur in hold fires, as the product of an explosion, in the waste gases of petroleum and oil-driven engines, and when refrigerated meat cargoes decompose. Refrigerant gases such as ammonia vapour, carbon dioxide, or freon, will displace oxygen, making the air unsafe to breathe. In the presence of an open flame, the properties of freon change, producing a toxic substance. Certain refrigerated cargoes, including fruit, vegetables, and cheese, generate carbon dioxide during normal storage. With failure of a refrigerating plant, food cargoes, especially meat, may generate poisonous and inflammable cargo space. This can be particularly dangerous if the cargo space is flooded. Carbon monoxide, ammonia, hydrogen sulphide, and hydrogen may be generated in addition to carbon dioxide. In any great concentration, these gases are extremely poisonous, and some are explosive.

NOTE:

Inhalation is the most common method of poisoning in the shipping industry. The toxic substance may consist of vapour, gas, mist, spray dust, or fumes.

Storage of Dangerous Goods on Board

Every hazardous substance stored, handled, or used in a workplace must be managed to ensure that the potential hazard to workers is minimal. This is accomplished by clearly marking and labelling packages and by placing warning placards on containers and transport units as indicated by national and international regulations.

Confined Space: Characteristics and Dangers

Crew members entering confined spaces where air cannot support life risk injury or even death. Such spaces may lack oxygen content; some may even contain asphyxiating or toxic gases. Pump rooms or tanks that previously contained petroleum or chemicals are a particular risk for toxic gases. Rusting, fire, and bacteria present in any enclosed space can also use up and deplete oxygen content.

> **NOTE:**
>
> *Never enter a confined space without the authorization of the master or a responsible officer.*

Only specially trained personnel are permitted to work in a confined space. When respiratory protection is required, workers in a confined space must wear a safety or body harness securely attached to a lifeline. A safety watch must be stationed outside the confined space to provide constant watch and maintain communication with the worker inside. The safety watch must activate a suitable alarm if a rescue in a confined space becomes necessary.

MEDICAL CARE OF RESCUED PERSONS

Immediate Care of Survivors

Survival in a rescue craft (lifeboat or raft) is one of the most strenuous ordeals a person can face (Figure 24–5).

Figure 24–5 A survival rescue craft.

Survivors must be cared for as soon as possible.

Rescued survivors may be found suffering from various injuries and ailments, including the following:

- Near-drowning
- Hypothermia and other cold-related injuries
- Emotional conditions
- Seasickness
- Sunburn
- Heat exposure (heat cramps, heat exhaustion, and heat stroke)
- Contamination with oil
- Dehydration and malnutrition
- Immersion foot (trench foot)

Emergency Care on a Survival Craft and on Board a Rescue Vessel

A medical survival kit and supplies may not always be available on a survival craft. Therefore, always establish a plan of action when caring for people in any emergency.

1. **Persons Rescued From Near-Drowning**

    In a near-drowning situation, the person survives submersion, although sometimes only temporarily.

The process of drowning begins when small amounts of water are inhaled into the lungs. As a result, the person may eventually suffocate and become unconscious. In some cases, those rescued promptly from near-drowning recover immediately. In other cases, however, your ABC check may reveal that treatment may consist of immediate resuscitation. You should attempt to resuscitate the person even if he or she has been submerged for a prolonged period. People have been successfully resuscitated even after having been submerged for longer than 30 minutes in cold water.

2. Generalized Hypothermia Due to Immersion or Other Cold-Related Injuries

(See Chapter 17 – Heat- and Cold-Related Emergencies)

3. Emotional Conditions

People who have abandoned ship or have experienced a traumatic situation have faced an emotional crisis. Provide emotional support by listening. Some survivors may require further crisis intervention. To ensure that you are prepared to deal with cases of crisis intervention, you should develop a local contact as a resource. To find local crisis intervention resources, speak to your Instructor, check the front of the phone book for numbers, or contact the local crisis intervention help line.

4. Seasickness

Seasickness (motion sickness) is an acute illness largely due to the motion of the ship or vessel. Signs and symptoms vary but include the following:

- Loss of appetite
- Headaches
- Nausea
- Cold sweat
- Dizziness
- Abdominal cramps
- Vomiting
- Exhaustion
- Dry mouth

NOTE:

Ginger tablets help settle the stomach.

Persons who are not accustomed to the sea are most susceptible; but even experienced seafarers may be affected in rough conditions (Figure 24–6).

- In mild cases, the condition will gradually wear off, perhaps during sleep, and no specific treatment may be necessary.

- Keep the person quiet and warm.

- Provide dry foods in small portions, such as crackers or toast, to help settle the person's stomach.

- Cracked ice may help relieve the person's thirst.

- More severe cases of prolonged vomiting may be managed with over-the-counter preventive medications in dosages recommended by the manufacturer. It is very important to note the contraindications and side effects of these medications before drug administration (see Pharmacology section in this chapter).

5. Sunburn

(See Chapter 11 – Soft Tissue Injuries)

Figure 24–6 Vomiting is a symptom of seasickness and can affect even experienced seafarers.

6. **Heat Exposure: Heat Exhaustion, Heat Cramps, and Heat Stroke**

(See Chapter 17 – Heat- and Cold-Related Emergencies)

7. **Contamination With Oil**

Survivors of shipwreck are sometimes covered in oil. If a person has suffered oil contamination, do the following:

- Clean the skin only after the person is warm and comfortable (clean the areas around the mouth and eyes immediately).

- Wipe the skin with a soft cloth or strong paper towels. You can also have the person take a warm shower using regular hair shampoo and body soap. If the person has any signs of burns, do not wipe that area directly.

NOTE:

Contamination with oil can lead to breathing difficulties, if inhaled, or nausea and vomiting, if ingested.

8. **Dehydration and Malnutrition**

Survivors who have been adrift for several days may be found suffering from dehydration. If they have been adrift for several weeks, malnutrition may also have developed.

- Remember to give food and water in small amounts at first to avoid reversing dehydration or malnutrition too rapidly.

- You should seek radio medical advice on how to treat the person.

- Initially, a diet of nourishing liquids (sugar and water combination, milk, or soup) will help satisfy nutritional requirements.

- This diet should continue until the survivor can be transferred to medical care ashore.

9. **Immersion Foot (Trench Foot)**

Immersion foot is caused by exposure of the lower extremities to water above freezing temperatures, but usually below 10°C for more than 12 hours. It typically occurs in shipwrecked sailors who have survived but who are, for the most part, inactive, in lifeboats or rafts in adverse weather conditions and with wet and constrictive clothing, and who have a poor diet.

Preventing Immersion Foot

- Keep your feet clean and dry.
- Wear proper-fitting boots.
- Wear wool or synthetic socks.
- Sleep in dry socks or barefoot.
- Dry and massage your feet twice a day.

Signs and Symptoms of Immersion Foot

Initial signs and symptoms include (Figure 24–7):

- Swollen, cold, waxy feet
- Peeling skin
- Reduced sensitivity to touch
- Wooden feeling in feet
- Delayed capillary refill time (nail beds stay white after you squeeze them)

After the foot warms up:

- Warm, dry, red skin
- Blisters
- Pain
- Tingling or itching
- Increased sensitivity to cold

Care for Immersion Foot

When caring for immersion foot, handle the area gently and warm it slowly. Raise the foot (or feet) and continue to monitor the person as well as the affected area.

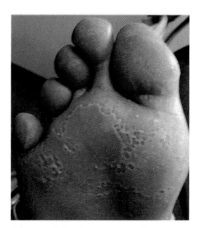

Figure 24–7 Signs and symptoms of immersion foot.

RADIO MEDICAL ADVICE

As a general rule, procedures beyond your training and ability as a marine first aid attendant should not be attempted. However, you should be aware that medical advice is available, especially in cases in which more advanced medical procedures are required. Medical advice can be accessed through a doctor by:

• cellular phone;

• direct radiotelephone contact with a shore radio station using a prearranged radio frequency (e.g., Rescue Coordination Centre [RCC]/Maritime Rescue Sub-Centres [MRSC] or the Marine Communications and Traffic Services Centre [MCTS]). You should request to speak to a doctor; or

• contacting a nearby port or nearby ship with a doctor on board. The advice received from a medical advisor will depend on the severity of the situation and the appropriate supplies and medical personnel available on board the ship. You should prepare for the medical advice by having the list of medications and supplies carried on hand during the call.

Preparing Information for Radio Medical Advice

When seeking medical advice, provide as much information as possible to the medical advisor. Remember to repeat the information back to the advisor to ensure that the information exchanged is accurate. You may want to record the exchange on tape to help clarify any written notes.

Prior to seeking radio medical advice, you should prepare key information about your ship, the ill or injured person, and treatment rendered (Table 24-5).

NOTE:

For medical-legal purposes, remember to transcribe your notes regarding the instructions given and the medical actions taken on to the person's and ship's records. Always keep a copy of the records on board.

Radiotelephone Procedures

Transport Canada provides a reference regarding radiotelephone procedures (TP 9878E: Safety and Distress Radiotelephone Procedures), which should be displayed next to your vessel's radiotelephone. The procedures in this reference advise that safety and distress radio messages should be made on Channel 16 (156.8 MHz) or on frequency 2,182 kHz, MF.

The normal procedure to obtain radio medical advice is as follows:

1. Make contact with the shore radio station and request medical advice (Figure 24–8).

2. Give the doctor all the information you can so that a medical assessment of the situation can be made.

3. The doctor will give advice on the immediate care of the person.

4. After the link call is over, the doctor will advise the Search and Rescue (SAR) authority or coast guard service (e.g., RCC) on the best method of evacuation.

5. If helicopter evacuation is determined desirable, the coast guard will keep in touch with the ship.

Figure 24–8 Obtaining radio medical advice.

TABLE 24-5 FORMS TO BE USED IN COMMUNICATING TO A DOCTOR INFORMATION ABOUT A PERSON'S ILLNESS (PART A) OR INJURY (PART B)*

(A) IN THE CASE OF ILLNESS

1. *Routine information about the ship*

   1.1   Name of ship

   1.2   Call sign

   1.3   Date and time (GMT)

   1.4   Course, speed, position, and cargo

   1.5.1   Port of destination _____

           which is _____ hours/days away

   1.5.2   Nearest port _____

           which is _____ hours/days away

   1.5.3   Alternative port _____

           which is _____ hours/days away

   1.6   Local weather (if relevant)

2. *Routine information about the person*

   2.1   Surname

   2.2   Other names

   2.3   Rank

   2.4   Job on board (specify kind of work, not just the trade)

   2.5   Age and sex

3. *Details of illness*

   3.1   When did the illness first begin?

   3.2   Has the illness occurred before? If so, when?

   3.3   How did the illness begin (suddenly, slowly, etc.).

   3.4   What did the person first complain of?

   3.5   List all the person's complaints and symptoms.

   3.6   Describe the course of the present illness from the start of the illness to the present time.

   3.7   Give details of past illnesses/injuries/operations.

   3.8   List serious illnesses of parents, brothers, sisters, if known (family history).

   3.9   List social pursuits and previous occupations, including hobbies (social and occupational history).

3.10   List all medicines/tablets/drugs that the person was taking *before the present illness began* and indicate the dose(s) and frequency of administration.

3.11   Does the person smoke? If so, how much and how often?

3.12   Does the person drink alcohol? If so, how much (on how many days a week, on average, and how many drinks a day, on average)?

3.13   Does the person take any herbal or folk medicines? If so, how are they taken?

3.14   Does the person use recreational drugs? If so, how are they taken?

4.   *Results of examination of person*

4.1   Note temperature, pulse, blood pressure, and respiration.

4.2   Describe the general appearance of the person (healthy, obviously ill, pale, etc.)

4.3   Describe the appearance of affected parts of the body (consider faxing or e-mailing a digital photograph).

4.4   Describe your observations about the affected parts of the body (swelling, tenderness, lack of movement, etc.).

4.5.1   What tests have you done (urine, blood, other) and what were the results?

4.5.2   Give the results, if available, of any previous blood tests, X-rays, or other investigations.

5.   *Diagnosis*

5.1   What is your diagnosis?

6.   *Treatment*

6.1   Describe care you have administered since the illness began.

6.2   List ALL medicines/tablets/drugs that the person has taken or been given, and indicate the dose(s), the number of times given, and frequency of administration.

6.3   How has the person responded to the treatment?

7.   *Problems*

7.1   What problems are worrying you now?

7.2   What do you need advice about?

8.   *Other comments*

9.   *Comments by the doctor*

(B) IN THE CASE OF INJURY

1.   *Routine information about the ship*

1.1   Name of ship

1.2   Call sign

1.3   Date and time (GMT)

1.4   Course, speed, position, and cargo

1.5.1   Port of destination _____

which is _____ hours/days away

1.5.2   Nearest port _____

which is _____ hours/days away

1.5.3   Alternative port _____

which is _____ hours/days away

1.6   Local weather (if relevant)

---

2.   *Routine information about the person*

2.1   Surname

2.2   Other names

2.3   Rank

2.4   Job on board (specify kind of work, not just the trade)

2.5   Age and sex

---

3.   *History of the injury or injuries*

3.1   Exactly how did the injury or injuries occur?

3.2   Did the person lose any blood? If so, how much?

3.3   When did the injury or injuries occur?

3.4   How long before the incident did the person last eat or drink?

3.5   What does the person complain of? (List the complaints in order of importance or severity.)

3.6   List all past illnesses/injuries/operations.

3.7   List all medicines/tablets/drugs that the person was taking *before the present injury or injuries occurred*, indicate the dose(s) and frequency of administration.

3.8   Has the person been taking any alcohol?

3.9   Do you think the person might have taken narcotic drugs, amphetamine, etc?

3.10   Does the person remember everything that happened? If not, how long before the accident is his last clear memory?

3.11   Did the person lose consciousness, even for a very short time? If so, for how long and when in relation to the injury?

4. Results of examination of person

    4.1   Note temperature, pulse, blood pressure, and respiration.

    4.2   Describe the general condition of the person.

    4.3   List what you believe to be the person's injuries in order of importance and severity.

    4.5.1   What tests have you done (urine, blood, other) and what were the results?

    4.5.2   Give the results, if available, of any previous blood tests, X-rays, or other investigations.

5. Treatment

    5.1   Describe care you have administered since the injury or injuries occurred.

    5.2   List ALL medicines/tablets/drugs that the person has taken or been given, and indicate the dose(s), the number of times given, and frequency of administration.

    5.3   How has the person responded to the treatment?

6. Problems

    6.1   What problems are worrying you now?

    6.2   What do you need advice about?

7. Other comments

8. Comments by the doctor

Source: Adapted with permission from World Health Organization, *International Medical Guide for Ships, 3rd Edition*. Geneva: World Health Organization, 2007.

NOTE:

The phonetic alphabet (see Table 24-6) may be useful in conveying information such as call signs or to clarify a person's medical condition or the name of a medication.

Communication With Doctors

A written letter or form should always accompany any person seeing a doctor. A clearly written communication in a foreign language is sometimes better understood than a spoken one (see Table 24-7).

TRANSFER AND TRANSPORT

Medical Evacuation From a Ship

People who require rapid transport to a hospital facility due to severe trauma or medical emergency are indications for medical evacuation from a ship.

Evacuation by Helicopter

Once helicopter evacuation is determined to be necessary, the following measures should be taken:

- Give the ship's position, description, and details of the person's condition.

- Advise the bridge and engine room watches that someone should maintain direct communication with the helicopter.

- If direct communication with the helicopter cannot be made, send a message via a shore radio station or coast guard station (on 2,182 kHz, MF or on VHF) and follow all instructions provided.

- Clear as large an area as possible on the deck and mark the area in white with a large letter "H" to identify the "hoist area." If possible, whip and wire aerials in and around the area should be taken down.

- Ensure that all loose articles are securely tied.

- In heavy shipping areas, it is helpful to identify

TABLE 24-6 PHONETIC ALPHABET

Use plain language whenever possible. However, due to differences in accents and pronunciations throughout the world, or when conditions for reception are not completely clear, it is standard procedure to use the phonetic alphabet for your call sign and for completing your communication.

Letter	Word	Pronounced as	Letter	Word	Pronounced as
A	Alpha	AL FAH	N	November	NOVEM BER
B	Bravo	BRAH VOH	O	Oscar	OSS CAR
C	Charlie	CHAR LEE or SHAR LEE	P	Papa	PAH PAH
D	Delta	DELL TAH	Q	Quebec	KEH BECK
E	Echo	ECK OH	R	Romeo	ROW ME OH
F	Foxtrot	FOKS TROT	S	Sierra	SEE AIR RAH
G	Golf	GOLF	T	Tango	TANG GO
H	Hotel	HOH TELL	U	Uniform	YOU NEE FORM or OO NEE FORM
I	India	IN DEE AH	V	Victor	VIK TAH
J	Juliette	JEW LEE ETT	W	Whiskey	WISS KEY
K	Kilo	KEE LOH	X	X-ray	ECKS RAY
L	Lima	LEE MAH	Y	Yankee	YANG KEY
M	Mike	MIKE	Z	Zulu	ZOO LOO

Example of Urgency Call and Message

PAN PAN, PAN PAN, PAN PAN

HALIFAX COAST GUARD RADIO, HALIFAX COAST GUARD RADIO, HALIFAX COAST GUARD RADIO

THIS IS CANCROSS VY1896, CANCROSS VY1896, CANCROSS VY1896

ONE OF THE RESCUED PERSONS HAS GONE INTO DEEP SHOCK REQUEST HELICOPTER AIR LIFT

MY POSITION IS 30 MILES SOUTH OF HALIFAX

CANCROSS VY1896 OVER

Example of Reply

PAN PAN

CANCROSS VY1896, CANCROSS VY1896, CANCROSS VY1896

THIS IS HALIFAX COAST GUARD RADIO, HALIFAX COAST GUARD RADIO, HALIFAX COAST GUARD RADIO

HELICOPTER HAS BEEN DISPATCHED

ESTIMATED TIME OF ARRIVAL IS 1215z
(say "zulu" for "z")

HALIFAX COAST GUARD RADIO OVER

If the vessel Cancross VY1896 had been asked to spell its name and call sign phonetically it would do so as follows: "CHARLIE, ALPHA, NOVEMBER, CHARLIE, ROMEO, OSCAR, SIERRA, SIERRA, VICTOR, YANKEE, one, eight, niner, six."

TABLE 24-7 MEDICAL REPORT FORMS FOR SEAFARERS*

Ship Master's Report Form

Date of report _____

****

Ship's Identity and Navigation Status

Name _____

Owner _____

Name and address of on-shore agent _____

_____

Position (latitude, longitude) at onset of illness _____

Destination and ETA (expected time of arrival) _____

_____

****

The Person and The Medical Problem

Surname and first name _____

Sex _____ Male ☐ Female ☐

Date of birth (dd-mm-yyyy) _____

Nationality _____

Seafarer registration number _____

Shipboard job title _____

Hour and date when taken off work _____

Hour and date when returned to work _____

****

Injury or illness

Hour and date of injury or onset of illness _____

Hour and date of first examination or treatment _____

Location on ship where injury occurred _____

Circumstances of injury _____

_____

Symptoms _____

Findings of physical examination _____

_____

Findings of X-ray or laboratory tests _____

Overall clinical impression before treatment _____

_____

Treatment given on board _____

_____

Overall clinical impression after treatment _____

_____

****

Telemedical Consultation (on-line medical control)

Hour and date of initial contact _____

Mode of communication (radio, telephone, fax, other) _____

Surname and first name of telemedical consultant _____

Details of telemedical advice given _____

_____

****

N.B. Attach all relevant medical reports to this report form.

Person Health Status Form

(To accompany person being evacuated)

Surname and first name _____

Age (years) _____

Sex _____

Time (hour) and date _____

Vital signs _____

      Blood pressure (systolic/diastolic) _____

      Pulse (beats/min) _____

      Body temperature (oral), note F or C _____

Presenting medical problem: symptoms, site(s) of pain or injury, time of onset, duration of problem, contributing factors _____

_____

_____

Treatment given (medication, dressings, etc.) _____

_____

Telemedical advice (on-line medical control) received _____

_____

Other current medical problems _____

_____

Past history of significant medical problems _____

_____

Current medication being taken (generic **and** brand names; dosage; time of last dose)

_____

Source: Adapted with permission from World Health Organization, *International Medical Guide for Ships, 3rd Edition.* Geneva: World Health Organization, 2007.

the ship to the flight crew with a signal (orange-coloured smoke, for example, which is often used in lifeboats).

- Never hook the hoist cable of the helicopter to any part of the ship.

- A helicopter can build up a significant charge of static electricity, so the winch wire should be handled only by personnel wearing rubber gloves.

- If the hoist is being carried out at night, point search lights vertically upward as aid in locating the ship. Light the pick-up area as much as possible. Be sure not to blind the pilot by shining any lights directly on the helicopter.

- Obey the helicopter crew instructions at all times.

NOTE:

See Chapter 23 for information on preparing a person for transfer, and ship-to-ship transfer.

PHARMACOLOGY

Medications and Health Supplies Carried on Board

In the *International Medical Guide for Ships, 3rd Edition*

(2007), the World Health Organization (WHO) recommends a list of medications and health supplies to be carried on board for the ship's medicine chest (see Table 24-8). The quantities of medications recommended depend on the:

- type of vessel;

- length of time the vessel may be away from port or port of call; and

- size of the crew complement.

Medical supplies and medications are most likely located in the ship's sick bay (ship's hospital). Cabinets and drawers in the sick bay should hold a working quantity of the recommended medications and should be clearly labelled. The contents of the ship's medicine chest should be inspected annually by a pharmacist.

NOTE:

Drug administration requires specialized training and is intended for those who provide advanced medical care. The following section, which describes medications found on ships, and their side effects, is intended to provide a basic overview only.

TABLE 24-8 WORLD HEALTH ORGANIZATION (WHO) LIST OF MEDICINES RECOMMENDED FOR THE SHIP'S MEDICINE CHEST*

Generic name	Acetylsalicylic acid
Dosage form, strength	tablet 300 mg
Indications (on board ship)	high dose (600-900 mg); to reduce pain, fever, inflammation
	low dose (100-150 mg) to inhibit formation of blood clots in angina pectoris, myocardial infarction, stroke
Contraindications	peptic ulcer, history of gastrointestinal bleeding, hemophilia, fever in patients under 18, trauma
Unwanted effects	indigestion
	gastric bleeding
	increased bleeding during surgery

Generic name	Aciclovir
Dosage form, strength	tablet 400 mg
Indications (on board ship)	treatment of primary or recurrent herpes simplex virus infection
	may be useful for severe varicella and herpes zoster (doctor should be consulted)
Contraindications	ND
Unwanted effects	ND

Generic name	Adrenaline
Dosage form, strength	ampoule 1 mL = 1 mg
Indications (on board ship)	to raise blood pressure in anaphylaxis
	to dilate airways in severe asthma or anaphylaxis
Contraindications	none in emergencies
Unwanted effects	palpitations
	cardiac dysrhythmia
	hypertension
	chest pain
	headache
	restlessness

Generic name	Amethocaine 0.5% eye drops
Dosage form, strength	single-use vial 1 mL
Indications (on board ship)	for eye examination and procedures
Contraindications	ND
Unwanted effects	transitory burning sensation soon after application

Generic name	Amoxicillin + Clavulanate
Dosage form, strength	tablet 875 mg + 125 mg
Indications (on board ship)	to treat infections responsive to this antibiotic
Contraindications	allergy to penicillin and beta-lactam antibiotics
	glandular fever (infectious mononucleosis)
	liver disease
Unwanted effects	diarrhea
	hepatitis due to clavulanate is rare but may be serious

Generic name	Artemether
Dosage form, strength	ampoule 1 mL = 80 mg
Indications (on board ship)	treatment of severe malaria
Contraindications	ND
Unwanted effects	pain at injection site

	slow pulse rate
	seizures
Generic name	Artemether + Lumefantrine
Dosage form, strength	tablet 20 mg + 120 mg
Indications (on board ship)	treatment of malaria
Contraindications	not to be used in women in early pregnancy without medical advice
Unwanted effects	headache
	dizziness
	sleep disorder
	palpitations
	anorexia
	nausea
	vomiting
	diarrhea
	itch
	rash
	arthralgia (joint pain)
	myalgia (muscle pain)
	weakness
	fatigue
Generic name	Atropine
Dosage form, strength	ampoule 1.2 mg/mL
Indications (on board ship)	to treat slow heart rate in myocardial infarction
	to treat organophosphate insecticide poisoning
Contraindications	none in emergencies
Unwanted effects	dry mouth
	blurred vision
	urinary retention
	hallucinations and psychosis (with very large doses)
Generic name	Azithromycin
Dosage form, strength	tablet 500 mg
Indications (on board ship)	to treat infections responsive to this antibiotic
Contraindications	allergy to erythromycin or similar (macrolide) antibiotics
Unwanted effects	diarrhea
	vomiting
	stomach pain

Generic name	Ceftriaxone
Dosage form, strength	ampoule 1 g powder for injection (dissolve in water for injection)
Indications (on board ship)	to treat infections responsive to this antibiotic
Contraindications	allergy to cephalosporin or penicillin antibiotics
Unwanted effects	diarrhea
	pain at injection site
	formation of biliary sludge and kidney stones

Generic name	Cetirizine
Dosage form, strength	tablet 10 mg
Indications (on board ship)	to treat allergy symptoms in hay fever, hives, allergic dermatitis, etc.
Contraindications	allergy to cetirizine
Unwanted effects	drowsiness (in 10-15% of cases)
	dry mouth
	headache
	nausea

Generic name	Charcoal, activated
Dosage form, strength	50 g in 300 mL purified water
Indications (on board ship)	to absorb ingested poisons
Contraindications	bowel obstruction
Unwanted effects	abdominal pain
	vomiting
	constipation

Generic name	Ciprofloxacin
Dosage form, strength	tablet 250 mg
Indications (on board ship)	to treat infections responsive to this antibiotic
Contraindications	allergy to quinolones
Unwanted effects	vomiting
	diarrhea
	depression
	ankle pain
	makes sunburn worse
	may increase the effect of caffeine, with headache, palpitations, and nausea

Generic name	Cloves, oil of
Dosage form, strength	oil
Indications (on board ship)	toothache
Contraindications	ND

Unwanted effects	irritation of the mucous membranes
Generic name	Dexamethasone
Dosage form, strength	ampoule 4 mg/mL
Indications (on board ship)	to treat life-threatening and severe asthma
	to treat anaphylaxis
	to treat severe allergic reactions
Contraindications	none in emergencies
Unwanted effects	with repeated doses exacerbates peptic ulcer
	euphoria or depression
	exacerbates diabetes mellitus
Generic name	Diazepam
Dosage form, strength	tablet 5 mg
Indications (on board ship)	to treat alcohol withdrawal
Contraindications	severe respiratory disease
	opioid intoxication
	severe liver disease
	myasthenia gravis
Unwanted effects	drowsiness
	confusion
Generic name	Docusate + Senna (or equivalent)
Dosage form, strength	tablet 50 mg + 8 mg
Indications (on board ship)	to avoid straining in patients with anal fissure and hemorrhoids
	to prevent constipation caused by opioid use
Contraindications	suspected bowel obstruction
	inflammatory bowel disease
	appendicitis
Unwanted effects	flatulence
	abdominal cramps (rare)
	diarrhea
Generic name	Doxycycline
Dosage form, strength	tablet 100 mg
Indications (on board ship)	as recommended in IMGS3 for the specific infection
Contraindications	allergy to tetracyclines
	severe liver disease
	not to be used in children under eight years or age or pregnant women
Unwanted effects	vomiting

diarrhea

makes sunburn worse

ulceration of the esophagus (rare)

Generic name	Ethanol 70%, hand cleanser gel
Dosage form, strength	gel
Indications (on board ship)	an alternative to hand-washing when hands are not obviously soiled
Contraindications	soiled hands
Unwanted effects	dryness, but less than with soap and water

Generic name	Ethanol 70%, liquid
Dosage form, strength	liquid
Indications (on board ship)	to disinfect instruments and surfaces
Contraindications	ND
Unwanted effects	ND

Generic name	Fluorescein 1%, strips
Dosage form, strength	ND
Indications (on board ship)	to detect damage to cornea: damaged area stains yellow/green
Contraindications	ND
Unwanted effects	ND

Generic name	Furosemide
Dosage form, strength	ampoule 4 mL = 40 mg
Indications (on board ship)	to treat severe fluid retention in lungs (pulmonary edema) due to cardiac failure
Contraindications	none in an emergency
Unwanted effects	dehydration
	loss of potassium
	hearing loss if given too quickly IV

Generic name	Glucagon, ready to use
Dosage form, strength	ampoule 1 mg
Indications (on board ship)	to treat low blood sugar (hypoglycemia) due to insulin when oral intake is impossible and intravenous glucose cannot be given
Contraindications	ND
Unwanted effects	ND

Generic name	Haloperidol
Dosage form, strength	ampoule 1 mL = 5 mg
Indications (on board ship)	to treat psychotic hallucinations and delusions
	to treat severe agitation and aggressiveness

Contraindications	coma of whatever cause
	severe alcohol intoxication
Unwanted effects	drowsiness
	low blood pressure
	confusion
	dry mouth
	urine retention
Generic name	Hydrocortisone 1% cream
Dosage form, strength	cream
Indications (on board ship)	to treat allergy and some other inflammatory skin conditions
Contraindications	open wounds or skin infections caused by bacteria, viruses or fungi
Unwanted effects	minimal with short-term use
	thinning of skin with long-term use
Generic name	Ibuprofen
Dosage form, strength	coated tablet 400 mg
Indications (on board ship)	to treat inflammation
	to reduce mild-to-moderate pain, especially if associated with inflammation
Contraindications	peptic ulcer
	gastrointestinal bleeding
	kidney failure
	liver failure
	history of exacerbation of asthma after taking aspirin
Unwanted effects	stomach pain
	vomiting
	diarrhea
	headache
	edema
	hypertension
Generic name	Isosorbide dinitrate
Dosage form, strength	tablet 5 mg
Indications (on board ship)	to treat angina pectoris
	to treat myocardial infarction
Contraindications	hypotension
	known heart valve disease
	head injury
	treatment with sildenafil (Viagra®) and similar drugs

Unwanted effects	headache
	flushing
	dizziness or fainting
	palpitations

Generic name	Lidocaine 1% (without adrenaline)
Dosage form, strength	ampoule 5 mL
Indications (on board ship)	for local anaesthesia when suturing wounds or performing minor surgery
Contraindications	allergy to local anaesthetics
Unwanted effects	stinging on injection

Generic name	Loperamide
Dosage form, strength	tablet 2 mg
Indications (on board ship)	to treat symptoms of diarrhea
Contraindications	bowel obstruction
	dysentery
	acute ulcerative colitis
Unwanted effects	abdominal pain
	bloating
	constipation

Generic name	Mebendazole
Dosage form, strength	tablet 100 mg
Indications (on board ship)	to treat intestinal worm infections
	not effective for tapeworm infection or hydatid disease
Contraindications	allergy to mebendazole
Unwanted effects	diarrhea
	stomach pain

Generic name	Metoprolol
Dosage form, strength	tablet 100 mg
Indications (on board ship)	to treat hypertension
	to treat atrial fibrillation
	to treat angina pectoris
	to prevent migraine
Contraindications	asthma
	shock
	heart rate less than 50 beats/min
	cardiac failure
Unwanted effects	tiredness

light-headedness

cold hands and feet

slow heart rate

shortness of breath

wheezing

fainting due to low blood pressure

Generic name	Metronidazole
Dosage form, strength	tablet 500 mg
Indications (on board ship)	to treat infections responsive to this antibiotic
Contraindications	allergy to metronidazole
Unwanted effects	metallic taste in the mouth
	nausea
	vomiting
	diarrhea
	nerve damage (rare)
Generic name	Miconazole 2% cream
Dosage form, strength	cream
Indications (on board ship)	to treat fungal skin infections
Contraindications	allergy to miconazole
Unwanted effects	ND
Generic name	Midazolam
Dosage form, strength	ampoule 1 mL = 5 mg
Indications (on board ship)	to terminate epileptic seizures
Contraindications	ND
Unwanted effects	sedation
Generic name	Misoprostol
Dosage form, strength	tablet 200 mg
Indications (on board ship)	to prevent post-partum hemorrhage
Contraindications	none if given according to IMGS3 recommendations
Unwanted effects	diarrhea
Generic name	Morphine (injectable)
Dosage form, strength	ampoule 1 mL = 10 mg
Indications (on board ship)	to reduce severe pain
	to reduce pain not relieved by other analgesics
Contraindications	coma, unless the patient is dying of a clearly-documented illness, such as cancer

Unwanted effects	severe liver disease
	asthma
	severe respiratory disease except pneumonia or pleurisy associated with severe pain
	to be used with caution in patients known to have epilepsy, head injury, acute alcohol intoxication, withdrawal, shock (of whatever cause)
	sedation
	confusion
	nausea
	vomiting
	low blood pressure
	respiratory depression
	small pupils
	constipation
Generic name	Morphine (oral)
Dosage form, strength	liquid 1 mg/mL
Indications (on board ship)	to reduce severe pain likely to last several days in patients able to eat and drink
Contraindications	as for morphine given by injection
Unwanted effects	as for morphine given by injection
Generic name	Naloxone
Dosage form, strength	ampoule 1 mL = 0.4 mg
Indications (on board ship)	to reverse effects of opioids, especially in cases of overdose
Contraindications	ND
Unwanted effects	ND
Generic name	Omeprazole
Dosage form, strength	tablet 20 mg
Indications (on board ship)	to treat gastro-esophageal reflux
	to treat peptic ulcer disease
Contraindications	ND
Unwanted effects	nausea
	diarrhea
Generic name	Ondansetron
Dosage form, strength	tablet 4 mg
Indications (on board ship)	to prevent vomiting
	to prevent seasickness

Contraindications	ND
Unwanted effects	headache
	fatigue
	constipation

Generic name	Oral rehydration salts
Dosage form, strength	sachets of powder for reconstitution
Indications (on board ship)	to prevent or treat dehydration, especially due to diarrhea
Contraindications	ND
Unwanted effects	vomiting

Generic name	Oxymetazoline 0.5% (or equivalent)
Dosage form, strength	drops
Indications (on board ship)	to treat nasal obstruction due to allergies or viral infection
	to improve sinus drainage in sinusitis
Contraindications	use of anti-depressants
Unwanted effects	stinging or burning in nose or throat
	dry nasal mucosa
	rebound obstruction

Generic name	Paracetamol (acetaminophen)
Dosage form, strength	tablet 500 mg
Indications (on board ship)	to reduce pain and fever (but not inflammation)
Contraindications	liver disease
Unwanted effects	rare at normal doses

Generic name	Permethrin 1% lotion
Dosage form, strength	lotion
Indications (on board ship)	to eliminate hair, pubic, and body lice
Contraindications	ND
Unwanted effects	increased likelihood of skin irritation in cases of scabies

Generic name	Permethrin 5% lotion
Dosage form, strength	lotion
Indications (on board ship)	to treat scabies
Contraindications	ND
Unwanted effects	increased likelihood of skin irritation

Generic name	Povidone iodine ointment 10% and solution 10%
Dosage form, strength	ointment, liquid
Indications (on board ship)	to disinfect skin and wounds

Contraindications	allergy to iodine
Unwanted effects	skin irritation

Generic name	Prednisone
Dosage form, strength	tablet 25 mg
Indications (on board ship)	to treat severe asthma
	to treat other inflammatory conditions (on medical advice)
Contraindications	ND
Unwanted effects	exacerbates diabetes mellitus, depression or euphoria

Generic name	Salbutamol aerosol
Dosage form, strength	inhaler 0.1 mg/dose with volume spacer
Indications (on board ship)	to treat asthma
	to treat chronic bronchitis
	to treat emphysema
	to treat other lung diseases
Contraindications	ND
Unwanted effects	dry mouth
	throat irritation
	tremor
	nervousness
	dizziness
	excitement
	rapid heartbeat
	headache

Generic name	Sodium chloride 0.9% infusion
Dosage form, strength	plastic bottle 1 litre
Indications (on board ship)	for fluid replacement
Contraindications	ND
Unwanted effects	cardiac overload and pulmonary edema if large doses are administered at a high flow rate

Generic name	Tetracycline 1% ointment
Dosage form, strength	ointment
Indications (on board ship)	to treat minor eye infections
	to prevent infection following damage to the cornea
Contraindications	allergy to tetracyclines
Unwanted effects	ND

Generic name	Vitamin K
Dosage form, strength	ampoule 1 mL = 10 mg
Indications (on board ship)	to reverse excessive or unwanted effect of warfarin or related drugs
Contraindications	ND
Unwanted effects	pain at the injection site if given IM
	anaphylaxis, if given IV
Generic name	Water for injection
Dosage form, strength	ampoule 5 mL
Indications (on board ship)	reconstitution of injectable drugs provided as powders
Contraindications	ND
Unwanted effects	ND
Generic name	Zidovudine + Lamivudine
Dosage form, strength	tablet 300 mg + 150 mg
Indications (on board ship)	prophylaxis against HIV infection after needle-stick injury
Contraindications	allergy to either component
	pre-existing HIV infection
Unwanted effects	Common: headache, fatigue and malaise, insomnia, nausea, vomiting, diarrhea or constipation, cough, loss of appetite, muscle soreness or weakness
	Uncommon but potentially serious: low white blood cell count, anemia, hepatitis, severe muscle weakness, pancreatitis
Generic name	Zinc oxide
Dosage form, strength	paste or ointment 20%
Indications (on board ship)	protection of irritated skin
Contraindications	ND
Unwanted effects	soiling of clothes

Source: Adapted with permission from World Health Organization, *International Medical Guide for Ships, 3rd Edition*. Geneva: World Health Organization, 2007.

Notes: • Medicines are listed in alphabetical order based on their generic name.

• The choice of medications recommended in this table is based on effect, unwanted effects, route of administration, shelf life, worldwide availability, price, storage conditions, and the medical skills officers on board are presumed to possess.

• A doctor needs to give permission to administer these medications, and will recommend dosages and frequency depending on the seriousness of the person's symptoms.
ND = not determined

QUALIFICATIONS REQUIRED TO ADMINISTER SPECIFIC MEDICATIONS

Medications can be beneficial but can also be dangerous if used incorrectly. Specialized training is required for those assigned to administer medications. This is particularly important for medications that are administered through an intravenous line (IV) or injection. Under certain circumstances, under medical direction, you may be able to provide a health product to a person or to assist a person with his or her own prescription medication. Medications require medical direction before they are administered to a person. The deck or staff officer assigned to the ship's medicine chest should be the only person (other than the ship's master) to hold the keys to the sick bay, medicine chest, and the locker containing the controlled medications.

Guidelines for Injections

Safe administration of medications through injection requires specific steps be followed before, during, and after administration of the medication.

SYRINGES AND NEEDLES MUST BE USED ONCE ONLY—if disposable syringes are not available, sterilize glass syringes and needles by boiling.

The steps for safe administration of injections are:

- Medicines for injection are supplied either in rubber-capped vials or in glass ampoules.

- The use of multi-dose vials carries a risk of contamination; a new needle and syringe **must always be used** when drawing medicines from a multi-dose vial.

- Check that the name and strength of the medicine is marked on the vial or ampoule.

- If you cannot see or decipher the name of the medicine, discard the vial or ampoule.

- Glass ampoules may have a coloured band around the neck indicating the level at which the top of the ampoule will break off cleanly.

- The rubber cap of a vial is held on by a metal cap with a small tear-off seal; do not remove this seal until the drug is required.

How to Give a Subcutaneous Injection

- Assemble the following items:

  - a disposable syringe

  - a 19- or 21-gauge needle for drawing the medicine into the syringe

  - a disposable 23- or 25-gauge needle for injecting the medicine

  - alcohol swabs

  - the medicine

- If the medicine is in a multiple-dose vial, clean the rubber diaphragm on the vial with alcohol. If the medicine is in an ampoule, tap the ampoule gently with a finger to ensure that all the liquid is below the neck of the ampoule, then break off the top with a sharp snap:

  - If you are not experienced in this procedure, hold the top of the ampoule with a cloth or swab to avoid being cut by the edge of the glass.

- Remove the guard from the needle without touching the needle. If the medicine is in a vial, inject into the vial an amount of air equal to the amount of medicine to be withdrawn, this will make it easier to withdraw the medicine. Withdraw the correct amount of medicine. Change the needle to the appropriate gauge for injection. Point the needle upwards and push the plunger to expel any air in the syringe. Select a site for the injection and disinfect the skin with an alcohol swab.

- Grasp between your thumb and forefinger a fold of skin large enough to offer plenty of space between the site of injection and your fingers. Insert the needle firmly and quickly at an angle of about 45°. Once the needle is under the skin, draw back the syringe plunger. If no blood appears in the syringe, inject the medicine and withdraw the needle. If blood appears, repeat the procedure at a new site, using new sterile equipment. Place the needle, together with the syringe, directly into a proper sharps disposal bin.

How to Give an Intramuscular Injection

- Assemble the following items:
  - a disposable syringe
  - a disposable 19- or 21-gauge needle
  - alcohol swabs
  - the medicine

- If the medicine is in a multidose vial, clean the rubber diaphragm on the vial with an alcohol swab. If the medicine is in an ampoule, break off the top of the ampoule. Remove the guard from the needle without touching the needle. If the medicine is in a vial, inject into the vial an amount of air equal to the amount of medicine to be withdrawn in order to make withdrawal easy. Withdraw the correct amount of medicine. Expel any air from the syringe.

- Select a site for the injection: the preferred sites are the outer upper quadrant of either buttock or outer thigh muscle: **do not use other parts of the buttock.** In infants use only the outer thigh muscle. Swab the skin at the injection site with alcohol swabs.

- Stretch the skin with thumb and forefinger and insert the needle at a right angle to the skin to a depth of about 2 cm (0.787 inches) so as to penetrate the subcutaneous fat and enter the muscle.

- Draw back the syringe plunger. If no blood appears, inject the medicine and withdraw the needle. If blood appears, repeat the procedure at another site, using new sterile equipment. Place the needle together with the syringe directly into a proper sharps disposal bin.

After You Have Given an Injection

- Place the needle together with the syringe, directly into a proper sharps disposal bin.

- **Never, under any circumstances, replace the needle guard on the needle or attempt to break the needle and syringe.**

DRUGS REQUIRING MEDICAL ADVICE

Safe drug therapy requires clear communication with the person and medical professionals. In some situations, first aid attendants must access radio medical advice before administering medication (see Radio Medical Advice Section). For example, nitroglycerin spray (Figure 24–9) is a medication restricted to "on the advice of a doctor" in DFO/5758. The *International Medical Guide for Ships, 3rd Edition* (2007), gives advice on other specific medications, with cautions stating, "Give only on radio medical advice from a doctor," "Should the patient be allergic to the drug, radio medical advice should be

Figure 24–9 Nitroglycerin spray is one of the medications requiring medical advice.

obtained for an alternative anti-infective treatment," or "Do not administer this drug before obtaining radio medical advice." Refer to the drug guide stored on your ship or check with local standards and protocols for clarification. For some medications, first aid attendants are likely to assist a person in taking medications from his own supply. Assisting a person with his medications includes:

- finding the medication bottle,
- getting water for pills, and
- helping the person hold a glass or read a label.

Each drug has several names. The two most important are the generic name and the trade name. The generic name is a simple or abbreviated form of the complex chemical name. The trade name (brand name) is a copyright name given to a drug by the company that manufactures the medication. For example, a common over-the counter medication found in local drug stores is acetaminophen. Acetaminophen is the generic name. Trade names for acetaminophen include Tylenol® (CAN/US), Atasol® (CAN), Excedrin® (CAN), and Paracetamol® (UK).

Use (Indications) and Cautions (Contraindications and Side Effects)

Indications, side effects, and contraindications are essential characteristics of each medication. The name, strength, dose, and directions are printed on the label of each drug container. The *International Medical Guide for Ships, 3rd Edition* (2007), provides a drug guide in the following format for each medicine: Dosage, Indications, Contraindications, and Side Effects.

Before taking a medication, read the caution(s) (contraindications and side effects) and note(s) relating to each of the drugs contained in the ship's medicine chest. If a side effect from a drug is pronounced, seek radio medical advice regarding appropriate care for the person.

The process for drug administration includes:

- assessing a person, both before and after a medication is taken;
- knowing the drug use;
- knowing the cautions of the drug; and
- obtaining authorization to administer the drug.

Assess signs and symptoms, and vital signs, and find out if the person has allergies, medical conditions, and medications. This is to determine if the person has a condition for which a medication might be helpful. The attendant may also find situations in which the person cannot take the medication (cautions) (e.g., no nitroglycerin if the person has taken an erectile dysfunction drug such as Viagra®, Cialis®, or Levitra® in the past 24 to 48 hours). Once you determine that an intervention with a medication may be required, you should obtain authorization for administering the drug by contacting a medical advisor for direction.

Disinfection

Instruments used in emergency care that pass through the skin of a person pose an increased risk of infection for the ill or injured person. For this reason, there are certain standards to follow when disinfecting surgical instruments. Disinfectants are solutions used to inactivate any infectious agents that may be present in blood or other body fluids. This will decrease the number of bacteria and viruses on an object, but not sterilize it, reducing the risk to people who will be handling the objects during further cleaning and sterilization. There are various types of disinfectant solutions, which also have varying degrees of effectiveness. Sodium hypochlorite, or bleach, is one of the most common worldwide disinfectant solutions.

- Disinfectant solutions must always be available for:
  - disinfecting working surfaces,
  - disinfecting equipment that cannot be sterilized further (such as in an autoclave),

- cleaning non-disposable items, or

- dealing with any spills involving body fluids or other known infectious material.

- All needles and instruments should be soaked in a disinfectant solution for 30 minutes before cleaning.

- If reusable needles are to be cleaned, they must be handled very carefully and should be placed in a disinfectant before being cleaned and sterilized.

- Gloves should always be used when disinfecting equipment, especially when working with soiled materials, such as linen. Soiled linen should be put in leak-proof bags for transport. Thick gloves should be worn when needles and sharp instruments are being cleaned.

- To further clean soiled linen, wash it in cool water first then disinfect with a diluted chlorine solution. After this, wash the linen with detergent at a temperature of at least 71°C for 25 minutes.

- Some situations, such as a large spill of infected body fluid, may require higher concentrations of disinfectant, as lower concentrations of solution will actually be inactivated by the large amount of organic matter. Not only should a higher concentration be used, but the solution should stay in contact with the infected material for a longer period of time. This is known as "contact time," and is the time the infectious material requires to become completely inactivated by the disinfectant solution.

- No matter what disinfectant solution is used, ensure it is used before its expiry date, and always follow the manufacturer's or other specific guidelines for that particular solution.

SUMMARY

Providing care on a ship brings special challenges, and marine first aid attendants require specialized training for the medical care of seafarers. This care covers a range of skills, in particular for administering oxygen, using airway adjuncts such as endotracheal intubation, administering medications, understanding hazardous materials, and working in confined spaces. It is important to be familiar with the equipment and safety precautions required for these specialized procedures.

You may be called upon to provide care for a rescued person who has suffered a near-drowning, hypothermia, or other illness or injury. Providing first aid treatment on a survival craft can present situations not encountered on land. You may also need to know how to radio for medical help or prepare someone for transfer to another ship or a helicopter.

Administering medications requires specialized training. However, under certain circumstances and under medical direction, you may be able to provide a health product to a person or to assist someone with taking their prescription medication.

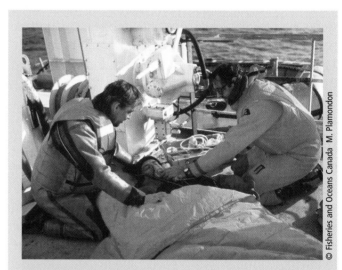

Once back on board he is sluggish and is having problems taking a deep breath without coughing. What do you do?

Appendix *A*

ADDITIONAL INTERVENTIONS:

Introduction to Basic Pharmacology

The following protocols have been developed for use by EMRs in applicable provinces and territories. This set of assessment models, treatment principles, and protocols reflects the accepted medical practice for EMRs in applicable provinces and territories. Each protocol follows the current direction of the medical community, taking into consideration the limitations and special circumstances that may exist in out-of-hospital care environments.

Protocols allow the EMR to perform medical procedures that are normally in the domain of a physician. This allows for the initiation of care that people would not otherwise receive until they arrived at a medical facility.

Pharmacology is the study of drugs and how they interact with the body. Drugs do not confer any new properties on cells. Drugs can be given locally or can be systemic. They tend to have actions at multiple sites, so they need to be thought of systemically even if administered locally.

Generally, all medications have indications, contraindications, and side effects to their administration. Indications are conditions that make administration of the drug appropriate. Contraindications are conditions that make administration of the drug inappropriate due to potential harmful effects. Side effects are any unfavourable or undesired reactions to the drug other than the contraindication. Indicated drugs include side effects, but the benefit of administering the drug is higher than the side effects.

Guidelines for Medication Administration

The provider has a responsibility to know the medication's potential effects, side effects, and actions that they are assisting with. (They are responsible for ensuring that they have knowledge of the drug, what it can do, and the appropriate circumstances as to when it can be administered.)

Drug Profiles

BROMIDE, IPRATROPIUM BROMIDE, ATROVENT

Classification: Anticholinergic, bronchodilator.

Mechanism: Anticholinergic (parasympatholytic) agent that appears to inhibit vagally mediated reflexes by antagonizing the action of acetylcholine, the transmitter released from the vagus nerve.

Indications: Bronchospasm associated with COPD. To be used either alone or in combination with other bronchodilators, especially beta-adrenergics (i.e., albuterol).

Contraindications: Ipratropium bromide is contraindicated in known or suspected cases of hypersensitivity to ipratropium bromide or to atropine and its derivatives. Precaution: should be used with caution in people with narrow-angle glaucoma.

Adverse Effects: Respiratory: coughing, sputum increased; central nervous system (CNS): dizziness, insomnia, tremor, nervousness; GI: nausea.

Dose: Give 500 mcg in 2.5 mL normal saline (1-unit dose vial) via small volume nebulizer (SVN) with a mouthpiece or in line with a ventilatory device. Repeat according to medical control preference. May mix one-unit dose vial of ipratropium with one-unit dose vial of albuterol.

Routes of Administration: Nebulized, mouth piece, or in-line inhaler (person's own).

Onset: 5 to 15 minutes.

Peak Effects: 60 to 120 minutes.

Duration: 240 to 480 minutes.

Dosage Forms/Packaging: Inhalation solution unit dose vial is supplied as a 0.02% clear, colourless solution containing 2.5 mL with 25 vials per foil pouch.

Note: Anticholinergics produce preferential dilatation of the larger central airways, in contrast to beta agonists, which affect the peripheral airways. May be more effective used in combination with beta agonists.

Should be kept out of light in a foil pouch; avoid excessive humidity.

EPINEPHRINE HYDROCHLORIDE (ADRENALINE, "EPI")

Classification: Sympathomimetic; natural catecholamine with alpha and beta effects.

Mechanism: Stimulates alpha- and beta-adrenergic receptors within the sympathetic nervous system.

Beta effects include:

- Increased heart rate
- Increased cardiac output
- Increased AV conduction
- Increased irritability
- Bronchodilation

Alpha effects include peripheral vasoconstriction at higher doses.

Indications: Bronchospasm, anaphylaxis, severe cardiac dysrhythmias as in asystole or idioventricular rhythm, fine ventricular fibrillation to increase the success of countershock.

Contraindications: None in cardiac arrest, known allergies, extreme caution when treating someone for bronchospasm if person has concurrent cardiovascular disease, narrow-angle glaucoma, caution in pregnancy (may decrease placental blood flow and can induce labour), caution with pre-existing tachycardias.

Dose, Route, and Routes of Administration:

1.0 mg bolus IV 1:10,000 q 3 minutes (cardiac arrest).

0.005 mg/kg SC 1:1,000 q 3 minutes to effect (bronchospasm).

0.005 mg/kg SC 1:1,000 one dose, call medical director for repeat doses (anaphylaxis).

200 mcg IV 1:10,000, maximum total dosage IV is 500 mcg (bronchospasm, anaphylaxis).

ET 1:10,000 solution via ET tube (follow ET drug administration guidelines).

Onset: IV: 1 to 2 minutes; SC: 5 to 10 minutes.

Duration: 5 to 10 minutes.

Metabolism: Rapidly metabolized by enzymes in the blood, liver, and other tissues and excreted in urine.

Adverse Effects: Respiratory: pulmonary edma (rare), dyspnea (rare); CNS: nervousness, tremor, anxiety, headache, cerebral hemorrhage, agitation; circulatory system: tachycardia, ventriciular fibrillation, palpitations, widened pulse pressure, hypertension, stroke, anginal pain; skin: pallor, sweating, necrosis due to vascoconstriction.

NITROGLYCERIN

Classification: Antianginal, vasodilator.

Mechanism: Reduces cardiac oxygen demand primarily by dilating blood vessels resulting in decreased blood flow (preload) to the heart from the body, decreased resistance to the heart's pumping (after load). Dilation of coronary arteries results in increased blood flow to cardiac tissue.

Indications: For cardiac chest pain when person has his own nitroglycerin and a systolic pressure of above 100. (Must take baseline set of vital signs.)

Contraindications: Systolic BP less than or equal to 100 mmHg, known allergy or sensitivity to nitrates, if person has used Viagra® or Levitra® in the past 24 hours or Cialis® in the past 48 hours.

Nitroglycerin

Onset, Dose, Route: Rapid onset via sublingual route (60 seconds) with 30-minute duration. Dose depends on strength of person's prescription. EMRs are to give one dose (q 5 min) to a maximum of three doses by the EMR in any 30-minute period.

Metabolism: Rapidly metabolized in the body by the liver and excreted by the kidneys.

Adverse Effects: Induces hypotension, dizziness, weakness, headache, nausea, vomiting, syncope, tachycardia, tingling or burning under the tongue.

Cautions: Hypotension frequently occurs, especially in older adults, and must be expected. Therefore, ensure that the person is not at risk of falling. Repeat vital signs and drug until pain is relieved, to a maximum of three doses (provided the systolic BP remains above 100; irrespective of any nitroglycerin taken by the person prior to your arrival), or follow local protocol. If the person has used Viagra® at any time in the past (beyond the 24-hour contraindication limit), there may be some cause for very careful monitoring of the person's blood pressure.

Notes: If pain is completely relieved for more than 5 minutes, you may initiate the chest pain protocol again if the pain returns. This is considered a new episode, and a total of three additional doses of nitroglycerin can be given. This is applicable even if three nitroglycerin doses have already been administered for the initial episode.

Nitroglycerin can be taken as a tablet sublingual (0.3 or 0.6 mg) or spray (0.4 mg). Do not shake the spray prior to administration.

Nitroglycerin comes in forms other than spray and/or tablet, none of which are approved for EMR use. If the person in your care has a nitroglycerin patch applied, it does not change the nitroglycerin protocol.

NITROUS OXIDE (ENTONOX)

Classification: An inorganic compound made of ammonium nitrate; analgesic.

Mechanism: Inhalation of a 50% mixture of nitrous oxide and oxygen produces CNS depression and rapid pain relief. Analgesic works specifically on the CNS.

Indications: Relief of moderate to severe pain from any cause: acute myocardial infarction, musculoskeletal trauma, burns, other indications (e.g., urethral colic, labour).

Contraindications: Any altered level of consciousness such as head injury (masks neurological signs one needs to monitor), chronic obstructive pulmonary disease, acute pulmonary edema (these people require 100% oxygen), known pneumothorax or chest injury (nitrous oxide collects in dead air spaces), abdominal distension (absent bowel sounds), major facial trauma, shock, decompression sickness, air embolism, person has taken a depressant drug, cyanosis develops during administration, air transportation, usage in an enclosed area with no ventilation, person has taken nitroglycerin within the last 5 minutes, inhalation injury with O_2 saturation less than 100%.

Dose: Self-administered. As the person becomes drowsy, the mask will drop away from the person's face. Person controls pain until pain is relieved.

Adverse Effects: There are nine common adverse affects in the use of Entonox:

- Aggravation of middle ear (increases pressure)
- Drowsiness
- Nausea
- Vomiting
- Giddiness
- Dizziness
- Amnesia
- Decreased level of consciousness
- Decreased cardiac output

Cautions:

Improper Storage: Separation of N_2O_2 and O_2 where N_2O_2 rises to the top of the cylinder.

Separation occurs when:

- The tank is stored below −6°C.
- Gas is stagnant over a long period of time.
- The tank has been stored in a vertical position.

Combustible: Supports combustion

Inhalation by EMR: Affects EMR's competency in caring for people and driving ability

Entonox Dependence: Addictive

Note: Information provided in the drug profile is generic. In any conflict in data between your protocols and the drug profile, your protocol will take precedence. In this case, those items currently listed as cautions in the Entonox protocol are not reflected as cautions in the drug profile.

ORAL GLUCOSE

Classification: Caloric.

Mechanism: Absorbed into the bloodstream, resulting in increased blood glucose levels, thereby providing an increased level of glucose for use by cells.

Indications: For some jurisdictions, oral glucose gel is indicated for someone with a decreased LOC with a known diabetic history.

Contraindications: If airway management cannot be maintained, oral glucose is contraindicated.

Onset, Dose, Route: Via the buccal/sublingual route, glucose is absorbed slowly into the bloodstream. EMRs administer approximately 12 g prior to transport. In approximately three to five minutes, administer another approximately 12 g of oral glucose inside the lower cheek, again being cautious of the person's airway. The effects of oral glucose are not immediate.

Metabolism: Glucose enters cells, where it is used to provide energy. It is oxidized (broken down) into carbon dioxide and water and excreted through the lungs and kidneys.

Adverse Effects: May increase airway management problems.

Oral Glucose

Cautions: People must be placed semi-prone prior to administration; if this position cannot be achieved due to other complications, administration is contraindicated due to the possibility of causing aspiration.

Notes: Place gel into a dependent buccal pouch (lower cheek).

A number of different brands of oral glucose containing 25 g 40% dextrose are available on the market.

Using a tongue depressor may help with administration.

If there is an initial improvement in the person's LOC, administer more oral glucose only if the LOC begins to drop.

Document the time, route (oral), dose, and result.

OXYGEN

Classification: Oxidizing agent (gas).

Description: Oxygen is an odourless, colourless, tasteless gas and is essential for life. It is one of the most important emergency drugs.

Calculating How Long an Oxygen Cylinder Will Last

Oxygen cylinder size is designated with a letter. If you know the size of your oxygen cylinder and the reading on the pressure gauge, you can calculate how long the supply will last. There are various protocols as to when to change your tank; however, in all cases, 200 psi is known as the safe residual pressure, and the tank should always be changed around this point.

The calculation is as follows:

$$\text{Duration of flow} = \frac{(\text{gauge pressure} - 200 \text{ psi}) \times C}{\text{Flow rate (L/min)}}$$

Where C = the cylinder constant

Cylinder constants

D cylinder = 0.16 L/psi

E cylinder = 0.28 L/psi

M cylinder = 1.56 L/psi

Indications: Hypoxia or anticipated hypoxia or in any person with a medical problem or in a trauma situation to improve respiratory efficiency.

Contraindications: There are no contraindications to oxygen administration.

Cautions: COPD and very prolonged administration of high concentrations in the newborn.

Dose/Route: Varies with route used.

SALBUTAMOL, ALBUTEROL (VENTOLIN®)

Classification: Bronchodilator, sympathomimetic.

Mechanism: Relaxes the smooth muscles of the bronchial tree and peripheral vasculature by stimulating beta-adrenergic receptors of the sympathetic nervous system; action is relatively selective, affecting primarily the $beta^2$ receptors, although $beta^1$-adrenergic receptors are stimulated. As the dose of the drug is increased, more and more $beta^1$ effects are produced.

Indications: Failing respirations with bronchospasm; bronchospasm in anaphylaxis.

Contraindications: Known sensitivity, allergy, caution in children, caution in people sensitive to sympathomimetic amines; caution in people with myocardial insufficiency, dysrhythmia, hypertension, diabetes mellitus, or thyrotoxicosis; should not be used concurrently with other beta-adrenergic drugs, such as isoproterenol; safety in pregnancy not firmly established.

Salbutamol, Albuterol (Ventolin®)

Dose: 2.5 to 5 mg in premixed ampoules.

Routes of Administration: Nebulizer mask, side port nebulizer (if person intubated).

Onset: 5 to 10 minutes for maximum effect.

Duration: 3 to 4 hours (half-life of 2.7 to 5 hours).

Metabolism: Metabolized in liver into inactive metabolites.

Adverse Effects: Respiratory: coughing, bronchospasm; CNS: restlessness, apprehension, tremor, dizziness, headache; circulatory system: palpitations, blood pressure changes, tachycardia, dysrhythmias—cardiac arrest, chest discomfort; GI: nausea; skin: pallor, flush, sweating.

Note: Careful charting of air entry, lung sounds, degree of respiratory distress, and use of accessory muscles should be done pre- and post-treatment.

PULSE OXIMETRY

A pulse oximeter is a device that measures the percentage of red blood cells that are saturated by oxygen.

Pulse oximetry is a simple, rapid, safe, and non-invasive method of measuring, minute by minute, how well a person's blood is oxygenated.

To ensure that the instrument is measuring arterial and not venous oxygenation, pulse oximeters are designed to assess only pulsating blood vessels. The pulse oximeter will also measure the pulse. A 100% saturation measurement means that all the red blood cells are oxygenated; 80% saturation means that only 80% of the red blood cells are carrying oxygen.

A healthy, non-smoking adult should have oxygen saturation on room air around 97 to 100%, whereas smokers can have oxygen saturation on room air around 94 to 96%. People with chronic lung disease may have oxygen saturation on room air as low as 90% when they are not ill. Oxygen saturation below 80% is considered incompatible with life.

> **NOTE:**
>
> *A pulse oximetry reading is the percent saturation, but the device cannot distinguish what molecule it is (e.g., CO versus O_2).*

CAUSES OF FAULTY READINGS OF PULSE OXIMETER

Cause	Rationale
Anemia	Fewer circulating red blood cells to carry oxygen
Carbon monoxide	CO binds to hemoglobin more easily than oxygen
Nail polish	Blocks the sensor light
Hypovolemia	Fewer circulating red blood cells to carry oxygen
Decreased circulation to the extremities	Insufficient blood flow to obtain an accurate reading

Oxygen saturation readings can be faulty when people are anemic, hypovolemic, or exposed to gases (such as carbon monoxide) that have a greater affinity to hemoglobin than oxygen.

How to Use the Pulse Oximeter

The unit should be used in accordance with the manufacturer's specifications.

WHEN IN DOUBT, LOOK AT THE PERSON

Remember, treat the person, not the pulse oximeter.

INTRAVENOUS THERAPY (IV THERAPY)

Indications: Where an IV has already been established, the responder may be required to monitor an IV as per medical direction or oversight.

Solution Types:
- Normal saline
- $2/3-1/3$
- Ringer's lactate
- D_5W

Calculating Flow Rates: To calculate flow rates for infusion of IV fluids, use the following formula:

$$\text{gtts/min} = \frac{\text{volume to be infused} \times \text{gtts/mL of administration set}}{\text{Total time of infusion (in minutes)}}$$

Changing an IV bag is indicated in the following circumstances:

- The bag is empty or has less than approximately 50 mL remaining.

- You are given instructions from the medical staff that the IV is to be changed en route during a transfer. In this circumstance, you can request that the nursing staff change the bag prior to the transfer or obtain a replacement bag from the hospital to be changed en route.

- Glass solution bottles are rare, but if a glass bottle is hanging and the person is going on an air evacuation, you will need to change to a plastic bag so that the IV will run at high altitudes. Remember that gas expands at higher altitudes.

The following procedure must be followed when changing an IV bag:

1. Wash your hands and ensure aseptic technique.

2. Remove a new bag of solution from the outer wrappings and inspect it for leaks, discolouration, and the expiry date. Ensure that it has the correct concerns and concentration as per hospital instructions and in accordance with the established protocols.

3. Close the flow clamp on the tubing.

4. Remove the spike on the administration set from the old bag. Taking care not to contaminate the spike, remove the protective cap from the IV port on the new bag. Insert the spike into the IV port on the new bag.

5. Fill the drip chamber one-half to two-thirds full; set the flow rate.

6. Document the procedure by noting the time you changed the IV bag and the amount and type of solution hung. Example: 930 to 1,000 mL N/S started at 500 mL/hr/ [your signature].

Complications

In the course of monitoring an IV, several complications may arise that require intervention. Seven complications of IV administration include the following:

Interstitial: Interstitial means that the IV fluid is flowing into the surrounding tissues instead of into the vein due to complete or partial perforation of the vein through the opposite wall. This is identified by swelling around the injection site, and the skin will be cool to the touch. Flow rate may be diminished and pain may or may not be present.

Interventions:

• Once you have identified that the IV is interstitial, discontinue the IV.

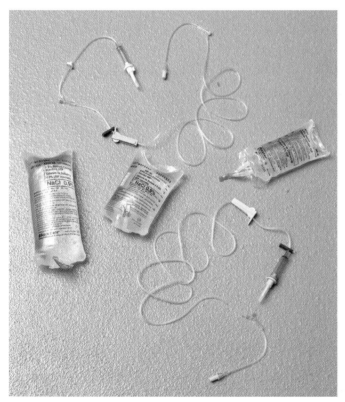

Intravenous Therapy

• Record the time at which the IV was discontinued and the amount infused.

• If the swollen area is small, apply a cold pack.

• If the swollen area is large, apply warm, wet compresses to promote reabsorption of the fluid.

Circulatory Overload: Circulatory overload occurs when the person's system is unable to manage the extra fluids administered, leading to cardiac and pulmonary complications similar to congestive heart failure or pulmonary edema. This can be caused by excessive fluid administration or rapid fluid delivery. Ensure careful monitoring of vital signs and IV flow line.

Interventions:

• Should the person develop signs of fluid overload, immediately slow the IV rate to keep the vein open (TKVO).

• Place the person in a semi-sitting position and apply oxygen.

• Transport the person as quickly as possible and give the hospital notification of your arrival.

• Closely monitor the person's vital signs en route and make sure you keep the person warm to promote peripheral circulation.

• Document your findings, including slowing the IV rate. Someone with circulatory overload should be treated as a person with CHF.

Thrombosis and Thrombophlebitis: Thrombosis is the formation of a clot and usually occurs at the tip of the catheter. Thrombophlebitis is inflammation of a vein due to the formation of a blood clot (thrombus = blood clot; phlebitis = inflammation of a vein).

Causes:

A clot may form if:

- The IV is running too slowly.

- There is injury to the vein wall during insertion or from mechanical irritation (e.g., excessive movement of the person).

- The catheter is too large for the lumen of the vein.

- The vein is too small to handle the amount or type of solution being administered.

- There is irritation to the vein by medications (e.g., drug infusions).

Thrombosis and thrombophlebitis can be prevented by choosing the appropriately sized vein for the gauge of catheter you are using and by ensuring that any potentially irritating medications are given through large veins with good blood flow. Keeping the infusion flowing at the established rate helps prevent the formation of a thrombus at the end of the needle. Stabilizing the IV site with an arm board or splint will prevent mechanical irritation.

Interventions:

- If thrombophlebitis develops, discontinue the IV.

- Record the time at which the IV was discontinued and the amount of fluid infused.

- Apply warm, wet compresses to decrease the pain and promote healing.

- Do not massage or rub the affected arm as this may dislodge the clot that has formed.

Catheter Embolism: Catheter embolism means that the catheter or a portion of it has broken off and is carried away in the bloodstream. Although rare, it can be caused by attempting to rethread the needle during insertion.

Interventions:

- Discontinue the IV but do not discard the catheter. Give the catheter to the hospital personnel for examination and follow-up.

- Record the time at which the IV was discontinued and the amount of solution infused.

- Apply a tourniquet above the insertion site to impede venous return and prevent further migration of the catheter. Be careful not to obstruct the arterial flow; check the distal pulse to ensure its presence.

- Apply high-flow oxygen to the person if necessary.

- Notify the hospital and transport the person as an emergency.

Infection of Site: Recognition of the infection will more likely occur in transporting people who already have IVs in place. The majority of infections are due to skin flora entering the wound when the IV is started because of poor aseptic techniques. Infection is usually recognized by redness at the area, swelling of the site, or possible discharge.

Interventions:

- If possible, notify the sending facility before transporting the person.

- Discontinue the IV and record the time.

- Document the amount of solution infused.

- Dispose of the catheter in a sterile container and give it to hospital personnel for testing.

- Dress the site with a sterile dressing and apply a warm pack.

Allergic Reaction: Caused by a hypersensitivity to an IV solution or an additive resulting in generalized rash, shortness of breath, rapid heart rate, and a drop in blood pressure.

NOTE:
Search for other substances that may have caused the reaction. If unable to find another cause of the reaction, discontinue the IV.

Interventions:

- Decrease the IV rate to keep the vein open (or discontinue the IV).

- Record the time the IV rate was changed.

- Notify the hospital.

- Administer oxygen if necessary.

Air Embolism: Air embolism can be caused by allowing an IV bag to run dry, air in the tubing, or loose connections between the IV tubing and the catheter or at the piggybacking sites. When setting up an IV, make sure you clear the tubing of all the air bubbles. Change the IV bags before they are empty and make sure all connections are secured.

Interventions:

- Turn the person on his left side with the head down 30°. If air has entered the heart chambers, this position may keep the air bubbles on the right side of the heart, where they can then enter the pulmonary circulation and be absorbed.

- Check the IV system for leaks.

- Administer oxygen.

- Notify the hospital and transport immediately.

Discontinuing an IV:

An IV-endorsed paramedic will decide to remove an IV in the event of:

- Interstitial when flow is impaired

- Thrombophlebitis

- Catheter embolism

- Infection at the venipuncture site (most likely will be seen on an inter-hospital transport)

Do not remove an IV catheter if a "do not remove" order has been given.

The procedure for discontinuing an IV is as follows:

1. Wash your hands, put on gloves, and ensure aseptic technique.

2. Turn off the flow control clamp.

3. Remove the transparent dressing and the tape from the site when minimizing IV and catheter movement. It helps if you stabilize the hub of the catheter with one hand while removing the tape with the other.

4. Hold a sterile gauze over the puncture site. Grasping the catheter by the hub, pull straight back. Do not use an alcohol swab for this procedure as this may interfere with blood clotting and be painful for the person.

5. Immediately apply firm pressure to the site and continue this for at least three to five minutes to stop the bleeding.

6. Once bleeding has stopped, cover the puncture site with an adhesive bandage.

7. Inspect the catheter for completeness.

8. Document the time the IV was discontinued and the amount of solution infused.

Common Abbreviations for Documentation

♀	Female
♂	Male
↓	Diminished, decreased, lower
↑	Elevated, increased, upper
>	Greater than
<	Less than
=	Equals
≠	Not equal
i, ii, iii	One, two, three
Ø	None, not present, not found
abd	Abdomen
ac	Before meals
AED	Automated external defibrillator
AE, A/E	Air entry
am	Before noon
ANU	Ambulance not used
AOB	Alcohol on breath
approx	Approximately
ASA	Acetylsalicylic acid, Aspirin®
ASAP	As soon as possible
bG	Blood glucose
bid	Twice a day
BM	Bowel movement
BP	Blood pressure
c̄	With
°C	Degrees Celsius
C-section	Caesarean section
C/C	Chief complaint
c/o	Complains of
Ca	Cancer
CABG	Coronary artery bypass graft
CAD	Coronary artery disease
cath	Catheter
CBC	Complete blood count
cc	Cubic centimetre
CCU	Cardiac care unit

CHF	Congestive heart failure
CIS	Critical incident stress
CO_2	Carbon dioxide
COPD	Chronic obstructive pulmonary disease
CP	Chest pain
CPR	Cardiopulmonary resuscitation
CSF	Cerebrospinal fluid
CT (CAT)	Computed tomography
CVA	Cerebrovascular accident
D_5W	Dextrose 5% in water
$D_{10}W$	Dextrose 10% in water
DNR	Do not resuscitate
DOA	Dead on arrival
DPU	Discharge planning unit
Dx	Diagnosis
ECG, EKG	Electrocardiogram
ECU	Extended care unit
EEG	Electroencephalograph
EP	Emergency physician
ER, ED	Emergency room, department
ET	Endotracheal
ETA	Estimated time of arrival
FR	First responder
Fx, #	Fracture
GI	Gastrointestinal
GOA	Gone on arrival
gtt	Drop
Hb	Hemoglobin
Hct	Hematocrit
Hg	Chemical symbol for mercury
H_2O	Water
hr	Hour
Hs	Evening, at bedtime
Hx	History

ICN	Intensive care nursery		PEARL	Pupils equal and react to light
IDDM	Insulin-dependent diabetes mellitus		PERLA	Pupils equal, round, react to light and accommodation
IM	Intramuscular		PO	By mouth, oral
IV	Intravenous		post-op	Postoperative
			pre-op	Preoperative
kg	Kilogram		prn	As needed, as required
			pt	Patient
L1	First lumbar vertebrae			
l, L	Litre		q am	Every morning
lg	Large		QID/qid	Four times per day
LLQ	Left lower quadrant		q1h, q2h	Every hour, every two hours
LOC	Level of consciousness			
LUQ	Left upper quadrant		R, resp	Respirations
			RBC	Red blood cells
MCG, mcg	Microgram		RLQ	Right lower quadrant
MCI	Multiple casualty incident		RUQ	Right upper quadrant
mEq/L	Milliequivalents per litre		Rx	Medications
mg	Milligram		R/O	Rule out
MI	Myocardial infarction			
ml, mL	Millilitre		s, w/o	Without
mmHg	Millimetres of mercury		SA	Sinoatrial node
MO	Mental observation point		SC, sc	Subcutaneous
MRI	Magnetic resonance imaging		SCN	Special care nursery
MVC	Motor vehicle collision		SIDS	Sudden infant death syndrome
			SL, sl	Sublingual
N/A	Not applicable/Not available		SOB	Shortness of breath
NIDDM	Non-insulin-dependent diabetes mellitus		stat	Immediately
nitro	Nitroglycerin		SV	Stroke volume
NKA	No known allergies			
N_2O	Nitrous oxide (Entonox)		T2	Second thoracic vertebrae
NPO	Nothing by mouth		tab	Tablet
NS	Normal saline		TIA	Transient ischemic attack
NYD	Not yet diagnosed		tid	Three times per day
			TKO, TKVO	To keep vein open
O_2	Oxygen		TPR	Temperature, pulse, respiration
OB, OBS	Obstetrics		TPN	Total parenteral nutrition
od	Once per day		Tx	Treatment
OD	Overdose		tx	Transmit
OR	Operating room			
OTC	Over the counter		U/K	Unknown
P	Pulse		vag	Vaginal
palp	Palpation			
PAU	Psychiatric assessment unit		yr	Year
pc	After meals, after food			
per	Through, by			

Glossary

A

Abandonment: Ending care of an ill or injured person without that person's consent or without ensuring that someone with equal or greater training will continue that care.

Abdomen: The part of the trunk below the ribs and above the pelvis.

Abdominal aortic aneurysm: A rupturing of the abdominal aorta.

Abdominal cavity: An area located in the trunk that contains the liver, pancreas, intestine, stomach, and spleen.

Abdominal thrusts: A technique for unblocking an obstructed airway by forcefully squeezing the abdomen.

Abrasion: A wound characterized by skin that has been scraped or rubbed away.

Abruptio placentae: A partial or complete detachment of a normally implanted placenta at more than 20 weeks gestation.

Absorbed poison: A poison that enters the body through the skin or mucous membranes.

Active listening: A process that helps you more fully communicate with a person by focussing on what the person is saying.

Acute pulmonary edema: Fluid buildup in the lungs.

Adolescent: A person between 13 and 18 years of age.

AIDS (acquired immune deficiency syndrome): A condition caused by the human immunodeficiency virus (HIV).

Airborne transmission: The transmission of a disease by inhaling infected droplets that become airborne when an infected person coughs or sneezes.

Airway: The pathway for air from the mouth and nose to the lungs.

Airway obstruction: A blockage of the airway that prevents air from reaching a person's lungs.

Altitude sickness: Illness due to a change in altitude.

Alveoli: Small air sacs in the lungs where gases and waste are exchanged between the lungs and the blood.

Alzheimer's disease: A progressive, degenerative disease that affects the brain, resulting in impaired memory, thinking, and behaviour.

Amniotic sac: A fluid-filled sac that encloses, bathes, and protects the developing baby.

Amputation: The complete removal or severing of a body part.

Anaphylaxis: A severe allergic reaction in which the air passages constrict and restrict the person's breathing.

Anatomic splint: A splint that uses an uninjured body part to immobilize an injured body part.

Anatomical obstruction: The blockage of the airway by an anatomical structure, such as the tongue.

Anatomical position: A position in which a person is standing erect with arms down at the sides, and palms facing forward.

Aneurysm: A condition in which the wall of an artery or vein weakens, balloons out, and ruptures.

Angina: Chest pain or pressure resulting when the heart needs more oxygen-rich blood than it is getting; pain or pressure usually lasts less than 10 minutes.

Anterior: Toward the front of the body.

Appendicitis: Acute inflammation of the appendix.

Arrhythmia: A disturbance in the conduction of electrical impulses within the heart; also called dysrhythmia

Arteries: Large blood vessels that carry oxygen-rich blood from the heart to all parts of the body.

Arthritis: An inflamed condition of the joints, causing pain and swelling and sometimes limiting motion.

Aspiration: Taking blood, vomit, saliva, or other foreign material into the lungs.

Assault: Abuse, either physical or sexual, resulting in injury and often emotional crisis.

Asthma: A condition that narrows the air passages and makes breathing difficult.

Asystole: The stopping of all electrical activity in the heart.

Atherosclerosis: A form of cardiovascular disease marked by a narrowing of the arteries in the heart and other parts of the body.

Atria: The upper chambers of the heart.

Aura: An unusual sensation or feeling a person may experience before an epileptic seizure; may be a visual hallucination; a strange sound, taste, or smell; or an urgent need to get to safety.

Auscultation: Listening to the internal sounds of the body; usually with a stethoscope.

Automated external defibrillator (AED): An electronic device that shocks a person's heart to stop certain arrhythmias.

Avulsion: A wound in which a portion of the skin, and sometimes other soft tissue, is partially or completely torn away.

B

Baby: Someone up to 1 year of age.

Bacteria: One-celled microorganisms that may cause infections.

Bag-valve-mask (BVM) resuscitator: A hand-held ventilation device consisting of a self-inflating bag, a one-way valve, and a face mask; can be used with or without supplemental oxygen.

Bandage: Material used to wrap or cover a part of the body; commonly used to hold a dressing or splint in place.

Behavioural disorder: Any of various forms of behaviour, resulting from situational, organic, or psychiatric causes, that are dangerous or disturbing to the person or those around him.

Biological death: The irreversible damage caused by the death of brain cells.

Birth canal: The passageway from the uterus to the vaginal opening through which a baby passes during birth.

Bladder: An organ in the pelvis in which urine is stored until released from the body.

Blast injury: An injury resulting from an explosion; caused by pressure waves, flying debris, or being thrown.

Blood-borne pathogens: Bacteria and viruses present in human blood and body fluids that can cause disease in humans.

Blood glucose level: The amount of sugar (glucose) in the blood.

Blood pressure (BP): The force exerted by blood against the blood vessel walls as it travels throughout the body.

Blood pressure cuff: A device used to measure a person's blood pressure.

Blood volume: The total amount of blood circulating within the body.

Body cavity: A hollow place in the body that contains organs, glands, blood vessels, and nerves.

Body mechanics: Using the body to gain mechanical advantage in the safest and most efficient way.

Body system: A group of organs and other structures working together to carry out specific functions.

Bone: A dense, hard tissue that forms the skeleton.

Bowel obstruction: An occlusion of the intestinal cavity resulting in blockage of normal flow of intestinal contents.

Brachial artery: A large artery located in the upper arm.

Brain: The centre of the nervous system that controls all body functions.

Breathing emergency: An emergency in which breathing is so impaired that life can be threatened.

Breech birth: The delivery of a baby feet or buttocks first.

Bronchi: The air passages that lead from the trachea to the lungs.

Bronchitis: A disease causing excessive mucous

secretions and inflammatory changes to the bronchi.

Burn: An injury to the skin or other body tissues caused by heat, chemicals, electricity, or radiation.

C

Capillaries: Tiny blood vessels linking arteries and veins that transfer oxygen and other nutrients from the blood to all body cells and remove waste products.

Capillary refill: An estimate of the amount of blood flowing through the capillary beds, such as those in the fingertips.

Carbon dioxide: A colourless, odourless gas; a waste product of respiration.

Cardiac arrest: A condition in which the heart has stopped functioning.

Cardiopulmonary resuscitation (CPR): A technique that combines rescue breathing and chest compressions for a person whose breathing and heart have stopped.

Cardiovascular disease: A disease of the heart and blood vessels; commonly known as heart disease.

Carotid arteries: Arteries located in the neck that supply blood to the head and neck.

Cartilage: An elastic tissue that acts as a shock absorber when a person is walking, running, or jumping.

Cell: The basic unit of all living tissue.

Cervical collar: A rigid device positioned around the neck to limit movement of the head and neck.

Cervix: The upper part of the birth canal.

Chemical burns: Burns that are caused by caustic chemicals, such as strong acids or alkalies.

Chest thrusts: Forceful pushes on the chest; delivered to a person with an obstructed airway in an attempt to expel any foreign object blocking the airway.

Child abuse: The physical, psychological, or sexual assault of a child, resulting in injury and emotional trauma.

Chocking: The use of items, such as wooden blocks, placed against the wheels of a vehicle to help stabilize the vehicle.

Cholesterol: A fatty substance made by the body and found in certain foods.

Chronic obstructive pulmonary disease (COPD): A disease characterized by a loss of lung function.

Circulatory emergencies: Sudden illnesses or injuries involving the heart or blood vessels.

Circulatory system: A group of organs and other structures that carry oxygen-rich blood and other nutrients throughout the body and remove waste.

Clavicle: See collarbone.

Clinical death: The condition in which the heart stops beating and breathing stops.

Closed fracture: A fracture in which the skin is left unbroken.

Closed wound: A wound in which soft tissue damage occurs beneath the skin and the skin is not broken.

Clotting: The process by which blood thickens at a wound site to seal an opening in a blood vessel and stop bleeding.

Collarbone: A horizontal bone that connects with the sternum and the shoulder; also called the clavicle.

Compassion: An understanding of the emotional state of another person, combined with the desire to alleviate or reduce the suffering of that person.

Competence: The state or quality of being adequately qualified for, or the ability to perform, a particular role; the ability of an ill or injured person to understand a responder's questions and the implications of a decision.

Concussion: A temporary impairment of brain function, usually without permanent damage to the brain.

Confidence: The state of being certain that a chosen course of action is the best or most effective.

Confidentiality: Protecting a person's privacy by not revealing any personal information you learn about the person except to law enforcement personnel or more advanced medical care.

Conflict: An internal or external state of unrest due to the opposition of one's needs, values, and interests.

Congestive heart failure: A condition in which the heart loses its pumping ability, causing fluid buildup in the body; results in heart failure.

Consciousness: The state of being aware of one's self and one's surroundings.

Consent: Permission to provide care, given by an ill or injured person to a responder.

Contraction: The rhythmic tightening of muscles in the uterus during labour; or the pumping action of the heart.

Coronary arteries: Blood vessels that supply the heart muscle with oxygen-rich blood.

Cranial cavity: An area in the body that contains the brain and is protected by the skull.

Cravat: A triangular bandage folded to form a long, narrow strip.

Critical burn: Any burn that is potentially life-threatening, disabling, or disfiguring; a burn requiring more advanced emergency care.

Croup: A viral infection that causes swelling of the tissues below the vocal cords; a common childhood illness.

Crowning: The time in labour when the baby's head is at the opening of the vagina.

Crush injury: An injury caused when a crushing force is applied to any part of the body over a short or long period of time.

Cyanosis: A bluish colouration of the skin and mucous membranes due to the presence of deoxygenated blood in the vessels near the skin surface.

D

Decomposition: The breaking down of the body's chemical composition after death.

Defibrillation: An electric shock administered to correct a life-threatening heart rhythm.

Depressants: Substances that affect the central nervous system to slow physical and mental activity.

Dermis: The deeper of the two layers of skin.

Designer drug: A potent and illegal street drug formed from a medicinal substance whose chemical composition has been modified ("designed").

Developmentally disabled: A person with impaired mental function, resulting from injury or genetics.

Diabetic emergency: A situation in which a person becomes ill because of an imbalance of insulin.

Diaphragm: A dome-shaped muscle that aids breathing and separates the chest from the abdomen.

Diastolic pressure: The pressure in the arteries when the heart is at rest.

Digestive system: A group of organs and other structures that digests food and eliminates wastes.

Dignity: The state of being worthy of honour and respect.

Diplomacy: Using tact and skill when dealing with people.

Direct contact transmission: The transmission of a disease by touching an infected person's body fluids.

Direct pressure: The pressure applied on a wound to control bleeding.

Discretion: The ability to make responsible decisions.

Dislocation: The displacement of a bone from its normal position at a joint.

Distal: Away from the trunk of the body.

Distal circulation: Blood flow below the site of an injury.

Downwind: In the direction in which the wind blows.

Dressing: A pad placed directly over a wound to absorb blood and other body fluids and to prevent infection.

Drowning: Death by suffocation when submerged in water.

Drug: Any substance other than food intended to affect the functions of the body.

Duty to act: A legal responsibility of some individuals to provide a reasonable standard of emergency care; may be required by case law, statute, or job description.

Dysrhythmia: A disturbance in the conduction of electrical impulses within the heart; also called arrhythmia.

E

Ectopic pregnancy: When a fertilized ovum implants anywhere other than in the uterus.

Elder abuse: Any of four types of abuse: the infliction of pain or injury (physical abuse); mental anguish or suffering (psychological abuse); financial or material abuse; or unnecessary confinement or willful deprivation (neglect) by an older adult's caretaker.

Electrical burn: A burn caused by an electrical source, such as an electrical appliance or lightning.

Embolism: A sudden blockage of a blood vessel by a traveling clot or other material, such as fat or air.

Emergency medical responder (EMR): a responder who has successfully completed a recognized training program in the care and transportation of an ill or injured person.

Emergency medical services (EMS) system: A network of community resources and medical personnel that provides emergency care to people who are injured or suddenly ill.

Emergency move: Moving a person before completing care; done only in certain necessary circumstances.

Emotional crisis: A highly emotional state resulting from stress, often involving a significant event in a person's life, such as the death of a loved one.

Empathy: Feeling or expressing emotion for another.

Emphysema: A disease in which the alveoli lose their elasticity, become distended with trapped air, and stop working.

Endocrine system: A group of organs and other structures that regulate and coordinate the activities of other systems by producing chemicals that influence the activity of tissues.

Epidermis: The outer layer of skin.

Epidural hematoma: Arterial bleeding between the skull and dura matter.

Epiglottis: The flap of tissue that covers the trachea to keep food and liquid out of the lungs.

Epiglottitis: A bacterial infection that causes a severe inflammation of the epiglottis.

Epilepsy: A chronic condition characterized by seizures that vary in type and duration; can usually be controlled by medication.

Epinephrine: A naturally occurring hormone; can be used to counter the effects of anaphylaxis.

Esophagus: The tube leading from the mouth to the stomach.

Ethical: Conforming to accepted standards of conduct.

Exhale: To breathe air out of the lungs.

External bleeding: Bleeding from an open wound in the skin.

Extremities: The limbs of the body.

Extrication: The freeing of someone or something from an entanglement or difficulty.

F

Fainting (syncope): A loss of consciousness resulting from a temporary reduction in blood flow to the brain.

Febrile seizure: A seizure caused by an elevated body temperature.

Femur: The thighbone.

Fibula: One of the bones in the lower leg.

Finger sweep: A technique used to remove foreign material from a person's airway.

First responder: A person trained in emergency care who may be called on to provide such care as a routine part of his or her job; often the first trained professional to respond to emergencies.

Flail chest: An injury involving fractured ribs that do not move normally with the rest of the chest during breathing.

Flowmeter: A device used to regulate in litres per minute (lpm) the amount of oxygen administered to a person.

Fracture: A break or disruption in bone tissue.

Freeboard: The distance between the top of a watercraft, or the deck of a ship, and the waterline.

Frostbite: A serious condition in which body tissues freeze, most commonly in the fingers, toes, ears, and nose.

Full-thickness burn: A burn injury involving both layers of skin and underlying tissues; skin may be brown or charred, and underlying tissues may appear white.

G

Gastric distention: Air in the stomach, causing it to bloat.

Gastroenteritis: A condition often resulting from an infection of the gastrointestinal tract.

Genitalia: The external reproductive organs.

Genitourinary system: A group of organs and other structures that eliminate waste and enable reproduction.

Glands: Organs that release fluid and other substances into the blood or on the skin.

Glasgow Coma Scale (GCS): A standardized system used to determine a person's level of consciousness; often performed on people with suspected head injuries.

Glucometer: A device used to measure a person's blood glucose level.

Good Samaritan laws: Laws that protect people who willingly give emergency care while acting in good faith, without negligence, and within the scope of their training.

H

Hallucinogens: Substances that affect mood, sensation, thought, emotion, and self-awareness; alter perceptions of time and space; and produce delusions.

Hazardous materials: Substances that are harmful or toxic to the body; can be liquids, solids, or gases.

Head-tilt/chin-lift: A method of opening the airway when there is no suspected head or spine injury.

Hearing impaired: A nonspecific term applied to a person who is either deaf or partially deaf.

Heart: A fist-sized muscular organ that pumps blood throughout the body.

Heart attack: A sudden illness involving the death of heart muscle tissue when it does not receive enough oxygen-rich blood; also called myocardial infarction (MI).

Heat cramps: Painful spasms of skeletal muscles following exercise or work in warm or moderate temperatures; usually involve the calf and abdominal muscles.

Heat exhaustion: A form of shock, often resulting from strenuous work or exercise in a hot environment.

Heat stroke: A life-threatening condition that develops when the body's cooling mechanisms are overwhelmed and body systems begin to fail.

Hemorrhage: A loss of a large amount of blood in a short time.

Hemothorax: A condition in which blood enters the pleural space as a result of a blunt or penetrating trauma.

Hepatitis: A viral infection of the liver.

Herpes: A viral infection that causes eruptions of the skin and mucous membranes.

HIV (human immunodeficiency virus): The virus that destroys the body's ability to fight infection. The resultant state is referred to as AIDS.

Humerus: The bone of the upper arm.

Hyperglycemia: A condition in which too much sugar is in the bloodstream.

Hypertension: High blood pressure.

Hyperventilation: Rapid breathing that upsets the body's balance of oxygen and carbon dioxide.

Hypoglycemia: A condition in which too little sugar is in the bloodstream.

Hypothermia: A life-threatening condition in which the body's warming mechanisms fail to maintain normal body temperature and the entire body cools.

Hypoxia: A decrease in oxygen in the blood.

I

Immobilize: To use a splint or other method to keep an injured body part from moving.

Immune system: The body's group of responses for fighting disease.

Immunization: A specific substance containing weakened or killed pathogens that is introduced into the body to build resistance to specific infection.

Impaled object: An object remaining in a wound.

Implied consent: A legal concept assuming that people who are unconscious, or so severely injured or ill that they cannot respond, would consent to receive emergency care.

Incident command system (ICS): A system used to manage resources, such as personnel, equipment, and supplies, at the scene of an emergency.

Indirect contact transmission: The transmission of a disease by touching a contaminated object.

Infection: A condition caused by disease-producing microorganisms, also called pathogens or germs, in the body.

Infectious disease: Disease capable of being transmitted from people, objects, animals, or insects.

Inferior: Toward the feet.

Informed (actual) consent: Permission the ill or injured person, parent, or guardian gives the responder to provide care. This consent requires the responder to explain his or her level of training, what the responder thinks is wrong, and the care the responder intends to give.

Ingested poison: A poison that is swallowed.

Inhalants: Substances inhaled to produce an effect.

Inhale: To breathe in.

Inhaled poison: A poison breathed into the lungs.

Injected poison: A poison that enters the body through a bite, sting, or syringe.

In-line stabilization: A technique used to minimize movement of a person's head and neck.

Insulin: A hormone that enables the body to use sugar for energy; frequently used to treat diabetes.

Integumentary system: A group of organs and other structures that protect the body, retain fluids, and help prevent infection.

Internal bleeding: Bleeding that occurs inside the body.

Interpersonal communication: The process of speaking and listening to other people at an emergency scene; can be verbal or nonverbal.

Intervention: A medication, device, therapy, or action that produces an effect or that is intended to alter the course of an illness or injury.

J

Jaw thrust: A method of opening the airway when there is a suspected head or spine injury.

Joint: A structure in which two or more bones are joined.

K

Kidney: An organ that filters waste from the blood to form urine.

Kidney stones: Solid concentrations of dissolved minerals found in the kidneys or ureters.

L

Labour: The birth process; beginning with the contraction of the uterus and dilation of the cervix and ending with the stabilization and recovery of the mother.

Laceration: A cut, usually from a sharp object; may have jagged or smooth edges.

Landing zone: The area where aircraft land.

Larynx: A part of the airway connecting the pharynx with the trachea; commonly called the "voice box."

Lateral: Away from the midline.

Level of consciousness (LOC): A person's state of awareness, ranging from being fully alert to unconscious.

Ligament: A fibrous band that holds bones together at a joint.

Lividity: Following death, a large pooling of blood in the trunk resulting in discolouration.

Lungs: A pair of organs in the chest that provides the mechanism for taking oxygen in and removing carbon dioxide during breathing.

Lyme disease: An illness transmitted by a certain kind of infected tick.

M

Mechanism of injury (MOI): The event or forces that caused a person's injury.

Medial: Toward the midline.

Medical control: The process that allows a physician to direct care given to an ill or injured person by pre-hospital professionals (may also be known as transfer of function, or medical delegation).

Medication: A drug given to prevent or correct the effects of a disease or condition or otherwise enhance mental or physical well-being.

Membranes: A thin sheet of tissue that covers a structure or lines a cavity, such as the mouth or nose.

Meningitis: An inflammation of the brain or spinal cord caused by a viral or bacterial infection.

Mental disability: Impaired mental function that interferes with normal activity.

Metered-dose inhaler (MDI): A device prescribed to many people with asthma, containing a medication that counters the effects of an asthma attack.

Miscarriage: The spontaneous termination of pregnancy before 20 weeks of gestation.

Multiple casualty incident (MCI): An emergency situation involving two or more ill or injured people.

Muscle: A tissue that lengthens and shortens to create movement.

Musculoskeletal system: A group of tissues and other structures that supports the body, protects internal organs, allows movement, stores minerals, manufactures blood cells, and creates heat.

N

Narcotics: Powerful depressant substances used to relieve anxiety and pain.

Nasal cannula: A device used to administer oxygen through the nostrils to a breathing person.

Nasopharyngeal airway (NPA): A curved tube inserted into the nose to assist in maintaining an open airway.

Near-drowning: A situation in which a person who has been submerged in water survives.

Negligence: The failure to provide the level of care a person of similar training would provide, thereby causing injury or damage to another.

Nervous system: A group of organs and other structures that regulates all body functions.

Nitroglycerin: A medication often prescribed to people diagnosed with angina.

Non-rebreather mask: A special mask combined with a reservoir bag, used to administer high-concentration oxygen to a breathing person through a mask covering both the nose and the mouth.

Nonverbal communication: Communication through body actions, such as assuming a nonthreatening posture or the use of hand gestures.

O

Occlusive dressing: A dressing or bandage that seals a wound and protects it from the air.

Open fracture: A fracture that results when bone ends tear the skin and surrounding tissue or when an object penetrates the skin and breaks a bone.

Open wound: A wound resulting in a break in the skin surface.

Organ: A collection of similar tissues acting together to perform specific body functions.

Oropharyngeal airway (OPA): A curved plastic tube inserted into the mouth and positioned at the back of the throat to keep the tongue from blocking the airway.

Osteoporosis: A disease characterized by low bone mass and bone tissue deterioration.

Overdose: A situation in which a person takes enough of a substance that it has poisonous or fatal effects.

Oxygen: A tasteless, colourless, odourless gas necessary to sustain life.

Oxygen cylinder: A steel or alloy cylinder that contains 100 percent oxygen under high pressure.

Oxygen delivery device: A device used to administer oxygen from an oxygen cylinder to a person.

P

Palpation: The method of feeling with the hands by a

responder during a physical examination of an ill or injured person.

Paradoxical movement: The movement of one part of the chest wall in the opposite direction from the rest of the chest wall.

Paralysis: A loss of muscle control; a permanent loss of feeling and movement.

Partial-thickness burn: A burn injury involving both layers of skin; characterized by red, wet skin and blisters.

Patella: The kneecap.

Pathogen: A disease-causing agent; also called a microorganism or germ.

Pelvic cavity: The lowest part of the trunk that contains the bladder, rectum, and the reproductive organs in females.

Pelvis: The lower part of the trunk, containing the intestines, bladder, and female reproductive organs.

Peptic ulcer: A small erosion in the gastrointestinal tract caused by the destruction of the gastric or intestinal mucosal lining by hydrochloric acid.

Perfusion: The circulation of blood throughout the body.

Peritonitis: An inflammation of the peritoneum.

Personal flotation device (PFD): A buoyant device designed to be worn to keep a person afloat.

Personal protective equipment (PPE): Specialized clothing or equipment worn for protection from a hazard.

Pharynx: A part of the airway formed by the back of the nose and throat.

Physical assault: Abuse that may result in injury to the body.

Physical disability: A serious injury that results in the loss of limb function or a condition with which there is an impairment that interferes with normal activity or movement.

Placard: A sign or notice; a poster.

Placenta: An organ attached to the uterus and unborn child through which nutrients are delivered to the baby; expelled after the baby is delivered.

Placenta previa: A condition in which the placenta is attached in the lower uterus.

Plasma: The liquid part of blood.

Platelets: Disc-shaped structures in the blood that are made of cell fragments; help stop bleeding by forming blood clots at wound sites.

Pneumonia: A group of illnesses characterized by lung infection and fluid of pus-filled alveoli, resulting in inadequate oxygen in the blood.

Pneumothorax: A condition in which air enters the pleural space usually as a result of a blunt or penetrating trauma.

Poison: Any substance that causes injury, illness, or death when introduced into the body.

Poison Control Centre: A specialized health centre that provides information in cases of poisoning or suspected poisoning emergencies.

Posterior: Toward the back.

Postpartum bleeding: Bleeding after the birth of a newborn; characterized by more than 500 mL of blood loss.

Pregnancy: A condition in which the egg (ovum) of the female is fertilized by the sperm of the male, forming an embryo.

Preschooler: A child 3, 4, or 5 years of age.

Pressure bandage: A bandage applied snugly to create pressure on a wound to aid in controlling bleeding.

Pressure points: Sites on the body where pressure can be applied to major arteries to slow the flow of blood to a body part.

Pressure regulator: A device attached to an oxygen cylinder that reduces the delivery pressure of oxygen to a safe level.

Primary survey: A check for conditions that are an immediate threat to a person's life.

Prolapsed cord: A complication of childbirth in which a loop of umbilical cord protrudes through the vagina prior to delivery of the baby.

Prone: A position in which a person is lying face down on his or her stomach.

Protocols: Standardized methods.

Proximal: Closer to the trunk of the body.

Pulmonary embolism: A blockage of a pulmonary artery by a clot or other foreign material.

Pulse: The beat felt in arteries with each contraction of the heart.

Pulse oximeter: A device used to measure the percentage of red blood cells that are saturated by oxygen.

Puncture: A wound that results when the skin is pierced with a pointed object, such as a nail, a piece of glass, or a knife.

Q

Quality assurance: Providing evidence needed to establish quality in work.

R

Rabies: A disease caused by a virus transmitted through the saliva of an infected animal.

Radial pulse: The pulse felt in the wrist.

Radiation burn: A burn caused by rays, energy, or electromagnetic waves.

Refusal of care: The declining of care by a person.

Reproductive system: A group of organs and other structures that enable sexual reproduction.

Rescue breathing: A technique of breathing for a non-breathing person.

Respiration: The breathing process of the body that takes in oxygen and eliminates carbon dioxide.

Respiratory arrest: A condition in which breathing has stopped.

Respiratory distress: A condition in which breathing is difficult.

Respiratory rate: The number of times a person breathes per minute.

Respiratory system: A group of organs and other structures that bring air into the body and remove wastes through a process called breathing, or respiration.

Resuscitation mask: A pliable, dome-shaped device that fits over the nose and mouth; used to administer oxygen and assist with rescue breathing.

Rib cage: The cage of bones formed by the 12 pairs of ribs, the sternum, and the spine.

Ribs: Bones that attach to the spine and sternum and protect the heart and lungs.

Right-of-way: The right of a vessel or vehicle to cross in front of other vessels or vehicles.

Rigid splint: A splint made of boards, metal strips, and folded magazines or newspaper.

Rigor mortis: The rigid stiffening of heart and skeletal muscle after death.

Risk factors: Conditions or behaviours that increase the chance that a person will develop a disease.

Roller bandage: A bandage made of gauze or gauzelike material used to wrap around a dressing.

Routine maintenance: Maintenance work that is planned and performed on a regular basis to ensure proper working order of equipment and/or vehicles.

Rule of Nines: A method in which to estimate the percent of body surface area burned.

Rule of Palms: A method in which to estimate the percent of body surface area burned.

S

Scapula: See shoulder blade.

School-age: A child between 6 and 12 years of age.

Secondary survey: A check for injuries or conditions that could become life-threatening if not cared for.

Seizure: A disorder in the brain's electrical activity, marked by loss of consciousness and often uncontrollable muscle movement.

Sexual assault: Forcing another person to take part in a sexual act.

Shock: A life-threatening condition that occurs when the circulatory system fails to provide adequate oxygen-rich blood to all parts of the body.

Shoulder blade: A large, flat, triangular bone at the back of the shoulder in the upper part of the back; also called the scapula.

Signs: Any observable evidence of injury or illness, such as bleeding or an unusually pale skin colour.

Skeletal muscles: Muscles that attach to bones.

Skeleton: The 206 bones of the body that protect vital organs and other soft tissue.

Skin: A tough, supple membrane that covers the entire surface of the body.

Sling: A bandage used to hold and support an injured part of the body; often used to support an injured arm.

Soft tissues: Body structures that include the layers of skin, fat, and muscles.

Spinal cavity: An area in the body that contains the spinal cord and is protected by the bones of the spine.

Spinal column: The series of vertebrae extending from the base of the skull to the tip of the tailbone (coccyx).

Spinal cord: A bundle of nerves extending from the base of the skull to the lower back, protected by the spinal column.

Spine: A series of bones (vertebrae) that surrounds and protects the spinal cord; also called the backbone.

Splint: A device used to immobilize body parts.

Sprain: The excessive stretching and tearing of ligaments and other soft tissue structures at a joint.

Standard of care: The minimal standard and quality of care expected of an emergency care provider.

START system: A simple system used at the scene of multiple casualty incidents to quickly assess and prioritize care according to three conditions: breathing, circulation, and level of consciousness.

Status epilepticus: A continuous seizure or two or more seizures without a period of consciousness.

Sternum: The long, flat bone in the middle of the front of the rib cage; also called the breastbone.

Stimulants: Substances that affect the central nervous system to speed up physical and mental activity.

Stimuli: Anything that rouses or excites an organism or body part to respond.

Stoma: An opening connecting a part of a body cavity to the outside environment.

Stomach: One of the main organs of digestion, located in the abdomen.

Strain: The excessive stretching and tearing of muscles and tendons.

Stress management: Techniques or interventions designed to help an individual cope with psychological stress.

Stroke: A disruption of blood flow to a part of the brain that causes permanent damage; also called a cerebrovascular accident (CVA).

Subdural hematoma: Venous bleeding in the subdural space.

Substance abuse: The deliberate, persistent, excessive use of a substance without regard to health concerns or accepted medical practices.

Substance misuse: The use of a substance for unintended purposes or for intended purposes but in improper amounts or doses.

Sucking chest wound: A type of penetrating chest injury in which a sucking sound is heard with each breath a person takes due to air freely passing in and out of the chest cavity.

Suctioning: The process of removing matter such as saliva, vomitus, or blood from a person's mouth and throat by means of a mechanical or manual device.

Suction tip: A rigid or flexible tubing attached to the end of a suction device and placed in the mouth or throat of a person to remove foreign matter.

Sudden infant death syndrome (SIDS): The sudden death of a seemingly normal, healthy infant that occurs during the infant's sleep without evidence of disease.

Suicide: Self-inflicted death.

Superficial burn: A burn injury involving only the top layer of skin, characterized by red, dry skin.

Superior: Toward the head.

Supine: A position in which a person is lying face up on his or her back.

Sympathy: Understanding another's emotions, and feeling concern for that person.

Symptoms: Something the person tells you about his or her condition, such as "my chest hurts," or "I feel sick to my stomach."

Systolic pressure: The pressure in the arteries when the heart is contracting.

T

Tact: Acting appropriately according to one's situation and environment; the ability to communicate without offending others.

Taking charge: Assuming control or command.

Tendon: A fibrous band that attaches muscle to bone.

Tension pneumothorax: The continual flow of air into the pleural space, which cannot escape.

Third trimester bleeding: Bleeding during the last three months of pregnancy. Usually caused by abruptio placentae, placenta previa, or uterine rupture.

Thoracic cavity: An area in the body that contains the heart and lungs and is protected by the rib cage and upper portion of the spine.

Tibia: One of the bones in the lower leg.

Tissue: A collection of similar cells acting together to perform specific body functions.

Toddler: A child 1 or 2 years of age.

Tourniquet: A constricting band used over an artery above the site of an open wound with severe bleeding to decrease blood flow to the injured area for a short period of time.

Trachea: A tube leading from the upper airway to the lungs.

Traction: A pulling force applied to a body part to care for specific musculoskeletal injuries.

Transient ischemic attack: A temporary disruption of blood flow to the brain; sometimes called a ministroke or TIA.

Trauma: Physical injury caused by an outside force.

Triage: The process of sorting and providing care to multiple people according to the severity of their injuries or illnesses.

Triangular bandage: A bandage that can be used as a sling or to hold a dressing or splint in place.

Tripod position: A position in which a person is sitting upright, leaning forward, struggling to breathe.

Trunk: The part of the body containing the chest, abdomen, and pelvis.

Tuberculosis (TB): A respiratory disease caused by a bacterium.

U

Umbilical cord: A flexible structure that attaches the placenta to the unborn child, allowing for the passage of blood, nutrients, and waste.

Universal precautions: Safety measures taken to prevent occupational-risk exposure to blood or other body fluids.

Upwind: In the direction from which the wind blows.

Urinary system: A group of organs and other structures that eliminates waste products from the blood.

Urinary tract infection: An infection, usually bacterial, at any site within the urinary tract.

Uterine rupture: A spontaneous or traumatic rupture of the uterine wall.

Uterus: A pear-shaped organ in a woman's pelvis in which an embryo is formed and develops into a baby.

V

Vaccine: A medical substance containing killed or weakened microorganisms that is introduced into the body to prevent, kill, or treat a disease.

Vagina: The lower part of the birth canal through which the baby passes during birth.

Vector transmission: The transmission of a disease by an animal or insect bite through exposure to blood or other body fluids.

Veins: Blood vessels that carry oxygen-poor blood from all parts of the body to the heart.

Ventilation: The process of providing oxygen to the lungs through rescue breathing or by other means.

Ventilation devices: Devices used to help with ventilation.

Ventricles: The two lower chambers of the heart.

Ventricular fibrillation: A life-threatening arrhythmia in which the heart muscle quivers rather than pumping blood.

Ventricular tachycardia: A life-threatening arrhythmia in which the heart muscle contracts too quickly for an adequate pumping of blood to the body.

Vertebrae: The 33 bones of the spinal column.

Virus: A disease-causing agent, or pathogen, that requires another organism to live and reproduce.

Visually impaired: A nonspecific term applied to a person who is either blind or partially blind.

Vital organs: Organs whose functions are essential to life, including the brain, heart, and lungs.

Vital signs: Important information about the person's condition, obtained by checking level of consciousness, breathing, pulse, skin characteristics, blood pressure, and pupils.

W

Wound: An injury to the soft tissues.

Index

Emergency response, components of, 4
Emergency response plans, 13
Emergency scene, 14-15
Emergency vehicle, 356-359
Emotional crisis, 328-332
Emphysema, 88, 89
Endocrine system, 41, 50
 age-related changes in, 308
Endoplasmic reticulum, 42
Endotracheal intubation, 371-373
Energy, 166
Engineering controls, 28-29
Entonox, 405-406
Environmental conditions and vehicle operation, 359
Epidermis, 49, 169
Epidural hematoma, 220-221
Epiglottis, 42-43
Epiglottitis, 306-307
Epilepsy, 270-271
Epinephrine auto-injector, 87-88
Epinephrine hydrochloride, 404
Equipment, 13
 on ambulance, 357
 cleaning/disinfecting, 29
 recommendations for, 334
Erectile dysfunction medications, 128
Erythromycin, 388
Esophagus, 42-43
Ethanol 70%, 391
Ethical responsibilities, 8
Exercise, 131, 198
Exhale, 42, 44
Exposure control plan, 30
 Health Canada recommendations for, 30
Exposure determination, 30
Exposure protocols, 31
External bleeding, 151-153
 with head/spine injury, 229
Extremity lift, 343, 345
Extrication, 227-228, 247-248, 334
 rapid, 228
Eye, 183-184
Eye drops, 387

Eye injury, 234-238
Eye opening, 63
Eye sockets. See Orbits
Eyelid injury, 237

Facial droop, 143
Fainting, 267
Falls
 in older adults, 309
 preventing, 240
FAST, 143-144
Fat, 169
Febrile seizure, 270, 271
 in child, 306
Femoral artery, 210, 211
Femur, 210, 211
Fetus, 317
Fibula, 210
Finger injury, 209
Finger sweep, 81-82
 in baby, 84-85
Fire danger, 17
First aid attendants, marine, 364
First aid kit, marine, 369-370
 international, 365-368
 on survival craft, 370
First aid station, marine, 364
First responders, 3
First-trimester emergency, 323
Fixed-wing aircraft, 359
Flail chest, 253
Flat bones, 192
Flexion, 224
Flow rate for IV, 408, 409
Flowmeter, 112, 114
Fluids, 298
Fluorescein, 391
Food cargo, 373
Foot drag, 343, 345
Foot injuries, 213-214
Football helmet, 230
Forces, 164-165
Fore-and-aft lift, 343, 345
Forearm, 208-209
Foreign object in eye, 235-236
Forms, marine, 379-381, 383-385
Fowler position, 344

Fracture, 195, 196
Freeboard, 362
French catheter, 104
Freon, 373
Frost nip, 295
Frostbite, 292, 295-297, 298
Full-face helmet, 240
Full-thickness burn, 169, 181
Fungi, 22
Furosemide, 391
Fused bones, 195

Gastric distension, 93
Gastroenteritis, 272
Gastrointestinal system
 age-related changes in, 308
 See also Digestive system
Gastrointestinal tract ulcer, 272
General impression, 56
Generic name, 401
Genital injury, 260
Genitalia, 51
Genitourinary system, 41, 51
 age-related changes in, 308
Glands, 50
Glasgow Coma Scale (GCS), 63
Globes, 237
Gloves, removal of, 27-28
Glucagon, 391
Glucometer, 269
Glucose, oral, 406
Golgi, 42
Good Samaritan Laws, 9
Grief, 329-330
Grieving process, 330
Guide dog, 311

Hallucination, 313
Hallucinogens, 286, 287
Haloperidol, 391-392
Hamstring muscles, 192
Hand cleanser gel, 391
Hand injuries, 208-209
Hand-washing technique, 28
Hantavirus, 280
Hard hat, 240
Hazardous materials, 18

NOTES:

NOTES: